PLEASE HELP TO UPDATE THIS BOOK

India and its fast-growing tourist industry are constantly changing. It is hard to keep track of, and impossible to test out each new bar, beach-hut, restaurant, theatre, elephant ride, bus journey...

And so we need your knowledge, thoughts and experiences to create as complete a picture as possible for each update. If you have had a particularly pleasing (or unpleasant) experience, we would like to hear about it. Similarly, if you feel that you have some ideas for the guide, send them in. Be as opinionated as you like. Writers of the best letters each year are awarded a complimentary guide of their choice from the series.

CADOGAN GUIDES

'Cadogan Guides really need no introduction and are mini-encyclopaedic on the countries covered...they give the explorer, the intellectual or culture buff—indeed any visitor—all they need to know to get the very best from their visit...and make a good read too by the many inveterate armchair travellers.'

—*The Book Journal*

'The quality of writing in this British series is exceptional...From practical facts to history, customs, sightseeing, food and lodging, the Cadogan Series can be counted on for interesting detail and informed recommendations.'

—*Going Places* (US)

'Standouts these days are the Cadogan Guides...sophisticated, beautifully written books.'

—*American Bookseller Magazine*

'Entertaining comparisons, with sharp insights, local gossip and far more of a feeling of a living author...The series has received plaudits worldwide for intelligence, originality and a slightly irreverent sense of fun.'

—*Saturday Telegraph*

Other titles in the Cadogan Guides Series:

AMSTERDAM
AUSTRALIA
BALI
BERLIN
THE CARIBBEAN
CENTRAL AMERICA
ECUADOR,
  THE GALAPAGOS
  & COLOMBIA
GREEK ISLANDS
IRELAND
ITALIAN ISLANDS
MEXICO
MOROCCO
NEW YORK
NORTHEAST ITALY
NORTHWEST ITALY
PORTUGAL
PRAGUE
ROME
SCOTLAND

SOUTHOF FRANCE: PROVENCE,
  CÔTE D'AZUR &
  LANGUEDOC-ROUSSILLON
SOUTH ITALY
SOUTHERN SPAIN: GIBRALTAR &
  ANDALUCÍA
SPAIN
THAILAND
TUNISIA
TURKEY
TUSCANY, UMBRIA & THE MARCHES
VENICE

Forthcoming:
CENTRAL ASIA
CYPRUS
GERMANY
MALTA
MOSCOW & ST PETERSBURG
PARIS
SICILY

CADOGAN GUIDES

INDIA

FRANK KUSY

CADOGAN BOOKS
London

THE GLOBE PEQUOT PRESS
Old Saybrook, Connecticut

Cadogan Books Ltd
Mercury House, 195 Knightsbridge, London SW7 1RE

The Globe Pequot Press
6 Business Park Drive, PO Box 833, Old Saybrook, Connecticut 06475-0833

Editor: Victoria Ingle (Managing)
Series Editor: Rachel Fielding

Third Edition, revised and updated in association with
Gulmohur Press Pvt Ltd, New Delhi, India

Proofreader and indexer: Sarah Israel

First published in 1987; Second Edition 1989
Third, revised edition 1993

A Catalogue Record for this book is available from the British Library
ISBN 0-947754-32-6

Library of Congress Cataloging-in-Publication Data
Kusy, Frank,
    India/Frank Kusy; illustrations by Pauline Pears.—3rd ed.
    p. cm.—(Cadogan guides)
    Includes index.
    ISBN 1-56440-004-2
    1. India—Guidebooks, I. Title. II. Series
DS406.K87   1992
                                        92-28244
915.404'52—dc20

Photoset in Palatino by Gulmohur Press Pvt Ltd, New Delhi
Printed and bound by BPC Wheatons Ltd, Exeter, Great Britain

ABOUT THE AUTHOR

Frank Kusy is a professional travel writer. The son of Polish-Hungarian immigrants, he first travelled abroad at the age of four, and has been wandering ever since. Born in England, he left Cardiff University for a career in journalism and worked for a while with *The Financial Times*. India is his first love, the only country he knows which improves on repeated viewings. He now visits for pleasure and on business, for at least three months every year.

This, the third edition of Frank's guide, has been updated with the help of Bikram Grewal and Toby Sinclair of Gulmohur Press, New Delhi, India. The company has been packaging specialist publications, on travel, art history and wildlife, for the home and international market for nearly 10 years.

ACKNOWLEDGEMENTS

There are many without whom the first, second and third editions of this guide would not have been possible. Special thanks go to Maggi Nixon and Oberoi Hotels and Pleasureseekers Ltd, Steve Pettitt, Nigel Berry and Pettitts India, Surendra Singh and Pushkar Hotel, Mr and Mrs Raju Shahani (Bhubaneshwar), Col. K. Fateh Singh and Indu Singh (Jaipur), His Highness the Maharajah of Jodhpur, Dr S. Dandapani, and the Government of India Tourist Office. I would also like to thank the many travellers, hoteliers, restaurateurs, tourist officers and local Indian people who have contributed information, experiences and anecdotes over the years. A final mention goes to my parents, for putting up with blaring Indian music and a humming word processor for over three years.

The editor would like to thank colleagues and friends at Gulmohur Press, who tirelessly collected and collated information for the best part of a hot, then very wet 1992. Bikram Grewal, for his untiring captaincy of the project in India, for letting us take over his home and his office, and for sparks of inspiration when others flagged; Toby Sinclair for sharing his knowledge and love of the country which has been his home for 18 years, for his hard work and support, and unfailing good humour; Surit Mitra for his invaluable help on the Nepal section; Reuben Israel and Narender Kumar for their professionalism and lightning keyboard skills; Sarah Israel, who flew from Bombay to proofread and index the guide, and whose impeccable standards set an example for us all; Shobita Punja for her company and her great hospitality; and Swapan, Ram, Jugal and Chotu for their kindness, their help, a parade of tea and nourishment, and the occasional, ice-cold beer.

CONTENTS

About the Author *Page v*

Acknowledgements *Page vi*

List of Maps and Tables *Page x*

Introduction *Page xi*

Part I: General Information *Pages 1–51*

Part II: Culture *Pages 52–72*

Part III: Topics *Pages 73–86*

Part IV: North India *Pages 87–261*

Part V: West India *Pages 262–337*

Part VI: East India *Pages 338–395*

Part VII: South India *Pages 396–488*

Part VIII: Nepal—the Kathmandu Valley *Pages 489–516*

Language *Pages 517–518*

Further Reading *Pages 519–520*

Index *Pages 521–530*

LIST OF MAPS

TABLES

INTRODUCTION

Travel in India is a total experience, one which no visitor ever forgets. A vast subcontinent of over 900 million people, it covers 25 states, stretches some 3200 km (2000 miles) north to south, and about 2700 km (1700 miles) east to west, and contains more different languages, religions, races and cultures than any other country in the world. It is also one of the oldest civilisations known, dating back approximately 5000 years, and was in its heyday one of the richest, known as 'The Golden Bird of the East'.

Whatever you want from a holiday, it's here in India: royal palaces, desert fortresses, beach resorts, hill stations, temples, mountains and lakes—you'll find them all, and a lot more besides. And India is still one of the cheapest tourist destinations in the world. Where else could you stay at a five-star hotel for less than £35 (US$70) per night, or dine out on the most sumptuous cuisine for less than £17 (US$14), or find such good shopping bargains—top-quality silks and brocades, furnishings and paintings, carvings and carpets, jewellery and gems? If you're into sports and recreation, there are good facilities in many cities for golf and fishing, for horse-riding and swimming, for tennis and squash, while in outlying areas you can explore wildlife parks on elephant-back or cross the remote Thar Desert on a camel-safari. Finally, don't forget India's rich cultural heritage. Here you can enjoy some of the best music, dance and theatre in the East.

But this is only one side of India. Yes, this is a place of exotic enchantment, of religious mystique, of great natural beauty. But it is also a place of incredible noise, squalor and poverty; a large country, with large problems. Everything here is on a grand scale—both good and bad. This powerful sense of contrast, this alternation between luxury and poverty, beauty and ugliness, efficiency and chaos, is the key to understanding India. It's something which can produce an ambivalent reaction, and many foreign travellers develop a love-hate relationship on their travels.

India is a very personal experience, and every traveller's impressions are different. But nobody returns unaffected or unchanged. It's an amazing and contradictory land, full of colour and vitality, hospitable and very friendly. Yet it's seldom peaceful, never private and often frustrating. But once it's in your bloodstream, you'll never get it out. You'll never fully understand it and you'll never see it all, but the compulsion to keep on trying will probably send you back time and again.

Perhaps the most absorbing part of India is not her 'sights' but her street-life. The typical Indian street is a living theatre of people shaving, hawking goods, gossiping, making clothes and preparing betel, of sacred cows, camels and dogs jostling for position with taxis, bicycles, rickshaws and pilgrims, of heaped mountains of colourful spices, fruits, vegetables and incense. It never seems to stop, and if you like 'street action', you'll never want to leave. Everywhere you look, every corner you turn, every person you meet, will make an indelible impression. If you're a keen photographer, you'll just love it. Even if you aren't, you'll still be hypnotised. In India, every glance is a picture.

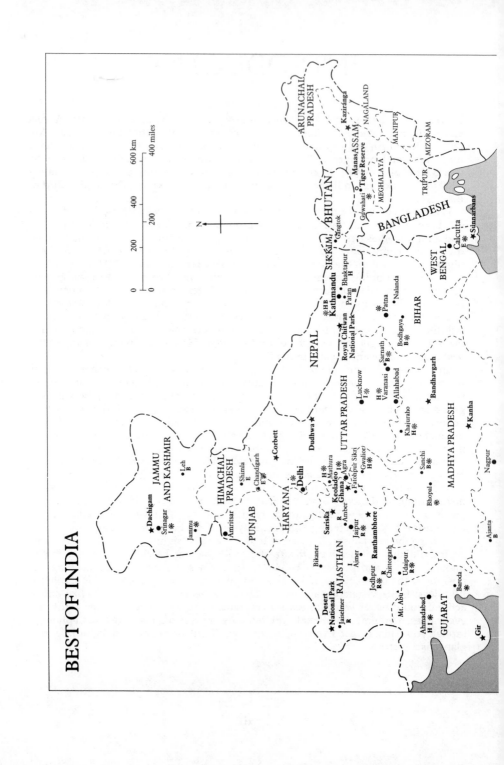

BEST OF INDIA

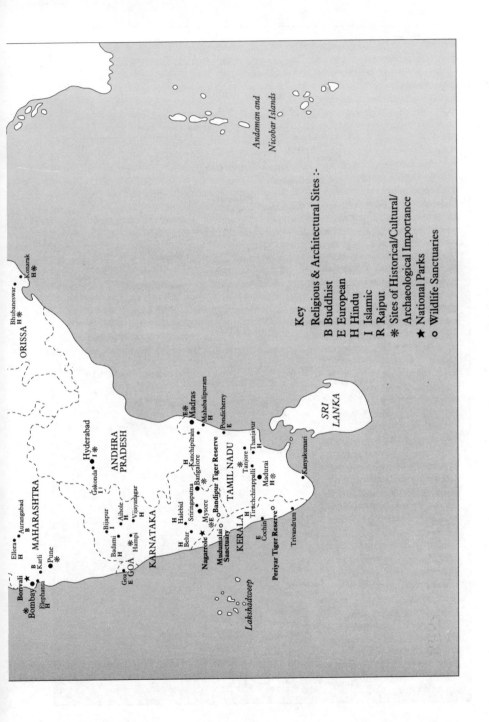

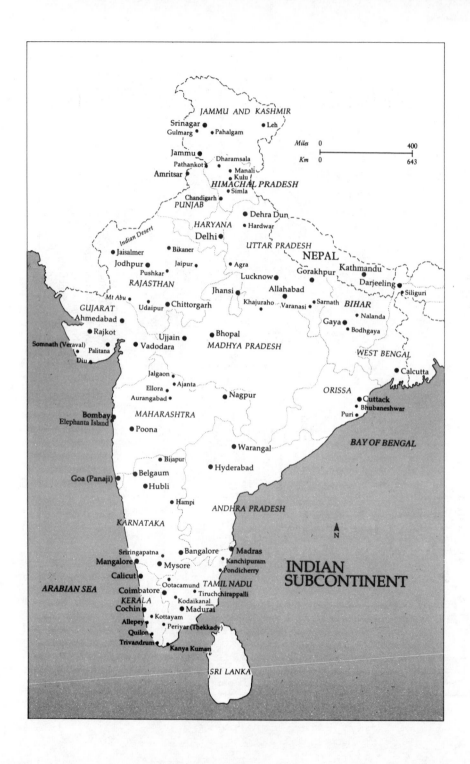

Part I

GENERAL INFORMATION

Victoria Terminus

Before You Go

India is vast, and travellers who have been wandering round this sprawling continent for two or three years still won't have seen everything. As a general rule, it is much better to see a little of India in depth than a number of places in haste. This is a country to appreciate at leisure; if you miss something the first trip, you can always go back.

There is no point going to India for less than three weeks, because the climate, culture and lifestyle can be overwhelming. It's an intense, overpowering place to begin with, and many travellers only just begin to enjoy it when they have to go home again. The ideal length for an introduction to India is therefore between four and six weeks.

Once you have decided how long you're going for, plan a route. Experienced travellers might grumble: 'You can't plan India—the best way of getting round it is just to flow with the tide!' That's all right if you've got a few months to spare, but if you only have a short amount of time at your disposal, select a certain area of India and see it properly. Once you've decided on a route, stick to it.

1

Route Planning and Selection

Good preparation is vital. Nothing in India is straightforward, and you can expect to see the best-laid plans come unstuck on occasion. The pace of life is also much slower than in the West. Those who just drift in with no clear idea of where they're going easily become discouraged by one or two failed hurdles (usually theft, illness or train-reservation queues). Those who arrive quite certain of where they're going either become distracted or meet a brick wall of bureaucratic resistance, with the result that they see only half the places on their itinerary. Travel in India is always an adventure but rarely so complicated that it cannot be done. However, for many things there are formalities to go through, paperwork to be processed, queues to be negotiated, and all manner of bizarre delays to be experienced—human, animal and mechanical. But those travellers who have a plan and persist with it, who remain patient and, above all, retain their sense of humour intact throughout, never regret coming.

There are 13 recommended routes in this book, covering over 70 places of major tourist interest. Each route is self-contained, has a separate travel itinerary, and can take anything between one and three weeks to cover at leisure. For travellers with more time to spare, there are additional options suggested on each travel itinerary which connect it with other nearby routes. In each town or city, at least one sightseeing tour is given, which suggests how to cover the main points of interest in the shortest time. And whether you are backpacking, or intending to travel in luxury, you'll find hotels and restaurants to suit your pocket, plus up-to-date information on shopping, recreation, entertainment, transport and tours.

The routes all begin from one of the four gateway cities—Delhi, Bombay, Calcutta and Madras. Choosing the right capital to land in can be just as important as selecting the best route. For example, arriving in sticky Madras if you don't like heat is just as unwise as turning up in Bombay when you don't enjoy big city hubbub. Similarly, if you're sensitive to poverty and crowds, you might find Calcutta a shock and should arrive in more sedate Delhi to acclimatise to the country. Each city has its pros and cons. Read the relevant sections, and make your choice.

The routes have been chosen to provide as much of a balance as possible. They all have a particular emphasis: beaches in Goa, temples in Tamil Nadu, desert fortresses in Rajasthan; and where possible at least one hill station or oasis is included, to supply some variation and a cool, relaxing break.

To select your route or routes, just decide what your priority is (beaches, wildlife, temples, palaces) and what you're likely to enjoy doing there most (sightseeing, shopping, recreation, sports, just relaxing). Don't feel you have to visit the time-honoured tourist spots. India is not just the Taj Mahal, and the 'Golden Triangle' of Agra, Jaipur and Delhi. These places are magnificent, yes, but so too are the Eastern Triangle of Bhubaneshwar, Puri and Konarak, and the Western Triangle of Diu, Somnath and Sasan-Gir. And they are much less touristy. Nor should Tamil Nadu and the 'deep south' be ignored either.

Climate and When to Go

Whatever the time of year, there is always somewhere in India where you can enjoy a relaxing and memorable vacation. But the climate varies, depending on season and

Weather Chart

T = Temperature in °C (°F)   R = Rainfall in mm (ins)

City			Jan	Feb	Mar	Apr	May	Jun	Jul	Aug	Sep	Oct	Nov	Dec
Ahmedabad	T	max.	29(84)	31(88)	36(97)	40(104)	41(106)	38(100)	33(91)	32(90)	33(91)	36(97)	33(91)	30(86)
		min.	12(54)	15(59)	19(66)	23(73)	26(79)	27(81)	26(79)	25(77)	24(75)	21(70)	16(61)	13(55)
	R	avg.	4(0.2)	0(0.0)	1(0.0)	2(0.1)	5(0.2)	100(3.9)	316(12.4)	213(8.4)	163(6.4)	13(0.5)	5(0.2)	1(0.0)
Aurangabad	T	max.	29(84)	32(90)	36(97)	38(100)	40(104)	35(95)	29(84)	29(84)	30(86)	31(88)	30(86)	29(84)
		min.	14(57)	16(61)	20(68)	24(75)	25(77)	23(73)	22(72)	21(70)	21(70)	20(68)	16(61)	14(57)
	R	avg.	3(0.1)	3(0.1)	4(0.2)	7(0.3)	17(0.7)	141(5.5)	189(7.4)	146(5.7)	179(7.0)	62(2.4)	32(1.3)	9(0.3)
Bangalore	T	max.	28(82)	31(88)	33(91)	34(93)	33(91)	30(86)	28(82)	29(84)	28(82)	28(82)	27(81)	27(81)
		min.	15(59)	16(61)	19(66)	21(70)	21(70)	20(68)	19(66)	19(66)	19(66)	19(66)	17(63)	15(59)
	R	avg.	4(0.2)	14(0.5)	6(0.2)	37(1.5)	119(4.7)	65(2.0)	93(3.7)	95(3.7)	129(5.1)	195(7.7)	46(1.8)	16(0.6)
Bombay	T	max.	31(88)	32(90)	33(91)	33(91)	33(91)	32(90)	30(86)	29(84)	30(86)	32(90)	33(91)	32(90)
		min.	16(61)	17(63)	20(68)	24(75)	26(79)	26(79)	25(77)	24(75)	24(75)	23(73)	20(68)	18(64)
	R	avg.	0(0.0)	1(0.0)	0(0.0)	0(0.0)	20(0.8)	647(25.5)	945(37.2)	660(26.0)	309(12.2)	117(4.6)	7(0.3)	1(0.0)
Calcutta	T	max.	26(79)	29(84)	34(93)	36(97)	36(97)	34(93)	32(90)	32(90)	32(90)	31(88)	29(84)	27(81)
		min.	12(54)	15(59)	20(68)	24(75)	26(79)	26(79)	26(79)	26(79)	26(79)	24(75)	18(64)	13(55)
	R	avg.	13(0.5)	22(0.9)	30(1.2)	50(2.0)	135(5.3)	263(10.3)	320(12.6)	318(12.5)	253(10.0)	134(5.3)	29(1.1)	4(0.2)
Cochin	T	max.	31(88)	31(88)	31(88)	31(88)	31(88)	29(84)	28(82)	28(82)	28(82)	29(84)	30(86)	30(86)
		min.	23(73)	24(75)	26(79)	26(79)	26(79)	24(75)	24(75)	24(75)	24(75)	24(75)	24(75)	23(73)
	R	avg.	9(0.3)	34(1.3)	50(2.0)	139(5.5)	364(14.3)	756(29.8)	572(22.5)	386(15.2)	235(9.2)	333(13.1)	184(7.2)	37(1.5)
Darjeeling	T	max.	9(48)	11(52)	15(59)	18(64)	19(66)	19(66)	20(68)	20(68)	20(68)	19(66)	15(59)	12(54)
		min.	3(37)	4(39)	8(46)	11(52)	13(55)	15(59)	15(59)	15(59)	15(59)	11(52)	7(45)	4(39)
	R	avg.	22(0.9)	27(1.1)	52(2.0)	109(4.3)	187(7.4)	522(20.5)	713(28.1)	573(22.6)	419(16.5)	116(4.6)	14(0.5)	5(0.2)
Delhi	T	max.	21(70)	24(75)	30(86)	36(97)	41(106)	40(104)	35(95)	34(93)	34(93)	35(95)	29(84)	23(73)
		min.	7(45)	10(50)	15(59)	21(70)	27(81)	29(84)	27(81)	26(79)	25(77)	19(66)	12(54)	8(46)
	R	avg.	25(1.0)	22(0.9)	17(0.7)	7(0.3)	8(0.3)	65(2.6)	211(8.3)	173(6.8)	150(5.9)	31(1.2)	1(0.0)	5(0.2)
Hyderabad	T	max.	29(84)	31(88)	35(95)	37(99)	39(102)	34(93)	30(86)	29(84)	30(86)	30(86)	29(84)	28(82)
		min.	15(59)	17(63)	20(68)	24(75)	26(79)	24(75)	22(72)	22(72)	22(72)	20(68)	16(61)	13(55)
	R	avg.	2(0.1)	11(0.4)	13(0.5)	24(0.9)	30(1.2)	107(4.2)	165(6.5)	147(5.8)	163(6.4)	71(2.8)	25(1.0)	5(0.2)
Jaipur	T	max.	22(72)	25(77)	31(88)	37(99)	41(106)	39(102)	34(93)	32(90)	33(91)	33(91)	29(84)	24(75)
		min.	8(46)	11(52)	15(59)	21(70)	26(79)	27(81)	26(79)	24(75)	23(73)	18(64)	12(54)	9(48)
	R	avg.	14(0.5)	8(0.3)	9(0.3)	4(0.2)	10(0.4)	54(2.1)	193(7.6)	239(9.4)	90(3.6)	19(0.7)	3(0.1)	4(0.2)
Jammu	T	max.	18(64)	21(70)	26(79)	33(91)	39(102)	40(104)	35(95)	33(91)	33(91)	31(88)	26(79)	21(70)
		min.	8(46)	11(52)	15(59)	21(70)	26(79)	28(82)	26(79)	25(77)	24(75)	19(66)	13(55)	9(48)
	R	avg.	71(2.8)	54(2.1)	57(2.2)	25(1.0)	17(0.7)	61(2.4)	321(12.6)	319(12.5)	151(5.9)	29(1.1)	8(0.3)	29(1.1)
Jodhpur	T	max.	25(77)	28(82)	33(91)	38(100)	42(108)	40(104)	36(97)	33(91)	35(95)	36(97)	31(88)	27(79)
		min.	9(48)	12(54)	17(63)	22(72)	27(81)	29(84)	27(81)	26(79)	24(75)	20(68)	14(57)	11(52)
	R	avg.	7(0.3)	5(0.2)	2(0.1)	2(0.1)	6(0.2)	31(1.2)	122(4.8)	145(5.7)	47(1.8)	7(0.3)	3(0.1)	1(0.0)
Madras	T	max.	29(84)	31(88)	33(91)	35(95)	38(100)	37(99)	35(95)	35(95)	34(93)	32(90)	29(84)	28(82)
		min.	20(68)	21(70)	23(73)	26(79)	28(82)	28(82)	26(79)	26(79)	25(77)	24(75)	23(73)	21(70)
	R	avg.	24(0.9)	7(0.3)	15(0.6)	25(1.0)	52(2.0)	53(2.1)	83(3.3)	124(4.9)	118(4.6)	267(10.5)	309(12.2)	139(5.5)
Madurai	T	max.	30(86)	32(90)	35(95)	36(97)	37(99)	37(99)	36(97)	35(95)	35(95)	33(91)	31(88)	30(86)
		min.	21(70)	22(72)	23(73)	26(79)	26(79)	26(79)	26(79)	25(77)	24(75)	24(73)	23(73)	22(72)
	R	avg.	26(1.0)	16(0.6)	21(0.8)	81(3.2)	59(2.3)	31(1.2)	48(1.9)	117(4.6)	123(4.8)	179(7.1)	161(6.3)	43(1.7)
Panaji (Goa)	T	max.	31(88)	32(90)	32(90)	33(91)	33(91)	31(88)	29(84)	29(84)	29(84)	31(88)	33(91)	33(91)
		min.	19(66)	20(68)	23(73)	25(77)	27(81)	25(77)	24(75)	24(75)	24(75)	23(73)	22(72)	21(70)
	R	avg.	2(0.1)	0(0.0)	4(0.2)	17(0.7)	18(0.7)	580(22.8)	892(35.1)	341(13.4)	277(10.9)	122(4.8)	20(0.8)	37(1.5)
Puri	T	max.	27(81)	28(82)	30(86)	31(88)	32(90)	31(88)	31(88)	31(88)	31(88)	31(88)	29(84)	27(81)
		min.	18(64)	21(70)	25(77)	27(81)	27(81)	27(81)	27(81)	27(81)	27(81)	25(77)	21(70)	18(64)
	R	avg.	9(0.3)	20(0.8)	14(0.5)	12(0.5)	63(2.5)	187(7.3)	296(11.6)	256(10.1)	258(10.2)	242(9.5)	75(3.0)	8(0.3)
Simla	T	max.	9(48)	10(50)	14(57)	19(66)	23(73)	24(75)	21(70)	20(68)	20(68)	18(64)	15(59)	11(52)
		min.	2(36)	3(37)	7(45)	11(52)	15(59)	16(61)	16(61)	15(59)	14(57)	10(50)	7(45)	4(39)
	R	avg.	65(2.6)	48(1.9)	58(2.3)	38(1.5)	54(2.1)	147(5.8)	415(16.3)	385(15.1)	195(7.7)	45(1.8)	7(0.3)	24(0.9)
Srinagar	T	max.	4(39)	8(46)	13(55)	19(66)	25(77)	29(84)	31(88)	30(86)	28(82)	23(73)	15(59)	9(48)
		min.	−2(28)	−1(30)	3(37)	7(45)	11(52)	14(57)	18(64)	18(64)	13(55)	6(43)	0(32)	−2(28)
	R	avg.	73(2.9)	72(2.8)	104(4.1)	78(3.1)	63(2.5)	36(1.4)	61(2.4)	63(2.5)	32(1.3)	29(1.1)	17(0.7)	36(1.4)
Trivandrum (Kovalum)	T	max.	31(88)	32(90)	33(91)	32(90)	31(88)	29(84)	29(84)	29(84)	30(86)	30(86)	30(86)	31(88)
		min.	22(72)	23(73)	24(75)	25(77)	25(77)	24(75)	23(73)	23(73)	23(73)	23(73)	23(73)	22(72)
	R	avg.	20(0.8)	20(0.8)	43(1.7)	122(4.8)	249(9.8)	331(13.0)	215(8.5)	164(6.4)	123(4.8)	271(10.7)	207(8.1)	73(2.9)
Varanasi	T	max.	23(74)	27(81)	33(91)	39(102)	41(106)	39(102)	33(91)	32(90)	32(90)	32(90)	29(84)	25(77)
		min.	9(48)	11(52)	17(63)	22(72)	27(81)	28(82)	26(79)	26(79)	25(77)	21(70)	13(55)	9(48)
	R	avg.	23(0.9)	8(0.3)	14(0.5)	1(0.0)	8(0.3)	102(4.0)	346(13.6)	240(9.5)	261(10.3)	38(1.5)	15(0.6)	2(0.1)

3

location, and you need to consider this when planning your holiday. The country has four seasons—spring, autumn and two monsoons. The south-west monsoon starts in June on the west coast and slowly wends its way northwards; the north-east monsoon takes place between October and December. This can actually be a most pleasant time to go. In between the sudden, short downpours of rain are periods of clear, brilliant sunshine, and all the foliage and flowers suddenly burst into colour. It's a photographer's dream, and the heat at such times is rarely unbearable.

The movements of foreign tourists tend to follow a set pattern. From November to January, you'll find many travellers in the south. It's always hot in the south, but this is the coolest season. By February, the annual migration northwards has begun. Travellers move slowly up the western coast, settling briefly in Kovalam and Goa between February and early March, before heading up to Bombay, Calcutta and Delhi by mid- to late March. These are the three main jump-off centres for, respectively, Kashmir, Darjeeling and Nepal. At the time of writing, continuing political unrest makes Kashmir an unsafe destination, but the cool mountain resorts of the north are where the bulk of travellers relax between April and June. Then come the monsoons, and it's only in the autumn, from October onwards, that tourists re-appear in any force, usually to take in the clear mountain views and beautiful plants and flowers that blossom in the wake of the rains.

As a general guide, **Delhi** and **Rajasthan** (along with the cities of the northern plains) are most pleasant from late September until late March, very hot during April and May, and receive the rains from mid-June. **Bombay** and **Goa** are best during November to February, thereafter hot and humid until the monsoons break in early June. **South India** is coolest from November to April, and gets the rains as early as late May. **Ladakh** is snowbound for half the year, and can be visited from May to October only.

Most foreign tourists visit India in season, to enjoy the best weather and facilities, and to meet other travellers. A cunning minority go off season—usually a week or two before everybody else—to take advantage of the 30–50% accommodation discounts offered by Goan beach-huts and hill station hotels. Travelling off season also means fewer crowds, more seats on buses, and no long queues for train tickets.

Don't travel north during May and June. In early May Indian schools break up. This is the cue for a mass exodus of home tourists to Darjeeling and Shimla, and practically everywhere else that qualifies as a holiday or honeymoon resort. Secondly, try to avoid Bombay, Calcutta, or Delhi during March. All three centres are crowded out with travellers then, and finding accommodation can be very difficult.

GETTING THERE

India is not a country to go into with your eyes shut. It's vital to plan ahead. A lot of travellers' initial problems, especially with regard to health and security, are due to little or no prior preparation. To get the best out of your trip, make sure all your arrangements are airtight.

By Air (International)

It's usually a good idea to book your flight to India six months or so before departure. This gives you a set date to work towards, and a firm reservation with the airline of your choice. Budget travellers might prefer to leave their booking till much later to take advantage of any last-minute bargains offered by cheap flight specialists.

From the UK

While the standard one-way fare from London to Bombay/Delhi is around £515 (2nd class, economy) and £1641 (1st class), £770 and £2983, respectively, return, shopping around can get you reductions of 50% or more. Many cheap bargains are advertised in magazines like *Time Out, LAM, TNT* and *Australasian Express,* and there are many cut-price travel agencies around Earl's Court, London. Bear in mind, though, that the cheaper you go the more likely it is that you'll end up on an Arab or Russian (Aeroflot) service which often makes interminable stopovers to refuel or to dump passengers in the middle of nowhere. It can often be far better to pay a bit extra for a direct flight with **Air India** or **British Airways.** Other airlines providing good, regular and reliable services to India include **Air France, Cathay Pacific, Emirates, Gulf Air, KLM, JAL, Lufthansa, Thai International, Alitalia, Swissair,** and **Singapore Airlines.** Students under 26 should enquire about the generous student discounts offered by some of these airlines, notably Thai International and Singapore Airlines.

Discount Air Travel

Cheaper fares are also available between London and both New Delhi and Bombay on many of these airlines. Restrictions, such as minimum and maximum length of stay often apply. The following offer good deals on flights:

Discount Travel, 8 Hogarth Rd, London SW5 (tel 071-835 1484)
Flamingo Travel, 24 Wardour St, London WC1 (tel 071-287 0402)
Flightbookers, 118 Tottenham Court Rd, London WC1 (tel 071-387 1550)
GSA Hindustan Travel, 30 Poland St, London WC1 (tel 071-439 9801)
STA Travel, 117 Euston Rd, London NW1 (tel 071-937 9971)
Trailfinders, 42–50 Earls Court Rd, London W8 (tel 071-938 3366)

Fares offered by these agents vary, according to season and availability, but they range from £380 (low season by Gulf Air), £399 (high season by Alitalia—with stopover in Rome), to £440 (low season by Singapore Airlines) and £525 (high season by British Airways and Air India).

High season to India usually denotes the months of July and August, and December and January, but this varies from agent to agent.

From the US

The cheapest round-trip scheduled flights are operated by **Air India,** at around US$1400 (2nd class), US$2500 (1st class) from New York (the best US base, with daily flights to Bombay, Delhi and Madras, and at least one flight to Calcutta per week). From other places like Chicago and Boston the fare is about US$1900. **STA Travel** in San Francisco (tel 416 391 8407) offers a return fare to Bombay of about US$1200. To save money, and to get best flight availability, many American travellers fly into New York on cheap internal flights from various other parts of the country. For those on the West Coast, it's worth checking the travel section in the Sunday edition of the *LA Times*, where many cheap flights to India are advertised.

While certain travel agents offer discounts if you're prepared to shop around, it is generally far more difficult to get decent fare concessions in either the US or Australia than it is in the UK. Many American visitors travel to India **via London**, where cheap flight deals are readily available, or **via Bangkok** where certain airlines—Singapore, United, Korean and North-west Orient—offer 'easy fares' or discounted package rates, especially if flying from New York, Los Angeles or San Francisco, the three 'cheapie' departure points in the USA (e.g. San Francisco–Bangkok US$535 one-way, US$780 return). Several of them ring **Trailfinders** 42–50 Earl's Court Rd, London W8 6EJ (tel 071-938 3366) to pre-book the connecting flight from the UK to India; others use one of the American equivalents of Trailfinders—**Adventure Center**, 1311 63rd St, Suite 200, Emeryville, CA 94608, (tel 510 654 1879; fax 510 654 4200), who specialise in round-the-world itineraries. Also worth looking into are good-value **Apex fares**, or the popular **SIA 'Inter-Asia' flights** which run in conjunction with several Asian airlines and which offer a wide range of cheap fares in Asia.

From Australia
It is often cheaper to fly to Bombay or Delhi from Darwin or Perth rather than from Sydney. Many Australian travellers get cheap or Apex tickets to Singapore or Bangkok, and fly on to India from there. **Jetset**, 99 Walker St, North Sydney, N.S.W. (tel 02 956 9333; fax 02 956 9500) offer attractive flight discounts. Possibly the cheapest Australia–India option of all is a flight hop from Perth to Bali, followed by an overland trek up through Southeast Asia.

Several cheap-flight agencies have now sprung up in Delhi, Bombay and Calcutta— offering heavily discounted fares *from* India to foreign destinations. Very handy, if you're flying out on a one-way ticket, and wish to carry on to Thailand, Nepal, Hong Kong or Australia.

One warning: if you stay in India over 180 days, you must now obtain income tax clearance. That means that you should regularly change money at banks rather than on the black market in order to have a few encashment certificates to present to the income tax office. Most airlines mark their discounted tickets 'subject to income tax clearance'.

Flight Booking (Domestic)

If your travel itinerary is going to include domestic flights within India itself, then you'll probably be dealing with **Indian Airlines** (a quite separate body from Air India), which runs an extensive network of flights connecting most major towns and cities in the country. In general, it's wiser to book all your domestic flights from home, as booking within India can be time-consuming, but in practice, this is not always possible. The computerisation of Indian Airlines reservations in 1985 has, in theory, made bookings far easier to confirm. Many international airlines are now linked by computer to Indian Airlines and most reservations should be confirmed instantly from any part of the world. Reconfirm all your domestic flights, though, as soon as you land in India with the nearest Indian Airlines office. Failure to do so could well jeopardise your entire travel itinerary. This can be done either by using an established travel agent—in the major cities most travel agents have direct access to the Indian

Airlines computer system—or by going direct to one of the Indian Airlines offices listed in Getting Around, p.27.

Computerisation has, however, made Indian Airlines' cheap 'package' deals much more attractive than in the bad old days of double-booked seats and foiled reservation requests. The 'Discover India' ticket (US$400) offers 21 days' unlimited economy class travel on all domestic Indian Airline services); the 'Youth Fare' ticket (75% of normal fare) offers 120 days' unlimited travel, if you're under 30); the 'Tour India' ticket (US$300) offers 14 days, over any six sectors), or there's the 'Wonderfare' ticket (US$200 for 7 days, also over any 6 sectors of your choice in one of the 4 regions). There is also a 'South India Excursion' which gives a 30% discount on the US$ tariff for travel on specified south India sectors. With all these schemes, you are allowed to visit no airport more than once, except for the purpose of a connecting flight or when in transit.

A third airline, **Vayudoot**, was established in 1981 as a feeder airline providing links with smaller airfields and towns. Covering a number of destinations within India not served by Indian Airlines, there are also plans for Vayudoot to operate international charters and haj flights to Saudi Arabia. Ask your nearest travel agent or Government of India tourist office for details.

Delays of one to three hours on popular domestic flights still occur but not as frequently as before. Wise travellers always check the current flight situation (i.e. phone ahead to the airport) before leaving their hotel. **Indian Airlines' route map is located on p.26.**

Since 1990, a more liberalised government policy has allowed private airlines and charter services to be set up. At the time of writing, these new operations are still in their infancy. **East West Airlines** operates Boeing 737s from Bombay to Ahmedabad, Calicut, Cochin, Coimbatore, Mangalore and New Delhi. **Jagson's Airlines** links New Delhi with Kulu, Shimla and Dehra Dun. From Bangalore **UB Air** links Madras, Tirupati and Mangalore.

Travelling in Style

It is still possible to recapture the magic, majesty and magnificence of pre-Independence India—to laze indolently by luxury swimming-pools, to sip hot toddies on verandahs of colonial bungalows, to enjoy a relaxing round of golf or tennis before 'tiffin' (lunch), to go fishing and have your catch brought in for you, to gain entry to privileged clubs and societies, generally to have your every whim and wish catered for, even anticipated. India really knows how to pamper and cosset her rich foreign guests. When you need them, there are chauffeurs, guides, porters, bearers, dolis (sedan-chair carriers), punkah-wallahs (to cool your fevered brow), waiters, personal servants, massage-men, 'khansamahs' (cooks), and hopeful shoe-shine boys. It's a totally different side of India from that normally seen by the budget traveller. Your hotel will take care of all your travel arrangements, arrange your sightseeing, confirm your flights, provide you with a packed lunch, cater for your guests, introduce you to the right people, arrange for sports and cultural entertainments, and make introductions for you.

The social life of the wealthy Indian is much the same as that of his counterpart in Europe and America. If anything, even more so. Dress, manners and general etiquette matter, and in the big cities the nightlife is a whirlwind of social engagements, introductions, club activities, luncheons and supper parties. The food often doesn't arrive till after midnight. Before this, it's whisky all round (bottles of it) on empty stomachs. You will be expected to be widely informed on all matters political and economical, and to have strong opinions. Do not be upset by blunt, forthright questioning. To earn respect, you'll have to give as good as you get—and stay sober.

Packaged and Special Interest Holidays

Packaged holidays have come a long way in recent years. Sensitive to travellers' dislike of group living, many companies now organise tailor-made tours for the individual. They also specialise in certain areas of India such as the Golden Triangle, Rajasthan, Kerala, Goa, Pilgrim's Trail and the Himalaya. It's true that if you go on a package, however special, you don't have the flexibility of the solo traveller, and some people do not feel they have gained the flavour or the true atmosphere of India from air-conditioned buses and hotels. Nevertheless, if you have limited time, and perhaps a little extra cash, and if you don't cope well with the anxieties and sheer hard work that inevitably accompany the organisation of your own trip to India, such a deal is probably best for you—as a introduction to the country, at least.

Your nearest India Tourist Office will supply a comprehensive (unbiased) list of tour operators covering India from all countries. The companies given below offer specialist and tailor-made tours.

UK Tour Operators

Abercrombie & Kent Ltd, Sloane Square House, Holbein Place, London SW1W 8NS (tel 071-730 9600; fax 071-730 9376)

Bales Tours, Bales House, Junction Rd, Dorking, Surrey RH4 3HB (tel 0306 885923). Escorted tours (Himalayan, trekking, wildlife and top-market) from £735.

Butterfield's Tours, Burton Fleming, Driffield YO25 OPQ (tel 026 287 230). Adventure and train holidays.

Coromandel Tours, operated by Andrew Brock Travel Ltd, 10 Barley Mow Passage, London W4 4PH (tel 081-995 3642; fax 081-742 1066; tlx 94193369). Private car tours of Rajasthan and southern India of between 15 and 17 days £1604 to £1716.

Cox and Kings Travel Ltd, St James Court, Buckingham Gate, London SW1 (tel 071-931 9106; fax 071-630 6038; tlx 23378). Runs a popular range of tours, including Forts and Palaces of Rajputana (17 days, around £2000), 'Southern Trader'(18 days, around £2000) and 'Indian Experience'(9 days, around £1100). Wildlife and adventure tours are also available.

Cygnus Wildlife Holidays, 57 Fore St, Kingsbridge, Devon TQ7 1P6 (tel 0548 856178; fax 0548 857537). Bird-watching and wildlife holidays.

Dragoman Adventure Travel, Camp Green, Kenton Road, Debenham, Suffolk 1P14 6LA (tel 0728 861133; fax 0728 861127; tlx 987009 DRAGOM). Overland adventure trips.

Encounter Overland, 267 Old Brompton Road, London SW5 9JA (tel 071-370 6951; fax 071-244 9737). Adventure holidays, camel treks.

Equinox Travel, 12 Beauchamp Place, London SW3 1NQ (tel 071-584 2244; fax 071-225 3894). Fishing and boating trips, wildlife and trekking tours, festival holidays.

Exodus, 9 Weir Road, London SW12 OLT (tel 081-675 5550; fax 081-673 0779; tlx 8951700 EXODUS G). Walking and trekking holidays to unusual areas such as Garhwal, Bhutan and Sikkim.

Explor Asia Ltd, 13 Chapter St, London SW1 (tel 071-630 7102; fax 071-630 0355; tlx 266774 EXPLOR G). Wildlife safaris (e.g. Tigertops), Himalayan river-rafting, trekking, mountain-climbing, trout-fishing, etc., also walkabouts of Rajasthan, south India and Nepal. Marketing office for the Ladakh Sarai outside Leh, and for the Corbett Jungle Lodge outside the Corbett National Park.

Himalayan Kingdoms, 20 The Mall, Clifton, Bristol BS8 4DR (tel 0272 237163). In association with Abercrombie & Kent's Indian offices, organises treks and tours into the Himalayan areas and the neighbouring countries of Bhutan and Nepal.

Jasmin Tours, 23 High Street, Chalfont St Peter, Bucks SL9 9QE (tel 0753 889577; fax 0753 886678). Long-haul specialists; archaeology tours.

Journeys, High Holborn House, 52–54 High Holborn, London WC1V 6RL (tel 071-405 5099; fax 071-404 5023). A new company established in 1992 with offices in Bombay and New Delhi. Organises special interest tours and trips 'off the beaten track'.

Kuoni Travel Ltd, Kuoni House, Dorking, Surrey RH5 4AZ (tel 0306-740888; fax 0306 884609). Largest UK operator to India. Two options: top-bracket Kuoni Worldwide range (expensive); Kuoni 3 range (economy). Speciality is their 'Palaces of India' tour, 16 nights, £1298.

Naturetrek, Chautara, Bighton, Nr Alresford, Hants SO 24 9RB (tel 0962 733051; fax 0962 733368). Wildlife reserves and National Parks (e.g.19-day tour of the National Parks of southern India £2190, with extension to Andaman Islands £790.

Pettitt's India, 14 Lonsdale Gardens, Tunbridge Wells, Kent TN1 1NU (tel 0892-515966; fax 0892 515966). Good, cheap tailor-made holidays for the independent traveller.

Pleasureseekers, 52 Haymarket, London SW1 4RP (tel 071-930 3803; fax 071-930 6331). Customised holidays for the traveller who wishes to journey alone or with a single companion. Itineraries on and off the beaten track. An 11-day tour of 'Classical India', beginning and ending in Delhi, costs £579 per person, assuming two sharing a twin room. You can mix and match your own price-labelled component diversions and excursions. Prices are inclusive of guide, chauffeur-driven car (when journeys are too short for air travel), and breakfast.

Renaissance Cruises, 11 Quadrant Arcade, Regent Street, London W1R5PB (tel 071-287 9040; fax 071-434 1410). Quality yachts carrying 100 passengers.

Trailfinders Travel Centre, 42–50 Earls Court Rd, London W8 6EJ (tel 071-938 3366; fax 071-937 9294). A clearing-house for the best, most economical tours to India (and other countries), both luxury and budget. Will advise on the best current bets.

The Travel Alternative, 27 Park End Street, Oxford OX1 1HU (tel 0865 791636; fax 0865 791732; tlx 83201 BIZCOM G). Crafts and textile tours of northern India (about £2000 for 17 days; optional excursion into Gujarat).

Woodcock Travel, Worldways House, Park House Lane, Sheffield S9 1WY (tel 0742 561666; fax 0742 722700). Photography holidays.

US Tour Operators

Because British tours tend to be much cheaper, although not necessarily better than American tours, the US traveller would do well to send off for some UK brochures to compare prices before making a booking. Flying into London to connect with a UK tour could still make economic sense.

Abercrombie and Kent Int. Inc., 1520 Kensington Road, Oak Brook IL 60521 (tel 708 954 4758).

Adventure Center, 1311 63rd Stret, Suite 200, Emeryville, CA 94608 (tel 510 654 1879; fax 510 654 4200). Provides a general 'round-the-world itinerary' service, and can advise on tours at the most favourable current rates.

InnerAsia Expeditions Inc., 2627 Lombard St, San Francisco 94123 (tel 415-922 0448; fax 415-346 5535; tlx 278716 TIGER UR).

Journeyworld International Ltd, 19 West 57th Street, New York, NY 10019 (tel 212 752 8308).

Mountain Travel-SOBEK, 6420 Fairmount Avenue, El Cerrito, CA 94530 (tel 510 527 8100; fax 510 525 7710).

Tours of Distinction, Room 706, 141 East 44th Street, New York, NY 10017 (tel 212 661 4680).

Passports and Visas

Make sure you have a full passport (a temporary or visitor's passport won't do for India), and that it has enough spare pages to take a visa stamp, an immigration stamp, and any liquor permit stamps, issued in 'dry' or non-alcoholic Indian states, which you may collect in the course of your journey. Also, check that your passport is up-to-date. If it isn't, you'll need to send it off for renewal a good two months before your holiday.

At the time of writing, all foreign nationals require a visa to enter India. There are several kinds of visa: the standard tourist visa is valid for 180 days and entitles the holder to multiple entries into India within that period. An extension can be obtained from various Foreigners' Registration offices in India. Visas can be applied for from any Indian consular office or High Commission. In the UK, a six-month multiple entry visa costs £16.00. A single entry visa, valid for 30 days from the date of issue, costs £3.00. In the US and other countries, it has been standardised to US$5.00.

In the UK, apply for visas to the High Commission of India, Consular Dept, India House, Aldwych, London WC2B 4NA (tel 071-836 8484/0990, 9.30 am to 1.00 pm; 071-240 2084, 2.00 pm to 5.30 pm). Application forms are available either from the High Commission or from the Government of India Tourist Office, 7 Cork St, London W1 (tel 071-437 3677/8; fax 071-494 1048). You can apply either by post, which can take up to four weeks to process (send passport, three passport photos and crossed postal order to 'High Commission of India'); or in person, which takes just 24 hours (arrive with passport, three passport-size photos and an application form at the High Commission building, 9 am latest, to avoid queues. It's open 9.30 am to 1.00 pm weekdays, and you'll have to return the next working day to collect passport and visa between 4.30 and 5.30 pm). Trailfinders, Thomas Cook and American Express have quick, efficient visa services for travellers, and for a small charge, will do all the waiting and queuing for you.

US visitors can use the Embassy of India, 2107 Massachusetts Avenue NW, Washington, DC 20008 (tel 202 939 7000/7069) or the Consulate-General of India, 3 East 64th Street, New York, NY 10021 (tel 212 879 7888). There are also consular offices in San Francisco, Chicago and Houston. **Canadians** should apply to 10 Springfield Road, Ottawa, KIM 109 (tel 744 3751). **French** visitors can apply to the Ambassade de l'Inde, 15 Rue Alfred Dehodencq, 75016 Paris (tel 4520 3930). **Germans** to Adenaverallee 262, 5300 Bonn (tel 540 50). **Australians** go to the consular office at 3–5 Moonah Place, Yarralumla, ACT 2600 (tel 062 733 999).

The Foreigners' Regional Registration Offices are based in **Bombay** (Annexe-2, Police Headquarters, Near Crawford Market, tel 2611169); **Calcutta** (237 Acharya Jagdish Bose Road, tel 443301, 440549); **Madras** (9 Village Road, Nungambakkam, tel 477036); and **New Delhi** (Hans Bhavan, Tilak Bridge, tel 3319489). Elsewhere all superintendents of police in all district headquarters also function as Foreigners' Registration Officers.

Medical Matters

You will need a course of vaccinations and a supply of malaria tablets for India. They are not essential requirements for entering the country, but are very strongly recommended. While sanitation and hygiene in India remain at their current levels, it's wise to take every possible precaution against ill-health.

Vaccinations
You'll need protection against typhoid, tetanus, polio, hepatitis and, if you intend to spend some time in Delhi, meningitis. The cholera vaccine is now considered ineffective against the strains prevalent in India. Diseases like malaria and hepatitis, which are both very easily contracted, can not only make your life a misery while you are abroad, but may also remain with you for the rest of your life.

In the UK, you can either make an appointment to see your local GP or use a local vaccinating centre. Your GP is likely to be the cheapest option, but make sure you leave yourself enough time. London has several quick and efficient drop-in centres: West London Vaccinating Centre at 53 Gt Cumberland Place, London W1H 7LH (tel 071-262 6456), open from 9.00 am to 4.45 pm; the London Hospital for Tropical Diseases, 4 St Pancras Way, London NW1 (tel 071-637 9899); Trailfinders, 194 Kensington High Street, London W8 7RG (tel 071-938 3939); Thomas Cook, 45 Berkeley St, London W1 (tel 071-408 4157); British Airways Travel Clinic, 156 Regent St, London W1 (tel 071-439 9584), open from 9.00 am to 4.15 pm daily, 10.00 am to 12.30 pm and 2.00 pm to 4.00 pm Saturdays. Expect to pay up to £40 for a full course of injections at a commercial travel clinic.

Vaccinations are best administered about two weeks before departure. This gives them time to take full effect (typhoid immunity takes 10 days to settle in properly), and allows you to get over any unpleasant side-effects before you travel. The commonly used vaccine against hepatitis A, gamma globulin, remains at peak strength for only a few weeks, so take it as close to departure as possible. If you are intending to stay in India for 6 months or longer, you might want to consider the newer, more expensive vaccine, which affords protection for up to a year. For frequent travellers, there is now a course which immunises you for life.

Malaria Tablets
You will need both the daily and weekly varieties of tablets. Start taking them 10 days before you leave for India. This gives you a chance to change them if the ones prescribed by the clinic or your GP don't agree with you; and it also allows your body to start building up some immunity before you arrive. Continue taking them for 6 weeks after returning home. Malarial parasites are extraordinarily resilient and many varieties are now found in India. Unfortunately, resistance to the currently

available drugs is now widespread, but this does not mean that you should not bother taking them; rather, equip yourself with a mosquito net (if you intend to spend a great deal of time out of doors), some coils (to burn in hotel rooms), and a good repellent such as **Jungle Formula**, to give you double protection.

Once you've seen the doctor, see your **dentist**. Ask for spare caps, plus glue kit, for any teeth presently capped. While dental treatment in the major cities is of a high standard and not expensive, facilities outside the major cities are often more basic.

Contact-lens wearers should seriously consider switching to specs for India, because of dust, heat, intense glare, etc. **Spectacle-wearers** should note down their prescription. Opticians in India are cheap, and the cost of prescription lenses and frames is often a fraction of the UK equivalent.

AIDS

AIDS in India is much more prevalent than is officially accepted. The problem is not confined to the 'red-light' areas of the major towns but is possibly spread throughout the country. Anyone seeking a working or student visa for more than one year must take an AIDS test and submit a copy of the certificate verifying a negative result along with the visa application.

Travel and Medical Insurance

You don't have to believe everything you hear about theft and illness in India, but you can't afford to ignore it either. Good travel insurance is essential for your peace of mind, and has saved many travellers a lot of heartache. Take great care when choosing your policy, and always read the small print. A good travel insurance should give full cover of your possessions and health. In case of illness, it should provide for all medical costs, hospital benefits, permanent disabilities and the flight home. In case of theft or loss, it should recompense you for lost luggage, money and valuables, also for travel delay and personal liability. Most important (and this could be a life-saver) it should provide you with a 24-hour contact number in the event of medical emergencies.

If your own bank or insurance company hasn't an adequate travel insurance scheme (they usually have), then try the comprehensive schemes offered by **Trail-finders** (tel 071-938 3939) or **Jardine's** (tel 061-228 3742), or the Centurion Assistance policy (linked to Europ Assistance) offered by **American Express** (tel 0444 239900). Travel companies often include insurance in the cost of a luxury tour, but this is not always adequate. Indian Airlines normally take responsibility for domestic flight delays or cancellations, and recompense travellers (eventually) for any inconvenience caused.

Whichever insurance you buy, take a copy of the policy with you to India. Most important, keep a separate note of the 24-hour emergency number.

Should anything be stolen a copy of the police report or FIR (First Information Report) should be asked for and retained. This is especially important if an item on a TBRE (Tourist Baggage Re-Export Form), issued by customs on entering the country, has been lost or stolen. A copy of the police report may also be required by your insurance company when making a claim.

Money and Travellers' Cheques

The important thing to remember is that you cannot take rupees into (or out of) India; you have to buy them there. Travellers' cheques and currency should be ordered from your bank or travel agency at least 7 days before departure. Some places, like Trailfinders, can process money and travellers' cheques in a couple of days, but they take only cash, not cheques. When ordering your currency for India, aim for a 50:50 split between travellers' cheques and pounds/US dollars. This kind of balance is best, because both forms of currencies are equally useful, and travellers' cheques can be refunded if lost or stolen. American Express travellers' cheques are the best bet, because they have a pristine reputation for swift, efficient refunding in the event of loss. This is very important. It is a common misconception that if you have travellers' cheques and lose them, they will be refunded immediately. But some banks only refund them when you return home (useless), while others don't offer any refunding facilities at all.

American Express have five solid refunding agents: in Delhi (Wenger House, Connaught Place, tel 3324119/3322868); Madras (Binny Limited, 65 Armenian Street, tel 840803, 845407); Bombay (Regal Cinema Building, Chatrapati Shivaji Road, Colaba, tel 2048291, 2851820); Calcutta (21 Old Court House Street, tel 289471, 282134); and Srinagar (Kai Travels Private Ltd, Tara Bhavan Place Blvd 2, tel 74366, 75373, 74180).

Thomas Cook has offices in Bangalore (55 MG Road, tel 566342); Bombay (Dr Dadabhai Naoroji Road, tel 2048556/8); Calcutta (12-B/1 Park Street, tel 298862); Hyderabad (Nasir Arcade, 6-1-57 Saifabad, tel 231988); Madras (112 Nungambakkam High Road, tel 473092 and 20 Rajaji Road, tel 589994, 534976); New Delhi (Hotel Imperial, Janpath, tel 3327135, 3322171 and 104/5 Bajaj House, 97 Nehru Place, tel 6419000, 6423035); and Pune (Thackers House, Shop No. 13, 2418 Gen Thimmaya Road, tel 667187/8, 667175).

If you order cheques from a bank, do choose one whose insurer gives you (in writing) the addresses of the refunding agents in India. Sign your travellers' cheques immediately on receipt. Then take a separate note of the cheque numbers to facilitate their refund in the event of theft.

How much you take is up to you, but don't leave yourself short. Having money sent over to you in India can be a very slow, awkward business. To be on the safe side, take all your credit cards with you. Most large hotels, restaurants, shops (and Indian Airlines) accept them, and you'll be surprised how long the bills take to get home to you. Some of the grander Indian hotels seem almost disappointed when you decide to pay cash.

A month spent in India can cost anything between Rs12 000 (on a shoestring) and Rs150 000 (all the luxury trimmings), exclusive of any shopping purchases. In the summer of '92 there were Rs55 to the pound and Rs29 to the dollar. Travelling in mid-range comfort, budget for around Rs30 000 a month. This includes eating and sleeping at good, moderate restaurants and hotels, travelling 2nd class by rail and bus, and all in-town taxi/rickshaw/bus transport. Make extra allowances for the inevitable shopping expeditions. For 'irresistible' bargains, carry a couple of personal credit cards. In India the American Express card justifies its additional expense by enabling you to raise cash readily from Amex offices, gets you into hotels if you've just lost all your money), and lets you use their mail-receiving facilities.

What to Pack

What to take and how to take it are prime considerations. Essentially, there are two kinds of traveller in India: those who can afford to have their bags carried around for them (hotel staff will always be pleased to help for a modest gratuity); and those who can't. But even if you are travelling in style, you'll want to take the most practical luggage possible. Unwieldy, insecure baggage has a habit of breaking open, or being broken into, at airports, stations or anywhere where there are jostling crowds. For the budget traveller, the priority is comfort and security. Travelling with your 'home' on your back or in your hands, you'll want to take as little as possible, in bags that are both easy to carry and relatively thief-proof. Don't give them to anyone else to carry. Indian porters are all right, but on the streets, and in buses and trains, never ever let them out of your sight.

Luggage

The best all-round choice is a good, strong shoulder-bag—a big one with lots of zipped compartments and an adjustable shoulder-strap. Samsonite and Globetrotter both do a very good range. If the bag isn't sold with a combination lock, buy one yourself (and a spare). Set the lock to a number you will remember, and keep a note of the number on a security list in case you forget it.

For backpackers, an internal-framed rucksack, with a top carrying handle and numerous pockets is most suitable. Backpacks are good because they leave the hands free (very useful for barging onto crowded trains and buses) and they give a lot of mobility to anyone expecting a lot of rough travelling. But they are easily cut into by would-be thieves and are not always socially acceptable. Rucksacks are commonly associated with 'hippies', whom many Indians regard as a breed apart, some kind of foreign 'untouchables'. Lastly, railway retiring rooms, a favourite repository for budget travellers, often won't store rucksacks without a lock. And how do you lock a rucksack?

Suitcases are a poor choice, unless you're travelling on business. They are bulky, uncomfortable to carry and, if soft-framed, easily broken into by dishonest baggage handlers. If you must take one, get the hard-framed variety, with a set of wheels.

Try to pack everything into one bag; you can always buy another one in India to hold any purchases. Second, leave your main bag underpacked so that you leave room for any airport purchases and for the inevitable 'spreading' of used clothes. Third, buy a small night-bag—one that will fold easily into the main bag—with a shoulder-strap, to take with you onto the plane. To conform with Indian Airlines' cabin-luggage regulations, this should measure no more than 45 ins (calculated by adding width to length to depth) and weigh no more than 11 lbs (5 kg). You'll find it not only useful on the plane to hold duty-free alcohol and tobacco, newspapers, camera film, etc., but also very handy as a day–bag later on, for side trips, picnics and outings in India.

Finally, be sure to label all bags.

Packing List

Make this up well in advance. It will give you peace of mind and it will greatly assist any insurance claims you may have to make for lost luggage. Make two copies, and leave one at home in a safe place. A good packing list can be used again and again (with amendments) for all future holidays abroad.

Keep the list short. Certain items like toiletries, sun-cream (particularly high-factor protection), radios, and personal medicines you'll have to include, because they're expensive or your brand may be unobtainable in India. Many other things, especially clothes, you can buy out there easily and at little cost.

Clothes

Indians go a lot by appearances, and it's very much a case of you are what you wear. This does not mean you have to dress ultra-chic or smart, simply that you should wear sensible, comfortable clothes and dress with a view to what is acceptable and appropriate in the circumstances.

Indian people do not smile upon hippy clothes (ragged old jeans, dirty old shirts, beads and headbands) and consider Western women's dress (short skirts, sleeveless and backless shirts, and cut-off trousers) both shameless and, in the case of Indian men, a big come-on. Long hair and drug-taking aren't likely to win you any medals either. You may get away with skimpy Western-style dress in some of the big cities, especially liberal Bombay, but in most of the country, notably in the deep south and in Rajasthan, old customs die hard and you may cause a lot of offence if you're not properly covered. When visiting a temple, *gurudwara* or mosque, it is important to be sensitive to the feelings of the regular worshippers and dress accordingly. Women should avoid baring their shoulders and arms, or wearing skirts that are too short. In gurudwaras, it is important for both men and women to cover their head: a clean handkerchief will usually do.

Cool, clean cotton garments which cover the chest, back and legs are the most acceptable wear in India. They are also extremely comfortable and very cheap to buy. Many towns have good street tailors who will make up clothes to your precise requirements both quickly and cheaply. For about Rs250 you can have a complete silk/cotton suit made up out there (*kurta* shirt and pajama for men; *salwar kameez* dresses or traditional saris for women), and you'll automatically escape half the unwanted attention experienced by travellers wearing normal Western dress. Experienced Indo-philes have two such suits made up—one to wear while the other is being laundered by a *dhobi*.

The larger cities often have a good range of export surplus or seconds of locally made clothes available in the local markets.

The few clothes you'll need to bring with you should be durable, comfortable and above all practical. A lightweight zipper **jacket**, with large, deep front pockets to accommodate passport and documents while in transit, is indispensable. Take a couple of cotton **shirts**, again with large breast pockets if possible. These are practical wear when it becomes too warm to wear the jacket. Two pairs of light, loose-fitting cotton **trousers** will be sufficient. They should have pockets secured by zips or velcro, and loops for a belt: you'll be amazed at how many inches drop off the waist and buttocks travelling in India). Jeans are bulky, hot and not always practical. **Shorts** are generally okay for men but, outside the smarter international hotel areas of the big cities, unacceptable for women.

A few **T-shirts** are a must. They are cool and comfortable, take up little room, and make an ideal quick change of shirt. They can also double as substitute pillow-cases in hotels or on overnight train or bus journeys.

15

If you are considering spending any time in the desert overnight, some thermal underwear is very useful: it may be extremely hot during the day, but the temperatures plummet at night.

For **underwear,** men should consider a few pairs of boxer-shorts. They provide better ventilation than jockey-style underpants, which means less risk of '*dhobi* itch'. They also make acceptable swimming trunks. Women may find that flimsy cotton underwear suffers rude treatment from enthusiastic dhobis. Some of it won't come back at all.

You'll need a few pairs of cotton **socks**—notably for visits to temples or mosques, where you have to take your shoes off (dancing around on white-hot holy ground in bare feet may be great entertainment for the locals, but you won't enjoy it). Socks are also useful for smart evening wear, or to ease in new pairs of sandals.

Take a pair of light casual **shoes** such as trainers plus a pair of sandals for hot places or the beach. Rubber flip-flops, which all the Indians wear, are sold everywhere. Women will also need a pair of decent shoes for evening wear. When selecting footwear for your journey, remember that feet tend to swell in hot climates, so choose a pair with wide fittings. Most travellers, however, buy their footwear in India itself: there's a great selection available.

Hotels are fairly liberal when it comes to **beachwear,** as are the more popular beaches such as Goa, and Westerners can get away with wearing few if any clothes. However, in other areas this is likely to attract attention and be insensitive to local custom. Men can usually get away with a pair of trunks or shorts; women should wear a one-piece suit.

You will need some warm clothing: a single medium-thickness sweater will be adequate for most occasions, including draughty train journeys, cool desert evenings, chilly hill stations, or (a big consideration) padding for bone-hard bus and train seats.

Unless you're going on business, a suit is not advisable. They are bulky and rarely travel well. If you must, select one that won't show up the dirt and remember to put a rumple-free tie or black bow tie in one of the pockets.

Everyone should consider taking a **hat** to protect the head, neck and face from the sun. The wide-brimmed floppy cotton variety, with string cord, is most suitable. In the south, a very practical alternative is a ladies'**umbrella**. You can buy these just as easily out there. A decent pair of **sunglasses** is also essential.

Equipment

The most vital piece of equipment is a **water-bottle**. In a country where uncontaminated drinking water is scarce, although bottled mineral water is now widely available, a guaranteed supply of sterilised water from a clean container is essential. Unless you're heading out to desert regions, in which case the large 2-litre size is a good investment, the standard 1-litre flask will be adequate. The 'thermal' model is the best because it keeps water fresh and cool, even in the most torrid external temperatures.

For personal security, you'll need either a **money-belt** or a zipped document-holder. A body-belt can be bulky, uncomfortable to wear, and surprisingly vulnerable to theft. Far better to buy a cotton neck-purse (from a camping shop) or a transparent document holder with zip (from stationery shops), and sew an elasticated armband into it. The pouch should be large enough to hold your passport, plane tickets, credit cards, currency and travellers' cheques, and should fit snugly out of sight round the upper arm. Nobody should underestimate the skill and enterprise of pickpockets. For your own peace of mind, carry your vital documents on your person at all times. If staying in budget lodges, get into the habit of sleeping with your security pouch nestling in the safe embrace of your armpit.

Another important security item to take is a strong **combination padlock**, hard to come by in India and useful in many different situations. Its mere presence deflects potential thieves from your luggage, and you can use them to bolt bags or rucksacks to train bunks, to hotel-room furniture, or to bus seats. Padlocks also give added security when fixed to the doors of cheaper lodges which either have poor locks, or no locks at all. If taking small ordinary locks for securing rucksack pockets, take two sets of keys.

A small powerful **flashlight**, together with spare bulb and a stock of batteries, is a worthwhile investment. In desert or village areas, there is often no electricity at night. And few places in India are exempt from power-cuts. A useful back-up to a flashlight is one of the squat 'everlasting' candles sold in many camping shops. Voltage in India is 220 (occasionally 230), and if you take a **travelling iron**, an **electric shaver**, or **hairdryer**, you'll need the appropriate **adaptor**.

Other useful inclusions are a **universal plug** because cheaper Indian hotels rarely have plugs in their wash-hand basins, a small **penknife** for peeling fruit, a cheap, tough **alarm watch** for catching those elusive early-morning trains and buses, a box of waxed earplugs to halve the initial shock of Indian traffic and double the chance of a good night's sleep, some **writing materials** (many Indian travellers become prolific diarists), and a small sewing kit, complete with scissors, buttons, thread, zips and needles. If you're off to the beaches, a **face-mask** and a **snorkel** come in handy.

Medical Kit

Apart from regular toiletries, this should include some **sterile gauze pads** (better than Band-aids), a good **moisturising cream**, some flat packs of **toilet paper** (rolls are too bulky) and a supply of **multi-vitamin tablets** (important in a country where one's diet tends to suffer). **Medical wipes** are also useful for keeping hands and equipment clean when washing facilities are not available.

Other useful inclusions are: **water-purification tablets**, to sterilise all drinking water; a small bottle of **antiseptic** liquid, for throat or mouth infections from which many Westerners tend to suffer in India (try Oraldene); and **zinc-based ointment** for fungal skin infections and below-the-belt 'dhobi itch'.

There is no medical 'cure' for diarrhoea, and you're probably best applying the traditional natural remedy (a rigid diet of tea, rice, bananas, papaya, bread and curd) and allowing the body to cleanse itself in one to three days. If, however, you've got a long bus or train journey ahead, this may not be practical. For emergencies like this, get your doctor to prescribe a small supply of suitable tablets, which will provide effective temporary relief. Sunstroke, vomiting and dysentery are all common causes of dehydration and loss of body salts. To combat this, take a few packets of **dioralyte rehydrate powder**. This is readily available in India too.

Take a good **mosquito repellent** such as Jungle Formula for protection in the daytime, the Indian-brand Odomos is good. Treat bites with soothing **antihistamine** cream, or try using toothpaste. A **mosquito net** is also worth considering: they fold up small and save a great deal of anguish. Even if you have a good net, shake it out well before retiring each night. Mosquitoes have an uncanny knack of climbing into bed with you, either buried in the net or in trouser cuffs.

Finally, take an additional supply of **contraceptive, malaria and vitamin tablets**. It's easy to run short after bouts of sickness and vomiting. To prevent such complaints, avoid drinking local water (even filtered or purified) for the first couple of days. Many travellers drink one of the many brands of purified and mineral water now available in most towns and adjust to local food and water very slowly.

Personal Luxuries

Always leave space in your luggage for a few personal luxuries: they can make all the difference to your holiday. A small pocket **cassette-recorder** and a collection of tapes can help break the monotony of long train and bus journeys, and you can also tape any good Indian music recitals or dance shows. A **light-weight shortwave radio** can also provide a respite from Indian music, which is often loud, insistent and blares from many street microphones. Cassettes of many popular Western groups and singers, along with a broad range of jazz and western classical music, are now available in all major towns and at remarkably cheap prices. Only a few CDs are available.

Another popular 'luxury' is a small, versatile and light automatic **camera**. India is an extremely photogenic country, full of varied and interesting sights and scenery.

For those who enjoy wildlife- or bird-spotting, a pair of miniature or full-size **binoculars** is recommended. Others, who fret in long queues (lots of these in India) or who like something to do on long, dull evenings (very few of these), take along a couple of **pocket-games** like chess, backgammon, pocket-scrabble or playing cards. Budget travellers, who are going to be sleeping in places with little or no bedding, or on beaches, take along a **sleeping bag**. This is a bulky addition to one's luggage, but there are excellent lightweight (1-kg) pure down bags available, which take up surprisingly little space. If heading up to cool, often damp, areas like the hill stations, a sleeping bag may even be a necessity. The place to sell them at a profit later on, if headed that way, is Kathmandu or Pokhara in Nepal.

Regular budget travellers to India opt instead for a **sheet sleeping bag**. This is a sewn double sheet, similar to those found in Youth Hostels, which you can either make yourself or buy in Bombay or other main centres. It is useful on overnight train journeys or when staying in forest department lodges; it is also much cooler than a regular sleeping bag, and takes up even less room in your luggage.

One luxury every traveller in India should allow himself is a small inflatable **pillow**. It guarantees you a comfortable night's sleep anywhere, even on bumpy buses and trains. Seasoned travellers prefer a down-and-feather pillow, and spend the bulk of their stay in India just sitting on it—bus, train, cinema and restaurant seats in this country are notoriously hard.

Souvenirs and Presents

A small stock of these can greatly smooth your journey. When you want to express your thanks to a good guide or driver, to a helpful hotelier, or to a kind Indian family, a small token of your appreciation is not only good manners but often elicits surprising offers of further help.

Duty-free whisky and cigarettes, spare camera film, cigarette lighters and bars of perfumed soaps are all good upmarket gifts. Popular with hotel staff, guides, porters and children are cheap pens, sweets, small-denomination English or American coins and postcards of the Royal Family.

Address List

India is a country you will dearly wish to share with friends and relatives back home, and an address list is better than a regular address book: it can be stashed away in your security pouch and is far less easily lost. Make a couple of copies of the list and keep them in separate places.

To enable people to write to you while you're in India, leave them the address of the *poste restante* in the capital you're making your base. If using an American Express card or their travellers' cheques, you can use the addresses of their offices in India as a *poste restante*.

Security List

This may be the last thing you get round to doing before you go, but it is the most important. If you lose all your vital documents in India, or have them stolen, you could be in big trouble. A comprehensive personal security list should detail:

a) your **name, address and telephone number;**

b) **person to contact,** in the event of accident or death (name, address, telephone number);

c) name, number and value of all travellers' cheques, plus details of **refunding agents** in India (helps with claims in case of theft);

d) number, date and place of issue of your **passport;**

e) numbers and issue dates of all international and domestic **flight tickets;**

f) 24-hour emergency number of your **medical insurance** and **credit cards** (plus policy and card issue numbers);

g) serial numbers of your **camera, binoculars and radio, prescription details for spectacles** and **personal medicines** (you'll need the generic title);

h) finally, since it is the Consular Department—not the Embassy—which is responsible for the welfare of travellers abroad, you'll need to take a note of the nearest **consular office** to your destination in India (e.g. for UK travellers, there are British High Commissions at New Delhi (Chanakyapuri, New Delhi, 110021, tel 601371); Bombay (Hong Kong Bank Building, Mahatma Gandhi Road, PO Box 815, Bombay 400023, tel 274874); Calcutta (1 Ho Chi Minh Sarani, Calcutta 700071, tel 445171/2) and Madras (24 Anderson Road, Madras 600006, tel 473136).

Once you've completed your security list, make one copy to leave at home and put the original in your document holder. Keep it on you at all times. Alternatively, many Indian hotels have safe-deposit boxes, and supply a receipt for anything left in their care.

19

Background Reading

The best general preparation for a trip to India is to read as much about her history, society, culture and religion as possible.

In the UK, there are a few bookshops which specialise in Indian literature:

Books from India, 45 Museum St, London WC1 (tel 071-405 7226).

The Travel Bookshop Ltd, 13 Blenheim Crescent, London W11 2EE (tel 071-229 5260). Also, an excellent programme of talks and events, and a useful noticeboard.

Trailfinders, 194 Kensington High Street, London W8 7RG (tel 071-938 3939), and for people booking flights through them, a marvellous library.

Daunt Books, 83 Marylebone High Street, London W1M 4AL (tel 071-224 2295), where a wide range of fiction and non-fiction titles are grouped according to their country or place of association.

Travellers' Bookstore, 25 Cecil Court, London WC2 (tel 071-836 9132).

Stanfords, 12–14 Long Acre, London WC2E 9LP (tel 071-836 1321) London's huge specialist store for maps and guides.

In the US travellers have recommended:

Pilot Books, 347 Fifth Avenue, New York, NY 10016, who produce their own list of travel books.

Tourist Information

For general literature—brochures, maps, hotel and festival lists, air/rail timetables etc., visit your nearest **Government of India Tourist Office**. Main offices are:

UK: 7 Cork St, London W1 2AB (tel 071-437 3677/8)

USA: 30 Rockefeller Plaza, Room 15, North Mezzanine, New York, NY 10020 (tel 212 586 4901) or 3550 Wilshire Boulevard, Suite 204, Los Angeles, CA 90010 (tel 213 380 8855)

France: 8 Boulevard de la Madeleine, 75009 Paris 9 (tel 42 65 83 86/77 06)

Australia: Level 1, 17 Castereagh Street, Sydney, NSW 2000 (tel 02 232 1600)

Canada: 60 Bloor St (West), Suite No.1003, Ontario M4W 3B8 (tel 416 962 3787)

Japan: Pearl Building, 9–18 Ginza, 7 Chome, Chuo–Ku, Tokyo 104 (tel 03 571 5062/63).

Maps

The best general map of the Indian subcontinent is still Bartholomew's one-page Travel Map (No. 15 in the series)—if nothing else, it gives you an idea of the sheer size of the country. Good maps of major Indian cities are sold by **Stanfords** (see above). **Books from India** (also listed above) stocks a useful compendium of 60 Indian city maps called *The City Atlas of India* (Tamilnad Printers Pvt Ltd, 1985), and the more comprehensive *An Atlas of India* (New Delhi, Oxford University Press, 1991).

On Arrival

Charminar Gate, Hyderabad

Customs and Currency Regulations

Coming into India, you're allowed the usual duty-free bottle of wine or spirits (0.95 litre) and 200 cigarettes. If you land in Delhi, these re-sell on the black market for twice what you paid for them, and touts hover hopefully just outside the airport exit. At other airports, don't bother. If you bring more than US$1000 into the country, in cash or travellers' cheques, you are required to fill out a currency declaration form. It's all right to bring in gadgets like radios, Walkmans, calculators, cameras, etc., but some people do get stopped at customs and are required to register them on a 'Tourist Baggage Re-Export' form to ensure that they take them back out of the country.

When changing money, **keep your encashment receipts**. These are required when you exchange spare rupees when you leave the country—as proof that the cash you are removing is your own—and when you pay the hotel bill, purchase an airline ticket or tour, or make any large purchase from a government emporium. If you stay in India for 180 days or more, you also have to obtain income tax clearance, for which encashment certificates are required. The Foreign Section of the Income Tax Offices in Delhi, Bombay, Calcutta and Madras issue these certificates on sight of passport, airline ticket, visa and encashment certificates.

21

Orientation

First impressions of India are often extreme. Wherever you decide to land, give yourself at least three days to get used to the heat, noise and crowds. The first couple of days are when tourists are the most susceptible to health, security and money problems, largely because they are too numbed and stunned to take proper care of themselves. This is when they are at the mercy of streetwise entrepreneurs. The important thing is to keep plugging away, to pass through the initial bombardment of touts, beggars, postcard-sellers, and rickshaw-drivers, and to develop the street knowledge necessary to enjoy India. There's so much going on, so much to absorb, that this has to be a fairly rapid process. After just one day, you'll feel like you've been here a week.

What is really strange about India is that all the frantic traffic, hurrying crowds, and feverish atmosphere is just an illusion. In reality, everything is incredibly slow. A good example is queues. Indians have an inordinate fondness for queues, and any two people waiting for something in one spot constitutes a queue. For example, you may think, looking at the eager hordes of people gathered round a cinema ticket office window, that their only aim is to get in and out as soon as possible. But then you get in that queue, and nothing happens. It appears to be moving forward in great haste, but in fact it's not moving at all. That's because there are probably 20 hands jammed under the ticket window, and the vendor can't make up his mind whom to serve first. So he isn't serving anybody. An hour or two later, just as you've fought and elbowed your way to the window yourself, he may well close up for lunch. All you can do is smile, and make sure you're the first one in the queue in the afternoon.

The two things you'll need above all else are humour and patience. There's no point in losing either here. The more angry you get, the less you'll get done. There are times, as when in a tide of people fighting for a couple of remaining seats on a bus, you'll have to go into battle like a Viking, sweeping all before you with your luggage. It takes time, though, to know when to stop and when to go. India must be about the only country in the world where it is accepted custom to both wait and push at the same time.

The simplest and best way of understanding the country, and of settling into it comfortably, is to make some Indian friends. This should be easy. The Indian people are very outgoing and curious. And Hinduism is based upon toleration of other races, cultures and creeds. India is also used to foreigners, having spent much of her history accommodating them.

The Indian View of the West

Indians are very eager to find out about Western culture. Just a few years ago there were only 40 000 television sets in the whole of India. Today the figure is over 10 million. With the advent of satellite broadcasting out of Hong Kong, hundreds of thousands of homes throughout the country can now watch BBC World Service Television or Star TV entertainment and sports channels 24 hours a day.

There's also been an influx of Japanese cars, American technology, Michael Jackson T-shirts, and in 1993, the return of Coca-Cola. The largest growth area for low-cost consumer items is in fact the huge rural community, as the recession affects the large middle class and urban population dependent on fixed wages and salaries. This produces an interesting situation. Many Western tourists visit India out of a fascination with the country's 'spirituality'. Yet many Indians themselves, especially the urbanised younger generation, are just as fascinated by Western materialism. A widely held belief is that all foreign visitors are well off. It doesn't matter if you're living here on the tightest budget; you have come from a part of the world that is rich by Indian standards, and you have certainly been able to afford the fare over here. You are therefore fair game for touts, salesmen and beggars.

Being stared at can be just as disconcerting to new foreign arrivals as being continually approached for money. Western notions of social distance and personal privacy don't exist here, and you'll almost certainly never be alone. Wherever you go you will be asked your name, where you come from, what you do, and (if you're female) whether you are married. These questions are aimed at placing you in their caste structure, and while some travellers find this intrusive and irritating, no offence is intended.

The best way of dealing with it is to ask a lot of questions back. Preferably in Hindi. Good ones are 'aap ka shubh naam?' (what is your name?), 'aap kaise hein?' (how are you?) and 'kya yeh sambhav hein?' (is it possible?). Essential responses are 'dhanyavad' (thank you) and 'meera naam——hein' (my name is——). A little local language, combined with an attitude of unruffled calm and friendliness, opens all sorts of doors. Suddenly, many of those things described to you as 'not possible' become very possible indeed.

Sometimes though, you just won't be in the mood for company. First, try ignoring it. If this doesn't work, 'chale jao' (pronounced 'chelay') means 'go away'. If this doesn't work, and you've still got a dancing silk emporium salesman on your hands, then you've got to steel yourself to walk right through him—sometimes right over him.

Asking Directions

There is no room for ambiguity or indecision in India. The first thing to learn is to make up your mind. Standing around looking lost or helpless, getting involved in complicated arguments or asking open-ended, woolly questions are all invitations to disaster. Indians are very polite people. If you ask them, 'Is this the way to Netaji Subhash Road?', they'll invariably reply 'yes', even when it isn't. They're not being awkward: saying 'no' would just be impolite. You must say, 'I want Netaji Subhash Road'. This compels a decent set of directions, or a (very) reluctant 'I don't know'. Don't be confused when a straightforward question evokes an apparently negative waggle of the head from side to side. This means 'okay' or 'this is possible'. It is affirmative, not negative. The word 'acha' means 'okay' too, and you'll hear it used everywhere, but sometimes it means 'yes—we have no bananas'. Complicated? Well yes, but this is India.

The solution is to decide in advance exactly what you want, and then to ask for it precisely and clearly. The fewer words you use, the better. By the same token, if you don't want something, just say 'nahin' (no) and stroll on.

The need for orientation to India has always been understated. My father, who visited Bombay in 1945 as part of the British armed forces, received the following circular:

Avoid exposure of your head to sun before 4 pm, eating over-ripe fruit or fruits not protected by skin; drinking water from street fountains or soft drinks from marble-stoppered bottles, walking barefooted, shouting or bullying, patronising beggars, mendicants, fortune-tellers and curio dealers, fraternising with low class people. Do not give alms to beggars, some of them are diseased.

The general intention was not to orientate, but to disorientate, the visiting soldier. Insulated from the country and its people, he never established any real relationship with it. The same could be said of tourists who hide in large hotels, who venture onto the streets only under duress, who fear contamination by the ugliness of India; they will never see its beauty, its poetry or its latent charm. In general, the more you face the country head-on and the less you rely on Western luxuries and reminders, the better your trip will be. Endurance gives way to enjoyment, and it is then, quite unexpectedly, that the real India reveals herself.

GETTING AROUND

In general, Indian towns and cities can be divided, for the purposes of quick orientation, into two categories: manageable and unmanageable. Major cities like Bombay, Calcutta and Delhi are impossible to know intimately in just three or four days, which is all most travellers allow. To cover the most ground, you'll need to take a sightseeing bus to acquaint yourself with the layout, main features and sights, then a taxi, rickshaw or cycle tour to fill in any gaps. The first things to do in a major city, therefore, are to visit the main tourist office and get a decent map, current brochures and details of any cultural programmes.

Tourist Information

There are national and state tourist offices in most of the larger cities in India which vary considerably in their degree of efficiency. In many states the tourist offices run tourist bungalows which usually offer extremely good-value accommodation; state tourist offices are normally located in these bungalows. There is also an organisation known as the Indian Tourism Development Corporation (ITDC) which often runs the city tour buses and a chain of hotels under the Ashok name. Government of India tourist offices include:

Agra: 191 The Mall (tel 363377)
Aurangabad: Krishna Vilas, Station Rd (tel 24817)
Bangalore: KFC Building, 48 Church St (tel 579517)
Bombay: 123 M. Karve Rd, Churchgate (tel 293144)
Calcutta: 4 Shakespeare Sarani (tel 221402)
Cochin: Willingdon Island (tel 340352)
New Delhi: 88 Janpath (tel 332005)
Jaipur: Khasa Kothi Hotel (tel 72200)
Khajuraho: Near Western Group Temples (tel 2047)
Madras: 154 Mount Rd (tel 869685)
Panaji (Goa): Communicade Building, Church Square (tel 43412)
Varanasi: 15B The Mall (tel 42744)

Most of the better hotels will be able to give you this information—and book a half- or full-day sightseeing tour, or hire a guide. Many Indian railway stations have tourist offices *in situ*, which means that you can plan your sightseeing schedule as soon as you arrive.

Bear in mind that the real sights of India are out there on the streets, not confined to monuments, palaces, parks and museums. Wandering off on foot or by cycle down small, narrow backstreets can turn up all sorts of delights—tiny local temples, quaint pavement shrines, colourful markets and bazaars, and out-of-the-way curio shops. Off the beaten track is usually where you'll find the real India—the small, yet lively communities of local people working, eating, resting, playing and praying. They are invariably interested in, and keen to meet, foreign tourists.

The smaller towns, villages, hill stations and beaches fall into the 'manageable' category. These places are rarely built up, have few major streets, and are difficult to get lost in. Sights may be limited, but so is the pressure to see them. Here, you can nearly always cycle or walk round the main points of interest in a day, and don't need to rely on tour buses or guides to get around.

Some places, like Agra and Jaipur, fall in between. They don't really merit a sightseeing tour by bus, yet can be very difficult to negotiate on foot or by cycle. The problem here is over-tourism, resulting in a crush of vehicles in and around famous places like the Taj Mahal or the old Pink City of Jaipur. One seasoned traveller remarked that he would never risk cycling in any town or city with a preponderance of traffic signs. Good examples are Bombay ('Hop along in life, or cross the road carefully'), Hyderabad ('Make up your mind what you are going to do, then cross the street') and Ahmedabad ('No elephants allowed'). The accident rate in some places is quite high—notably in towns with notorious 'Stop-Go' signs (nobody stops, everyone goes) or with lots of cross-walks.

Getting Around by Air

Most of the air traffic inside the Indian subcontinent is handled by **Indian Airlines**. Their network covers the entire country with daily, interconnecting flights. The Indian Airlines timetable contains details of all their domestic flights, and should be available from their offices, listed below. In practice, demand exceeds availability. Otherwise there are two private publications which are generally available from hotel travel desks and bookshops: *Divan* and *Excel*. These list both domestic and international Indian Airlines' flights, as well as the domestic stations covered by **Vayudoot**, the third national airline, which links several of the more remote or out-of-the-way centres not covered by Indian Airlines.

Domestic flights are surprisingly good value. For long-hauls, as from Delhi up to Srinagar (an exhausting 2-day journey, mainly by bus), paying out Rs1650 (less than £35) for a beautiful 2-hour air journey over the Himalaya is money well spent. Indian Airlines are also useful for hopping back and forth between the four main capitals, greatly extending your holiday options. The prices are reasonable: Bombay–Delhi, Rs2201; Bombay–Calcutta, Rs2960; Bombay–Madras, Rs2080; Calcutta–Delhi, Rs2488; Calcutta–Madras, Rs2603; Delhi–Madras, Rs3086. Meals are supplied on most domestic flights. Special tickets and package deals are also available; see p.7.

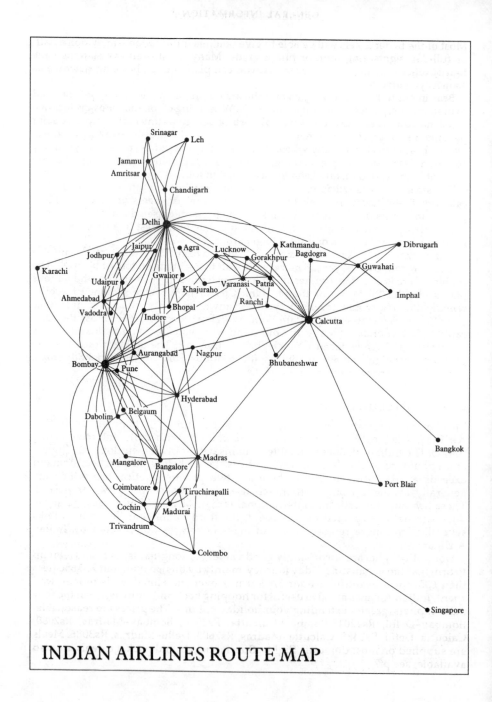

INDIAN AIRLINES ROUTE MAP

Foreign tourists are now required to make payment for their air tickets at a price based on a dollar tariff, which may be up to 30% higher than the rupee rate paid by residents. Some hole-in-the-wall travel agents may offer to get round this problem for you.

It is relatively easy to arrange internal flights, but seats on some major trunk routes are not always instantly available, especially during the holiday periods, and you may find yourself on a wait-list for up to two weeks. And you'll have to pay in foreign currency or produce an encashment certificate when buying a ticket (see p.21). If you have booked them from home, you'll need to reconfirm your entire itinerary immediately to be sure of keeping your reservations. You can do this by going directly to one of the **Indian Airlines offices** listed below. (Airport abbreviated to apt.)

Agra: Hotel Clarks Shiraz, 54 Taj Rd (tel 361421/9, apt 360153)

Ahmedabad: Airlines House, Lal Darwaja (tel 353333/9, apt 319233/6)

Aurangabad: Amikar Building, Adalat Road (tel 24864, apt 83442)

Bangalore: Housing Board Building, Kempe Gowda Rd (tel 211211, apt 566233)

Bhubaneshwar: V11-C/8 Raj Path, Bapuji Nagar (tel 400544, apt 401084)

Bombay: Air India Building, Ist Floor, Madam Cama Rd, Nariman Point (tel 2876161, apt 6114433)

Calcutta: Airlines House, 39 Chittaranjan Ave (tel 263135, apt 569841–5)

Cochin: Durbar Hall Rd, Ernakulam (tel 353901, apt 364433)

Delhi: Safdarjang Airport (24 hours) (tel 4624332); Kanchenjunga, Barakhamba Rd (tel 3313732, apt 142/143)

Goa (Dabolim): Dempo House, Cample, Panjim (tel 4067, apt 2568)

Hyderabad: Saifabad, near Legislative Assembly Building (tel 243333, apt 844433)

Jaipur: Nehru Place, Tonk Rd (tel 70724, apt 142)

Jodhpur: Rupali Tourist Bungalow, High Court Rd (tel 28600, apt 30617)

Khajuraho: Khajuraho Hotel (tel 2035, apt 2036)

Madras: 19 Marshalls Rd (tel 8251677, apt 142/2344433)

Srinagar: Tourist Reception Centre (tel 71918, apt 30334)

Trivandrum: Near Mascot Hotel, Museum Rd (tel 62288, apt 72740)

Udaipur: LIC Building, Delhi Gate (tel 28999, apt 142)

Varanasi: Mint House Motel, opposite Nadesar Palace, Cantonment (tel 44537, apt 142)

In Bombay and New Delhi the Indian Airlines offices at Santa Cruz Airport (tel 6114433) and at Safdarjung Airport (tel 4624332), respectively, are open 24 hours a day.

Queues at the Indian Airlines offices can be formidable, and in the larger cities, particularly, you may have to get a travel agent to arrange reservations, cancellations and confirmations. Some of the larger hotels (usually Taj or Oberoi) have travel desks, and a few have Indian Airlines extension counters which can deal with bookings very quickly.

It's a good idea to check in at each airport on your route a good hour before the scheduled time of flight departure. **Flight information** is available by telephone from the following airports:

Bangalore: 566233, 564433, 562533, 572605
Bombay: 142, 143, 2023262, 2876363
Calcutta: 569841/42/43/44

Dabolim (Goa): 2568, 2788, 3863
Delhi (arrivals):141,142; (departures):143 Guwahati: 82221, 82235, 82279
Hyderabad 844422, 844433
Madras: 2344433
Trivandrum: 72740, 73537, 72228.

One last tip: if you are travelling to India on an open return (no fixed date for your international flight home), go to the airline office dealing with your booking as soon as you can and pick a flight near to your intended departure date, and book it. In high season, many international flights are heavily subscribed, and failure to advance-book a seat may leave you stranded abroad for weeks. Don't worry about being held to a provisional booking: you can always change it later on, should you wish to extend your trip.

Getting Around by Rail

Since the days when it was developed to link the commercial and military centres of the Indian Empire, and ambitious young officers fanned out to take up their posts across India, the Indian Railways system has expanded considerably. By the close of the 19th century, there were 40 000 miles of track, stretching to the remotest parts of the country. Today, Indian Railways is the largest system in Asia, and the second largest in the world. Each day, over 11 million people travel to and from a total of 7021 railway stations. Included in every passenger list are a number of foreign travellers, most of them convinced that the Indian train is the only way to travel round the subcontinent.

A separate book could be written about India's rail service. The network itself is extremely extensive, always a madhouse and yet (after a fashion) amazingly efficient, although few trains leave on time.

If you're going to be spending any length of time on trains in India, invest in a copy of the *Indian Bradshaw*, the complete timetable of every rail service in India, which costs about Rs20. Smaller, and easier to decipher, is the *Trains at a Glance* booklet, sold for Rs6 at most large rail stations.

There are five basic classes of passenger rail travel: air-conditioned first class (operates on certain trains and routes only); two-tier air-conditioned sleeper; air-conditioned chair-car; 1st-class non air-conditioned and 2nd-class reserved. The most cost-effective method of travel is air-conditioned chair-car. This guarantees you a seat of your own, which no one can pinch, squat in or otherwise usurp. For long journeys (say, anything over a day) a two-tier air-con sleeper is half the price of the over-rated 1st-class AC sleeper, far more private and comfortable.

Always travel with a reservation, and always in the quicker mail, express or superfast trains. Never catch a local passenger train (takes ages), or travel in crowded 2nd-class unreserved carriages.

Mahatma Gandhi, newly arrived in India after his sojourn in South Africa, chose to explore the country in 3rd-class train accommodation. Travelling many thousands of miles, he shared heat, dust, overcrowding and general discomfort with untouchables, beggars and pilgrims, and pronounced it the most authentic way of discovering India. Certainly, Indian trains capture the essence of the country: a vast, sprawling and diverse organism chugging along, sometimes fast, sometimes slow, always managing to function in one way or another.

Rail travel is a leisurely way of taking in the varied scenery—mountains, lakes, rivers, forests and (except when the doors and windows are bolted against bandit attacks) dense jungles and hill terrains. You'll also meet a great many people. And time passes very quickly when you're sharing food, jokes, gifts and conversation. Whenever the train pulls into a station, platforms are an explosion of noise and colour: cries of 'chai-ya!' and 'om-elette!' float invitingly over the general hubbub. Here you can buy fresh(ish) fruit and vegetables, a hot samosa or a *'chaat'* snack, chapatis and parathas for next to nothing. Or you can wait until the daily shipment of *thali* suppers is loaded onto the train, and dine in civilised fashion later on. Train food is cheap (e.g. omelette and chapatis for Rs5), though rather bland. If on a marathon journey, it's a good idea to bring along supplies of your own—chocolate, biscuits and mandarin oranges. They help break the monotony of *dhal* and rice, peanuts, cucumbers and chips. Drinks are never a problem. At practically every station you come to, a man with an aluminium teapot will be beetling up and down the platform doling out *chai*. This often comes in little earthenware pots, which you are expected to lob out of the window when empty.

Perhaps the most economical mode of rail travel is the night sleeper. A Rs12 2nd-class sleeper reservation is a very cheap night's accommodation. And they save you time (while you are asleep, you are often covering a lot of ground). If you can stretch out, there's a good chance that you'll get a comfortable night's sleep. The middle bunks are often best: top bunks can be too hot or too draughty; the bottom ones can be dusty, and are favourite resting places of all-night squatters. Lights generally go out at 10.30 pm, but passengers can take a long time to settle down.

Because of the enormous volume of traffic, you can't just buy a ticket and get on a train, and you may really have to fight for a ticket. The reservations queue, winding out of a station concourse onto the street like a long, meandering snake, is the special dread of the foreign tourist. If you meet one, you've four choices: a) get a travel agent to reserve your ticket for you; b) hire a boy for a rupee or two to wait in the queue while you relax elsewhere; c) if you are male, find a woman tourist to buy your ticket for you—women are always allowed to the front queues in India; d) queue up yourself. If you have to do this, you'll need to get a **reservation slip** and fill it out first. At better organised stations, there is a system of number stamping, whereby a platform official (usually a ticket collector) writes your number in the queue on your ticket. This means that you can wander off and barge to the front of the queue when (often hours later) your number is called.

Sometimes, you'll get the doleful shake of the head and the apologetic words, 'So sorry, all full'. This means you'll have to apply for the **tourist quota** of tickets, usually issued by the District Commercial Superintendent of the railway department. His office is often miles away from the station, but you'll be surprised how easily he'll supply you with a ticket. Other 'quotas' are hidden away in all sorts of subterranean places in and out of the station complex. If you are really stuck, ask the nearest tourist office if there's a 'tourist quota' on the train you want. Or approach the stationmaster and try and break into his **VIP quota**. If nothing works, it's worth paying a few rupees baksheesh to a station porter to get a seat in an unreserved compartment.

Your reservation ticket will have the numbers of your carriage and berth written on it. Your sleeper reservation ticket (yes, probably another queue) will have your bunk number on it. If you arrive at your berth to find someone already sleeping in it, you may have to track down the reservation ticket officer (always somewhere on the train) to remove him. Alternatively, remind the offending person that 'Ticketless travel is a social evil' (a priceless sign at Kanwar rail station) and remove him yourself.

Arriving on a crowded, seething series of platforms looking for your train can be a problem. If you ask for directions from passengers or even station officials you may not be given the correct information. One couple arrived at Delhi station for the 4.20 pm train to Madras. They arrived an hour early to be sure of catching it. They were told by the station master, the platform guards, the ticket collector and half-a-dozen assorted railway officials that their train would certainly depart from platform 13. But it didn't; it left from platform 12, and they missed it.

And newly-arrived tourists may find themselves pestered by spurious 'guides' who will see you to the train and then try to extort as much money as possible out of you. A couple of rupees will get you a porter. He will not only carry your bags through the maelstrom, but will locate the right train for you.

A good way of checking that your reservation is all right, and that you've got the right train, is to look at the 'reservation sheet' posted on the sides of each carriage. This—a wonderfully efficient Indian device—will have your name and berth number scrawled on it.

Indian railway stations themselves are fascinating. They often have a collection of interesting old steam engines huffing and puffing in and out—a gricer's dream—and they often have very good waiting-rooms, with a decent restaurant and sometimes a bathroom. Tourists can use both 1st- and 2nd-class waiting-rooms, and even sleep free in them, provided they have a valid train ticket. Most stations also have a left-luggage room, where you can leave your bags for just Rs1 per day—very useful if you're only spending a few hours in a town, and don't want to book into a hotel.

Luxury Train Travel
The *Palace on Wheels* attempts to recreate the lifestyle of the old colonial rulers and their princely Indian counterparts. Offering an 'unparalleled luxurious mode of travel' through Rajasthan—Jaipur, Udaipur, Jaisalmer, Jodhpur—and Bharatpur, Fatehpur Sikri and Agra, it leaves Delhi every Wednesday between October and March. The one-week tour costs £1200/US$2375 for two persons, £890/US$1750 for single persons in twin-bedded cabins. The *Palace on Wheels* is now marketed abroad, at the Indrail branch offices given overleaf.

A similar train has recently been launched in south India linking Bangalore, Mysore, Hassan, Hospet, Badami, Bijapur and Goa. Cheaper, and by all accounts more satisfactory, is the Indian Rail Rover ticket sold by Trailfinders (see p.5). Facilities are much more basic, but it is valid for 18–32 days, allowing the bearer to cover a lot more territory.

Indrail Passes
If you're going to be doing a lot of rail travel, the Indrail Pass can be very good value. Valid for one year from purchase date, it gives unlimited travel on Indian trains, and allows you to go where and when you like without ever (if travelling unreserved) having to join a ticket queue.

If you do want a reservation, you'll still have to queue but the Indrail Pass carries a bit of weight and often produces quotas denied to other ordinary rail travellers. It is also very useful for gaining access to 1st-class station waiting-rooms and retiring-rooms. To make the best use of your Indrail Pass, pick up a copy of *Indrail India Rail Rovers* booklet, issued free at general sales agents (e.g. the foreigners' booking office in New Delhi rail station). It lists all trains, discusses all rail travel options, and generally helps you plan your itinerary.

The main offices which handle Indrail passes are located at:

New Delhi: Railway Tourist Guide, New Delhi Railway Station; and Central Reservation Office, Northern Railway, Connaught Place.
Bombay: Railway Tourist Guide, Western Railway, Churchgate, and Railway Tourist Guide, Central Railway, Victoria Terminus.
Calcutta: Railway Tourist Guide, Eastern Railway, Fairlie Place, and Central Reservation Office, South-Eastern Railway, Esplanade Mansion.
Madras: Central Reservation Office, Southern Railway, Madras Central.

Indrail Pass Costs (US$)

Validity	Air-con	1st class	2nd class
7 days	220	110	55
15 days	270	135	65
21 days	330	165	75
30 days	410	205	90
60 days	600	300	135
90 days	800	400	175

Indian Rail Fares (Rs)

Distance (km)	Air-conditioned First Class	Air-conditioned Sleeper	First Class	Air-conditioned Chair Car	Second Class Mail or Express	Second Class Ordinary
1	122	89	25	25	7	1.5
20	122	89	25	25	7	1.5
25	123	89	34	34	8	4
50	144	113	63	44	13	9
75	184	137	81	51	20	13
100	231	159	97	62	22	14
200	350	221	156	95	42	24
300	490	294	218	134	57	33
400	627	365	279	163	61	40
500	741	470	327	194	87	46
750	1018	583	464	255	118	57
1000	1212	670	534	256	143	67
1500	1640	891	717	396	177	84
2000	2039	1072	891	481	201	101
2500	2438	1232	1065	569	225	117
3000	2838	1389	1238	653	249	134
3500	3234	1546	1410	741	273	150
4000	3634	1706	1587	826	298	167
4500	4034	1863	1761	914	312	183
5000	4432	2019	1934	999	347	200

Children aged between 5 and 12 years are charged only half the adult Indrail fare. In India, Indrail Passes are sold by many travel agents or Central Reservations Offices at major railway stations (New Delhi, Madras, Calcutta and Bombay). Payment in India must always be in UK£ or US$ cash, or travellers' cheques. In the UK, you can now buy the Indrail Pass from S.D. Enterprises Limited, 103 Wembley Park Drive, Wembley, Middlesex HA9 8HG (tel 081-903 3411); in France, from Carrefour, 15 Rue Des Ecoles, Paris; in the USA, from Hari World Travels, 30 Rockefeller Plaza, shop No. 21, Mezzanine North, New York; in Australia, from Penthouse Travel, Suite 5, Level 13, Commercial Union House, 109 Pitt St, Sydney.

Passenger Fares

You can work out the approximate cost of your journey by using the table of fares listed on p31. For example, the overnight sleeper from Delhi to Shimla—a journey of 221 miles (354 km) would cost Rs52 in 2nd-class (plus a Rs15 sleeper reservation) and Rs183 in 1st-class. There tend to be regular increases in fares, so bear this in mind when estimating the cost.

Getting Around by Bus

India has a very extensive and comprehensive bus system. Each state offers its own service—usually a combination of local, deluxe, super-deluxe and video buses—and tickets are usually purchased direct from the state bus-stands. Buses are often cheaper and more exciting than the trains, and go to several places, such as Leh, not linked by rail. They can also be a lot quicker. Most buses in India, whether local, state, or privately run, roar to their destinations with reckless verve and daring. Their drivers seem to have a particular grudge against 'public carrier' trucks, which often carry provocative logos like 'Owner is God—God is Grate'. All bus drivers have a little box containing their personal gods above their seat. From time to time, often when stopped by the police for not paying a speeding fine, they will pray to these. At other times, they will pull up at a roadside Hindu shrine and pay a priest to ring a bell to summon the major deities; this is often to give thanks for avoiding a major collision.

Every bus journey is an experience in itself, especially the ones which wind round an escalating series of hairpin bends on their way up to remote hill stations. And when the interior is full your only option is to sit on the roof. But there are always entertaining road-signs to keep your mind off the perilous drive. These signs are the creation of Public Works Department (PWD) poets, who are notoriously sexist. 'When you approach a corner, get horny', is one of their classics. 'Don't gossip—let him drive' is another. 'Family Awaits—Please Oblige', a direct appeal to the paternal instinct, is the only thing likely to make him slow down at tight corners.

Buses often stop at spots of great natural beauty, which makes a pleasant change from the hurly-burly of railway platforms. Another good thing about buses is that they leave so frequently, often every hour or half-hour, and they are much less trouble to book and board than trains. Buying a reservation slip often gets you onto buses where seats are likely to be at a premium, but you will need to turn up at the bus-station at least 40 minutes in advance to be sure of getting one.

Local buses are incredibly cheap and will often run you from one end of a state to another for less than Rs35, but they are also crowded, occasionally smelly and usually uncomfortable. Air-conditioned 'deluxe' buses are slightly less so. Video bus journeys can be something of a nightmare: constant disco music and blaring video shows can grind you down, especially when sharing a two-seater built for one. It's almost impossible to hear yourself think, let alone read, but Indian travellers adore the video bus, and the more distorted the sound, the more they like it.

Whenever leaving a bus to go to the toilet or to eat, leave a newspaper or something on your seat. This will reserve it. Take any other hand luggage off the bus with you. Backpacks and large cases are usually strapped under tarpaulin on the bus roof,or stored in the hold-all. If you're looking after them under your seat, make sure they are securely zipped and locked (padlocking to a bolted seat is best) before vacating the bus.

Bus stops can be either very short or very long (driver wanders off to visit his family). Passengers have been known to be left holding full cups of tea or squatting in ditches while the bus roars off without them. The only way of tracking its movements is to keep one eye constantly on the driver. As soon as he's back in his seat, you've got approximately 5 seconds to get back in yours.

Bus travel is best over short distances; for long journeys take the train. The roads are badly surfaced, full of yawning potholes, and always seem liable to collapse. So are the back axles of the overloaded buses. The hard, cramped seating, the draughty, rattling windows, the screaming children, the infrequent toilet stops, and the constant blare of the air-horn as the bus ploughs inexorably towards its destination, may leave you blinded, shell-shocked and with your nerves (and your backside) shot to pieces. But the network is extensive, and you can always reduce your discomfort by a) inserting earplugs; b) sitting on a soft pillow or sweater; c) jamming a sleeping bag into window gaps; d) wearing a hat and scarf (or crash helmet).

Prices

A seat on a deluxe bus is approximately 2 to 3 times the price of one on an ordinary bus—but some large Europeans literally cannot *fit* into the space offered in the latter.

Prices vary, but it is almost always the case that they will be a fraction lower than the fare for a 2nd class rail ticket along the same route. The longer the journey, the lower the rate per kilometre.

To anticipate your fare on a deluxe bus, divide the distance you wish to travel, in kilometres, by 3—and that's your approximate fare in rupees.

Sample bus fares:

> Delhi–Simla (9 hours, 354 km) Rs125
> Delhi–Jaipur (4 ½ hours, 259 km) Rs100
> Delhi–Agra (4 hours, 204 km) Rs85

Tour Buses

As a quick, cheap and comfortable introduction to larger Indian centres, sightseeing coach tours operated by government and state tourist offices are unbeatable value. Costing around Rs45 for a half-day, Rs80 for a full-day, they work out far less expensive than sightseeing by taxi or rickshaw, and of course you see more in less time. Their main advantage is their rapid orientation of foreign visitors to large, sprawling cities. There are rather too many stops at obscure temples and holy shrines for most Western passengers, and the deluxe buses themselves are sometimes draughty and dilapidated, but you'll cover an incredible amount of ground in just a day and other forms of in-town transport can be even less comfortable. Sightseeing buses can also be a great way of meeting people because you'll often be the only foreign tourist on board and it's common to be adopted for the day by friendly home tourists and fed large quantities of Indian picnic lunches. When booking your tour, ask for a seat at the front of the bus; it's far less bumpy, quicker to get to the toilets, and you'll hear more of the guide's talk.

Getting Around by Taxi and Auto-rickshaw

These are the two most common forms of in-town transport, most popular for short-distance hops to and from bus and rail stations when loaded down with luggage, or for solo sightseeing in smaller towns where tour buses aren't such good value. Taxis are usually black, with yellow tops, cost around Rs5–6 per kilometre with a minimum fare of Rs5.60, and are quite comfortable. Auto-rickshaws are three-wheeled scooters (a two-stroke motorcycle engine with two-seater canopy strapped behind it), which are noisy, less comfortable, but very nippy. They cost anything between Rs3.00 and Rs3.50 per kilometre.

Taxis and rickshaws are usually metered, but the meters are often not working. As soon as you walk off in search of another taxi, they suddenly begin working again. But even when the meter's returned from the dead, you're wise to fix the cost of your journey before setting off. A succession of recent fuel price increases has left taxi meter-readings way out of date. You'll often be handed a fare adjustment card indicating a far higher journey-fare than that shown on the meter. This isn't so bad in places like Delhi, where you'll be expected to pay only 15% on top of the meter-reading; but in places like Bombay and Ahmedabad, where taxi meters haven't been recalibrated in ages, surcharges of 400% and 500%, respectively, can come as a real shock to the penny-wise traveller.

If overcharged—if you've agreed a fair rate for the journey in advance, and the driver wants more at the end of it—don't get angry. Just write down the taxi number, and announce in a calm, determined voice that you're going to the police. There are stiff fines for extorting money from tourists, and your driver will usually 'remember' the correct fare instantly.

Another popular con used by taxis and scooters alike is to drive you miles out of your way, in order to collect a decent fare. Take a good city map with you and as soon as it's apparent that you're being taken miles out of the way, tell the driver firmly 'wrong way!' and manually reset his meter back to zero. But don't be too hasty to jump to conclusions, sometimes he will genuinely lose his way, or won't be able to understand where you want to go. Again, a city map is useful because you'll be able to point out your exact destination. In case you're totally lost in a big city, and need to get back to your hotel, always keep a hotel card handy. Drivers will usually take one look at the card, and take you straight home.

If hiring a taxi or auto-rickshaw between 11 pm and 5 am, be prepared to pay an additional 15% (up to 25% in some cities) on top of the usual daytime fare.

Some major airports, including both terminals at Delhi and Bombay, Bangalore and Madras, have introduced a system of 'prepaid taxis'. Before leaving the arrival terminal go to the police-manned taxi booth and purchase a ticket to the area of town you need to reach. There is a small charge of a few rupees but this service ensures new arrivals are not going to be over-charged and that they generally reach their destination without detours.

Getting Around by Cycle-rickshaw

These rather antiquated vehicles can be found only in certain places, usually in smaller towns. They provide a useful open mode of transport, and although rather slower than motorised transport, they are cheap—usually just Rs3 per kilometre—but again, always fix a total rate for your journey in advance. Drivers are notorious for trying to overcharge. This is often because they are unable to afford their own vehicles and are just hiring them out for a few rupees a day from someone else. Cycle-rickshaws are often ridden by some loquacious old pirate who hasn't the slightest idea of where he's going. It's accepted custom to get off and give him a push up steep hills. You'll probably also have to give him lots of directions and prompts. Many cycle-rickshaw drivers are skilled raconteurs, mines of local information (much of it embroidered), and extremely friendly.

Getting Around by Hire Car

Car hire in India is relatively new and even Hertz, Budget and EuropCar offer both self-drive cars and ones with drivers. One problem confronting all drivers are the mad streams of crazy traffic, aimless herds of sacred cows, pigs and goats and generally poor road surfaces which make driving something of an endurance test. Some people bring their own cars or motorbikes into the country. If you choose this option, you'll need to: a) fill out a customs declaration form (called a carnet) requiring you to bring the vehicle out again at the end of your stay; b) be in possession of an International Driving Licence. In 1989, a Swiss couple who'd bought an Enfield motorbike in Delhi for Rs16 000, motored all round India on it, and sold it in Srinagar for Rs13 000. They had no problems.

An expensive but good way of seeing India by car is to hire a chauffeur-driven Hindustan Ambassador (an unashamed replica of the mid-50s British Morris Oxford). In fact a range of cars (including Toyotas and Mercedes), with drivers, are available for hire in most cities. Prices are quite reasonable considering the freedom and flexibility it gives your itinerary. The driver often doubles up as a trained guide, as well as useful interpreter and watchman.

Getting Around by Bicycle

In many towns, cities and villages cycles are the basic form of transport. Cycling is often an ideal way of seeing the sights, and is cheap. Your hotel will always be able to recommend a hire place nearby, if they don't hire them out themselves—many of them do—and the daily rate is never going to be more than Rs10–20. When choosing your conveyance, always check the state of the tyres—if you get a puncture, you'll have no difficulty finding a repair man (they're all over the place—but you may well be hanging around for an hour while he spends over-long fixing it. You can usually speed him up by offering twice the correct Rs2 repair charge. The one thing your bike *must* have is a bell. In dense traffic you'll be ringing this continually (like everybody else) to avoid being mown down. Women in India travel side-saddle on cycles, so there is a great shortage of ladies' bikes. To snap up the few there are, be at the cycle-hire shop first thing in the morning.

Getting Around by Boat

The most famous Indian boat journeys are the ferry trip from Bombay to Goa, and the many small-boat trips through the backwaters of Kerala. Unfortunately, the former is not in operation at the time of writing, although there are plans to reinstate it. The latter should not be missed, and details are given in Route 12.

Disabled Travellers

India is not a country which is easy to travel around if you have limited mobility, despite (and possibly because of) the fact that so many of her own population are disabled. Airlines and some major hotels are often helpful, but you can never rely on special facilities being available. For example, wheelchair ramps do not exist and access to bathrooms, restaurants and even hotel bedrooms is often impossible for those who cannot use stairs or pass through narrow doorways and passages. It may be possible to overcome these problems with the help of a companion.

Travelling Alone

Even if you've agreed to tour in company, do spend a few days travelling on your own. India is very much a country for the individualist, which quickly brings out all your hidden resources. For a start, there is no room for doubt, indecision or complacency. Without the insulation of a boon companion (a permanent reminder of home) you'll feel compelled to attune to the country, its people and its customs, at top speed. It's also an excellent spur to making new friends. There should be no worry about feeling alone. In India, nobody's alone for very long. The beauty of travelling alone is that you can go exactly when and where you please, with a growing sense of freedom and confidence. The perfect place for a modern-day walkabout, India rewards the solo traveller with a rich variety of intense experiences—some good, some bad, none dull—and brings him or her to a deeper understanding of the country. The reason so much more happens on your own is simple—you have to *make* it happen.

Women Travellers

Indian society is still not very emancipated, and Western women travelling alone (or in pairs) are regarded with a mixture of fascination and puzzlement. They ought to be married, they should be wearing decent clothing which covers the upper arms, chest and back. The common misconception among young (and not so young) Indian men is that all Western women are available. Certain precautions, like wearing a wedding ring and firmly rebuking any over-zealous male, usually deter any unwelcome advances.

Indians are not inhibited and show their appreciation or interest by staring. They also have no notion of 'personal space', and this behaviour can sometimes be very intrusive as far as a Westerner is concerned, but is rarely threatening.

A great many women travellers visit India each year, and most have a thoroughly enjoyable time. There are strong advantages and drawbacks to travelling in India as a woman. A lack of adequate toilet facilities and occasional difficulty in getting accommodation are among some of the disadvantages. Some lodges in India (notably in Muslim areas like Hyderabad) refuse outright to give single women rooms, simply because it goes against the landlord's whole morality. On the other hand, women are rarely required to queue for anything: they can generally walk straight to the front of train, bus or cinema queues and buy their ticket. There are often special ladies' carriages in trains and sometimes seats reserved for women on buses. Many other places, including some cinemas, have special ladies' facilities. Finally, being young, single and even remotely attractive is the passport to all sorts of freebies, and will often secure hospitality, offers of help, and all manner of introductions.

Where to Stay

Prices
Hotels recommended in this book are divided into four categories—Luxury, Expensive, Mid-range and Budget—according to the facilities on offer. These categories are described below.

Indian hotels vary greatly in price and quality according to where in the country you are. As a general rule, the further south you go, the cheaper accommodation becomes.

Prices may vary according to season and during festivals; and rates in hotels vary according to whether they have pretty views or are in the quieter parts of the building. Prices quoted in this guide are for a double room with bath in high season at 1 October 1992. You can expect increases in the range of 5–10% for the '92/'93 season.

Effective from October 1992, an expenditure tax of 20% is levied on all hotel bills when a single-room charge is more than Rs1200 or US$50. This effectively places some hotels out of the mid-range—against their marketing policy—and it is likely that many will actually reduce their single-room rates, removing the necessity for any guest to the hotel to pay this tax.

Officially, foreign guests in all hotels in India are charged according to the dollar tariff, residents are charged in rupees. In practice, many mid-range and budget hotels only have a rupee tariff, although visitors will still be asked to pay in foreign exchange or in rupees against an encashment certificate. In the expensive hotel bracket, the dollar tariff applies. Moreover, as a result of currency fluctuations, tourist rates in these major hotels have become considerably higher than the equivalent rupee rates.

Expensive/Luxury (US$35–100 plus per room night)
In terms of atmosphere and location, India has some of the world's most spectacular hotels. Former palaces such as Shiv Niwas and the Lake Palace in Udaipur and the Rambagh Palace in Jaipur have been converted into excellent hotels. In the major cities some extremely good properties have appeared over the past decade or so. Some, such as the well-run Oberoi Grand in Calcutta, have been excellently renovated and reflect the grandeur of an older era. And the Taj Mahal Hotel in Bombay has never lost its place among the best of Indian hotels. Newer 'five-star plus' hotels include the Leela Kempinski and the Oberoi in Bombay, the Taj Bengal in Calcutta; the Hyatt, the Oberoi, and the Taj Mahal in New Delhi. The prices now tend to match the international quality of the hotels, but off-season discounts are

sometimes available. Thus, in Bombay, a night in a top hotel can cost as much as Rs4500 (around £90, US$45)—for this you could expect a smart air-conditioned double suite (probably with private balcony and view), access to a good swimming-pool, and a number of useful facilities like shopping arcade, travel agency, bank, two or three restaurants, in-house entertainments, car park, beauty parlour and health club. Car hire and sightseeing tours are also often arranged, and so are a selection of sports and activities. Out of the main cities, the standard of luxury hotels varies markedly, but so do the prices.

Mid-range (US$10–35/Rs250–1000 per room night)
The big problem with Asian countries gearing themselves up for tourism is a near vacuum of good hotels in the middle price-range. India is no exception. In many parts of the country, you've a straight choice: live in style, or nearer the bottom line. The situation is gradually improving, with an increase in the number of good to moderate hotels, and as hoteliers renovate and equip basic lodges to mid-range standards.

A double room in a decent moderate hotel, with air-conditioning, attached restaurant, some sort of room service and (occasionally) a lift and room telephone, will cost in the region of Rs1250 (around £25) in Bombay or Delhi, as little as half that in the south.

Budget (under US$10/Rs250 per room night)
Economy lodgings are often very good value in India, but the quality is very variable. In one town, you may find a clean, quiet double room with a fan, a shower and a toilet for Rs75–100 (around £1.50 or US$3). Until you're used to looking out the better places, it's generally advisable to stay at the state-run **Tourist Bungalows**. Most towns and cities have them, and though often drab and uninspiring, they are usually clean and well run. Like the popular YMCAs, they often have cheap dormitories which are ideal for meeting people and swapping experiences (and books).A typical double room in a Tourist Bungalow will cost between Rs100 and Rs200, though a dormitory berth can cost as little as Rs15.

Before you take any room in the cheaper range of hotels, give it a thorough once-over for cleanliness and for facilities. In economy places, you can perhaps overlook the chipped basins,the peeling plaster and old coffee stains on walls. What you can't overlook are a) dirty bed linen; b) bedbugs under mattresses; c) roaches in bathrooms and waste bins; d) overhead fans that don't work or which have only one (turbo) speed; e) dead electric lights; f) no hot water (or no water at all) in showers; g) no lock on the door or no latches on windows. In practice, a lot of travellers put up with basic, even unfriendly, accommodation, and rarely give rooms a proper check. This is often because they arrive in towns too tired to really care, or too late to have much choice in the matter. Others put up with really awful dives, on the basis that they're going to be out and about all day, and will only need a room to sleep in.

As a general rule, if you're just staying in a town for one or two nights, you're not going to have time or energy to traipse around looking for a decent hotel. If the recommended ones are full or unsatisfactory, you may have to take the first adequate place that comes along. This often means hiring a local hotel tout. There is no problem finding them; they find you. Bear in mind that they get a tidy commission for placing you, so don't pay them more than a couple of rupees.

A big con worked by hotel touts, rickshaw and taxi-drivers, seeking commissions from their hotels, is to deny that the hotel you want has any vacancies. 'Oh no, sahib', they will say, 'all full up'. But they're often not full up at all. And even if they are, you can probably find something else much better without their help. If the popular places have no room, take the time to wander round a few streets directly adjoining them. Remember, a lot of new hotels are opening all the time, and they're often just off the main tourist areas.

If you're going to spend a week or so in one town or city, it's worth tracking down a really decent place to stay, somewhere with a quiet, cosy atmosphere where you can just collapse, read, or write letters. If it has little luxuries like a writing-desk, a balcony, an easy chair or (rare) a clean waste-paper bin, then all the better.

One final tip: when you've really had enough of budget lodges, and putting up with depressing decor and constant heat, noise and draughts, it's time to give yourself a break. Splash out and book into a 1st-class or luxury hotel for a night or two. It works wonders for the morale.

Eating Out

It's a cliché, but true, that the best food you will eat in India is in private homes. And it is likely, given the enormously hospitable nature of the country, that you will be given the opportunity to discover this for yourself.

Food in Indian restaurants tends to be fairly basic, although a number of excellent speciality restaurants have sprung up in the gateway cities over the past 10 years. However, if you're expecting the same standard of cuisine that you find in Indian restaurants (mainly Punjabi) in the West, you're likely to be disappointed. In fact, if you're on budget and haven't got a taste for spicy or mushy food, it could be rather difficult to eat well in India. If you are a confirmed carnivore, travelling in the south, where restaurants serve almost exclusively vegetarian food, might be difficult. And even in the large northern cities, where meat is more available (generally stringy mutton or emaciated chicken) you should eat it only in larger restaurants; in the small ones, it's often re-cooked and not fresh.

Many people return from India dedicated vegetarians. If this is something you've been planning to do for years, this is just the place to do it, both because meat is in short supply, and because there's such a wide range of tasty vegetarian food. Indian fare may be very simple, but what there is of it is good, and consistently good. It's also very cheap and widely available. It has been said that the Indians invented the concept of fast food. Their ability to feed a whole busload of people at a roadside *dhaba* in under 10 minutes is quite remarkable. Western-style food—available in the bigger cities—is much more expensive. So is 'Kwality' Indian food, which you can find in the better restaurants of most Indian cities. Simple, but good, 'meals' (another word for *thali* are served in trains and in railway canteens for as little as Rs10 (25 pence) and in the *dhaba*. Many books warn against eating at the latter, and if you are newly arrived in India, it is probably wise to steer clear of this type of food for the first few weeks until your stomach has had a chance to acclimatise.

At a high-class restaurant, particularly in the large international hotels, you can expect to pay anything beween Rs150–400 for a meal which outside would probably cost a quarter of that. Smart hotel restaurants also levy a 20% expenditure tax. But it's sometimes worth paying out for proper food. Etiquette in basic eating-houses, especially in the south, requires that you eat with your fingers. Local people will often stop at your table to advise that you mix your meat/vegetables in with your rice—this is necessary, they will say, 'to get the full flavour of the spices'. They will also give you a pitying/disgusted look if you're scooping mushy *thali* into your mouth with your left hand. The left hand is used for something else entirely. Eat only with the right.

Restaurant Categories

Restaurants in the guide are grouped according to type of cuisine—where you have a choice. All food in India is comparatively cheap for the foreign visitor, and it is true to say that excellent food need not be expensive. In fact, above the most basic restaurants, you tend to pay for the decor; this is especially true of restaurants in hotels.

Restaurants often have long and wonderfully mis-spelt menus. Items like 'Sour and Acrid', 'Scream Bled Eggs' and 'Lemon Sod' will keep you entertained while you are waiting for your food. When ordering, you'll often find it a waste of time asking for what you want from a menu. It will probably be 'off'. Far simpler to ask your waiter what he's got. If you're lucky, this may line up with something you want. As a general guide, the longer the menu, the more likely it is that you'll end up with a *thali*.

Indian Cuisine

Northern Indian cuisine is characterised by a greater use of dried spices; the dishes of southern India rely more heavily on green spices. Combining these spices for any particular dish, you have a *masala*. The most common northern Indian variety is called *garam masala*, a (hot) mixture of cardamom, cinnamon, black pepper, cumin, cloves and coriander seeds, all freshly ground into a powder with a mortar and pestle. Indian curries (actually a British term, covering the full range of spiced Indian foods) are prepared from any combination of about 25 spices. The most widely used are cardamom (used a lot in Kashmiri tea, Indian sweets, and to flavour meat dishes); chillies; coriander (a cooling agent), garlic and ginger (digestive aids); and sometimes cinnamon, fenugreek, mace and cloves. A dish of caraway seeds is often placed at your table, to cleanse your mouth after meals. Sometimes, so is a wad of *paan* (a mixture of spices, lime paste, and mildly addictive areca nut wrapped in a betel leaf), another popular aid to digestion.

Vegetarian dishes usually appear on a *thali*, a steel tray on which are ranged a number of small *katori* bowls. These contain an assortment of vegetable or *dhal* (lentil) preparations—commonly potatoes, carrots, beans and cauliflower, plus a chutney of chillies, onions, tamarind, coconut and mint. Every *thali* should include a dish of *raita* or curd (yogurt). Most people eat *thali* with their fingers, and use *pappadam* or *chappati* to mop up the drippy mush and carry it to their mouths. These breads come with the *thali*, and again, you get as many as you want.

A bread that is particularly associated with the south is *dosa*, a papyrus-thin or doughy-thick pancake made from rice and lentils. Filled with spicy potato and vegetable curry, it is called a *masala dosa*—the staple diet of many southern Indians, and also incredibly cheap. In the north, the most popular breads are wheat-based *roti*, butter or ghee-basted *paratha* or deep-fried *poori*. Nearly everywhere, you will find the delicious oven-baked *naan* bread and the flat cupcake *idli* breads made from rice flour.

Meat-dishes can be good, if you don't mind paying out for them. Recommended main courses are *biriani*, usually chicken or mutton cooked in spices, mixed in with saffron-yellow rice; meat-based curries like lamb *roganjosh* with tomatoes, *do-piaza* with onions, *vindaloo* (Goan pork speciality) with hotly spiced meat, marinated in vinegar, and *korma* which contains only mild spices; finally (in the north) *tandoori*, usually chicken deliciously marinated in herbs and spices, baked in a clay oven. *Biriani* and *tandoori* make a pleasant change from curries, being on the whole, much milder.

The quality of soups is erratic—you're generally safe with *sambhar*, a filling soup of vegetables and lentils, spiced with tamarind; or with the very hot and savoury *rasam*, a popular southern consommé with a lentil base; but beware of ordering 'veg soup' in backwoods places; it can be nothing more than a bowl of green water, with a single cabbage leaf floating in it.

You can eat excellent seafood, notably at Goa,in Kerala, near Mangalore and other coastal resorts, where lobster, prawn, crayfish, crab and shark are often served fresh off the beach.

Indian desserts or sweetmeats are very sweet. But nobody makes ice-cream like they do here. Major brands like Vadilal, Milkfood, Cadbury's and Gaylord do a wide, mouthwatering range of flavours—as good as anything you will find in the West. Traditional desserts like *kulfi* (similar to ice-cream), *jalebi* (small cartwheel-shaped pancakes, dripping with syrup) and milk/curd-based sweetmeats like *rasgulla* and *sandesh* are all widely available, though best sampled in Calcutta. Indian sweets are often sold in elegant little boxes, with each item individually covered in wafer-thin silver foil. You can eat the silver, but eating the sweet itself is not always pleasant. Many have a high content of cardamom, and this spice is very much an acquired taste.

Fresh fruit—mangoes, pineapples, melons, pichots (like dates), bananas, coconuts and tangerines are widely sold in markets in most parts of India. And it's all ridiculously cheap. It's often a bad idea to buy fruit and vegetables (e.g. tomatoes) cut into segments and sold on the street because they attract too many flies.Always buy complete fruits, and peel them yourself.

Drinks

The most popular beverage by far in India is tea or *chai*. Brewed up on every street corner, price just 50 paise, it usually appears as a glass of filmy, dark brown liquid strong enough to stand a spoon up in. *Chai* is commonly made from boiled buffalo milk, and is loaded with sugar. If you haven't a sweet tooth, one of the first Indian phrases you'll learn will be *'ek chai—chini neh'* (one tea, no sugar). In restaurants, a good idea is to order a pot of boiling water with your pot of tea so that you can dilute it. If this doesn't work, order 'tray tea' where the tea, milk and sugar are served separately. Some travellers give up on *chai* completely, and switch to coffee. This is nearly always good, especially in the south (where it is the main drink), and is available from Indian coffee houses in most towns and cities.

Excellent natural fruit juices and curd-based *lassi* are widely available, as are a vast selection of carbonated bottled drinks. These go under names like Gold Spot (orange), Limca (lemon), Citra, Campa Cola and Thums Up. Pepsi-Cola and 7Up were introduced to the Indian market in 1990. Coca-Cola (which was banned in 1977) promises to be back in 1993. In general, they are too sweet to be a satisfactory thirst-quencher, and in hot climates you're probably better off with a kilo of oranges (around Rs10, and they last longer).

Alcoholic drinks can be very expensive—especially imported wine. Beer is popular and widely available, and generally sells as largish bottles of chilled, gassy lager for around Rs20–25, though in Goa and a few other states the price is lower. Popular brand names include Golden Eagle, Black Label and Kingfisher. In Bangalore and Bombay, draught beer is readily available. Indians are very much into whisky, which sells in 'wine' shops. It's very raw, and hasn't got much of a bouquet, but at around Rs40 per half-bottle it's very cheap. Indian rum is generally of a high standard and locally made gin and vodka are in most cases good. In the 'dry' state of Gujarat, you can buy beer or whisky for consumption in the darkness of your hotel room, or in a few hotels and restaurants with permits. For this you need to have a 'liquor permit' stamped in your passport. These can be issued by the main tourist offices. Desert villages, notably in Rajasthan, produce some interesting rum—usually ex-army issue and strong enough to blow your head off—while in Goa and the ex-Portuguese enclaves of Diu and Daman, you can find the coconut-extract *toddy*, the cashew-nut *feni*, and often some 'country wine' of unknown origin.

Health

India does not have to be a survival experience—something to be endured rather than enjoyed. Eating sensibly, drinking clean water, keeping clean, and getting enough rest are the keys to health in India. All too many cases of illness (and theft) reported by travellers come back to exhaustion caused by living too cheap too long. And it's easy to do: the tendency to save money is infectious (even compulsive) in a country where poverty is the general rule.

The most common afflictions are diarrhoea, amoebic dysentery, giardiasis (drastic stomach upset) and hepatitis. The best prescription for **diarrhoea** and any stomach complaint is a strict diet of black tea, boiled water, plain boiled rice, curd and bananas. This is a lot more effective than taking tablets, which simply block up the infection in your stomach.

If you have **giardiasis**, the best remedy is a course of the antibiotic Tinidazole: it may be worth getting your GP to give you a prescription to use just in case, but if you do this, don't use the tablets for anything else; you could end up with another infection.

The best protection against **hepatitis** is to get yourself inoculated with gamma globulin before you go; or better still, to take the new course of injections which immunises you against hepatitis B (the worst kind) for life. But if you do get it, you won't have much option other than to ship yourself home as soon as you can.

Amoebic dysentery is probably the worst thing you can expect. It's the same as diarrhoea, with the added attractions of fever plus blood or pus in the stool. Indian doctors may be able to provide temporary relief by prescribing a course of Flagyl, but again you're best going straight home and getting it dealt with properly. The longer you leave hepatitis and amoebic dysentery, the more difficult they are to cure.

The same could be said of **malaria**, which is caused by mosquito bites and which can lie dormant for a long time. This is why it is important to keep taking the tablets for up to six weeks after your return home.

Rabies, caused by bites or scratches from 'friendly' stray dogs and temple monkeys, should be dealt with on the spot. Go straight to the nearest Indian hospital (better than a doctor) if any animal draws blood. Few dogs (and no monkeys) have 'owners', and it will be impossible to apply a saliva test to see if they're rabid or not. Rather than take the chance, take a full course of rabies injections. You'll have to stay in one place for 14 days to have them administered by the doctor/hospital. The only alternative is to buy the whole course of vaccine (about Rs50) plus sterilised needles from a street chemist, and administer them yourself. If travelling about, this raises one big problem: the vaccine must be kept at a constant temperature of between 2° and 10°C (35° to 50°F). This means finding fresh ice each day to keep it in. A new vaccine is available in the major cities, which involves a course of just three injections, but it is expensive. In the final analysis, the best preventive against rabies is to be aware (not paranoid) of animals, and be especially careful in places like Pushkar, Jaisalmer and Kovalam beach.

How to Stay Healthy

1) Keep a flask of fresh drinking water handy at all times. Top it up each morning before you leave your hotel. This saves you having to drink local (often insanitary) water. Most diseases out here are water-borne.
2) Never drink any water (even in restaurants) that has not been filtered, sterilised with Puritabs or with water-purification tablets, or boiled for at least 10 minutes. Bottled water, such as **Bisleri**, is now widely available, price about Rs 10.
3) If no fresh water is available, stick to hot tea (or buy some oranges).
4) Brush your teeth with boiled or bottled water. Take care not to swallow water in showers.
5) Strictly avoid ice-cubes, and go easy on local ice-cream, delicious though it is. Many germs survive being deep-frozen.
6) With aerated drinks or fruit juices, never drink from the bottle; always ask for a straw. Be especially careful with soda-water: it's often made in somebody's backyard, loaded with typhoid germs. Stick to popular brands and avoid anything slightly suspect.
7) Always peel your own fruit and vegetables and steer clear of raw vegetable salads, raw sugar-cane or (a major cause of amoebic dysentery) iced cane-juice.
8) Adjust slowly to Indian food. At the start of your journey, when the stomach is likely to be ultra-sensitive, stick to mild foods, such as boiled rice, yogurt (*raita*), breads and boiled eggs.
9) Avoid street food unless you've been in India for a couple of months, and it is freshly cooked and still hot.
10) Eat three square meals a day. In hot, dry climates, like Rajasthan, travellers often go right off solid foods and live on a watery diet of fruit salads, curd, and loads of bottled drinks. The inevitable result is diarrhoea. To soak up all that excess liquid, eat some solids (bananas, breads, biscuits, etc.) immediately.
11) In very dry climates, the best way of quenching thirst is to drink deeply and seldom, not little and often. This applies especially to people tackling the Rajasthan and Ladakh routes.

12) When eating with your fingers (which is the Indian custom), clean them first—most restaurants have a wash-hand basin. Better, use moistened medicated tissues or orange-skin peelings. It is very difficult to keep clean in India, though the Indian people themselves are among the cleanest in the world.

13) Avoid throat and chest complaints by rationing visits to fiercely air-conditioned luxury hotels and restaurants, and go easy on sunbathing or bathing in cold swimming-pools. Walking along dusty streets, get into the habit of breathing through the nose, not the mouth. In hot, humid places like Bombay and Madras, wear a vest or absorbent under-garment to soak up excess perspiration.

14) Keep your medical kit regularly replenished. Before you head off into remote places, visit a local pharmacist and stock up on first-aid essentials.

15) Make sure that you have adequate protection against the sun, such as a long-sleeved shirt, a hat, and sun-cream.

Observing these precautions should see you returning home fitter and healthier than when you set out. You will almost certainly lose a lot of weight. If illness does strike, remember that Indian doctors are generally excellent, and your hotel should be able to recommend the best local one. Most main cities also have good hospitals and superior nursing facilities. This said, medical treatment abroad is expensive for those used to the European welfare state. One poor man contracted typhoid by drinking local soda water: his doctor's bill for just one week was over £200.

Security

This is a very personal matter—some travellers go completely overboard and clank their way into India loaded down with more padlocks, chains, zips and clips than Marley's ghost. Others take the opposite line, and lounge about in crowded bazaars with wads of money sticking out of every pocket. Both approaches attract the attention of every beggar and would-be thief in town. Very few Indians are villains, but if you make a show of wealth, it's an invitation to trouble. Westerners can be rather insensitive to the poverty around them; whipping out a ripple of 100-rupee notes in search of small change for a rickshaw man, will not only magnetise a whole street, but is an appalling demonstration of bad taste. Far safer and kinder to keep a small amount of money sufficient for the day's expenses in a small neck-purse separate from your main stash.

India is actually a very safe country indeed. Unlike many ex-colonial countries, there is minimal anti-British feeling here, and (for some reason) the local people will often go out of their way to help British travellers. This said, it is tempting providence to stroll off down dark backstreets at night or to sleep out alone on lonely beaches or in empty fields.

General Security Points

1) On the streets, wear shoulder-bags across the body (impossible to snatch), and keep all money and valuables out of sight (never in unzipped pockets). Beware of being frisked by beggars pretending a friendly hug. Never give anyone your camera, radio or Walkman to 'look at', unless you feel quite sure of getting it back again.

2) On Indian trains, where robbery is common, use your rucksack or bag as a pillow (or stash it under your knees) when sleeping. If going to the bathroom, bolt your bag

to a fixed compartment attachment or to a window bar.

3) On crowded local buses, keep a constant eye on your luggage. You may be asked to put your bags under a seat to make room for other passengers. Don't do it. One woman who did lost a £300 camera lens—and it wasn't insured.

4) In cheap lodgings, double-lock the door (with combination padlock) and secure all windows before retiring for the night. Thieves are adept at creeping into unsecured hotel rooms.

5) If leaving your luggage anywhere, for any reason, padlock it to a pipe, a bedstead, or anything that can't be moved. Some hotels will mind it for you, but always get a receipt, and always check nothing's missing on your return.

Your best security is yourself. Fear, anger or carelessness all attract theft; calm confidence and alertness deter it. If you become a victim, report your loss to the police by all means (you'll need their report for any insurance claim), but don't expect a lot of sympathy. India is for the self-reliant—a quality that some travellers have to learn the hard way.

Communications

Post offices in India provide a good, reliable service, and are open from 10 am to 5 pm on weekdays, and Saturday mornings. The cost of postage from India is Rs11.00 for a letter, Rs6.50 for an aerogramme, and Rs6 for a postcard. Enterprising postal staff have a peculiar talent for 'disappearing' unfranked (uncancelled) stamps off letters and postcards, which then go precisely nowhere. Either have your mail franked (cancelled) before your very eyes in a post office, or (better) buy a stack of pre-stamped aerogrammes, which can't be interfered with.

The post office's answer to the courier companies has been the introduction of Speed Post which links over 60 towns in India and serves most countries. For sending documents this service is generally as quick as a courier but considerably cheaper.

Postes restantes (general delivery offices) are usually located in main post offices, but not always. Notable exceptions are New Delhi, Jodhpur and Udaipur. In some cities there are two *postes restantes*—New Delhi's office is located at the end of Baba KharakSingh Marg, near Connaught Place, whereas Delhi's office is located between Kashmir Gate and the Delhi railway station. They also provide a good service, and your expected mail is nearly always waiting for you when you call. If it isn't, check not only under the initial of your surname, but under that of your christian name (misfiling is common). When collecting mail from a *poste restante*, you'll need some sort of identity document (e.g. a passport) to claim it. And if you don't claim it within a month, it's often returned to the sender. Have all letters and cards addressed to you as follows:

Bloggs, J.
Poste Restante
New Delhi 110001
India

If for some reason, you want your mail from home to be redirected to a different *poste restante* from the one originally specified, then visit the latter and fill out an instruction slip. This procedure takes only a minute, and will save you from having to write home to all your friends and relatives to tell them you've moved.

Posting parcels home can be difficult. If possible, get someone to do it for you—there are excellent postal packing services in Delhi and Bombay. Otherwise, allow a whole morning to: a) take parcel to a local tailor, ask him to stitch a linen bag for it, with the seams sealed with wax. This service is usually also available from people sitting outside the major post offices, such as the one in A Block of Connaught Place, New Delhi. This will cost around Rs8–10, and you'll need to press a mark into the wax (a ring or foreign coin is best) to identify it as your property; b) fill out two customs declarations forms at a post office, stick one to the parcel with glue (messy), write your passport number and 'bona fide tourist' somewhere on the forms, describe the parcel contents as a gift, and its value as not more than Rs1000; c) have the parcel weighed, and establish the cost (airmail is nearly three times the cost of seamail, around Rs200 per 1 kg sent, but gets home three times quicker, in around three to four weeks); d) buy the appropriate stamps, and glue (not stick) them on; e) give the package in to the parcel counter, and ask for a receipt.

Telephones tend to be rather unreliable; the quality of the line often depends on the weather. The system is improving but many exchanges are overloaded and this leads to numerous problems. With local calls, you'll either get through immediately, or not at all. Even if you are lucky, you may not be able to hear anything. A friend who had similar problems speculated that if his hotel was burning down, he wouldn't phone the fire station—he would write them a letter instead. If you don't get straight through to someone on a local call, hail a taxi and visit them personally instead: it could be much quicker.

For long-distance calls, you can make a regular call through the operator, direct dial by Subscriber Trunk Dialing (STD), make a Demand Call (more expensive, but quicker), or buy a Lightning Call (much more expensive, but you can get through immediately).

International calls can be made from the GPO, STD shops, or from your hotel. But don't expect immediate results. You might have to wait anything between a half-hour and a day before anything happens. You've always got a better chance of success in big hotels, where you can dial at leisure away from public-booth crowds.

In most towns, small shops with phone booths providing quick, efficient and generally reliable STD and IDD services have sprung up. Some of these 'shops' also provide fax services.

Telex messages are also best sent from the larger hotels (if they let you use their service—subject to a hefty service charge) or from the main post offices, and are relatively cheap. The advantage of the telex is that it gives you a record of any hotel bookings or airline confirmations made—a wise precaution in a country notorious for double-booking suites and seats.

Money

The Indian rupee (Rs) divides into 100 paise (p). There are coins of 5, 10, 20, 25 and 50 paise, Rs1, 2 and 5. Notes are Rs2, 5, 10, 20, 50, 100 and 500. The approximate exchange rates at the time of writing are:

£1   = Rs55
US$1 = Rs29
A$1 = Rs22

You will have to buy your currency in India, supposedly at banks or official money-changers. Indian banks can, however, be exceedingly slow. There is a black market for foreign currency, and you are likely to be approached by various unofficial money-changers during your trip. You can extend your money by changing it in this way, but it's always something of a risk, and you must change some foreign currency in the banks because it's the only way you'll get currency exchange forms (yes, more forms). You'll need these for a) any re-exchange of Indian currency when leaving the country; b) any airline-ticket purchases; c) settling hotel bills; d) any application to extend your visa.

When changing money, don't get stuck with worn or torn notes, because you'll never get rid of them, except at banks; or with only large-denomination notes, because nobody in India will change them down—even when they can. Change only small amounts at a time—£50/100 is the norm—and always keep a US$100 bill tucked away somewhere very safe. This ensures that if you ever get robbed, and lose your main stash of money, you're not at a complete loss. You can book into a hotel, and wire home for more cash—though even by cable this could take weeks. Always keep encashment certificates: you will need these when paying for your hotel bill and purchasing an air ticket—amongst other things (see Customs and Currency Regulations, p.21).

Transferring money is best done through a foreign bank: Indian banks often have to receive money at a main foreign exchange dealing branch, which may not be either evident or the most convenient to you. They have been known to deny that long-awaited money has arrived, sometimes weeks after they've received it.

Consulates

If you find yourself in serious trouble, contact the Consular Section of your embassy or high commission, which will be in New Delhi. Many countries also have consulates or deputy high commissions in Bombay, Calcutta and Madras. These are listed in the respective city sections.

Shopping

India is one of the great markets of the world. You can find a remarkable range of fabulous produce—silk, cotton, leather, jewellery, carving and handicrafts—at real bargain prices, sometimes four or five times cheaper than abroad. The quality of craftsmanship can be excellent, and even if what you want is not in stock, it can invariably be made up for you—either done on the spot, or sent on later. Tailors can run up clothes overnight, and although cuts tend to be a little out-moded for those with more fashionable tastes, they will copy any design you provide to perfection, and it's worth bringing along a favourite piece of clothing for that very purpose. Bulky purchases, such as carpets and large ornaments, can be shipped home for you. Expensive jewellery buys can be verified for you at gem-testing laboratories. Large hotels have their own shopping emporia, packed with a wide variety of goods, where you can shop in air-conditioned comfort.

Always try to start your shopping tour with a visit to a government or state emporium. These stock the full range of local produce and handicrafts, sometimes also a selection of goods from neighbouring states. Because all prices are fixed, you are able to establish exactly what is available, and how much it should cost. This knowledge can be invaluable when it comes to buying things in less scrupulous high-street shops, markets or bazaars.

The best all-round places to shop are the huge Central Cottage Industries Emporia, currently located in Delhi, Bombay, Calcutta, Jaipur and Bangalore. These are the places you can do all your shopping in one place—very popular with people making last-minute purchases before flying back home. Of the smaller state emporia, make a point of visiting those of Gujarat and Rajasthan: these provide the most colourful, attractive and exotic variety of handmade goods.

On the streets, you'll have to bargain hard when buying anything. The big thing to bear in mind is that there is an Indian price and a tourist price for everything. Never accept the first price given; it will always be too high. You can try the 'walk away' technique to bring it down, but many Indians have got wise to this, and you may end up walking away from something you really want, and never being called back. It is often far more effective to pretend interest in something you don't want, haggle over it a bit, affect to lose interest, then pick up the article you do want almost as an afterthought. To make some sort of sale, the vendor will often give a half-decent price immediately. If he doesn't, some well-chosen Hindi phrases will always improve your chances of getting the local price. Asking *kitne paise?* (how much), grumbling *bahut paisa hai!* (too much) and wheedling *kum karo* (come down a bit) often have the desired effect. It is also helpful to have asked a local Indian the correct price of the item even before entering the shop.

Bargaining can be great fun. Once you've got the hang of it, it's possible to buy things in markets and bazaars even cheaper than in fixed-price emporia. But beware, travellers do get carried away by success, and it's not uncommon to meet someone stuck with £2000 worth of useless carpets, the result of being sweet-talked into visiting some street-tout's 'uncle's shop' or 'brother's silk emporium'. With big buys, you really do have to know what you're talking about. Don't let anyone take you anywhere you can't afford to go. In any shopping situation, as soon as you've lost the initiative, you're halfway to buying something you don't even want. Even worse, you may have to lug it halfway round India until you find some way of sending it home.

Most decent shops and emporia a) give you a certificate of origin with major purchases and a receipt (essential for when the article hits customs; very expensive if you can't produce them); b) arrange for the item(s) bought to be shipped home for you. In case a completely different article turns up at your front door, it can be a good idea to photograph or mark the item at the time of actually purchasing it.

Unless you have to, don't make all purchases in one place. Different areas of India are famous for different things. You'll always get a better choice and quality of when you buy at source, rather than from a central government emporium.

Go to Agra for sublime marble inlay work, to Jaipur for gems and jewellery, to Mysore for incense and sandalwood, to Varanasi for silks and brasswork, to

Hyderabad for silver inlay and for pearls, to Udaipur for miniature paintings and for wall-hangings, and to Rajasthan in general for chunky folk-art jewellery, colourful mirror-embroidery and white-glazed pottery.

If you want to know more about these products, manufacturing processes, general prices, and how to tell the real McCoy from cheap tourist tat, read the appropriate shopping sections in the main body of the text. If this only whets your appetite, there are ample opportunities in many handicraft centres to visit local crafts factories and see carpets, miniature paintings, tapestries, carvings and even incense being made. There is no obligation to buy at these places—just a lot of friendly pressure.

Sports and Leisure Activities

Not many people come to India in pursuit of sports, but Indians are keen followers of sport (especially hockey and cricket), and many towns have facilities for games such as tennis, squash, golf, riding and swimming. And of course the countryside in its vastness and infinite variety offers an inexhaustible range of adventures: trekking, camel-safaris, white-water rafting and game-viewing are just some of the activities on offer.

If you want to take exercise of an organised nature, the tourist office or your hotel should be able to guide you. There are few public recreational facilities; most are attached to clubs or hotels, and access may be limited to members and guests. Specific details are given where possible in the text, but you will find that the best way to gain access to facilities is via your local friends.

Opening Hours and Admission Times

Most government organisations and private businesses follow a 5-day week, from 9.30 am–5.30 pm. Some state government offices are open on Saturdays, but often take the second Saturday of the month as a holiday. All offices are closed on Sundays.

Most airline offices are open 6 days a week, also from 9.30 am to 5.30 pm; the four major international airports are open 24 hours. Banking hours are 10 am–2 pm for 5 days a week and 10 am–12 pm on a 6th day. Sundays are generally but not invariably the day of rest. You can usually find a bank open every day of the week in the major cities.

Post offices open 10 am–4 pm, Mon–Sat; in the major cities one branch will stay open 24 hours. Shops will normally be open 10 am–8 pm 6 days a week, although in some towns such as Pune or Goa shopkeepers take a siesta. Most of these organisations will be closed on Sundays, but in major cities one shopping area is generally open and takes a compensatory day off during the week.

Festivals and Public Holidays

The Indian calendar is an ongoing procession of thousands of festivals, each year. Nearly everywhere you go, some sort of temple celebration, religious pageant, or colourful arts festival will have just started or just ended. They are always worth going out of your way to see, most being highly spectacular and great fun. All Indian festivals have a strong cultural, artistic and religious theme and flavour, and the major ones attract some of the best exponents of music, dance and theatre in the country. Also vast crowds of hysterical devotees, so be careful.

There are no fixed dates for many of these festivals. Their timing is determined by the Indian lunar calendar, and is calculable only during the previous year. Around October, your nearest Government of India tourist office should have the full list of festivals and dates for the forthcoming year. There are, however, a few national holidays when shops, banks and government offices are closed. Republic Day on 26 January, Independence Day on 15 August and Mahatma Gandhi's birthday on 2 October are three days when everything is closed.

Some major religious rites and rituals, like **Dussehra** and **Diwali**, are celebrated (in differing regional forms) all over India. Other celebrations, like the popular **International Film Festival**, are held in different locations every other year but are held in New Delhi in alternate years (1993, 1995, etc.).

A new series of festivals have been started by the state government tourist departments to promote tourism. They are organised at well-known historical sites such as the cave site of Elephanta near Bombay, Mahabalipuram near Madras, Konarak and Khajuraho. The festival is usually a 5-day affair consisting of evening dance recitals. Eminent exponents of the many dance forms are invited to perform, among others, *Bharatnatyam* from south India, *Kathak*, from northern India, *Odissi*, from Orissa, *Kuchipudi* from Andhra Pradesh and *Kathakali* from Kerala. These festivals provide an excellent opportunity to see a major historical site and good dance at the same time.

The more interesting and worthwhile festivals and fairs, together with their approximate dates, are listed below. You'll find more details of them in the relevant route sections in this book.

Pongal (Sankranti)—Mid-Jan. A 3-day harvest festival, best seen in Tamil Nadu and Karnataka (south India). Lively processions, bull-fights, and much decorating of sacred cows. *Pongal* is the sweet rice preparation prepared from the freshly harvested paddy.

Republic Day—26 January. Important national festival celebrated all over the country, notably in New Delhi. On 27 and 28 January, a big folk-dance festival takes place in Delhi, and on 29 January the famous 'Beating Retreat' ceremony below the magnificent Secretariat buildings.

Vasant Panchami—Jan/Feb. All across India, especially in the north (marks first day of spring) and in West Bengal, where the celebrations are public and include colourful kite-flying. This Hindu festival is held in honour of Saraswati, goddess of learning.

Float Festival—Jan/Feb. Madurai. Commemorates birth of Tirumalai Nayak, the city's 17th-century ruler.

Desert Festival—Jan/Feb. With the magnificent Jaisalmer Fort as the background, this festival gives an opportunity to listen to the music of the desert, see local craftsmen at work and watch dance performances.

Carnival—Feb. Held in Goa, and very popular. Goa is also a great place to be at Christmas.

Shivratri—Feb/Mar. All over India, especially at important Shiva temples at Khajuraho, Varanasi, Mandi, Chidambaram and Kashmir. Devotees perform all-night vigil and fasting, then a 'break fast' of fruits, nuts, sweet potatoes and rice.

Holi—Feb/Mar. This is the big one. Throughout northern India (best in Mathura and Rajasthan), everybody pelts everyone else with coloured water and powder. It's their way of celebrating the advent of spring.

Khajuraho Dance Festival—early March. Unmissable display of performing arts at Khajuraho in authentic temple surroundings.

Gangaur—Mar/Apr. Rajasthan, especially Udaipur and Jaipur. The festival is held in honour of Parvati and is named after a mythical embodiment of wifely devotion called Gangaur. Therefore, it is the culmination of marriage ceremonies (very colourful) in these parts. Also held in West Bengal and Orissa.

Spring Festival and Baisakhi—Apr/May. Two celebrations, with a horticultural theme, best seen in Punjab. The latter marks the Hindu solar New Year.

Meenakshi Kalyanam—Apr/May. Madurai. Spectacular annual solemnisation of Meenakshi's marriage to Shiva, held at the end of a 10-day non-stop festival in and around the famous Meenakshi temple. Excellent music.

Buddha Purnima—May/Jun. Commemorates date of Buddha's birth, death, and enlightenment. Best at Sarnath and Bodhgaya.

Rath Yatra—Jun/Jul. Held at Puri, this is the temple festival to beat them all. Three gigantic temple chariots, containing the deities Jagannath, Balabhadra (his brother) and Subhadra (his sister), are dragged in awesome procession through a living sea of pilgrims. Unbelievable atmosphere.

Independence Day—15 August. Celebrated all over India.

Ganesh (Ganpati) Chaturthi—Sept. The elephant-headed god of good luck is feted in many areas, but especially in Bombay where huge processions are taken out to take clay images of the deity into the sea.

Dussehra—Sept/Oct. A 10-day festival of national importance, celebrated everywhere. Most colourful and entertaining in Mysore, Kulu and West Bengal. Also in Delhi and Varanasi. At Ramnagar, across the river Ganga from Varanasi a many-night-long theatrical performance called **Ram Lila** draws many thousands of visitors.

Diwali—Oct/Nov. The liveliest and noisiest of all Indian festivals, a night-long revel of firecrackers, illuminations and general pageantry. In some parts of the country, Diwali marks the start of the Hindu New Year. Best seen in Delhi and the north.

Cattle Fair—Nov/Dec. Pushkar's annual fair, held on the very edge of the desert. A real tourist favourite.

Christmas Day—25 December. All over India, but best in Goa, Delhi and Bombay. Many music and dance festivals.

Madras Dance and Arts Festival—Mid-Dec to early Jan. Held in Madras, and getting better every year.

Be warned: Indian festivals may be wonderful, exciting occasions most of the time, but some do go way over the top, and you would be well advised to check the festival diary before you travel. A common culprit is Holi, during which foreign tourists are a favourite target not only for the usual coloured powders, but also (on occasion) less pleasant things like paint, ink, axle grease and even car battery-acid. The place not to be when things go out of control is on the open streets, or in trains. Excited crowds are common, and can be frightening. At such times, police find it difficult to keep public order.

Part II

CULTURE

Bronze c. 2500 BC, National Museum, New Delhi

People and Society

India is a wide-ranging amalgam of races, religions and cultures. There are Tibetans up in Ladakh, Kashmiris of central Asian stock in the far north, Bengalis in the east, negroid aboriginals in the Nicobar Islands, dark-skinned Dravidians in the south, and all manner of Aryan, European, Arab, Semite and Mongol permutations throughout the north and down the western coast. They are dissimilar in hundreds of ways, but have succeeded in becoming a single nation.

This unity has been achieved (even more impressively) in the face of a dramatic population explosion. The current figure of around 900 million increases at a rate of 18 million a year—that's the size of the population of Australia, and the size of the workforce on Indian Railways. Following the unfortunate experiment in enforced sterilisation in the mid-70s, subsequent Indian governments have adopted a very low profile on population control. It is probable that by the end of the century, there will be one billion Indians.

The unexpected (to Western prophets of doom) national unity of India following Independence was largely due to the age-old moral and spiritual unity of the people.

The essential beliefs and social institutions which marked Indians as a self-contained people originated long before the time of Buddha; their domestic rituals and ceremonials were inscribed three centuries or more before Christ; and their legal system was codified two millennia ago. Little wonder, therefore, that Indian society, morals and laws resisted and often absorbed the civilisations of numerous foreign invaders, or that they formed the strong, solid basis on which to unite modern, free India.

Hindu society, from the earliest times, was distinguished by three characteristics: the caste system, the joint family, and the codified system of law.

Caste

The caste system is highly complex, dividing the whole of society (in theory at least) into four castes—**Brahmins** (priests, men of learning, and general arbiters of morals); **Kshatriyas** (soldiers and administrators); **Vaisyas** (traders, men of commerce); and **Sudras** (farmers, peasants and the great mass of the working people). In practice, with social evolution these basic four divisions have fragmented into hundreds of sub-castes, and the original definitions have lost their meaning. Only the Brahmin class, by virtue of its exclusiveness, can be said to have clung, more or less, to its original function. This is perhaps appropriate, since it was the Brahmins—doubtless to preserve their privileged rights and position in society—who seem to have developed the caste system in the first place. The more romantic explanation is that the four castes sprang from the mouth (Brahmins), arms (Kshatriyas), thighs (Vaisyas) and feet (Sudras) of the creator, Brahma.

Joint Family

The joint family was a system under which property was held in common, and brothers and sons lived together under one roof: lacking in privacy, yes, but also productive of great community spirit and strength, as can be seen in many of the village areas of India today. A less satisfactory consequence of the joint family arrangement, however, was that all property was inherited not by succession to the eldest son, but divided equally between all sons. In the long term, this led to wide and disparate fragmentation of the land, each successive generation inheriting less property than the last.

Law

The system of law was a complicated batch of rights and obligations based on ancient texts and local customs. Eventually associated with Hindu religion, it was archaic in the extreme, particularly where women were concerned. An independent life for women had never been contemplated under Hindu law, and their economic dependence on men (including only limited right to property) was at all times heavily emphasised.

Then came the social revolution. At Independence, the new constitution set itself the task of bringing India up-to-date with the rest of the modern world. It abolished untouchability, redesignating the *harijans* as a 'scheduled caste' with full democratic and human rights; it offered a secular law for all Indian citizens to opt for while allowing all communities to retain their own traditions; it broke down the joint family system with new inheritance laws, giving daughters equal rights to inherit with sons;

it offered a unified marriage law all over India, not only permitting marriages between different castes and religions, but allowing women the right of remarriage and divorce.

In theory, modern India is no longer a socially backward country, dominated by caste and anachronistic customs, denying millions of people social rights. It has promised itself a major revolution, and would like to think of itself as moving rapidly towards it. In practice, however, India has always been slow to change. To understand why this is so, one has to appreciate the great social emphasis of the country. Far more than in the West, Indian life is governed at all levels by the extended family, a system of favours and obligations, of communal identity and sharing, by age-old social ethics and morality.

Marriage Act

The 1952 Marriage Act, for instance, gave women the right of remarriage, but very few young widows, even today, take advantage of it. The customs of thousands of years that have proved for some reason beneficial to society are very difficult to break, and even if these women were to declare themselves available, few Indian men would have them. Arranged marriages are still the general rule, and 'love matches' the notable exception. Marriage in India always was, and still is, a social phenomenon first, and a matter of personal preference seccnd. In most cases, parents and relatives continue to select the bride from similar background with some political, financial and social benefit; in some states (notably Rajasthan) child marriages still go on, despite being strictly illegal; and it is still rare today for the bridegroom to be left alone with his betrothed before the marriage ceremony. The pertinent traditional argument in favour of arranged marriages (and a major stumbling block to social liberation in the Western sense) is that the bride and groom have to make the alliance work. Both parties are responsible not so much to each other, but to society, for a successful married life. To fail in marriage is to fail in society, and the divorce rate is consequently low. Because Indians can't think simply of their own needs, but must also take into account their wider responsibility to society, they generally make far greater efforts to make marriages work that Westerners. But when they do break down, it can be very tough on women. To leave a marriage is, effectively, to step right out of society. Disownment by the family, loss of caste and social identity, and, in the absence of any social security arrangement, financial deprivation, are all problems faced by women seeking divorce in India today. And modern Indian marriages are by no means as stable as before. The tradition of dowries—whereby the prospective bride's father practically gives the shirt off his back, persists despite being against the law. Today, the average dowry demanded by middle-class parents for their often overpriced boys can be anything from Rs10 000 to Rs1 000 000, which often puts the bride's family into debt for the rest of their lives. The scale peaks for boys living and working abroad, with those holding US green cards fetching the best price. IAS officers (the senior cadre of civil servants), doctors and lawyers receive higher bids than idealistic teachers or publishers. Worse, 'kitchen accidents' still occur: young wives who disappoint greedy in-laws are doused in kerosene and incinerated in locked kitchens. This leaves the husband free to remarry and collect another handsome dowry. Such practices reflect the temptations generated by an increasingly consumer-oriented society.

Distribution of Wealth

Another thorn in the side of social progress is the unequal distribution of wealth in the country. As one young Brahmin remarked: 'For many ages past, the rich have been lazy and the higher castes spoilt, leaving the lower castes to work all day long for practically nothing.' At present, about 2% of India's population are rich, with some 25% salaried; the remaining 60% are the homeless, jobless and often landless poor, who live mainly in the villages. Indians of education and vision point out that the same state of affairs existed in England and the USA a century ago, when similar socio-economic inequalities existed, yet were quickly harmonised after the triumph of democracy. The more optimistic of them predict the same rapid improvements in India. But others, more realistically, fear that India will make the same mistakes as the West and that society will lose its cohesiveness.

Society still tends to determine every facet of an Indian's life: the kind of work he can do, the woman he will marry, the people he will (and won't) mix with, and the type of religious observances he will perform. This gives him a strong social identity, a certain sense of 'belonging', and a definite role in life. All these things contribute to the great openness, lack of social inhibition (no neuroses here!) and personal confidence of the Indian people. Yet caste, despite its great social value, can be construed as a severe restriction on individual growth and national progress. Many well-qualified and professional Indians, for example, find caste a real block to incentive, and prefer to work abroad. It is still possible that a man might wait 10 years for promotion, working in the same low-paid job, and then when his superior leaves or dies finds that someone of a higher caste but less experience has been promoted above his head. On a wider level, the lack of social mobility created by caste is 'free' India's most complex challenge. Whether or not it is productive of widespread apathy among the people is open to debate, but it is certainly no spur to individual incentive.

Cracks in the armour of caste have started to appear. Curiously, these are less the result of legislation than of the powerful stimulus of the West. The new Indian middle class which arose in the 19th century was formed as a result of Western education and industrialisation with its attendant economic changes. The powerful Indian business class that had gained power over centuries became concentrated in the big capitals of Bombay, Calcutta and Delhi during the rapid industrial growth after Independence. The critical factor, though, was the legacy of the British Raj. When the English moved out in 1947, they left behind the élitist and influential traditions of the armed services, the civil service, the judiciary, the universities, the press and the political structures. This new Indian élite was brought up with alien concepts of Western clothes, ideas, food and social customs. For the previous century at least, this created a market and a dumping ground for all sorts of Western produce. Even India's street lamps were imported from Britain.

But it is in the continuing tradition of English education that the Raj continues to influence every level of Indian life. Those who can afford an English education for their children are the 'haves', while those who can't are the 'have nots'. All sorts of doors—social, political and economic—open to people with the right (English) education, especially in the British heritage of clubs and societies. This breed of snobbishness, a direct hangover from the Raj, is Britain's own contribution to the Indian heritage of class and caste. In effect, the Raj created a completely new caste, one that was particularly relevant to modern industrial India—of the privileged, British-educated ruling élite.

Small wonder, then, that Indians are so keen to communicate with English-speaking visitors. For English is the chosen *lingua franca* of India's upper classes. It has status value, it is a passport to senior jobs, it is the language of central government, of the higher law courts, of business and of the professional classes. Most important of all, it is a language of opportunity, unfettered by traditional caste and social restrictions, to which anyone with enough enterprise and money can aspire. Not that this is a desirable situation. Advancement, restricted to the urban middle classes on which the Raj pinned their hopes, is still denied to the great mass of the poorer people who flock to the great towns and cities of British India—notably Bombay and Calcutta—in search of food and work.

History

As late as 1920, it was believed that civilisation in India dated back only to the time of Alexander's invasion in the 4th century BC. The problem was that the Hindu people, unlike the Greeks, the Europeans, the Chinese and the Arabs, never developed the art of historical writing. India did have a considerable historical tradition, embodied in both its literature and its semi-religious works known as the *Puranas*, but until the early 1800s little was known of the history of the Hindu people before the Muslim invasions of the 11th century AD.

Ancient India

Then came the discovery of the ancient Indus civilisation. Some time in the mid-19th century, British engineers laying a rail track between Karachi and the Punjab stumbled across a vast quantity of ancient sun-baked bricks, which were being used by locals to provide solid foundations for the track. It was later found that these bricks were over 5000 years old. Intrigued, archaeologists visited the area in the 1920s and presently came up with two buried cities—Mohenjodaro (mound of the dead) along the Indus, and Harappa on the Ravi. A rapid series of other discoveries, in the Punjab and in Gujarat, confirmed that an ancient civilisation with well-planned cities, large-scale commerce, skilled craftsmen, knowledge of mathematics and script, and sophisticated social structure existed in India as long ago as 3000 BC. This was a timely discovery. To know that they belonged to one of the earliest areas of civilisation in the world, contemporary with ancient Egypt and Sumer, provided the modern Indian people with just the kind of national pride and feeling they needed to achieve unity, and with it Independence.

The Indus civilisation was created by the 'original' Indians whose descendants still inhabit the south of the country today. This civilization then spread to northern and western India while the original cities fell into disuse. Around 1500 BC the Aryans came from the north, mounted on horses and riding in chariots. They were a Caucasian people who brought a rich language tradition to India, later to result in the Sanskrit literary classics of the *Vedas*. Around 800 BC they learned how to make iron tools and weapons, and then pushed further east and south-wards to the Gangetic plain where they founded villages, tribal republics and well-governed powerful states. These communities developed agricultural and mercantile wealth.

Under Cyrus, then Darius (521–485 BC), the Persians conquered the Indus Valley regions of the Punjab and Sind. Theirs was a passing visit, but they left some interesting influences on religion, art and administration. The Greeks, under Alexander the Great, spent even less time in India—Alexander overthrew Darius III in 331 BC, advanced as far as the Beas River in 326 BC, conquered King Porus and his elephants, and was then compelled by his troops to return home, leaving behind a series of garrisons and administrative systems to keep the trade links open with west Asia and the consequent exchange of ideas and art.

The powerful Maurya dynasty of Magadha (present-day Bihar) which rose under the monarch Chandragupta, cut out an extensive swathe of territory across the Indo-Gangetic plain, from Bengal in the east into the heart of Afghanistan in the north-west. By this time the religious legacy of the first Aryans, Brahmanical Hinduism, had laid down firm roots, and the 6th-century BC protest movements of Buddhism and Jainism, were also well-established. The caste system, interest-ingly, was starting to splinter—by Chandragupta's time, the original four castes had given way to at least seven definite classes of Indian society: priests and scholars, graziers and hunters, artisans and traders, tillers, police and bureaucrats.

The Mauryan empire reached its zenith under Ashoka (268–31 BC), who con-solidated the north, conquered as far south as Mysore, and then drove east to Orissa. His fateful battle here, at Kalinga, caused him to renounce warfare forever (so appalled was he by the carnage that he had wrought) and to espouse Buddhism. He had messages of peace inscribed on rocks and pillars all over his domain, notably in Orissa, in Gujarat, at Sarnath and Sanchi, and in Delhi. He also sent his son Mahendra over to Sri Lanka (armed with a sapling of the Bodhi Tree) to spread the message of Buddhism.

The Mauryan power collapsed within a century of Ashoka's death. In its heyday though, this empire probably ruled over more of India than any other until the time of the British. In its wake, came a number of different dynasties—Brahmin rulers in the Indo-Gangetic plains, Telugus in the Deccan plain, and Cholas (round Madras), Cheras (Kerala) and Pandyas (Tamil Nadu) in the south. While the Tamils busied themselves in exporting Hinduism, Buddhism, Jainism and Indian philosophy, art and medicine to Ceylon, Cambodia, Java, Rome and the Far East (either by invasion or trade), the Telugus—self-styled 'Lords of the Deccan'—were mainly engaged in building Buddhist *stupas* (burial mounds). During their rule Hinayana Buddhism, in which the Buddha was represented by *stupas*, footprints, elephants and trees, flourished. This form of Buddhism continued to around AD 400, but had been effectively supplanted by the Mahayana form at least a couple of centuries earlier. The Buddhist influence at this time was so strong that when the Greeks revisited, occupying the Punjab and invading the Mauryan capital of Pataliputra (Patna) in

150 BC, their king (Menander) promptly converted to Buddhism. But what was happening in the north of India was invariably a very different story to what was happening in the south. In the north, Hinduism continued to flourish more or less unaffected.

Invasions

As foreign invasions became more and more frequent, India became a virtual melting pot of different cultures. Some say it was simply born to be invaded, its geography certainly points that way. The northernmost zone of the country—the soaring Himalayan range of mountains—gave Indians the illusion of being guarded by an impassable wall. But there was always a series of accessible passes—the Khyber, the Bolan and the Khurram in the northwest, and others linking India to Tibet—and these were the routes which for three millennia at least brought invader and trader across the Afghan-Punjab saddle. They came in the main to loot the vast Indo-Gangetic plains, an apparently inexhaustible granary. They were marauders from the north, who crossed over the passes in the autumn before snowfall, descended to the Indian plains just as the crops began to ripen, fought the traditional big battle in the Punjab, spent the winter methodically looting the rich cities and raiding winter crops, and then—unless they decided to found an empire—disappeared back across the mountains before the hot season arrived.

As such invaders continued to make their inroads through the northwestern passes, India received visits from western China, from the Scythians (around 130 BC), from the Parthians, and from the Kushans of central Asia. Then came a century-long free-for-all, followed by the rise of India's greatest Hindu dynasty—the Imperial Guptas. This empire was founded by Chandragupta II in AD 319, and for the ensuing three centuries (ending in AD 647) ruled an extending domain which eventually included the whole Indo-Gangetic plain down to the northern boundaries of the Deccan. During this period of peace and stability, art and literature flourished (polished Sanskrit replacing Pali script) and extremely fine painting and sculpture were executed at Buddhist centres like Ajanta, Sarnath and Sanchi. By the end of the Gupta period, however, the popularity of Buddhism had begun to wane, and the star of Hinduism rose once again. The break-up of the Gupta Empire meant the general splintering of north India into a number of separate Hindu kingdoms. Prominent amongst these were the Prathiharas of central India, Gangas of eastern India, the western and eastern Chalukyas and further south the Cholas, Cheras and Pandyas. By the 10th–11th centuries these powerful dynasties had created vast kingdoms, built impressive capitals and magnificent temples. In eastern India the temples of Bhubaneshwar and the Sun Temple of Konarak are a reminder of the splendid Ganga kingdoms. The temples of Khajuraho, which draw thousands of tourists to their erotic sculptures, are the best surviving examples of central Indian temples. While many thought that India was in a state of decadence thus paving the way for the advent of Islam it appears that this was not the case. It was during the 9th–13th centuries, and in some case the late 15th century, that the greatest achievements of Hindu art, music, literature and philosophy were made.

The Muslims

The Muslim conquest of India had far-reaching effects on the political, social and cultural life of the country. Between AD 1001 and 1027, the infamous Mahmud of Ghazni mounted 17 separate attacks, eliminating Hindu armies, ransacking temples, and sacking cities on each occasion. His most notable victory was the capture of the holy city of Somnath—the wealth and booty he found here were so great that even he couldn't carry it all away. Mahmud also picked up the nasty habit of collecting severed Hindu fingers, one for each chieftain vanquished. But he was never anything more than a glorified bandit, who returned home to Ghazni in Afghanistan after each individual raid. The real conqueror-founder of Islam in India was Mohammed of Ghor, who mounted the first wholesale invasion of the country in 1192, and brought Muslim power to stay. The Hindu kingdoms of the Gangetic Valley fell without effective resistance to his attacks within a single decade. One of his generals, Mohammed Khilji, swept through Bihar in 1193 and effectively destroyed Buddhism overnight—razing all the monasteries and massacring all the monks. Another general, Qutb-ud-din, became Mohammed of Ghori's direct successor, and after the latter's death in 1206 became the first Sultan of Delhi. But it was left to the Khilji monarchs, notably Ala-ud-din Khilji, to consolidate the Muslim conquest. He ruled for 20 years (1296–1316).

The next Turkish dynasty, the Tughlaqs, ruled from 1320–97. It had two great kings—the first, Mohammed Tughlaq was very potty; the second, Mohammed Firuz, was a great patron of the arts and architecture. His successor, Nasir-ud-din, fell victim to the encroaching Mongol hordes. In 1397 Timur (known as Tamerlane to the Europeans) swept over the Indus, massacred 100 000 Hindu prisoners captured in the Punjab, and toppled the Delhi Sultans. The direct result of his invasion, which nobody could withstand, was to sever India into two parts. Parts of northern India returned to the Turks and the Afghan princes; the south regained independent status under Hindu kings. The latter development was significant. Even while the Muslim Sultans of Delhi were in control of parts of the North, in south India the mighty Vijayanagar Empire was founded in 1336 with its capital at Hampi.

The Mughal Emperors

Of all the invading dynasties, the Mughals were the most influential. A succession of six Mughal emperors left behind a powerful legacy of magnificent buildings, including the Taj Mahal. Their rise was quick and dramatic. The first Mughal monarch, Babur, ruled from 1527 to 1530. He believed it his duty to conquer India and release it from the rule of the Turks. But he started with the Afghan Lodhi rulers of Delhi, employing superior tactics to defeat an army 10 times stronger than his own. Then he advanced, with some trepidation, against the Hindus. The reason for his nerves was that for once the Hindu forces had buried their differences and managed to form a united confederacy under the Rajput monarch, Rana Sanga. This redoubtable individual was a living tapestry of warlike wounds—he had lost an eye and an arm, and had 80 battle scars on his body. But Babur won the day, and raised himself to the status of 'Ghazi', slayer of infidels.

He had intended to stay, but then found he didn't much care for India after all. He liked its countryside, its monsoon and its gold, but he was plagued by its heat, winds and dust. He died, still dreaming of a return to the cool, fragrant air of Kabul, and

India passed to his even more hesitant son, Humayun. This young man was a natural recluse, more interested in scholarly pursuits than in administering an empire. Seizing on this weakness, the brilliant chieftain Sher Shah attacked and retook parts of the empire for the Afghans (1540). He was an enlightened ruler, who ruled only 5 years but achieved more in them—far-reaching administrative, financial and transport improvements—than his three weak successors (1545–56) put together. Then, after 15 years of exile, Humayun finally recaptured Delhi and Agra for the Mughals (1556). His honour vindicated, he enjoyed a few weeks of power, then tripped down some steps hurrying to prayer, and fractured his skull.

Humayun's son, Akbar (1556–1605) was only 14 when he came to the throne. It took him 6 years to remove power-hungry guardians (one was flung off the ramparts of a Delhi fort) and to become the real ruler. He then revealed himself to be the greatest of the Mughal emperors. A man of culture, intelligence, wisdom and equity, he was also a military genius with a practical motto: 'A monarch should be ever intent on conquest, otherwise his neighbours will rise in arms against him.' Instead of trying to subjugate the Hindus (an impossible task, in view of their numbers) he went far to integrating them into his empire with a policy of effective administration. To start the ball rolling, he married a Hindu and raised her Rajput kinsmen to high rank. Then he recruited several Hindu advisers, generals and administrators, abolished a number of taxes on Hindus, and evolved his concept of a secular state with an eclectic faith combining the best of Islam, Hinduism, Jainism, Christianity, Zoroastrianism and Buddhism. This enlightened experiment failed (with Akbar himself as the supreme god-head, it could only be short-lived), but the memory of it still lives on in Akbar's greatest monument, the ghost city of Fatehpur Sikri.

On Akbar's death, his son Jahangir (1605–27) took over. He was an excellent builder, who left fine marble tombs and mosques in and around Agra (and in his beloved Kashmir), but his achievements were obscured by two things: his craving for alcohol and women, and his sadism. Gifted with none of his father's vision for a united people, he put down the Hindu Rajputs and the Deccani Muslims with calculated ruthlessness.

The fifth Mughal, Shah Jahan (1627–58), spent half his reign campaigning against the Rajputs and the Deccan kingdoms. Merciless in his dealings, he gave his Hindu subjects very short shrift (even destroying their places of worship), but in his case military shortcomings were obscured by architectural triumphs. Shah Jahan created the greatest Mughal monuments, including the Taj Mahal, the famous Pearl Mosque in Agra Fort, the Royal Mosque (Jama Masjid, biggest and best mosque in the world) and the Red Fort in Delhi. But this passion for building eventually led to his downfall, and his son Aurangzeb had him imprisoned for the last 7 years of his life—partly to stop him spending any more money.

Aurangzeb (1658–1707) was the last and the dullest of the great Mughal emperors. He was a pious puritan, who dressed simply, lived frugally and died having given strict orders for a modest tomb. Aurangzeb was also a single-minded religious zealot, who systematically murdered his brothers and their sons, extended the empire's boundaries even further in order to replace as many Hindu temples with Muslim mosques as possible, and reduced his non-Muslim subjects to second-class citizens. In later years, after much spilling of blood, he realised that he had sown the seeds of the Mughal Empire's destruction.

After Aurangzeb, came a long line of insignificant, wastrel and weak kings. The dynasty devolved, and finally came to an end under the profligate Mohammed Shah, nicknamed the 'Merry Monarch', who was still drinking, fornicating and generally having a ball in Delhi's Red Fort when the Persian invader, Nadir Shah, suddenly dropped in. He arrived in 1739, stripping Delhi clean of its wealth, massacring 150 000 of its civilian population, and in 5 short months' stay, wrecking her system of administration. To load all the booty he had collected and take it back home to Persia, he employed 1000 elephants, 7000 horses and 10 000 camels.

The Mughal king he left behind now ruled just the four walls of Delhi's Red Fort, but the bell had tolled for the Mughals a lot earlier. When the blood-thirsty Aurangzeb began to assert his Islamic stamp on the Mughal Empire he provoked the Hindu revival—under the Maratha monarch Shivaji—which was to lead to its downfall. By the middle of the 18th century, authority over practically the whole of Hindustan outside the Punjab had passed to the Marathas. It was only when Arthur Wellesley (later Duke of Wellington) broke their power at Assaye (1803) that the British finally became the leading power in India, and only when the Maratha Empire was finally extinguished (1818) that the East India Company became the effective sovereign of the country.

The Mughals, a sad postscript, had come to blows with the British some time earlier, in 1757, at the battle of Plassey. Their defeat here signalled the birth of a new (and final) imperial power in India—the British Raj.

The Raj

The British were not the first Europeans to arrive in India—that privilege went to the Portuguese. In 1498 Vasco da Gama landed at modern-day Kerala, commencing a century-long trade monopoly for the Portuguese, and establishing the base for their later conquest of Goa (1510), then Daman and Diu. The British first appeared in 1612, establishing a trading-post at Surat in Gujarat. For the next 240 years Britain's interest in India was administered not by the crown or the government, but by the London-based East India Company. This founded bases at Madras (1640), Bombay (1668) and Calcutta (1690). To consolidate them, and to establish its trade dominance in India generally, the British had to deal with the Dutch and the French, both of whom had similar trading-posts in the country. The French took Madras in 1746, but lost it back to the British in 1749. Their power in India ended with the surrender of Pondicherry in 1761. The Nawab of Bengal took Calcutta in 1756, but lost it back to Robert Clive in the following year. In the south, the 'Tiger of Mysore' Tipu Sultan (and his father Hyder Ali) inflicted a series of defeats on the British, then were overcome in 1799. With the defeat of the Marathas in 1803, it only remained for the Company to fight the two Sikh Wars and gain control of the Punjab (1849) to put the final seal on empire. The British had come to trade but the need to seek more markets and protect sources of supply lead to an imposition of an alien administration supported by an ever expanding army.

The success of the British was partly the result of Mughal collapse and subsequent Hindu disunity, but owed more to their policy of toleration towards the conquered. Following Akbar's lead, they made little attempt to interfere in Hindu religion, customs or culture; rather, they made it quite clear that they had come just for trade. Many Indian princes no doubt threatened by the disciplined British army, decided to take a break from in-fighting and to accept British suzerainty. They included most of the Rajput princes, the relics of the Mughal Empire like the Nizam of Hyderabad (at that time, and for a long time to come, among the richest individuals in the world) and various survivors of the defeated Maratha confederacy.

The British achieved the closest thing to an Indian empire yet (even the most powerful of prior civilisations had not encompassed all of present-day India), but the country remained just a motley of separate states, each one ruled in name by a Prince, Nawab or Maharajah, but in actuality by the residing British Viceroy or Governor-General. The first of these crown-appointed officials, who replaced the old Company Governor-Generals, which had begun with Warren Hastings in 1774, was Lord Canning in 1859; the last was Mountbatten in 1947. With their rule established, the British went into large-scale iron and coal mining, tea production, coffee and cotton growing, and generally exploited India's vast, largely untapped natural resources. In order to facilitate this exploitation they developed an extensive system of railways, massive irrigation and agricultural programmes, and (some say most importantly) a code of civil law. Actually, it was far from democratic since the conquerors always held the privileged position, but it did ensure an element of equality among the Indians themselves. And this was in a country where Hindu law had previously differentiated strictly between Brahmin and non-Brahmin, where Islamic law had one set of codes for Muslims and quite another for 'kafirs' or infidels. The British also instituted the bureaucracy of the civil service and—while keeping the Indians at a comfortable distance from any real power within it—set about creating an Indian middle class with an increasing responsibility for it. Ultimately, knowledge of ideas and institutions brought an intense desire for self-government.

But the first sign of Indian disaffection against British rule probably had little to do with Independence. The Indian Mutiny of 1857–8 had, in fact, no real discernible cause apart from greased bullets. Somehow, a rumour spread among Muslim and Hindu troops serving with British forces that new bullets being issued were greased with pig (unclean to Muslims) and cow (sacred to Hindus) fat. Too slow to deny this rumour, the British soon had 47 mutinying Indian battalions on their hands. The Mutiny erupted at Meerut, near Delhi, and spread rapidly across north India. The sepoys, actively assisted by disaffected Sikh forces, visited Delhi, dug up the phantom Mughal emperor there (Bahadur Shah) and appointed him reluctant Emperor of Hindustan. His rule lasted just 6 months. There were repeated massacres and sieges on both sides before the Mutiny ran out of steam. In January 1858 Bahadur Shah was sentenced by a British military tribunal to life imprisonment, and with his departure into exile the great Mughal dynasty came to an ignominious end.

The Mutiny was the cause of the transfer of India from the rule of the East India Company to sovereignty of the British Crown. It had been an unexpected blow to British confidence, and it was one which both sides never forgot. The Indian Mutiny had been crushed, but the spirit of rebellion remained alive and slowly began to grow. Resistance was centralised in a sudden, wholesale reform of Hinduism itself. Previous attempts to rally Indians round the banner of the Hindu religion had always foundered on the rocks of caste—the exclusiveness of the Brahmins gave them no feel for the mass popular pulse. But a few determined visionaries—Ram Mohun Roy, Ramakrishna, Swami Vivekananda, Dayananda and even the European Mrs Annie Besant—led a series of important reforms designed to revive Hinduism as a truly modern religion, and thus to totally reorganise (and standardise) totally Hindu society. The movement for social reform ran alongside a parallel movement for national identity and freedom. The latter was fed by a number of timely developments, including the discovery of India's antiquity (excavation of Indus Valley civilisation); the revival of Sanskrit and renewed appreciation of its classics like the *Bhagavad Gita*; and the repatriation of Buddhism, with the coming to light of its long-lost literary, artistic and philosophical achievements. Hindu history and heritage was refound, largely through the researches (ironically) of Western scholars, and this contributed significantly to the evolving national self-image of India as a whole. Other groups, such as the Muslims, also began to develop a sense of national pride and seek self determination.

The Indian National Congress, founded in 1885, was destined to give the British their most prolonged opposition. It began by trying to unite all the communities in India under one banner, but this was not always possible. The Muslims, in particular, still regarded themselves as a race apart, with their traditions rooted outside India, and were alarmed by the growth of Indian nationalism and its demands for political freedom. Faced by the prospect of a Hindu-dominated free India, they founded the Muslim League in 1906 and began making demands for a separate communal electorate for themselves. The Anglo-Muslim alliance of 1906 was a decisive development: it split India into two nations, and Hindus and Muslims were embarked on two entirely different courses. In 1909, perhaps the greatest mistake the British ever made, the Morley-Minto reforms initiated the creation of separate Muslim electorates which directly paved the way for the partition of the Indian Empire.

Gandhi and Independence

The cry for independence, which had become nationwide by the turn of the century, was muted by the arrival of the First World War. Then it burst forth again—this time as an insistent roar—under the charismatic leadership of Mohandas Karamchand Gandhi. Soon to be styled the Mahatma (Great Soul) of the nation, Gandhi arrived in India in 1915, following a long period of fighting on behalf of human rights in South Africa. Gandhi fervently believed in Hindu-Muslim unity: at no time did he contemplate India as an exclusively Hindu state. His life and thoughts were a direct reflection of the 'Karma Yogin' (saint in action). His campaign for the abolition of untouchability, his famous fasts compelling Hindus and Muslims to live together in harmony, his ideals of *ahimsa* (non-violence) and *satyagraha* (passive resistance), and his own life of extreme austerity were all in strict accordance with Hindu traditions. He focused on the movement for independence after the disgraceful massacre of peaceful protesters by armed British troops at Amritsar in 1919, and turned the movement from an ineffective middle-class one to a village-based one of irresistible power.

As the clamour for independence reached its peak, Gandhi was forced to fight a rearguard action against the revived Muslim League under Mohammed Ali Jinnah. After 1936 a demand began for the creation of an independent homeland for Islam, and the fight was on for a partitioned India. The Second World War brought matters to a head. When in 1942 the Mahatma launched his last great struggle, two things became clear: first, that independence was the only settlement possible with Indian nationalism after the war; second, that partition was inevitable. Jinnah out-manoeuvred both the British and the Indian Congress. When, on 9 August 1942,

Gandhi uttered the words in every Hindu's heart and told the British to 'Quit India', Jinnah followed with the demand to 'Divide and Quit'. Against their better judgement, the British were forced to do just this. It was a simple case of partition or civil war. As bloody clashes between Muslims and Hindus mounted in frequency and intensity, even the Congress—after a few months' experience of coalition government (1946–47)—realised that partition was inevitable. As the new British Viceroy, Lord Louis Mountbatten, issued the date for Independence—14 August 1947—the old Indian spokesman, Mahatma Gandhi, left the political scene, darkly predicting chaos.

It was worse than chaos. In 1947, the Indian subcontinent had its eastern and western extremes sliced off to form the two wings of Pakistan, one of which is present-day Bangladesh. But at the time of partition, the new India contained over 35 million Muslims, while the new Pakistan housed vast numbers of Hindus. The problem was worst in the new border states of Bengal and the Punjab, which had very mixed populations and a long history of intercommunal antagonism, and which were both neatly chopped in two by partition. The situation was explosive, and when, during the weeks following Independence, the mass exodus of Hindus and Muslims, uprooting homes in now 'alien' states and travelling to their new homelands, began, it was the signal for bloody and prolonged carnage on an unimaginable scale. Trainloads of Hindu and Sikh emigrants going east were stopped and butchered by Muslims, while parties of Muslims fighting their way west suffered the same fate from Hindus and Sikhs. Around 10 million people were 'exchanged' following Independence; some 500 000 perished *en route*.

Such was the extent of the holocaust that Jawarhalal Nehru, Gandhi's political disciple and the first Prime Minister of India, made an unexpected plea for help to the ex-British Viceroy, Mountbatten. 'Ours is the politics of agitation, not of government!' he declared. 'Please come back and help us out till we find our feet!'. Mountbatten returned and the crisis was soon overcome. Only in Kashmir was a satisfactory long-term solution not found. The region was claimed by both Pakistan and India, and since neither would give way over it, the UN was forced to step in and divide it with a demarcation line. But Kashmir continues to be a strong bone of contention, neither side having ever agreed to an official state border.

On 30 January 1948, the last act in the bitter-sweet drama of Independence, Gandhi was assassinated. Shot three times by a Hindu fanatic, he died a disappointed man—his dream of an undivided, free India never realised.

Since Independence

Fortunately for India, Nehru was a capable successor. Following Independence, he steered the country on a balanced course which made the initial transition to self-government both quick and painless. His favourite word may have been 'dynamic', but his political, economic and social outlook was basically conservative (some say, even static). 'The developing countries need peace for their development', he stated. 'They need at least two decades of uninterrupted peace.' To ensure this, he adopted a strict policy of non-alignment with other world powers. For the first 9 years of his premiership, it worked. But at heart Nehru was a convinced socialist, more than somewhat influenced by Marxism, and he tended to lean markedly in favour of the communist world rather than the democracies. For a non-aligned country to align itself heavily on one side put India at a disadvantage, and lost her both friends and influence over the years. Then in 1956 Russia invaded Hungary. Nehru was forced to show his hand (India was the only non-aligned country to support the USSR's move), and henceforth nobody took his non-alignment seriously. The final humiliation took place in 1962, when Sino-Indian border clashes led to the threat of a Chinese invasion. Nehru made pleas for military aid to both East and West, but while Britain and the US promised immediate help, the USSR stood on the fence of 'non- alignment' and simply advised restraint.

Domestically, Nehru's record was far better. He used a charismatic persona and an unchallenged majority to build up a strong, cohesive central government and thus to consolidate the nascent unity of India. He also made important, progressive social changes, especially with regard to the liberalisation of policies for women. Despite criticism, he also retained good relations with the British ex-colonisers, and encouraged both a free press and an independent judiciary.

He was succeeded by Lal Bahadur Shastri (for just 20 months), a meek but (when the occasion called for it) surprisingly strong-willed leader. His premiership was overshadowed by Pakistan's twin attack on India—in the Rann of Kutch and in Kashmir—in 1965. Shastri, who had never felt that Nehru was militant enough, abandoned India's long-standing policy of peaceful neutrality and retaliated with force. But he was essentially a man of moderate views, and his untimely death—shortly after the Pakistan armies had withdrawn—spelt the advance of extremism in the country.

A feature of Indian politics is its emphasis on 'personality' leaders. A second has been the failure of these leaders to surround themselves with strong, capable lieutenants. Mahatma Gandhi was an exception. He had begun grooming Nehru for power as early as 1929, realising perhaps the truth of the old Buddhist precept, that a master's prime duty is to create a disciple even stronger than himself. But Nehru himself failed to do this and the vacuum of young generation leaders in the Congress following his death left it seriously out of touch with the masses. Inevitably, the old and the new had to fall out, and Congress was doomed to split.

Into the political breach created by Shastri's death, stepped Indira Gandhi, Nehru's only daughter. She was elected Prime Minister in 1966. Her landslide victory at the polls was partly due to her extravagant promises of bread for the masses, but doubtless owed more to the magic of the name 'Gandhi' (though no relation to the Mahatma), coupled with the right amount of forceful 'personality'. Subsequent re-election in 1971, swept in on a tidal wave of war-fever created by Pakistan's treatment of East Pakistan and the subsequent creation of an independent Bangladesh, confirmed her in a dangerous situation of unchallenged power. By 1975, as attempts to suppress the free press and to muzzle the judiciary gave way to more openly fascist policies, serious opposition to her rule surfaced. She retaliated with the so-called state of emergency, freeing herself of regular parliamentary restraints and functioning virtually as an unchallenged ruler. This enabled her to push through a number of positive economic reforms and generally improve efficiency. On the other hand, the imprisonment of protesting elements and the disastrous sterilisation and 'people's car' programmes initiated by her son, Sanjay, set the nation against her. (The idea behind this was to produce a car made in India costing Rs10 000, but the programme failed and the enterprise was nationalised in 1978. Suzuki now own 50% of the factory.) Under the illusion that the people would support her whatever she did, she unwisely went to the polls in 1977 and lost.

In the place of Indira and Congress came the conservative Morarji Desai and his uncohesive Janata 'People's Party'. Inadequate to the task of government, unable to stop inflation spiralling, Janata broke apart in 1979, and Indira Gandhi returned triumphant in 1980. She tried and failed to deal with escalating social problems including rife corruption, police brutality, persecution of untouchables and Hindu/Muslim/Sikh intercommunal unrest. And her drastic solution to Sikh unrest in the Punjab, culminating in the armed occupation of the Golden Temple in Amritsar, eventually cost her her life. She was shot by an assassin's bullet in October 1984.

The circumstances of her death ensured her son, Rajiv Gandhi, an unprecedented victory at the polls in December 1984. In early 1985, everyone was confidently predicting great things of the young Rajiv. 'If the man is not assassinated first,' joked one prominent official, 'he will challenge caste, remove poverty and rid us of corruption.' Within three years Rajiv Gandhi was under attack in his own country. People were skeptical of his promise to usher India into the 21st century by means of a technological revolution. Many Indians see technology as a threat to jobs, and it was almost with glee that Delhi newspapers announced, in 1987, that two defence scandals had surfaced: the Swedish Bofors company admitted paying millions of pounds in 'commission', and a 7% 'agent's fee' had been involved on a German submarine deal. Members of Rajiv Gandhi's own family were implicated, and his own image as 'Mr Clean' was tarnished beyond repair. To make things worse, he embroiled himself in several regional conflicts, starting with Tamil Nadu (where his peacekeeping force sent to Sri Lanka, was nicknamed 'Indian people-killing force' by resentful Tamils), and later with Pakistan, West Bengal, Kashmir and the Punjab, where his soft approach brought forth a growing voice of disapproval. Rajiv Gandhi lost the next general election in 1990.

For the second time since Independence the Congress Party found themselves in opposition. A coalition government lead by V.P. Singh, who had earlier been Finance Minister and Defence Minister under Rajiv Gandhi, tried to form a united government and weather the storm created by Congress rule. Failing miserably in its task, the National Front government was replaced by an interim minority government under Chandra Shekhar. This led to fresh elections in May 1991. Congress under Rajiv Gandhi, were confident of winning because the National Front government had been unable to govern, and many of its policies were thought to have divided the country. Congress saw themselves as a party of unification. What the result would have been under normal circumstances will never be known, for Rajiv Gandhi was assassinated on 21 May 1991. Congress was returned to power as the largest party in Parliament but was without a majority. P.V. Narasimha Rao, an elderly, experienced Congress politician became the next Prime Minister and has had to face the effects of years of misrule. The new government instituted major economic reforms to stabilise and open the Indian economy to the world market.

Today India is still struggling towards a clear, solid identity—with unity as its prime objective. No amount of self-criticism, however, can disguise some truly remarkable achievements since Independence in 1947. India is presently one of the top industrial powers in the world. Her government and her legal, educational, and military institutions are strong. She is agriculturally self-sufficient, and making rapid strides in space-age technology (in Delhi, computer technology now helps the railways make 45 000 seat reservations a day).

Religion

Westerners have difficulty understanding the importance of religion to the average Indian. It governs his every thought, regulates his every action, and gives him his strong sense of identity—his 'dharma', or personal course in life. Religion is everything in India, and there are just as many different faiths to be found here—Hinduism and Buddhism, Jainism and Sikhism, Christianity, Zoroastrianism and Islam—as there are different peoples, tongues and cultures.

Some 80% of Indians are Hindus; another 10% follow the Muslim faith; Sikhs and Christians, combined, make up a further 5%. All the others—Jains, Parsis, Buddhists, Bahai, etc.—comprise the remainder. Social traditions differ among the Muslim, tribal, Christian, Sikh, Parsi and other communities that constitute more than 20% of India's population today. Each of these communities is governed by its own social mores and traditions.

Hinduism

An ancient repository of Indian spiritual consciousness, Hinduism is the oldest surviving religion in the world, and has more adherents than any other religion in Asia. Hinduism went through various periods of prosperity and decline, but demonstrated the most amazing capacity for absorbing and assimilating all competing faiths, and was never down for long. One of its earliest scriptures, the *Upanishads* (400–200 BC), stated 'The Great God is One, and the learned call Him by different names'—and it was this aphorism which encapsulated the unique talent for Hindu religious toleration. It never destroyed other beliefs, just synthesised them into its own philosophical system.

Although all forms of worship are acceptable to Hinduism, there are a few basic beliefs which tie the various creeds together. The main three are Samsara, Karma and Dharma. **Samsara** is the eternity of life in which the soul is believed to pass through a cycle of births and deaths on its way to perfection, and to union with the Supreme Being (Brahma). **Karma**, or the law of cause and effect, is where every thought, word and deed produces a consequent reaction (good or bad) in this or in a subsequent incarnation. **Dharma**, the code of living, is where every person has a specific role or set of moral duties to perform in life, through which he can break the cycle of rebirth and attain *nirvana* (heaven).

There are many thousands of gods in the Hindu pantheon. The Aryans were a nomadic people, worshippers of the natural elements. They had a Supreme Being, a central figure who controlled everything in life, but they also had gods to represent all forms of natural energy (sun, moon, wind, water, etc.) and all facets of human life and endeavour (courage, faith, luck, beauty, etc.). The total number of gods was calculated from the estimated population of the known world round the time of the mythical *Mahabharata*. This was the classic battle between good and evil in which five good brothers, aided by the god Krishna, defeated 100 wicked cousins. It was written down between 200 BC and AD 500, and Indian literature is full of references to it. Over the centuries, many stories and legends grew up round the various gods and goddesses. The main group—the Puranas (AD 500–1500)—became the base of all art in India. Most sculptures and paintings told a 'purana' story, and through such legends and parables, Hindu morals, customs, manners and traditions slowly became crystallised. It was the only way in which the common people received any social education, for the Brahmin priest caste had exclusive access to the ancient Vedic scriptures and holy books, and never transferred this knowledge to the masses, except in such symbolic form.

The one supreme God of Hinduism, **Parabrahma**, has three physical manifestations—**Brahma** the Creator, **Vishnu** the Preserver, and **Shiva** the Destroyer. Representing the three basic processes in human life (birth, life and death), this main trinity rules over all the lesser gods. All three deities are normally depicted with four arms, but Brahma also has four heads to show his omniscient wisdom. Unlike the other two, however, he has had very few temples built for him. Each god has a 'carrier', an animal or bird who transports him about.

Vishnu is often seen sitting on an eagle with human features called a *Garuda*. He has visited earth in 9 incarnations (avatars), and is due to pay one last visit, as the horse-headed Kalki. He has already appeared as a fish, a tortoise, a boar, a half-man, a beggar-dwarf, and in human form carrying an axe. On his seventh call, he came as **Rama** with an impossible mission to destroy the demon king Ravana of Lanka (Ceylon). The dramatic story of his success, aided and abetted by the faithful monkey-god **Hanuman**, became one of the world's greatest epics, the *Ramayana* (350 BC–AD 250). Vishnu made his eighth appearance as **Krishna**, the dark-skinned boy of the Mathura milkmaids, whom he married 'en masse' after releasing them from the demon king Naraka. A good start for any religious debate with a Hindu is to ask him what he makes of Krishna having 16 000 girlfriends. The ninth incarnation of Vishnu, an imaginative ploy to reabsorb Buddhism back into the Hindu religion, is supposed to have been the **Buddha** himself.

Shiva's main symbol is the cobra, the virulent snake of death and destruction, though he generally rides out on the bull *Nandi*. His creative/sexual function is symbolised by the stone lingam. He is often shown with a third eye (sometimes used as a death-ray), and is believed to spend a lot of time in his Himalayan mountain home smoking the holy weed (*ganja*). When roused, Shiva has a very nasty temper. First he chopped off Brahma's fifth head, and had to wander round as a beggar until the severed skull unstuck itself from his palm. Then he lopped off the head of his younger son, **Ganesh**, for refusing to let him visit his wife **Parvati** while she was having a bath. Repenting of his error, Shiva looked round for a new head for his offspring, and came up with one of an elephant. Thus, 'lucky' **Ganesh**, god of good fortune (and divine remover of obstacles) was born. His animal vehicle is the bandicoot, or rat.

Each of the Hindu trinity has a consort, representing the feminine side of their energy. Brahma is married to **Saraswati**, the goddess of learning, and her vehicle is the swan. Vishnu's consort is the beautiful **Lakshmi** (Laxmi), goddess of wealth and prosperity. Shiva started out with **Sati** (who burnt herself to death—the original 'sati' victim), then acquired **Parvati**, symbol of cosmic energy in the form of **Shakti**, the World Mother. She is also symbol (in her dark aspect) of destruction in the form of either **Kali**, wearing a wreath of skulls, or **Durga** the terrible, riding a tiger and waving weapons from 10 hands. In addition to Ganesh, Parvati had one other son by Shiva, the six-headed God of War, **Kartikkeya** (Murugan in south India or Subramanhya).

The good-humoured, indulgent, even playful attitude of many Hindus to their gods is something that mystifies many Westerners, used to religion as rather a solemn business. But while Hinduism is a strict faith, with many rituals, ceremonies and practices geared towards keeping the individual on the general straight and narrow, it has a great inbuilt sense of fun and spectacle. This is especially true on a social level, where births, marriages and even deaths are all an occasion for colourful, noisy bands and processions, complete with caparisoned elephants, performing monkeys, lots of firecrackers and entertainments, and (of course) plentiful free food. It's all a perfect reflection of, and a tribute to a pantheon of gods who may be gaudy, boisterous, flamboyant but never dull.

Jainism

Jainism was the first major sect to break away from Hinduism, and was founded around 500 BC by Vardhamana Mahavira. He was the last of the 24 Jain saints or **Tirthankars**, and was an older contemporary of the Buddha. The schism from Hinduism came from his belief that there was no Supreme Creator of the universe, but that it was infinite and eternal. The Jains did believe in reincarnation (like the Hindus), but their method of achieving salvation was much more extreme. Mahavira preached the total subjugation of the senses as the most direct path to the world of the spirit, and Jain monks became noted for their great asceticism. They wandered about in a loin cloth, with just an alms bowl and a stave as possessions. In this, they resembled the Shaivite Hindu ascetics called *sadhus*, but their strict doctrine of *ahimsa* (non-violence to any living creature) caused them to go even further—thus, they also carried a broom to sweep the ground before them clear of any insects, and wore a muslin mask to prevent them swallowing any flying parasites. The Jains found little problem finding a sanctuary in India—for the simple reason that the Hindus considered them even better Hindus than they were.

Around the 1st century AD, the Jains split into two sects: the white-clad **Shvetambaras** and the sky-clad **Digambaras**. The latter were literally 'sky-clad', being so contemptuous of material possessions that they wore no clothing at all. Jain temples are often quite beautiful, with highly ornate carvings on columns and ceilings. The best of these can be seen in Rajasthan (Mt Abu and Ranakpur), Gujarat (Palitana and Junagadh) and Bombay, the main Jain centres. Jainism is particularly strong in Rajasthan, for it is believed that the tirthankars were also Rajput princes. The Jains themselves are today few in number, but have great commercial and business influence. Many of them are successful traders, bankers and philanthropists.

Buddhism

The Buddhist religion was the second reformist offshoot of Hinduism, and presented it with a far greater threat. Founded by **Siddhartha** (Shakyamuni) **Gautama** (during the 5th century BC) in northern India, it was a dynamic force which thrived for 1700 years before slowly being won back to the Hindu fold by the revivalist movement started by Sankara in the 8th century AD.

Buddha was a Kshatriya prince who, preoccupied by the human problems of old age, sickness and death, forsook riches to embark on a long quest for the Truth. After several years of rigorous ascetic practice, he attained his enlightenment at Bodhgaya and spent the final 45 years of his life teaching his new philosophy. This incorporated Hindu elements, like the doctrines of *karma* and reincarnation, but reinterpreted them in a far more dynamic form. As far as Buddha was concerned, *karma* had nothing to do with fate or predestination. It was a strict causal law of dynamic action. He taught that every living being (not just priests or ascetics) could aspire to enlightenment in this lifetime, without passively awaiting better circumstances in a future incarnation. His central doctrine, whereby enlightenment could be achieved and the cycle of rebirth extinguished, was the eightfold path of the 'middle way'. This put the case for moderation in all things, and rejected as harmful the rules, regulations and general extremism of Hinduism and Jainism (Buddha had tried ascetic starvation, and found it more likely to lead to death than enlightenment). It was a simple, optimistic message, but the Hindus rejected Buddhism as a religion of compromise. With the 'middle way' discarded, India became progressively a land of extremes and stark contrasts.

Buddhism took its big leap forward in India when adopted by the great emperor Ashoka (3rd century BC). It was carried outwards to every part of his extensive empire, and spread in time to Burma, Thailand, Sri Lanka, Korea, China, Vietnam, Nepal, Tibet, Central Asia and Japan. But in India, it quickly experienced a schism, leading to two main schools. The **Hinayana** or 'lesser vehicle' held that enlightenment was an individual pursuit; the **Mahayana** or 'greater vehicle' held that it was a collective one, with the ultimate aim of bringing all humanity to salvation. After Buddhism's collapse in India, the centre of Mahayana transferred to Japan, where the essence of Gautama's final teaching (the *Lotus Sutra*, or *Myoho Renge Kyo*) was revealed by the 13th-century monk Nichiren. Unlike the Hinayana sect, who always referred to the Buddha in terms of external symbols (the lotus for his birth, the tree for his enlightenment, the wheel of law for his first sermon, and the *stupa* for his final *nirvana* or salvation), the growing realisation of the Mahayana sect was to seek Buddha nowhere else but in themselves, and in every living thing.

Islam

There are more Muslims in India (around 100 million) than any other religious minority group. The most recent and successful Asian religion, it was founded by the prophet **Mohammed** in the early 7th century AD. The Muslim canon, the **Koran**, is a collection of apocalyptic messages delivered to Mohammed by Allah (God). A keynote of the faith was its militancy, its evangelical zeal to spread the good word—by the sword, if necessary. Starting in Arabia, Islam extended its influence east for several centuries, and was eventually firmly established in three continents. Conversion was easy—to become a Muslim required only saying the words, 'There is no God but Allah and Mohammed is his prophet'. It was especially easy in India, where the Muslims came in the 11th century AD, for there were a great many low-caste Hindus seeking escape from the discriminations of Brahmanical Hinduism. They could no longer turn to Buddhism (there were no Buddhists left), so their only recourse was Islam. But in the long term Hinduism was too strong to be dislodged.

There are two types of Muslim, resulting from an early schism. These are the **Sunnis** (the majority), whose allegiance is to the succession from Mohammed's direct successor, the Caliph; and the **Shias** or Shi'ites who follow the descendants of the prophet's son-in-law, Ali. For both, the big objective is to make the pilgrimage to **Mecca** (Mohammed's birthplace in AD 570) and become a *haji*. The Muslims may have come to north India first as ruthless, iconoclastic conquerors, but their contribution to Indian civilisation is still prevalent in art, architecture and culture.

Sikhism

The Sikh religion is comparatively new, having broken away from Hinduism as late as the 15th century. It was born of the frictions between Hindus and Muslims in the Punjab, and was founded by **Guru Nanak** (1494–1538). Originally a pacifist movement, aimed at synthesising the best of the Hindu and Islamic religions, it turned into a militant brotherhood under the tenth Guru of the line, Guru Gobind Singh, in the 17th century. This was a reaction to the extreme persecution which the Sikhs of those times were suffering, and all of them thereafter bore the surname Singh or 'Lion'.

The Sikh Bible is called **Granth Sahib**. It is opposed to several Hindu tenets, including the caste system and the dominance of the Brahmins. It differs from other Hindu-based faiths in its unique rejection of non-violence, and it condones the killing of animals for food. The Sikhs believe in one god, have temples known as **gurdwaras**, and have had a total of 10 Gurus whose collected writings (plus various Hindu and Muslim scripts) form the Granth Sahib.

Sikhs are instantly distinguishable by their five symbols or *kakka*, introduced by Guru Gobind Singh: *kesa* or unshorn hair (normally wrapped under a turban); *kachcha* or short trousers; the steel bracelet or *kara*; the wooden or ivory comb called *kangha*; and the *kirpan* or sword.

Although just 2% of the Indian population follows the Sikh religion, Sikhs dominate the army, and the transport and light engineering industries. They have a well-earned reputation for a no-nonsense attitude, a capacity for hard work, and skill in mechanical matters—they are said to be the best car mechanics in the world.

In the early 1980s a section of Sikh extremists took up the call for a separate country, called Khalistan. This led to the political and economic decline of the Punjab, the most prosperous state in India. The terrorists converted the Golden Temple, the most venerated Sikh shrine, into their headquarters, and this led to army action in 1984. This further alienated Sikhs from the rest of the country, and ultimately resulted in the assassination of Indira Gandhi by her Sikh bodyguards. The subsequent riots, during which several thousand innocent Sikhs were massacred, led to an even greater rift.

At the time of writing, the political situation has yet to be resolved, but personal relationships between Sikhs and other members of the Indian community remain relatively unscathed.

Zoroastrianism

The tiny community of Zoroastrians, commonly known as **Parsis**, are concentrated in Bombay. Theirs is one of the oldest religions known, founded by the prophet

Zoroaster (Zarathustra) in Persia, around 800 BC. Forced to flee their native country by a Muslim invasion of Persia, they were given sanctuary in India. Their scripture, the **Zend-Avesta,** describes the ongoing battle between good and evil, and their god is **Ahura Mazda** who is symbolised by fire. Parsis revere the elements of nature, but are not fire-worshippers: they keep the sacred flame burning in all their temples only as a symbol of their god. To preserve the purity of the elements they do not defile fire, earth, water or air by burying or cremating their dead. Instead, they leave the bodies atop the 'Towers of Silence' (Bombay) to be devoured by vultures.

As a community, the Parsis are distinctive, enterprising and have contributed much to modern India. They have an extraordinary talent for commerce, and the Tatas, a highly respected Parsi business group, has wide-ranging and extremely profitable interests in the oil, steel, automobile, computing and tea industries, amongst others. The Taj Group of Hotels is run by Tatas, and Air India was a Tata enterprise which was later nationalised. Parsis are also renowned for their philanthropy, and run a range of trusts to look after the interests of their own community.

Only if the father is Parsi can the children be Parsi, and you cannot join Parsi ranks through conversion. This, combined perhaps with the apparent reluctance of well-educated and increasingly independent Parsi women to settle down, has resulted in a marked decline in numbers of the Parsi community.

Christianity and Judaism

There have been Christians in India since St Thomas, one of Christ's Disciples, arrived in Kerala in AD 54. The Syrian Church he founded here is the second oldest Christian Church in the world, after that in ancient Palestine. During the mid-4th and 8th centuries, two waves of Christian immigrants arrived from the Middle East, and a substantial community of 'Syrian Christians' grew up in Kerala.

Later still, in the 16th century, Catholic and Protestant missionaries made a number of converts from various Portuguese, Dutch and English settlements. In the Indian community, they concentrated mainly on areas where large numbers of labourers were gathered, such as tea gardens and oil fields, and on the tribal areas of Bihar and north-east India, where they experienced considerable success. The lower castes were naturally more susceptible to conversion, as a means of escape from their unchangeably low status in the Hindu caste system.

However only in Goa, where the Portuguese left a sizeable Christian community of relatively influential men, were the efforts of the missionaries longlasting; though the Syrian Orthodox Church in Kerala is still fairly strong. Amongst the disaffected Hindus of the lower castes, the religion could not find the power it needed to become widespread. Nevertheless Christians in India have made their mark in social, medical, educational and philanthropic fields.

In Kerala once more, the Jews of Cochin deserve a special mention—their ancestry goes back to the 6th century BC. They were a highly influential community in their time and the Cochin synagogue is the oldest in the Commonwealth, but at present there are only about 28 Cochin Jews remaining, most of whom are in their 70s.

A more ancient, larger and more significant Jewish community called the Bene Israel exists in and around Bombay. It is estimated that there are about 4000 Jews in the whole country but, like the Parsis, their community is declining.

Part III

TOPICS

Baksheesh

Unlike tipping, baksheesh is something you pay to get things done, not to reward things done already. Discerning use of baksheesh, usually just a few rupees, can save you hours (even days) of waiting and queuing. You can use this subtle form of bribery to hire a boy to wait in an endless rail reservation queue; while you go sightseeing; or to buy the services of a station porter to find a seat on a train which doesn't apparently have any. You can also use it to make sure that you get a berth on the roof of the boat for the magnificent 8–hour trip up the Kerala backwaters from Quilon to Alleppey.

The trouble about baksheesh is that once you start paying it out—to gain decent room service in hotels, for example—it's very difficult to stop. There is a tradition of tipping in Indian hotels and restaurants; it generally works wonders and a little goes a long way. Asking for things firmly, politely and with a big smile will nearly always get you what you want.

But you must abide by the unspoken rules. An English couple were spotted trying to board a packed train without tickets. They were carrying heavy packs, including unwieldy fishing-rods and full tackle. Instead of taking the ticket-collector off somewhere private, they loudly offered him baksheesh for berths in front of half the platform. The ticket-collector began dancing up and down in a frenzy of affected affront, and even called the station police. The point is, baksheesh is strictly against the law, so be discreet.

Beggars

You'll see lots of beggars, mainly around temples, holy places and railway stations. The Indian people themselves respect their beggars and few of them will enter a temple without a handful of small change to give to the less fortunate. To give to the poor is considered a necessary accumulation of personal good fortune.

This unofficial form of social security ensures that at least some apparently desperate beggars are better off than they appear. Some of them are experienced professionals, who shed their grime and rags for new, clean clothes when 'off duty'. Unfortunately for the foreign tourist, faced by armies of identical skinny women toting dirty babies and identical old men wearing doleful expressions, there is no way of knowing who really needs help and who doesn't.

Giving money to beggars is a very personal matter. Some travellers, stricken by conscience, give all their money and possessions away hours after arriving in the country. Others go to the opposite extreme, and treat the haves and the have-nots with equal indifference.

The Indian point of view is to give nothing to a man who is able-bodied, because he can make more money from begging than from working, and that giving to children may encourage them to leave school. Many give to the elderly, sick, or disabled, either small change or food. If you feel strongly about this issue, there are, of course, many charities in India which will always be grateful for anything you are able to give.

The Black Market

India has a small but strong black market, mainly for hard foreign currency and Western gadgets. It is most prevalent in the big cities, where no matter where you go, someone will eventually sidle up to you and mutter the words 'Change Dollar?' He is either a black marketeer, or a police informer masquerading as a black marketeer. Sometimes he is both. You will be offered a little more than the going bank rate for your dollars, a temptation many travellers find hard to resist. Foreign currency is much in demand in India, especially among rich Indians travelling abroad who may be limited by how much they can officially take out of the country. But whatever dollars they do take, they have to supplement with what they buy on the 'black', often at very inflated prices. Whether or not you decide to supply this demand is up to you.

Changing money on the streets is generally a bad idea. It is common to be palmed off with torn or ripped notes, or to end up with a stack of Rs10 notes instead of Rs100s (a cunning sleight of hand). Also, if the police turn up, you'll have to run in both directions at once to avoid a big fine or imprisonment. Shops are much safer—if they turn you in, you turn them in.

Selling cameras, tape-recorders, watches, Walkmans and even Western clothes on the 'black' is much easier, and there is usually a reasonable profit to be made. But don't bring too many gadgets into the country for intended sale as they may all be entered into your passport at Indian customs. This means you can't sell them, but must take them all back out of the country at the end of your stay.

Cinema

No visit to India is complete without seeing at least one Hindi film. More films are made here than in Hollywood, mostly in Madras and Bombay (known locally as 'Bollywood').

Top matinee idols can command a salary of over Rs4 million a film, which places them amongst the highest earners in the country. Indian movie stars are also role models for the cinema-going youth, which is the vast majority of the male population especially aged between 15 and 30. Their idols still tend to owe something of their dress sense to John Travolta in 'Saturday Night Fever', or the early Engelbert Humperdinck. Female stars are sexy, extravagant, heavily made up, and dress like no one else on the planet. Bollywood-style films are about love—always star-crossed, but with a Happy Ending— and invariably feature song and dance sequences, action scenes in which the hero can show off his physical prowess, and an astounding number of costume changes.

By contrast, the serious Indian film industry produces an increasing number of high quality and popular films, which deal with serious social concerns often ignored by all other sectors of Indian society. For example, such films may address the problems of slum dwelling, over-population, police and political corruption, and prostitution (in Bombay alone there are 60 000 Nepalese women working the streets for less than Rs10 a time). Directors such as the late Satyajit Ray and Mrinal Sen (both from Bengal, which has its own thriving and distinctive art cinema), and Mira Nair (who directed and produced 'Salaam Bombay') have achieved both international recognition and commercial success.

The huge success of the Indian film industry owes something to the low taxation levied on its profits, but is mainly due to the mass popularity of colourful, fantastic and escapist entertainment provided on the celluloid screen. Any première of a major new film is the cue for massed crowds and blockaded ticket offices. Prices for seats are extremely cheap. Many cinemas are well-equipped, with comfy seating and air-conditioning. Before the main feature, which usually runs for around 3–4 hours, there is an obligatory documentary 'short'.

Many cinemas also show matinee performances of English-speaking films, often spicy Western imports with 'lots of killing' and 'hot sexy encounters'. Full current programmes are listed in local newspapers, and the advertisements are sometimes just as entertaining as the films.

Video prints of new films are available within hours of release—from both the Indian and the import markets, of America especially. Every residential area and market in both big cities and small towns have video libraries where films can be hired for Rs10 per day. Door-to-door video salesmen will frequently supply films for purchase or hire to residential areas. It has to be said that most of this business is conducted without the knowledge or permission of the distributors, and many pirated prints are of poor quality. Some may even be camera prints, taken by a video camera hidden during the first public showing of a film.

This illegal practice has deprived film producers of rightful income, but it has to be said that it has created an enterprise industry, and a vital and knowledgeable band of screen enthusiasts.

In fact, in India video is ubiquitous: you will encounter it in buses, shopping centres, restaurants and homes. Monthly video magazines—on news, sports, lifestyles, commerce and the film industry (of course) are big business.

Cows

Cows are an integral part of life in India; sacred to Hindus, who constitute the bulk of the population. The animals' foreheads are painted with *bindi* spots, their horns are adorned with sweet-smelling jasmine, little bells are tied around their feet, and they wander wherever they please.

Ironically, cows are the unofficial rubbish collectors of India. They eat anything from newspapers to oil-soaked doormats. They are particularly fond of cardboard boxes. Because they are so numerous, and because they like wandering the streets, they constitute a major traffic hazard. Even non-Hindu drivers would do anything to avoid hitting a cow—crowd reaction can be fast and vengeful.

Indian myths and legends abound with cows. The cow draws its mythical and religious sanctity from the multitude of nourishing products that can be drawn from its body. Being largely a vegetarian country, India relies on the cow for the proteins in its milk, its dung for fuel and fertilizer, and its strength for ploughing the farmers' fields. Cows extend their influence to every aspect of Indian life.

Creepy-crawlies

In some areas, like damp and humid Kerala, you'll see more insects than elsewhere. The numbers of vermin and rodents are always worse in the big cities, where they can feed on abundant litter and refuse. But everywhere you'll find flies. They are an intrinsic part of India, buzzing round your face, going up your nose, and sitting hopefully on restaurant tables. In the evenings, there are fewer flies and more mosquitoes. Local repellents/smoke rings like Odomos/Tortoise keep them at bay for a while, but they always get you in the end.

The problem is worst in basic budget lodgings. These places are notorious for ants, bedbugs, cockroaches, rats and practically anything else that buzzes or scurries around in the dead of night. If you don't want to be a sleeping lunch for these creatures, never leave any food (biscuits, chocolates, sweets or cakes) or fluids lying around. It brings them all running. So do clean bodies. Mosquitoes just love the smell of shampoo and soap. Seasoned travellers have their shower/bath early in the morning, and go to bed covered in a protective layer of grime and dust.

To find out how many hidden 'guests' you've got in your room, put some insect powder down at night—round toilet cisterns, waste bins, and any dark or damp corners. Other useful safeguards are to hang up your shoes on a wall-nail (or shake them out in the morning), and to zip up all your bags at night.

Another species of persistent room-guest, found mainly in the south, are the small lizards called geckos. These are quite harmless and spend most of their time plastered to walls and ceilings, sound asleep. They can actually be beneficial, by eating insects. If they do disturb you, a bright torch-beam usually guides them out of the window. Summoning a roomboy to do this for you is fatal. He'll just fling open all doors and windows, run around with a large broom, and let in hordes more of the creatures.

One of the simplest ways of preventing too many insects coming into your room is to make sure all windows are closed at least half an hour before sunset and they remain closed for at least an hour after sunset. Mosquitoes are also very active at first light, and can wake you up unpleasantly at sunrise.

There are many theories about insects being attracted to certain colours, most of which are apocryphal, but they do seem to find soft, white flesh completely irresistible.

Dhobi

India doesn't have launderettes, but it does have dhobis, who spirit away your dirty clothes first thing in the morning, and usually have them back sparkling-clean and immaculately pressed the next day. The cost is rarely more than Rs2/3 per dress, shirt, trousers, Rs1 for socks and underwear. Every hotel has one, or can send out to one.

Your *dhobi* will take your clothes down to a *'dhobi ghat'*, a public washing area, where they will be pounded mercilessly with a big stick, or be flogged viciously against a washing stone. Not a speck of dirt survives this kind of treatment. In time, neither do your buttons, so take some extras. Once washed, the clothes are hung out along with miles of other wet togs to dry in the sun— and the sun will eventually bleach out any colour your clothes may have had. Then they go to the ironing sheds to receive knife-edge creases from conscientious ironers. Finally, and this is the miracle, they are picked out from millions of other garments and returned to your room, looking as good as new, albeit somewhat thinner!

When asking your hotel if they do *dhobi*, always get a total price for the washload before handing it in. Prices tend to increase dramatically 'after the event'. Second, never pay in advance. This gives you leverage if (and this is rare) clothes return from the *dhobi* stained or dyed a different colour. Last, be quite sure the person you hand your washing to is the *dhobi*, or you may never see your clothes again.

The larger hotels generally have an excellent laundry and dry-cleaning service. Most towns have 24-hour dry-cleaners. One word of warning: if buying new clothes in India the colours tend to run so it may be better to wash them separately yourself or at least advise the *dhobi* to do so.

Hippies

Some parts of India are still hippy havens. The beach resorts of Goa and Kovalam, the hill stations of Kodai and Dharamsala, the pilgrimage centres of Varanasi and Pushkar, and the mountain valley resort of Manali all have resident populations of happy hippies. Bob Dylan, the Doors, Hendrix, Jefferson Airplane and Cream— familiar friends long forgotten—rise eerily from the grave, and sing once again. Bright, patterned clothes, headbands and joss sticks, beads and bangles and bracelets are all back in style. Beach parties, skinny dipping and lazy, mystic encounters with bearded or bald-headed gurus are still the rage. It's all very transcendental (man), and a tremendous nostalgia trip, if you like that sort of thing.

Since the late 60s, hippies have found all the best beaches, settled in the most atmospheric holy spots, and established communities in remote hill and desert areas. Indians tend to regard them with some distaste, and in a serious attempt to attract a more respectable class of foreign tourist, the Indian government is enforcing two laws. The first one requires all hotels in India to register their guests, and makes it very difficult for foreigners to remain anonymous and outstay their welcome in the country. The second enforces stringent penalties against the smoking of, or possession of, dope. If anyone is caught, they go straight to jail. In the main hippy centres, if you look the part, it is still not uncommon to be spot-searched by police. One unfortunate, caught with half a kilo of best Kerala grass up his kaftan, was given a straight choice: 10 years in jail, or a Rs10 000 fine.

Loos

Old habits die hard, and many Indians still prefer squatting in the street. Public urinals (only for men and often overflowing due to lack of maintenance) and signs announcing 'Please do Not Commit Urine!'are largely ignored. Western-style lavatories are still usually found only in relatively upmarket hotels, and in the better restaurants. Squat toilets are the norm and usually have no facilities for washing hands. Toilet paper is a rare find in public toilets but is available in general stores.

On the open road, conveniences are where and when you can find them. Bus and rail stations usually have them, but to say they are basic would be a compliment. Women travellers certainly can't use them, and it is a common complaint (outside big cities) that toilet facilities for women just don't appear to exist. The problem is always worst on long bus journeys, when the two or three daily stops made are at ill-equipped *chai* places with no toilet at all, just a public urinal wall for men. Disgruntled women travellers always ask the same question: 'Where *do* women shit in this country?'

Photography

India is a very photogenic country, and most people take a lot more photographs than they had anticipated. At certain spots, like the magical Kerala backwater, you'll find yourself shooting everything that moves, flies, crawls and swims, as well as the green, semi-tropical jungles themselves.

Intense glare, hazy atmosphere, powerful light and deep shade all present the serious photographer with problems. Sometimes, the more sophisticated the camera you bring, the more difficult it is to line up a shot and to get a sharp result. Polarised filters improve your chances, but not as much as you might expect. Always take special care with photos taken in mountain or hill station regions—over-exposure is a common problem.

A light fully-automatic 35 mm camera has three distinct advantages over big expensive models: it's easier to carry and less prone to theft; you don't have to spend time setting up a shot, and risk missing it; and it's most suitable for photographing people.

In general, it's neither necessary nor sensitive to take furtive snaps of local people from roof tops or balconies, with the aid of a giant telephoto lens. The direct, personal approach always produces the best results. Some of the best 'people' shots you'll get will be in *chai* shops where locals soon lose their inhibitions in the presence of foreigners, and often ask to be snapped.

Indians are pretty security-conscious, and it's always worth asking before pointing your camera. Photography at airports, military bases, railway stations, bridges, even public notices and interesting old steam engines can cause problems and is in many cases prohibited. Women in general are shy of being photographed, and snapping Muslim women in black purdah can cause offence. So can flashing away at funeral pyres or the inner sanctums of certain temples. Most other things are fair game. Indeed, many Indians just love being photographed, and are often very disappointed when you run out of film. But they're horrible posers! A camera poked out of a tour bus window in Delhi can bring an entire street of rickshaws, cars and pedestrians grinding to a halt and standing to military attention.

You can buy film in India, but in small towns it tends to be expensive and often past its sell-by date. A lot of it is surplus stock bought off returning tourists, and resold to the incoming lot at inflated prices. Slide film is less easy to find, so bring stocks from home.

In Delhi and Bombay film is available from many photographic stores at rates comparable with those in Europe. In Calcutta, Madras and other cities it is slightly more expensive. Kodachrome, however, is rarely found unless a traveller sells his surplus stock. Fujichrome, Fujicolor, Kodacolor and Konica films are the most readily available.

Processing quality of E6 colour slides and black and white film varies. Kinsey Bros or Mahattas in Connaught Place, New Delhi, are two of the best studios. The best black and white printing is generally thought to be done by the Mitter Bedi Studio, behind the Taj Mahal Hotel in Bombay. Colour prints are usually well processed in most towns.

The X-ray machines at international airports do not damage film on the first few occasions, but since the fogging effect is cumulative you may prefer to have them checked by hand. The Indian heat may also damage your film.

Video cameras are stamped in your passport on entry to India. They are not always welcome at tourist spots like the Taj Mahal or Fatehpur Sikri at Agra. Permission to use a video camera and a tripod for stills photography at archaeological sites of national importance requires prior written permission from the office of the Director General, The Archaeological Survey of India, Janpath (next to the National Museum), New Delhi. This may take some time to obtain, and in practice it is sometimes possible to gain permission on the spot from the guards at the respective sites.

Temples

There are temples all over India. Every street and backstreet in every town, city or village has at least one. To absorb their atmosphere, quietly observe the pilgrims filing into prayer, the beggars moaning for alms, and the priests intoning complicated rituals. You must take off your shoes when visiting Hindu or Muslim shrines, and cover your head when entering a Sikh one. It is also customary to have a bath before entering a temple but this is not expected of tourists. Women should be appropriately dressed, and many temples like to ensure leather articles including handbags and camera bags are not taken into the shrine.

In general, foreigners are welcome to all parts of temple complexes, although none but the priest is allowed in the inner sanctum. However, a few temples including the

Jagannath at Puri, the Lingaraj at Bhubaneshwar, and most of the temples in Kerala completely bar entrance to non-Hindus (who are of course by birth 'untouchable').

In Hinduism the most revered gods are Vishnu and Shiva and their incarnations—the popular figures of Lords Krishna and Rama are both avatars or incarnations of Vishnu. The Vishnu priests often have vertical lines of sandal paste on their foreheads; the Shaivaites have horizontal lines. It is often possible to work out the main resident deity of the temple by the presence of his or her *vahan* or animal 'carrier'. A large kneeling bull (*Nandi*), for example, is Shiva's *vahan*; an eagle-like *garuda*, half-bird, half-man, denotes a Vishnu temple. At the base of an image of Ganesh is a mouse or rat. The goddesses Ganga and Yamuna, whose figures often flank a temple doorway, ride crocodile- and turtle-like animals respectively. However, many temples have statues of numerous gods both within and on the outer walls. The temple is dedicated to the image housed in the *garbha griha*—literally 'womb chamber'. The image in most Shiva temples is a *linga* representing the supreme power of the god.

At temples, *ghats* and many holy areas devotees perform private *puja* or prayer. Communal worship does take place but most worship is an individual communion between the devotee and his or her god. Quite often at the conclusion of *arti*, literally 'surrendering and glorifing the lord' at the end of the day, or after you have paid respects to the temple, the *pujari* or priest offers you *prasad*, consecrated food which could be fruit, rice, coconut or, most often milk sweets. It is also usual to tie a piece of string round your wrist, and place vermilion paste or powder onto your forehead; both indicate that the wearer has performed *puja*. It is customary to place a small offering at the foot of the image—Rs5 or Rs10 would be sufficient, and it is best to have this ready before entering the temple rather than having to fumble with a money belt in front of the *pujari*.

Many Hindu temples are not supported financially by the government. This means that most of the cost of their repair, renovation or maintenance is borne by the public. And that's why donations are sought and most holy places have a donation box. Temples that tourists frequent are often surrounded by touts and less than scrupulous priests who will take you around and show you what to do and ensure you receive *darshan*.

It is not unusual for a young, happy Hindu with a carefree spirit to want to be a priest. And while many priests are people of scholarship and considerable intellectual skills, this is not a precondition. There are numerous temples open to people with ambition and many 'part-time priests' manage to pursue a job during the day while officiating at a temple in the mornings and evenings.

Wildlife and National Parks

India's extensive natural heritage includes 443 protected areas that are administered by the forest departments of each state. Many of these areas are protected more in name than in reality, but scattered throughout India are some startlingly beautiful areas with a broad range of animal and bird life.

As with so much in India, the country has an ambivalent relationship with its vast natural resources and biological wealth of plants and animals—torn between fond respect and admiration and the relentless demands of an ever expanding human population.

As early as 2000 years ago Emperor Ashoka understood the need to husband his empire's natural wealth with codes to protect animals and forests. In about 300 BC Emperor Kautilya, who ruled a large area of north-western India, established protected areas as 'forests free from fear' for both animals and humans. The Mughal emperors designated certain areas for their hunts and protected them from other disturbances for long periods. Similarly during the 19th century the British administrators and many princely states designated and managed areas exclusively for *shikar*, hunting, and banned all other exploitation of the areas. Today many of these old hunting reserves have become the nucleus of India's national parks and wildlife sanctuaries. Less formally, groves and forests around temples are often protected by the sanctity of the shrine they embrace. The wildlife that inhabits such places find protection in local beliefs. For example, Bishnoi villagers in Rajasthan and Haryana believe their ancestors' souls, in their reluctance to leave the area they have lived in, take temporary refuge in the wild animals that surround the village. The herds of **blackbuck** and **chinkara** that roam freely on the outskirts of towns and villages in Rajasthan are protected by this belief; and the **nilgai** or bluebull is protected by its resemblance to the cow.

Natural Wealth Under Threat

India's forests and plains are home to 2094 species and sub-species of birds of which about 1750 are resident (the balance being migrants). The country sustains over 350 species of mammal and 353 species of reptile. The diversity of amphibians, insects, plants and trees is equally impressive. The small Himalayan state of Sikkim has recorded over 600 species of wild orchid.

At the apex of India's biological pyramid is the **tiger**—a supreme predator whose numbers fell to the alarmingly low figure of 1830 in 1972. A few years later the government with support from the World-Wide Fund for Nature (WWF), launched Project Tiger. This plan originally brought 7 areas under a coordinated management scheme and by 1989 the number of reserves had increased to 18 and the country's tiger population had risen to 4334. However, by no means all tigers live safely in the protected areas. Some estimate a third live outside protected areas and India's great conservationist, 'Billy' Arjan Singh refers to them as the 'forgotten tigers'.

In the late 1940s large herds of **blackbuck** still grazed large areas throughout northern and western India. Now the herds are greatly reduced and confined to a few Bishnoi villages and sanctuaries such as **Tal Chappar** near Bikaner in Rajasthan, and **Velavader**, near Bhavnagar in Gujarat. Earlier this century herds of **swamp deer** thrived in the *Terai* (riverine grasslands and forest) region along the border between India and Nepal, but the malaria eradication programmes of the 1950s allowed the area to be farmed and the northern races are now restricted to **Kaziranga** and **Dudhwa National Parks**, and a few areas of south-western Nepal.

Officially 13% of the country is under forest cover but the actual figure, including marginal lands, is more likely to be 8%. As the human population increases at the rate of approximately 18 million a year, the needs of villagers for grazing land and fuel has put enormous pressure on the country's forest and has begun to threaten the protected areas. The axe and the chainsaw have accelerated the destruction of wilderness areas, and pessimists feel that much of what is left is doomed. However, Project Tiger is an example of what can be done. The country has a range of overlapping conservation plans, many of which have been successful and there is no reason that, with the correct administrative and political will, India's national parks and reserves should not at least remain to be as rich as they are today.

Major Conservation Areas

The parks of the Gangetic plain and peninsular India are the easiest to visit, and have guest accommodation. Small forest rest houses built and run by the forest department provide basic shelter for visitors but rarely food. Some of these, built in the late 19th or early 20th centuries, command spectacular views of forested hills and valleys which more than compensate for the lack of facilities. With the exceptions of parks such as **Bandhavgarh** and **Kanha**, in Madhya Pradesh, hospitality for visitors is often basic and there are few lodges or camps run along the lines of those in Africa. A few tour operators based in Delhi and Bombay have an understanding of the needs of a tour of wilderness areas and can help make arrangements. Try **Mountain Travel India**, 1/1 Rani Jhansi Road, New Delhi (tel 7533483, tlx 31-63016 TREK IN, fax 011-777483) and **Abercrombie & Kent**, Chiranjiv Tower, 43 Nehru Place, New Delhi (tel 6436207, fax 011-6444966). Going through a travel agent often makes a tour more expensive but is of great help if your time is limited. Most private camps and lodges are located on the borders of national parks and provide board and lodging. Some include visits into the park by jeep or on elephant back within their charges; others can provide this but charge separately for it. Almost all protected areas close during the monsoon and only reopen in October or occasionaly November—exceptions include Keoladeo Ghana at Bharatpur, Sariska and Nagarhole.

North-western India
In the Kashmir Valley **Dachigam National Park**, only 22 km (14 miles) from Srinagar, is the last viable refuge for the **hangul** or Kashmir stag. The park can be visited with prior permission from the Chief Wildlife Warden's office at the Tourist Reception Centre in Srinagar. However, the political situation in Kashmir is extremely unstable at the time of writing and at present a visit to the area is not recommended. Other Himalayan areas don't present the same problems, although access may involve trekking. The **Great Himalayan Park** in Himachal Pradesh is a 3-day trek east of Kulu. Covering a vast 1736 sq km, it includes some relatively undisturbed areas and a good population of many endangered species of pheasant. **Nanda Devi National Park** in the Garhwal Himalaya protects the natural sanctuary ringed by many peaks of 6000 m to 8000 m.

Uttar Pradesh
Here the habitat varies from the lush mixed deciduous forest and riverine grasslands of the *Terai* to dry scrub. Along the foothills of the Himalaya are two important Project Tiger reserves. The larger of these, **Corbett National Park**, has grown from India's earliest park founded in 1935. A 7-hour drive from Delhi, Corbett can also be reached by train via Moradabad and Ramnagar. **UP Tourism** (Chandralok Building, Janpath, New Delhi) run regular buses to the park from November through to April or May. The reserve includes several ridges of the Shivalik foothills of the Himalaya through which the Ramganga river flows; the region is extraordinarily beautiful. Apart from the occasional glimpse of a tiger, or the more elusive leopard, there are numerous prey species and herds of elephant migrate through the area. Because of the varied

topography and habitat and the large intrusion of the Ramganga reservoir, Corbett has an extraordinary range of birds—quite possibly more species than any other park in the subcontinent. **Forest rest houses** and a small 'tourist complex' at Dhikala, within Corbett, can be booked through **UP Tourism offices** in Lucknow or New Delhi. Outside the park boundary, overlooking the Kosi river are two lodges. The better of the two, with trained naturalists and a high level of service is the **Tiger Tops Corbett Lodge**, with rooms, food and game-viewing costing US$120 per person per night. (Book through Tiger Tops India, 1/1 Rani Jhansi Road, New Delhi (tel 7771055, 7525357, tlx 31-63016 TREK IN, fax 011-7777483). The second lodge has a better location slightly beyond the park entrance but the lodge is not of the calibre of Tiger Tops. The **Quality Inn Corbett Jungle Resort** with rooms from Rs500, is booked through Quality Inns, 51 Vasant Marg, Vasant Vihar, New Delhi (tel 675347).

The other tiger reserve in Uttar Pradesh is located on the south-west border of Nepal, 260 km (162 miles) north-west of Lucknow and a long 9-hour drive from Delhi. **Dudhwa National Park** owes its creation and continued existence to the work of one of India's foremost conservationists, Billy Arjan Singh. Arjan Singh's farm, **Tiger Haven**, on the edge of the park, can accommodate small groups or individuals subject to prior confirmation. Travel agents in Delhi can help or write directly to Tiger Haven, PO Pallia, Dist Kheri, Uttar Pradesh 262902).

Assam
In the north-eastern states of India is a rich faunal and floral diversity of species; along India's borders with Burma and China there is a meeting of species from the Malayan region. The troubled state of Assam has long been associated with the **one-horned rhinoceros**, and **Kaziranga National Park** on the southern bank of the Brahmaputra river, in the state was first protected in 1908 when the rhino population fell to about a dozen. Today, despite poaching for horn, the population has risen to almost 900. **Kaziranga Forest Lodge** has reasonable rooms from Rs300 but a new private lodge, **Wild Grass** with rooms from Rs450 and well-organised jeep-safaris into the park started operating in 1991. Bookings are handled by **WG Resorts**, Uzanbazar, Guwahati. **Manas Tiger Reserve**, 176 km (110 miles) north of Guwahati, is one of the country's most beautiful parks and Asia's most important wildlife areas. Straddling the international border with Bhutan, the park contains representatives of at least 20 of India's most endangered species and a magnificent bird life. Accommodation is limited and political problems in the area since the late 1980s have limited the management efficiency of the park authorities.

Permits to travel to Assam must be applied for through an Indian Embassy, along with a visa application, at least 6 weeks prior to visiting the area. It is sometimes possible to get permits from the Foreigners' Section of the Home Ministry in New Delhi (Lok Nayak Bhavan, Khan Market). Any travel in Assam should be coordinated through a specialist travel agent or arranged through one in Guwahati such as **Sheba Travels** G.N. Bordoloi Road, Guwahati (tel 43280).

Rajasthan and Gujarat
In complete contrast to the lush habitats of the north-east, forest cover along ridges and in the valleys of the Aravali hills in Rajasthan is largely dry scrub. Home to a small tiger population, the state has two reserves under Project Tiger. Both are subject to considerable pressure along their peripheries from villagers seeking grassing and

fuelwood. **Sariska National Park** near Alwar is only a 3-hour drive south of Delhi (180 km; 125 miles) and 2 hours from Jaipur (110 km; 68 miles). Although not a good area for seeing tiger the protection given to the area under Project Tiger has benefited the large populations of antelope and deer as well as an extensive bird life. Opposite the park entrance is the **Sariska Palace Hotel** (tel Sariska 222) with rooms from Rs600 and organises jeep trips into the park (tel. Delhi 739712). Also at the park entrance is a forest rest house and Rajasthan Tourism's **Tiger Den** tourist bungalow with rooms from Rs250. Further south is **Ranthambore National Park** 132 km (82 miles) southeast of Jaipur and well connected by train with Delhi and Bombay. Sawai Madhopur station is 13 km (8 miles) from the park entrance and most express trains between Delhi and Bombay stop here. Jeeps are available at the station and the Park Director's office is just opposite. Ranthambore is considered by many as one of the two best places for seeing tiger although in the summer of 1992 reports of poaching in the area has probably made this more difficult. One kilometre from the station is the Taj Group's **Sawai Madhopur Lodge** (tel 2541, 2247) with rooms including food at US$70 single, US$85 double. RTDC **Castle Jhoomar Baori** (tel 2495) is midway between the park entrance and Sawai Madhopur and has rooms from Rs400. Two other small camps are located toward the park entrance.

Rajasthan is, perhaps surprisingly for the 'desert state', home to one of the world's most important wetland sanctuaries. The **Keoladeo Ghana National Park** at Bharatpur, 53 km (33 miles) west of Agra and only 184 km (125 miles) south of Delhi. About a third of the park's 29 sq km is flooded during the monsoon and is host to tens of thousands of resident breeding birds from August to November. In October large groups of migratory waterfowl, waders and birds of prey arrive from Siberia, Central Asia, Tibet and the Russian Steppes. The rarest visitor by far is the tiny relic population of **Siberian crane** that winters each year in the park—during the 1991–92 winter only 9 arrived. To the far west of Rajasthan, near Jaisalmer, is the **Desert National Park** (see p.178) covering over 3000 sq km of sand dune and scrub and sustaining a very different range of wildlife to most of India's other parks. Permission to visit must be sought from the Forest Department and District Magistrate's office in Jaisalmer.

In Gujarat, **Gir National Park** is internationally famous as the last refuge for the **Asiatic Lion**. The dry, hot Kathiawar Peninsular has one sizable tract of forest remaining and since the 1920s has been protected. Today's lion population are descendants of the 20 or so individuals that survived into the 20th century. **Forest Lodge** (see p.332) on the edge of the park provides reasonable accommodation. In northern Gujarat, at the edge of the Little Rann of Kutch is the **Dhrangadhra Sanctuary**. The flat saline wilderness of the Rann has a population of **wild ass** and good numbers of chinkara and blackbuck. The small private **Camp Zainabad** near Dasad, Gujarat 382751, organises trips into the area and provides comfortable accommodation.

Madhya Pradesh
Some of the country's largest tracts of forest are in the central state of Madhya Pradesh. Large areas are sparsely populated and it is these jungles that formed the backdrop to Kipling's *Jungle Book*. There are many protected areas in the state but two national parks are among the best in the country. **Bandhavgarh National Park** 220 km (138 miles) south-east of Khajuraho, is probably the best place in the country

to see tiger. The original park area was relatively small and had a high density of tigers—22 in 105 sq km. Apart from tiger the park has a good mix of prey species and a large number of bird species. A private, deluxe camp run on the line of the luxury camps in East Africa, operates near the park entrance. **Bandhavgarh Jungle Camp** has inclusive rates of US$105 per person and includes accommodation, food, game-viewing, elephant rides into the park and all fees (book through a travel agent or directly to B-21 Greater Kailash Enclave II, New Delhi 110048 tel 6411619, 6412501, fax 011-6428311).

Kanha National Park, 220 km (138 miles) south of Bandhavgarh, has long been considered one of the best in Asia. It was one of the first parks to come under Project Tiger management and flourished. One of the park's success stories is the reestablishment of a viable breeding population of the Central Indian race of **Swamp deer**. Near Kisli on the western edge of the park are various private camps including **Kipling Camp** with accommodation and all services from Rs1500. Book through Kipling Camp, c/o Tollygunge Club, 120 D.P. Sasmal Road, Calcutta.

South India

The Western Ghats are the range of hills that stretch parallel with the west coast and rarely more than 100 km inland. Large areas of forest still survive although the pressures of development are as strong here as anywhere in the country. The Western Ghats have an isolated fauna with many species of birds, insect and fish common with those in the eastern Himalaya but not found in the intervening area. Along the length of the range are various small and little known sanctuaries, but where the Eastern Ghats and the Nilgiri Hills meet the Western Ghats there is one of India's richest areas for wildlife. The three southern states of Karnataka, Kerala and Tamil Nadu also meet here and protected areas in all three have been loosely joined to form a large biosphere reserve. In Karnataka **Nagarhole National Park** and **Bandipur Tiger Reserve** are two of the constituent areas. Apart from a tiger population and a healthy range of prey species, the area is refuge to the largest number of India's threatened **elephant** population. Perhaps 5000 out of an estimated 20 000 elephants in the subcontinent thrive and migrate through these forests. Nagarhole also has perhaps the best government-managed tourist infrastructure. **Kabini River Lodge** (book through Jungle Lodges & Resorts, Shrungar Shopping Centre, 2nd floor, M.G. Road, Bangalore, tel 575195) is beautifully located in a large well-wooded compound on the bank of the Kabini Reservoir; rooms with food and game drives are from Rs950. Only 75 km (47 miles) south-west of Mysore (see p.477) the park is one of the easiest to visit. Across the reservoir is Bandipur where the forest is slightly thinner and drier. The park is bisected by the Mysore–Ooty highway which continues through to the **Madumalai Sanctuary** in neighbouring Tamil Nadu. There are two private farms on the edge of the sanctuary at Masinagudi, 18 km (11 miles) from the park headquarters at Madumalai. **Bamboo Banks** and **Jungle Hut** (tel Masinagudi 40—via Ooty), Masinagudi PO, Nilgiris 643223, provide good accommodation with food, and organise game-viewing trips. West of Bandipur, and also merging with both Nagarhole and Madumalai, is the **Wynad Sanctuary** in Kerala.

The Western Ghats in Kerala are never far from the sea and the forests and sholas in the area are extremely well watered. **Eravikulam National Park** is little known and has no accommodation in or nearby the park. Sixteen kilometres (10 miles) from Munnar, the park has India's largest population of **Nilgiri tahr** which graze on the rolling hills above the tree line. These highlands interspersed with sholas or small woods in the valleys, lead to south India's highest peak, Anaimudi (2695 m; 8853 feet). Further south, the century-old lake on the Periyar river forms the nucleus of the **Periyar Tiger Reserve**, 190 km (118 miles) east of Cochin. The lake covers 26 sq km (10 sq miles) and its catchment area is among the densest tropical forest in the country. The total park area covers 777 sq km (299 sq miles) but most game-viewing is from boats of animals coming to the water's edge—elephants (the park supports a population of almost 1200 and it is a common sight to see a herd feeding, bathing and swimming), gaur, wild pig, sambar deer, cheetal, and very occasionally wild dog or perhaps even a tiger. The forest has an abundant range of woodland birds but drives into the forest have to be specially arranged with the park authorities. Kerala Tourism run three lodges within the park providing mid-range accommodation at **Aranya Niwas Hotel** and **Edapalayam Lake Palace** beside the lake, and budget accommodation at **Periyar House**. All can be booked through the **KTDC office**, PB No 46, Behind Secretariat, Trivandrum (64705, 64261). A new property at 950 metres (3000 feet) on the edge of the park, **Spice Village** (tel 2314) at Kumily (book through the Casino Hotel, Cochin tel 340221, tlx 0885-6314, fax 484-340001) has cottages from Rs575 single and Rs 775 double. The drive from Periyar to Madurai (see p.419) 145 km (90 miles) to the east is among the most interesting in southern India; a visit to the reserve is included in route 12 and can easily be added to route 11.

Many of India's protected areas have survived because of their remoteness or because they were originally protected as areas for hunting. Almost all hunting has now been banned but poaching in some areas does unfortunately continue. While some of the obscurer parks can take a day to reach from a major city you may be travelling through, others can be incorporated in a tour without too much difficulty and show yet another facet of this fascinating country.

Part IV

NORTH INDIA

The Lion Capital, emblem of the government

DELHI

Capital of India, Delhi is two cities in one—first the Old Delhi of the Mughals, created by Shah Jahan and still a medieval place of forts, mosques and bazaars; second, the New Delhi built by the British, an elegant metropolis of broad avenues, stately homes and landscaped gardens. The coexistence of the old and the new, a common feature of modern Indian cities, is nowhere more obvious than in Delhi; with the poor inner city leading a life of its own, the rich and the political élite retire to the sophisticated diplomatic enclaves, and debate the encroaching poverty from behind closed doors. Delhi is the seat of Indian government, and what visitors see here is a reflection of what is happening in the country as a whole.

When the great coastal cities of India were still mud-flats, Delhi was already a thriving capital of an ancient empire. Legend has it that the Pandavas, heroes of the *Mahabharata* epic, founded a city on this site, called Indraprastha, around 1200 BC. Certainly, it has for many, many centuries exerted a powerful influence on the history of the country. Its strategic situation between the Aravali hills, known here as the Ridge, and flanked to the east by the river Yamuna, was one that no prospective Hindu ruler or northern invader could afford to ignore. Consequently, it was built, fought over, defended, destroyed, deserted and rebuilt on several occasions over the ages. In the process, it absorbed many different cultures and became uniquely cosmopolitan in its outlook.

No fewer than 15 different cities are said to have risen and fallen in and around Delhi since the 11th century. The first four 'Dillis' were Rajput structures, erected in the southern hills near the present situation of the Qutb Minar. The first historically recorded citadel was Lal Kot, built by the Tomar Rajputs (founders of 8th-century Dillika) in AD 1060. Taken by the Chauhan Rajputs in the 12th century, it was enlarged and renamed Qila Rai Pithora. Then came the Turk slave-king Qutb-ud-Din Aibak, the first Sultan of Delhi (1206), who built India's first mosque (Quwwat-ud-Islam) and her symbolic tower of victory, Qutb Minar. Under the Khilji dynasty, Islam's influence spread and the prosperous city of Sir゛ ∠prang up (Delhi II, 1290–1320) near to present-day Hauz Khas. Next came the Tughlaqs, a bulldog breed who built no fewer than three new cities here in the 14th century—first Tughlaqabad, a massive 13-gate fort 10 km (6.3 miles) south-east of Qutb Minar (used for only five years), then Jahanapanah (rapidly abandoned by the mad Sultan Mohammed, who marched the whole population off to distant Daulatabad, near Aurangabad and then marched them all back again 17 years later), and finally Ferozabad (creation of Mohammed's more stable successor, Feroz Shah), in its day the richest city in the world. This fifth version of Delhi marked the critical move north to the river settlement along the river Yamuna. It lasted a remarkably long time (Delhi's turbulent history considered), the Tughlaq's successors (Sayyids and Lodhis) being too busy building tombs to construct new cities. Emperor Sher Shah, the Afghan usurper, displaced the Mughals just long enough to build a sixth Delhi, Shergarh, before they won it back again (1555). But it wasn't for another century that the seat of Mughal power transferred back to Delhi from Agra. The move took place under Emperor Shah Jahan, who built Shahjahanabad (the present Old Delhi) between 1638 and 1648, obliterating most of old Ferozabad and Shergarh to provide building materials. His son, Aurangzeb, made some improvements to the new capital, but the succession of weak Mughal rulers who came afterwards only paved the way for the infamous invasion of Nadir Shah (1739) when 30 000 Delhi inhabitants lost their lives overnight. After this, the Mughal emperor could only sit sadly in his sacked Red Fort (Lal Qila) and utter the epitaph of his conquered dynasty: 'My kingdom extends no further than these four walls.' Delhi then fell to the British, returning only briefly to Mughal rule during the Indian Mutiny. The last Mughal emperor, Bahadur Shah, was reluctantly persuaded out of retirement for this, and suffered for his decision by being marched off into exile in Rangoon. It was the end of the great Mughal Empire in India.

Under British rule, Delhi remained in the backwaters until 1911, when The King-Emperor announced the creation of a new city, New Delhi and the transfer of the government from Calcutta, and became a capital once more. To mark its new status as a brand-new city, the eighth (New) Delhi was constructed. The creation of two British architects—Edwin Lutyens and Herbert Baker—it was designed in magnificent style to reflect the might of the British Empire in India and to accommodate 70 000 people. The new, modern city sprang up from out of a bare wilderness previously inhabited only by wild animals—a mirage of planned gardens, noble monuments and enormous avenues. Completed in 1931, on the very eve of Independence, it is today considered either the blindest folly of the British Raj or (being generous) its finest gift to modern, free India.

Today, New Delhi remains distinctly British. The old imperiousness of the Viceroys has become the political élitism of the Indian ruling-class, and many of the parliamentary, legislative and educational procedures of the Raj remain not only intact, but reinforced by the Indian love of red tape. In Connaught Place, while young gum-chewing Delhiites queue with foreign tourists in fast-food Wimpy bars, politicians and place-hunters jostle with filmstars and media types in swanky upmarket hotels and restaurants, and at private dinners. It's not difficult to detect the ghost of the Raj.

Delhi elicits strong likes and dislikes amongst foreign travellers. On the plus side, it's an easy introduction to India, with some of the best hotels, restaurants and facilities in the country, and it's a very convenient base for sightseeing: from here you can jump off to Rajasthan, Varanasi, Kashmir (if the political situation allows) and the ever-popular Golden Triangle. But many find it lacking in colour, character and expression—a city without a face, not like real India at all. In an important sense, what started out being considered the Raj's greatest contribution to free India—the splendid new city of Delhi—could well become a long-term hindrance, a continuous reminder of a past best forgotten.

WHEN TO GO
If you arrive in early January, don't expect warm tropical sun: it can be as cold here as in London. The popular season here may be October to March, but it gets decidedly chilly in December and January. Delhi is most pleasant and green in October–November and February–March. A popular attraction is Republic Day (26 January), celebrated here as nowhere else, with a whole week of festivals, dance performances, massed bands and ceremonial displays. The highlight is the military parade on the day itself along the length of Rajpath and on to Connaught Place and the Red Fort. In October, the emphasis shifts from a military to a cultural show of strength, the big Dussehra festival coinciding with plays, classical dance, music recitals and readings of epic poems. The festival to avoid is Holi (March), when unwary tourists, along with everybody else, are pelted with coloured powder, water and even paint. Another time to avoid is late May and June when the temperature soars and power-cuts become more frequent. The fierce white heat of a June afternoon, when the temperature can reach 46°C, is only partly redeemed by the widely available fresh lime and soda or a cold beer.

ARRIVAL/DEPARTURE

Air
Delhi's Indira Gandhi International Airport now has two separate terminals. The international terminal (Terminal I, tel 5452011) is 22 km (13 miles) from Connaught Place, and is a newer, more efficient airport used only for international flights. The domestic terminal (Terminal II, tel 5483535, 3295121) at Palam, 17 km from Connaught Place, is exclusively for the use of Indian Airlines, Vayudoot flights and the new private domestic airlines and charter operators such as East West Airlines.Both airports have retiring rest rooms (handy if your plane is delayed/cancelled), and desks for air/rail/hotel bookings. Delhi is well connected by International carriers including Air India.

Delhi airport is fairly efficent although it can take up to an hour for baggage to arrive on the conveyor belts as all incoming suitcases are X-rayed. It is therefore wise to carry film and computer disks in your hand luggage. You can use the time between waiting for your checked bags and clearing immigration, which usually takes about 40 minutes, by changing money at the bank in the arrivals hall. At the bank insist on some small denomination notes (Rs5, 10 and 20). These are useful for tipping porters, and taxis often never have enough change.

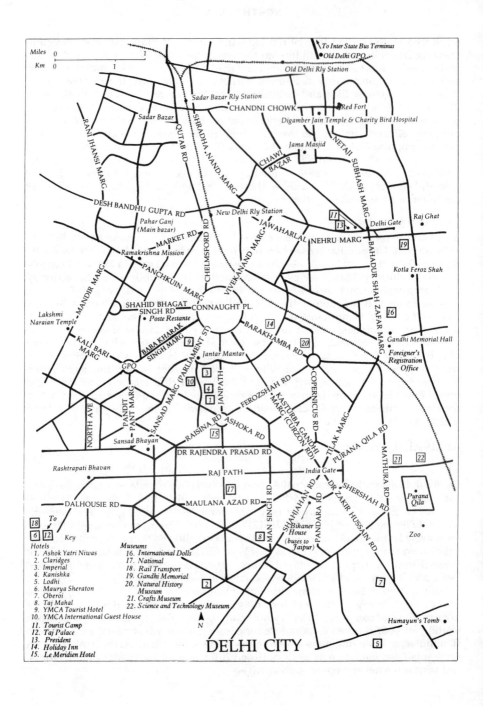

Miles 0 _____ 1
Km 0 _____ 1

To Inter State Bus Terminus
Old Delhi GPO
Old Delhi Rly Station

Sadar Bazar Rly Station
CHANDNI CHOWK
Red Fort
Digamber Jain Temple & Charity Bird Hospital
Sadar Bazar
Jama Masjid

RANI JHANSI MARG
QUTAB RD
SHRADDHA NAND MARG
CHAWRI BAZAR
NETAJI SUBHASH MARG

DESH BANDHU GUPTA RD
New Delhi Rly Station
[11]
[13]
Delhi Gate
Raj Ghat
Pahar Ganj (Main bazar)
MARKET RD
JAWAHARLAL NEHRU MARG
[19]
Ramakrishna Mission
CHELMSFORD RD
BAHADUR SHAH ZAFAR MARG
Kotla Feroz Shah
PANCHKUIN MARG
VIVEKANAND MARG

MANDIR MARG
SHAHID BHAGAT SINGH RD
CONNAUGHT PL.
[16]
Lakshmi Naraian Temple
Poste Restante
[14]
Gandhi Memorial Hall
KALI BARI MARG
BABA KHARAK SINGH MARG
[9]
BARAKHAMBA RD
[20]
Foreigner's Registration Office
GPO
Jantar Mantar
[10]
[3]

NORTH AVE
PANDIT PANT MARG
SANSAD MARG (PARLIAMENT ST)
JANPATH
FEROZSHAH RD
COPERNICUS RD
[4]
[1]
KASTURBA GANDHI MARG (CURZON RD)
PURANA QILA RD
MATHURA RD
Sansad Bhavan
RAISINA RD
ASHOKA RD
[15]
TILAK MARG
[21]
[22]
DR RAJENDRA PRASAD RD
Rashtrapati Bhavan
RAJ PATH
India Gate
Purana Qila
[17]
DALHOUSIE RD
MAULANA AZAD RD
MAN SINGH RD
SHAHJAHAN RD
Bikaner House (buses to Jaipur)
PANDARA RD
DR ZAKIR HUSSAIN RD
SHERSHAH RD
Zoo
[18] To
[6] [12] Key
[8]
[2]
[7]
Humayun's Tomb
[5]
N

Hotels
1. Ashok Yatri Niwas
2. Claridges
3. Imperial
4. Kanishka
5. Lodhi
6. Maurya Sheraton
7. Oberoi
8. Taj Mahal
9. YMCA Tourist Hotel
10. YMCA International Guest House
11. Tourist Camp
12. Taj Palace
13. President
14. Holiday Inn
15. Le Meridien Hotel

Museums
16. International Dolls
17. National
18. Rail Transport
19. Gandhi Memorial
20. Natural History Museum
21. Crafts Museum
22. Science and Technology Museum

DELHI CITY

The three cheapest forms of airport to city transport are a) air-con 'Fly Bus' service (Rs20, drops at major hotels and Connaught Place, *returns* to airport from Madras Hotel, Radial Rd 2, Connaught Place); b) non air-con EATS bus service (Rs17, drops at major hotels, *returns* to airport from Malhotra Building, next to Indian Airlines and opposite Palika Bazaar, Connaught Place); c) Delhi Transport Corporation bus service (Rs30, goes to New Delhi and Interstate Bus Stand, *returns* to airport from Super Bazaar, Connaught Place). For the first-time visitor the pre-paid taxi service (more expensive, around Rs6 per km) may be the easiest way of getting out of the airport. However you travel, the trip from airport to city centre takes around 30 minutes.

Rail
Trains run from Delhi to all major tourist destinations—sometimes, as with Agra (*Shatabdi Express, Taj Express*) and Jaipur (*Pink City Express*), they can work out even quicker than air travel. There are two main rail stations: Old Delhi station, in the heart of the old city, and New Delhi station, just north of Connaught Place on Chelmsford Road. Rail reservations are now relatively quick and easy to obtain from the special tourist counter on the 1st floor of New Delhi Station. It's air-conditioned, fully computerised, and you can—if you have an Indrail Pass (also sold here)—book your rail itinerary weeks ahead. However, many travellers report long queues. To tap the tourist quota, apply to the Railway Tourist Guide. He's at the counter between 10 am and 5 pm (except Sunday), and has tickets for every train out of Delhi.

Bus
Most long-distance buses (to Haryana, Himachal Pradesh, Jammu & Kashmir, Uttar Pradesh) leave from the Interstate Bus Terminal (ISBT) at Kashmiri Gate, north of Old Delhi rail station. Popular destinations are Agra, Jaipur, Dharmsala, Jammu (for Srinagar) and Chandigarh (for Shimla). Deluxe state buses to Rajasthan leave from Bikaner House, near India Gate. Deluxe buses to Himachal Pradesh leave from outside Chandralok Building in Janpath. Seats on most of these services can be booked in advance.

GETTING AROUND
Orientation in New Delhi is fairly easy: most roads are well- signed, and street names are uniform (no confusing post-Independence duplications). Budget travellers collect in three major 'pockets': in and around the central-city hub of Connaught Circus (for airline offices, tourist offices, banks, travel agents, cheap hotels and better restaurants); in the Paharganj area 2 km (⅓ miles) north of Connaught Place (for New Delhi rail station and more budget accommodation); and in places like Tourist Camp in the old city (for Old Delhi rail station, Red Fort and the bazaars). A fourth pocket, reserved for the rich and influential, is round Lutyens' imperial complex and the new post-Independence colonies of south Delhi where most of the five-star hotels are along with the smarter residential and shopping areas.

In New Delhi, you can hire taxis, auto-rickshaws and local buses. In Old Delhi, there are also cycle-rickshaws. The latter are slow, but open and airy, and you can get right across town (e.g. from Paharganj down to the YMCA, Jaisingh Rd) for Rs8–10. Expect to pay twice this for auto-rickshaws, but at least they don't get lost so often. If you're in a hurry, and simply can't afford to get lost, always take a taxi. Don't go anywhere until you've either agreed a fair price, or (better) have persuaded your driver to use his meter. Theoretically, you can report him to the police for

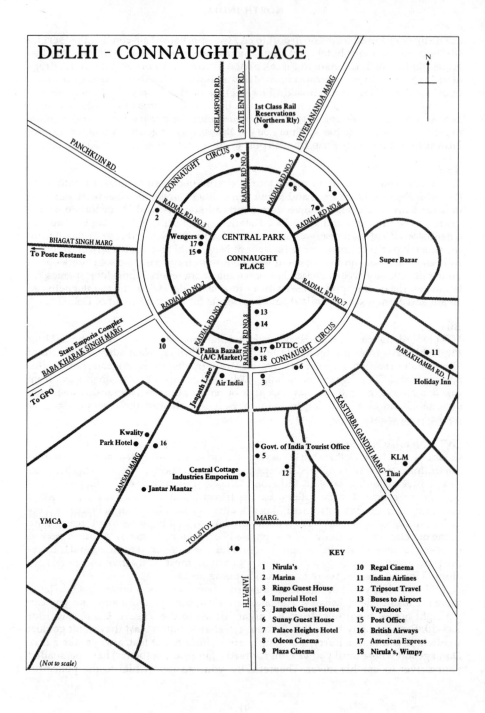

DELHI - CONNAUGHT PLACE

N

CHELMSFORD RD.
STATE ENTRY RD.
VIVEKANANDA MARG

1st Class Rail Reservations (Northern Rly)

PANCHKUIN RD.

CONNAUGHT CIRCUS

RADIAL RD NO.4
RADIAL RD NO.5
RADIAL RD NO.3
RADIAL RD NO.6
RADIAL RD NO.2
RADIAL RD NO.1
RADIAL RD NO.8
RADIAL RD NO.7

9 ●
8 ●
1 ●
7 ●
2 ●

BHAGAT SINGH MARG
← To Poste Restante

Wengers ●
17 ●
15 ●

CENTRAL PARK

CONNAUGHT PLACE

Super Bazar

State Emporia Complex
BABA KHARAK SINGH MARG

10 ●

13 ●
14 ●

Palika Bazaar (A/C Market)

17 ● DTDC
18 ●

CONNAUGHT CIRCUS

BARAKHAMBA RD.
11 ●

Holiday Inn

← To GPO

Janpath Lane
Air India

6 ●
3 ●

KASTURBA GANDHI MARG

Kwality ●
Park Hotel ●   ● 16

Govt. of India Tourist Office
5 ●

KLM
Thai

SANSAD MARG

Central Cottage Industries Emporium ●

12 ●

● Jantar Mantar

YMCA ●

TOLSTOY

MARG.

4 ●

JANPATH

KEY

1	Nirula's	10	Regal Cinema
2	Marina	11	Indian Airlines
3	Ringo Guest House	12	Tripsout Travel
4	Imperial Hotel	13	Buses to Airport
5	Janpath Guest House	14	Vayudoot
6	Sunny Guest House	15	Post Office
7	Palace Heights Hotel	16	British Airways
8	Odeon Cinema	17	American Express
9	Plaza Cinema	18	Nirula's, Wimpy

(Not to scale)

overcharging, but hardly any travellers have time for that. The threat is usually sufficient. Meters should be flagged down before setting off, and should read Rs5.60 (for taxis) and Rs3 (for auto-rickshaws). This covers you for the first 2 km. A surcharge of 12.5% is payable on the final meter reading, in respect of recent fuel-price increases. Up-to-date tariffs are obtainable from the police booth opposite the Government of India tourist office. One warning: every rickshaw and taxi driver in Delhi will want to buy your duty-free whisky, foreign currency, Walkman, watch, or camera. Some of them are police informers. The local bus service has improved but buses are not recommended before about 10 am or after 4 pm when they become impossibly crowded.

WHAT TO SEE
Delhi has more sights than any other Indian city, so you'll need to be selective. As a new arrival, your best bet is probably to take a full-day or two half-day conducted tours. Delhi's tours aren't the best—far too much time is wasted on picking up passengers before hitting the sights—but at least you cover a lot of out-of-the-way spots which would cost much more time and money to see by taxi, rickshaw or car. And you can always return to spend more time at places you particularly like.

One tip: before taking on a tour, give yourself a day or two to get over jet-lag. Like all major Indian cities, Delhi can be pretty overpowering and during the summer incredibly hot.

City Tour (conducted sightseeing coach, 4 hours)
Jantar Mantar–Laxmi Narayan Temple–Rashtrapati Bhavan–India Gate–Safdarjang Tomb–Qutb Minar–Humayun's Tomb

Leaving Connaught Place down Parliament St, you'll first see the salmon-pink astronomical observatory of **Jantar Mantar**. Built in AD 1724, this was the first of five brick-and-mortar observatories created by the starstruck Maharajah Jai Singh II of Jaipur. It consists of four differing masonry instruments designed to predict eclipses and to plot the course of the planets, stars and sun. The big feature is the huge 'Prince of Dials' sundial. But Delhi city-dwellers come here mainly for picnics on the pleasant garden lawns. Open sunrise to 10 pm daily.

The next stop is **Laxmi Narayan Temple** on Mandir Marg, 2 km (⅓ miles) west of Connaught Place. This is a colourful pink and gold 'modern' Hindu temple, erected by the philanthropist G.D. Birla (1938) and commonly referred to as **Birla Temple**. It's an interesting place, not least because it's so different from normal Indian temples: first, it's composed of several different-coloured stone materials (instead of the traditional red sandstone); second, it's open to all Hindus, including the *harijans* (ex-'untouchables'); third, it's a mixture of various Hindu architectural styles instead of just one; finally, it's dedicated to a number of other gods (notably Ganesh, Hanuman and Durga) in addition to the focal deities of Vishnu, god of preservation, and his consort Laxmi, goddess of wealth. The ecumenism of the temple even extends to other religions, and inside you'll find not only some fine Buddhist and Sikh wall-frescoes, but also a huge bronze bell and a huge marble globe presented by Chinese Buddhists. But it's Krishna's shrine which visitors come to see—an ingenious mirror-chamber where, everywhere you look, Krishna's reflection is staring back at you. In the courtyard, you'll see the fine equestrian statue of Arjuna and the other Mahabharata brothers who helped Krishna defeat the forces of evil in times of old.

Rashtrapati Bhavan, the former Viceregal Lodge, now the official residence of India's President, is the next place on the itinerary. It is the best example of Lutyens' expansive, imperialist vision, built—like the massive complex of government buildings and offices it overlooks—of red sandstone in the Indo-Saracenic (eastern baroque) style. It was once irreverently described as 'a British matron in fancy dress'. Covering 330 acres of Raisina Hill, it's a huge place which (since the tour bus only speeds past) you may want to see properly another day. You won't be allowed into Rashtrapati Bhavan, but you can visit the beautiful 10 acres of Mughal gardens behind it (open February–March) on production of a pass obtained from the tourist office. There are two new museums at Rashtrapati Bhavan; the first at 1 Willingdon Crescent contains a documentary and photographic history of the building. A second museum in the Marble Hall within the building is only open on certain days and is more of a portrait gallery. You can also, with an introduction from your Embassy, visit nearby **Sansad Bhavan** (Parliament House)—the vast, circular, colonnade-rimmed building designed by Baker on the south end of Sansad Marg.

A scenic drive down stately, tree-lined **Rajpath** brings you to **India Gate**, the symbol of modern Delhi. A 42-m (136-ft) high, white-sandstone monolith, it was built by the British to salute the 90 000 Indian soldiers who lost their lives in the Great War of 1914–18. The small eternal flame or *Amer Jawan Jyoti* beneath it was added later by Indira Gandhi, in memory of Indian casualties of the 1971 war with Pakistan. Modelled on the Menin Gate in Belgium, India Gate is today a favourite tourist attraction—another place where Delhiites come to wind down after work.

A long drive south (8 km; 5 miles from the city centre), is **Safdarjang Tomb**, built between 1753 and 1774 for Mohammed Shah's prime minister, Safdar Jang, the second Nawab of Oudh. The mausoleum is set on a raised terrace in fountain-sprinkled gardens, and comprises a 12-m (40-ft) high central hall supporting a bulbous dome, with marble minarets. It is notable for being the 'last great flicker in the lamp of Mughal architecture at Delhi'.

Towering over the ancient monuments of Lal Kot is Delhi's most famous landmark, the **Qutb Minar**. Situated some 15 km (9.4 miles) south of New Delhi, it is the highlight of the tour: a soaring tower of victory, commenced in AD 1199 to mark the Muslim defeat of the last Hindu king, and once used as a minaret by the muezzins. It has five storeys—three of red sandstone, two of marble and sandstone—and tapers up to a height of 72.5 m (236 ft). Despite earthquakes, lightning, and the general ravages of time, it remains in remarkably good condition. A masterpiece of perfect proportion, with exquisite embellishments adorning the walls (intricate carvings of quotations from the *Koran*, growing ever-larger the higher up the tower you look, so that the words are equally easy to read at both the top and the bottom), it has been called one of the wonders of the ancient world. Until recently, visitors were allowed up the tower stairway to enjoy views from the top balconies—but there were a few suicide attempts, and the stairway was closed.

Below the Qutb Minar stands the earliest extant mosque built in India, the **Quwwat-ul-Islam** ('Might of Islam') Mosque. Commenced in AD 1193 on the site of an old Hindu temple, it was plastered and richly ornamented with floral designs and text from the *Koran*, to cover over the old Hindu decorations. But time has eroded the plaster and you can now see some of the original carving, and the places where the faces of the Hindu gods have been hacked away.

Within the mosque is the famous **Iron Pillar**. Probably cast in the 4th century AD, nobody knows where it came from nor what it's doing there and why it hasn't gone rusty. A popular myth is that if you can clasp your hands standing with your back to the pillar, you'll get your wish. This pillar is so strong that someone once fired a cannon at it, and it wasn't even dented. Leaving the mosque, you'll come across the enormous base of the **Alai Minar**—an attempt by the Afghan Sultan Ala-ud-Din to build another tower of victory *twice* the size of Qutb Minar. The surviving 27 m (88 ft) base was as far as he got, because after his death (1315) nobody had the courage to continue the work. He did, however, complete the **Alai Darwaza** (1310), a richly ornamented gateway of red sandstone, with two huge marble-latticed window screens. It has been described as the most beautiful specimen of external polychromatic decoration in the world.

Tour buses sometimes slot in **Humayun's Tomb** on the way back north. This first substantial example of Mughal architecture lies on the edge of the new city, on the Delhi–Mathura road. It was built in AD 1556–69 by Bega Begum, the widow of the second Mughal emperor Humayun, and employs various prototype features of Mughal architecture—octagonal plan, lofty arches, pillared kiosks, bulbous dome and gardens with fountains—which were later to culminate in Agra's Taj Mahal and Itmud-ud-Daulah's Tomb. Bega Begum is buried here, along with Humayun and a few unlucky (murdered) princes. This was also the place where Bahadur Shah II, last of the Mughal emperors, hid out in the wake of the Indian Mutiny, until captured by a British officer.

The tour over, take a walk round **Connaught Circus**, built by Robert Tor Russell and opened in 1931. A double concentric circle of colonial-style buildings with colonnaded verandahs centred round a park, it is New Delhi's original shopping and entertainment centre. A series of broad 'radial roads' run out from it like spokes on a cartwheel, and getting lost here is a foregone conclusion. Even taxi drivers who have been working here for 20 years haven't got the hang of it, and to do a full tour round you'll need a lot of stamina and a good map. Head for the inner circle for lunch at one of the Western-style restaurants, then head off down Radial Road 8 for a relaxing afternoon's swim in one of Janpath's luxury hotel pools.

Old Delhi Tour (rickshaw/taxi, 4–5 hours)
Dolls Museum–Feroz Shah Kotla–Raj Ghat–Jama Masjid–Chandni Chowk– Red Fort

Start around 3 pm with a cab or rickshaw over to the **International Dolls Museum** in Nehru House, Bahadur Shah Zafar Marg. It is located 2 km (⅓ miles) east of Connaught Circus, and is easy to find—being practically the only non-newspaper building in Delhi's 'Fleet Street'. Open 10 am to 6 pm daily except Monday, it features a beautiful collection of 6000 dolls from all over the world (85 different countries represented), plus the new display of dolls in traditional Indian costumes. Admission is Rs1.

Further up the same road (rickshaw ride, or hair-raising 15-minute walk), you'll find **Feroz Shah Kotla**, the historic fifth city of Delhi, just outside Delhi Gate on the Mathura Road. Built in AD 1354 by Feroz Shah Tughlaq, most of the structure, including much of the original 9-m (30-ft) high wall, was knocked down to provide materials for the later city of Shahjahanabad, but what remains is nevertheless impressive. Worth seeing are the ruins of the old mosque, the Baoli (well) and the Wazir's house (near northern wall). Best of all, there's the striking monolithic **Ashoka Pillar**, a 13-m (42-ft) high sandstone column, inscribed with Ashokan edicts, which dates back to the 3rd century BC, brought here by Feroz Shah from Ambala. When the traveller Finch visited Delhi in 1601, the pillar was surmounted by a glittering globe and gilded crescent, but these were destroyed by lightning in 1715–19.

Leave Feroz Shah Kotla at the eastern end for Mahatma Gandhi Road. A 10-minute walk left brings you to **Raj Ghat** (appears on right), the simple, black marble platform commemorating the place of Mahatma Gandhi's cremation. Set in green, tranquil gardens, it is a popular pilgrimage spot—especially on Friday evenings, when a special ceremony is held (Gandhi was assassinated on a Friday, 30 January 1948). Just opposite, and along to the left, is the small but interesting **Gandhi Memorial Museum** (open 9.30 am to 5.30 pm, except Monday). There's a film show on Gandhi in English here every Sunday, commencing at 5 pm.

From the museum, it's a short stroll left to **Delhi Gate**, then a fascinating 30-minute walk up Netaji Subhash Road (site of a remarkable pavement bazaar) to the **Jama Masjid**. This is India's largest mosque, approached via a grassy maidan. The massive red sandstone structure—only rivalled by the similar mosque at Fatehpur Sikri—was initiated by Shah Jahan (his final extravagance) in 1644 and completed by Aurangzeb in 1658. The Jama Masjid has three great gateways, entrance usually being via the grand flight of stairs at the Eastern Gate. Women not accompanied by a 'responsible male relative' are instantly ejected. Inside the massive cloistered courtyard (it holds up to 20 000 worshippers on important festivals), fend off enterprising nobodies trying to sell you (unnecessary) Rs1 camera tickets, and head for the small booth left of the entrance to buy a (necessary) Rs2 'Meenar Ticket'. This gains you access to the 46-m (150-ft) South Minaret, which provides superlative views of the Red Fort and old city. This is one of two minarets here—both built of strips of red sandstone and white marble—which flank the imposing 61-m (200-ft) high central dome. On your way up the narrow 122-step staircase to the top, firmly discourage so-called guides. All they'll do is wander up there with you, follow you back down, and demand Rs20 for doing precisely nothing. The best day to visit the Jama Masjid is Friday (Muslim holy day), or during the annual festival of Ramadan.

Leaving the mosque by the Northern Gate, you'll soon enter the crowded 'moonlit crossroads' of **Chandni Chowk**. Constructed in 1648, this 21-m (68-ft) wide road was once the richest street of India and the most famous bazaar in the East. Today, it is a crowded, frantic shopping-centre—full of covered arcades, tiny roadside temples, lucky palaces, suiting and shirting shops and novelty stores—with a quite electric atmosphere. For minimal shell-shock, do a short reconnaissance by rickshaw before getting swallowed up in the crowds. Ask to be put off near the excellent gold and silver jewellery market at the red sandstone **Fountain** (the big landmark), then either wander down one of the numerous backstreets (lots of little curio shops, get pleasantly lost for hours) or visit the **Digambar Jain Mandir** (1656) at the top of the chowk, near Red Fort. This elegant Jain temple has a charming marble courtyard and a profusion of paintings and gilded carvings in its interior, but most visitors come here out of curiosity—to see its kitsch Charity Hospital for Sick Birds.

Across the road is the mighty red-sandstone **Red Fort** (Lal Qila), overlooking the river Yamuna. This was built by Shah Jahan (1638–48) as his personal royal residence within his new capital of Shahjahanabad. Deposed by his son Aurangzeb, he hardly ever used it, but left behind one of the most magnificent of all Indian royal palaces. The battlements alone are 2.4 km (1½ miles) long and (at certain points) 18.5 m (60 ft) high. There are two massive gates: Delhi Gate to the south, Lahore Gate to the west. Visitors' entrance is via the Lahore Gate (admission Rs0.50, free on Fridays), which leads directly into the vaulted shopping arcade of **Chhatta Chowk**. Once the province of quality court jewellers and weavers, it is now full of tourist shops. Run this gauntlet to emerge at the 2-storeyed palace entrance gate, the **Naubat Khana**. It opens out into pleasant gardens—look out for bullocks mowing the lawn—and the public audience hall of **Diwan-i-Am**, where the Emperor heard commoners' complaints from a 3-m (10-ft) high marble recess, fronted by a huge *shamiana* decorated with pearls, jewels and golden embroidered work. All this finery, together with the beautiful bird, flower and fruit mosaics of the Emperor's Seat itself, was picked out and looted in the aftermath of the 1857 Mutiny.

Beyond is an open courtyard with serene, green gardens and six palace *mahals*. To the far right is **Mumtaz Mahal**, now a small museum (open 9 am to 5 pm, except Friday), and next to it the **Rang Mahal** (Painted Palace), which once had a rich silver ceiling ornamented with golden flowers, later melted down to augment the royal coffers. The lotus-shaped marble tank here was the starting-point of the 'Stream of Paradise' (**Nahr-i-Bashisht**) which ran through the centre of the mahals and kept them cool. Moving left, there are three connecting marble apartments, where the Emperor used to pray, sleep and live, known as the **Khas Mahal**. But it's the adjoining **Diwan-i-Khas** (private audience hall) that was the centrepiece of the complex. A magnificent marble pavilion supported by 32 richly carved pillars, inlaid with precious gems, it was stripped of its magnificence (including the solid-silver ceiling) by Jat looters in 1779. Some time earlier (1739), it had lost its greatest treasure, the priceless **Peacock Throne** to the Persian invader Nadir Shah. A fabulous work of art, the throne was made of solid gold and constructed in the shape of two dancing fantailed peacocks. Their eyes were studded with rubies and diamonds, and between their tailspreads stood a parakeet carved from a single huge emerald. Clusters of diamonds were set into the throne's legs, and on either side of it were two human figures made of gold, pearls and precious stones. The Diwan-i-Khas has just one 'treasure' left—the famous (though as it turned out, premature) sentiment of Shah Jahan: 'If on earth there be a paradise of bliss, it is this, it is this, it is this.' You'll find it inscribed in gold Persian lettering, over an arch in the central hall.

Next door are the three Royal Baths (**Hammams**), where the emperor and favoured guests took hot saunas round perfumed fountains, fed by the marble 'stream of paradise'. Pause here to look over the fort wall towards the Yamuna. There's normally some sort of entertainment taking place for the benefit of tourists—rope-climbers, magicians, fakirs, contortionists.

From the mahals, cross over to the charming **Moti Masjid** (Pearl Mosque), constructed by Aurangzeb (1622) for private worship. It's a little gem. The original gilded copper domes vanished during the Mutiny, but the present marble ones are a good substitute and it's a small-scale masterpiece throughout, right down to the small, handsome entrance gate of worked brass.

By now, if you've timed things right, it should be early evening and time for the excellent **Sound and Light Show** at the Red Fort. Timings vary according to the season so check at the tourist office. It's worth spending out on a Rs8 luxury seat. The cheaper Rs4 'garden seats' seem to attract all the mosquitoes. The show runs for an hour, and you're expected to stand up at the end for a stirring anthem.

City Sights Round-up (rickshaw/taxi, 5 hours)
National Museum–Zoological Gardens–Purana Qila–Crafts Museum–Rail Transport Museum–Hauz Khas Village

Delhi's lesser-known sights don't get seen often enough, partly because there are so many of them, but also because 2 days' sightseeing is more than enough for most people. But some places are well worth a third day's outing. To find all places on this tour open, go any day except a Monday or a Friday.

Start with a ride down Janpath to the **National Museum**, just below the Rajpath crossing. This is one of India's newer museums (opened round 1950) and has one of the most comprehensive collections of Indian art and artefacts to be found anywhere. It has been recently enlarged, and is undergoing a change in layout as new galleries are opened and others expanded. The ground floor has magnificent miniature paintings on silk and paper, copies of murals, stucco figures dating back to the 7th and 8th centuries, exhibits from the Prehistoric and Indus Valley civilisations, and bronzes/sculptures from the Maurya, Gandhara and Gupta periods. On the first floor is an excellent Central Asian gallery. Rather less dusty and musty, the new wing has a fine collection of folk, classical and tribal music instruments. Open from 10 am to 5 pm (except Mondays) the museum shows good films on 2nd Saturdays and Sundays, at 11 am and 3 pm and has occasional lecture programmes.

Another short ride (3 km, 2 miles) east brings you to the **Zoological Gardens** on Mathura Road (open 9 am to 5 pm, except Fridays). Founded in 1959, this is one of the largest zoos in Asia, and the most important in India. A vast array of species including descendants of the rare white tiger of Rewa live here in acceptable surroundings, and you can wander round the large, open area for hours watching not only the many representative species of India's extensive fauna but also many species from other parts of the world, including a magnificent pair of jaguars. If you're here in the autumn, you will witness large flocks of migratory birds. Above the zoo, to the north, there soars the old fort or **Purana Qila**, the broken shell of Sher Shah's ex-capital. It is believed to have been erected on the site of the first Delhi, Indraprastha, and is worth a visit. Enter the fort by the south gate to find the **Sher Mandal**, a small, red-sandstone octagonal tower the original purpose of which is unknown but was probably built by Sher Shah. It is chiefly remembered today as the place where Emperor Humayun, who had converted it into a library, tripped down the stairs on his way to prayer and sustained mortal injuries. Just north of the tower, see **Qal'a-i-Kunha Mosque**, a fine Indo-Afghan structure of red-sandstone also incorporating marble, slate and coloured stonework. Open from 8 am to 6.30 pm daily, the fort has a small Field Museum, housing a good collection of archaeological site recoveries.

Set within the main exhibition grounds, **Pragati Maidan**, slightly to the north of Purana Qila is the National Handicrafts and Handlooms Museum better known as the **Crafts Museum**. As a homage to the craftspeople and artists who keep alive India's artistic tradition, the museum has been a great success. The complex is made up of replicas of village houses from the various regions of India with a central building used for both permanent and special exhibitions. From September to April craftspeople from throughout the country work at the museum displaying and selling their products which may vary from a clay pot to a sari that has taken a full month to weave. Open daily from 9.30 am to 5 pm. The museum has a small shop and an excellent book about its collection.

A 5-km (3-mile) ride west to Shanti Path, Chanakyapuri, brings you to Delhi's marvellous **Rail Transport Museum**. This features a superb collection of old trains and rolling stock, dotted around a pleasant garden compound. The exhibits include the charming 1908 Memorial Engine with its single steamroller wheel, the mammoth 1923 Bombay Mail with fog-lamp the size of a dinner table, and the elegant 1908 Viceregal dining-coach with gilded wood-panelling interior (and baize-covered card tables). At the back of the compound, there's the showpiece Beyer-Garratt locomotive: 35 yards of gleaming green majesty, with silver-rimmed wheels and vermilion piston shafts. Climb the hump-back bridge at the rear of the compound for the obligatory photograph. Then take in the museum, full of interesting brass engine-plates from all over the world, lots of exotic silver and ivory dinner cutlery, and photographs illustrating the development of India's historic rail network (some of the mountains cut through to lay track claimed the lives of 30% of the workforce). There are some lovely model locomotives, including one of the Rocket itself, and don't miss the prize exhibit—the skull of a wild elephant which charged a Calcutta-bound train in 1894 and lost. The train-driver kept one of the tusks; the other is in the British Museum. Keen gricers can choose from a selection of original builders' plates sold at the entrance. The museum is open 9.30 am to 5.30 pm (except Mondays). Admission is Rs1, and the extra Rs5 camera charge is worth it.

Delhi's newest and most interesting shopping-centre is in the old **Hauz Khas** village about 10 km (7 miles) south of Connaught Place. An old village adjacent to a deer park and the site of a great 13th-century tank built by Ala-ud-din Khilji, Hauz Khas has been absorbed by the southward spread of New Delhi. While remaining a village many of the buildings have been converted into chic and glitzy shops for Delhi's élite and fashionable. On entering the village, the first shop you see is **Dastkar**, a sort of mini Cottage Industries emporium with traditional village crafts from throughout the country on sale. Other shops are more 'high fashion' outlets with expensive designer items. Some good restaurants have been opened (see below), including Delhi's only jazz club. Walk through the village and explore the extensive ruins of the *madrassa*, or religious school, built in 1352 and Feroz Shah's tomb nearby.

RECREATION
Delhi offers a very good choice of cultural entertainments. For a full listing of forthcoming dance shows, music recitals, art exhibitions etc., buy a weekend copy of the *Indian Express* or Friday's *Times of India*; for a short précis of what's going on, pick up a *This Week in Delhi* handout from the tourist office. Two other small publications are available in most hotels; *Delhi Diary* and *The City Guide*. Most music and dance performances commence at 6 pm or 6.30 pm, and there's a central ticket office at the Cottage Industries Emporium, Janpath. The regular *Dances of India* programme at **Parsi Anjuman Hall**, Bahadur Shah Zafar Marg, Delhi Gate (tel 3318615) is a popular introduction to Indian culture for new tourist arrivals. Advertised as '75 minutes of Music, Dance and Song in all their exquisite finesse', it starts

at 7 pm daily and costs about Rs85. Tickets are sold at the door, but you can book from a travel agent or your hotel. Serious dance shows take place at the **Kathak Kendra**; best Bengali and Punjabi plays at **Sapru House**. For cinema, try the **Odeon** in Connaught Place for 10 am matinee films in English, or the swank **Sheila** opposite New Delhi railway station for the latest releases and maximum comfort. Delhi is film-crazy: to avoid awesome queues and 'House full' signs, always buy seats well in advance.

In the daytime, escape from Delhi's heat, dust or noise at a luxury hotel **swimming-pool**. The Ashok (Chanakyapuri) and Claridges (12 Aurangzeb Rd) allow non-residents to use their pools for around Rs75 per day, though most travellers seem to prefer the Imperial in Janpath (which is a nice pool, if crowded) at Rs95 per day. Hardly anyone goes swimming in December/February (too cold) and hotel pools are usually emptied out.

As in Calcutta, the best sports are concentrated in the clubs. There's horse-riding (Rs150 per hour) at the **Delhi Riding Club**, Safdarjang Rd (tel 3011891; book the day before); golf (US$25 weekdays, US$35 weekends) at the **Delhi Golf Club**, Dr Zakir Hussain Marg (tel 4361236 for temporary membership; clubs for hire; green fees US$35); polo, by invitation of a member, or riding at **President's Estate Polo Club**, Willingdon (tel 3015604 for temporary membership); flying at **Delhi Flying and Gliding** (and hot-air ballooning) **Clubs**, Safdarjang Airport (tel 3319679 for temporary membership); and tennis, squash and swimming at the **Chelmsford Club**, Raisina Rd (tel 3714692). Few of these clubs are as welcoming as those of Bombay or Calcutta, however, and serious sports enthusiasts should select a luxury hotel with recreational facilities geared to their special requirements.

SHOPPING
You can buy practically anything in Delhi. It has the best selection of goods from all parts of India, often sold more cheaply than at their point of origin. For instance, smart leather shoes sell here for 20–30% less than in Agra, where many of them are produced.

All the major co-operatives have stores in Delhi. The best is **Central Cottage Industries Emporium** in Janpath. This sells all types of products and craft items, at fixed prices, and is a useful place to check what's available (and how much it should cost) before hitting the bazaars and shops. It offers a fine range of fabrics, crafts and furniture, including silk for Rs80–300 per metre, leather and suede jackets for Rs1000–2000, and Kashmiri carpets from Rs6000. Having seen the range, you can walk two roads clockwise round Connaught Place to Baba Kharak Singh Marg (on radial road 2) for the local specialities of the various **State Government Emporia** (Orissa for crafts, Tamil Nadu and Bihar for silks, Rajasthan for mirror-work embroidery, Gujarat for high-quality carvings and lacquered items). Many other bazaars are worth visiting: notably the **Tibetan Bazaar** in front of the Hotel Imperial on Janpath; **Khadi Gramodyog Bhawan**, 24 Regal Building, Connaught Place (for nice hand-loomed textiles); and the **Antique Market** round Sunder Nagar Square, by the Zoo (for bronze, brass, curios and jewellery).

Also good for jewellery are the bazaars of **Chandni Chowk** in the old city. You can pick up brass, rugs, paintings and antiques here at knockdown prices. It's a good idea to take any big art buys to the National Museum to have them authenticated. It's also worth having expensive jewels verified at the Government Gem Laboratory at New Delhi House in Barakhamba Rd. Two other good markets, particularly for saris, sandals, block-printed fabrics, are **Khan Market** in New Delhi, and **South Extension**. Both have good tailors who can run up dresses, shirts, suits both quickly (usually within a few hours) and cheaply. A slightly more costly but excellent tailoring service is provided by the Maurya Sheraton Hotel, Sardar Patel Marg.

Finally, a special mention for the underground **Palika Bazaar** on Connaught Circle. This busy, air-conditioned market, open 10 am to 8 pm (except Sundays) is a great place for general shopping. **Lal Behari Tandon** (shop 20) has well-priced clothes and furnishings: men's *kurta*-pajama sets (Rs95–250), ladies' *kurta*-pajama/*salwar* sets (Rs95–500), embroidered tablecloths (Rs250–700) and table-mat sets. Several other shops, like **Godfather** (shop 206), have regular 'fashion' clothes sales. In all markets there are shops selling music cassettes which in India are remarkably cheap (Rs40-60 and most of them are legal.

Hauz Khas Village (see p.105) is one of the newer shopping areas with a good range of craft shops, fashion clothes and leather goods. There are also two interesting art galleries with regular shows.

Serious shoppers should look in the advertising columns of daily newspapers for details of forthcoming sales and exhibitions, at which many items are often heavily discounted.

Most shops in Delhi are open from around 9 am to 7 pm Monday to Saturday, closed on Sunday. Some areas such as South Extension and Greater Kailash are open on Sunday but closed Mondays.

WHERE TO STAY
Accommodation in Delhi is very good, if expensive. As in Bombay, budget travellers stay here just long enough to acclimatise to the country or recover from it, before moving out to cheaper regions. The busy time for Delhi hotels is October to March; during these months, if you want a decent room it's *essential* to advance-book. During the low season (May to September), many larger hotels offer 10-25% discounts, though you'll still find the usual 20% expenditure tax on rooms costing more than Rs1200/US$50 per night, and a 5–10% service charge on all hotel bills. A good many high-class hotels are located away from the city centre, in and around the select Diplomatic Enclave. They are, however, not particularly convenient for sightseeing or shopping.

Prices
In the gateway cities, tariffs are naturally higher. That said, it is possible to live in a great deal of style in the moderate price range; budget hotels are more difficult to find—harder still to recommend. We have listed those cheap lodgings which have managed to retain their reputation; others will come and go. If you are on a budget, keep your ear to the travellers' grapevine.

Prices listed below do not include tax.

Expensive–Luxury (US$100–250 per room night)
The Taj Mahal Hotel, 1 Mansingh Rd (tel 3016162, tlx 31-61898, fax 011-3017299) combines quality, comfort and service. It is remarkably restrained and 'personal' for a five-star hotel, and is geared very much to the general traveller. There's a good choice of restaurants, a nice pool exclusively for guests, and cosy (if smallish) rooms

101

at US$160 single, US$175 double. India's first modern luxury hotel, **The Oberoi**, Dr Zakir Hussain Marg (tel 4363030, tlx 31-63222, fax 011-4360484), is still the smartest place in town, with the swishest pool, and the most livable rooms. There's a wide range of facilities, including an executive centre for business visitors. You have a choice of views, of the golf course where peacocks strut on the putting greens, and of Humayun's Tomb.

Two deluxe hotels next to each other on Sardar Patel Marg are the **Taj Palace Inter-Continental** (tel 3010404, tlx 31-61673, fax 011-3011252) and the **Welcomgroup Maurya Sheraton** (tel 3010101, tlx 31-61447, fax 011-3010908). The Taj Palace is a popular conference venue, with excellent rooms from US$140, good restaurants and what is probably the best hotel shop in India; **The Khazana**. The Maurya Sheraton is well known for its two Indian restaurants, its discotheque and the new **Jazz Bar**. Rooms are from US$135. Also in south Delhi is the **Hyatt Regency** (tel 6881234, tlx 031-61512, fax 011 78833) with rooms from US$140.

Nearer to the centre of town, on Janpath, at Windsor Place is **Hotel Le Meridien** (tel 3710101, fax 011-3714545) with views over Lutyens's city. Rooms range from US$140. At the southern tip of Janpath is **Claridges Hotel**, 12 Aurangzeb Road (tel 3010211, fax 011-3010625) with a friendly atmosphere and large rooms. Rooms at US$70 upwards are excellent value for this price category.

Even closer to the centre, the **Holiday Inn Crowne Plaza**, Barakhamba Avenue (near Connaught Place) (tel 3320101, fax 011-3325335) is a smart new property with a wide range of restaurants and facilities. Rooms from US$140.

Mid-range (US$25–100 per room night)
In the city centre itself, there are a variety of mid-range hotels. **Hotel Kanishka**, 19 Ashok Rd (tel 3324422, tlx 31-62788), has 3 restaurants, 24-hour coffee shop, many facilities, and comfy rooms at Rs1350 single, Rs1500 double. **Hotel Imperial** in Janpath (tel 3325332, tlx 31-62603 HIMP IN, fax 011-3324542) is famous for its colonial flavour and for its popular pool. A great many Westerners stay here. Friendly staff, good food, a nice shopping arcade, and charming rooms with floral wallpaper, Victorian furniture and TVs, make this a real favourite. Tariffs are US$54 single, US$60 double.

Other centrally located mid-range hotels with rooms from Rs800–1200 with a good reputation include **Hans Plaza**, 19 Barakhamba Rd (tel 3216861, fax 011-3314830); **Connaught Palace**, Shaheed Bhagat Singh Marg (tel 344225, fax 011-310757); and **The Ambassador**, Sujan Singh Park (tel 690391) which has a good vegetarian restaurant.

In Old Delhi, the **Oberoi Maidens**, 7 Sham Nath Marg (tel 2525464, tlx 31-66303) is a jewel of colonial architecture set amidst 8 acres of emerald-green lawns, and the only viable hotel in this area. It offers spacious old-style rooms for Rs1350 single, Rs1550 double and a quaint 'peppermint pool', tennis courts, and a restaurant with a good reputation for Western food.

Budget (under US$25/Rs750 per room night)
Nirula Hotel, L Block, Connaught Circus (tel 3322419) is central and relatively cheap. The famous restaurant is just upstairs, the hotel is centrally air-conditioned, with pleasant rooms at US$24 single, US$36 double. It is noisy, though. Travellers speak well of the **Asian International**, Janpath Lane (tel 3321636), which offers smart

singles/doubles at Rs380/580). Good mentions too for the **Ashok Yatri Niwas**, 19 Ashok Rd (tel 3324511), which has a nice air-conditioned bar, passable canteen, popular restaurant specialising in south Indian food, and good- value single/double rooms at US$11–US$15. A friendly place, modest and quiet, is **Roshan Villa Guest House** (tel 3311770, 3317240), 7 Babar Lane, 1 km south-east of Connaught Place. Food is good here, and staff take care of all your travel arrangements. If you're new to the country, the best inexpensive place to use as your base while you adapt is the **YMCA Tourist Hostel**, Jai Singh Rd (tel 311915). Comfortable and clean, it has useful facilities including money exchange, travel agency, restaurant, swimming-pool, tennis courts, baggage room, and well-priced rooms at Rs235 single, Rs400 double (with air-conditioning, Rs420–700). It is wise to advance-book this one, or be at the desk at 12 noon sharp to reserve vacated rooms.

Cheaper rooms, in the high season, can be hard to find. As in Bombay, you often have to be at the better budget lodges *very* early in the morning to snap up any rooms going. The main cheap hotel area is around Connaught Place—**Ringo's, Gandhi's** and **Hotel Palace Heights**—all with rooms from less than Rs50 a night. In Paharganj, popular cheapies include hotels **Vivek, Vishal** and **Navrang**. You can get a Rs25 shared-dorm bed at several places near Old Delhi Railway Station.

In many residential colonies of south and west Delhi private homes have been converted into small hotels and guest-houses with rates of about Rs450 and upwards. As many are located in residential areas they are usually quiet and mostly used by businessmen from out of town. Almost all have a limited form of room service and most rooms are air-conditioned and have cable TV. The main tourist office in Janpath has an up-to-date list of guest-houses but a few worth noting are **Shervani Fort View**, 11 Sunder Nagar (tel 611771); **Jukaso Inn**, 50 Sunder Nagar (tel 690309), and **Panchsheel Inn**, C-4 Panchsheel Enclave (tel 6433874).

EATING OUT
Delhi is a fiesta of good food. Many restaurants specialise in Mughlai and Tandoori dishes, but others offer a wide variety of cuisine: Continental, Chinese, so-called North-west Frontier and even Polynesian.

Unfortunately, in the mid- to upper-price ranges few Delhi restaurants that are not attached to hotels have a repuation for fine food. And expenditure tax is levied on restaurant bills in major hotels. However, as is the case almost everywhere else in India, you can eat very well in the budget categories.

Prices listed below are per head, exclusive of alcohol and tax.

Indian Food
Maurya Sheraton's **Bukhara** (tel 3010101) and Oberoi Hotel's **The Kandahar** (tel 4363030) specialise in the currently very popular North-west Frontier food, which is largely meat dishes often prepared and marinated with yogurt, and cooked in a large clay oven or *tandoor*. The Bukhara certainly wins on atmosphere and only takes bookings upto 8.30 pm; thereafter a wait of up to 30 minutes for a table is a reflection of this restaurant's popularity and high standards. The most original Indian restaurant is the Maurya Sheraton's **Dum Pukht** (tel 3010101) with superb service, and an intriguing menu of delicate, unusual dishes. For these three restaurants, expect to pay Rs300 per person.

Two popular south Indian restaurants are the **Coconut Grove** at the Ashok Yatri Niwas Hotel, Ashok Road and **Dasaprakash** at the Ambassador Hotel, Sujan Singh Park. While the Dasaprakash is part of the chain of the same name specialising in vegetarian food, the Coconut Grove has a mixed menu of Malabar (Kerala) vegetarian and non-vegetarian cuisine. Meals in both restaurants cost from Rs100 per person and expenditure tax does not apply in either.

Gaylord's restaurant, next to the Regal cinema (between Radial Rds 1 and 2, outer circle of Connaught Circus) is the Indian equivalent of Continental Nirula's with stylish decor and exceptional service. Just round the corner, in Parliament St, there's the cheaper **Kwality** restaurant, serving popular Indian, Chinese and Continental food.

Continental

La Rochelle at the Oberoi, **The Orient Express** at The Taj Palace, **Valentino's** at the Hyatt, **Captain's Cabin** at the Taj Mahal and the **Grill Room** at the Holiday Inn are considered the best. Dinner at any of these will cost from Rs400.

The Taj Hotel's roof-top restaurant, **Casa Medici**, is famous for Italian food—especially its flamed pasta dishes. Come here for the good-value buffet lunch (Rs225, 1 to 3 pm daily), and enjoy superb high-rise views of Lutyens's imperial city. In the evening, there's a good live band (you will either love Indian-style pop music or hate it) and a small dance floor. Dinner from Rs300.

There is an excellent Rs110 buffet lunch at the Imperial Hotel's **Garden Party** restaurant. This is where most Westerners come to eat all they can before getting on the train out of Delhi. Cuisine here is a blend of continental, Indian and Tandoori.

Delhi is renowned as the capital of American-style fast-food parlours. Around a dozen of these have sprung up in the vicinity of Connaught Circus alone. First and foremost amongst these is **Nirula's** on L Block, at the top of Radial Rd 6. This is the original all-in-one food palace—with an excellent Chinese Room, a Hot Shoppe, Pastry Shop, Dayville's Ice Cream Parlour, and an upstairs **Potpourri** restaurant with popular salad bar, local wine by the glass, pizzas, shakes, burgers and chocolate cake, which is the backpacker's favourite haunt. At the bottom of Radial Rd 8, you'll find **Wimpy** and (another) **Nirula's**, while over on Radial Rd 3 there's **Wengers** with superlative pastries and cakes but no seats. Next to Wengers is **Keventers** for popular flavoured milk-shakes and ice-cream shakes. Nirulas have branches in many of New Delhi's residential areas and Wimpy plan to open more branches in 1993.

Other

Chinese cuisine is popular and many residential areas have restaurants. However, the better and gastronomically correct, menus are those found in some hotels. The two Taj hotels (see above) have *Szechwan* restaurants. **The Tea House of the August Moon** at the Taj Palace and the **House of Ming** at the Taj Mahal have remained popular with both visitors and locals since they opened. At the Oberoi the **Tai Pan** restaurant also specialises in *Szechwan* cuisine. Situated on the roof it has magnificent views over the golf course and Lutyens's Delhi. A meal at each of these restaurants would also cost from Rs250 per person. **The Silk Orchid** at the Holiday Inn is Delhi's only Thai restaurant. From Rs250 per person.

All major hotels have 24-hour coffee shops. **The Machan** at the Taj Mahal and the **Pavilion** at the Maurya Sheraton are popular. The Hyatt coffee shop has an excellent buffet lunch for Rs150 and holds regular food festivals.

The **Bistro** and its neighbouring restaurants in the centre of Hauz Khas Village (see p.101) have good European, Indian and Chinese menus with meals from Rs100, and are popular with a young, creative local crowd. It's the nearest Delhi gets to café society, and the Bistro has a Singles' Night on Tuesdays (which men have to go to with a partner).

GENERAL INFORMATION

Delhi is *the* place to gather information—wherever you're heading for next, gather all relevant maps, brochures and transport details here. Also use Delhi to do as much advance travel-planning as possible, especially air and rail bookings.

Tourist Offices

Government of India Tourist Office, 88 Janpath (tel 320005) open 9 am to 6 pm except Sundays, supplies good information on all parts of India, also (at last) an up-to-date map of Delhi. This is the place to book your city tours for New Delhi (morning) and Old Delhi (afternoon), operated by both ITDC (Rs35 per tour) and DTDC (Rs20). There are also tourist information desks (ITDC) at the domestic (tel 3291171) and international (tel 3291351) airports.

Maps: The Survey of India, headquartered in Dehra Dun, has a branch office in the old Janpath Barracks next to the Cottage Industries Emporium. City maps and plans, trekking maps and survey sheets of much of India are available here. Maps of border areas are not available.

Delhi Tourism Development Corporation (DTDC), N-36 Bombay Life Building, Connaught Place (Middle Circle) (tel 3315322), open 7 am to 9 pm daily, is mainly useful for sightseeing tours. In particular, city tours (mentioned above; cheaper than ITDC, but no guide aboard) and the excellent 'Delhi by Evening' tour (5.15 to 9 pm, every Monday, Wednesday, Friday and Sunday). This is Rs50 well-spent: you see the Diplomatic Enclave prettily illuminated by night, then the *son et lumière* at Red Fort; sometimes, there's even a free meal thrown in! DTDC has a 24-hour desk at the international airport (tel 391213) only. American Express Travel Service (tel 3325963, 3324119) operates daily tours, both half- and full-day, starting at the Holiday Inn at 9 am and finishing at 6 pm.

State Tourist Offices, useful for collecting specialised information on places you're going to visit, are collected at three separate locations: Chanderlok Building, 36 Janpath (Haryana, Himachal Pradesh, Rajasthan, and Uttar Pradesh); Kanishka Shopping Plaza, 19 Ashok Rd (Bihar, Jammu & Kashmir, Kerala, Madhya Pradesh and Punjab); and State Emporia Building, Baba Kharak Singh Marg (Gujarat, Karnataka, Maharashtra, Orissa, and Tamil Nadu).

Airline Offices

Domestic: Indian Airlines, Safdarjung Airport (this is an old airfield near the Safdarjung Tomb and not the operational airport at Palam) for 24-hour bookings and reconfirmations (tel 4620566, 690366), Kanchenjunga Building, 18 Barakhamba Rd (tel 3313732), pre-recorded arrival information tel 142, departure information tel 143; East West Airlines, DCM Building, Barakhamba Road (tel 3755167), Jagson Airlines, 12E Vandana Building, Tolstoy Marg (tel 3711069); Vayudoot, Malhotra Building, Janpath (tel 3312779, apt 3295126, 5481216), Safdarjung Airport (tel 4623056, 4622122).

International: Air France, Atmaram Mansion, Scindia House, Connaught Circus (tel 3310407, 3317054, apt 5452099); Air India, Jeevan Bharti Building, 124 Connaught

Circus (tel 3311225, apt 5452050); Alitalia, Surya Kiran, 19 K.G. Marg (tel 3311019, apt 5483174); British Airways, DLF Centre, Parliament Street (tel 3327428, 3327630 apt 5452078); Cathay Pacific, 123 Tolstoy House, Tolstoy Marg (tel 3325789); Delta (tel 3325222, 3321571) and Japan Airlines (tel 3322409, 3327608) both at Chanderlok Building, 36 Janpath; Emirates, Kanchenjunga, Barakhamba Road (tel 3324803, apt 5482861); Gulf Air, Indraprakash, Barakhamba Road (tel 3323352, apt 3294486); KLM, Prakash Deep, 7 Tolstoy Marg (tel 3311747, apt 5482894); Lufthansa, 56 Janpath (tel 3323310, apt 5452064); Royal Nepal Airlines, 44 Janpath (tel 3320517); Singapore Airlines, G-11 Connaught Circus (tel 3321292, apt 5452011); Swiss Air, DLF Centre, Parliament Street (tel 3325511) and Thai, Ambadeep, K.G.Marg (tel 3323608, apt 5482672).

Travel Agents
For big travel deals use **Sita World Travel**, F-12 Connaught Place (tel 3311133); **Thomas Cook**, Hotel Imperial, Janpath (tel 33322468); **Cox & Kings**, Indra Place, Connaught Circus (tel 3320067) or **American Express**, Wenger House, A Block, Connaught Place (tel 343946).

Consulates
Most High Commissions and Embassies are in Chanakyapuri (Diplomatic Enclave) unless stated otherwise, and include UK (tel 601371), USA (tel 600651), Australia (tel 601336), Canada (tel 6876500), France (tel 604004), and Germany (tel 604861), Nepal, Barakhamba Road (tel 3328191), New Zealand (tel 6883170), Pakistan (tel 600601). Others in telephone directory.

Miscellaneous
Foreigners' Registration Office is 1st floor, Hans Bhavan, Tilak Bridge (tel 3319489). For quick, painless visa extensions, turn up at 9.30 am, armed with your passport and four photos. There's a useful photo booth on the ground floor.

Main **GPO** is at Sansad Marg (tel 344111). Open 10 am to 8 pm weekdays, from 10 am to 5 pm Sundays and holidays. Most travellers use the Post Office at A Block, Connaught Place (tel 344214). It's more convenient and has facilities outside for wrapping parcels in cloth as required by the post office.

Poste Restante (curiously, in neither of the above) is at Bhai Vir Singh Marg, about 1 km (½ mile) from Connaught Place behind Irwin Road. Opening hours are 9 am to 5 pm Monday to Friday, 9 am to 1 pm Saturday, closed all day Sunday. Tell your friends/family to write to you at *New* Delhi. Mountains of letters marked simply 'Delhi' are sitting unclaimed in the old Delhi post office near Kashmiri Gate.

Bookshops you'll find scattered all around Connaught Place and in Khan Market, excellent for stocking up on big novels to pass away long, boring bus/train journeys. Two good ones are Oxford Book Shop in N Block, and New Book Depot at 18B Block, Connaught Place; in Khan Market The Bookshop and Bahri Sons are two of the best in Delhi. Down in Palika Bazaar, there's Book World (Shop 7). Look out for ITDC's *1982 Guide to Delhi*, Louise Nicholson's Odyssey Guide to *Delhi, Agra & Jaipur* and Gaynor Barton and Laurraine Malone's *Old Delhi—10 Easy Walks*.

Two city magazines—*Genesis City Guide* (monthly, Rs7) and *Delhi Diary* (weekly, Rs5)—are sold at many street bookstalls. Packed with useful up-to-date information on hotels, restaurants, sights, transport, and entertainment, they are essential reference reading.

Two good libraries, nice places to spend a civilised afternoon reading newspapers and catching up on home news, are the **American Library**, 24 Kasturba Gandhi Marg and the **British Council Library**, Kasturba Gandhi Marg (tel 3711401).

Parcel-Packing Service, T298 General Market, Main Bazaar, Paharganj (tel 777008, 778298) is very useful for sending home loads of presents, souvenirs, camera film and useless stuff that you thought you'd need in India but don't. Much better than lugging it all over the country. Send everything by airmail—it may be three times more expensive than seamail, but it's three times quicker. And your goods will arrive home in one piece!

Route 1—Forts, Palaces, Temples and the Taj

Situated close to historic Delhi, cradle of numerous civilisations and cultures, the corner-stones of this trip—Agra, Khajuraho and Varanasi—witnessed astonishing bursts of creative energy from various dynasties. For this reason, they represent many of the images India has projected over the centuries. The finest quintessence of medieval and Mughal art and architecture in the northern states, they are major tourist attractions. Consequently, the pace of life is generally hectic and crowded, but in Agra and Khajuraho transport and hotels are a marked improvement on those in many other parts of the country. The sights themselves are consistently good, and rarely disappoint. Within the same region are other less well-known towns worth the effort of taking a small detour to visit.

Agra is the Mughal city of the Taj Mahal, one of the wonders of the world, and the most extravagant monument to love ever built. Also at Agra, magnificent palaces and mausoleums, gardens and handicrafts, an imposing fort and (at nearby Fatehpur Sikri) a ghost city of poignant grandeur. At least two days for each city is recommended as a minimum stay.

South of Agra is the Maratha city of Gwalior, dominated by one of the finest forts in India. A further 120 km (75 miles) south from Gwalior, and a slight detour from the road to Khajuraho, is the charming and little changed 16th-century town of Orchha on the banks of the Betwa river.

South-east of Agra, below the great central plateau of Madhya Pradesh, are the graceful temples of Khajuraho, creation of the eclectic Chandella kings. Once seen, never forgotten. To the north-east of Khajuraho, and back in Uttar Pradesh, is the holiest of India's sacred cities, Varanasi or Benares. The cities are well connected to each other by air and there is a daily flight in both directions (IC407/408) that links Delhi–Agra–Khajuraho–Varanasi–Kathmandu.

Season: October to March.
Climate: 11°–48°C (summer); 2°–32°C (winter).
Monsoons: Mid-June to September.
Route duration: 5 to 8 days.

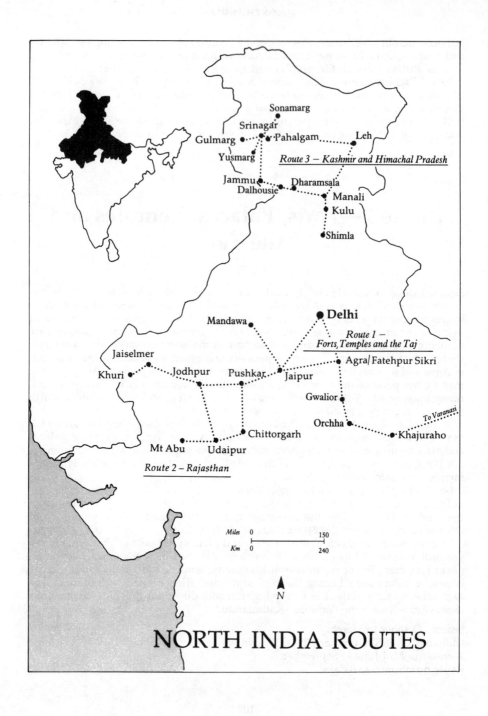

Route 3 – Kashmir and Himachal Pradesh

Sonamarg
Srinagar
Gulmarg • Pahalgam • Leh
Yusmarg
Jammu • Dharamsala
Dalhousie • Manali
Kulu
Shimla

Delhi

Route 1 –
Forts, Temples and the Taj

Mandawa
Agra/Fatehpur Sikri

Jaiselmer
Khuri • Jodhpur Pushkar Jaipur
Gwalior
Orchha To Varanasi
Khajuraho
Mt Abu Udaipur Chittorgarh

Route 2 – Rajasthan

Miles 0   150
Km 0   240

N

NORTH INDIA ROUTES

TRAVEL ITINERARY

Delhi to Agra 204 km (127 miles)

Air
One flight daily—IC407 at Rs525 throughout the year and between October and March there is usually a second flight. From Agra airport to town centre (8 km; 5 miles) it costs Rs10 by airport bus (which is not always available), Rs30 by cycle-rickshaw, Rs40 by auto-rickshaw, Rs80/90 by taxi. Bargain hard for these rates.

Rail
Agra is on the main line between Delhi and southern India. Numerous trains stop throughout the day and night but there are two excellent express trains connecting the two great Mughal capitals. Both these are considerably more reliable than the flights and a lot less traumatic than the drive.

The fast *Shatabdi Express* and *Taj Express* can work out even quicker than the plane. Both leave New Delhi Station early in the morning and return at about 10 pm. Tickets are purchased in advance from the Tourist Counters at the respective stations, or from an agent. He is always advisable to both the return leg in advice too. Jhansi is the best rail connection for Khajuraho.

Shatabdi Express Timings

NEW DELHI		AGRA CANTT		GWALIOR		JHANSI		BHOPAL
0615	→	0810	→	0930	→	1040	→	1400
2220	←	2013	←	1855	←	1750	←	1440

Taj Express Timings

0700	→	0950	→	1150
2220	←	1835	←	1700

Shatabdi Express Train Tariffs (Rs: Executive class/1st class)

DELHI	-	200/400	255/510	300/600	420/840
AGRA	200/400	-	115/230	165/330	325/650
GWALIOR	255/510	115/230	-	110/220	275/550
JHANSI	330/600	165/330	110/220	-	240/480
BHOPAL	420/840	325/650	275/550	240/480	-
	DELHI	AGRA	GWALIOR	JHANSI	BHOPAL

Road
Various deluxe bus services now operate from Delhi to Agra. The Travel House Express (US$33) leaves the Maurya Sheraton Hotel at 7 am every day and provides a packed breakfast *en route*, stopping at Sikandra and the Taj before lunch at the Mughal Sheraton. In the afternoon the tour goes to the Agra Fort before departing for Delhi at 5.30 pm. Book through **Travel House** in New Delhi (tel 3010101 extn 2929).

Hourly buses from Delhi's Interstate bus-stand (5 hours, Rs45). If returning to Delhi, hourly buses from Agra's Idgah bus-stand (no need for advance-reservation—

buy tickets half an hour before departure). Deluxe buses ply in both directions (4 hours, Rs50). There are also regular buses to Jaipur, Bharatpur, Gwalior and Jhansi.

Agra to Gwalior 118 km (74 miles)

Air
Gwalior is not connected by air to Agra but has daily flights (IC433/434) linking it with Delhi (Rs738), Bhopal (Rs773), Indore (Rs1083) and Bombay (Rs1940).

Rail
The *Shatabdi Express* leaves Agra Cantt at 8.10 am reaching Gwalior at 9.30 am and the *Taj Express* leaves Agra at 9.50 am reaching Gwalior at 11.50 am. The return journeys to Agra and New Delhi leave at 7 pm and 5 pm respectively Tariffs, p. 109.

Road
There are regular buses from the Idgah bus-station in Agra and services to and from Delhi, Jhansi and Bhopal.

Agra to Khajuraho 395 km (247 miles)

Air
The one flight daily—IC407 (Rs767) originating in Delhi is routed via Agra. In the winter there is a second direct flight from Delhi which continues to Varanasi before returning to Delhi. From Khajuraho airport to town (5 km) is Rs50 by taxi. There is no airport bus.

Rail/Road
The *Shatabdi Express* (see p.109) is the best train to Jhansi, leaving New Delhi at 6.15 am and Agra at 8.10 am, reaches Jhansi at 10.40 am. A bus to Khajuraho takes between 5 and 6 hours although a new deluxe service operates in the winter and takes 4 hours. Private taxis meet the *Shatabdi* at the station and after a little haggling cost about Rs1200 and take slightly over 3 hours. From Khajuraho, there are five buses daily (Rs40) to Jhansi, for the rail connection to Delhi. The evening *Shatabdi* leaves Jhansi at 5.50 pm and there are numerous other trains heading north to Agra and Delhi.

Road
One direct bus daily, departs 5 am, arrives 3 pm (Rs55). Quick, popular. From Khajuraho, there are daily buses back to Agra and Delhi.

Khajuraho to Varanasi 408 km (255 miles)

Air
IC407/408 connects Varanasi with Delhi (Rs1394), Agra (Rs1106) and Khajuraho (Rs767).

Rail
There is no direct rail connection between Khajuraho and Varanasi. There are regular connections with Delhi, Lucknow and Calcutta. There are regular trains from Satna which is 117 km (74 miles) east of Khajuraho.

Road
There are no deluxe buses for the 10- to 12-hour bus journey via Satna, Rewa and Allahabad or Mirzapur. By country bus, it's a long and uncomfortable haul.

CONTINUATIONS
From Agra, you can take a train, bus or flight (not operating at the time of writing) to Jaipur 237 km (148 miles) to the west. Another side trip from Agra is a visit to one of the world's most important wetland bird sanctuaries on the outskirts of Bharatpur 50 km (32 miles) to the west.

AGRA

Little is known about the city's early history but a small settlement was possibly first established some 5000 years ago. Agra's strategic situation on the right bank of the Yamuna made it an ancient frontier defence of the Aryans. At one time it may have been known as *Agrabana* ('Paradise' in Sanskrit), a possible corruption of the name of its founder, Maharajah Ugersen. But the city achieved fame and wealth as the capital of the Mughals. Today, it is famous as the home of the Taj Mahal, the most popular tourist attraction in India.

Agra rose to sudden prominence in the early 16th century, when the Mughals seized it from the Hindu Lodhi dynasty. In 1566 the modern city of Agra was

Red Fort, Agra

established by the Emperor Akbar, and was made capital of the Mughal empire. Fabulously wealthy, it soon rose to great importance. The commentator Abul Fazal reported:

> A great city having esteemed healthy air. Pleasant houses and gardens inhabited by people of all nations and exhibited with the production of every climate are built on both banks of the river (Yamuna). A castle of red sandstone, like of which no traveller has ever seen, has been created by the Emperor. The fort alone contains five hundred wonderful stone buildings in the Bengal, Gujarat and other styles. Formerly Agra was only a village depending upon Bayana, where Sikander Lodi [founder of Sikandra, 8 km (5 miles) out of present Agra] held his courts. At the same spot His Majesty has laid the foundations of a most magnificent city.

Under Akbar's son, the talented drunkard Jahangir, Agra became a major industrial and commercial city. But it was Shah Jahan, Jahangir's successor, who left Agra her most enduring monument—the Taj Mahal. This most beautiful (and most costly) monument to love remains today the finest wonder of the modern world. Having created it, Shah Jahan moved his capital from Agra to Delhi, and the city, and the fortunes of the Mughals in general, fell into slow decline. In 1803 (after a long period of being ransacked and pillaged by local Maratha and Jat forces) it came under British rule and, until 1877, became the capital of North-western Province (now Uttar Pradesh). It never, however, regained its former glory. Agra remained trapped in time, a bitter-sweet reminder of the peak of Mughal power and glory.

Today Agra is a city of over a million people, a busy centre of education and commerce. Its main industry, by virtue of its many well-preserved Mughal monuments, is tourism. The area around, but luckily not within, the three principal sights—the Taj, the Fort, and the ghost town of Fatehpur Sikri—are flooded with touts, beggars and touristy emporia. By contrast, the old British cantonment with its wide, spacious streets, its peaceful parks and gardens and its several lesser palaces and monuments, is surprisingly relaxing.

WHEN TO GO

Most people visit Agra during the cooler winter months of October to March. Possibly the best month is October, when the town is wreathed in crimson bougainvillaea and yellow mustard, there is no dust, and the Taj, washed by the rains, gleams like a new pin.

ARRIVAL/DEPARTURE

Air
Indian Airlines flies daily from Agra to Delhi (Rs525), Khajuraho (Rs767), and Varanasi (Rs1106).

Rail
There are daily trains from Agra Cantonment station to Delhi, Jaipur, Varanasi, and Jhansi (for Khajuraho).

Road
Buses to Delhi, Jaipur and Khajuraho leave from Agra's Idgah bus-stand. Cars can be hired from hotel travel desks or one of the larger travel agents in the town.

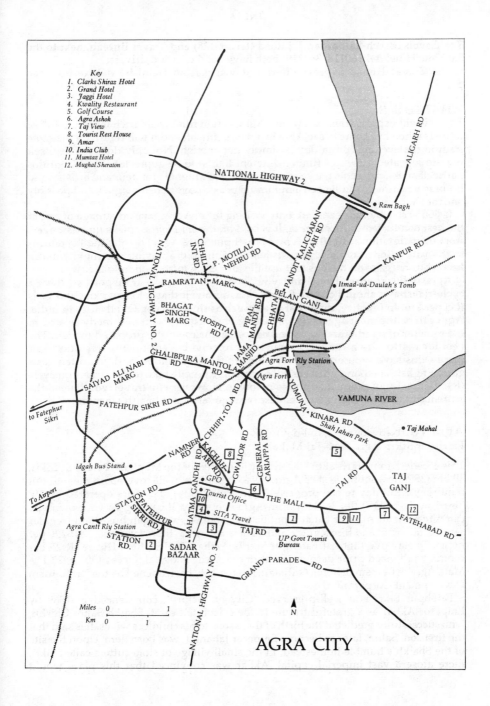

Key
1. Clarks Shiraz Hotel
2. Grand Hotel
3. Jaggi Hotel
4. Kwality Restaurant
5. Golf Course
6. Agra Ashok
7. Taj View
8. Tourist Rest House
9. Amar
10. India Club
11. Mumtaz Hotel
12. Mughal Sheraton

NATIONAL HIGHWAY 2

ALIGARH RD

• Ram Bagh

NATIONAL HIGHWAY NO. 2

KANPUR RD

CHHILI INT RD

P. MOTILAL NEHRU RD

PANDIT KALICHARAN TIWARI RD

RAMRATAN MARG

BELAN GANJ

• Itmad-ud-Daulah's Tomb

BHAGAT SINGH MARG

HOSPITAL RD

PIPAL MANDI RD

CHHATTA RD

SAIYAD ALI NABI MARG

GHALIBPURA RD

MANTOLA RD

JAMA MASJID

Agra Fort Rly Station

to Fatehpur Sikri

FATEHPUR SIKRI RD

TOLA RD

Agra Fort

YUMUNA

YAMUNA RIVER

KINARA RD

Shah Jahan Park

• Taj Mahal

Idgah Bus Stand •

NAMNER RD

KACHAHRI RD

GWALIOR RD

CHHIPI TOLA RD

GENERAL CARIAPPA RD

8

5

TAJ RD

TAJ GANJ

To Airport

STATION RD

FATEHPUR SIKRI RD

GPO

6

THE MALL

MAHATMA GANDHI RD

Tourist Office

10

4

SITA Travel

1

9 11

7

12

FATEHABAD RD

Agra Cantt Rly Station

STATION RD.

3

TAJ RD

UP Govt Tourist Bureau

2

SADAR BAZAAR

NATIONAL HIGHWAY NO. 3

GRAND PARADE RD

Miles 0   1

Km 0   1

N

AGRA CITY

Taj Travels, Beech-ka-Bazaar, Taj Road (tel 360128) and **Travel Bureau,** next to the Taj View Hotel (tel 360118, 360719) both have good cars and drivers.

The **Travel House Express** offers a day trip from Delhi by deluxe bus (see p.109).

WHAT TO SEE

The efficient express trains draw into Agra station from Delhi each morning, full of tourists who have come to see Agra in a day, many of whom will return on the same train in the evening. But a day is simply not enough. Not only does the Taj itself require repeated viewings (under different lights) to be appreciated fully, but this particular city represents the very quintessence of Mughal grandeur and artistry, and is not to be rushed. You'll need a minimum of two days here for sights, and possibly one for shopping.

If you arrive by train, and are only visiting for one day, take advantage of one of the best conducted tours in India. It is sold on the *Taj Express*, picks up passengers from the rail station at 10.10 am, covers Fatehpur Sikri, Agra Fort and the Taj, returns to the rail station at 6 pm, and costs just Rs45. If you're staying overnight you can keep your luggage on the bus and use the tour as an introduction to the city.

Agra is fairly spread out, and you'll need to use local transport. In theory, cycle-rickshaws should charge Rs1 per km, auto-rickshaws Rs3 per km, and taxis Rs5 per km. In practice, they charge as much as they can get. Of all cities in India, Agra can be the most aggressive. The cost of transport is often directly related to the number of handicraft shops and carpet factories you're prepared to visit. The best idea is to hire a car from your hotel or travel agent for the day at a fixed price—this saves you endless diversions to tiresome shops, and you often get a good English-speaking guide as a driver. Some people take to the streets on cycle (Rs10–15 per day, many hire places in town). However you travel, you'll need the patience of a saint—Agra's touts deserve a government health warning.

Agra Tour (by tour bus, full-day)
Fatehpur Sikri–Agra Fort–Taj Mahal

This excellent tour starts at the legendary ghost city of the Mughals, **Fatehpur Sikri,** 40 km (25 miles) south-west of Agra. It's a huge place, well-covered on the tour but requiring a full day to see properly. There are also regular tours operated by **UP Tourism** (UPSTDC) (tel 360140) from Agra every day. If coming on your own you can hire a car in Agra or catch a public bus from Agra's Idgah bus-stand (regular service, fare Rs5) and hire a guide at the entrance (get a 'first-class' one, Rs15/20 per hour). To stay overnight at Fatehpur Sikri's **Archaeological Rest House** (Rs25 per room), you'll need prior permission from the Archaeological Survey Office, 22 The Mall, Agra. A new small hotel, **Gulistan,** has recently been opened by the UP Tourism Development Corporation.

Fatehpur Sikri is a well-preserved 'City of Victory', commenced in 1569 by Emperor Akbar as a grateful tribute to the celebrated saint, Shaikh Salim Chishti, who successfully predicted the birth of three sons to his childless wives. It is said that the first son, Salim, later to become Emperor Jahangir, was born here. Upon the site of the Shaikh's humble homestead, in the small village of stonecutters called Sikri, there arose a vast imperial capital. Akbar was convinced that this place would

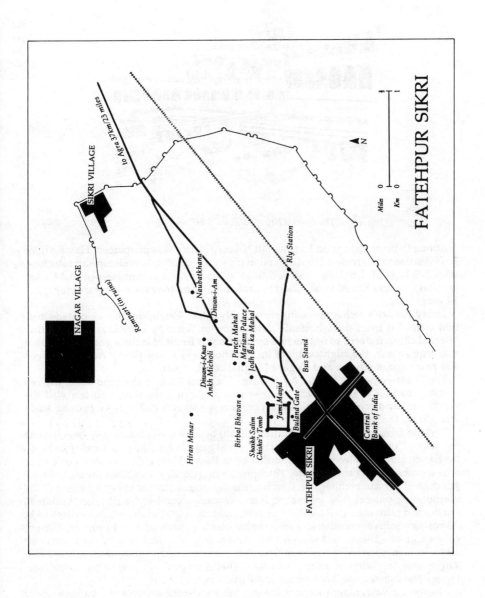

FATEHPUR SIKRI

N

Miles 0
Km 0

SIKRI VILLAGE

to Agra 37 km / 23 miles

NAGAR VILLAGE

Rampart (in ruins)

Hiran Minar

Diwan-i-Khas
Ankh Micholi

Naubatkhana
Diwan-i-Am

Panch Mahal
Mariam Palace
Jodh Bai ka Mahal

Birbal Bhavan
Shaikh Salim
Chishti's Tomb

Jami Masjid
Buland Gate

Bus Stand

Rly Station

Central
Bank of India

FATEHPUR SIKRI

The deserted city of Fatehpur Sikri, near Agra

continue to bring him good fortune but his confidence was misplaced. Having used 10 000 artisans to create a Hindu-Persian masterpiece of red-sandstone architecture, with 500 beautiful palaces and buildings spread over a circumference of 14.4 km (9 miles), he was forced to abandon it, probably owing to severe water shortage, just 14 years later.

Today, his achievement remains remarkably intact. Fatehpur Sikri's isolated situation spared it from the wholesale destruction inflicted by later invaders on other Mughal cities. Indeed, so untouched by time is this finest of India's ghost towns, that you require only the slightest bit of imagination to visualise how it must have been 400 years ago, a refined and elegant Mughal court capital.

You'll enter the fort by the **Agra Gate**. There's a fork in the road here, the left turning leading to the modern town where (if staying the day) you can visit the workshops and see the traditional art of Sikri stonecutting. The right turning leads straight up to the royal palaces.

Past the **Diwan-i-Am** (Public Audience Hall) beyond the entrance gate, you'll come to **Pachesi Courtyard**, where Akbar played sexist games of *pachesi* (similar to chess) with his harem ladies as pieces. A little further on is **Panch Mahal**, the five-storeyed edifice which probably best encapsulates Fatehpur Sikri. Its design combines the best of both Hindu and Persian architecture. Climb to the top of this elegant tower for views of the surrounding palaces. The interesting blend of architectural styles (Persian, Buddhist, Hindu and Jain) seen in Panch Mahal runs right through the city—it is a reflection of Akbar's definitively ecumenical philosophy. Having met with Hindu priests, Muslim elders, Catholic fathers and various gurus and monks of other faiths, he concluded that all paths in religion led to the same God. A brave attempt to synthesise all beliefs into a single, unifying religion, called 'Din Ilahi' (Religion of God), was sadly short-lived, though the architecture that typified it still lives on.

Through a vast, magnificent maze of pink-sandstone courtyards, palaces, royal chambers, meeting-halls, balconies, colonnades, baths and minarets, one comes at

116

last to the huge quadrangle south of the fort. This is the city's largest and grandest structure—the **Jami Masjid**, constructed in 1575 to hold 10 000 worshippers. Facing it is India's 'grandest gateway', the massive 54-m (176-ft) **Buland Gate**, erected in 1602 to commemorate Akbar's victory in Gujarat. Once the highest gate in the world, it bears the Arabic legend, 'The world is a bridge; pass over it but build no house'.

Inside the vast congregational courtyard is the city's finest treasure—the glittering white marble **Tomb of Shaikh Salim Chishti**, an important Sufi shrine. Visiting pilgrims from all faiths seal their prayers by binding pieces of string to the beautiful marble screens encircling the cenotaph, returning to remove the threads when their wish has been granted. The canopy of *shishma* wood above the inner shrine is exquisitely inlaid with mother of pearl, and the air is sweet with the heavy scent of attar of roses.

The Victory Gate is the normal exit from the fort, and provides fine general views over the village of Sikri. The gate, however, was designed as an entrance so it is worth looking back as you walk away. If visiting in spring, watch out for dead bees on the way out.

Returning to Agra, the tour next visits **Agra Fort**. Built by Akbar between 1565 and 1573 on the site of an earlier Lodhi fort, and much added to by Jahangir and Shah Jahan, this 'Red Fort' is just as interesting as the one in Delhi, and is far better preserved. In Mughal days, this massive red-turreted fortress with its 24-km (15-mile) circuit contained some 500 stone buildings within its sturdy double wall, and was encircled by a wide moat. It served a dual function, housing both residential palaces (for the royal family) and defensive military quarters (for the Mughal, then the British, now the Indian armies). Part of the fort is open from sunrise to sunset, admission is Rs2, and there are guides for hire at the entrance (about Rs50). Entry is through the Amar Singh Gate, the only one of three gates open to the public, at the southern corner.

The great Mughal emperors ruled India for a century from this fort, and within it you will find their palaces: Akbar's (broken foundations, situated behind a small tree), Jahangir's (to the front, with its rich carvings and marble inlay work) and Shah Jahan's (simpler, white marble effort). At the great Hall of Public Audience, **the Diwan-i-Am**, they held court for the common people. When, as was common, proceedings dragged on too long, decorated elephants paraded up and down in front of the emperor to bring matters to a speedy conclusion. Also near the Diwan-i-Am is the exquisite little **Pearl Mosque**, named after the large, priceless pearl which used to hang by a golden chain from the ceiling. It is widely considered the most beautiful mosque in India but is currently being restored, and is closed to the public.

For the perfect preview of the Taj Mahal, pass round the flower-laden garden of the central courtyard and climb the stairs up to the **Musamman Burj**. It was here, in this small octagonal, turreted room, that Shah Jahan may have spent the last eight years of his life, a prisoner of his son Aurangzeb, looking over the Yamuna to the shrine of his beloved Mumtaz—the Taj Mahal. This 'Jasmine Tower', so-called because of its adornment of jasmine blossoms, is surrounded with marvellous marble filigree screens. The adjoining **Diwan-i-Khas** is remarkable for its mosaics, their original colours intact, and for its flower-wreathed columns, inlaid with precious stones. Outside, on the palisade, are the two marble thrones of Shah Jahan (white) and Jahangir (black). One feature common to all Mughal gardens was the use of water. The fountain and sunken courtyard opposite the lovely **Sheesh Mahal** (Mirror Palace) are fine examples of water engineering. The palace itself, composed of two

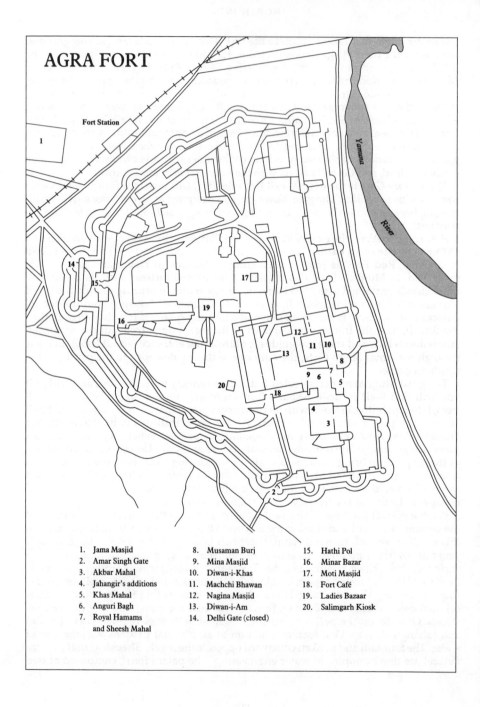

AGRA FORT

Fort Station

Yamuna River

1. Jama Masjid
2. Amar Singh Gate
3. Akbar Mahal
4. Jahangir's additions
5. Khas Mahal
6. Anguri Bagh
7. Royal Hamams
   and Sheesh Mahal
8. Musaman Burj
9. Mina Masjid
10. Diwan-i-Khas
11. Machchi Bhawan
12. Nagina Masjid
13. Diwan-i-Am
14. Delhi Gate (closed)
15. Hathi Pol
16. Minar Bazar
17. Moti Masjid
18. Fort Café
19. Ladies Bazaar
20. Salimgarh Kiosk

The Taj Mahal

rooms, artificial fountains and a cascade, the walls enriched with badly renovated mirror-work, was once the bath-house of the zenana (women's) quarters.

The final stop of the day is the 'Crown of Palaces', the **Taj Mahal**. Many people visit this essential symbol of India fully prepared to be disappointed. But few are. The most photographed, filmed, drawn and described building in the world, it is one of those few rare places in India which consistently meets (even exceeds) expectations. The secret of its success lies largely in its simplicity. True beauty, as its architect Shah Jahan proved, needs no ornament; it is essentially pure and simple.

The Taj is the most accomplished monument to love the world has ever seen. It was the creation of Shah Jahan, built to immortalise the memory of his beloved wife, Mumtaz Mahal, who died tragically in 1631 giving birth to her 14th child. He intended it to be the culminating masterpiece of his many buildings and so used the best artisans to ensure the highest possible quality of design and craftsmanship. An incredible 20 000 workmen laboured day and night for 22 years to bring it to completion. One of the less charming myths surrounding its construction is that many of the principal architects and sculptors lost their hands afterwards lest they should ever build such a masterpiece again.

The main mausoleum went up first, 22 tons of white marble inlaid with semi-precious stones. Then, because no tomb was complete without one, a mosque was added. A 'dummy' mosque, to provide symmetry, appeared on the right side. Then the gardens were laid out, and the gigantic red-sandstone entrance gate was built. It was inscribed with Koranic texts in letters that appeared totally uniform in size, whether viewed at the top or the bottom. And on the tomb itself was inscribed Shah Jahan's tragic prayer: 'Help us, O Lord, to bear that which we cannot bear'.

You don't have to be a romantic to fall in love with the Taj—it moves even hardened cynics. The smooth white marble has a supple, sensual quality that has visitors compulsively stroking and touching it or standing back to photograph it. Much of the attraction, as one traveller observed, has to do with coming face-to-face with something which one always has associated with India, ever since a child reading storybooks, yet somehow never expected to be real. It's one of those few times in life when fantasy and reality perfectly coincide.

The Taj is something to be seen at leisure, not rushed. Instead of bolting down to see it at close quarters, start with a general appreciation from the mammoth entrance gate: first the beautiful canals, fountains and tanks (sometimes with water in, sometimes not); next, the sweeping green lawns (minus the original fruit trees and gardens, but still pretty); then the two red-sandstone side buildings including the mosque; finally, the huge domed mausoleum in the centre. The Taj Mahal stands on a raised marble platform, with a tall, narrow minaret at each corner. The minarets were built to lean very slightly outwards, to save the tomb from damage should they ever topple. The huge bulbous dome atop the main structure is surrounded by four smaller domes. The four sides of the Taj are identical, and the building itself sits against a backdrop of empty sky, a conscious device producing the illusion of a floating palace seemingly suspended in the air.

The approach to the mausoleum is via long paths separated by a long central watercourse, in which (when there is water) it is beautifully reflected. The illusion of perfection is maintained even when viewing the structure at close range. The walls and arches are elegantly engraved with screen and mosaic work, the exquisite tracery and carving more like lace than sculpture. Semi-precious stones have been inlaid into the marble in incredibly precise patterns, a distinctive process of craftsmanship called *pietra dura*.

Inside the cool cenotaph chamber decorated with emeralds, jaspers, sapphires and other precious stones, a plain marble screen runs round the two dummy tombs of Shah Jahan and Mumtaz (the real ones, to avoid looting, were placed in the dark, humid basement chamber below). The original gem-studded gold screen was replaced by the present plain one in 1642—because Shah Jahan didn't want to encourage grave-robbers! But the Taj was a natural target for looters, and the real tombs below were stripped of all their gold and jewels by Jats from Bharatpur in 1754. The chamber itself has fine inlay work—mainly floral designs on red, green, gold or black marble. The Cairene lamp hanging from the dome of the cenotaph was donated by Lord Curzon in 1909.

After exploring the mausoleum, stroll outside to view it at leisure from the cool, shaded gardens. It's all been said before, but the Taj is quite unique—a rare master-piece of perfect proportion, symmetrical construction and harmonious form. Blinding-white at noon, the stark Macrana marble mellows by dusk to a sultry orange-cream, only to adopt a deathly blue-white pallor at night. Nights of a full moon used to be a popular viewing time, but in 1985 security precautions caused the building to be closed after dark. There are plans to re-open it on moonlit nights but until that happens, the only way you're going to see the Taj at night is to book a room at The Taj View Hotel directly overlooking it.

Midway along the western wall of the garden is the small **Taj Museum** with an interesting collection of Mughal items and 19th-century photographs of the Taj.

For the time being, the Taj Mahal is open from sunrise to 7.30 pm only. Admission is Rs2, and last tickets are sold at 6.30 pm. Like all sites managed by the Archaeological Survey of India, it is free on a Friday. This, however, is the one day not to visit—delirious hordes of pilgrims and local tourists. If visiting during March/April, avoid daydreaming by the cenotaph entrance: the ceiling is full of hives, and the floor carpeted with dead honey-bees. Shoes aren't allowed.

Peripheral Attractions (by rickshaw/taxi or cycle, half-day)
Itmud-ud-Daulah's Tomb–Chini ka Rauza–Ram Bagh Gardens–Sikandra

For day two, first visit Agra's most underrated sight: **Itmud-ud-Daulah's Tomb**, 4 km (2½ miles) upstream from the Taj and across the Yamuna River. The journey along one bank to the road bridge across the river and down the opposite bank can be slow. It is worth allowing 3–4 hours to visit the three places of interest on this bank of the river.

The tomb of a Persian nobleman, Ghiyas Beg, who became Jahangir's chief minister and took the title Itmud-ud-Daulah, was built in just 6 years (1522–8) by his powerful daughter, Empress Nur Jahan (Jahangir's consort). It was the first monument in India to feature Persian mosaic-style inlay work, or *pietra dura*. Greatly resembling the Taj in its use of inlay on white marble, its twin sandstone mosques, and its (smaller) ornamental sandstone gate, this elegant tomb in fact directly preceded it, the extensive use of *pietra dura* here being simplified and brought to its most elegant flowering in the construction of the Taj Mahal.

If anything, the quality of precise, delicate workmanship at Itmud-ud-Daulah is far superior to that of its more fêted rival, making its popular pseudonym of the 'Bibi-Taj' (little Taj) rather unfair. Like the main Taj, it is a simple white mausoleum, but its four minarets are far more sturdy and broad, and instead of a dome it has a Chinese palanquin-type top, with two spires. Though beautifully preserved, it receives very few visitors. A pity, since the elaborate inlay patterning (mainly floral) on the exterior is quite remarkable. The yellow-and-white inlay is Indian, the grey and multi-coloured stonework Persian. The ceiling of the edifice was originally decorated with gold and silver paintings, later scraped off or plastered over by looters or defilers of fine art. Lord Curzon achieved a partial restoration in 1905, preceding the Prince of Wales' visit, notably on the floor and ceiling. The four sandstone gates of the tomb are perfectly symmetrical, and the plaster interior has attractive hand-painted floral designs. Within are the tombs of Nur Jahan's parents (brown marble) and of Mumtaz's parents and various relatives. The surrounding gardens are well-kept and tranquil, full of blooms, plants and birds. Admission to the tomb is Rs2, and it's open from sunrise to sunset.

From here, you can return north and 1 km away is the once blue-tiled, but now heavily damaged, **Chini ka Rauza**. This Persian-influenced tomb was built by Afzal Khan (who died in 1639) for his own use. Carry on a further 2 km (1½ miles) north to **Ram Bagh**—the rather unkempt prototype of future Mughal gardens, built by Emperor Babur in 1528.

Ten kilometres (6 miles) north of Agra, along the Grand Trunk Road to Delhi, at Sikandra is **Akbar's mausoleum**. Combining architectural themes and motifs from both Islam and Hinduism. Akbar tried to bring these together in his Din Ilahi (religion of God). Although the tomb lacks the grace of either Humayun's tomb in Delhi or the Taj Mahal, it is interesting and set in extensive gardens.

RECREATION
Swimming is available at the larger hotels, though the non-resident fees are quite heavy—Rs150 per day at the Mughal Sheraton, Rs80 at the Taj View (best), and Rs55

at the Agra Ashok (worst). **Folk dance/puppet show programmes** are held most nights at the Mughal Sheraton and Clarks Shiraz hotels. The Agra Club, just down the road from the tourist office, offers a whole host of Raj-style recreations. It's a typical **British club**, with badminton and squash courts, billiards and cards rooms, and an 18-hole golf course nearby. For more relaxed entertainment, there are at least three good **cinemas**—the Natraj, Shah, and Mehar—which show English-speaking matinees.

SHOPPING

Agra is a positive mecca of handicraft shops and emporia, selling a wide range of goods from marble curios, brassware and embroidery to ivory, wood carvings, saris and ready-made garments, and carpets and jewellery. Every taxi and auto-rickshaw driver will try to punctuate an afternoon's tour of monuments with one or more visits to an emporium. The best general shopping area is **Sadar Bazaar**, below the tourist office, where you can pick up good marble, leather and clothes bargains. Before buying anything, however, get a list of approved shops from the Government of India tourist office.

Agra has a particularly fine **handicrafts** pedigree. When Humayun returned here from his exile in Persia, he brought with him a retinue of captive artisans and weavers. His son Akbar gave these craftsmen, painters, jewellers a royal commission. At this point, Agra became the handicrafts centre of north India, and the country's very first carpets came into being. Inevitably, these were of Persian design. There are many **carpet wholesalers** in Agra today, the two main ones being **Cottage Industries Exposition**, 39 Fatehabad Rd, and **Manglick & Sons**, 5 Taj Rd. CIE is located in an old haunted castle, and its motto is 'if you buy a carpet here, you're sure to fly!'. Trouble is, their carpets are Kashmiri (unlike Manglick, which has the authentic Agra produce) and the only thing likely to fly is your credit card. Try **Harish Carpet Co.**, in Vibhav Nagar Rd (tel 75594) , who have a wide range. For the time being, this is the best-deal carpet wholesaler in town—a standard 5 × 7 ft example (pure Agra wool, choice of Persian or Punjabi designs, 280 double-knots per sq in). Beautiful wool dhurries, in the same size, are very reasonably priced at Rs650. Guarantees are supplied with all purchases, and shipping home is no problem.

Other famous Agra products are **marble** *pietra dura* and *papier mâché*. There are several factories dotted around town where you can watch these items being made, with no obligation (just a lot of pressure) to buy.

Agra Marble

Agra is especially famous for its high-quality marblework, the presence of the Taj having encouraged the local people to develop a real expertise in it. There are presently hundreds of factories in Agra working on marble, most of them in the Balu Ganj area, just up from the Mall. Every one of the workers seems to have had an ancestor who worked on the Taj Mahal itself.

Though shopping for marble is best done at a fair-price shop like **Subhash Emporium** (in Gwalior Rd, opposite the Central Telegraph Office), it's worth visiting a place like **Marble Art Palace** (159 Garden Road, Balu Ganj) to see the complex marble-inlay process. So neatly do the little mosaic pieces of semi-precious stones fit into the marble surrounds, that you can't help wondering how the stone has been so perfectly incised. Well, it hasn't. Instead, the marble has been given a coating of orange henna, on which the major axes of the design are carefully scratched out, leaving the stone below exposed as white lines. Only when an exact, symmetrical design has been achieved is it drawn onto the marble. Then the semi-precious stones are cut to the exact shape of the pattern, using judgement of eye alone (templates are used nowhere in the process), and are glued together on a sheet of molten plastic. The resulting jigsaw mosaic of precious stones is then settled into recesses etched into the marble, and polished off with emery until the whole surface is uniformly smooth. The hard, durable, non-staining marble used comes not from Agra, but from Macrana, south-west of Jaipur. The process of working it (as described) has remained more or less unchanged since the days of the Taj.

Particularly fine marble gifts are the beautiful mosaic plates, inlaid with semi-precious stones, which sell at places like the emporium boulevard leading into the Taj itself. Expensive perhaps, but much better than the inferior soapstone rubbish (posing as marble) sold at less reputable places. An easy way of telling marble from soapstone (alabaster), by the way, is to scratch the item being sold against a piece of wood. Soapstone marks, marble doesn't.

Two last points about shopping in Agra. Be careful when paying for anything by credit card and always keep copies of the bill and voucher copy—shop-owners are very skilled at adding a couple of zeros to the price shown on receipts. Second, don't go into any shop with touts or rickshaw men. They get up to 30% commission on any purchases you make.

WHERE TO STAY

Luxury/Expensive (US$50–150 per room night)
Agra's most expensive hotel, the five-star **Mughal Sheraton**, Fatehabad Rd (tel 361701, fax 0562-361730, tlx 0565-210), is a somewhat pretentious place with a resident elephant, a resident camel, and an astrologer in the lobby. Still, it has a lovely pool, good facilities, six (nice) speciality restaurants, and a few superb Taj-facing rooms with imagined Mughal decor at US$125–165. The Taj Group's venture, **Taj View Hotel**, Fatehabad Rd (tel 361171, fax 0562-361179, tx 565-202), is a worthy alternative—if anything, the rooms here (US$90 single, US$100 double) are even classier than at the Sheraton. They certainly have better views of the Taj. All other features—food, facilities, service and (twin) swimming-pool—are just fine. No complaints either about **Hotel Clarks Shiraz**, 54 Taj Rd (tel 361421, tx 0565-211). This old-style hotel with cosy and personal service is located a little further, but still within sight of the Taj. It has a popular roof-top restaurant, decent pool, efficient room service, and large Taj-view suites. Rooms range from US$65–147. Nearby, the new **Hotel Agra Ashok**, 6B The Mall (tel 361223, tx 565-313) is friendly, but tacky. It's supposed to have the best air conditioning in town, and rooms range from US$35–60.

Mid-range (US$10–35/Rs250–1000 per room night)
The best mid-range deal is **Hotel Amar**, Fatehabad Rd (tel 360695, tlx 0565-341), with good bar and restaurant, new swimming-pool, useful amenities, and well-furnished rooms at Rs450 single, Rs650–750 double. All rooms have TVs, with in-house movies. The **Mumtaz**, Fatehabad Rd (tel 361771, tlx 0565-222) has more rooms with views of the Taj than the Amar, rates are the same and it is a good alternative. Also recom-

mended is **Grand Hotel,** 137 Station Rd, Cantonment (tel 74014), a large bungalow-style place with lots of character. One of the oldest hotels in town, it has a cosy TV lounge, a cheap air-conditioned restaurant (try 'Les Oeufs of Pates', 'Aloo Stuff' or 'Choke Bar'), cheap beer, some swish air-con rooms with TV/fridge at Rs400, and many other rooms from Rs280–450. The Grand is well-located—close to airport, rail and bus-stations—and has a useful ticket-booking service. Like all the above hotels, 25–30% discounts are possible in the low season.

Budget (Under US$10/Rs250 per room night)
The priority in Agra is a room with a view, but surprisingly few upmarket hotels have them. If anything, it is the small group of budget lodges round the back of the Taj South Gate that fill the need. **Shanti Lodge** has air-cooled rooms, three of them with unequalled sunset/moonlight views of the Taj Mahal. There's also one nice 'suite', with private bathroom. The nearby **India Guest House** is rather more basic, but rooms are cheap and it's run by someone who keeps all touts at bay. Down by the tourist office, **Jaggi Hotel,** 183 Taj Rd, is a modest, serviceable option with great advertising ('homelike care and moving honour from Welcome to Au Revoir') and clean single/double rooms.

EATING OUT
If you can afford about Rs200 per head excluding tax, you can eat very well in Agra. The lunchtime buffets at the **Mughal Sheraton** (Chinese or Continental), at the **Taj View** (variety of cuisines) and at the **Clarks Shiraz** (Chinese, Continental and Indian) are all good value. The breakfast at the Clarks is an experience. Travellers return here in the evening, for live music, *à la carte* specialities (try the steaks), and relaxing atmosphere.

For cheaper fare (Rs70), try **Zorba the Buddha** below the tourist office. It's a Rajneesh place, serving pure vegetarian food in air-conditioned comfort. Music and service are well above par. At the bottom of Sadar Bazaar, the **Kwality Restaurant** has a real café feel—like a Joe Lyons transplanted from London. It's a rather dim, dingy place, but there's nothing wrong with the food, the pastry counter, or the air-conditioning (Rs60). Over the road, the cheaper **Prakash** does popular Indian-style snacks. **ITDC Cafeteria & Restaurant** is very handy for Taj Mahal day-trippers (it's just outside the entrance). Food though is limited to sandwiches, omelettes, snacks (Rs45).

GENERAL INFORMATION
Government of India Tourist Office, 191 The Mall (tel 72377) is open 9 am to 5.30 pm Monday–Friday, 9 am to 1 pm Saturday, closed Sunday. It's a small, helpful office with plenty of printed information in five languages. You can hire a guide here (Rs100 per day, one to four persons) or book one of the conducted sightseeing tours (half-day tour of Fatehpur Sikri or full-day, continuing on to Agra Fort and Taj Mahal). Tours start from the tourist office at 9 am, then go to rail station to collect people off the *Taj Express*. It's best to join tours here—they only leave the station at 10.10 am.

GPO and *poste restante*, opposite the tourist office, is open 9 am to 6 pm weekdays, 9 am to 3 pm Saturday, closed Sunday. Indian Airlines, Air India and (good) TCI travel agency all have desks at Clarks Shiraz hotel. Best bookshop is Modern Book Depot, on the Mall.

GWALIOR

The strategically important fort at Gwalior dominates the city and for centuries controlled one of the major routes between north and south India. Its history goes back 2000 years, with rock inscriptions from the 5th century still to be found. From the 12th century control of the fort and surrounding area passed through a succession of Muslim, Tomar Rajput, Afghan, Mughal and finally Maratha rulers. During the 12th century Qutb-ud-din-Aibak was the first Muslim ruler to hold it but eventually the Tomars took possession. Perhaps the most famous was Man Singh who came to power in 1486. It was during this period that many of the great battlements and interior palaces were built. After a short period of control by the Lodhis (Afghans), the first Mughal Emperor Babur took the fort, and described it as 'the pearl among the fortresses of Hind'. During the slow collapse of the Mughal empire the Scindia line of Marathas conquered the area in 1754. At times during the Maratha wars the British took control of the fort. They held it for 30 years after capturing the Rani of Jhansi within its walls in 1858, thus bringing to a close the Indian Mutiny.

Once one of the largest and richest of the Indian Princely States, Gwalior is the main city of a rich agricultural region with an expanding industrial base. The new town, Lashkar, is south of the fort; the very smart railway station, to the south-east.

ARRIVAL/DEPARTURE

Air
Gwalior is not connected by air to Agra but has daily flights (IC433/434) linking it with Delhi (Rs738), Bhopal (Rs773), Indore (Rs1083).

Rail
Gwalior is on the main line between Delhi and most of the important centres in central and south India. The *Shatabdi Express* leaves New Delhi at 6.15 am and Agra Cantonment Station at 8.15 am reaching Gwalior at 9.30 am, and the *Taj Express* leaves Delhi at 7 am and Agra at 10 am arriving at 11.50 am. The return journeys to Agra and New Delhi leave at 7 pm and 5pm, respectively. Tariffs, p.109.

Road
There are regular buses from the ISBT in Delhi (Rs150), Idgah bus-station in Agra, and services to and from Jhansi and Bhopal.

WHAT TO SEE
The best place to start a tour of Gwalior is at the fort: its commanding view of the city and environs is the best introduction to the area. Pick up a locally produced guide; the fort is immense and a map will prove valuable. (The old city lies to the north and north-east.) There are two ways of entering the fort: by car, the road skirts the fort and passes the **21 Jain sculptures** carved out of the rock between the 8th and 15th centuries. These were mutilated by the first Mughal armies on Babur's orders. Partial restoration in recent years has replaced the statues' faces but not their private parts. The road then enters the fort through the **Urwahi Gate**. On foot, the easiest entrance is via the **Alamgir Gate**. Taxis and auto-rickshaws can drop you at the top

so you can walk down. There is no refreshment stall within the fort so it is advisable to carry a water-bottle—essential in summer.

The fort walls and the buildings within were constructed by different generations of rulers. The **Suraj Kund**, inside the outer walls, is an ancient tank at the site of the original pond where Suraj Pal was supposedly cured of leprosy by Saint Gwalipa in AD 8. The **Teli-ka Mandir**, dedicated to Vishnu and built by the Pratiharas (8th–11th centuries) is one of the oldest buildings in the fort. Intricate stone carvings decorate the doorway. Two 11th-century temples known as the **Sas-Bahu ka Mandir**, are also dedicated to Vishnu. Their open design contrasts with the Teli ka Mandir. The 16th-century **Gujri Mahal Palace** near the **Hindola Gate** now houses a small **Archaeological Museum** (open 10 am–5 pm, closed Mondays). One of the finest buildings in the fort is the four-storey **Man Mandir Palace** built in the late 15th century by Raja Man Singh. A blue and patterned tile decoration dominates one side of the fort's exterior wall. Other buildings of interest within the fort are the interconnected **Vikramaditya** and **Karan Palaces**.

Some of the buildings complex are only open at certain times of the day and it is worth checking before starting the climb.

In the town is a huge 19th-century palace. The enormous **Jai Vilas Palace** includes what are supposedly a pair of the world's heaviest chandeliers in the **Darbar Hall**, and a crystal staircase. The dining table is fitted with an electric train made of silver with which the Maharajah delivered cigars, port, brandy and other items in crystal wagons to favoured guests. Thirty-five rooms have now been converted to a museum filled with the family's memorabilia—open 10.30 am–5 pm, closed Monday.

There are two notable tombs in the old town. The early Mughal tomb of **Muhammed Ghaus** is built as a hexagonal tower with a dome, once covered in blue tiles. The tomb of **Tansen** nearby commemorates the great musician who played at Akbar's court. Both are located in wasteland about 15 minutes' walk from the northeastern gate of the fort. The **Royal Chhatris** or cenotaphs, are near Jayaji Chowk market.

RECREATION
Son et Lumière at the Man Singh Palace in the fort plays every night. There is both a Hindi and English language version, and the timings vary so check locally for details.

SHOPPING
Fine saris of a mixed cotton and silk weave from **Chanderi**, 239 km (148 miles) south of Gwalior, are available from Kothari and Son, Sarfa Bazaar (tel 23333).

WHERE TO STAY
The most expensive hotel in Gwalior is the bland **Welcomgroup Usha Kiran Palace** next to the Jai Vilas Palace, (tel 23453). Originally the Maharajah's guest-house, the hotel has an attractive garden and location with all major facilities. Rates Rs1200 upwards. The MP Tourism **Hotel Tansen** has both air-conditioned and non air-conditioned rooms; centrally located at 6A Gandhi Road (tel 21568) the room rates range from Rs200–Rs650. Other hotels in Gwalior include the **Hotel Gwalior Regency** on the Bus-stand Road (tel 29516) with air-conditioned rooms ranging from Rs400–650; the **Metro Hotel** in Ganesh Bazaar (tel 25530) is much simpler and cheaper (Rs200 for an air-conditioned room.)

EATING OUT
The **Kwality Restaurant** in Motilal Nehru Marg and **Wengier's Restaurant** near-by are both in the Lashkar area of town (Rs75). The **Tansen Hotel** and **Usha Kiran Palace** both have restaurants open to non–residents (Rs80 and Rs100 respectively).

GENERAL INFORMATION
Madhya Pradesh Tourism have an information office at the Tansen Hotel (tel 21568). Cars are available for local excursions and trips to Orchha, Jhansi and Shivpuri—from MP Tourism at Hotel Tansen and from S.S. Travels at the Usha Kiran Palace (tel 26636).

ORCHHA

The quiet town of Orchha was between 1531 and 1783 the capital of a locally powerful Rajput kingdom. The city was founded by a local Rajput chieftain, Rudra Pratap, in the early 16th century, who sited his new capital on a large rocky island in the Betwa river. Subsequent rulers added to the city before the capital was shifted to Tikamgarh. Orchha today is little more than a village with a population of only a couple of thousand. Rarely visited, but in fact fairly easy to reach from Delhi, Agra or Khajuraho, Orchha is one of India's many surprises. You should enjoy wandering gently around.

ARRIVAL/DEPARTURE

Air
The nearest airport is Gwalior, 116 km (74 miles) to the north. Khajuraho is 178 km (110 miles) to the east (see p.110).

Rail
Jhansi, 19 km (12 miles) to the west is the most convenient railhead. The *Shatabdi Express* links Jhansi with Delhi, Agra and Gwalior and arrives at 10.40 am. Tariff, p.109. The return train leaves at 5.50 pm. All major trains between Bombay and Delhi (on the Central Railway) and Madras and Delhi stop at Jhansi.

Road
There are regular buses from Jhansi to Orchha and taxis are available from Jhansi railway station (Rs200–250). The road from Gwalior passes the **Datia Palace**, built in 1620 and described by Edwin Lutyens as the finest building in India. Don't stop, you cannot visit.

WHAT TO SEE
The fort occupies much of a low-lying, rocky island in the Betwa river, reached by an arched bridge. Three palaces set in an open courtyard within the fort are the first buildings to explore. The tiered **Jahangir Mahal** was built to commemorate the visit of Emperor Jahangir in 1606. The **Raj Mahal**, to the right of the courtyard, was built by Madhukar Shah. Its plain exterior does not give any indication of the bold and

colourful murals inside. The third palace, **Rai Praveen Mahal**, is a two-storey brick structure set in the gardens of **Anand Mahal**.

Of the many temples within the fort, three are especially worth visiting: the Ram Raja, the Chaturbhuj and the Lakshminarayan Temples. The **Ram Raja Mandir** was originally a palace and became a temple more by accident than design. An image of Ram was installed while the temple being built for it, the **Chaturbhuj**, was under construction. For some reason the image could not be moved from the palace so the building despite its spires and ornate decoration became a sacred place. Linked to the Ram Raja Mandir is the **Lakshminarayan Temple**, the interiors of which have some of the best-preserved murals and wall paintings in Orchha. Much of the fort area is a ruin, but with sturdy shoes and trousers, to avoid the thorns, it is worth walking around.

From across the river, there is a marvellous view of the royal chhatris. On winter evenings they are silhouetted against the setting sun.

WHERE TO STAY
There are two or three private guest-houses and small hotels, all in the budget range, but the best place to stay is the charming **Sheesh Mahal** (tel 224). Run by MP Tourism, and with only eight rooms, Sheesh Mahal is tucked away at one corner of the Jahangir Mahal. The service is slow but courteous and the room rates range from Rs100–450. Advance-booking through the MP Tourism office in Delhi (Kanishka Shopping Plaza) or Bhopal is advisable.

KHAJURAHO

The famous temples of Khajuraho are a major tourist magnet, partly because, situated in the dry, hot plains of Madhya Pradesh and miles from anywhere, they have an alluring quality of romantic isolation; partly because they include the most sublime, sensuous and erotic temple sculpture in India; and finally, because they are remarkably intact, their remote situation having spared them the customary desecrations inflicted by Muslim invaders on other northern temples.

Over 80 temples, of which 22 survive, were built by the mighty Chandella dynasty, which claimed descent from the legendary moon god Chandra. The bulk of them appeared in a single, sudden burst of creative and religious energy, between the mid-10th and mid-11th centuries. The much reduced Chandella kingdom lasted almost 500 years; their capital at Kalanjar having fallen in 1203 they remained at Ajaygarh until the early 18th century. When their ancient religious centre of Khajuraho was deserted is not known. But the sculptures live on. Though the 'dirty postcard' touts at Delhi would have you believe otherwise, Khajuraho is not a place for the thrill-seeking voyeur. It is, rather, just a frank expression of joy in life, a remarkable symphony in stone erected in praise of love and women. And the purpose of the sculptures has been an object of discussion and academic debate since the temples were 'rediscovered' by Capt T. S. Burt in 1838. The skill and the vivacity of the carvings themselves have rarely been equalled.

Khajuraho today is a small peaceful village of some 5000 inhabitants. Many of them continue to tend their fields and animals. It comes as a real surprise to many visitors to find such a green, well-maintained garden environment, though even the park benches and the pastoral setting can't take your mind off the heat. Khajuraho has an extreme climate—very hot in summer, very cold in winter. The most comfortable months are November to February. If you don't like crowds, come in March. The special **Dance Festival**, which takes place every year (end February/early March) over seven days is a marvellous opportunity to see some of India's top dancers and musicians performing in an original setting (the floodlit temple grounds) for a nominal cost of between Rs10 and Rs100 per seat.

ARRIVAL/DEPARTURE

Air
Indian Airlines flies daily between Khajuraho and Agra (Rs767), Delhi (Rs1031) and Varanasi (Rs767). IC408 continues from Varanasi to connect with Kathmandu. A new twice-weekly flight links Khajuraho with Bombay.

Rail
Khajuraho has no direct rail connections. The nearest station is Satna, 117 km (74 miles) east of Khajuraho, from which there are regular connections with Delhi, Varanasi, Lucknow and Calcutta. Jhansi, 176 km (109 miles) to the west, is connected to Delhi, Agra, Gwalior and Bhopal by the superfast *Shatabdi Express* (see p.109).

Road
There are daily buses to Agra and Delhi, and to Jhansi (for the rail connection to Delhi; see p.109). There are also regular local buses to Chhatarpur and Satna.

WHAT TO SEE
Khajuraho is small enough to see in a day, and this is exactly what most visitors do. They fly in from Delhi or Agra in the morning and continue to Varanasi the next day (a taxi from the airport is Rs50). But a few short hours simply aren't enough. You'll need at least two days here, to see the temples at leisure and to appreciate fully the glorious sunrises and sunsets.

There are three groups of temples. The larger Western Group is conveniently near the modern part of town, with its hotels, restaurants, shops and bus-station. The unkempt but interesting Eastern Group is 1.5 km (1 mile) away in the old village. The Southern Group is 4 km (2½ miles) below the new town. You can walk to all these places, or tour round by cycle available opposite the bus-stand or from many of the hotels for approximately Rs10 per day. If it's too hot, or you're short on time, it's a good idea to hire a taxi (Rs100 per half-day) or a rickshaw.

Temple Tour (on foot or cycle/rickshaw, full-day)

The temples are all open from sunrise to sunset, and you can get right round them in 5/6 hours. To make best use of your time, hire out a proper badge-carrying guide from the tourist office. Touts and unofficial guides are prohibited inside the Western Group of temples, which is a good thing. Every temple, however, has a guard with a large store of anecdotal information to impart. If you happen to miss any of the sex scenes, they'll eagerly point these out to you. And they'll be very happy with a rupee or two for their (unsolicited) services. Khajuraho was recently declared a World

Heritage Monument, under the UNESCO scheme. The temples are well maintained by the Archaeological Survey of India and in very good condition. They are interesting, even if there is a lot of apparent repetition in the sculptures. The erotic carvings are well distributed, but not exclusive. As one archaeologist observed: 'Khajuraho's temples belong to that stage of development of the religious art of India, when sculpture and architecture were perfectly integrated'.

Most tours start at the **Western Group** of temples. The Rs1 admission covers entry to the **Archaeological Museum** across the road, which you can visit later when the day becomes hotter. Open 9 am to 5 pm, except Friday, it houses a beautiful collection of sculpture from the temples both ruined and existing. The museum takes just 20 minutes to walk through.

The Western Group of temples make particularly easy viewing—they are all contained in one compact area (not spread out, as at Bhubaneshwar) and are surrounded by gardens beautifully maintained by the Archaeological Survey. A leisurely tour round them should take about 2 hours.

As a general introduction, the architecture of the three main temples follows a five-part pattern: each temple having an *ardhamandapa* or entrance porch, leading into a pillared *mandapa* hall, then an *antarala* or vestibule, and finally an enclosed corridor or *pradakshina* which runs around the inner sanctum or *garbha griha*. Each of the Khajuraho temples stands on a high masonry platform, the primary exterior features being the distinctive spires or shikaras, which move vertically upwards in rhythmic stages, giving a total effect of grace and lightness, reminiscent of an ascending range of Himalayan peaks.

Inside the gateway, just to the left, is the first group of four temples. The largest one, the **Lakshmana** (*c.* AD 930–50) is a very early example, also the only Khajuraho temple to have remained completely intact. The decorative sculpture includes fine figures of apsaras (heavenly nymphs), erotic scenes, and a frieze running right round the base which includes some of the more explicit erotica. The **Devi** and **Varah** temples are two small shrines opposite the Lakshmana; the Varah being dedicated to Vishnu in his incarnation as a boar. Outside the enclosure is **Matangesvara**, the fourth of the group, which is still used for worship. Each evening between 6.30 pm and 7.30 pm, depending on the time of year, is the evening *arti* or prayers to which all are welcome.

At the back of the Western enclosure, you'll find the biggest and best of all Khajuraho temples, **Kandariya Mahadev** (1025–50). The zenith of Chandella art, its main spire soars to a height of 31 m (108 ft), and every inch of its surface is covered in intricate carvings, each one a masterpiece. Among the 872 statues between 60 and 75 cm high within and without, very few can be termed erotic. Kandariya is the showpiece temple of Khajuraho—its carvings turn up on all the naughty postcards touted round India. Two other temples share the same extended platform; the small **Mahadeva** (largely ruined, but houses famous sculpture of lion being fondled by androgynous figure) and the **Devi Jagadamba** with some of the finest sculptures.

At the north-east corner of the enclosure, you'll find **Chitragupta Temple**, dedicated to Surya, the sun god. Despite poor condition, some fine processional, dancing and hunting sculpture reliefs remain. So does an 11-headed statue of Vishnu (10 incarnations, plus Vishnu himself) and a lintal relief of Surya being pulled along in his chariot by seven spirited steeds. Completing your circuit of the compound at the south-east end, there's the **Parvati Temple** and **Vishvanath Temple**, dedicated to Shiva, with its large **Nandi** bull. Steps are flanked with elephants (south) and lions (north), sculptures are devoted almost exclusively to women, engaged in all types of daily activity. Take a rest, then head out by taxi or cycle to the **Eastern Group** of temples, situated beside the original Khajuraho village.

This group divides into two: three Hindu temples lie on the northern side of the village, then three Jain shrines within a walled enclosure. The **Parsvanatha** is unlike any other temple surviving at Khajuraho in that it lacks a platform base and the sculptures are at eye level. The two other Jain temples are the **Adinatha** (apart from the Jain image within, looks very Hindu) and the **Santinatha** (modern, but houses fine collection of older sculptures). Outside this group, there's a little museum set up by the local Jain community (entrance Rs1). Back in the village are the Hindu shrines, the **Javari Temple** (*c.* 1075–1100, fine small-scale architecture, dedicated to Vishnu), the **Vamana** (a little further north, dedicated to Vishnu's incarnation as a dwarf, exterior adorned with profusion of 'celestial maidens'), and the **Brahma Temple** (stylistically older and probably originally dedicated to Vishnu, although it contains a four-faced Shivalinga). Look out for the large **Hanuman Statue**, now within a modern shrine on the road between the Western and Eastern Groups.

If you've timed things right—wisely visiting the Eastern temples from 4 to 6 pm, when the heat is down—you'll just be strolling back into town for the glorious sunset over the western temples, their range of soaring *shikara*-spires haloed by the bright crimson sky.

If you've finished earlier than expected at the Jain enclosure visit the **Duladeo** temple a few hundred metres south of the road and next to the Khodar stream. The most remote temple, nearer the airport, and easily visited *en route* if you allow an extra 30 minutes, is the **Chaturbhuj** temple. The Chaturbhuj temple is isolated from the other remaining temples and seldom visited but it houses one of the most impressive statues at Khajuraho. The 2.7-m high image of the four-armed Dakshinamurti Shiva must be an example of the size of image originally enshrined in all the temples.

A punishing, but rewarding, day **excursion by cycle** is out to the river 23 km (14½ miles) out of Khajuraho. Here, walk along the rocks for 10 minutes, to find the large waterfall (plus crocodiles). It's an excellent situation for bathing. Other popular excursion spots are **Panna National Park** (40 km) and the Hunting Palace of the Maharajahs (20 km). Both are best visited by taxi, arranged by Mr Lavania of Khajuraho Tours, just opposite the entrance to the Western Group, or by the tourist office.

RECREATION
Chandella Hotel's swimming-pool is just the place to cool off after all those hot, dusty temples. Oberoi has a pool too, but it has little shade and you'll burn. In the evening, there's live sitar music and dance at the Chandella, and good cultural programmes in the Oberoi's lobby.

SHOPPING
Lots of thellas (push-cart stalls) and hawkers sell postcards, 'old' coins and artefacts. There is one shop near the Western Group called 'Junks and Jewels' which sums up the general standard.

WHERE TO STAY

Expensive (US$50–100 per room night)

The peaceful **Jass Oberoi** on By-pass Rd (tel 2066, cable OBHOTEL) is a comfortable option. Pleasant decor, cultural shows, good service, and stylish rooms (all with balconies) at US$70 single, US$80 double. It has air-conditioning and a swimming-pool. Taj Group's **Hotel Chandella** (tel 2054) is nearby on the way to the airport. The original hotel in Khajuraho, it has done much to make Khajuraho the popular destination it has become. Popular with travellers, it's an attractive building surrounded by landscaped gardens. The pool is excellent, and there's a choice of three restaurants. Rooms are air-conditioned, with balcony or patio, and cost US$49 single, US$80 double. Interesting facilities include 'camel and elephant for joy rides'.

Moderate (US$10–35/Rs250–1000 per room night)

Payal Hotel (tel 2076), 1 km behind the Western Group of temples, is excellent value. It's a homely accommodation—lovely bright rooms, with balconies, at Rs350 single, Rs400 double (non-air-conditioned rooms are about Rs100 less). No pool, but running hot and cold water, chatty staff, and good food. Tariffs are inclusive of breakfast. The new **Hotel Jhankar** (tel 2063) to the south of the town has similar facilities as the Hotel Payal, but without the atmosphere. The rates are the same as the Payal. Both hotels can be booked through the MP Tourism offices in Delhi and Bhopal.

Budget (Under US$10/Rs250 per room night)

Best budget lodges are **Hotel Harmony, Sunset View** (good reputation, fine temple views from terrace), **New Bharat Lodge**, and **Jain Lodge** (old, popular)—all charging between Rs75 and 150, and all near the bus-stand. The **Tourist Bungalow** (tel 2064) is an overpriced fallback.

EATING OUT

Jass Oberoi's **Apsara** restaurant offers good buffet lunches (Indian, Chinese and Continental) for about Rs150. The favourite local-style dish is rahu—fresh river-fish, served with special sauces. It's not on the menu though—you have to advance-order. The Chandella's Coffee Shop is reasonable (Rs100) but not exciting. Meals at the Payal are superb—two can have an excellent meal for around Rs80. New Bharat Restaurant, down the road from the hotel, does pure vegetarian food only; it's very cheap and very good. The 'Swiss-run' Raja's Cafe is a popular meeting place, but meals are mediocre.

GENERAL INFORMATION

The Government Tourist Office (tel 2047), opposite the Western Group, is open 9 am to 5.30 pm weekdays, 8 am to 12 noon Saturday, closed Sunday. Information is poor, but come here for maps and to book guides. Khajuraho now has a proper Guide Association—approved guides speaking German, Spanish, Japanese, Italian, French and English. They charge Rs50 half-day, Rs100 full-day for up to four people. The ASI guide to the temples is an excellent introduction costing Rs6, available at the entrance to the Western Group. A recently published study of Khajuraho: *Divine Ecstasy* by a young academic, Shobita Punja (Viking 1992) gives a scholarly yet highly readable survey of the many interpretations of Khajuraho, the temples and their sculpture, and puts forward an exciting and original theory as to the Chandella's original concept.

The post office is housed in a charming, rustic old building, near the bus-stand. It's open 9 am to 5 pm Monday to Saturday, closed Sunday. Indian Airlines have an office near the Chandella Hotel. State Bank of India have a branch opposite the Western Group of temples.

VARANASI (BENARES)

The centre of Hinduism, and most important pilgrimage place in the country, Varanasi is one of the seven ancient Sacred Cities of the Hindus. The spiritual heart of Uttar Pradesh state, this is a city of colourful bazaars, bright quality silks, festivals, temples, mosques and palaces—all centring round the teeming ghats of the Holy Gange (Gangas). Nearby **Sarnath** is a total contrast—a peaceful Buddhist centre of *stupas*, shrines, monasteries and museums, where the Buddha came to preach his first sermon. Ancient capital of Hindu faith and learning, Varanasi is one of the oldest living cities in the world and certainly the most fascinating.

In many ways this is India in a nutshell—an inextricable maze of narrow, winding streets and alleys, domes and minarets, pinnacles and towers, derelict 18th-century palaces and hundreds of temples, the whole a continuous riot of noise, colour and clanging temple gongs. A haunting city of dignified buildings, many crumbling and sliding inexorably into the holy Ganges, the old 'eternal' city retains a very special vitality.

Varanasi's early history is lost in antiquity. Ancient accounts like the *Mahabharata* and *Skanda Purana* mention its existence at least 3000 years ago, though traditionally it was founded around 1200 BC. The Chinese pilgrims Fa-Hsien and Hieun Tsiang, writing in the 5th and 7th centuries AD respectively, give the first historical accounts of its many Hindu temples and monasteries, but it had long since become a flourishing centre of religion, education and commerce. The Buddha came to Sarnath, just 10 km (6 miles) north of the city, to preach his eight-fold path to truth and enlightenment. And along the holy ghats by the Ganges, numerous shrines and temples arose, dedicated to Shiva, the presiding deity. Rich and powerful, Varanasi became an inevitable bone of contention between local rulers, and an irresistible lure to northern invaders. From the 11th century on, it was regularly looted by the Muslims, and later on by Aurangzeb, the Mughal Emperor (he destroyed nearly all the temples and rebuilt the most famous one as a mosque). Few of the present Varanasi shrines, therefore, are older than the 18th century. Only in 1738, with the accession of a strong Hindu monarch, was firm rule reestablished. Ceded to the British in 1775, Varanasi finally entered an era of consolidation and rehabilitation. Mark Twain, who visited India in the late 19th century, wrote that 'Benares is older than history, older than tradition, older even than legend, and looks twice as old as all of them put together'.

The present name of Varanasi is a restoration of its ancient title meaning the city between two rivers—the Varuna and the Asi. Its spiritual name is Kashi, meaning the city that shines with *kasha* (divine light). The city's other name of **Benares** by which it was known for the last 300 years or so, is probably a corruption of Varanasi. Most visitors are pilgrims making the requisite once-in-a-lifetime Hindu visit to clean

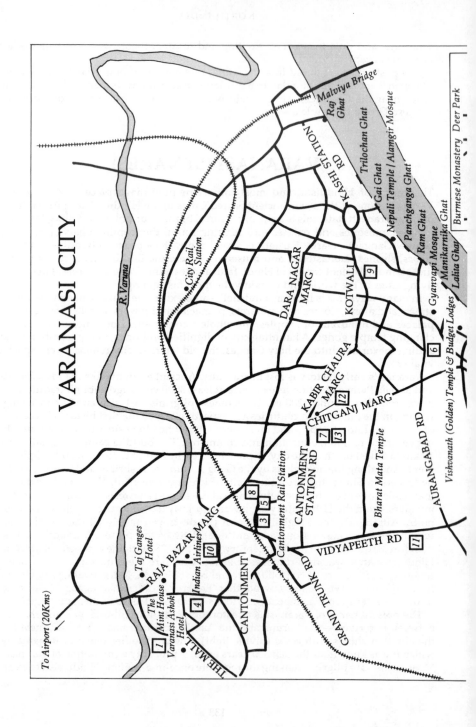

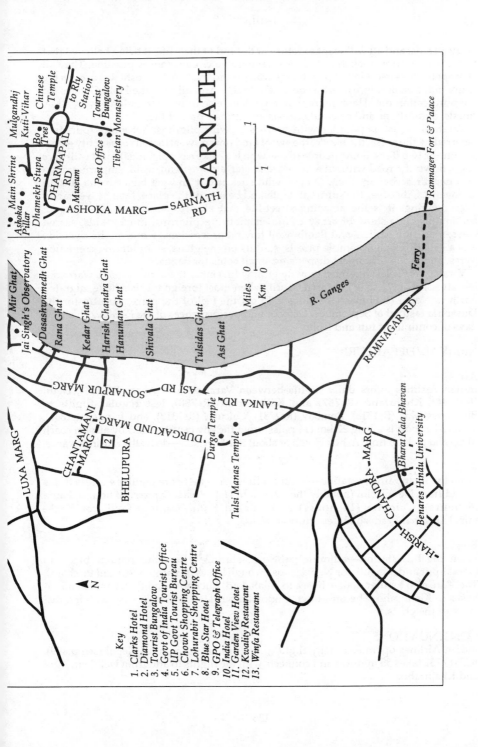

SARNATH

Chinese Temple
to Rly Station
Tourist Bungalow
Mulgandhi Kuti-Vihar
Bo Tree
DHARMAPAL RD
Tibetan Monastery
Main Shrine
Ashoka Pillar
Dhamekh Stupa
Post Office
Museum
ASHOKA MARG
SARNATH RD

Mir Ghat
Jai Singh's Observatory
Dasashwamedh Ghat
Rana Ghat
Kedar Ghat
Harish Chandra Ghat
Hanuman Ghat
Shivala Ghat
Tulsidas Ghat
Asi Ghat

R. Ganges

Ferry
Ramnager Fort & Palace

Miles
Km

LUXA MARG
CHANTAMANI MARG
BHELUPURA
SONARPUR MARG
ASI RD
DURGAKUND MARG
Durga Temple
LANKA RD
Tulsi Manas Temple

RAMNAGAR RD

HARISH CHANDRA MARG
Bharat Kala Bhavan
Benares Hindu University

N

Key

1. Clarks Hotel
2. Diamond Hotel
3. Tourist Bungalow
4. Govt of India Tourist Office
5. UP Govt Tourist Bureau
6. Chowk Shopping Centre
7. Lohurabir Shopping Centre
8. Blue Star Hotel
9. GPO & Telegraph Office
10. India Hotel
11. Garden View Hotel
12. Kwality Restaurant
13. Winfa Restaurant

away all sins; and all will want to return at the end of their life, it being believed that to die here ensures rebirth in the most favourable circumstances possible. They all attempt the 55-km (36-mile) pilgrimage walk round the Panchakroshi Road, even the many old, sick and infirm who come here to die. And all visit the Holy Ganges for the purification dip. Here, more than anywhere else in India, religion—with all its rituals, dedications and celebrations—is an intrinsic part of life.

Varanasi is just as popular with tourists as with pilgrims. Yet many tourists—deterred by the noise, the hassle, the sweet (and not so sweet) smells of sanctity—stay just one or two days. Some people (those who look like easy pickings) can't walk five paces down the road without a money-changer, a dope fiend, a silk emporium man or a beggar accosting them. Others, who stick it out and get beneath the surface annoyances, discover the spiritual depth and beauty of the place. Intense, yet rarely overpowering, it is the amazing street-life that absorbs visitors most—a rapid, continuous slide-show of crazy traffic, clamouring pilgrims, mucky kids, sacred cows, road-side barbers and flamboyant funeral processions; while on the riverside it is a kaleidoscope of temple priests, sadhus on the ghats, smouldering cremation pyres, and money-changers dispensing small coins for beggars.

Varanasi is coolest but most crowded from November to February. For a warm but less stressful stay, come in March/April, when most foreign tourists have migrated north to Nepal or Himachal Pradesh. To get the feel of the place, turn up for the **Dussehra** festival of September/October and performances of the *Ramlila*. This is 30 days of continuous fun and frolic.

ARRIVAL/DEPARTURE

Air
Indian Airlines offers daily flights between Varanasi and Agra (Rs1106), Delhi (Rs1394), Khajuraho (Rs767) and Kathmandu (Rs788); less regular flights to Bhubaneshwar (Rs1313), Bombay (Rs2781), Calcutta (Rs1313), and Jaipur (Rs1831). Varanasi airport is a long 22 km (14 miles) from the city centre—Rs25 by airport coach (drop and pick up from Ashok Hotel) or about Rs100 by taxi—do fix the rate in advance.

Rail
From the main railway station—Varanasi Junction—there are regular express trains to and from New Delhi (notably the overnight *Upper India Express*, 13 hours), Patna (6 hours), Calcutta (12 hours) and Chakki Bank/Jammu Tawi, for Kashmir/Himachal Pradesh (3 departures a week).

Bus
From the bus-station—adjoining the rail station—there are regular buses to Gorakhpur and Sonauli, for Nepal (plus through buses to Kathmandu and Pokhara). There are also regular deluxe buses to Allahabad, Lucknow and Patna and standard buses to Khajuraho. The mid-town Godowlia bus-stop is within easy walking distance of the ghats.

CONTINUATIONS
Indian Airlines operates a daily flight to and from Kathmandu, Nepal (see p.489). IC751/752 takes 55 minutes and connects with the flights to and from Delhi via Agra and Khajuraho.

WHAT TO SEE

Sightseeing is pretty informal in Varanasi. A good proportion of travellers come less for the city's sights (fine though they are) than for its unique atmosphere, and for some kind of personal spiritual experience.

All the 'action' takes place in the old city, which sprawls out along the west bank of the Ganges and falls back from the riverside ghats in a twisting maze of narrow alleys and medieval old ruins; losing one's way is not uncommon but it is difficult to be truly lost as there is always someone to guide you back to a familiar landmark. The new city, centring on the Cantonment area beyond the rail station, is a total contrast of quiet, civilised tree-lined avenues.

Getting round is easiest by non-metered auto-rickshaws who charge about Rs2.50 per km and can be hired for the whole day. Cycles can also be hired by the day (Rs15); There are many hire places around Lanka bus-stop, near Benares Hindu University. Cars can be hired from hotel travel desks, for the day or by the hour.

You can see all the principal attractions—Ganges, ghats and old city, plus Sarnath in just two days. But this is one place in India to linger longer if necessary.

Varanasi Tour (by boat, on foot; full-day)
River Ganges–The Ghats–Nepalese Temple–
Vishvanath Temple (Golden Temple)–Gyanvapi Mosque–Durga Temple–
Tulsi Manas Temple–Benares Hindu University–Bharat Kala Bhawan

The essential Varanasi can be found on the river-front at dawn—when Hindu pilgrims flock to the ghats (stepped embankments) on the bank of the Ganges to perform their ablutions, do their gymnastic exercises, have a ritual bath in the river, and perform *puja* to the rising sun, all rituals evolved and derived from thousands of years of worship and tradition. A rich and fascinating sight.

Book a morning tour from hotel or tourist office, and arrange to be woken at least an hour before dawn in order to take a rickshaw from anywhere in the new town down to the tour boat. It usually leaves from the central **Dasashwamedh Ghat**, which offers a splendid view of the river-front. This is the ghat of the 10 (*das*) horse (*aswa*) sacrifice (*madh*), performed by Brahma, which paved the way for Shiva's return to Varanasi after a brief spell of banishment by the then ruler. If not taking an organised tour, boats can be hired for between Rs25 and Rs75 per 2-hour trip from many of the ghats.

From the ghat steps, watch the huge red orb of the sun creep over the horizon and cast its rosy warm glow over the holy Ganges (a uniquely memorable sight), then board your boat and work silently up the river. With the coming of dawn, the lonely mist-grey ghats suddenly burst into lively, colourful activity. The faithful flock down to the riverside, and the Venice-like vista of ruined temples (many sliding into the sea) and bathing ghats is filled with priests invoking the dawn, young men practising yoga exercises, people washing clothes or having the ritual morning bath, and pyres being lit for the first cremations of the day. On a particularly auspicious day, as many as 30 000 pilgrims may show up at Dasashwamedh Ghat to greet the dawn.

Whether you take an organised boat-trip or hire a private boat is up to you. There are always young lads patrolling the river, offering to show tourists the ghats as part of a private boat excursion (2 hours). Going solo certainly has its advantages: tour boats attract a lot of unwelcome attention from 'fake' Sadhus (holy men) wanting money, or from insistent trinket salesmen. Yet the conducted tour gives good information, and guides you round the principal old city temples off the river. Perhaps best, therefore, to use this for orientation and to take a private boat-trip at leisure later on.

Tour boats take you up-river first, proceeding south from Dasashwamedh Ghat (with its shrine to Sitala, goddess of smallpox) to **Kedar Ghat** (fine lingams and temple), **Harischandra Ghat** (secondary burning ghat, bodies cremated by *chandal* outcastes), **Dandi Ghat** (used by ascetics), the popular **Hanuman Ghat** (used by worshippers of the monkey god), **Shivala** (Kali) **Ghat** (owned by the Maharajah, has a famous lingam), **Tulsi Ghat** (dedicated to the poet Gosain Tulsi Das; now sliding into the river), and **Asi Ghat**, the furthest ghat upstream and one of the holiest. It marks the confluence of the Asi and Ganges waters, and is the first of the five special ghats pilgrims must bathe in (during a single day) to fulfil the purification ritual. The other four are Dasashwamedh, Barnasangam, Panchganga and Manikarnika.

From Asi Ghat, you'll return back downstream to Dasashwamedh to see the northern ghats. First, next to Dasashwamedh, is **Jai Singh's 1710 observatory** built within Mansingh's old palace (1600) at **Man Mandir Ghat**. The observatory is one of three surviving (see Jaipur, p.154). Much of the palace was restored in the 19th century and the fine north-corner stone balcony is original. Then **Lalita Ghat**, below the **Nepalese Temple** and (further back) the **Vishvanath Temple**. At the adjoining **Jalsain** and **Manikarnika Ghats** (main burning ghats), photography is strictly forbidden. Jalsain is named after Vishnu's incarnation as Jalsai, sleeper on the ocean. Manikarnika is most sacred because Shiva dug a tank here, filling it with sweat as he tried to recover an earring Parvati had dropped in it. Between the tank and ghat is the **Chandrapaduka** and a slab of stone with Vishnu's footprints. Further on is **Dattatreya Ghat** (with the footprints of a Brahmin saint, in a small temple), the huge **Scindia Ghat**, the **Ram Ghat** built by the Rajah of Jaipur, and above this Aurangzeb's small **Alamgir Mosque**, which incorporates earlier Buddhist columns. Further north, **Gai Ghat** is marked by its stone figure of a cow, and **Trilochan Ghat** by its two turrets (between which pilgrims bathe in the extra-holy water). These last two ghats are also where most of the vultures hang out, waiting for lunch to float by. From here, enjoy close-up views of the stately new **Malviya Bridge**, then return to Dasashwamedh Ghat.

Off the boat, it's up the steps and to the right for the marvellous little **Nepalese Temple**, recently renovated and full of exotic wood carvings depicting Shiva, Parvati, Hanuman and various other deities. Diving into the tunnel backstreets of the old city, you emerge presently at Varanasi's famous **Vishvanath** (Golden) **Temple**. You can't go in but if you climb the stairs of the old house opposite, you can get reasonable views from the balcony. The solid-gold plating of the temple towers was donated by Maharajah Ranjit Singh of Lahore in 1835. Dedicated to Shiva as Vishvanath, Lord of the Universe, the present temple was erected by Rani Ahalyabai Holkar of Indore in 1776. Adjacent to it is the site of the original temple, built in 1600, which Aurangzeb destroyed to make way for his Gyanvapi Mosque in the 17th century. The foundations and rear of this mosque still display rare examples of temple design and the columns in front also came from the earlier building. The two minarets rise 71 m (233 ft) above the river and dominate the skyline of this part of the city when seen from the river. The **Gyan Vapi** (Covered Well) to the side of the mosque is a favourite resting place of pilgrims.

Though the tour continues on to **Benares University**, you may well decide to remain in the old city. There's good shopping at the innumerable tiny shops and stalls round the Golden Temple (buy anything from attractive silk and sarees to old coins and curios, elegant glass bangles to novelty fly whisks and toy-boats chugging away in washing-up bowls). Then take a short walk south to the blood-crimson stained **Durga Temple**, commonly known as the Monkey Temple owing to its resident population of mischievous monkeys. Built in the North Indian Nagara style by an 18th-century Bengali Maharani, it is dedicated to Parvati's manifestation as the 'terrible' Durga, and goat sacrifices are common. Entrance to the temple is prohibited, but you can look down on it (quite enough for the queasy) from the walkway above. Next door is the modern **Tulsi Manas Temple**, built in 1964 to commemorate the place where the poet-saint Tulsidas lived. The marble walls of this *shikhara*-style temple are inscribed with the entire text of the epic *Ramacharitamanas* (expounding the history and deeds of Rama, one of Vishnu's incarnations), composed by the poet. A further 20 minutes' walk south down Asi Rd (or a short rickshaw ride) brings you to Benares Hindu University, some 11 km (7 miles) from the city centre. This turn-of-the-century university is a vast complex 5 sq km (2 sq miles in area) featuring one of India's finest museums, the **Bharat Kala Bhawan**. This houses a superb collection of Indian miniatures, sculptures and terracottas. Open 11 am to 4 pm July–April and 7.30 am to 12.30 pm in May and June, daily (except Sunday).

After a rest, use the afternoon for a return visit to the old city. If you get lost wandering through the bazaars, shops and stalls, and can't find your way back to the ghats, hire a guide; follow a sacred cow or just ask for directions. There are over 100 ghats to explore, so no fear of getting bored. But be careful around the Manikarnika 'burning' ghat; the cremation pyres can unsettle some people. People are understandably sensitive about the ghats and visitors have had their cameras destroyed for trying to take photographs. Every local who sidles up to you in this area—usually pretending to be a guide to holy Hindu rituals—is likely to be a silk emporium tout. But the funeral ceremonies themselves are fascinating—here in Varanasi, more than anywhere else in India, life and death are on constant public view.

If you still have time (and energy) to spare, finish the day off with a rickshaw ride out to **Bharat Mata Temple** 1.5 km (1 mile) south of Cantonment station where, instead of the usual images of gods and goddesses, there is a relief map of 'Mother India' engraved in marble. This temple was inaugurated by Mahatma Gandhi.

Sarnath (by bus, half-day)
Chowkandi Stupa–Archaeological Museum–Ashoka Pillar–Dhamekh Stupa–Mulagandhakuti Vihara

The ancient site of Sarnath, situated 10 km (6 miles) north of Varanasi, is a principal centre of Buddhism. It was here, around 530 BC, that the Buddha came from Bodhgaya after gaining enlightenment and preached his first sermon in the large garden known as Deer Park. This initial message of the 'Middle Way' (the path of moderation leading to *nirvana*) became the corner-stone of the Buddhist religion.

Sarnath probably gets its name from Saranganath, Lord of the Deer (one of the Buddha's titles) and was for long known simply as the Deer Park. From the remains of the famous **Dhamekh Stupa** here, originally a 31-m (100-ft) high memorial tower or *stupa*, it seems probable that the first monk communities came to the site around the 3rd century BC. Ashoka, the warlord turned man of peace, patronised Sarnath as a centre of the Buddhist religion and erected several magnificent stupas and buildings. Visiting Sarnath in AD 637, the Chinese pilgrim Hieun Tsiang described its structures as:

> In eight divisions, all enclosed within one wall with tiers of balconies and rows of halls, extremely artistic, inhabited by 1500 monks. Within the great enclosing wall was a temple above 61 metres high, surmounted by an embossed gilt *amra* (mango); in the brick portion above were more than 100 rows of niches, each containing a gilt image of the Buddha; inside the temple was a bellmetal image of the Buddha in the attitude of preaching, as large as life.

But as early as the 3rd century AD Buddhism had fallen into decline, the squabbles of the various splinter sects paving the way for its eventual reabsorption into the mainstream of Hindu faith and philosophy. The last of Sarnath's great monasteries, built by the devout Kumara Devi, Queen of Varanasi (1114–54), fell quick victim, along with the rest, to the Muslim invasions of the 12th and 17th centuries. Today, the ruins of Sarnath afford only a glimpse of the magnificent monastery of the Turning of the Wheel of Law described by visiting Chinese pilgrims.

The good conducted tour round Sarnath leaves from the tourist office daily (the alternative is to go there by local bus, regular departures from Varanasi station). It stops just before Sarnath at the modest **Chowkandi Stupa**. Buddhist stupas fall into three main categories: commemorative, relic and votive. This one commemorates the place of the Buddha's reunion with his five ascetic friends. They had earlier deserted him when he accepted milk from a cowherd's daughter, breaking his fast. The *stupa* is a simple redbrick octagonal structure, situated on a small hillock and erected by Akbar in the 16th century to mark an original 5th-century site.

Sarnath itself is a pleasant and peaceful place. A charming **Chinese Temple** opposite the bus-stand points the way to the outstanding **Archaeological Museum** (open 10 am to 5 pm, except Friday, admission Rs0.50). This houses several fine recoveries from the Sarnath ruins, notably the **Lion Capital** which originally surmounted the huge Ashoka Pillar. Adopted by free India as her state emblem, this well-preserved capital was carved from a single block of stone. It features four back-to-back lions, beneath which is a four-panel band. The panels have spirited sculptures of a lion (Buddha as 'lion king'), an elephant (Buddha's mother, Maya, dreamt of a white elephant before his birth), a horse (the one he rode away on, abandoning princely comforts to search for truth) and a bull. The base of the capital is an inverted lotus flower, symbolic of the seven lotus blossoms which sprang from the waters on Buddha's death. It was constructed, along with its ex-pillar, by Ashoka in the 3rd century BC. Most of the museum's exhibits—mainly Buddhas, 2 life-size Bodhisattvas, flowers and animals in carved sandstone—date from the Mauryan period of 3rd to 1st centuries BC, though there is also a selection of later Hindu images from the 9th to 12th centuries AD.

Sarnath's ruins are pretty ruined. Of the towering Ashoka Pillar only a short jagged shard remains. The inscription on it directs the community of monks to 'act in such a way that the *sangha* cannot be divided by anyone. Verily, that monk or nun who shall break up the *sangha* should be compelled to put on white robes and to reside in what is unfit for the residence of a recluse.'

Of the two magnificent ancient stupas for ceremonial public worship, only the Dhamekh remains standing (the other, the Dharmarajika, was dismantled in the 18th century by the Benares ruler Jagat Singh). The **Dhamekh Stupa** dates back to around AD 500, is 338 m (110 ft) high, and is covered with interesting swastika and floral motifs. It commemorates the spot where Buddha gave his first sermon. He delivered it to his five closest disciples, and in it he preached the doctrine of the four 'noble truths' (suffering is part of life, there is always a cause for suffering, suffering can be overcome, and there are eight righteous paths by which to achieve this).

Near the Dhamekh Stupa is a **Jain Temple**, built in the 19th century in honour of the 11th Jain tirthankar, Sriyansanath. Also nearby is the elegant **Mulagandhakuti Vihara**, erected by the Mahabodhi Society in 1931. This is a modern temple enshrining ancient relics. The silver casket within is said to house the original relics of the Buddha, as recovered from a 1st-century BC temple during a 19th-century archaeological dig. Consequently, it is a major Buddhist pilgrimage spot, second only in importance to the Bodhi tree at Bodhgaya. The interior has a series of frescoes, depicting scenes in the Buddha's life, painted by a famous Japanese artist. The main shrine has a graceful gold replica of the Buddha, modelled on an original 5th-century AD statue.

There is a **Tourist Bungalow** at Sarnath (tel 42002, 42515) rooms Rs50 single, Rs80 double for those who wish to stay here overnight.

Ramnagar

If there's time, the Sarnath tour bus continues on to **Ramnagar Fort** on the far bank of the Ganges, once the residence of the Maharajahs of Benares. The palace Durbar Hall has been converted into a rather dilapidated 'museum' (open 10 am to noon, 1 to 5 pm, admission Rs1) containing textiles, ivory coaches, duelling pistols, elephant-foot stools and moth-eaten tiger-skin rugs.

During the Dussehra festival each October the story of Lord Rama is retold in a traditional play, the *Ramlila* over a period of a month. The version enacted at Ramnagar is considered an important interpretaion of the story and if you are visiting Varanasi during this period it is worth spending an extra day to see an episode.

RECREATION

After a long, dusty day's touring, there's nothing to beat a cool dip in a luxury swimming-pool. The Taj Ganges and Clarks Varanasi hotels both have nice pools and can be used with temporary membership (about Rs50 per day).

Varanasi is home to some of India's best musicians. For details of upcoming recitals (and other entertainments), pick up a copy of *Northern Patrika* newspaper. Clarks Varanasi hotel offers good live music as part of its set buffet dinners. Apart from organised recitals it is occasionally possible to spend an informal evening with a group of musicians in their homes. This can sometimes be arranged through the front office of your hotel or through the local tourist office. Other than this, you're at the mercy of local rickshaw-men, who always happen to know of a music show going on locally.

SHOPPING

Varanasi's silks—brocades and cloth—have been famous for centuries. Even the Buddha, when a royal prince, is known to have valued them. Today, the world's finest dressmakers use Varanasi brocades for making elaborate garments. The most beautiful handwoven silk brocades are called *kinkhab*, and are exquisitely decorated with *kalabatun* (gold thread) and embellished with all-over designs of tiny motifs. All Varanasi's top products—saris, stoles and brocades—are individual works of art, accomplished by master weavers. Expect to pay accordingly.

There is a very wide price range for silk items. Cheap to moderate cushion-covers, wall-hangings, and bedspreads can be found but on the whole it is far better to splurge on something of real quality. The best *kinkhabs* are incredibly flashy and incredibly expensive—the ones incorporating real gold thread can cost up to Rs25 000, those with silver thread 'only' around Rs3000–5000.

In the absence of any decent government emporia, it can be very difficult to get a fix on what's available in Varanasi, and how much it should cost. This makes tourists very vulnerable to the onslaughts of persistent, smooth-talking operators whose 'uncle' always has a silk shop. This is a major problem in Varanasi and the only way to avoid it is to make up your mind exactly what you want, where you're going to look for it, and how much you're prepared to spend. Be quite firm with anybody who tries to change your mind.

If you must visit a particular shop (generally a bad idea), try **J. Aurora**, 42 Cantonment, next to the tourist office (tel 43796). At least you get a free cup of tea and no hassle to buy. This place sells nice ethnic jewellery and wonderful Turkish-style 'folk' rugs and dhurries at low prices. Also inexpensive batiks, wall-hangings, cushion-covers and silk materials.

Far better than shops, since you can compare prices and bargain better, are the bazaars of the old city. The central Chowk Bazaar, which runs between (and behind) the two main burning ghats, is good for everything—especially silk saris (from around Rs400), silk by the metre (from Rs160), beautiful carved walking sticks, cheap ready-made cotton clothes and wooden toys. At night, the atmosphere here is electric. For better-quality silk, try Satti Bazaar, and for ornamental brass work (Varanasi's other speciality) the Thetary Bazaar. For fabulous glass bangles (often lacquered, between Rs20 and Rs100 per set) and other ornamental/novelty items, the city market around the Golden Temple is best.

When shopping in Varanasi, apply the 'burning test' on p.221 to tell real silk from common 'banana' cotton-silk. Also, steer clear of any so-called Moradabad brass which does not show a good pink colour, denoting high copper content. If possible, spend a whole day looking around, comparing quality and price of all produce, before buying anything.

Although the items on sale are mainly Kashmiri the **CIE** shop at the **Mint House** is worth visiting in order to see the building. The Mint house was established by James Princep in 1820–21 when he was appointed Mint Master by the East india Company.

WHERE TO STAY

Expensive (Over US$35/Rs1000 per room night)
In high season, Varanasi's few luxury hotels are constantly full, and you'll need to advance-book. In low season (April–June) both the Clarks and Ashok hotels offer

attractive 20–30% discounts. All the top hotels are conveniently located near the rail station, in the new Cantonment area. The most expensive one, **Hotel Taj Ganges** (tel 42480, tlx 545-219 TAGA IN, fax 0542-322067), is a friendly place with good food, nice pool, and rooms at US$49 single, US$75 double. Many people, however, favour the well-established **Clarks Varanasi** (tel 46771, tlx 0545-204) on the Mall. This pleasant old-fashioned hotel has been recently renovated to look brand-new. Centrally air-conditioned, it has a relaxing pool, chummy staff, snug bar, and probably the best Chinese food in town. Standard single/double rooms are Rs1200/1750, but ask for one of the delightful old-block garden rooms. Somewhat underrated, ITDC's **Hotel Varanasi Ashok** (tel 46020, tlx 0545-205 ITDC IN), is a cut above the usual government-run luxury hotel. Bright-white stucco interior, and rooms with balcony and river-view. Singles Rs1000, doubles Rs1200. Useful travel agency in lobby, handy airport coach service.

Mid-range (US$10–35/Rs250–1000 per room night)
Many of the mid-range hotels are concentrated in the Lahurabir area, between the rail station and Gowdolia bus-stand. Choose from **Diamond Hotel**, Bhelupura (tel 310696), **Gautam Hotel**, Ramkatora (tel 44015), and the newish **Pradeep Hotel** (tel 66363) at Jagatganj. Room prices vary between Rs200–250 single, Rs250–400 double with air-conditioning. All three places are well-run and friendly, though the Diamond and Gautam certainly have the best food. Other properties in this range include the spacious **Hotel de Paris** (tel 46601, tlx 0545-323), located in the Cantonment with an extensive garden and large rooms from Rs450. In the bazaar the **Pallavi International** (tel 54894, 56939), Hathwa Market, Chetganj has air-conditioned rooms from Rs375 single, Rs450 double.

Budget (Under US$10/Rs250 per room night)
Varanasi has a glut of cheap budget lodges/hotels, which are changing all the time. In the Cantonment area the **Tourist Dak Bungalow** on the Mall with a pleasant garden and camping facilities has rooms from Rs125. Also in the Cantonment area the **Hotel India**, 59 Patel Nagar (another nice garden, rooms at Rs100) and **Hotel Surya**, behind Clarks Hotel (popular, quiet rooms at Rs100). Near the rail station **Hotel Blue Star** is popular, with good information and food. Rooms are from Rs70, and you'll want one at the back, away from the noisy main street. More out of the way (halfway between station and ghats) is **Hotel Garden View**, Sigra Crossing, Vidyapeth Rd. Nice clean rooms from Rs65 single, Rs90 double; good information and travel/tour service; decent restaurant although service is erratic. Down in the old city/ghats area—where the bulk of shoestring travellers stay—there are a wealth of cheap and often dirty places huddled round the Vishvanath Temple, or overlooking the Ganges from the various ghats. **Trimurti Lodge** has a couple of 3rd-floor rooms directly overlooking the Temple. Close by is **Sri Venkateshwar Lodge** with a pleasant courtyard, very genial manager, and quiet rooms. Two recommended riverside places are **Shankeri Tourist Lodge** a nice old house at Mir Ghat, with friendly people, great food, big double rooms; and **Tandon Lodge**, near Gai Ghat, with good-value rooms. Both these places offer marvellous views over the Ganges.

EATING OUT
For a big night out, go to **Hotel Clarks Varanasi**. The Indian restaurant here lays on very special buffet dinners—with great live music thrown in from 7.30 to 10.30 pm

daily (Rs125). **Hotel Taj Ganges** probably has the best Indian food in town but it is more expensive. For Chinese fare, check out the **Chinese Mandarin Restaurant** next to Tourist Bungalow (near rail station) or the friendly **Chinese Garden** next to the Cantonment tourist office. They're both quite cheap (Rs50). For mid-range Indian/Continental cuisine, try **Diamond Hotel** in Bhelupura. Less expensive food at **Tulasi Restaurant** (vegetarian) or at Pradeep Hotel's **Poonam Restaurant** (Indo-Chinese), both in Lahurabir area. Down by the ghats, the better budget restaurants are conveniently (inevitably) close to the better budget lodges. **Street View Restaurant** is near Tandon Lodge, Sudha Hotel's **Ajanta Cafe** and (opposite) **Ayaars Cafe** are both near Shankheri Lodge, and **Sindhi Restaurant**. All these places do good, reliable Indian-style snacks.

GENERAL INFORMATION
Government of India Tourist Office, 15B The Mall, Cantonment (tel 43744) is good for information, hires out guides for the old city, and runs decent sightseeing tours where you spend more time at sights than in shops. Morning tours cover sunrise at the Ganges, river trip, temples, Benares University (5.30 am to noon); afternoon tours cover Sarnath and Ramnagar Fort (2 pm to 6 pm). The Tourist Office can also help guide you to any music recitals that might be taking place.

Indian Airlines is at Mint House Motel, opposite Nandesar Palace, Cantonment (tel 44537, 45959); other office at Babatpur Airport (tel 142, 62411). State Bank of India has branches at Varanasi Ashok Hotel (tel 46020) and Varuna Bridge, also at airport.

Post office is at Bisheswarganj, in Kotwali area. There's a good parcel-packing service outside it. Good travel agent is Travel Bureau (tel 46771) in Clarks Hotel, useful for air, rail and bus bookings. The well-stocked Nandi bookshop in Ashok Hotel has a wide range of fiction and non-fiction titles, also nice postcards. There is a locally printed map of the ghats, available in most hotel bookshops.

Route 2—Rajasthan

Exotic 'Land of Princes', Rajasthan is a barren desert territory—dotted with battle-scarred forts and palaces—whose harsh climate and rough terrain gave birth to a proud, warrior people of legendary courage and valour. Over the centuries, the Rajput chieftains resisted all and any foreign invaders, and whenever faced by certain defeat invariably preferred glorious death to ignoble surrender. But martial traditions coexisted with love of colour, culture and pageantry—and today Rajasthan is just as famous for its gardens and lakes, festivals and handicrafts as for its fortress theatres of war. It's also the only state where one feels compelled to learn some Hindi—the proud Rajputs often won't speak to you in English. Once the ice is broken, however, they are among the friendliest and most hospitable people in India. You'll love them.

The bustling state capital of Jaipur is most often classed as the third city of India's Golden Triangle but is in fact the entry point to a large and fascinating state. The towering fort of Jodhpur, with the finest palace museum in the country, leads out to the rolling dunes of the Great Thar Desert, where you can take camel-safaris from Khuri village. The medieval mystery of Jaisalmer, a desert city of filigree merchants' houses, Jain temples and charming bazaars, gives way to cool, refined elegance at Udaipur, a famous 'lake city' of charming gardens and palaces. The sole hill station of the state, Mount Abu, is famous for its sunsets and its Dilwara temples—the most exquisite examples of Jain architecture in the country. Nearby Chittorgarh, 'City of Valour', is the fortress site of the Rajputs' most glorious hour. Finally there's Pushkar, a peaceful oasis in the desert, with one of the few temples to Brahma in India, and where pilgrims and travellers gather to pray, to relax, to simply hang out.

Season: October to March.
Climate: 17° to 45°C (summer); 7° to 32° C (winter).
Monsoons: July to September.
Route duration: 14 to 21 days (but very easy to stay longer).

TRAVEL ITINERARY

Delhi to Jaipur 261 km (164 miles)

Air
Two flights daily (IC491/493) Rs646.

Rail
The *Pink City Express* leaves Delhi Station at 6 am reaching Jaipur at 11.05 am. Other trains operate throughout the day and take 5–6 hours.

Road
Rajasthan State Transport buses leave Bikaner House near India Gate every 1–2 hours from 6 am to 9 pm every day. Other buses operate from New Delhi's Interstate Bus Terminal.

Jaipur to Jodhpur 332 km (208 miles)

Air
Two flights daily—IC491/493 (Rs767). Both originate in Delhi. At Jodhpur airport, it's Rs50 by taxi or Rs20 by auto-rickshaw into the city (5 km).

Rail
The *Jodhpur Mail* daily from Delhi—dep 8.30 pm, arr 11.05 am. is quick and reliable. From Jaipur the *Mandore Express* departs at 11.45 pm (it originates in Delhi at 6 pm) and arrives the following morning at 6.05 pm.

Jodhpur to Jaisalmer 287 km (179 miles)

Air
Three Vayudoot flights a week—Tuesday, Thursday, Saturday—PF117, are scheduled but seats are rarely available and the flights often cancelled. Vayudoot bookings through Mayur Travels, Kalyan Singh Building, Sojati Gate (tel 20909).

Rail

Overnight sleeper—dep 10.45 pm, arr 7 am—is the most comfortable option (day trains very hot, dusty and dull). Essential to reserve tickets as soon as you reach Jodhpur, from the excellent Tourist Assistance Booth (open 5 am to 11 pm daily) on the station platform. It has a tourist quota of tickets. It also has good information, baggage store, easy chairs, air-cooling, free use of fridge, and free high-pressure showers. On the journey to Jaisalmer, watch your belongings—there's always a thief or two aboard this night train.

Bus

One bus daily (dep 1.30 pm, arr 9 pm) from Raika Bagh bus-stand, 3 km (1¾ miles) from Jodhpur rail station. It's something to consider when (and this does happen) the train is cancelled.

Jaisalmer to Khuri 45 km (28 miles)

Road

Shared taxi from rail station into Jaisalmer town. Head straight for the Collectorate office (see p. 179) for your Khuri permit. Then catch the 10.30 am bus (1½ hours) to Khuri, from bus-stand just outside the fort walls, near Trio Restaurant. To ensure a seat on this (one and only) bus, turn up 10 am latest. Later, you can climb on the roof for cool breezes and good views.

Khuri to Jaisalmer 45 km (28 miles)

Road

One bus daily, leaving at 4.30 pm. Khuri villagers make sure you catch it.

Jaisalmer to Jodhpur 287 km (179 miles)

Air

Three flights a week—Tuesday, Thursday, Saturday—on Vayudoot PF118. These flights continue on to Jaipur and Delhi. For bookings, contact Vayudoot's office in Mangla Hotel, near Bank of Baroda, Jaisalmer.

Rail

The overnight sleeper—dep 9.15 pm, arr 7 am—is best. Most Jaisalmer landlords handle reservations. Two tips—first, there are no refreshments at stations to Jodhpur, so take lots of oranges, food and water; second, get off at Raika Bagh Palace Junction, 2 km (1½ miles) before Jodhpur Central station, if you want the tourist office, the Tourist Bungalow, or the bus-station (i.e. to advance-book an onward bus to Udaipur).

Road

Two buses daily—at 5 am and 4 pm (8 hours). The earlier bus is the cooler, comfier option.

Jodhpur to Udaipur 275 km (172 miles)

Air
One flight daily—IC491 (Rs767). Quick, dull. It's an expensive Rs100 taxi ride from Udaipur airport into town (25 km).

Rail
Regular trains daily—but few people take them. They're 4 hours slower than the bus.

Road
One express bus (7 hours), leaving Jodhpur's Raika Bagh bus-stand (near Tourist Bungalow) at 5.30 am daily. No advance reservations possible—when the bus arrives, simply toss your bags through the window to 'reserve' your seat, then buy your ticket.

This early bus makes an unmissable stop at **Ranakpur**, for some of the biggest and best Jain temples in India. Do spend some time here. You'll arrive from Jodhpur at 10 am, and can cover Ranakpur's temples at leisure before catching the 1 pm or 3.15 pm buses on to Udaipur. Still better, stay overnight at Ranakpur (at the budget *dharamsala*, the mid-range RTDC Tourist Bungalow, or the plush Maharani Bagh Orchard Retreat), and see the sights in the cool of the morning. Later on, when the heat gets up, you'll have to hot-foot it round the temples—footwear isn't allowed in any of them. Ranakpur's temples are beautifully preserved, and compare favourably with Mt Abu's Dilwara group. See the three temples outside the main complex first. The central temple is open to non-Jains from 11 am only. It has 1440 columns, no two the same, and is absolutely fantastic. Admission is free, and you can photograph anything except Jain deities.

There are a few slower buses from Jodhpur to Udaipur at 7.30 am, 3 pm and 10.30 pm. If carrying straight on to Pushkar, there are hourly buses from Jodhpur to Ajmer.

Udaipur to Mt Abu 185 km (116 miles)

Road
One deluxe bus daily, dep 8 am, arr 12.30 pm. Book from Taldar Travels (tel 28160), opposite Town Hall, Highway No. 8, Udaipur. Ordinary public buses to Abu (from Udaipur's ST bus-stand) are much slower and give their passengers slipped discs.

Udaipur to Chittorgarh 98 km (61 miles)

Air
From Udaipur, IC492 flies daily to Jodhpur (Rs583), Jaipur (Rs767) and Delhi (Rs1129).

Road
One express bus on to Chittorgarh (dep 8.30 am and 1.30 pm, arr 12.30 pm and 4.30 pm respectively) from Udaipur bus-stand. Journey is both pretty, and pretty uncomfortable.

Chittorgarh to Pushkar 198 km (124 miles)

Road
Hourly deluxe buses to Ajmer (4½ hours, from Chittor's RTC bus-stand, below the Fort; then Rs5 cycle-rickshaw from Ajmer bus-stand to rail station; from here, half-hourly buses up to Pushkar (30 minutes). The Chittor/Ajmer run, be warned, is one of the most dangerous stretches of road in India.

Pushkar to Delhi 371 km (232 miles)

Road
One express bus daily—dep 10.15 am, arr 6.15 pm—from Marwar bus-stand (nr Pushkar post office). This is the cheap 'pilgrim special', complete with noisy videos, delirious passengers, and a holy mission to reach Hardwar (its eventual destination) as soon as possible. Have some prayers of your own ready. Or take a slower, more relaxing deluxe bus instead. These leave from the Ajmer bus-stand (nr Pushkar Hotel) at 7.15 am and 7.45 am daily.

Pushkar also has daily buses to Ajmer (30 minutes), to Jaipur (3 hours), to Udaipur (8 hours) and to Jodhpur (8 hours). Ajmer has quick hourly buses to Jodhpur (5 hours), and good rail connections to Delhi, Agra, Jaipur, Ahmedabad and Udaipur. All bus/rail timings are posted at the Pushkar Hotel. If stuck in Ajmer overnight, stay at the Tourist Bungalow—it's adequate.

CONTINUATIONS
From Udaipur, you can fly to Aurangabad (IC491 daily, Rs1221) for the Maharashtra route. From Mt Abu, there's a nippy 6½-hour express bus down to Ahmedabad, for the overnight *Gurdinar Express* to Veraval/Diu in Gujarat. The 6 am or 7 am bus from Abu is best—make the reservation desk in Ahmedabad station before 2 pm closing. From Pushkar/Ajmer, there are many buses and trains to Jaipur.

JAIPUR

Surrounded on three sides by the rugged Aravali hills, Jaipur is the picturesque capital of Rajasthan. It takes its name from the prince, soldier and astronomer Jai Singh II, who moved his capital here in 1727. The old capital, Amber (or Amer), had long been a stronghold of Rajput power, but had become too cramped at its mountain site. Although it had been attacked by various rulers of Delhi the Kachhwaha rulers were secure in the Jaigarh fort. When the Mughals arrived Maharajah Mansingh (the then ruler of Amber) guaranteed the safety of his kingdom on becoming a general and minister in Akbar's court and by giving his sister to the Emperor in marriage. With his new position and wealth Man Singh built the imposing fort-palace of Amber below the earlier fort. But the Kachhwahas of Amber were seen by other Rajput rulers as having sold out, a blot on her record which transferred to Jaipur, and which time has not erased.

Jai Singh built Jaipur as a planned city. It is divided into seven rectangular blocks, built on a grid of nine squares as detailed in the *Shilpa Shastra*, an ancient Hindu architectural treatise. The broad well-laid-out main streets (33.8 m: 110 ft wide) cut the side lanes at sharp right-angles. The entire city is encircled by fortified, crenellated walls, and guarded by seven gates.

An attraction of Jaipur is its distinctive pink-orange colouring. The whole of the old city, including many fine palaces and buildings, was constructed from solid blocks of sandstone or faced with the same stone. But it was only in 1853, when Prince Albert visited and the city was painted pink for the first time that it gained its famous title of the 'Pink City'. The soft glow of its buildings and monuments, most magical at sunset, have fascinated visitors for over two centuries.

Jaipur is the real gateway to Rajasthan. Though a very busy, commercial capital, the underlying Rajput spirit stubbornly lives on. The traditional dress, decoration and colour can be seen everywhere—the station porters in bright red turbans and jackets, the veiled women in loose-flowing robes of red, orange and yellow, the tiny *khol*-eyed infants in swaddling clothes of rich, embroidered silk. Inside the old city, the atmosphere is electric—a bustling, jolly round of ringing bicycle bells, teeming traffic, itinerant sacred cows, busy bazaars and tourist-hungry rickshaws.

Situated on the plains, Jaipur gets pretty hot. Coolest from October to February, busiest and most popular from January to March, it remains pleasant to mid-April (not too hot but less crowded). Two important dates for your diary are the Elephant Festival just before Holi in March and the spring festival of Gangaur in March/April which culminates on the 17th day after Holi when the Goddess Gauri (Parvati) is paraded from the City Palace and through the city streets. The Teej festival during early August is an important festival for local women and celebrates the monsoon.

ARRIVAL/DEPARTURE

Air
Indian Airlines has daily flights between Jaipur and Ahmedabad (Rs1083), Aurangabad (Rs1221), Bombay (Rs1848), Delhi (Rs646), Jodhpur (Rs767), and Udaipur (Rs767). Flights to Agra operate during the winter months. There is also a flight to and from Calcutta via Varanasi.

In August 1992 East West Airlines started a daily Boeing 737 service between Bombay and Jaipur each evening (flight no 4S 767/8). The Jaipur office tel 512961.

Jaipur airport is a long 14 km (8¾ miles) out of town—Rs20 by airport bus, Rs90 by taxi.

Rail
There are daily trains between Jaipur and Agra and Delhi, and to Jodhpur (7 hours). From Delhi the *Pink City Express* leaves Delhi Station (Old Delhi) at 6 am reaching Jaipur at 11.05 am. The return departs Jaipur at 5 pm arriving in Delhi at 10.10 pm. The *Pink City* continues to Ahmedabad via Ajmer, Jodhpur and Abu Road. The *Chetak Express* to Udaipur also stops at Jaipur and Ajmer. There are numerous other trains, many of them slower, throughout the day and night. The 22dn *Superfast Express* departs from Agra fort station at 5 pm, arriving in Jaipur at 10 pm. It returns from Jaipur at 6.10 am daily. Advance-booking is necessary in both directions—this is a popular train.

Road
Deluxe buses link Jaipur with Delhi (5 hours, 259 km: 162 miles), Agra (5 hours–237 km: 148 miles), Udaipur (9 hours), Jaisalmer (14 hours), Jodhpur (7 hours), Ajmer

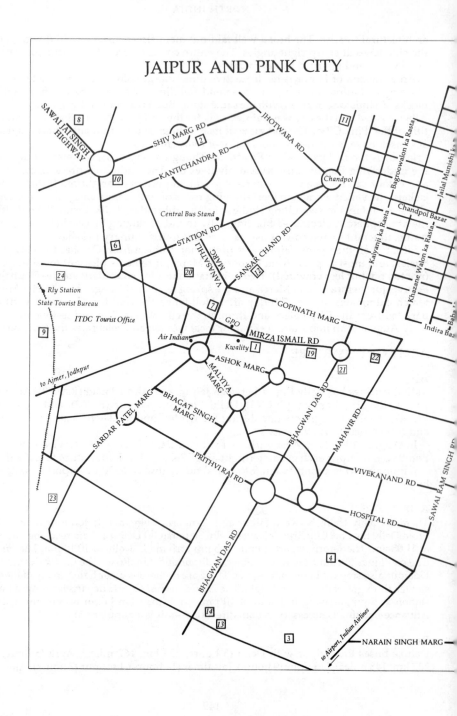

• Gaitor

To Amber 11 Kms

Gobind Devji Temple

Nahargarh Fort Rd

Gangauri Bazar

Jalebi
Chowk

City Palace & Museum

Hawa Mahal Bazar

[16]

Jantar
Mantar

Jantar Mantar

Chhoti
Chaupar

Isarlat

Tripolia Gate

Hawa
Mahal

Tripolia Bazar

Ghora Nikas Rd

Badi
Chaupar

Gopalji ka Rasta

Ram Ganj Bazar

Kishan Pol Bazar

Chaura Rasta

Haldion ka Rasta

Ramganj
Chaupar

Johari Bazar

[5]

Surajpol Bazar

Nehru Bazar

Bapu Bazar

Ghat Darvaja Bazar

Pahar Ganj ka Rasta

Elephant Owners Area

[18]

Rasta Balaji ki Kothi

AGRA RD

[17]

Zoo

To Agra

[15]

LAL NEHRU MARG

MOTI DOONGARI RD

Govt. of Rajasthan
Tourist Office

N

Miles 0   1
Km   0   1½

Key

Hotels
1 Evergreen
2 Jaipur Inn
3 Rambagh Palace
4 Lakshmi Vilas
5 L.M.B.
6 Teej Tourist Bungalow
7 Mansingh Hotel
8 Megh Niwas
9 Jai Mahal
10 Jaipur Ashok
11 Bissau Palace
12 Arya Niwas
Miscellaneous
13 Golf Club
14 Polo Club
15 Central Museum
16 City Museum
17 Modern Art Gallery & Ravindra Rangmanch
18 Rajasthan Govt. Handicrafts
19 Central Cottage Industries
20 Sita World Travel
21 Raj Mandir Cinema
22 Niro's Restaurant
23 Raj Mahal Palace
24 Welcomgroup Rajputana Palace

(regular service, 2½ hours) and Kotah. These must be booked a day in advance, at the Tourist Information Booth, Platform 3, Sindhi Camp bus-stand, Jaipur. Cheaper, slower express buses are bookable from Ashok Travels, next to ITDC Tourist Office. Traffic along the main Delhi–Jaipur highway and on to Ajmer is becoming increasingly heavy and the journeys are often delayed by truck accidents *en route*.

CONTINUATIONS
From Jaipur, you can join the **Rajasthan circuit** either at Ajmer (by bus or train) or at Jodhpur (by bus 7 hours; by train 10 hours; or by IC491/493 daily flights).

WHAT TO SEE
Jaipur is divided into the 'old' city, with its many sights enclosed behind high pink-sandstone walls; and the modern commercial 'new' city (many hotels, bus and rail stations, the tourist office) which has grown up to the south. Most visitors stay in the new town—it's much quieter and far less humid. Cycles are a good way of getting round (Jaipur has some of India's best paved roads) and can be hired for Rs10–15 per day from many places, including the rank outside the rail station. Auto-rickshaws don't have meters. You'll have to bargain hard for a fair fare, and as often as not, you'll end up at a gem or carpet shop instead of your required destination. Taxis have meters, but rarely use them. Cycle-rickshaws are cheap (around Rs1/50km) and slow, and their drivers talk business constantly. Local buses, if you can handle them, are far less trouble. They are especially useful for visiting Amber Fort. Cars can be hired from most hotels at fixed rates for half or a full day.

To cover the main sights, and fit in some shopping, you'll need two full days in Jaipur. Plus an extra day to recover. Sightseeing is most comfortable by RTDC's *morning* conducted tour, but does not include the Central Museum which is closed on Friday. Full-day tours are very tiring, not recommended. Both RTDC and ITDC tours start from the rail station, and pick up from Teej and Gangaur Tourist Bungalows.

City Tour (by tour bus, morning)
Nawab Sahib Ki Haveli–Hawa Mahal–Amber Palace–Gaitor–
Jantar Mantar–City Palace and Museum

This tour starts in the heart of the old city, at the high 18th-century merchant's house called **Nawab Sahib Ki Haveli**. The remarkable panoramic views of the whole city from its vantage-point roof-top terraces make it the ideal introduction to Jaipur (but have the exact Rs5 entrance fee ready: they never have change). From here, you can look down onto bicycle-infested Tripolia Bazaar, the wide central avenue which cuts right through old Jaipur, starting at Surajpol Bazaar at one end and finishing at Chand Pol Bazaar at the other. Look over to **Jai Singh's Observatory**, the **Clock Tower**, the **Jai Mahal**, the **City Palace** and, up on the hill opposite is **Nahargarh** or Tiger Fort once Jai Singh's treasury. This is also a good place to appreciate the unique city-planning of Jaipur: all those symmetrical main streets, neatly intersected by little narrow side-roads. There's a clear guide service at the Haveli, followed by a charming roof-top puppet show.

Just down the road, at the junction of Tripolia Bazaar and Siredeori Rd, is the high pyramidal façade of **Hawa Mahal**. This famous landmark of Jaipur, nicknamed

'Palace of Winds' (the cool westerly winds blow through it), was built by Pratap Singh in 1799. It comprises five storeys of semi-octagonal overhanging windows, with domes and spires. From the windows, the ladies of the court used to view the city below. There's a modest museum behind the façade, with a good 'Jaipur Past and Present' exhibition. Open 10 am to 4.30 pm daily (except Fridays), entrance Rs1 (free on Mondays).

Leaving the pink city by the Zorawar Gate, it's an 11 km (7 mile) journey north to the old capital of **Amber**, with its majestic hilltop fortress. Local buses ply back and forth there from the Hawa Mahal, at 15-minute intervals (fare Rs1). About halfway to Amber, look out for Pratap Singh's cream-yellow **Water Palace** (Jal Mahal). The vast rainwater reservoirs are now often dry, and visitors aren't allowed in.

Amber Palace has a spectacular location, built below the older Jaigarh Fort, overlooking the **Moata Lake**, surrounded by a wide ring of craggy watchtowers and fortifications. The Jaigarh Fort itself dates back to the 11th century. An elegantly harmonious construction, it is most beautiful at dawn and dusk, when it glows with a yellow, luminous quality. To reach Jaigarh, take the turning to the left soon after passing the Jal Mahal and follow the road up the hill. Entry to the fort costs Rs6 and it is open from 9 am to 4.30 pm.

At Amber, you can either walk up to the Fort via the narrow, cobbled path (10–15 minutes), or you can take the popular (but overpriced) elephant-ride. If you walk it, there's a perfectly adequate elephant-ride round the *chowk* (square) at the top but you will have to bargain hard. Below the fort, just over the small bridge, there's a place to hire boats on Moata Lake, although in recent years there has been insufficient rain to keep the lake more than a quarter full.

Up at the fort, pass through the main entrance gate (**Suraj Pol**) and enter the small, busy square with its monkey-infested banyan tree, colourful spice stalls, and rank of elephants. Proceed up to the left for the visit to **Kalimata Temple**, constantly full of jostling pilgrims. This temple, with its silver doors, beautiful carved pillars and walls, contains an image of Shila Devi brought here by the grateful Maharajah Man Singh from East Bengal, following his successful defeat of the warlord Kedar in 1604.

If here on your own, hire a guide from near the elephant rank, Rs20. Otherwise, follow the tour into the palace (entrance Rs6) with the Mughal influenced **Diwan-i-Am** to the left of the courtyard. From the courtyard enter the private quarters of the palace via the ornate **Ganesh Pol** (Elephant Gate), a façade of colourful frescoes constructed by Jai Singh in 1639. Beyond the gate is the inner court with the royal apartments, a glittering array of mosaic, marble and mirrors, all grouped around a central ornamental garden. The main attraction is the showpiece **Sheesh Mahal** or Mirror Palace, built by Jai Singh. The exterior is a studded jewel-box of polished mirror fragments, set in plaster. Within, glass mosaic panels and highly ornamented plaster reliefs, inlaid with glass and marble carvings, vie for attention. Pass stained-glass windows to lookout points, affording fine views down over the lake and old palaces.

Proceed next to the magical **Chamber of Mirrors**, which used to be the Maharajah's bedroom. The whole ceiling is a glitter of tiny mirrors which, when illuminated by the guide's candle, produces a spectacular illusion of a galaxy of stars traversing a night-black sky.

Above the Jai Mandir is a cool pavilion, the **Jas Mahal**, from which there are good views over Amber town, the lake and palace.

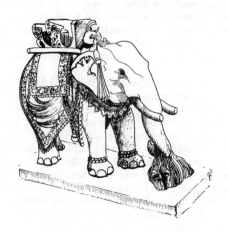

Stone elephant, Jaipur City Palace

Across the formal garden is the **Sukh Niwas,** or Hall of Pleasure. The main chamber has decorative relief work in plaster and a marble cascade to the rear. Together with the breeze passing through its perforated marble screen, this water cascade served as a cooling device during the summer. The pavilion doors still retain some of the original ivory and sandalwood inlay work. On the way out, steal a minute or two to appreciate the beautiful gardens.

From Amber, the tour returns to town via **Gaitor,** the royal cremation ground. This site, located some 8 km (5 miles) out of Jaipur, contains a number of elegant chhatris or cenotaphs of various kings and queens. The white marble structure of Jai Singh II, with its intricately carved dome and 20 supporting pillars, is the most beautiful. Members of the royal family, mainly the ladies, are still cremated at Gaitor, a new cenotaph being erected for each fresh casualty.

Back in the walled city of Jaipur enter the precincts of the City Palace covering one-seventh of the original city's area. Begin with a visit to Jai Singh's most interesting legacy, the **Jantar Mantar** observatory. The starstruck young ruler first conceived the idea in 1718, and sent out scholars to study foreign observatories in Britain, Greece, Arabia and Portugal and gather information. An experimental prototype at Delhi (1724) was followed by others at Ujjain, Benares and Mathura. Then, in 1728, he realised his dream of India's greatest astronomical observatory here at Jaipur. It is the largest of the series, and has the unique *Rashi Valaya* instrument in which Jai Singh himself used to sit to make his observations.

Renovated in 1901, this strange collection of surreal, yellow-sandstone sculptures each has a specific astronomical function, be it to measure the sun's declination, azimuth or altitude, or to determine eclipses or the declination of fixed stars and planets. The tall sundial, with its 30-m (97-ft) high gnomon, is the most notable instrument. It casts a shadow which moves some 4 m (13 ft) each hour, giving the time down to 2-second accuracy—though only, of course, when the sun is shining. Hours are 9 am to 5 pm daily. Entry is Rs1, free on Mondays.

154

From the observatory enter the **City Palace,** an imposing blend of traditional Rajasthani and Mughal architecture. Some of the buildings within the Palace have become the Sawai Man Singh II Museum. The first building is the two-storey **Mubarak Mahal** the first floor of which now contains the Textile and Costume Museum. To the north-west of the courtyard is the Arms and Armour Gallery with an impressive array of weapons. From the first courtyard enter a second area passing through an impressive gateway, the *Singh Pole*, with huge doors covered in patterned brass. In the Hall of Private Audience, **Diwan-i-Khas** (complete with antique carpets and chandeliers which are unrolled and unbagged for holy festivals) facing the gateway, are two huge silver urns built for Sawai Madhu Singh in 1902 to carry water from the River Ganga on his visit to London for Edward VII's coronation.

Through a small portrait gallery to the north of the Diwan-i-Khas, watched over by a Chinese Buddha, you come out into the spacious courtyard. Here dancing used to take place, watched by the Maharanis in the balconies above. The seven-storey Chandra Mahal is today the home of the present Maharajah and his family. The ground floor is open to the public and leads onto a lawn with the 356 fountains still in working order, which perfectly complement the beautiful gardens. So do the green, violet and red chandeliers and the plain marble doors leading off the mosaic courtyard.

The Art Gallery and main Museum are housed in the Hall of Public Audience to the south-east of the inner courtyard. The gallery has some of India's largest and richest carpets, most of them from Herat (Afghanistan) and Lahore (Pakistan). Several date back to AD 1625 and the largest is 18 m (58 ft) long. Also in this section are a collection of ivory elephant howdahs, and the second largest chandelier (Czech) in the country. The art gallery is famous for its Jaipur and Mughal miniature paintings, and for its 20 000 handwritten Sanskrit manuscripts (only a few on show—you'll have to ask if you want to see more).

The palace and museum are open 9.30 am to 4.45 pm daily (art gallery closed Sundays). Entrance is Rs6 (half-price for students and teachers).

For most people, this will be quite sufficient for one day. The afternoons are often sticky and hot, and are best spent relaxing or at the pool. Dusk is the time to venture forth again, either for rowing round Moata Lake and enjoying the sunset at Amber Fort, or for climbing the huge sundial at Jantar Mantar to see an equally fine sunset over the pink city.

In town, one final sight not to be missed is the **Central Museum** (Albert Hall). It forms part of the sprawling **Ram Niwas Garden** in the new city (10 minutes' walk down Chaurasta, off Tripolia Bazaar), which is also the site of a modest **Zoo**. The museum's **Durbar Hall** was built in 1887, a pleasant blend of Oriental and Victorian architecture, and houses a vast collection of portraits, miniatures, works of art (top floor) and costumes, woodwork, brassware, jewellery and pottery (bottom floor).

RECREATION

Jaipur has the best sports facilities Rajasthan can offer. It is most famous for polo (elephant, horse, camel, even bicycle polo!) and most big hotels can arrange a game. Spring is the polo season: five major tournaments are held here between January and March.

For horse-riding the **Rambagh Palace Hotel** can arrange horses of mixed calibre.

Go swimming at the Rambagh's heavenly indoor swimming-pool—it's well worth the Rs60 non-resident fee, especially during the mid-afternoon 'quiet time'. Two other hotels with good pools are the Khasa Kothi, near the rail station and the Mansingh.

Fishing is possible at Ramgarh Lake 30 km (19 miles) away but poor monsoons in recent years have led to a reduction in the level of the lake; permits from Gangaur Tourist Bungalow (tel 74373). Most major hotels can arrange tennis, squash and good sports activities.

For cultural shows and entertainments, buy a *Rajasthan Echo* (for current programmes) or visit Ravendra Manch, near Albert Hall. Jaipur has one of India's best cinemas—the Raj Mandir. A few others, like the Prem Prakash and the Mayur, show English matinees at 10 am on Sundays.

SHOPPING

Jaipur is a shopper's paradise, even for Indian people. They come here from all over the country, to buy tie-and-dye *bandhini* bed linen, handwoven blankets, *dhurrie*, mirror-inlaid bangles, enamelled and blue pottery, gold and silver jewellery. Most of these things can be bought at reasonable prices at the many bazaars south of the old city, or at the several shops in Mirza Ismail (M.I.) and Agra Roads. Bapu Bazaar and Nehru Bazaar are where to buy textiles, local perfumes and camel-skin shoes (Bapu closed Sunday, Nehru Monday), and Johari Bazaar is the best place to window-shop for jewellery (here live most of the city's silversmiths, goldsmiths and jewellers), to find traditional tie-and-dye saris and textiles, and to buy practically anything at much cheaper prices than high-street shops (closed Sunday, and Tuesday afternoons). Before hitting the markets though, make a visit to Rajasthan Government Handicrafts Emporium in M.I. Rd. This is a fixed-price place, open 8 am to 8 pm daily, where you see what's available and how much it should cost. In a town like Jaipur, where hordes of tourists are ripped off daily, an hour or two spent here could save you a lot of money!

Jaipur's best buys are gems and jewellery. This city is one of the centres of the jewellery industry in India, and attracts dealers from all over the world. Sapphires, emeralds, rubies, diamonds and every other kind of precious and semi-precious stone sell at a fraction of what they fetch when they get to Cartier or Tiffany. Gems are still mined in India, but roughstones are brought here to be processed from all over the world, because the craftsmen here can get a better yield. They examine and sort roughstones into three main categories: the clearest, finest stones, which are cut and polished into gems; the second-grade stones, which are made into necklaces and bracelets; and the lowest-quality which are generally ground down into powder, to furnish durable mineral paints and dyes for textiles and miniature paintings.

Jaipur has hundreds of gem 'factories', most of them located in the Parganj area of the old city (near Suraj Old Gate). These factories are usually small household concerns, run by families who polish and hand-cut the gems, then deliver them to the 'big man' who oversees each area. The workers are generally children, who start their apprenticeship at about age 8 and are fully skilled by about 20. Watching them at work is a fascinating experience. To produce small gems, they glue the rough stone to the end of a long cane, which enables them to manoeuvre it easily while they use an electric rotating wheel to cut in the faces. To produce the facets on larger stones, they use a manual cutting-machine which resembles a saw.

Nearly every street tout and rickshaw driver in Jaipur will try to steer you to a gem factory. They will tell you that you save 20–30% by buying 'at source' rather than at a high-street shop. Rickshaw men are the worst—insist (if you can) that they remain in their vehicle while you go shopping. If they get in the shop with you, expect to pay 20–30% more, not less. Recently, as tourists have got wise to this con, touts have become more cunning.

If you must visit an emporium, at least go to a reliable one. The largest and best selection of loose stones and ready-made jewellery is at **Gem Palace** on Mirza Ismail Rd. This is a treasure trove with everything from strands of garnets at Rs50 to a Maharajah's collection of original Mughal pieces for a good deal more. You won't make a killing here, but you're not going to be ripped off. The same goes for the three 'name' jewellers in Johari Bazaar—**D.Y. Durlabhji, Surana**, and **Ratnasangam**—all of which specialise in high-class gems, particularly emeralds. Jaipur is the emerald centre of the world. Unfortunately, the mark-up is fabulous. Before you buy an emerald ring in the UK, at least seven people have made money on it. Emeralds which sell at Durlabhji's for Rs1000 per carat, are sold in London for at least five times as much. But if you think you can, as a foreigner, buy cheap emeralds in Jaipur you're mistaken. You really have to know what you're talking about. If you do, check out the small alley between 264 and 268 Johari Bazaar. This is the recognised 'gem centre' of Jaipur, where you can pick up all kinds of loose stones at rock-bottom prices. But you *must* know what you're looking for. As soon as you enter the alley, you're assaulted by a scrum of urgent, insistent guys screaming 'Buy my packet!'. Their packets contain glittering arrays of random rough-cut stones, offered at low, low prices. Often, the reason why these guys are so urgent to sell (and why the gems are so cheap) is that they are factory workers who have pocketed stones they've been working on and have to get rid of them in their lunch breaks. It's an ideal market for a young jeweller who has some knowledge of gems, but even the average tourist can't go far wrong—*provided* he or she makes no 'offer' until ready to buy. Once you've made an offer, you've got to buy. No offer should be made until you've had a good look at several packets, and have compared price and quality. When making your selection, bear in mind that these stones are not sized—you'll have to pay extra later on, to have them made up into rings, necklaces, pendants, cufflinks etc. This is best done at a reputed jeweller like **Beg Gems**, Mehdika Chowk, Badi Chopa (near Wind Palace).

Actually, gem-buying is not as specialised a business as one might think. Following a few basic rules, you're bound to win. Take emeralds, for instance. Shades vary from dark to light green. The darker and greener the stone is, the more value is placed on it. Next, look at its opaqueness. A transparent stone has more value than an opaque stone. But the 'colour' should be primarily clear, giving it 'brilliance'. Next, you take out your eyeglass (something which always impresses street-traders) and examine the stone for 'cut'. The cut should be even, and the number of 'carats' not less than 16 to 18. This means the stone will contain 125 facets, giving it a good colour and lustre. A stone with few facets will have little transparency, and this will detract significantly from its value. A lot of 'street-cut' jewellery is of dubious quality—with gems, the facets may be uneven, the colour poor (look out for flecks and impurities), and there may even be unsightly scratches and chips. You're fairly safe with semi-precious stones, like garnets and lapis lazuli, but a number of the so-called emeralds you may be shown will look more like cheap green malachite. With an eyeglass, you should be able to detect any flecks, flaws and hairline cracks. Sometimes, you'll come across a stone which is absolutely brilliant—no impurities whatsoever! In 99% of cases, it will be synthetic. Fortunately, however, the human eye is very accurate—given a choice of several rough stones, it will usually select the very best one. If you don't trust your judgement, nip over to the **Gem Testing Laboratory** off M.I. Rd (near New Gate), where for a nominal sum (around Rs25) you can have your purchases verified and valued. Steer clear of diamonds, by the way—they must be paid for in foreign currency, carry special setting restrictions, and require an export certificate. Silver is excellent value in Jaipur. You should, however, never pay over the bullion price per gram for silver bangles—they rarely have over 50% silver content. For a reliable shop, try **Balaji Silvercraft**, 102 Siredeori Bazaar (just off Johari Bazaar). Otherwise, check out the silver market in Johari Bazaar, or wander round the (innumerable) silver shops in Choti Chopa square. Forget about buying gold—it's even more expensive in India than in Europe.

Other popular buys in Jaipur are Persian-style carpets, stone carvings and Krishna-art miniature paintings. One look in the government arts emporium is all it takes to convince you that prices are too high. You'll find cheaper, better carpets in Pushkar and Jaisalmer, and miniature paintings in Udaipur. Jaipur does, however, have a good name for saris, fabrics and bed-linen. **Kadar Bux Patel**, 10 Havamahal (beyond Johari Bazaar), sells featherlight cotton quilts—the traditional winter bedding of the region—at Rs250 single-size, Rs500 double-size. Similar quilts can be found at **Anokhi**, 2 Tilak Marg, but in a much greater variety of colours and designs, with prices from Rs450. They also stock a mass of interior furnishings and fine-quality cotton clothes at ridiculously low prices—unique cotton appliquéd bedcovers from Rs550, dresses from about Rs180. Over at **Kin Fabrics**, Station Rd, you can pick up *atamsookh*—quilted dressing gowns once worn by the maharajahs—from Rs350. Also kotah *doria* muslin—fine handloomed cotton, sometimes studded discreetly with tiny rhinestones or delicately threaded with gold—at Rs240 for the plain lengths, and between Rs400 and 600 for the decorated pieces.

WHERE TO STAY

Luxury/Expensive (US$50–150 plus per room night)

Jaipur has a good range of clean, civilised places to stay at all levels. Far and away the best hotel is the Taj Group's **Rambagh Palace** (tel 521241, tlx 0365-2254 and 2147, fax 0141-521098) on Bhawani Singh Marg, to the south of town. A delightful old palace of delicate cupolas and fretted screens, amid sprawling and landscaped gardens. Fully air-conditioned, it features a marvellous indoor pool, famous Polo Bar, regency-style French dining hall, a coffee shop, branches of many of Jaipur's best shops in the arcade—and an exercise bicycle in every bathroom. Choose between small, but cosy rooms at US$115, and opulent suites at US$150–450. Pricey yes, but living like a maharajah never was cheap. The Rambagh offers 20% discounts in May/June, but even then you're wise to advance-book—it's nearly always full.

Taj's other palace hotel is the smaller **Jai Mahal Palace** in Jacob Rd, Civil Lines (tel 68381, tlx 365-2250, fax 0141-65237). The original building dates from 1772 when it was constructed as the residence of royal physicians and dewans (ministers).

Expanded, altered and totally renovated by the Taj in the mid-80s, it has 18 acres of landscaped gardens, a nice restaurant overlooking regal lawns, a quaint haveli-style bar, and lots of useful facilities. It may lack the character of the Rambagh, but is newer and more functional. Rooms here are only cheaper than the Rambagh, from US$90 and suites start at US$175. Other upmarket options include the out-of-town **Clarks Amer**, Jawaharlal Nehru Marg (tel 822616, tlx 0365-2276) with rooms at US$50, and Welcomgroup's **Rajputana Palace**, Atul Ban, Kaiser-i-Hind Road (Station Road) (tel 64613, 72170, tlx 0365-2489) opened in late 1992 as Jaipur's most modern five-star property with room rates from US$100. At the **Hotel Mansingh**, Sansar Chandra Rd (tel 78771, tlx 0365-2344) rooms cost upwards of US$70.

The Taj Group have two other properties in and nearby Jaipur. **The Rajmahal Palace** (tel 521757, tlx c/o 0365-2176, fax c/o 0141-65237) with 11 rooms and swimming-pool was prior to 1947 the British Residency. Rooms cost US$60. The 11-room **Ramgarh Lodge**, 30 km (19 miles) from Jaipur costs US$70 upwards per room and is booked through the Rambagh Palace.

Mid-range (US$10–35/Rs250–1000 per room night)

It's in the mid-range hotels that Jaipur really comes into its own. And in India this is a real rarity. Take for instance, the fine **Hotel Megh Niwas** at C-9 Jai Singh Highway, Bani Park (tel 74018, tlx 365-2110). Run in ultra-efficient manner by Col. Singh (retired) and wife, this is a very large private house with lawns front and rear. Meals (which are excellent) are all taken out in the garden, where you can also enjoy an evening beer or gin. The Singhs handle all your travel arrangements, drive you round town, and even help you out with shopping. Rooms are well-furnished, extremely comfortable, and very reasonably priced from Rs300. If staying here, enquire about car tours of Rajasthan and trips to Pushkar's Desert Festival—they're good value too! **Hotel Bissau Palace**, outside Chand Pol Gate (tel 74191, 67728) also gets rave reviews. 'It's a real throwback to the days of the Raj—you half-expect Julie Christie or Greta Scacchi to appear out of the woodwork!' The pre-war residence of a Rajput chieftain, this place has a quaint library cum museum, traditional food and service, lawn tennis and badminton courts, and bags of old-world charm. The pool's nice, and rooms are pleasantly air-cooled (Rs350/Rs425). Many other private homes have been converted into pleasant, friendly hotels or guest houses. The Rajasthan Tourism office in Jaipur has published a most useful directory of Paying Guest Accommodation in Jaipur (and Jodhpur and Udaipur) available from Paryatan Bhawan at the end of M.I. Road (tel 70180, 70181). **Narain Niwas**, Narain Singh Road (tel 563448, 561291, tlx 0365-2482) has large airy rooms from Rs750. This is one of the first of the smaller hotels that travellers will book into if they can't get into a hotel in the upper range. **Achrol Lodge**, Jacob Road, Civil Lines (tel 352347, 343510) has a bed and breakfast service. **LMB Hotel** in Johari Bazaar (tel 565844, tlx 0365- 2617) offers 'five-star amenities on two-star tariff', and is unique in its prime old-city location. Centrally air-conditioned—like the famous attached restaurant—it has singles/doubles at Rs450/575. Top-floor rooms, while a bit noisy, have excellent views over the pink city. Rajasthan Tourism Development Corporation (RTDC) have the **Gangaur Tourist Bungalow** centallly located on M.I. Road (tel 60231) with a restaurant and coffee shop (3 Rooms from Rs350). **Teej Tourist Hotel**, Collectorate Road (tel 74206, 743734) is another well-run RTDC property, with clean rooms from Rs350).

Budget (under US$10/Rs250)
If on a budget, you'll have to fight hard to get to a decent lodge. Scooter drivers and Rickshaw-wallahs are highly inventive when it comes to placing you in dives which pay them commission. Upon persuading him to drive you to a good place, like **Jaipur Inn** (tel 66057) in Bani Park, he will feign astonishment, unable to believe that it has not (as previously stated) burnt down.

Jaipur Inn is a wonderfully eccentric lodge, run by a retired squadron leader who wanders round in a tweed jacket, looking for new ways to make it more English. He's even planning an English pub—without alcohol! The dorm beds have poor security (lockers broken), but there's nothing wrong with the rooms, which run from Rs70. The all-you-can-eat *thali* suppers are good value, and the whole place is as friendly and helpful as you could wish. **Hotel Arya Niwas** (tel 73456, tlx 0365-2423), behind the Amber Cinema, Sansar Chandra Rd, has a lovely family, good vegetarian food ('Breakfast with Egg Preparations'), pleasant verandah and garden area, and clean single/double rooms from about the same price. It's very handy for the GPO and bus-stand.

EATING OUT
Rambagh Palace's dining hall, the **Suvarna Mahal**, is magnificent but the food unfortunately is the hotel's weakest link. There's a good-value fixed menu at both lunch and dinner (Rs150). In the evening, get your seat by 7.30 pm—that's when the Rajasthani culture show starts. In the old city, **LMB Hotel** (Johari Bazaar) is where to go for Indian *nouvelle cuisine*—wacky food and ultra-kitsch 1950s decor, but it makes a change! Famous for its vegetarian food and sweetmeats, LMB also has a popular snacks/ice-cream counter. The sit-down three-course meals are excellent value (Rs70) and the service is superb. For Chinese and Tandoori fare the same price bracket try **Niro's** on M.I. Rd. It's a surprisingly cheerful place for an upmarket Indian restaurant, with soothing sounds, pleasant decor, and bubbly atmosphere. Right next door is **Surya Mahal**, serving outstanding vegetarian food at very low prices. Lots of Jaipuri families come here—it's spotlessly clean, staff wear smart uniforms, and service is quick. The mid-priced **Chanakya**, also on M.I. Rd, is another well-run vegetarian restaurant, heavily patronised by locals and very centrally located. **Kullu Islami** in Ramganj Bazaar is where to go for cheap non-vegetarian food. **Golden Dragon**, just off M.I. Rd, is a reliable Chinese restaurant—not as good as Niro's perhaps, but cheaper and well known for its *Szechwan* specialities. Jaipur's **Kwality Restaurant**, M.I. Rd, is probably the best of the whole chain—fabulous decor (like a Maharajah's mahal!), select atmosphere, mellow sounds, and multi-national cuisine. Food is a long time coming, but you can help yourself at the (good) lunchtime buffets.

GENERAL INFORMATION
RTDC Tourist Information Bureau, inside the rail station (tel 69784), is open 6 am to 8 pm daily. Come here for good information and handouts (even posters), for badge-carrying guides (Rs25 half-day, Rs50 full-day), and for useful city tours (Rs20 half-day, 8 am to 1 pm, or 1.30 pm to 6.30 pm; Rs35 full-day, 9 am to 6 pm). There's also a Government of India tourist office at State Hotel, Khasa Kothi (tel 72200) which runs similar ITDC tours.

The post office on M.I. Rd is (apparently) open 24 hours, and has an international phone facility. State Bank of India is at Sanganeri Gate (very quick currency exchange on the 1st floor), and has a small branch near the tourist office. Both offices are open 10 am to 2 pm, except Sundays. Indian Airlines is at Nehru Place on the Tonk Road to the airport (tel 74500, 70624, airport tel 822519, 822222, 822718); East West Airlines is at Hotel Jaipur Palace, Near Laxmi Mandir, Tonk Road (tel 512961, tlx 0365-2615). Foreigner's Registration Office is behind Hawa Mahal (Raj. Police Head Office) (tel 49391), and Rambagh Palace Hotel has a good bookshop.

JODHPUR

Situated close to the edge of the Thar Desert, Jodhpur is the second city of Rajasthan. It was founded by Rao Jodha in 1459, following the capture of the nearby old capital of Mandore, home of the Rathore Rajputs since the 12th century. Lying on the rich camel caravan routes, it became a very wealthy city indeed, with stately palaces, beautiful buildings and gracious temples. Up until recently, it was capital of the state of Marwar.

Jodhpur's pride is her mighty 15th-century fort, which stands on a low range of sandstone hills. It lies within the 10-km (3-mile) long stone wall encircling the old city and has eight immense gates. Facing the fort, on the other side of the city, is the magnificent Umaid Bhawan Palace. A modern creation (completed 1945), it was the then Maharajah's way of keeping his population busy during a time of severe famine. Today, it is another of Rajasthan's fantasy hotels.

Jodhpur is one of India's most interesting cities, especially in the narrow, bustling streets and bazaars of the old city, and there is a great deal to see and do. Yet it remains curiously unappreciated. Most travellers use it simply as a jumping-off point to nearby Jaisalmer (west), Udaipur (south) and Jaipur (north-east), and rarely linger here more than a day or two. This may have something to do with the heat (pretty severe, except from December to early March), but doubtless has a lot to do with Jodhpur's notoriety as a 'hassle' centre. Women travellers have a particularly difficult time here, and everybody is plagued by kids chanting 'Wottis your nem?' and begging school pens. This is a shame, since few places in India have finer palaces or bazaars, and Jodhpur's fort is perhaps the best-preserved and most attractive in the country.

ARRIVAL/DEPARTURE

Air
Indian Airlines has daily flights between Jodhpur and Ahmedabad (Rs893), Aurangabad (Rs1480), Bombay (Rs1629), Delhi (Rs1083), Jaipur (Rs767) and Udaipur (Rs583). Vayudoot offers occasional flights to Jaisalmer.

The Indian Airlines office is at the Ghoomar Tourist Bungalow (tel 28600, airport tel 20617). Vayudoot handling agents are Mayur Travels, Kalyan Singh Building, Sojati Gate (tel 20909). The general airport enquiry tel. is 30617.

Rail
There are daily trains to Delhi, Jaipur, Udaipur and Jaisalmer. See travel itinerary (pp. 145) for more details. The railway enquiry office is open from 10 am to 5 pm (tel 32535).

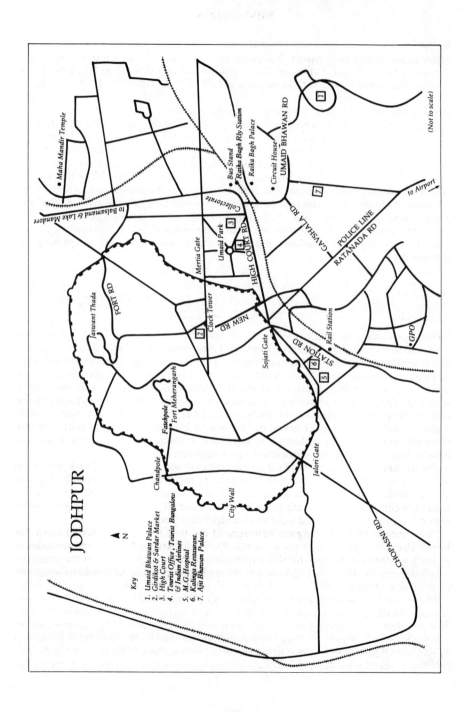

Road
Daily buses to Bikaner, Jaipur, Jaisalmer, Mt Abu, Ajmer, Ranakpur, Udaipur and Chittorgarh leave from Jodhpur's Raika Bagh bus-stand. The State Road Transport Corporation office is open 10 am to 5 pm (tel 44686).

WHAT TO SEE
For a large city, Jodhpur is quite easy to negotiate. The central market cuts through the centre of town, with the tourist office, bus-stand and railway station to the south, the fort and the old city to the north. For in-town transport, you have auto-rickshaws (real bandits: even locals have a hard time getting anywhere for less than Rs5), tempo minibuses (useful for visiting Mandore, and horse-drawn tongas (slow and expensive, around Rs4/km). There are few taxis but cars can be hired from Umaid Bhavan Palace and other hotels. The best (cheapest) way of getting round is by cycle. There are many bike-hire places near the rail station, charging only Rs10 per day.

Count on spending three full days in Jodhpur—it's worth it. If you can't digest all the suggested tours at one sitting, do a couple during your first visit, and pick up the last one on your return here from Jaisalmer.

City Tour (by rickshaw, or on foot; 4–6 hours)
Meherangarh Fort–Meherangarh Museum–Jaswant Thada–Umaid Gardens–Government Museum–Umaid Bhawan Palace and Museum

From Jalori Gate, at the old city entrance, it's a short auto-rickshaw ride (or 30-minute walk) up to Fatehpol, the entrance to the fort. The drive north takes you through the old city market, a teeming thoroughfare of narrow, winding lanes crammed with bicycles, carts, cows and camels. What you won't see here isn't worth mentioning— it's a wild, colourful pot-pourri of street tailors, candle-makers, incense sellers, sugar-cane presses, glass and lantern shops, all casually observed by old men sitting in doorways propped on silver-topped cane sticks. If you get stuck in the narrow-lane traffic (and this is common) watch out for young lads playing games with live rats (they throw them back and forth, the aim being to catch them by the tail, losers get bitten). Flying rodents sometimes end up in stationary rickshaws.

The **Meherangarh** (Majestic) **Fort** is Rajasthan's finest. Built on solid rock, towering 400 ft above the plains, this massive 15th-century fort was once described by Kipling as 'the work of angels, fairies and giants'. It was never captured, and once you've made the climb up there—a crippling 30-minute ascent, via huge gates pocked with cannonball scars and daubed with *sati* handprints—you'll know why.

The remarkable **Meherangarh Museum** at the top, recently converted from the Fort Palace, is worth every paisa of the Rs10 admission. This charge includes a smartly uniformed guide, who will explain the history and contents of the museum in impeccable English. The Rs25 camera charge is a bit stiff but there is some excellent photography here.

The museum is open 9 am–5 pm daily in winter and 8 am–6 pm in summer, and houses 18 different sections, full of well-displayed antiquities. Nowhere else in India will you find so much opulence, ostentation and fine craftsmanship concentrated in one place. Starting with the chamber full of baby-carriages (home of many fledgling Maharajahs), moving on to the haveli-type ladies' quarters with their stone-carved balconies, you'll pass through a whole series of palaces and courtyards to reach the amazing royal bedroom (coloured Christmas balls dangling from the ceiling, wall-to-wall exotic carpets, mirrors and mosaics instead of wallpaper) with its truly amazing centrepiece—the vast bed where the Maharajah entertained his 35 wives. Below is Maharajah Bhai Singh's 18th-century **Dancing Hall**, with its famous pure gold ceiling (80 kg: 176 lbs of it), the Fort's principal attraction. The armoury section has a brace of gigantic elephant guns, and leads on to a rich assortment of elephant howdahs, folk music instruments, palanquins, furniture and costumes.

This palace museum is in superb condition throughout. Unlike so many of India's palace attractions, the mosaics of jewels and semi-precious stones painstakingly inlaid into marble walls, ceilings and floors have not been picked out by invaders (or tourists), leaving it in pretty much the same condition as when first built. In the tent room is a huge Mughal tent made of silk and velvet for Emperor Shah Jahan. If you've only time for one 'sight' in Jodhpur, make it this.

Outside the museum entrance, beggar musicians play for money. There's one especially colourful gentleman decked out like a Rajput Acker Bilk, with bright red turban, orange-sleeved army jacket, and the most decorated trumpet I've ever seen. Take time to appreciate these artists—they're great fun, and well worth a photo.

Certain sections of the fort (notably the ladies' quarters inside the museum) give fine views down over the tenements and houses of the Brahmin quarter of town, unmistakable because they are painted bright blue. Blue is the pigment of Lord Krishna, and you'll see a lot of Brahmin women here wearing blue clothing). But to see all this royal blue to best advantage, head out of the museum past the **Sun Goddess (Chamundi) temple** until you reach the fort rampart. This gives the best overall view over Jodhpur city, and has one of the rarest displays of cannon in India.

The exit from the fort is to the left as you leave the museum. Just above the **Hero's Chhatri** (monument to brave hero who fell out of a window), there's a sharp bend in the road. It's the favourite pitch of boy musicians, on the fiddle. Here you can choose between heading left, down to the marble cenotaph of **Jaswant Thada** (cremation ground of the royal family, with translucent marble tombs and portraits of the 12 rulers of old Mandore, before the capital moved to present Jodhpur), or taking the crumbling stairway (on the bend) to the right, which takes you down into **Sadar Market**. This has a lively central square, with a clock tower, a barber's circle and an umbrella-shaded cobbler's corner. Beside the left-hand gate (one of three), there's **Sri Mishri Lal Hotel**—famous for its *makhania lassi*, a rich, creamy drink made with cow's milk, butterballs, cardamom and ice.

Outside the square, you can either head right into the festive **Central Market** or hire a horse-drawn tonga down New Road towards the Tourist Bungalow. Ask to be dropped off at the **Umaid Public Gardens**, a popular and attractive picnic spot. The green and well-maintained gardens are full of mango, bougainvillaea, roses and other flowering plants. The small **zoo** has some lethargic lions, who come out for a swim in the open-air pool when bored of sleeping. At the north-eastern end of the gardens, you'll find the **Government Museum**. Open 10 am–5 pm (except Fridays), admission Rs1, this has some nice porcelain and pottery pieces, some boring bits of old rock from Mandore, and some stuffed predators and reptiles restlessly roaming the walls. Above the old iron British turnstile at the entrance is a sign stating: 'Dogs and Hobnail Boots Not Allowed' The museum has not seen much renovation in the last 40 years.

From the gardens, it's a 20-minute walk south (via the Circuit House) to the stately **Umaid Bhawan Palace**. This was commenced in 1929 by Maharajah Umaid Singh, probably as 'famine relief work' for his drought-stricken subjects, and took the next 13 years (with 3000 labourers working day and night) to complete. Its architect, H.V. Lancaster, was told to build a structure to rival, if not equal, that of Lutyens' Delhi, then under construction. The result was an exquisite example of the Art-Deco style of the '30s, covering a built-up area of 3.5 acres. Many features, notably the side-minarets, are reminiscent of Lutyen's Rashtrapati Bhavan in New Delhi. The palace is a masterpiece of construction, fashioned completely of interlocking sandstone blocks—like a giant Lego set, it can be dismantled any time and reassembled anywhere. The structure is dominated by a central dome which rises 56 m high and provides a natural source of light and cross ventilation. Today, the palace is part hotel, part maharajah's residence, and part museum. The sophisticated young Maharajah still lives in, making this the largest private residence in India. It's also the most recent palace to be built in India.

There are guided tours of Umaid Bhawan Palace and Museum every hour or so from 8.30 am to 5 pm daily. Entrance fee is Rs5. The museum has an illuminated model of the palace (prepared in England as a design model for the actual building), beautiful miniature paintings, elegant Grecian-style paintings (by the famous Italian painter E. Norblin, 1946), delicate Japanese/Chinese china and pottery, an exquisite collection of clocks, and a 3-D portrait of Maharajah Umaid Singh. Wandering round the palace, you'll find a weird Roman Bath and a stuffed bear waiter (with white gloves and wine tray) standing outside the restaurant. The whole thing is one big memory trip for anyone who remembers the Raj, and a real eye-opener for anyone who doesn't.

Mandore Tour (by town bus, half-day)
Mandore–Mahamandir Temple

For the next day, take a 20-minute minibus ride (regular buses from the top of High Court Rd, opposite the Hospital) to Mandore (10 km: 6 miles north), the old capital of **Marwar**. Probably founded in the 6th century, it was mostly ruled by the Rajput Rathore clan, but was periodically captured by the Delhi sultans and other invaders. Originally an important centre of architecture and culture, as indicated by the many ancient sculptures found here, Mandore is today a popular local picnic spot with extensive gardens and high rock terraces.

The famous **gardens of Mandore** are most beautiful in March/April, when all the flowers are in full bloom, though the magnificent rose garden comes into its own in February. A riot of bougainvillaea, sunflowers, azaleas, tobacco plants and wall flowers, the general overall effect is that of an English country garden, and the air is heavy with the scent of flowers. As you stroll around, you'll find many unusual species of cacti, a greenhouse with no glass in it, several species of birds and monkeys, and flocks of strutting peacocks. At the top of the gardens are the impressive cenotaphs of the old Jodhpur rulers, most of them in excellent condition. They are raised on high terraces, their soaring spires and exquisite sculptures a tribute to Mandore's high architectural tradition. Mostly constructed of red-sandstone, these devals or royal cenotaphs were built in the form of temples, to immortalise the memory of Maharajah Jaswant Singh, Maharajah Ajit Singh (with a dominating four-storey masterpiece, with beautifully carved domed ceiling) and other rulers.

Entrance to the gardens is Rs1, and this includes access to the strange **Government Museum** (open 10 am to 4.30 pm except Friday). This has an elegant, tasteful display of lacquer, wood and ivory crafts. It also has a giant model ear, an odd montage of human entrails, a boil-ridden child, and a ghastly flayed traffic policeman. Pick your way down a dark, dank tunnel to locate the art gallery of miniature paintings, and don't trip over the stuffed bullocks and crocodiles lurking in the gloom. Emerging at the other end, you'll find the **Hall of Heroes**. These are 16 brightly-painted life-size figures carved out of the rock wall, fashioned in the 18th century to depict various kings, saints and cult heroes who displayed extraordinary courage, valour or chivalry (the traditional Rajput virtues). Also here is the temple of 330 million Hindu gods, full of painted deities, spirits and divinities.

Out of the museum, it's a short 15-minute walk up to the hills beyond the lake to the ruins of old Mandore fort and palaces. The **Balsamund Lake Palace**, site of the Maharajah's beautiful fruit orchards, is located 1.5 km (1 mile) right of the museum. The reservoir was first created in AD 1159. Mandore's own gardens, illuminated in the evenings (in season), are worth staying back to see.

Returning from Mandore, get down from the bus 2 km (1¼ miles) before Jodhpur city for the small walled town of **Mahamandir** (Great Temple). A hundred pillars support the roof of this unique structure, and the interior is richly ornamented with bas-relief designs depicting various postures of yoga.

Kailana Lake (cycle, half/full-day)

This is a good day excursion, the ideal escape from the hot, dusty inner city. **Kailana** is a delightful picnic spot, with a small artificial lake and gardens. Situated 11 km (7 miles) west of Jodhpur (an hour by cycle), it supplies part of Jodhpur city's water. To get there, cycle west from Jalori Gate, via State Bank of Bikaner, down the main Chopasni Road for about 1 km (⅔ mile). Then turn right, cycle another 2 km (1¼ miles), take first major turning left for Kailana Lake (3 km: 1⅔ miles). On the way, look out for **Eklinji**, a large hilltop Shiva temple, with a 'natural' swimming-pool (wash your sins off before climbing up!) and bags of mystic atmosphere. Kailana itself is actually two lakes in one—the one on the left is 5 km (3 miles) long, and very suitable for swimming (when there's water in it.). Lock your bike, have a dip in the cool, clean water, then (leaving bike behind) enjoy a scenic 1-km (⅔-mile) stroll up to the nearby **Bheem Bharak Caves**. At these two beautiful caves (one above, one underground) lives an old hermit who practises yoga. He looks 50, is actually well into his 80s, and has been here for the past 60 years. These natural caves are a popular picnic spot, and an ideal situation to enjoy the scenery—especially at sunset, when the lakes are a vivid, unforgettable splash of romantic colour. If going out for the day, ask your hotel for a packed lunch—Kailana has no refreshments.

RECREATION
The most popular recreation in hot, sticky Jodhpur is swimming. Umaid Palace Hotel has its novelty underground pool, available to non-residents for daily charge. The Ratanada Polo Hotel has its cosy open-air pool (with cool, shady garden surround).

The Palace hotel also offers golf—on a full 18-hole course which nobody ever completes. Given the recurrent drought situation, the Maharajah was asked how one could play with anything but a sand-wedge. 'It's a very interesting course', he replied, 'Very dry. To give you an even lie, you're permitted to use a piece of doormat. It works very well!' Also, this must be cheapest game of golf in the world.

Jodhpur has three or four cinemas, showing English films on Sunday mornings. See a local newspaper for details.

SHOPPING
While traditional Rajasthani handicrafts are best bought in Jaisalmer or Pushkar, Jodhpur is good for 'novelty' items—ranging from the quite useless (flick-knives made from lollipop sticks and elastic bands) to the very useful indeed (Rs30) ladies' umbrellas for long, hot camel-treks. The famous 'Jodhpurs' (polo pants) are now out of fashion, and you'll be hard pressed to find a tailor in town who can make them. Try **Arjun's** shop, outside Sowati Gate. Alternatively, ferret around in the market. One girl came up with a perfect pair of faded antique jodhpurs—complete with silver buttons and royal stains—for only Rs50. They were repaired by **Roopali** tailor, opposite the New Tourist Hotel.

Jodhpur is a shopping attraction less for its handicrafts than for its large, vibrant Central or Old Market, now known as the **Ghasmandi Bazaar.** This clean, colourful and friendly market is many people's favourite in India. There is no pressure on you to buy, the atmosphere is relaxing and civilised, and the air is sweet with spices and perfumes. Also, a big plus, the bazaar is divided into sections: starting from the Clock Tower, there is first a general market, then a cloth market, then an ivory and bamboo market, then a market for jewellery, silks and spices, fruit and vegetables, and finally sweets. Look out for the old haveli-type stone-carved houses above the shop-fronts, and for the charming modern Krishna Temple (lovely ceiling watercolours and 'scientific quartz clock') through a small gate on the left, halfway down the market.

WHERE TO STAY
Luxury/Expensive (over US$35/Rs1000 per room night)
Welcomgroup's **Umaid Bhawan Palace** (tel 22316, tlx 0552-202 UBP IN) has been tastefully converted from a palace into a luxury hotel, without losing either its character or its regal ambience. Here, as the brochure says, you really *can* live like a Maharajah. This place has one of the largest collections of 1930s Art-Deco in the world, and every room and suite is immaculately furnished. Actually, you have a choice of deluxe rooms (old-style period pieces), royal chambers (even better) from US$85, and regular/deluxe suites at US$200–660. The new air-conditioned rooms are small and rather ordinary. Facilities include underground pool (built to stop the royal ladies being spied on), two dining rooms, badminton and tennis courts, and lavish flare-lit buffets on the sweeping lawns. It's a great place to send a postcard home from, if you can afford to stay. And in the low season, when rates are discounted by up to 40%, this becomes quite possible!

The new **Hotel Ratanada Polo**, Residency Rd (tel 31910-14, tlx 552-233 POLO IN) is Jodhpur's only centrally air-conditioned hotel. It lacks the character of the Palace hotel, but is certainly cooler. There's a nice pool, an air-conditioned restaurant, a smart tennis court, and large bright rooms at Rs1200 single, Rs1400 double.

Mid-range (US$10–35/Rs250–1000 per room night)
The cheaper, more personal **Ajit Bhawan Palace**, near Circuit House (tel 20409), is very popular. A self-styled 'legendary resort', it is the family home of the Maharajah's uncle—Maharajah Swaroop Singh. Room rates vary and the best buy are the well-furnished little cottages—each with a different theme (ask for the 'milkman's room' or 'the room with the tree')—set around a desert-village compound. There's a pond, a courtyard, an antique bullock 'chariot' on the lawn, cosy dinners in the garden, and a constant store of cold drinks in your fridge. The hotel organises jeep-safari trips out to neighbouring villages (9 am–5 pm daily); Maharajah Swaroop Singh often tags along for the ride. Another nice place, also near Circuit House, is **Hotel Karni Bhawan** (tel 20157), owned by the Maharajah's private secretary. Here you can enjoy Rajasthani campfire suppers in the *dhani* (village-hut complex), or sip exotic local cocktails on the immaculate green lawns. Cosy and peaceful, this is a good getaway from the heat and dust of Jodhpur. Rooms are excellent value.

Budget (below US$10/Rs250 per room night)
Cheaper lodgings are mostly disappointing. The RTDC **Ghoomar Tourist Bungalow** (tel 44010, tlx 552-254) is on High Court Rd, next to Umaid Gardens. It's rather a shabby place, mainly useful as somewhere to stow your gear (for free) while you go sightseeing, but ideal if you're only here for the day. Single/double rooms range from Rs100 (depressing) to Rs300 with noisy air-conditioning. Best deal are the quiet, non-depressing, air-cooled rooms at Rs150/200. A much better deal is **Adarsh Niwas Hotel** (tel 26936, 23658) opposite the railway station. This has pleasant air-cooled rooms with tiled bathrooms, colour TV/video, and lots of space. The attached restaurant is a real bonus, and it's very convenient for early morning departures. So are the clean **Railway Retiring Rooms** (tel 22741), costing Rs30/40. But the best budget bet is still **New Tourist Hotel**, Lakshmi Bhawan, near Jalori Gate. This is run by a friendly Brahmin ex-teacher, Allen, who really looks after his 'dear fatigued foreign friends'. Most rooms are fairly basic, but there's one nice one on the roof. Allen makes delicious chocolate tea, rose-water *lassi*, and Rajasthani Royal Food. His friend is an ex-Maharajah's barber whose body-massage is the talk of Jodhpur. His city information is first-rate, and his sun-roof a real treat.

The **RTDC directory** of paying Guest accommodation in Jodhpur is available from the tourist office (tel 45083, 44010).

EATING OUT
Jodhpur's only real traditional fare, incorporating the heavy local millet (millet Sogra *chapati*, Sohita mutton cooked with millet), is a speciality. For a good blowout, try the special buffet supper at Umaid Bhawan Palace's **Marwar Hall**. This palatial 'restaurant', the scene of so many RAF parties in the 1940s, started life as a royal banqueting hall. Today, it serves excellent Indian, Continental and Rajasthani cuisine in true Maharajah style. The buffet runs from 7.30 to 10.30 pm, and includes live entertainment. Great value with meals from Rs150, but bring some Alka Seltzer—the desserts are incredibly rich.

Slightly cheaper, the **Khamaghani** restaurant at Hotel Ratananda Polo offers á la carte Indian, Chinese and Continental food. Some evenings, live entertainment is thrown in. The mood is very relaxed, and the food good. For convenience (it's opposite the rail station), try **Kalinga Restaurant**, something of a traveller's favourite. This is a cool air-conditioned place, serving Continental, Tandoor and Mughlai cuisine. Service is very patient (they're used to dithering foreigners) and vegetarian fare is very cheap (try 'Stuff Omelette' or 'Potato Chop'). The favourite local snack is Baked Beans on Toast. Cross the road for low-budget Indian meals at the small **New Restaurant**. For strictly vegetarian meals and good coffee, try **Pushpa Dal Bati**, outside Jalori Gate. Or the nearby **Pankaj**—also good, but pricier. Near Sojati Gate, you'll find **Jodhpur Coffee House**, full of *thali/dosa* afficionados and coffee-slurping locals.

GENERAL INFORMATION

RTDC Tourist Office, inside Tourist Bungalow, High Court Rd (tel 44010), is open 8 am to noon, 3 to 6 pm except Sundays (in theory.). Poor information, irregular conducted tours (8.30 am–1 pm, 2–6.30 pm), and no decent city map. Hires out tourist guides for half-day and full-day tours.

Universal Book Depot, Jalori Gate, sells the useful *Jodhpur—a Traveller's Guide*, full of detailed city information. State Bank of Bikaner is near Jalori Gate (open 10 am–2 pm). The post office is a few minutes' walk south of the main rail station.

JAISALMER

Jaisalmer, the 'Oasis of Jessal', was founded in 1156 by the Bhati prince, Jaisal, to replace the old capital of Lodawa, 17 km (11 miles) away, which had proved too vulnerable to attacks from neighbouring tribes. Perched on a high hill within the powerful embrace of the Meru mountains and enfolded by solid yellow-sandstone battlements and fortified walls, it was built to last. Best of all, it lay directly on the camel caravan routes leading out to Sind (now in Pakistan), which brought its Jain merchants and bankers great power and wealth between the 14th and 16th centuries. In thanks for their good fortune (and as an external depiction of status), they spent heavily on domestic architecture—leading to the creation of the famous Jaisalmer havelis or merchants' houses, with their intricate trellis-work balconies, ornamented windows and domed arches; and the equally distinctive Jain Temples in the Old Fort, with their elaborate carvings and decorations, and their numerous statues depicting 'Dieu' or the Jain god.

Throughout the centuries, the 6.4 km (4 miles) of ramparts at Jaisalmer Fort repelled all prospective invaders, including the Mughals, and trade prospered. Then, in 1947, it experienced a sudden crisis: India was partitioned, and the camel caravan trade routes to Sind were abruptly severed with a new international border only 55 km away. Only between 1965 and 1971, when the Indo-Pakistan wars revealed its strategic importance, did its fortunes revive. Rapidly connected to the rest of Rajasthan by road and rail, to support a military base, it was inevitable that this remote, exotic desert township would soon be discovered by tourism. In the hard days of the 1940s and 1950s, the people of Jaisalmer had turned for survival both to cattle-farming and (more relevant) to the production of high-quality woven handicrafts—notably camel-wool rugs, special wool carpets and fine hand-embroidery. When, therefore, the tourists began to trickle in in the early 1970s, there was a ready-made handicrafts industry waiting for them. But times were hard, and Jaisalmer couldn't rely on

The desert city of Jaisalmer

tourism alone. As a back-up, its age-old trading tradition smoothly channelled itself into large-scale smuggling. Conveniently situated less than 100 km from the Pakistan border, the old merchant's town has become a modern-day den of thieves. The deal is, Jaisalmer sends silver, whisky and beedies to Pakistan, and receives in return gold and heroin. The heroin goes to Delhi, Bombay and Jaipur, and an amazing amount of it ends up in Europe. The whole drugs scene, however, is very low profile. All Jaisalmer will be interested in selling you is carpets and camel-treks.

Travellers never forget their first impressions of Jaisalmer, a high rugged hill with a golden-walled city shimmering on top of it. Jaisalmer's principal attraction is its very real feel of antiquity—the majestic sand-coloured fort up on the hill, the atmospheric medieval town of lace-like havelis and narrow cobbled back-streets, the proud Rajput men in their bright turbans and patterned slippers (many bearing rifles or bandoleers), the elegant women in their coloured scarves and skirts, beautifully complemented by slim embroidered waistcoats. And all around an ethereal ambience of subdued yellow-sandstone, mellowing to pale gold by the light of the setting sun.

Today, Jaisalmer is poised for rapid tourist development. Three major hotel chains—Taj, Oberoi, and Welcomgroup—have all bought plots at Amarsagar, and are only waiting on the weather. Successive years of no rain in Jaisalmer had caused severe water shortages. By the late 1980s, 100 cows were dying every day—a critical situation for the outlying villages. Fortunately, 1991 and 1992 monsoons were bountiful and many dried-up lakes were replenished. The situation remains fragile and plans are afoot to turn Jaisalmer into a lake city once more—an underground pipeline should reach Gadisar Tank and neighbouring lakes soon.

Monsoons don't often get to Jaisalmer. In high summer, the thermometer bursts at temperatures of up to 47°C (117 ° F) and many locals retire, bleeding at the nose, to cooler climes. The pleasantest months are September to March—not too windy, not too hot. The high-spot of the year is the big **Desert Festival** of January when the plateau below the Fort is a rich, lively extravaganza of camel caravans, acrobatics and races, traditional music and dance shows, tug of war and turban-tying competitions. According to the brochures, it culminates on Full Moon Night (*purnima*) with a sound and light spectacle 'like Blood, Blade and Romance'. Of late, this event has become rather expensive (book through RTDC at Moomal Tourist Bungalow) but still remains a popular favourite. Another good event, if you can bear the heat, is the **Gangaur Festival of early April.** Here the Jaisalmer ladies take the floor for a colourful, attractive spectacle of dance and song within the fort walls, performing to the god Isht Dev for happy marriages, and for the happiness of their menfolk.

ARRIVAL/DEPARTURE
Air
The Vayudoot connection only operates intermittently and is not reliable.

Rail
The overnight sleeper is the most reliable and practical way of reaching Jaisalmer (and leaving): Departs Jodphur 8.30 pm, arrives 7.35 am. The long, dusty day journey departs 8.20 am, arrives 6.30 pm.

Road
Regular buses ply the 8-hour route from Jodphur. The one that leaves at 5 am is the cooler and more comfortable option.

WHAT TO SEE
Real Jaisalmer is no longer in the small town (which is already becoming plugged into tourism, albeit in a pleasant way), but out in the desert-villages. That is why it is important to get a taste of the traditional way of life in Khuri first. A number of villages covered on camel-treks from Jaisalmer, be warned, are now over-exposed to tourists. The result is a strong accent on money, rather than hospitality. Hassle is the name of the game in the fort area, where every hotel owner and every restaurateur seems to have 'the best camel-trek in town'. A few places like Fort View Hotel, New Tourist Hotel and Hotel Paradise offer cheap day treks (inclusive of fairly uninteresting meals) out to the old capital of **Lowada**, with its impressive ruins and fine Jain temples, or to the modern village of **Rupsi**. But if you want to see the 'dunes', it's a long, hard 4-day trek.

The best thing about camel-trekking from Jaisalmer is the spectacular view coming back into town. Emerging from the empty wilderness, the towering hilltop fort suddenly looms up out of nowhere, a fantastic mirage straight out of the *Arabian Nights.*

Some travellers just stroll off into the wilderness on foot. Beyond Jaisalmer town, there's absolutely nothing out there: just barren landscape relieved by a bit of scrub. It's a case of you against the elements. But you don't get lost—just follow the camel trails, pass the old ruins beyond the fort, and travel through a succession of local villages. Such solo walkabouts are, however, only for the very self-reliant or the very foolhardy. It's far safer and more comfortable to explore the desert round Jaisalmer by means of an organised camel-trek.

The fort city of Jaisalmer itself merits a good couple of days' stay—there is not a lot to see, but what there is is top-quality. Every building is a masterpiece of fine craftsmanship, and even the new havelis (commissioned by those who have grown

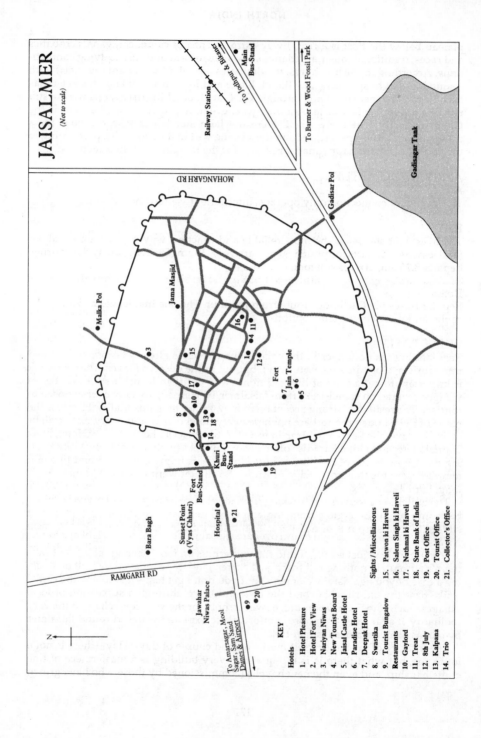

JAISALMER
(Not to scale)

MOHANGARH RD

To Jodhpur & Bikaner
To Barmer & Wood Fossil Park

Main Bus-Stand
Railway Station

Gadisar Pol

Gadisagar Tank

Malka Pol

Jama Masjid

3

15

16
4 11
1
12
6
5
7 Jain Temple
Fort

17
10
8
2
13 18
14

Khuri Bus-Stand

19

Fort Bus-Stand

Sunset Point (Vyas Chhatri)

Bara Bagh

Hospital

21

RAMGARH RD

Jawahar Niwas Palace

9
20

To Amarsagar, Mool Sagar, Sam Sand Dunes & Airport

N

KEY

Hotels

1. Hotel Pleasure
2. Hotel Fort View
3. Nariyan Niwas
4. New Tourist Board
5. Jaisal Castle Hotel
6. Paradise Hotel
7. Deepak Hotel
8. Swastika
9. Tourist Bungalow

Restaurants

10. Gaylord
11. Treat
12. 8th July
13. Kalpana
14. Trio

Sights / Miscellaneous

15. Patwon ki Haveli
16. Salem Singh ki Haveli
17. Nathmal ki Haveli
18. State Bank of India
19. Post Office
20. Tourist Office
21. Collector's Office

rich on tourism) have been designed to blend in perfectly with the old—resulting in a total absence of the usual Indian contrast between traditional and modern architecture.

In town, you have a choice of wandering around the narrow streets and bazaars on your own (the town is small enough for it not to matter if you get lost) or hiring a guide (from the fort entrance) to point out buildings and places of special interest. When in Khuri, Bhagwan Singh can generally suggest someone—usually an educated, informed friend of his—who will take you right round Jaisalmer with no expectation of reward beyond your friendship, yet another example of the remarkable Rajput hospitality.

Local transport is pretty thin. Cycles can be hired at Rs10/day from Dayal Cycle Service, opposite the fort entrance. Outside the fort area, you have a choice of taxis and jeeps (Rs5/km), or auto-rickshaws (Rs2.50/km). The main bus-stand is now opposite the rail station—inconvenient, if you're staying at the fort. All buses to Jodhpur, however, start from the Fort bus-stand, just outside Amritsagar Pol.

Fort and City Tour (on foot, 4/5 hours)
Gadisar Tank–Fort–Jain Temples–Salim Singh Haveli–Patwon ki Haveli–Nathmal ki Haveli

This tour is best done on foot, and in the cool of the morning. Set out around 7 am, taking a 10-minute stroll down Ashni Rd (from the fort entrance) to **Gadisar Tank**, just below the city walls to the south-west. This is the large natural oasis which lured Jaisal to the site 800 years ago, and which was the city's main source of water until the recent drought. Nowadays, it's just a shallow depression in the surrounding desert, strewn with beached cenotaphs. While waiting for the planned pipeline to fill it with water again, enjoy the desolate atmosphere, the splendid views of the battlemented fort from atop the temple roofs, and the beautiful arched gateway said to have been erected by Tilo, the famous prostitute. Her nemesis, the then Maharajah, threatened to knock this immoral structure down, until Tilo outwitted him by setting up a Krishna temple right next to it. Don't leave without paying a visit to Gadisar's quaint little **Folklore Museum**. Open from 7 am to 12 noon, 3 pm to 7 pm daily (admission Rs2), this houses a curious assortment of fossils, dolls, coins, ancient inscriptions, folklore artefacts, and 'ceremonial toilet boxes'. While here, pick up a copy of N.K. Sharma's local guidebook (Rs15), full of useful information and amusing titbits:

> Question: What is the 'Great Indian Bustard of Jaisalmer'? Answer: 'This is beautiful and extremely popular bird found over area Jaisalmer. It attains the height of 2 to 3 ft. Its neck is long like that of a camel. Which it moves side ways while walking. It is of grey colour. Its eyes shine like the eyes of a deer. Its voice is very sweet. It feeds on gravel. At the approach of the men it takes to flight. It's a very scarce bird found in the world.

A description of one of the world's rarest birds, which breeds in the large (3162 sq km, 1220 sq miles) Desert National Park (40 km, 925 miles) to the south-west of Jaisalmer.

From the museum, stroll up to the Gadisar Gate to re-enter the walled city. The powerful fort within the city, perched on the Tricuta (three-peak) hill of antiquity, is also known as 'Sonar Qila' or **Golden Fort** because all its fortifications and residential buildings are made of yellow-sandstone. Built over a period of 7 years (and much added to in the subsequent 700 years), its meandering, snakelike wall is buttressed by 99 bastions and corner towers. The unique feature in its construction is that no mortar or cement was used to join the huge blocks of stone, only sand. It was only in the mid-18th century that the fort's inhabitants began to come off the heights and settle on the downslope below. Over a century of flurried building ensued—and it was during this period that the wealthy city merchants formed their mohallas or guilds (after their clans and professions), laid their streets, and erected their imposing havelis (literally 'big houses'). The fort was attacked many times during its long history, notably by the Tughlaqs and the Mughals, and was captured on at least three occasions. Its walls bear the telltale scars of fireball and cannonball attack, and the battlements within are still littered with original cannon and stone balls. Red *sati* handprints at each of the gates are the sad legacy of doomed Rajput wives who went to join their husbands on the funeral pyres.

Just within the stout gateway, you'll see the soaring 7-storey palace. Ascend the sloping stone ramp until—many twists and bends later—you come to the large open square in the centre of the old Castle Fort. At the top of the square is the old **Diwan-i-Am**, a beautiful marble throne atop a high series of steps, from where the Maharajah used to hold open court with his subjects (no, you can't sit on it). Behind it, a low arched tunnel-gateway leads up to the **Jain Temples**. Open 7 am to noon daily, this highly decorative group of seven temples, constructed between the 14th and 16th centuries, contain a total of 6666 images of the Jain *tirthankars* (prophets), mythological figures and gods. The carvings are uniformly magnificent. There's a small library with a rare collection of miniature paintings, books and manuscripts. There's also a priceless emerald statue of the Jain deity in the temple of Mahavir Swami. But it's only open to view from 10 am to 11 am daily. Photos aren't allowed in any of the temples, and all leather articles (including belts and bags) must be left at the entrance.

A short walk left out of the temple complex brings you to **Dop Khana** ('place of cannon'), providing marvellous views down over Jaisalmer town. To the right of this rampart can be seen the fanciful **Salim Singh Haveli**. This palatial structure with its peacock-motif arched roof was built by the powerful late 18th-century prime minister Salim Singh. A man of overweening ambition, he earned his notoriety by wiping out two nearby villages (3000 people) in a single night. Then he set about building a house high enough to permit a bridge running across to the Fort itself, to give him private access to the king's ear. But his plans went awry, the other Rajput courtiers persuading the king to fire on Salim Singh's high-rise *haveli*, blowing the top two levels clean away.

To see it at close range (excellent façade, disappointing interior), leave the fort and cross over the central market to the north part of town. Near the *haveli* you'll also find the huge 19th-century **Mandir Palace**, with its beautiful silver furnishings. Just north of this is the finest example of Jaisalmer's architecture—the group of five ornate merchant's houses collectively known as **Patwon ki Haveli**. Contracted by the wealthy jeweller Patwon for his five sons, and built between 1800 and 1860, they represent the finest achievement of Jaisalmer's fastidious silavats or stone-carvers. Every pillar, bracket, window and balcony is an intricately carved masterpiece. The graceful filigreed windows in particular, remind one of the similar merchants' houses of Venice. From the top terraces, you have the best views of all—both of the yellow-gold fort, and of the tiny medieval backstreets. Of the five havelis, three are now government-owned, and only two are open to the public (10.30 am to 5 pm daily).

Finish off with a visit to nearby **Nathmal ki Haveli**, built as a prime minister's residence in the late 19th century. The right and left wings of this beautiful house were carved separately by two Muslim brothers, yet exhibit only minimal differences. The front door, guarded by a brace of elegant sandstone elephants, is a *tour de force*. The first floor is magnificently painted. The archway of this 5-storey edifice presents the best views. Outside, explore the countless other mansions and houses dotted round town—every bend in the road turns up fresh delights!

After a siesta, you'll be ready for a 'sunset experience' at **Sam Sand-Dunes**, 40 km (25 miles) west of Jaisalmer. Check out the sunrise/sunset timings at the tourist office, then arrange a jeep ride. Your hotel should handle this, and if you get a group together it should only cost about Rs50 per head. On the way to the dunes, stop off at **Mool Sagar** (7 km out of Jaisalmer) to see the Maharajah's 15th-century country house. When not stricken by drought, this is a popular picnic spot with beautiful gardens. There is an interesting camel pulley on the (now bone-dry) deep well, and some nice carvings on the walls. At Sam Sand, take a camel onto the dunes, pick one with no noisy home tourists on it, meditate on oneness with the desert, and pray for a decent sunset.

RECREATION

Traditional Jaisalmeri music employs varying themes of *maand* (Rajasthani chamber music) songs, which are usually depressing. As a local guidebook explained: 'When rains were over, the men went out along with their caravan for commercial purposes, leaving their better-halves behind who let out effusions of love in their separation. The variety of love-songs of separation are the glorious proofs thereof.' Street musicians and camel drivers prefer cheery *ghoomal* (dancing) melodies or lung-bursting *bharat* chants, used by warriors of old to summon the terrible power of Durga before each battle. Several hotels lay on traditional folk-music shows, performed by the guild of fort musicians. They normally play for marriage ceremonies, but they play just as well for tourists.

SHOPPING

Jaisalmer produces more wool than any other Indian town. Together with two neighbouring Rajasthan townships—Bikaner and Barmer—it also produces perhaps the best-quality camel and sheep wool in India. The best buys, therefore, are woollen carpets. Because they are locally produced (by skilled Mohammedan refugees who fled into India from Pakistan after the 1971 war, settling 150 km (94 miles) south of Jaisalmer, at Gadera, near Barmer) they are relatively inexpensive. The wool is gathered, sorted and spun in Jaisalmer, then sent to Gadera for weaving. The finished carpets return to Jaisalmer for sale. While the chance of getting an original carpet is pretty slim (patterns are generally copied from traditional designs, and the only real variations are those of colour), the quality of workmanship is quite high. At about Rs5000 a standard 5 × 7 ft (2.2 × 1.5 m) carpet (288 knots per sq in) is very good value.

Shopping in Jaisalmer can be a hassle. There's a lot of pressure on you to buy, and prices are hiked up depending on how dumb you look. The golden rule still applies: don't accept any recommendations from hotel owners or street touts. They are all helping themselves, not you. If you can face the heat, April–May is the best shopping season—there are few tourists about, and even hardened traders are forced to drop their prices. A good year-round shop is **Damoder Handicrafts** up in the fort (near 4th gate). Bargain hard here for wall-hangings, bedsheets, embroidery, paintings and leather goods at rock-bottom prices. To see the complete range of Jaisalmeri produce—Mughal-design carpets (a mix of Australian and Gadera wool), pastel woollen dhurries, mirrored wall-hangings and beautiful cushion-covers—check out **Jaisalmer Rugs 'n' Arts**, inside Chirriya Haveli, near Patwon ki Haveli. For now, its prices are very competitive indeed. Similar fair play is to be had at **Kamal Handicrafts Emporium**, near the Jain temples in the fort, famous for its embroidery items from Barmer. A lot of the hand-embroidered crafts sold in Pushkar, Jaipur and even Delhi originate from Barmer—where they were traditionally produced as heritage items handed down from father to son, or as marriage gifts.

Jaisalmer's sprawling **Bhatia Market** runs all the way down from the fort entrance to the State Bank of India. Here you can buy just about anything—cool *kurta*-pajamas (from **Khadi Gramodyog,** near July 8th Restaurant), good, cheap silver (from **Krishna Jewellers,** near Kalpana restaurant), patterned mojaris or desert slippers (from **Vijay Leatherwork,** Ashni Rd), bright 14-m (45-ft) turbans, handy for lowering down water-wells, or for covering yourself in sandstorms—their traditional desert use), and huge 7-m (23-ft) gathered skirts.

WHERE TO STAY

Expensive/Mid-range (US$10–35/Rs250–1000 per room night)
Jaisalmer now has a staggering total of 42 hotels—all but two of which are aimed at the budget traveller. Until the Taj and Oberoi set up shop, the only comfy option is **Narayan Niwas Palace** (tel 2408) with cool air-conditioned rooms at Rs700 single, Rs950 double. It's a converted caravanserai at the foot of town (near State Bank of India), with friendly family atmosphere and good food. Princess Anne once stayed here, and (if you believe the staff) she has already entered the pantheon of minor Hindu deities. The new **Heritage Inn** on Sam Road has rooms from Rs1200 upwards. The other place with air-conditioned rooms (Rs355 single, Rs400 double) is the gloomy **Moomal Tourist Bungalow** (tel 2492, 2392). The cheaper village-style huts (Rs100) are unbearably stuffy. The **Himmatgarh Palace**, 1 Ramgarh Road (tel 2213) and **Jawahar Niwas Palace** (tel 2208) are two mid-range hotels with all basic services but in need of renovation.

Budget (under US$10/Rs250 per room night)
Jaisalmer's reputation for personalised hospitality comes into its own in the budget lodges. Most of these make a point of reserving train tickets back to Jodhpur for you, regardless of whether or not you take their camel-trek. Rooms are generally spartan, but there's often good information, free guide services, a sun-roof (with views), and as much of the delicious local tea as you can drink.

A few of the better ones are **Fort View Hotel** (tel 2214) near the fort entrance, good information, overseas calls service, and superb views of the fort; **Hotel Pleasure,** opposite State Bank of India, with an informative manager, family atmosphere; nearby **Swastika Guest House,** with clean, comfortable rooms, cheap dorm beds.

Many people prefer to stay up in the Fort itself. It's cooler and quieter, and the views are just as good looking down as they are looking up. Shop around before taking a room though—old favourites like **Jaisal Castle Inn** (tel 2362, on the fort ramparts) have suffered badly from over-publicity, while new finds are coming up all the time. Best of the current crop is **Hotel Paradise** (tel 2569), originally the home of the Maharajah's family. The breezy sun-roof gives views of the main royal palaces to the north, while many rooms have the south-facing views over the town and desert (ask for No. 105). There's even a 24-hour chilled beer service.

Finally, for a rare opportunity to stay in a Prime Minister's *haveli*, check out **Shree Nath Palace Hotel**, situated in the oldest part of the fort. This is a 600-year-old house, with first-rate views of the Jain temples from the roof, and very cheap. Staying here is a real experience.

EATING OUT

Food is very cheap (you'll rarely pay more than Rs25 for a meal) but rather dull. Jaisalmeris are intractably vegetarian, the staple diet being boiled vegetables, fried *roti*, and green milos or wheat balls. And there's a dearth of good restaurants. **Jaisal Castle Hotel** offers superior food, but doesn't actually provide it. This goes for a good number of (unhygienic) budget restaurants too. But few people are really interested in food. Jaisalmer's air is so dry and hot, that most travellers live on a diet of Limcas, *lassis* and lime-sodas. Even local people aren't immune—they drink an average of 10 litres of liquid a day.

Up in the fort, at the 4th gate, **Arvind Cold Drinks** has a regular clientele of heat-blasted travellers guzzling ice-cold beers and mineral water. It also offers some of the cheapest camel-treks. Below the fort entrance, opposite Salem Singh *haveli*, there's **Treat**—a popular roof-top restaurant with an astonishing 347 items on its menu. It doesn't like to rush meals—'short time destroyed the cooking!'—but they're worth waiting for. Rajasthani specialities like desert beans and millet seeds, mutton and green vegetables, must be ordered 2 hours in advance. Nearby **Monica** roof-top restaurant offers the same royal Rajasthani fare, and is just as cheap and laidback. Another recomended restaurant near the main gate is **Gay Time**. Moving down into Bhatia market, a minute's walk from the fort entrance, find **8th July** restaurant. This is a good breakfast spot with a popular roof-top section. Come here for the best Chinese food, capucchino, and *lassi* in town. There are 25 varieties of ice-cream on offer, also 'items such as Vegemite, Marmite Toast, Mussielie, Brown Brade, Garlic Cheese and Peanut Butter'. A minute below 8th July, down an alley to the right, **Kanchan Shri** is famous for its *manikarnia lassi*—it doesn't seem to do much else. A 10-minute stroll down to the bottom of the market (past **Kailash Juice Centre**, good for fresh juices and *lassis*), you find Jaisalmer's better restaurants. **Kalpana's** is a pleasant open-air place, popular with locals and travellers alike, which stays open till late. It's a bit rough and ready, but the food—Indian, Continental and Chinese—is cheap and tasty. Service is quick, and the menu ('Chee's Ball', 'Omelette with Sours') is tantalising. **Hotel Narayan Niwas** has fairly upmarket cuisine—good for a minor blowout. The new **Trio**, a minute's walk below Kalpana's (and just inside the fort walls) is the only 'proper' restaurant in town—table service and napkins, tasteful decor, pots of weak English tea and superior Indian/Continental fare. When you've drunk enough mineral water to fill up the Gadisar Tank, come here to soak it up!

GENERAL INFORMATION

Government of Rajasthan Tourist Office (tel 2406, 2392), at the tourist bungalow between rail station and town, is open 8 am–12 noon, 3–6 pm (except Sundays). Fair information, poor handouts, and expensive (Rs75) jeep tours of the city. Far better tours are given by local guides, who wait at the entrance to the fort. They speak good English, and for about the same price will walk you right round Jaisalmer from 7 am to noon. If staying in the fort area, there's very good information at Fort View Hotel.

Vehicles are of no use within the city but can be hired for trips to Sam, Khuri, the Desert National Park and Lodurva. Rates are negotiable and should be agreed on in advance. **Jaisal Tours** in Hotel Narayan Niwas (tel 2408, 2397) can book cars and jeeps.

KHURI

Khuri lies in the heart of the Great Indian Desert, 40 km (25 miles) south-west of Jaisalmer. It is the central village of about 100 smaller settlements ruled by the Rajput Sodhas, a 'fire' caste who hail their origin from a mythological hero called Parma (one of the founders of the Rajput clans, who sprang from the holy flame at Achalgat, Mount Abu).

The Sodha family have ruled Khuri for some 400 years. There are about 2000 inhabitants, though about half of these are wandering nomads who travel far afield in search of water and fodder for their cattle. Noble, dignified Father Singh is the head man, but the real power behind the throne is 'Mama' Singh—a large, charismatic lady with a heart of gold and a real talent for cooking. Her two charming, well-educated sons—Bhagwan Singh and Tane Singh Sodha—are both perfect gentlemen, and take responsibility for looking after tourists. The service here is quite incredible: if they like you, you are instantly adopted into the family and simply nothing is too good for you. People they don't like are given a meal, then politely but firmly sent back to Jaisalmer on the next bus. As Tane Singh comments:

'Here in Khuri we are not out to exploit tourists—we want them to see the real way of the desert. And we are determined to keep our traditional customs and values, even if this means living somewhat in the past with simple means and few luxuries. Visitors who do not respect our culture, or who press business on us, we turn away.'

For the past 12 or so years, Western tourists have made the arduous trip out to Jaisalmer with one main objective—to do the big camel-trek into the Great Thar Desert. But the best part of the desert, the rolling sand-dunes, don't actually appear till some 40 km (25 miles) *out* of Jaisalmer.

To see the dunes, you'll have to go to Khuri. Jaisalmer hoteliers know this, and do everything in their power to stop travellers going there. They tell them awful fibs like 'Khuri is restricted area', or 'Khuri is in Pakistan', or even 'Khuri is out-of-bounds army post'. If this fails, they put a boycott on travellers returning from Khuri, and refuse to put them up in Jaisalmer. The best policy is to tell no one you're coming here, and (on your return) to tell no one where you've been.

Come to Khuri for an authentic desert experience. As one traveller wrote: 'When planning the culmination of your Rajasthan journey, try to find yourself here. Khuri is the gateway to the real Rajput people, folklore and customs. If you can, spend a week or so here, learn about the people, and become part of their extended family and way of life. Here, you can really become one with the desert and its tribes.'

The best time to visit is between September and February, when the desert is most cool and pleasant. The Sodhas run camel-safaris from October to March. Long treks of between 12 and 15 days—for enthusiasts who want a 'complete' experience of the desert—are really only practical from November to January. Bhagwan Singh runs a special 2-week camel-safari to connect with the annual **Cattle Fair** (100 000 cattle, 200 000 people) at Tilwara. This event, which takes place at the end of March, is even bigger and more spectacular than the famous Camel Fair at Pushkar.

Important Note: At the time of going to press, in September 1992, there were reports that Khuri was to fall within the inner line, and so become out of bounds to tourists. Permits to visit the area may be given by the District Commissioner's office in Jaisalmer. Permits are also required to visit the National Park in addition to making prior arrangements with the park authorities in Jaisalmer.

ARRIVAL/DEPARTURE
Negotiate the line of a jeep for the 40-km (25-mile) drive, or take the mid-morning bus which takes about 1½ hours. (Buses return at about 4.30 pm.)

WHAT TO SEE
Khuri is the place to come for a once-in-a-lifetime experience: a camel-trek across the white, rolling dunes of the Thar Desert. How long you stay is up to you. For maximum enjoyment, aim to spend at least 3 days here: one day to see the village, followed by a 2-day camel-trek. For those bothered by heat (and that applies to anybody coming here after end of March) a day excursion will be quite sufficient.

Khuri camel-treks are rather more expensive than Jaisalmer's. Charges vary a lot, depending on whether or not Mama takes to you. After all, the best thing about Khuri is Mama's cooking—a wide range of traditional breads and vegetarian dishes, and lots of it—and she doesn't tolerate skimpy eaters. All meals, and endless pots of thirst-quenching cardamom tea, are included in the price. So is one of the small beehive-shaped guest huts in the village. So are very mild-mannered, obedient camels and incredibly obliging camel-drivers. And—most important—so is the overwhelming hospitality of the villagers. A testimonial book of satisfied customers, the first thing you're shown on arrival, speaks for itself.

Bhagwan Singh always meets the morning bus from Jaisalmer at Khuri. He escorts you to the reception building, pumps you with tea and hospitality, settles you in your hut, and sends Mama over to greet you. Then you get lunch—about 10 courses of it. Later, after a siesta, a tour is arranged for you round the village. This takes place round dusk, when the heat is down and the desert sky is at its most beautiful.

Khuri village is a charming, modest settlement of small mud-and-stone beehive dwellings and stone huts, many painted with Aztec-like patterns by the women, interspersed with a few wicker cattle-pens. The tough old village elders squat or sit outside their huts, pounding flax for wool or spinning rough thread, while the younger men and boys pound straw and mud between the bricks of newly rising walls and huts. They are shy of visitors, but invariably friendly. Ask to be shown Khuri's small 'shop'—you'll need it to stock up on supplies for your morning trek. The desert tribes are heavily into 'guest-gifts', and you will do well to buy in a good stock of cigarettes, bidis, pens and sweets here. All these things are cheap, and go down well. So do small presents like English/American coins, and postcards of the Royal Family.

At sunset, climb to the roof of the hospitality/reception building and watch the evening sky turn deep, silky velvet-blue, and the thin cloud tissue burn a vivid rose-pink before fading suddenly into darkness. Night falls very quickly, and there is no electricity, only oil-lamps. The evening is generally spent with Bhagwan Singh and his chums in the courtyard below, supping the desert 'country wine' and listening to the low, atmospheric women's songs and village drums, as yet another marriage hut is ritually prepared for the bride and groom. Your bed is made up for you outside your hut, and you drift off to sleep under a glittering canopy of stars.

In the morning, after a substantial breakfast, you are introduced to your camel and your driver. Before leaving, check your equipment and dress: you'll need a flashlight (for sleeping out in the dunes), a good pair of sun-glasses (for desert glare), lots of camera film (photos are a great way of making friends in the villages) and as many oranges (best thirst-quenchers) as you can carry in from Jaisalmer. All food, water and bedding is provided for you, and a comfortable seat is made up on the camel. Despite this, many people suffer aching thighs and backsides on trek, so make sure your seat has as much padding as possible. Strong, comfortable shoes are a must—and they need to be narrow to fit in the camel stirrups. Sandals are no good. As for clothing, wear long trousers/skirts and long-sleeved shirts—not only because the Rajputs are a very modest people, but also because any exposed flesh is burnt red-raw after a few hours in the intense desert sun. Men should consider two pairs of underpants; women will certainly need bras. Both sexes should bring some sort of protective headwear (brimmed hats are best). An excellent alternative is a Jodhpur umbrella. Take the minimum of luggage on trek—leave your pack or bag with Mama Singh under lock and key.

Every camel comes complete with an experienced driver, who sits behind you and anticipates your every need. He is often a burnt-black, brightly turbaned character who grins a lot and speaks better camel than English. Many camel-drivers while away the hours singing plaintive desert songs (which is pleasant) and giving their foreign guests regular body-massages, both on and off the camel. Whatever you do, don't complain of an aching rear. This will only get you hurled face-down on the sands and pummelled rudely on the buttocks until you are screaming for mercy.

Camel-safaris from Khuri start off about 8 am, and you ride for about 4 hours (stopping at the most attractive dunes) until the heat becomes too intense, round noon. Lunch, and a long siesta, is spent at one of the nearby villages. Then, around 4 pm, you set off again. By now, you're probably used to the peculiar rocking, rolling sensation of camel-riding. Your kidneys have had a jolly good shuffle, and if the long siesta hasn't calmed you down, then the slow, soothing desert pace of life soon will. The vista is a silent, empty yellow-white wasteland of rolling sands, interspersed with bare rock and desolate scrub. From time to time, you may see a chinkara or Indian gazelle springing across the flatlands, or a flock of bright-plumed peacocks out for a stroll, or the occasional mongoose, fox, desert rat or the Great Indian Bustard, but otherwise there is absolutely nothing out there. A few hours of this, and the mind switches off and begins to play tricks. The most common mirage is of a five-star hotel with a refrigerated swimming-pool and ice-cold beers.

Sudden electric storms, dust storms, sand storms and rain storms tend to break the spell. So does the periodic emergence from the bleached-white desert of small local villages. They all look identical, and most of them are keen to trade or barter presents. The best thing to ask for is a bottle of Black Panther Triple X Rum (army canteen issue), which is the perfect way of ending a hard day's trek.

Sleeping out on the dunes is a magical experience. The night sky is crystal-clear, the desert goes quite silent, and the bunched cacti and brush lie in stark relief against the moonscape of the marble-smooth sands, giving the sinister aspect of giant surreal spiders frozen to the desert floor.

The sunrise, like the sunset, is another desert spectacle. It heralds the arrival of a huge breakfast, cooked by the drivers, and a glorious pot of steaming cardamom tea. Three more hours on the camel, and you're back in Khuri—to be met by Mama with a special lunch, and treated to as many cold showers and liquid refreshments as you can handle. The Sodha family crowd around to make their farewells, and see you safely onto the 4.30 pm bus out to Jaisalmer. You will remember their hospitality for years to come.

SHOPPING

Khuri has no tourist handicrafts business, and that's the way the Sodha family wish to keep it. There is a thriving cottage industry of pottery, blankets camel rugs and embroidery, but all these things are made by the villagers either for their own use or for barter with neighbouring villagers. Only if you supply your own materials your own camel, sheep's or goat's wool from Jaisalmer) will they consider taking orders for carpets, rugs or blankets. Tane Singh Sodha believes: 'Once greed, money and trade comes into a village, it turns the people bad. We don't want that.'

UDAIPUR

The lake city of Udaipur—'City of Dreams' or 'Venice of the East'— is perhaps the most beautiful of all Indian centres. With a relatively low population, it is certainly one of the quietest. A romantic collection of exotic gardens filled with blossoming trees, and fantasy island palaces shimmering in mirror-calm lakes—it is a firm favourite with travellers.

Udaipur was founded by Maharajah Udai Singh, who moved the Mewar capital here following the third and final sack of Chittor in 1567. Udai Singh was ruler of the foremost Rajput clan, the Sisodias, who claimed direct descent from the sun. He was also a keen gardener, and he chose this site not only because of its excellent natural protection (encircled by the rugged Aravali mountains), but because it had a good water supply. Under his auspices, Udaipur quickly gained fame as a place of colourful, scented, landscaped gardens, island parks, pavilions and fountains.

But the city's history is mainly one of blood and glory. Udai Singh left his son, Maharana Pratap, a difficult legacy—the new city of Udaipur fell under immediate attack from Akbar, the Mughal emperor of Delhi. Pratap was a stubborn, yet courageous man. Angry at the capitulation of Jaipur's Mansingh to the Mughals, he made it a matter of personal honour to resist the northern invaders. With only meagre resources at his disposal, he kept the Mughals successfully at bay for 25 years, before finally being overpowered in 1576. Subsequent Maharanas were involved in constant intrigue, warfare and bloodshed, and Udaipur regained its peace only in 1818 when it came under British control, like much of the rest of Rajasthan.

The City Palace at Udaipur from Lake Pichola

Today, Udaipur is still very much a traditional 16th-century Rajput town, proud of the fact that throughout its turbulent history it never succumbed to foreign cultural influences. Here, most families still cook, wash, pray and eat together as a family unit, and the city's strong heritage of community life remains pretty much intact. Only during the past decade or so, has the social structure suddenly shifted—with a growing number of people breaking the tradition of centuries and moving out of the quiet, safe old city walls to settle in the busy, densely populated commercial centre of the modern new town.

For the visitor, this development is reflected by the sharp contrasts in the way of life here. Down by the lakes, and especially round the old city to the east of Lake Pichola, Udaipur is a picture of peace and tranquillity. Outside the old city walls, however, and especially round the rail/bus stations to the southeast, it is the same old Indian story of mad, feverish traffic, dust and smoke. The odd thing is that such semi-rural romanticism and such urban chaos can so harmoniously coexist.

Situated in the shade of dark green hills, and cooled by its three lakes—the Pichola, Fateh Sagar and Udai Sagar—Udaipur has a uniquely refreshing climate. Pleasantly dry and cool from Sept to March, it is a nifty getaway from the rest of Rajasthan's heat and dust. But even here, it's hot by April. Only a hardy few make it for the June/July monsoons, and they see Udaipur at its best—all the lakes and gardens a rich, luxuriant burst of colour.

ARRIVAL/DEPARTURE

Air
Indian Airlines offers daily flights between Udaipur and Aurangabad (Rs1221), Bombay (Rs1348), Delhi (Rs1129), Jaipur (Rs767), and Jodhpur (Rs583).

Dabok Airport is 23 km (14 miles) from the city and taxis cost approximately Rs125–150 for a oneway transfer. The Indian Airlines office is near Delhi Gate (tel 28999, 23952) Dabok Airport flight information (tel 23011, 24433, 142).

182

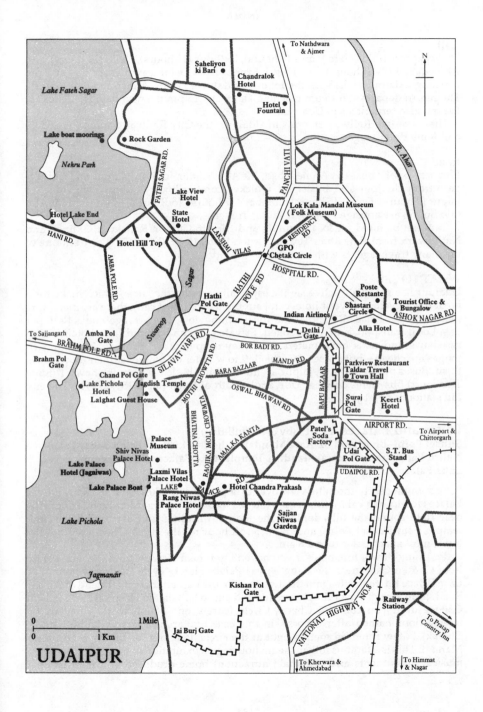

UDAIPUR

Rail

Daily express trains go to Jaipur (8 hours), Jodhpur (11 hours), Delhi (21 hours), and Ahmedabad (9–10 hours). The *Chetak Express* from Delhi leaves every day at 1 pm reaching Udaipur at 9.15 am the following day via Jaipur, Ajmer and Chittorgarh. The return departs at 6.15 pm reaching Delhi at 2.15 pm the next day. The *Pink City Express* also terminates in Udaipur.

There are two Railway Stations in Udaipur; the City Railway Station (tel 23535) and Rana Pratapnagar Station (tel 23425).

Road

Frequent public buses to Ahmedabad, Mt Abu, Ajmer, Jodhpur, Jaipur and Chittorgarh from Udaipur's ST bus-stand. Quicker, comfier luxury buses (often video) to Jaipur (9 hours), Delhi (15 hours), Bombay (17 hours), Jodhpur (7 hours) and Mt Abu (4½ hours) are arranged through Taldar Travels.

Cars can be hired for local running and trips to Chittor, Ranakpur, Eklingji and Nathdwara from **Rajasthan Tours**, Garden Hotel (tel 23030, 25777) or from one of the many travel agents with branches in the city.

WHAT TO SEE

Udaipur has many attractive sights, especially around the lakes, which make for a great day's cycling. If your hotel can't supply a bike (most can), there are many hire places in Lake Palace Rd and at the Tourist Bungalow. The average rate is Rs10 per day. Local transport is pretty crooked. Private cars can be hired from hotels. Auto-rickshaws and taxis have meters—but they're invariably 'broken'. Horse-drawn tongas are cheap—but horses are often left to wander off wherever their mood takes them. Buses out to Jodhpur, Jaipur, Delhi and Mt Abu leave from the new ST (State Transport) bus-stand down at Udiyapol, south of town (tel 27151, 27191). The city rail station is nearby.

Lakes and Palaces Tour (by cycle, full-day)
Sunset Point–Bhartiya Lok Kala Mandal–Sahelion-ki-Bari–Fateh Sagar Lake–Nehru Park–Pratap Smarak–Jagdish Temple–City Palace and Museum–Lake Palace

For a stunning early-morning view over Udaipur and its lakes, be at the Rang Niwas Palace Hotel, Lake Palace Rd, at 7 am latest. Head down the garden avenue opposite, bear right round the hillside, take the footpath leading up (just behind the pink temple, near **Sunset Point**) and allow a full hour for the climb. The view from the top is most spectacular round 8 am.

Returning down, hire bikes if you haven't got them already from the rank below Roof Garden Cafe (near the Rang Niwas Palace Hotel), cycle left to the bottom of Lake Palace Rd, then left again through the narrow Bapu Bazaar. At the end of Bazaar Road, head straight over the crossroads and curve left via the Hospital and Medical College until you come to Chetak Circle (surely one of the world's few traffic intersections named after a horse, in this case Maharana Pratap's faithful steed, Chetak). A few hundred metres right at the circle, look out for **Bhartiya Lok Kala Mandal**. This is a famous folk museum housing an exhibition of tribal knick-knacks, musical instruments and (the main attraction) home-produced and international puppets. Rajasthan is said to be the birthplace of Indian marionettes, and the Kala Mandal (established 1952) is the place responsible for reviving this traditional art form after centuries of neglect. It was set up primarily to preserve various folklore traditions, but once puppets began to catch on again (mainly as a children's education aid, though also for village family-planning programmes) it began running puppet training camps for aspiring artistes, not only in Udaipur but all over India. Here you can see string and 'lalua' puppets from Rajasthan, rod puppets from Bengal, shadow puppets from Andhra, and Orissan marionettes. Also a variety of muppets and puppets from America, Sweden, Romania, Czechoslovakia and many other countries. There is a charming 'puppet show' every hour or so, and if you are interested in seeing how the puppets are made, just drop into the small training centre left of the entrance. The Kala Mandal (tel 29296) is open 9 am to 5.30 pm daily, and admission is Rs2.

To see one of Udaipur's finest gardens, cycle right out of the museum and then left at Sukhadia Circle. The first major turning right along this road brings you to **Sahelion-ki-Bari** (garden of the maids of honour). This striking example of Hindu landscape gardening features a picturesque lotus pond (turfed with radiant yellow blossoms in the spring), round which are ranged four magnificent marble elephants and myriad fountains. The pretty pool pavilion (within small enclosure) has been much-photographed, but you should save your photos for the curious **Community Science Centre**. This is just behind the pavilion, and is unmissable: sea-monsters in milk bottles, neanderthal heads, moulting stuffed bats, and a skeleton in a sari! Rest awhile at **Sahelion-ki-Bari**. It's a peaceful, restful picnic spot—ideal for a packed lunch. Open from 9 am to 6 pm daily, admission Rs1, camera charge Rs5.

Cycling out left, then right (a short, exhausting ascent) you come presently out on **Fateh Sagar Lake**. The pretty island garden shimmering in the middle of it is **Nehru Park**. Leave the cycle at the foot of Moti Magri Hill, and take the Rs1 tourist boat over. The island is visually stunning: a riot of bright orange and maroon blossoms among green landscaped lawns. It has a small (bizarre) restaurant. Back on land, proceed along the lakeside a further 0.5 km (⅓ mile) and visit the **Pratap Smarak** monument on the left. Here, atop the Moti Magri or 'Pearl Hill', stands the ebony-black statue of Maharana Pratap (1540–97), mounted on his 'loyal and faithful mount' Chetak. The climb up is a bit wearing, but is relieved by pretty gardens, and at the top there is a marvellous view down over the lakes. If here between 3.30 and 6 pm, you can use the telescope observatory. The memorial itself is open 7 am to 7 pm daily, admission Rs2.

Below the entrance, hire a rowing boat (Rs35 per hour) to laze awhile on the tranquil Fateh Sagar Lake (scooped out by Maharana Fateh Singh after the original 1678 construction was destroyed by torrential rains). Then recover bikes, head back inland via the **Lake Swaroop Sagar causeway** (just keep to the left) and take directions for Hathipol, where the Rajput princes used to house their elephants in times of war. Past this, up the hill, visit the **Jagdish Temple**. This is the biggest and best temple in Udaipur, built in the Indo-Aryan style by Maharana Jagat Singh in 1651. The black stone image enshrined within depicts Vishnu as Jagannath, Lord of the Universe, the brass Garuda outside representing his animal-carrier, the man-eagle. The exterior walls are notable for their beautiful elephant-motif carvings. A good time to arrive here is late afternoon, when you may be lucky enough to find local ladies singing prayer-songs and traditional hymns, accompanied by lively temple musicians. The foot of the temple steps is the favourite pitch of Udaipur's best drinks vendor, with a selection of about 20 differently-flavoured fruit cordials—a real treat after all that hot cycling.

Just up the road, you'll find the grandiose **City Palace and Museum**. This largest of all Rajasthani palace complexes stands on the crest of a ridge, poised over the serene Pichola Lake. You'll enter from the northern end, through the triple **Tripolia Gate** (1725), with its eight exquisitely carved marble arches. This is where the Maharanas used to be weighed in gold or silver on their birthdays, the largesse later being distributed to the populace. Study the exterior—a breathtaking array of white filigreed balconies and windows, ornate arches and cupola-topped octagonal towers—then purchase the useful guide book at the entrance, and go exploring. The museum actually takes up most of the sumptuous palace complex, and is full of delights: the glorious peacock mosaics (depicting India's national bird at different seasons of the year) of the **Mor Chowk**, the mirror-encrusted **Moti Mahal**, the porcelain and glass of **Manak (Ruby) Mahal**, the fine collection of miniatures in **Krishna Vilas** (and **Zanana Mahal**) and the ornamented Chinese tiles of **Chini Mahal**. Climbing through a maze-like succession of staircases and small rooms (many decorated with mirrors, stained-glass windows, latticed balconies, ostentatious columns), enter a small second museum, with more superb miniatures, toys and royal knick-knacks, via the **Rai Angam** or Royal Courtyard. The views down over the Pichola, with its coronet backdrop of gaunt desert mountains, and of the glittering bone-white Lake Palace (framed perhaps, in an ornamented palace window) are something you'll remember for years to come. The Palace museum is open 9 am to 4 pm daily, admission is Rs10, camera fee Rs5 (Rs20 for video cameras!). There is an extensive and well illustrated catalogue available

Next, cycle down to **Bhansi Ghat** (below City Palace), and buy a boat ticket (includes coffee and biscuits) over to **Jag Niwas** island on the Pichola Lake. Built around 1740 as a summer palace for the Maharana, the **Lake Palace Hotel** on Jag Niwas is a utopian fantasy in dazzling white marble—the place to be at sunset, sipping a cool cocktail or an ice-cold 'deluxe' beer perhaps, watching the bird-scarers on the top terraces lassooing pigeons (they spoil the paintwork) and waiting for the still waters of the lake to turn first coppery-yellow, then a fiery blood-red. After dusk, flocks of giant fruit bats sweep over the lake, like a scene out of Hitchcock's 'The Birds'. On the subject of films, the nearby **Jag Mandir** island—another summerhouse of the Maharana—was used in James Bond's 'Octopussy'. Its other famous guest was the Emperor Shah Jahan, who apparently got the idea of building the Taj Mahal while imprisoned here.

Unless staying for supper at the Lake Palace Hotel, finish off with an evening meal at **Roof Garden Cafe** in Lake Palace Rd. From the roof top, you have a marvellous view of the City Palaces (beautifully illuminated by night) up on the hill, also a ringside seat for any marriage ceremonies going on at the small **Sitala Mata** (mother goddess) temple below. In March/April—the usual marriage season—the streets of Udaipur are alive with uniformed bands, colourful processions, and disco rickshaws. They generally all end up here, around 8 pm, since all marriages require the blessing of the goddess—not just before the wedding, but afterwards too.

The new West Zone Cultural Centre was one of seven centres set up in 1985. Established in the splendid **Bagor ki Haveli** near the main ghat on Fateh Sagar. Open daily from 10 am to 5 pm there is a small museum and regular theatre and music performances (tel 23305, 23858). The centre has also developed a crafts village known as **Shilpgram** near Havala 3 km (1¾ miles) away which hosts a festival each winter.

RECREATION

Udaipur offers Rajasthan's best cultural entertainments. In addition to the programmes organised by the Cultural Centre there are many other regular events. Here you can see traditional folk dancing performed by professionals—either at Meera Kala Mandir ('culture evenings' on Tuesdays, Thursdays and Saturdays, 7 pm start, tickets Rs20) and at Lake Palace Hotel (folk dances on the top terraces at 9 pm nightly). The Lake Palace also has fun puppet shows in the courtyard at 7 pm daily. A better 'puppet circus' takes place from 6 to 7 pm each evening at Bhartiya Lok Kala Mandal (Rs5).

There's fishing at Jaisamund Lake (permits from tourist office); free horse-riding (for guests only) at Pratap Country Inn and Shikarbadi Hotel; and swimming for Rs30–50 for non-residents at various hotel pools including Laxmi Vilas Palace, Shikarbadi and Hotel Lake End

SHOPPING

To see the full range of attractive handicrafts—dainty wooden folk toys, hand-printed textiles, tie-and-dye saris, wall-hangings, miniature paintings and chunky silver jewellery—start at **Rajasthan Government Handicrafts Emporium** in Chetak Circle. Then visit **Hathipol Market**, the best general area for shopping, to make your purchases. This market is especially good for antiques, paintings on silk, and clothes. It's not so good for batiks, picchwais and jewellery, which sell for up to 50% less at small local factories. Don't worry about finding these places—their touts will find you.

Best buys are *batik* (same both sides) wall-hangings, a traditional art form of the Muslim community. The special dyeing using various applications of wax to the cloth process produces a unique cracked, marbled effect on the cloth. There are many con-artists around producing inferior examples, so play safe and buy from a reputable shop like **Apollo Arts**, near Hathipol. It's run by the family who actually introduced batiks into Udaipur, and prices are quite reasonable. Apollo also sell attractive miniature paintings on bone, now that ivory has been banned, which apparently keep their colour and quality far longer than paintings on cotton, paper and silk.

Udaipur is also the base for picchwais—colourful wall-hangings painted with durable mineral colours on cloth or silk. This art form originated in nearby Nathdwara (48 km: 30 miles to the north), when a holy image of Krishna arrived from Mathura (to save it being destroyed by Aurangzeb) and a series of 'atmosphere' painted backdrops were created—to help Krishna play out his half-dozen daily roles. At 9 am, for instance, he appears as a cowherd—and a *picchwai* of cows, meadows and rolling hills would be hung out. In time, these temple wall-hangings became popular souvenirs for pilgrims, depicting Krishna in his varying moods. Today, there are many 'schools' of *picchwai* painters (many of them cowherds themselves), and there is little point recommending any single one—they just move around in the wake of tourist traffic. Prices range from Rs60 all the way up to Rs10 000 and more, and the more reliable shops are in the area of Lake Palace Road.

This is also a good area to buy tie-and-dye saris, bedsheets and shawls (try **Maharana Art Emporium**, 9 Lake Palace Road for well-priced items, cordial service). Tie-and-dye patterns are created by tying pinched clumps of the material round with thread, and dyeing the remainder. It is a familiar Rajasthani technique.

There are several good shops in City Palace Rd, leading past Jagdish Temple. **Ganesh Handicraft Emporium** has loads of good stuff—mirror-embroidered skirts, colourful needle-worked wall-hangings, appliquéd double bedspreads, and cheap bags, purses and cushion-covers. **Jagdish Emporium** has a similar range of produce, and is useful for comparing prices. **Queen Sarees & Art** sell quality scarves, bed-covers and silk pajama suits at very attractive rates. **Soni Jewellers** and **Silver Art Palace**, both below Mayur Cafe, sell beautiful silver jewellery and curios. Best buys are lovely enamelled silver boxes 'for any small thing'.

For novelty presents, try **Paiyabi Kilona Stores** under Hathipol Gate. This very old shop (sadly modernised) sells wonderful hand-carved wooden toys and puppets—the favourite buy of visiting Indians—and attractive old-style furniture.

WHERE TO STAY

Luxury/Expensive (over US$35/Rs1000 per room night)

If you're on a budget, and can afford just one night in an Indian luxury hotel, treat yourself to a 'touch of class' at Udaipur's **Lake Palace Hotel** (tel 23241-5, tlx 0335-203 LPAL IN, fax 0294-25804). It's a fabulous place, with sumptuous decor, excellent facilities, and indelibly memorable views over Pichola Lake. Food and in-house entertainments are good, and the 'ordinary' rooms (US$95) are truly palatial. The suites range from US$185 to US$450 for the opulent Maharajah's Suite. The dinky pool is disappointing. The magnificent **Shiv Niwas** within the City Palace complex (tel 28239-41, tlx 0335-126, fax 0294-23823) is the former royal guesthouse and has been refurnished with treasures from the royal stores, including a room with Belgium crystal furniture. Less exotic, but with great pool and lake views, is **Laxmi Vilas Palace**, Fateh Sagar Road (tel 24411, tlx 0335-218), with air-con singles/doubles from Rs1200. All rooms and furnishings are perfectly colour-matched, and the whole palace is a model of architectural symmetry. The Maharana was so concerned with perfection, that he knocked it down and started again whenever defects in workmanship appeared!

Mid-range (US$10–35/Rs250–1000 per room night)

Another royal establishment is **Hotel Shikarbadi** (tel 83200, tlx 0335-227, fax 0294-23823), some 5 km (3 miles) out of town on the Ahmedabad road. Remote perhaps, but this is the Maharana's personal hunting lodge—with swimming-pool and gardens, smart uniformed retainers, horse-riding and elephant-trekking in the Deer Park. Some travellers even go on wild-boar hunts with the Maharana! Rooms are air-conditioned and good value at Rs500/750.

Somewhat run-down but very charming, is the Maharani's old guesthouse, **Rang Niwas Hotel**, Lake Palace Rd (tel 23891) which caters for both middle- and budget-range travellers (old suites, with huge tub baths and antique furniture, cheap dorm beds in the ping-pong lounge). Lovely gardens and courtyard, homey service and atmosphere, friendly and informative staff. Other mid-range properties include **Hotel Rajdarshan**, 18 Pannadhai Marg (tel 29671-73, tlx 0335-310) with rooms from about Rs500; **Chandralok Hotel**, Saheli Marg (tel 29011) with rooms from Rs450; **Hotel Hilltop Palace**, 5 Ambavgarh, Fateh Sagar (tel 28708) and **Anand Bhawan**, Fateh Sagar Road (tel 23256). The RTDC property is **Hotel Kajri**, Shastri Circle Tel 29509, tlx 0335-239) with air-conditioned and air-cooled rooms from Rs250. RTDC have a small property at **Jaisamand**, 48 km (30 miles) to the south-east.

Budget (under US$10/Rs250 per room night)
Economy accommodation in Udaipur is often extremely good value. RTDC have published one of their directories of Paying Guest Accommodation for Udaipur— available from the Tourist Office (tel 23605). Of **Lalghat Guest House**, behind Jagdish Temple, one guest remarked: 'Why pay Rs1000 for a room at the Lake Palace, when you can have the same lake views for Rs50 here?' Actually, only the two roof-top rooms have the views, and you'll want the big Rs100 'suite' (with own bathroom) to qualify for luxury. Lalghat is a friendly family place, with popular sit-out terrace and 24-hour room service. Even better (say some) is the nearby **Jagat Niwas Hotel**, overlooking Lake Palace. If you get past the Canadian labrador (he only goes for people he doesn't know), you're in for a treat. This is a lovely traditional house, with great views and relaxing courtyard. If anything, the rooms, from Rs100, are better than Lalghat—especially the two on the roof with balconies. Ask for Room No. 1, with its stained-glass windows, tiled flooring, German chandeliers and huge Mughal-style double bed. Again, there's a lovely sun-terrace and cosy family-style atmosphere.

The novelty place to stay is **Pratap Country Inn** (tel 23638) at Titadhia village, 6 km (3¾ miles) out of the city. This used to be the Maharana's country house, and is now owned by his brother (a raconteur of epic proportions, full of stories about tiger shoots and the good old days of the Raj). The manager, Mr Singh, is one of life's true eccentrics. He offers free camel- and horse-riding, free transport to and from rail station, free (but empty) swimming-pool, lovely country walks (there's a great lake nearby), and a variety of rooms from Rs250. The speciality 'horse-safaris' are apparently fun, and if bored you can 'meet member of Udaipur's Ancient Royal Family of more than 1500 years'.

EATING OUT
A natural progression from sunset beers at Lake Palace is a meal at its pleasant **Neel Kamal** restaurant. The menu is wonderfully pretentious, offering you a wide choice of 'Royal Repasts' and 'International Celebrations'. The coffee shop and pool-side food are also good.

Reliable eating places on land include **Parkview** restaurant opposite Town Hall, and **Berry's** (tel 25132) near Chetak Circle. Both offer good mid-priced Indian, Chinese and Continental fare, and Berry's has great ice-cream. Over in Lake Palace Rd, there's **Roof Garden Cafe** with its umbrella-shaded roof patio (with views), wound-down sound system, friendly manager, quick service and 'exotic, delicious, hygienic food'. It's a find. So is **Mayur Cafe** up at Jagdish Temple. Run by a live-wire

14-year old gourmet (a self-confessed 'specialist in apple struddle'), this is a popular breakfast spot with banana cake, brown bread, great lassis and coffee, even decent porridge. The Mayur is also a good place to experiment with Indian food. By contrast, the **Kwality** opposite Rang Niwas Hotel is pricey, and pretty boring.

GENERAL INFORMATION
The Government of Rajasthan Tourist Office (tel 23605), at the Tourist Bungalow off Shastri Circle, is open 10 am to 5 pm (except Sunday). Helpful staff, fair information, useful city tours in the morning (8 am–1 pm), and excursions to Nathdwara/ Eklingji temples in the afternoon (2–7 pm). The RTDC Beer Shop outside (open 10 am–11 pm) is a real bonus. Guides for sightseeing can be hired at either the tourist office or at the City Palace— bargain hard.).

Indian Airlines (tel 24433) is at LIC building, outside Delhi Gate. State Bank of India is in Hospital Rd. GPO is behind the cinema at Chetak Circle (open 10 am to 5 pm, except Sundays), but *poste restante* is at the small sub-office in Shastri Circle, opposite the Tourist Bungalow.

MOUNT ABU

Rajasthan's only hill station lies on a 1200-m high plateau, in pleasantly green and lush surroundings. Principally a place of pilgrimage, it has recently come up as a summer retreat for honeymooning Indian couples (mainly from nearby Gujarat) and is strongly geared to home tourism.

Abu derives its name from 'Arbuda', the serpent son of the Himalaya who rescued Shiva's bull Nandi from a watery grave. Hindus revere the site because the sage Vashishta, from whose sacrificial fire the four original Rajput warrior clans first sprang, had his home here, and also because of its Nakki Lake, said to have been dug by the sage Balam-Rasiya using just his 'nakkhs' or nails. Holy dips in the waters of Nakki are held to be as spiritually purifying as bathing in the Ganges. Great numbers of Jain pilgrims visit Abu too, primarily because of its world-famous Dilwara Temples, possibly the finest examples of Jain architecture to be found in India.

An important religious centre since the times of Ashoka and before, Abu acquired its principal architecture and stone carvings only during the Parmer period, which came to a sudden end between 1302 and 1311 with the invasion of the Chauhans. Much later, the British purchased a site for a sanatorium here (1917), but Abu remained largely undeveloped and uninhabited until the home-tourist boom suddenly started in the 1970s.

Abu is today the most Indian of all hill stations—a lively little place of ice-cream parlours, omelette and *pau bhaji* stalls, 'fun' and novelty shops, and an awful lot of ponies. There is a pretty lake, several good hill walks, a refreshing mountain breeze, and a festive party atmosphere. The sight of Indians abroad—laughing, joking, taking endless photographs, swarming to and from Sunset Point, generally having a ball—has Western visitors completely mystified. It's not like India at all. It's not even like an Indian hill station: there's no hassle, no dirt, no drugs and no unemployed refugees. The very worst or best thing that can happen to you at Abu is being adopted by an Indian family and deluged with food and presents throughout your stay. They just love foreign tourists here, partly because they see so few of them. And their cordiality and friendship is genuinely infectious.

Abu is most pleasant from March to June, and from September to November. Avoid May–June when it's overcrowded, and the October Diwali festival (D-Day and Christmas rolled into one). Aim for March/April—quiet, relaxing, and half-price accommodation.

WHAT TO SEE

As hill stations go, Abu is very small and self-contained. You can get around very easily on foot, and walking is nearly all on the flat—there's none of that endless tramping up and down steep steps and winding declines that exhausts visitors to Darjeeling or Shimla. Also convenient, most restaurants and hotels, plus post office, bus-stand and tourist office, are all on the main road. This is directly in front of you as you step off the bus. At the bus-stand, you'll be met by Abu's *baba-gadis* (porters) with their brightly coloured prams, eager to wheel your luggage off to your hotel for a rupee or two. Later, their day's work done, they climb into their prams and go to sleep.

Abu's main sights and activities can be covered comfortably in a day—but stay a second day to pick up on the fun atmosphere. See all the pilgrimage places, including the Jain temples in the morning, by conducted tour (often crowded, book as soon as you arrive); leave the local walks and activities for the afternoon. Get around locally on foot, by pony, or by taxi/ambassador car (fixed charge for all journeys).

Temple and Town Tour (by sightseeing bus, morning; on foot, afternoon)
Adhar Devi–Guru Shikhar–Achalgarh–Dilwara Jain Temples–Nakki Lake– Sunset Point

Abu Town may be on the flat, but all the surrounding sights are not. Every place covered on tour involves a stiff, steep climb. When you've had enough exercise, hire dolis (palanquin men) to carry you up.

First stop of the morning is **Adhar Devi Temple** 3 km (1⅔ miles) out of town, dedicated to the patron goddess of Abu. To reach this 500-year-old Durga temple, you'll need to climb 220 steep steps, a taster of what's to come. The black-faced deity at the top is secreted in a cave under the rockface, and you'll have to do a bit of potholing to visit her. This temple is considered the oldest place of pilgrimage in Abu. It is called *adhar* (without support) because Devi's statue is believed to be not man-made but rather a mystical manifestation, resulting from the fervent prayer of saints and sages. Set in pleasant woodland, full of the sound of singing crickets, it gives fine views down over Abu. Back at the bottom, try a plate of sliced tomatoes (popular thirst-quenchers) before reboarding the bus— they're delicious.

On next to **Guru Shikhar** (15 km: 9½ miles), the highest peak in Rajasthan at 1772m. There's a small Vishnu temple with a 15th-century brass bell at the summit, offering fine views of the surrounding valleys and hills. It's at the top of 300 steps. Hire a palanquin if you are worn out. Still better, return to Guru Shikhar at sunrise (taxi from Abu 5 am, arrive 6 am)—the views are spectacular then.

191

The next stop is **Achalgarh** (11 km: 6⅔ miles)—site of an ancient Shiva temple (AD 813), and a slightly less ancient Parmer fort (AD 900) partially restored). Instead of the usual lingam, the main temple contains Shiva's toeprint (he once stood on Abu mountain to stop it moving away). This is at the bottom of a pit said to extend all the way down to the underworld. Pilgrims of three faiths pay their devotions here: the Hindus for the toeprint, and for the holy spring where the Devi goddess helped the 15th-century Rana to summon water from the rock and relieve a severe drought; the Jains for the richly-carved Jain arch and architecture; and the Muslims, because it was a Muslim warlord who built the new Shiva temple on this site after an attack of guilt over destroying the original one. There are lots of charming little temples and shrines containing bright-eyed gods, also a fine brass Nandi and a huge old champa tree in the courtyard. Outside, near the car park, is **Mandakini Kund**, a huge tank with a stone archer and three striking stone buffaloes. These figures face onto ancient cave dwellings of Jain monks, hidden up on the densely foliaged mountainside. According to legend, the tank was once full of *ghee* and three demons came in the form of buffaloes to drink at it each night. To stop them, the Parmer ruler Adipal killed all three with arrows. To see the pretty Jain temples above, take directions for the path up the hillside (10 minutes' climb).

Finally, you come to the small village of **Dilwara** (5 km: 3 miles) with its five famous Jain Temples. Two of these, the Vimal Vasahi and the Luna Vasahi (Tejpal), represent the finest Jain architecture in India. They are open to non-Jains from 12 noon to 6 pm daily, and there's an excellent free guide service. Security is a bit stiff though. Leather articles (and any 'arms and ammunition') must be left at the 'clock room'. A prominent sign declares: 'Women on their monthly course must not enter—those who do may suffer'. As a female visitor, be prepared to be quizzed at the entrance—

Jain temple, Mount Abu

often in front of a crowd of inquisitive Indians. There's a Rs5 camera charge and you can't take photos of any Jain deities.

See first the **Vimal Vasahi** (Adinath) temple, built completely of white marble and dedicated to the first Jain *tirthankar*, Adinath. It is the earliest temple of the group, built in AD 1031 by the minister Vimal Shah for the Gujarat ruler Bhim Deva. Measuring 30 m long and 13 m wide, it took 1500 sculptors and 1200 labourers (working continuously) 14 years to complete. Entering via a series of 48 carved pillars, you'll come to a room full of marble elephants, on one of which is mounted Bhim Deva himself. The central courtyard, a vision of sublime ornamentation and sculpture, houses the large bronze image of Adinath, with eyes of precious stones and a necklace of gems. Around it are ranged 52 identical cells, each with its small resident Jain figure. Everywhere you look in this temple, there's a beady-eyed cross-legged deity staring right back at you. In a rear chamber, you'll find the ancient blackstone statue of Adinath (said to have risen from the earth from below a peepal tree) which was the original cause of a temple being built on this site.

Move on to the **Luna Vasahi** (Neminatha) temple, built by two brother-ministers of the Gujarat ruler Viradhawaler in 1231, and dedicated to the 22nd *tirthankar*, Neminath. This has the same profusion of sculpture as the Adinath temple, but is notable for its technical perfection: every inch of marble is a masterpiece of intricate and delicate carving. Since each worker was paid in solid gold, and in direct proportion to the weight of marble covered, such attention to detail is perhaps not surprising. What is surprising is that this filigree fantasy-temple—with its cluster of translucent lotuses dripping from the porch dome, its glorious overhead panels of deities and attendants, its high-towered prayer hall and its massive statue of Neminatha—were all carved from a single massive block of Macrana marble. The overall effect is stunning. Other temples in the group include a 14th-century Adinatha temple and a 15th-century Parshvanatha temple.

Either take the tour bus back to Abu town (it stops only an hour here), or stay longer—the temples are worth it—and return back down by the regular jeep service.

In the afternoon, go boating on **Nakki Lake**, perhaps the finest hill station lake in India. It is an artificial sheet of water, studded with tiny islets, fringed by beautiful woodland, and overhung by the famous **Toad Rock** (a natural toad-shaped boulder). Paddle-boats are a waste of time—currents are too strong. Hire a rowing-boat, battle out to the centre of the lake, then relax.

Dusk marks the great exodus of tourists out to **Sunset Point** (2 km: 1¼ miles). It's the accepted thing to do—now practically a tradition. To get there in comfort (i.e. avoiding the multitudes), hire one of Abu's resident camels from the pony-rank at the town-end of Sunset road. This is great fun, and gets you noticed by every Indian tourist in town. At Sunset Point (it's here you realise you're on a mountain, the open plains stretching out for miles below) many of them are going to be far more interested in photographing you (with or without the camel) than the glorious sunset.

In the evening, Abu comes into its own. It is one of the few places in India with any claim to relaxed nightlife. People return from Sunset Point to take a long, leisurely evening promenade, and the town streets are a mass of gaily twinkling electric lights. Sweet buns, ice-creams, 'genuine Bombay omelettes', *pau bhaji* snacks and ice-cold beers are peddled on the roadside, and below the pony-rank is a row of stalls brewing up Abu's remarkable ginger tea. Nearby, ladies can buy the attractive *mendi* patterns (henna palm-paintings, traditionally painted on, but here sold as stencils: the pattern lasts 5 days) or colourful bangles, bracelets and *bindi* beauty-spots. There are numerous street tailors, photography shops, *paan* stalls and cheap novelty-gift emporia. There's even a 'Character Building World Spiritual Museum', where uninvited guides show visitors round the (strange) exhibition depicting the evolution of the world, then tell them how Lord Shiva will manage things after it has been blown up. If you need some light relief after this, try a short pony-ride round town.

RECREATION
Apart from pony-riding and boating, there's swimming at the Savera Palace Hotel's pool (nominal charge for non-guests) or pleasant walking to local viewpoints including Lover's Point, Honeymoon Point. For the best views, take any of the paths leading up from behind Nakki Lake to the hilltop (a 40-minute, 154-m climb). Abu also has a small wildlife sanctuary. To visit it, contact the Forestry Office (just up from the tourist office, open 10 am–5 pm).

SHOPPING
Abu's many 'fun shops' sell some of the worst tat in the world—useless plastic toys, ghoulish funny masks, hideous plaster gods, and 'breakable educational zoological animals'. To see something better, visit **Rajasthan Handicraft Emporium**, near the bus-stand. Or **Khadi Gramodyog Bhavan**, opposite the pony-rank. To see something completely different, visit **Cha Cha Museum**, Abu's biggest and oldest emporium. It is called a museum because most of its bizarre curios and antiques hang around for ages before finding a buyer.

WHERE TO STAY
Before the mid-April tourist rush, most of Abu's hotels offer generous 30–50% discounts. After that, prices soar and you can't (unless you advance-book) find a decent room for love or money. At any time of the year, the better hotels are full of noisy honeymooning couples, so take earplugs.

Mid-range/Expensive (US$10–35/Rs250–1000 per room night)
If you want a good night's sleep, book into **Hotel Hilltone** (tel 3112-5, tlx 0365-2700), opposite the bus-stand. Refreshingly quiet, it has a number of useful three-star facilities: lovely gardens, good room service, smart, courteous staff, nice restaurant, even a complimentary shoe-shine. Rooms are well-priced at Rs450 single, Rs700 double, and you'll want one on the 2nd floor, with sun-balcony. To live in the style of the Raj, try **Connaught House** (tel 3360, cable CONNAUGHT), a 5-minute walk up the hill opposite the bus-stand. This is a typical British hill station house, formerly the private residence of Sir Donald Field (the PM of Jodhpur state), and now owned by the Maharajah of Jodhpur. Attractions include nice gardens, traditional Rajasthani-style meals, and quaint cottage-style rooms (from Rs350), packed with Victorian memorabilia and period furnishings. For peace and quiet, ask for a new block room (with verandah). For prestige, plump for Room 2 in the old block—this is where the Maharajah stays!

The similar **Bikaner Palace** (tel 3121, 3133) was once the summer residence of the Maharajah of Bikaner, and has delightfully antique rooms from Rs450. It's rather out of the way, being 3 km (2 miles) north-east of town, towards Dilwara temples, and is often heavily booked. If the above places are full, it's a big step down to **Savera Palace**, Sunset Rd (tel 3354), with its ethnic cave-decor rooms (Rs450 double), roller-skating rink (with 'Automatic Baby Car'), steam bath ('hot water pudle'), blaring videos in the TV lounge, and the only swimming-pool in town. The Savera offers three-star facilities, and has no-star service.

More cheaply, **Hotel Madhuban** (tel 3121), next to the Hilltone. Friendly and comfortable, it has nice single/double rooms for Rs350. Alternatively, there's **Mount Hotel**, Dilwara Rd (tel 3155), with good-value doubles from Rs250 to 450, and a superb restaurant. **Mount Abu Hotel**, Mount Rd, also has good food and is owned by friendly Parsis. RTDC **Hotel Shikkar** (tel 3129, 3169) has rooms and independent cottages from Rs250.

Budget (under US$10/Rs250 per room night)
One of the really strange things about Abu is the lack of good hotels near beautiful Nakki Lake. The only one worth a mention is **Hotel Lake View** (tel 3240), with friendly management, a few lake-view rooms, and a monkey on the roof at 6 am, serving breakfast. Back in town, budget accommodation is pretty grim. **Hotel Surya Darshan** (tel 3165), near the taxi-stand, is undeniably seedy. But it does have some nice top-floor doubles for Rs100, overlooking the polo-ground.

EATING OUT
Abu's only 'traditional' food (actually a Bombay import, like the omelettes) is *pau bhaji*—a savoury vegetarian snack (tomatoes, potatoes, spices and lemon tossed about in a banana leaf, generally eaten with buttered toasted rolls) best sampled at the big open-air place beyond the Hotel Maharajah. Abu actually has a wide range of Indian cuisine, catering to its wide cross-section of Indian tourists. Thus, Bombayites have their omelette/*pau bhaji* stalls; Tamils have their *dosa/thali* places (try **Madras Cafe** next to Cha Cha Museum South Indian snacks, ice-cream, and coffee); Gujaratis dine out at **Hotel Sarswati** in front of the polo-ground for amazing Gujarati *thalis*), or at **Kanak Dining Hall** near the bus-stand; Punjabis enjoy tasty non-veg snacks at **Sher-Punjab**; and Rajasthanis tuck into spicy 'desert food' at **Jodhpur Bhoj Nalay** (signed in Hindi), opposite Abu's popular **Government Beer Shop**. This establishment serves cheap chilled beer from 10 am to 10 pm, and is located next to the police traffic circle, facing onto the polo-ground. Chinese food is best at the small restaurant next to Gujarati Travels. Western food is a real rarity, but at Hilltone Hotel's excellent **Handi** restaurant with its airy outdoor section, you can enjoy continental 'sizzlers' along with a bottle of 'Drought Beer'—very aptly named in view of Abu's perennial water shortage.

GENERAL INFORMATION
Tourist Office (tel 3151), opposite bus-stand, is open odd hours (8–11 am; 4–8 pm), and doesn't quite know what to do with Western tourists. Its half-day minibus tour (8.30–1.30 pm, or 1.30 pm–sunset) gets very mixed reports.

The post office is on Raj Bhavan Rd, open 10 am–5 pm except Sundays. State Bank of India is nearby, but Hotel Hilltone gives a better rate of exchange.

CHITTORGARH

The ancient Mewar capital of Chittorgarh (or Chittor) represents the quintessence of Rajput valour and chivalry. Three times in its long and bloody history, faced by overwhelming odds, its menfolk dressed up in the saffron robes of martyrdom and rode out to certain death, while its women walked into the sacrificial bonfire and committed *jauhar* or mass ritual suicide. Carved marble memorials to heroes and *sati* victims litter the broken ruins, making this oldest and most famous of all Rajasthani fortress towns perhaps the closest to the warrior Rajput's heart.

A great deal of Rajasthan's history centres round Chittor. The origin of this powerful hilltop fort, situated on a 180-m high precipice, is shrouded in romantic mystery. The legend goes that it was a fort since prehistoric times, having been founded by the hero Bhim, one of the five Pandava brothers of the *Mahabharata* epic. Two Lower Palaeolithic sites have been excavated at the nearby River Berach. But the fort probably only dates back to the 7th century AD. In the year 734 it was discovered as a strategic site by Bapa Rawal, founder of the Mewar dynasty, and made his capital. It was Bapa Rawal who thought up the clever idea of calling himself the *dewan* (minister) of Shiva, which sidestepped any possible accusation of tyranny and made possible the unity of the (clannish) Rajputs under a single leader. Much later, after a long period of steady growth, in 1303 Chittor was suddenly attacked and sacked by the ruthless Ala-ud-din Khilji, Sultan of Delhi, who fell in love with its beautiful princess Padmini (one fleeting glance of her face in a mirror was all it took) and determined to have her, whatever the cost. He walked in on an empty fort—Padmini having committed *jauhar* with all her royal ladies. Ala-ud-din ruled Chittor for just 23 years. Then the valorous nobleman Hamir retook it for the Rajputs, earning himself and all his descendants the 'premier' title of Maharana (at Independence in 1947, there were 532 Rajahs and Maharajahs in India, but only one Maharana).

Chittor's glorious revival had one unfortunate repercussion: now confirmed as the ruling seat of the Rajputs, it became the lodestone attracting every prospective invader of Rajasthan. Only when they had conquered this city, could they lay any real claim to rulership of the state. For a time Chittor met all attacks successfully—it was quite impossible to storm, and its everlasting water supply (from the fort's natural springs) meant that besieging enemies had to camp out for months on the hot, bone-dry plains waiting for its food to run out. But then came two more crippling defeats. First, in 1535, at the hands of Bahadur Shah, the Sultan of Gujarat (a disastrous engagement: 32 000 Rajput warriors slain, 13 000 of their women went up in *jauhar* smoke); then, in 1567, by Akbar, the Mughal emperor (and the orange saffron of 8000 more warriors bled red). It was shortly after this third and final sack of Chittor that Maharana Udai Singh decided enough was enough, and moved 110 km (69 miles westward to found the new Rajput capital of Udaipur.

Today, while a few hundred families still live on up in the fort, Chittorgarh is just another of India's deserted ghost cities—a silent, lonely expanse of arches, gates, memorials and cenotaphs which stand testament to a proud, heroic people to whom honour and valour meant more than life itself.

WHAT TO SEE

Apart from the fort, there's little to see or do. So arrive early from Udaipur, see the sights by auto-rickshaw or by the tourist office's morning tour (8 am–11.30 am), and arrange to be back in time for the afternoon bus on to Ajmer or return to Udaipur. Few people stay overnight in Chittor.

Fort Tour (3/4 hours)
Rana Kumbha Palace–Fateh Prakash Palace–Tower of Victory– Gaumukh Reservoir–Padmini's Palace–Tower of Fame

The ascent up to the fort, which contains all Chittor's interest points, is via a steep, winding 1-km (2/3-mile) long road. This takes you through seven gateways up to the western (main) gate of **Ram Pol** at the top. Ask your driver to stop on the way up at the **Hero's Chhatris**, marking the points where Jaimal and Kalla, two valorous victims of the 1567 conflict with Akbar, fell fighting.

Within the fort, see first the 15th-century **Rana Kumbha Palace**, with its Shiva temple, horse and elephant stables, and vaulted cellars believed to be site of Padmini's *jauhar*. In the more modern **Fateh Prakash Palace** opposite, visit the small and interesting museum with its collection of archaeological treasures recovered from the fort.

A short distance east, you'll find the **Tower of Victory** (Vijay Stambh), erected between 1458 and 1468 to commemorate Rana Kumbha's victory over the Muslim and Gujarat rulers in 1440. Climb this finest remainder of Rajput glory—nine storeys of noble yellow-sandstone, rising 37 m high—for nice views over the fort area. Outside, to the right, is the grim **Mahasati** area where ranas of olden days were cremated (there are several *sati* stones and tablets here). Straight ahead, and down some steps, is the **Gaumukh Reservoir,** a deep tank full of leaping fish situated right at the edge of the cliff. It takes its name from the carved cow's mouth which feeds the tank a constant supply of fresh spring water.

At **Padmini's Palace**, up on the eastern end of the fort, you can wander through the green gardens and flower-bordered courtyards to the balcony where Ala-ud-din got his fatal glimpse of the lovely Padmini, her face reflected in a silver mirror as she promenaded in the small water-bound island pavilion opposite. Then proceed by the **Deer Park** and the **Suraj Pol** to the **Tower of Fame** (Kirti Stambh), dedicated to Adinath, first of the Jain tirthankars. It was built in the 12th century (making it older than the Tower of Victory) by a wealthy Jain merchant. Covered in decorative nude figures of the Jain pantheon, it is a *digambara* or 'sky-clad' monument, and rises to a height of 22 m. You can climb the seven storeys to the top, for fine views.

WHERE TO STAY
If necessary, stay at the RTDC **Panna Tourist Bungalow** (tel 3238), close to the railway station, with air-cooled and air-conditioned rooms from Rs250. The nearby **Government Circuit House**, Udaipur Rd, has far more character, but is usually reserved for government officers. When it isn't, this lovely old-style palatial building lets out clean 'deluxe' quarters to travellers at cheap rates (Rs75–125). **Janta Avas Grah** (tel c/o 3238), at the tourist office, has spartan cells (Rs50). It will be difficult to find anything any better.

EATING OUT
An unappetising prospect. Good, cheap vegetarian fare at the new **Rituraj** restaurant, near the bus-stand. Nice chilled beers at the **RTDC Beer Shop**, outside the

tourist office. Basic, uninteresting food at **Panna's restaurant**, or at the **Railway Canteen**. In restaurants, as in hotels, Chittor seems resigned to tourists flitting in and out, with no desire to stay overnight.

GENERAL INFORMATION
The tourist office (tel 9) is in the Janta lodge, near the railway station. Open 8 am–12 noon and 3 pm–6 pm (except Sundays). In practice, the tourist officer is often at the Panna Tourist Bungalow. You might as well go there first anyway: Panna has better infornation and sells the conducted tours of the fort (8 am–11.30 pm, 3–6 pm daily, starting at 7 am and 4 pm respectively in summer; Rs15). As for English-speaking guides, you can pick up one of these (a useful companion for your tour) at the main entrance gate of the fort, outside the Archaeological Survey office. Guides all charge a fixed rate (currently about Rs40 per hour) and are often worth it.

PUSHKAR

A charming oasis on the very edge of the desert, Pushkar is the perfect place to wind up one's tour of Rajasthan. It is a tiny pilgrim town, fronting a holy lake, separated from nearby Ajmer by the 'Snake Mountain' of Nag Pahar.

Pushkar has one of the few Brahma temples in India. The legend is that a lotus fell from the hand of Brahma while he was searching for a place to perform *yagna* (sacrifice), and a lake sprang up. Brahma decided to make his home here, and a temple was built in commemoration. For ages past, Hindu pilgrims have flocked to Pushkar. Rama, hero of the Hindu epic *Ramayana* (1500 BC) is said to have paid his respects here, and the journals of Fa Hsien, the 4th-century AD Chinese

traveller confirm it as a major pilgrimage centre. The palaces and temples around the lake were a later addition of the Rajput maharajahs. Man Mahal, the palace built by Rajah Mansingh I of Amber, stands on the bank of the lake, and has been converted into the present Tourist Bungalow. Today, there are over 400 temples in Pushkar, and 90% of the population are said to belong to the community of priests.

For much of the year, Pushkar is a peaceful place with the emphasis on relaxation. Travellers come here for a total break from the rest of India. But at the annual **Cattle and Camel Fair** each November, it's a different story entirely: up to 200 000 traders and 50 000 cattle pour into town, along with numerous festooned camels and colourful pilgrims. After 10 hectic days of livestock-dealing, camel-racing, and colourful festivities, everybody goes for a big holy dip in the lake on the night of the full moon (*Kartik Purnima*). An explosion of fun, frolic, games and laughter', the fair provides some wonderful photographic opportunities. Also a rare occasion to see the Rajasthani women decked out in all their traditional jewellery, dress and finery. If this sounds your idea of fun, go for the last 5 days of the festival, and contact the Rajasthan Tourist Office, which organises traditional dance programmes, cultural events and tented accommodation. The next fairs will be 26–29 November 1993, 15–18 November 1994 and 6–8 November 1995.

WHAT TO SEE
Sightseeing is probably the last thing on your mind when you come here. Pushkar is a tiny, sleepy desert town which instantly envelops visitors in a calm embrace of inertia. The little activity there is—shops, restaurants, markets—centres on the single long street which tracks round the northern end of the lake, parallel to the bathing ghats. There are no taxis or rickshaws, nor any need for them. Cycles can be hired at Rs10/day from the rank near Pushkar Hotel, but most people prefer to walk. There's a regular parade of travellers trooping up and down the high street—trying on hippy clothes, buying silver bangles, drinking endless lassis, doing *puja* at the ghats, or simply collecting strange signs. A few examples are: 'Donate for Cow Saint and Words' (a temple), 'Welcome to see the real Mac Coy—Men at Work' (a handicrafts shop), and 'Surprising how a Single Name can change your Outlook' (a cigarette advertisement).

Spend your first day or two simply winding down—sunbathing, shopping, swimming and making new friends. Then, when you're up to some activity, try the following early morning jaunt.

Desert/Town Tour (on foot, 3/4 hours)
Savitri Temple–Brahma Temple–Bathing Ghats –Old Pushkar

Set out early (8 am latest, to avoid the heat) down at the lakeside, below the Tourist Bungalow. While crossing the narrow causeway to the peaceful southern ghats, look out for holy turtles (sacred to Brahma) swimming below. On the far bank, visit the marshy wetlands behind the thin forest—it's a birdwatcher's paradise. Back at the bridge, walk along the ghats by the lakeside until (quite unexpectedly) you emerge at the edge of the desert. Up ahead, atop a high peaked hill, is the small white **Savitri Temple**, dedicated to Brahma's first wife. The legend goes that after Brahma dropped his lotus flower at Pushkar, he returned to do *yagna* (purification ritual) here. Unfortunately, he didn't wait for his wife Savitri to show up. Instead, he took a substitute bride called Gayatri to help him officiate at the ceremony. Gayatri (who has a temple of her own, above Marwar bus-stand) was an untouchable, and to make her holy, she was apparently 'put into the mouth of a cow and removed from the anus'. Drastic, but apparently effective. When Savitri finally put in an appearance, she was not amused. She began cursing people. First she cursed Vishnu with everlasting estrangement from his wife. Then she cursed Shiva with eternal unhappiness. Then she cursed the Brahmins with never-ending poverty. She even cursed Gayatri's cow. Then, having cursed everyone who had approved the marriage, she turned on Brahma himself, saying, 'Take Pushkar. But it's going to be the only home you ever have!' With this, she stormed off up to the hill, and has been sulking there ever since. Brahma tried to cheer her up with the present temple, but she's still upset. Going up to see her involves a marvellous 20-minute stroll across the rolling dunes—a real compensation if you didn't see any at Jaisalmer—followed by a half-hour hike up an ancient, crumbling stone stairway (built around the 4th century AD), with the views getting better the higher you go. The temple itself dates back some 2000 years, and is a small, well-kept affair. If you make it to the top, you'll probably be rewarded with a cup of refreshing mint tea. Get your breath back, then get out your camera—the views down over Pushkar and its lakes are spectacular, while to the rear the white, undulating sands stretch back for as far as the eye can see.

Walking back across the dunes, re-enter Pushkar to the west for the pink-domed **Brahma Temple**. This is a bright, Disneyish effort—a riot of blue, green, yellow and red paint. It is immaculately clean, has great atmosphere, and sits within a small enclosure backing directly on to the desert. Over the entrance gateway, you'll find the *hans* or goose symbol of Brahma, while below it (facing into the shrine) there is his 'carrier', a silver turtle. This is inset into the marble floor, together with neat serried rows of old silver coins. Walk to the rear of the temple, through the small chamber with 'Donate to Cows' moneybox, for picture-postcard views of the desert.

The main road leading back into town runs alongside a succession of roadside temples (mainly to the left) and lakeside ghats (the northern series, all to right). You can visit any of these ghats, where you'll be expected to do *Brahma Puja*. This is a devotional exercise which commences with the giving of flowers, fruit, rice and coconut, and is expected to end with the giving of money.

Pushkar town is actually larger than may at first appear. Walking north of the touristy main street takes you into an extensive maze of charming old houses, sleepy backstreet temples, often guarded by aggressive monkeys, smart pilgrims' dharam-salas and shady banyan trees parked with dozy dogs, camels and cows.

Return to the Tourist Bungalow for a swim in the lake. The water is fairly clean and, since the removal of the resident crocodile, who ate a visiting official, very safe. The small island in the lake centre is Guru Ghat—a popular target for bathers, since you can stand on it.

For better swimming, you'll want to take a camel/jeep excursion out to **Old Pushkar** lake, 5 km (3 miles) north across the desert. But first you'll need to know a little more mythology—because there is not just one Pushkar, but three! When Brahma let fall the lotus blossom (*pushpa*) from his hand (*kar*)—giving rise to *Pushkar*—it fell at three separate places, like the Barnes-Wallis bouncing-bomb. **Senior Pushkar**, where all the pilgrims and tourists stay, is considered the most holy spot because the lotus fell here first. After that, it fell on **Middle Pushkar**, 2 km up the road, and then on **Junior (Old) Pushkar**, 3 km further north. Pilgrims visit all three spots. After that, they hop on buses bound for other holy venues like Badrinath and Hardwar. A lot of elderly Hindus spend their waning years roaring from one holy lake to the next in ghastly video buses.

Ram's Camel Adventures (motto: 'Me enjoy people') is located just up from the Pushkar Palace Hotel, and runs camel- and jeep-treks out to Old Pushkar and other surrounding beauty spots, and they're usually great fun. You can stop off at Middle Pushkar, which has a small **Hanuman Temple**, a 200-year-old banyan tree, and a natural ground-water well. Despite years of successive drought, this tank has not run dry. Middle Pushkar is where the incurably insane come twice a year, at auspicious full moons to recover their minds. It is otherwise unremarkable. Old (Junior) Pushkar has a small **Krishna temple**, a charming village (with *very* friendly people) and a large ex-lake. The ex-lake has been sadly reduced by successive droughts—and by the pipeline sunk here, which supplies water to Ajmer railway depot. It is now planted with sugar-cane, and you can for the time being forget all about swimming. The legend of Old Pushkar is that Aurangzeb came here once, intent on destroying more temples. After washing his face he saw his reflection, however, 'his hair turned grey and he began to look like an old man'. This experience apparently cured Aurangzeb of iconoclasm for life.

Pushkar (senior) is best at sunset when the dry heat is relieved by a cool breeze, the glare of the sun dies away, and the fading desert lights turn the lake a fiery blood-crimson. As the time approaches for worship, the hundreds of little temples by the lakeside come to life, and the air is filled with the clanging of bells, the beating of drums and the hypnotic drone of prayer. For many, this is the most authentically spiritual experience of their entire Rajasthan tour.

SHOPPING

Pushkar is an excellent shopping venue. Unlike Jaipur or Jaisalmer where anyone who 'shows you his shop' gets 30% under the table, there's usually no middleman here to stop you getting a sensible price. The most popular buys are cheap, colourful cotton clothes—either ready-made or made-to-measure by the town's excellent tailors.

All Pushkar's shops are concentrated in the single main street running along by the northern ghats: very convenient, and very difficult to resist. If you can run this colourful, inviting gauntlet without buying something (or anything), you're either very strong-willed or very poor. Two particularly good places for Rajasthani embroidery and clothes are **Swami Lilashah Cloth Store** and **Nathu Ram's Chilum Shop**, both near Gau Ghat. Clothes are very cheap (bright shirts, dresses, trousers and embroidered waistcoats), and mirror-embroidered items go for a song (wall-hangings, large bags, cushion-covers). Most of this stuff is second-rate, so do check all seams. They're often poorly finished.

Something *not* to buy in Pushkar is silver. A lot of so-called pure silver is actually 60% copper, and will tarnish quickly. Be equally suspicious of 'antique' silver, which is rarely more than a month old.

On a rather more mundane note, Pushkar is also a good place to sell things. The market is full of second-hand bookshops—every one of them obsessed with the idea of buying your camera, Walkman, or spare film. Selling you a book may not occur to them.

WHERE TO STAY

Mid-range (US$10–25/Rs250–750 per room night)
Pushkar's two reasonable hotels both have desert-palace architecture, overlook the lake, and are the first places you come to walking into town from the bus-stand. RTDC's **Sarovar Tourist Bungalow** started life some 500 years ago, as the summer palace of the Maharajah of Jaipur. Today, it has a lovely garden terrace, a relaxing sun-roof, and a choice of cosy old-style rooms (from Rs100) and modern, characterless rooms with air-cooling. Meanwhile, the adjoining **Pushkar Hotel** (tel 1) goes from strength to strength. Another old palace, built for the Maharajah of Kishangarh, it has gone—in the space of a few years—from dopehead den of iniquity to the smartest, most select place in Pushkar. Completely renovated, it now boasts several deluxe suites, with modern tiled bathrooms from Rs250, in addition to its many cheaper rooms. Again, you have a sun-roof, nice gardens, and ethnic decor throughout. But there's also excellent food, reliable service, and superb transport information. Owner Jagat Singh, and manager Mr Saxena take care of all rail/bus reservations and offer great camel-/jeep-treks out into the desert. Pushkar Palace has the best and most reasonably priced travel desk in town.

An okay fallback is **Peacock Holiday Resort** (tel 18), located 200 yards *back* from the bus-stand, on the fringe of town, with a pleasant little swimming-pool and an unpleasant manager.

Budget (Under US$10/Rs250 per room night)
There are many cheapies, most extremely basic. Current favourites include **The Om**, **The Royal Guest House** (very central), **The Lakeview** and **The Shiva**.

EATING OUT
You'll be glad to get back to Delhi. The food here is very plain and simple. This is a religious centre and vegetarianism is carried to an extreme. Meat, even eggs, are only obtainable on the black market. **Pushkar Hotel's** buffet suppers are from 6 to 9 pm daily, and are excellent value. The nearby **Sunset Cafe** is popular with the young crowd, mainly for pancakes, omelettes, snacks, good music and lake view, but is dirty. A little further on, directly opposite the Brahma Temple, **R.S. Restaurant** is cosy with some dishes that are 'very, very special', but for the past years or so travellers have favoured the **Om Sitiva** roof-top restaurant, especially for its cheap and varied buffet meals. Meals in Pushkar are never expensive and range from Rs30 to 70.

GENERAL INFORMATION
The nearest tourist office, in Ajmer at Khadim Tourist Bungalow (tel 20490), is hopeless. Much better information at Pushkar Hotel, courtesy of Surendra Singh.

Main GPO (open 10 am to 5 pm except Sundays) is near the Marwar bus-stand at the far end of town, but most travellers use the small sub-post office in the Sadar Bazaar. It used to be the most unpredictable post office in India, with days when it would sell stamps and days when it wouldn't. 'We used to have a crazy postman who stamped letters or not according to his whim', explained Mr Singh, 'but now we have a postman who does his duty'.

State Bank of Bikaner & Jaipur, 5 minutes down the road from Pushkar Hotel, is the only place in town to change foreign currency legally.

Route 3 —Valleys of the Gods: Kashmir, Ladakh and Kulu

'Who has not heard of the Vale of Cashmere?' suggests the poet. The Mughal emperors certainly had—each one that left this cool valley of mountain charm to go empire-founding forever dreamt of going back. To the far north of India is a land of sparkling rivers and placid lakes, flowery gardens and saffron meadows, deep valleys of emerald green and soaring mountains of snow-capped splendour. Two beautiful states, Kashmir and Himachal Pradesh, provide a rich selection of sports and activities (hiking, trekking, fishing, boating and skiing) together with the very best climate and natural scenery that India can provide. The people, a colourful friendly mix of hookah-smoking Muslims, Tibetan refugees and festival-loving hill folk, produce some of the finest handicrafts in India. If you've time or money enough for just one shopping spree, look no further.

Srinagar, the summer capital of Kashmir, has mirror-calm Dal Lake, a backdrop of Himalayan peaks, Mughal gardens and mosques—and, of course, carpets. Within easy striking distance is Gulmarg, famous 'Meadow of Flowers', summer golfing centre and popular winter sports resort; also Pahalgam, a place of great natural beauty at the head of the Kashmir vale, with pony-trekking, fishing, and many scenic walks. Though the flower season is mid-March, the meadows of Pahalgam and Gulmarg are at their finest in June. Beyond the Kashmir valley lies Ladakh, a miniature Tibet of insurmountable mountains, rich art treasures, exotic dance festivals, and ancient monasteries carved into the hillsides. Situated at the roof of the world, its flat lunar landscape and wild, unearthly scenery offers spectacular photography. Down in the cool river valleys of Himachal Pradesh, there is severe Dharmsala, present home of the Dalai Lama, with lovely walks, cheap handicrafts, and authentic Tibetan atmosphere. Manali, at the head of the Kulu Valley or Valley of the Gods, is a hill resort of rare charm. It is a popular trekking base with direct access to the snow-clad Rohtang Pass. Nearby Kulu, the quiet hill-town after which the valley is named, is host to Lord Jagannath (honoured by a vivid annual festival), and produces famous woollen handicrafts. Shimla, by contrast, is a lively, very British hill station resort, a place to enjoy scenic walks and, maybe, to hark back to the Raj.

Since late 1989, a popular movement demanding independence from India has grown stronger in the Kashmir Valley. Backed by various militant groups, the movement has disrupted daily life and restricted movement in the valley. Consequently the 70% of the population who were in one way or the other directly related to the tourism and handicraft industries are now experiencing a major slump. The level of tourism in 1991 was almost nil and in 1992 only slightly better. At present travel to Srinagar and into the valley is not recomended but one hopes the situation will improve quickly.

Season: April to October (summer); December to February (winter).
Monsoons: July to September.
Climate: 14° to 33°C (summer); 0° to 15°C (winter).
Route duration: 10–20 days.

TRAVEL ITINERARY
At the time of writing, the political situation in the Kashmir Valley makes travel to
Srinagar difficult, if not unwise. However, travel to the areas on the itinerary is not
affected.

Delhi to Srinagar 880 km (550 miles)

Air
Indian Airlines offers at least one flight daily (Rs1894). Views from the air are
spectacular, making this option very attractive. It is essential, however, to book.

Rail/Road
There are 3/4 trains daily to Jammu Tawi (the *Jammu Mail*, 12–13 hours, is best,
but be careful of theft at Old Delhi station); then bus up to Srinagar (10/12 hours
by luxury/ordinary bus; 8 hours by nippy super-deluxe minibus). Buses should
be booked immediately on arrival in Jammu from the J & K State Transport Office,
behind the Tourist Reception Centre. Jeeps can also be hired in Jammu. At present
it is unlikely the security forces would allow tourists to travel between Jammu
and Srinagar although the road is open to the military and convoys of domestic
traffic under escort.

Srinagar to Leh 434 km (271 miles)

Air
Indian Airlines have in recent years operated 3 flights a week (Tues, Wed, Fri) on
IC429 (Rs663) but in autumn of 1992 suspended them due to lack of bookings caused
by the disturbances in the state. It is possible that one weekly flight might continue
to operate. Book well in advance, and be prepared for delays/cancellations—planes
can only land in Leh in the morning, and when the weather is fine. From November
through to late May, an average of one in every three flights is cancelled. The same
goes for flights back to Srinagar—so reconfirm your return leg (at Indian Airlines'
office in Srinagar) before flying out.
    The half-hour flight from Srinagar to Leh offers stunning mountain scenery—
book a seat on the right-hand side of the plane, and look out for the Nun and Kun
peaks (K2 is to the left of the plane). At Leh airport, it's a Rs60 jeep ride into town
8 km (5 miles) away.

Road
The Leh–Srinagar National Highway is officially open from mid-May to late-
October—though weather conditions can hasten or delay the opening date. The
journey takes two days, and the overnight stop is made at Kargil. Nowadays buses
from Srinagar are rarely full but it is advisable to book a few days ahead at the
Tourist Reception Centre in town. Jeeps take up to 6 people, and cost around
US$250. They are a far more comfortable option.
    Since the problems in Kashmir began, people wishing to visit Ladakh by road do
so along the Manali–Leh road, which is open from late-July to mid-September (see
p.225).

Srinagar to Jammu 290 km (180 miles)

Air
At least one flight daily (Rs543), continuing on from Jammu to Chandigarh and Delhi. Again, because of glorious Himalayan views and because of the current security problems, this flight is heavily subscribed.

Road
State buses leave early each morning—ordinary-class and luxury-class (best). One of the great Indian bus journeys: 10–14 hours of stunning scenery, perilous roads, and astonishing road-signs. It is necessary to book at the Tourist Reception Centre, as soon as you arrive in Srinagar.

Jammu to Dharmsala 203 km (127 miles)

Road
Two direct buses daily—at 5 am and 6.10 am (5/6 hours). They roar out of Jammu bus-stand like crazed juggernauts, ignoring 'Dashing means Danger' road-signs, and upsetting passengers horribly.
   Jammu also has regular buses to Pathankot (2 hours), from where you can jump off to Dharmsala (half-hourly buses from 4.40 am to 7.30 pm take 3 hours); to Dalhousie (regular buses throughout the day travel the 80 km (50 miles) or to Kulu/Manali (buses at 4.45 am, 7 am, 8 am, 6.30 pm 7.30 pm; take 10–12 hours). If you miss all these buses, and are faced with an overnight stay in Pathankot (an awful prospect), consider the fast 6.33 pm and 11.25 pm trains back to Delhi. There are regular buses linking Dalhousie with Dharmsala.

Dharmsala to Kulu 214 km (132 miles)

Road
Two buses daily—at 5.15 am and 11 am. The earlier bus is a slow 'local', taking 10 hours. The 11 am bus zips to Kulu in just 7 hours, and continues on to Manali (9½ hours).

Kulu to Manali 42 km (26 miles)

Road
Very regular buses from 3.30 am to 11 pm take 1–2 hours. The scenery is beautiful, and road-signs fun—'Peep! Peep! Don't go to Sleep!'. Taxis ferry between Kulu and Manali and are worth considering for a group.

Manali to Shimla 247 km (154 miles)

Road/Air
Bus/taxi to Bhuntar airport (50 km), then Vayudoot flight PF148 (Tuesday, Thursday, Saturday only (Rs545) to Jubbarhatti airport, 20 km (12½ miles) below Shimla. Jagson Airlines also operate flights most days of the week between Delhi, Kulu and Shimla. Choice of airport coach or taxi up to the Tourist Lift on Shimla's Cart Rd.

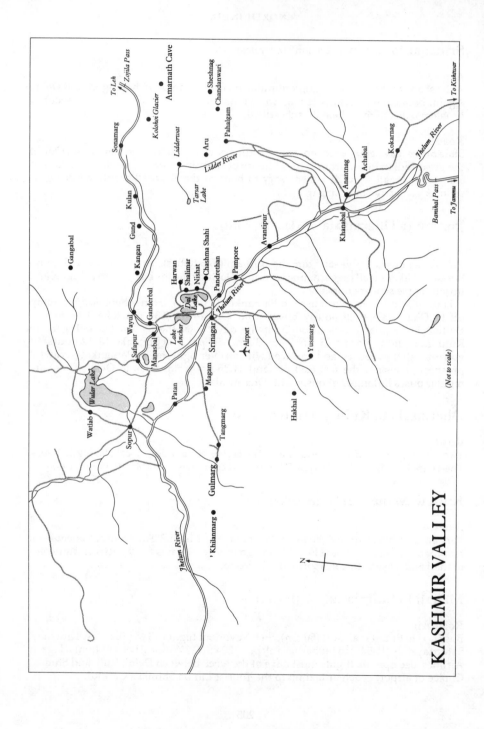

KASHMIR VALLEY

(Not to scale)

Road
One express bus daily—at 8 am (9 hours). Buy tickets in advance, from the tourist office.

Shimla to Delhi 354 km (220 miles)

Air
One flight daily—PF144 (Rs1637). Book tickets from Vayudoot desk at Shimla tourist office. Jagson Airlines have flights to Delhi most days.

Rail
The charming narrow-gauge toy train leaves Shimla's station at 5.30 pm daily, changing on to broad gauge at Kalka at 11.30 pm, arriving Delhi 6 am next morning. To reserve your comfy 2nd-class sleeper berth on this train, apply (*at least* 24 hours in advance) to the Northern Railway office, below the post office on the Mall. This is the only rail reservation place in India where I've been offered a cup of tea with my ticket.

Road
Several state and luxury coaches to Delhi daily—bookable from the tourist office or the Hotel Mayur. The best option is the 6.30 pm luxury bus (9 hours from the Interstate bus-stand on Cart Rd.) It's quicker and cheaper than the train, but a much less enjoyable experience.

CONTINUATIONS
Other hill resorts in Himachal include the quiet town of Dalhousie with its neighbouring towns of Khajjiar and Chamba. In central Himachal Pradesh there are villages and small towns such as Chail which are worth visiting for greater peace than one can now experience in Shimla.

If you want to stay in the cool, clear mountains, continue on from Delhi to Bagdogra (IC489 daily, Rs2406) for Darjeeling.

SRINAGAR

Srinagar is the summer capital of Jammu and Kashmir state, and a major tourist attraction for over a hundred years. Lying deep in the heart of the Kashmir valley, it offers beautiful mountain and lake scenery, also a wide range of activities including boating, fishing, trekking, pony-riding, water-sports and golf. An ideal holiday situation, it is especially popular as a cool, refreshing break from the summer heat of the Indian plains. Travellers come here to relax, to wind down and to spend at least a few days languishing on a luxury houseboat on Dal Lake. Then they go touring or trekking. Srinagar is the perfect base from which to explore the rest of Kashmir.

The origin of Srinagar is obscure. It was probably founded by the Emperor Ashoka some 2000 years ago, following his pilgrimage to the area. It is said that his daughter Charumati fell in love with Dal Lake, and that to please her Ashoka built a small *vihara* on the site. A small township grew up round it called Srinagar or 'city of beautiful scenery'. The present city was established by Rajah Pravarasen II in the 6th century AD though it was during the reign of the great Badshah (King Zain-ul-Abidin, 1421–72) that Persian and Central Asian artisans were brought in, and Kashmir's famous traditions of carpet-weaving, shawl-making and handicraft production originated. Later, under the rule of the Mughals, Srinagar acquired its remarkable mosques, its gardens and waterways, and its popular label of 'Paradise on Earth'.

The houseboats came into being during the British Raj. The Dogra Maharajahs of Kashmir were just as appreciative of Srinagar's cool, scenic climate as the British (who had ceded them sovereignty of Kashmir in 1846), and forbade them to build or to own land here. Undismayed, the British officers took to the lakes instead, living on the waters of the Dal in fully-equipped, beautifully ornate houseboats. The first one was constructed in 1875. Today, there are over 1300 houseboats on Srinagar's lakes.

In 1947, Jammu and Kashmir became part of the Indian Union. Since then, the area has been continually under dispute. Both Pakistan and India want Kashmir, but all Kashmir wants is to be left alone. Her main industry is tourism, and its success depends much on a quick and regular turnover of her famous handicrafts. But the recent troubles have blocked this. In part, this is Kashmir's own fault: all houseboats, land and even *shikara* canoes in the state are Kashmiri-owned, and no Indian is allowed to own land. 'In return', observed one Kashmiri journalist, 'the Indians retaliate by denying high-ranking posts to Kashmiris seeking influence outside of Kashmir. Also, the Indian press use every small disturbance in Kashmir as an excuse to stop tourists going there—knowing full well that Kashmir depends on tourism for its prosperity. We want our independence. Kashmir is so strategically important. Bear in mind, it sits on the borders of five countries—India, Pakistan, Afghanistan, China and the erstwhile Soviet Union.'

Shikara, Srinagar

While this kind of anti-Indian feeling remains strong, government restrictions on tourist development will remain stringent, producing considerable hardship and poverty in the region. But Kashmir's territorial isolation does have one compensation—it remains relatively unspoilt by tourism. Its traditional identity and culture have remained pretty well intact. The mainly Muslim inhabitants are a warm, simple and hospitable people, with a keen intelligence and a real love of foreigners. And hard times certainly haven't spoiled their enjoyment of a good bargain. Srinagar is not exactly relaxing for the first day or two—the Kashmiris are very business-minded, constantly hassling you to buy, buy, buy. But they do this with a smile, and you can always escape to the calm, peaceful haven of your houseboat if it gets too much.

The people themselves are a tall, fair and regular-featured race, and their traditional dress—the long, heavy woollen *pheran* (poncho), often with a little *kangri*, fire-pot braziers ('winter wives') carried round inside them, and woollen shepherd's caps—and with the ever-present hubble-bubble or *hookah*—are instantly recognisable.

Kashmir's climate is very British. It blows hot and cold throughout the year, and is highly unpredictable. Even in high summer, showers come out of nowhere, and are just as soon replaced by brilliant sunshine. The best time to visit Srinagar is April–May, when the snows on the upper reaches above Dal Lake start to melt, the willows turn green, and all the flowers and blossoms of the valley burst into brilliant colour. If you like a party, turn up for the new moon in May, when the big Muslim festival called Id takes place. Sports enthusiasts should come in June–July, the best months for boating, swimming, hiking and water-sports. October is quite pleasant (though a bit cold) and the post-monsoon mountain views are spectacular. By November, the winter has set in and the only real reason for coming is to enjoy the skiing at nearby Gulmarg from mid-December.

ARRIVAL/DEPARTURE

Air
There are daily Indian Airlines flights between Srinagar and Delhi (Rs1465) and Jammu (Rs843); less frequent flights to and from Amritsar (Rs865), Chandigarh (Rs1250) and Leh (Rs663). Road travel is not always available, so you should book tickets in and out of Srinagar in advance.

From the airport, it's a 13-km (8-mile) journey by airport bus which terminates at the Tourist Reception Centre, or by taxi into the city centre. Travel is usually under police or army escort. Srinagar airport has hotel/houseboat booking desks, and a tourist assistance desk. It also has the most stringent security of any of India's airports. The only hand baggage allowed is a book, your passport, boarding pass and ticket. No bags or even cameras are currently permitted.

Road
There are regular buses to Jammu (for the rail connection to Delhi) from the main bus-stand at Srinagar's Tourist Reception Centre. Buses to local interest spots like Gulmarg, Pahalgam, Sonamarg, Yusmarg (and, between June and September, Leh) also leave from here. It's a good idea to book all tour buses, in addition to the Jammu bus, as early as possible.

In 1991 and 1992 the few foreign tourists entering Srinagar were largely trekkers in organised groups. The army would escort them to the trek start directly from the airport and rarely would they visit Srinagar.

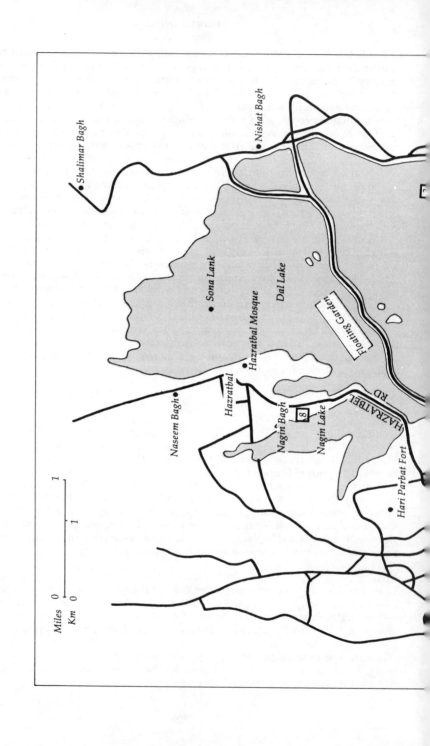

WHAT TO SEE

At the time of writing, it was not possible to check or update all the tours in this section on the Kashmir Valley. There may be lulls in the present disturbances when some tours may be possible. The publishers however strongly advise people wishing to travel to Srinagar to check first with the nearest Indian High Commission or Embassy or with their own country's mission in New Delhi.

If you're coming into Srinagar by plane, you're in for an unforgettable experience. Flying over a mirage range of rolling, snow-capped mountains, Kashmir suddenly bursts into view—a bright gem glittering in a valley of green meadows, rivers and lakes. From the airport, you'll proceed into town along wide avenues of tall chinars (oriental plane trees) overlooking lush green paddy fields. It is best to arrive with at least your first night's accommodation booked and confirmed. The police at the airport on arrival register where you will be staying. However, due to the current problems it is also possible to get bargain rates from houseboats.

Srinagar itself is very spread out, and can take some getting used to. The town is situated on a loop in the narrow, winding Jhelum River, with the Dal Lake (actually three lakes in one) stretching out to the north-west. Most of the cheaper houseboats are located at the south (bottom) part of the lake, opposite Dalgate and Boulevard Road. The higher class ones are in the more restful and scenic areas round Nehru Park and Nagin Lake.

In town, the major landmark is the Tourist Reception Centre which is the first place most tourists get taken to. It's located below Dalgate, and everybody knows it. Follow the bend running left of the Centre to reach the Bund, where the Post Office, the Government Arts Emporium, and most of the better restaurants are located.

It really helps if your houseboat owner speaks English, and can supply directions. Don't, however, accept any directions to his 'uncle's' shop!

Prior to the current problems getting round town was cheapest and most enjoyable by cycle. Taxi rates are fixed; rates are posted to a tree outside the Tourist Reception Centre. Tourist taxis can be hired from the reception centre itself. On the lakes you can be paddled almost anywhere by *shikara*, hired from any one of the many ghats running up the Boulevard. *Shikara* rates are fixed (rates are posted at the ghats) but are like 'fixed' taxi tariffs, never observed. Bargain hard here. If out-of-town excursions to Pahalgam, Gulmarg are possible, use the tour buses laid on by the Tourist Reception Centre.

The suggested sightseeing routes require 5 full days, and can be done in any order. Weather is variable in Kashmir, so do the delightful *shikara* ride on the first clear day that comes along. The excursions to Pahalgam, Gulmarg, Sonamarg and Yusmarg all require advance-booking, and are probably best left to last. If the weather looks tricky, don't do them at all.

Gardens and Lakes (by car or bus, morning; by *shikara*, afternoon)
Nehru Park–Shalimar–Nishat Bagh–Dal Lake–Floating Gardens

Set out early in the morning for the **Mughal Gardens**. There are three of them worthy of note: the Shalimar, the Nishat Bagh and the Naseen Bagh, but only the first two are worth going out of your way for. In spring and autumn these pleasure gardens are a continual delight of terraces, water-channels, fountains and cascades. Out of season (before April) they are as bleak as any city park on a rainy day.

The dawn mist clings to the ghostly hulks of houseboats, projecting like irregular rows of dominoes along the waterfront. The soaring mountain backdrop is a stately line of snow-capped peaks, glowing rose-pink by the light of the morning sun. In Srinagar this is the most beautiful time of day.

By bus, it's a half-hour journey (15 km: 9½ miles) up to **Shalimar Gardens** at the top of Dal Lake. This beautiful 'Garden of Love' was conceived by the Emperor Jahangir as a private recreation area for his wife Nur Jahan in AD 1616. Like the other Mughal gardens, it is open from sunrise to sunset. In the evenings from May to September, it offers a picturesque 'son et lumière', in English (timings are variable so check at the tourist office). On Sundays, the beautiful fountains are turned on.

Shalimar is a sophisticated garden comprising four shallow terraces, each rising above the other, and a canal—lined with polished stones and supplied with water from Harwan Lake—running through the centre. The top terraces used to be reserved for the royal ladies. The garden is full of clipped hedges, flower-beds and avenues of chinar trees. In the centre, there is a small marble palace.

From Shalimar, drive on to **Nishat Bagh**, 5 km (3 miles) down the road. This 'Garden of Bliss' was laid out for the public in AD 1633 by Nur Jahan's brother, Asaf Khan. It is a bigger and better version of Shalimar, with steep escalating terraces, lovely walkways, waterfalls, pavilions, a popular picnic park and superb views over the lake. In the distance, you can see **Hazratbal Mosque** (with its white dome) against a glorious backdrop of the Zabarwan mountains. Nishat Bagh has a total of 13 terraces, and is the largest Mughal garden of all.

In the afternoon, take a relaxing *shikara* ride round **Dal Lake**. This is the high spot of any visit to Srinagar. A trip round the south section of Dal Lake, encompassing the **Floating Garden**, **Nehru Park** and **Char Chinar**, will take 3 hours. If you want to visit the northern section as well (another **Floating Garden**, then **Sona Lank**, **Hazratbal Mosque** and **Naseen Bagh**), it will take 5 to 6 hours. A rather longer but very rewarding day-trip by *shikara* (6 hours there, 2 hours' stay, 3 hours return) is up to the bird sanctuary on the northwest of **Nagin Lake**, with miles upon miles of lotuses and glorious mountain scenery.

Once you have climbed into the low-canopied, exotically decorated *shikara*, and sunk into the plush silk-cushioned seats, prepare yourself for the only non-relaxing part of the trip—a sudden, unexpected onslaught from an armada of '*shikara* shops'. They come from the banks of Boulevard Road; first one, then two, then a whole convoy of wildly paddling boats manoeuvre into position alongside. They are manned by grinning, waving, hallooing traders with unlikely names like 'Tasty Tailor', 'Crocodile' and 'Nick the Jeweller' (Crocodile's cousin), and they are determined to sell you something, anything. Reeling under a simultaneous bombardment of saffron men, *papier-mâché* men, Buddhist-bell men and kebab-stick men, you will need to run this exhilarating gauntlet with a very clear idea of what you do or don't want to buy. The very best purchase is red saffron, followed by semi-precious stone necklaces (jade, tiger-eye and turquoise) and pretty *papier mâché* boxes. There's a flower man who sells beautiful hyacinths, and flower seeds. But be careful. The ready smiles and self-effacing sales patter conceal some of the sharpest business minds around. You can buy practically anything on Dal Lake: cigarettes, chocolate, Tibetan prayer-wheels, Kodak film, and toilet rolls. There's even a floating fruit market. But you have to be quite firm when you don't want to do business. Otherwise, you'll never get beyond the Boulevard.

Past all the *shikara* salesmen, it's a quiet, undisturbed ride up to **Nehru Park**. This is a small island at the foot of Shankaracharya Hill: a popular spot for evening walks and prettily illuminated at night. The *shikara* drops you here for a while; to have a drink at the small restaurant and enjoy views over glass-smooth Dal Lake, with **Pari Mahal** (a Buddhist monastery converted into a School of Astrology by Dara Shikoh, Shah Jahan's son) up in the hills, and below it the Hotel Oberoi Palace. Five-star 'deluxe' houseboats parked nearby bear amusing names like *Noah's Ark*, *New Neil Armstrong*, *King's Thrown*. And *Dongola Super Duper Deluxe with Water Skiz*. Shikara gondolas drift past with honeymooning Indian couples. They have titles like Indian Dream Disco Ha-Ha, and are followed by young lads propelling small dugga-boats with heart-shaped paddles. These budding entrepreneurs pause briefly to offer you a Pepsi or a choc-ice, then continue on.

Your boat will visit next the **Floating Gardens**, drifting silently through a wonderland of winding water-corridors carpeted with meadow-green lichen and pink-red water lilies. The 'old market', a floating bazaar which moves its site daily, is to be found in this quarter, and your *shikara*-man will gladly guide you to the best places for shopping (bear in mind, however, his commission) before slowly steering you homeward. Back at base, your houseboat owner will almost certainly be anxiously waiting for you, with a hot shower and a substantial meal prepared. If he isn't, change your houseboat.

Mosques and Temples (by cycle, 4–6 hours)
Shah Hamdan–Jamia Masjid–Hari Parbat–Shankaracharya Temple– Hazratbal Mosque

Under present circumstances it is probably not possible to do this tour. But it's included in the belief that the situation will improve. This is a pleasant cycle-excursion, best done on a Friday (Muslim holy day) when the town is a blaze of colourful, action-packed markets and bazaars. But it's worth doing any day—just to explore Srinagar town and catch some of the local atmosphere.

Start from Dalgate, cycling down the Maulana Azad Road (the long avenue running past the Tourist Reception Centre) and over the Jhelum river. At the far side, head right, keeping parallel to the river, and turn right again at the second bridge you come to. This will bring you, in 15 minutes or so, to **Shah Hamdan Mosque**. This is one of the city's oldest mosques and is dedicated to the 14th-century 'apostle of Kashmir', a Persian fakir called Shah Hamdan who was the best theologian and Sufi of his day and who did much to promote arts, crafts and learning. The mosque itself is remarkable for its *papier mâché* work which adorns all walls and ceilings.

Unless you are accompanied by a Muslim guide (your houseboat man is a good bet) you will only be allowed to admire the richly decorated external doorway. Inside, however, is some of the finest *papier mâché* decoration in the world. Also beautiful carpets, chandeliers from Portugal, Spain and France, lacquered pillars, walls and balconies, and floral latticed staircases.

Continuing on, head right over two small bridges until the **Jamia Masjid**, the largest mosque in Kashmir, appears on your left (5 mins). Originally built by Sultan Sikandar in AD 1400, and enlarged by his son Zain-ul-Abidin, it was destroyed by fire on three separate occasions and was rebuilt each time. But its massive original pillars, made of solid beams of polished pinewood, were spared the flames. Today (remarkably) they look as good as new. The mosque can accommodate 10 000 worshippers and, on the last day of Ramadan each year, it does so. You can climb to the top of the unusual, square-shaped meenars for a fine view of the whole city. Outside the mosque, there's often a lively bazaar in progress.

From the mosque, it's a 10-minute ride right (then left) until **Hari Parbat Fort** comes into view. This is situated on top of **Sharika Hill**, an ancient Hindu holy site. The wall around the hill was built, along with the almond orchards around it (beautiful in spring), by Akbar in AD 1592–8. The fort atop it was an 18th-century addition, constructed by Atta Mohammad Khan, an Afghan Governor. Presently occupied by the Indian army, there is little to see inside except crumbling ruins. Permission to visit must be sought from the Director of Tourism.

Directly opposite the fort, on the other side of Dal Lake, you can see the gleaming-white **Shankaracharya Temple**. Situated at 1000 ft directly over Srinagar, it is believed to be one of the oldest Hindu shrines in the valley, and is dedicated to Shiva. Previously known as Takht-i-Sulaiman (Throne of Solomon), after a local holy man who, like Francis of Assisi conversed with animals and birds, it was originally built by Jaluka (son of Ashoka) round 200 BC, and added to by an anonymous Hindu devotee during the tolerant reign of Jahangir. It makes a fine early-morning climb offering marvellous views of the town, the valleys and the mountains (0.5 km: ⅓ mile from Srinagar, 1-hour ascent. The hill path commences off Boulevard Road, opposite Nehru Park.)

Coming alongside the fort, by the jail, turn right, then sharp left, to proceed down the long Gurudwara Naidyat Road. This brings you out on the western bank of the Dal Lake, and (after 5 mins by cycle along the lakeside to **Hazratbal Mosque**, 7 km 4½ miles) from town. This elegant white-marble shrine—with its perfectly proportioned single-domed façade and single accompanying minaret has been compared to the Taj Mahal. The cone-shaped dome (not round, as in Mughal structures) and overlapping terraces define it, however, as a typical example of Kashmiri architecture. Its particular importance lies in the single hair of the Prophet Mohammed enshrined here. The original mosque on this site dates back some 600 years; the new building was erected from voluntary subscriptions very recently. The best time to visit is Friday, for 1.30 pm prayers. There are hordes of people, and an amazing bazaar complete with grizzled mountain men sucking hookahs, women in black purdah haggling expertly over meat and bread, vast cauldrons bubbling with bright-red holy food, and street dentists and opticians fitting old dentures and specs onto hopeful passers-by; and lots of dust, smoke and noise. The market closes at 4 pm.

Pahalgam (by tour bus, full-day)

Pahalgam lies 96 km (60 miles) east of Srinagar at 2130 m, in a pretty valley surrounded by 12 snow-covered peaks and deep pine forests, at the junction of the Sheshnag and Liddar rivers. Originally a small shepherd's village, it is now a popular holiday resort, with good facilities for walking, pony-trekking, trout-fishing and trekking. It makes a fine day-outing, though if you wish to stay longer, there are hotels and lodges available.

The Tourist Reception Centre, Srinagar, runs a good day-tour out to Pahalgam. You only get 3 hours in the village, but it's enough. And the 4-hour outward bus journey makes some interesting stops. There is no guide attached to the tour, but the glorious scenery of majestic mountains, green pine forests and meadows of bright yellow saffron, speaks for itself.

The tour first visits **Avantipur**, the old capital of Kashmir before earthquakes in the 14th century prompted a move to Srinagar. Here is the old ruined **Avantisvamim Temple**, built by King Avantivarman (AD855–83) and dedicated to Vishnu. Originally a masterpiece of perfectly proportioned architecture and art, graced with exuberant, graceful sculptures and carvings, it is now a heap of old ruins. But the main shrine, in the centre of a spacious oblong courtyard, is worth a look. So are the few fine carvings of Ganesh and Parvati near the entrance. Moving on past Sangram (where many of India's cricket bats are made), you'll come to the pilgrim centre of **Ramakrishna Mahasannalam Ashram**, where the god of rain, Indra, cured himself of some horrid disease by bathing in the holy sulphur springs. Of more interest is the medieval Muslim town of Islamabad (Anantag). During the recent troubles the town has been a centre of disturbances and many buildings have been burnt.

Coming into **Pahalgam**, lines of bearded, weather-worn, *hookah*-smoking shepherds appear by the roadside and gangs of local youths leap on to the side of the bus for a free ride into town. Off the bus, you are deluged by friendly, insistent youngsters wanting you to hire guides or ponies, or to buy handicrafts.

It's best to eat first—either at the **Pahalgam Hotel** (for civilised food) or at the **Lhasa** or **Tabela** restaurants (for cheaper civilised food). All three places are close together, 5 minutes' walk up the hill from the bus-stand.

The thing to do in Pahalgam is pony-trekking. There are over 1500 ponies in the valley, and ponies have been ferrying visitors for the last 100 years. If you can't find a pony (and this is rare, for they invariably find you) enquire at Pahalgam's tourist office, by the bus-stand. This office is open 24 hours a day except Sunday during the high season, and posts the correct rates. You can either trot off on your own or take on a pony-trek. These go on 1- to 3-day jaunts to nice spots like **Lidderwat**, a beautiful valley of flowers, best around May/June; **Aru**, a small valley with a charming meadow, deep forests, good fishing, and a few Dak Bungalows; and **Kolahoi Glacier**, an amazing year-round glacier, most accessible from May to September. If you're only here for the day, your best option is the hour-long **Four Points** pony-trek. This takes you out of town via the beautiful Nehru and Shail parks (in May–June, a riot of red, blue and yellow), and up to the four spots of optimum beauty overlooking the valley. Riding along conifer-lined mountain paths and over shallow rushing streams of leaping trout, you'll come at last to the higher ridges, offering superb alpine views. On your return, leave time for a short stop by the river bridge (just before re-entry to the village) to meet the shepherds and their flocks.

Before the troubles, there were two comfortable hotels in town: **Pahalgam Hotel** (tel 26, 52, tlx 0375-345) with centrally heated rooms, good food, lovely views, dinky pool, and disco; and **Woodstock Hotel** (tel 27), with the best views, nice gardens, and a good restaurant. The latter used to be a bit run down; both may no longer be operating. Rates used to be in the mid-range (about Rs700). The cheaper hotels are on or near the Liddar River, about a half-hour walk from the bus-stand. It's best to hire a pony. Property that opened just before the troubles is the **Senator Pine-N-Peak** (tel 11, tlx 0375-343).

Things to do in Pahalgam include golf (May–June season) on the lovely 9-hole course overlooking town from a high plateau; apply for temporary membership at the Golf Club; 1 km above the bus-stand. There's fishing from April to September with lots of trout in the Liddar and Sheshnag streams; and even more at Aru village, a one-day 11-km (7-mile) trek away. Permits are issued by the Fisheries Department at the Tourist Reception Centre in Srinagar, Trekking guides and ponies are for hire anywhere in town. For longer treks to Kolahoi Glacier (4 days), Sonamarg (7 days) and Ladakh/Zanskar (8 days) it is advisable to book through one of the major trekking agencies in Delhi, such as **Mountain Travel**, who will make all arangements. If you're around in August, try the trek up to the holy cave of **Amarnath**, located 48 km (30 miles) from Pahalgam at an altitude of 4154 m. Every year, thousands of pilgrims make the gruelling week-long trek up here to see the famous natural ice linga of Shiva that waxes and wanes with the moon. The July/August full moon is especially auspicious, and attracts a biblical exodus of devotees.

Gulmarg (full-day)

Situated 52 km (32½ miles) from Srinagar, this beautiful mountain resort is famous for its flowers (Emperor Jahangir once collected 21 varieties here), for its outstanding natural golf course (at 2650 m it claims to be the highest 18-hole course in the world), and for its winter skiing centre. Originally named Gaurimarg (after Shiva's wife), its spectacular beauty prompted Sultan Yusuf Shah to rename it Gul (flower) Marg (meadow) in 1581. Its 11.2-km (7-mile) circular road offers a magnificent view of the entire Kashmir valley.

Because of Gulmarg's high elevation (2730 m), the passes are often blocked by snow. The day-tour buses from Srinagar only operate between April and October. High season at Gulmarg is May to July, and it's wise to advance-book a hotel room from Srinagar tourist office if planning to stay overnight.

The tour bus takes 1½ hours to reach the village of Tangmarg, 13 km (8 miles) below Gulmarg. This is a good place to hire guides for day hikes up to Khilanmarg (June to October only). They wait in Tangmarg's quaint **Mahajan Restaurant** at the bus-stand. There are trekking equipment shops at Tangmarg, also a tourist information office. In the winter, when snow blocks the passes, buses can't get up to Gulmarg and you'll have to hire a pony. In summer, when dairy cows graze lush green meadows of beautiful flowers, the journey up by bus is a real delight.

In high season, Gulmarg is chaos. To avoid the rush leave the main road at the chair-lift, and follow the quiet pony trails straight up the mountain to **Khilanmarg**, 6 km (3¾ miles) from the bus-stand. This bright flower-meadow valley is a blaze of colour and fragrance in the springtime, and gives stunning views over the peaks, Wular lake and the Kashmir valley. It is also the principal location for Gulmarg's ski-runs. The return journey to Khilanmarg takes around 2 hours by pony and around 3 hours on foot. The walk's the thing: a pleasant 680-m ascent through meadows of wild flowers, azaleas and buttercups, dusted with butterflies. Come in May/June to see the scenery at its best.

If staying over at Gulmarg, take the right-hand fork from the bus-stand and walk 0.5 km down to the Tourist Office. Nearby are the better hotels. If it's hasn't been requisitioned by the army, **Hotel Highland Park** (tel 230, 207, tlx 0375-320) is a classy place to stay, colonial-style with nice views, interesting food and centrally heated rooms (big discounts out-of-season).

Gulmarg has probably the best range of recreational facilities in Kashmir. You can go pony-trekking round Outer Circular Walk, an 11-km (7-mile) circular road

Gulmarg

running right round Gulmarg and offering views down to Srinagar and up to Nanga Parbat, the fifth highest mountain in the world (8137 m). You can enjoy pleasant walks out to **Ningle Nallah** (10 km: 6¼ miles), **Alpather Lake** (13 km: 8 miles) and the Muslim shrine of **Ziarat of Babareshi** (5 km: 3 miles). Also exhilarating toboggan runs through the wooded snow passes, golfing on the highest 18-hole course in the world (near the tourist office), some of the best skiing in India with runs up to 10 km (6⅓ miles) and beginners' slopes (best January/February, when the snow is hard and compact), and an ice-skating rink, with skates for hire. For trekking, hire a guide/porter and travel out to Tosha Maidan, one of Kashmir's most beautiful meadows, a 3-day 50-km (31-mile) walk. On the way, stop at Ferozpore Nallah (5 km: 3 miles out of Gulmarg) for some superior trout-fishing (permit from Srinagar). This is also a marvellous picnic spot. Gulmarg, it's worth noting, also has a small post office and a very helpful J & K Bank.

Sonamarg (by tour bus, full-day)

Some 80 km (50 miles) north-east of Srinagar, Sonamarg is a wide, open valley of golden flowers and pine forests, ringed by high mountains and glaciers. Sonamarg literally means 'meadow of gold', and in spring—when the wooded glades are ablaze with bright orange marigolds—you can easily see why. The scenery here is much more dramatic than at Gulmarg or Pahalgam. All across the wide open plain, scattered rock outcrops testify to the retreating glaciers which once covered this beautiful terrain. The valley itself is full of huge rock deposits and moraine left behind by old glaciers; the lines of pine trees forming the banks of the ski run lie on an ancient lateral moraine. A massive hanging glacier (broken by the cliff) descends from the mountain saddle at the head of the vale. Standing at the foot of the ski run, you can see how the glacier has retreated.

218

You can visit Sonamarg from Srinagar between May and October only. The rest of the year, the passes are covered with snow. Best months to visit are July/August (for trekking) and May/June (for best views of the glaciers). September is very nice too.

The big thing to do at Sonamarg is the 3-hour (return) pony-trek up to **Thajwas Glacier**, the main attraction in these parts. If you want some exercise (the air is very bracing) you can get there just as quickly on foot—cutting over the hills, and avoiding the crowded main thoroughfare. It's about 5 km (3 miles) from the bus-stand to the glaciers/ski-run, and in the winter you may need to hire snow-gear from the trekking shops in town. It can get *very* cold here—Drass, one day's walk from Sonamarg, is the second coldest place in Asia, recording temperatures of about 65°–70°F in January.) You'll certainly need some warm clothes, and good walking shoes. At the ski-slope, you can hire toboggans or engage coolies to hike your ski-equipment up to the top of the glacier.

Trekking out of Sonamarg is extremely cheap. You should be able to pick up a guide for about Rs50 a day and a pony for Rs75. Sonamarg is the best base from which to trek to **Amarnath Cave**—15 km (9 miles) by jeep to Baltal, then 15 km (9¼ miles) up to Amarnath and back by pony.

Sonamarg is also the national highway to **Ladakh**. In 1974, the Sonamarg road was thrown open to Ladakh-bound tourists. No buses ply from Sonamarg to Leh, but it is possible—even as early as May (when the pass is still partly snowbound) to hire lifts in pick-up trucks as far as Kargil. Probably the best local trek from Sonamarg is to the beautiful high-altitude lake of **Gangabal**, situated at the foot of a year-round glacier. This trek can take anything between 5 and 7 days.

As the smallest of Kashmir's resorts, Sonamarg has rather limited accommodation. For the time being the most comfortable option is the **Tourist Bungalow**, with two-bedroomed huts (with bathroom, hot and cold water) and double tents (with bedding). Sonamarg's tourist office, before the troubles, was open 24 hours a day from May 1st to November 15th (closed Sunday), well-run, and very helpful.

Yusmarg (full day)

Yusmarg has been described as one of the best places in Kashmir to have peace of mind. It's a small valley set in the heart of the mountains, some 47 km (29 miles) from Srinagar. Much underrated, it has beautiful meadows to rival Gulmarg, rolling hills, forests and spectacular scenery. If you can find a guide, this would be ideal trekking territory. Otherwise, hire a pony (very cheap) and visit nearby **Nilnag Lake**. There are a few cheap guest houses near the lake, also a Tourist Bungalow with good food at the bus-stand. On the way in to Yusmarg the town of **Jari Sharif**, situated right at the head of the valley offer splendid views from its famous mosque. Cheap, high-quality Kashmiri pherans (winter-coats) are sold in the market.

RECREATION

Back in Srinagar, you can enjoy a game of golf. The ball may not fly as far as it does in Gulmarg, but the 18-hole course (near Nedou's Hotel) is quite respectable. For beginners, there is a small 6-hole mini-course below Oberoi Palace Hotel.

For water-sports, take a *shikara* out to the 'recreation' boats moored in the centre of Dal and Nagin lakes. From here you can go swimming, water-skiing, motor-boating and 'surf-riding' (lazy man's water-skiing on wide wooden boards) at low rates.

The small Nagin Club on Nagin Lake offers water-skiing and sailing. Swimming is also good at Nehru Park.

Fishing is good in several nearby rivers, and at Gulmarg/Pahalgam. Apply for permit (and good information) at the Tourist Reception Centre.

There is a strong tradition of folk music and dance in Srinagar, but surprisingly little evidence of it. Until recently, every evening in the summer a sound and light show at Shalimar Gardens recreated the era of Emperor Jahangir's court in Kashmir. It may be reinvested by the time you read this. The gardens were beautifully illuminated for these shows.

TREKKING

Trekking is traditionally 'big business' in Kashmir, and despite the current unrest, groups escorted by the army are still spending time here. Many treks are only possible from June to September, when the passes are clear of snow.

SHOPPING

Srinagar sells Kashmir's finest traditional produce: light Pashmina and Shahtoosh shawls, hand-knotted carpets, chain-stitch rugs, walnut-wood carvings, jewellery and gems, *papier mâché* and rare red saffron. Also leather and furs, coarse-knitted woollen sweaters, and tailor-made clothing. Kashmir has an old fur trade but many of the items offered and sold are illegal both in India and elsewhere in the world. Despite what you might be told, the trade in most wild animal furs is banned by international treaty.

Buying anything in Kashmir is always an experience, generally involving a preparatory cup of spiced Kashmiri tea, a lot of inconsequential banter, then a sudden, remorseless sales attack which has you pinned to your seat. The Kashmiris love bargaining, and have a real zest for communicating their love of their handicrafts to tourists. This often results in you buying a lot more stuff than originally planned. The general rule is either to be sure of exactly what you want, and then barter hard for it, or not to buy anything at all until you've got a fix on prices at a reliable government emporium. **Kashmir Government Arts Emporium**, Residency Rd, is a good one—especially for walnut-wood furniture, *papier mâché* items, chain-stitch materials, and carpets. It's open 10 am to 5 pm daily. The **Government Central Market**, across Badshah Bridge, stocks a wide variety of Kashmiri handicrafts and you can bargain yourself some very good deals. It's open 9 am to 9 pm, except Sundays. Also worth a visit is the **Cottage Industries Village**, some way out of town (cycle there, or get a taxi). This is where most of the local crafts of the area are produced, mainly *papier mâché*, silk and carpets. When you visit the large showroom upstairs, make sure you do so alone. Anyone who accompanies you gets a hefty commission on all your purchases.

One last shopping complex of note is the **'Old Market'** on the Dal Lake itself. It's actually a fruit, flower and vegetable market, but a lot of other interesting items turn up. Arrive early (5 am) to buy everything sold on the shikaras, but more of it and much cheaper. This market is elusive: it moves around the lake, settling on a new location every day, but your *shikara*-man will always know where to find it.

Your houseboat man will always 'happen to know' a good woodwork man or a good carpet factory nearby. The owner will be his 'brother' or his 'cousin', and he will be deeply offended if you buy anything from anybody else. Visit these places by all means—at the woodwork places you'll see beautiful walnut-wood jewellery boxes, employing the same carving designs as used on the intricately-worked awnings and balconies of the better houseboats, and you can watch them tracing the patterns onto the wood and then carefully chipping them out—but don't feel obliged to buy. It is always worth learning about the traditional processes by which such handicrafts are produced.

There are lots of small family-based 'factories' operating from housefronts, both on land and on the lake. Dalgate has some worthwhile *papier mâché* factories. For jewellery, curios and Tibetan/Nepali handicrafts, look in on **Tibetan Gift House**, at the junction of Dalgate and Boulevard.

The Boulevard itself is one big hassle of carpet sellers, gem dealers, fur houses and handicraft shops—to be avoided at all costs.

A lot has been written about Kashmiri carpets, the item that tourists instinctively make a beeline for in Srinagar. Cynics claim that the industry has been ruined by mass-purchase business mughals flooding the European and American markets with Kashmiri carpets, so that they cost more to buy here than abroad. This is a fable. What has happened is that the Kashmiris, like the Rajasthanis, have recently become only too aware of the true market value of their goods and prices have risen to about half current London prices.

Most Kashmiri carpets employ old Persian designs, and are made by true descendants of the old Persian families. The composition of silk carpets is usually 80% silk (to give them durability and sheen) and 20% wool. The wool is from Rajasthan and the silk from Mysore or China (Kashmiri silk, being so expensive, is now used only for saris). The dyes are generally chemical, imported from Germany. The feature of the Kashmiri 'magic' carpet is its special weave which produces two entirely different shades: viewed from one side, light; from the other side, dark. This effect is produced by cutting each knot downwards when filling it between each pair of threads, resulting in a dark intermediary pattern running through the primarily light weave.

Kashmiri carpets are still the best handmade carpets in the world. They are usually produced on large wooden looms by teams of young boys, and, depending on size and quality, take anything from 6 months to 4 years to make. Because they are so popular, a lot of inferior stuff is regularly produced, simply to meet the demand. You need to be very careful when buying carpets. Regardless of what the salesman tells you, check first the content of the carpet: the only real way of telling if it's silk, or just a poor 'staple' (cotton derivative) substitute, is to take out a knot and burn it—cotton has a relatively slow burn, but real silk goes off like a quick fuse, leaving a small 'knob' on the end of the thread. Second, count the number of knots in a sample inch of carpet. A good silk carpet should have a minimum of 324 knots per sq in. Really good ones go up to 900 knots, but most people can't afford them. Anything less than 299 knots is probably not worth buying. Third, check the colour and pattern of the carpet—both should be in perfect symmetry. Finally, make sure the vendor has an export licence and can supply you with a certificate of origin (this saves you heavy VAT/customs payments). It's also a good idea to photograph or mark any carpet being shipped home for you. This reduces the risk of being sent a completely different, inferior carpet to the one purchased.

WHERE TO STAY

At the time of writing many hotels are being requisitioned by the army; others have closed down because of local violence or lack of trade. Tourism however is

Kashmir's main industry and, as soon as it can, the industry will undoubtedly reinstate itself.

Hotels you can get anywhere in India. Houseboats you find only in Kashmir. They come in all shapes, sizes and categories, and are wonderfully relaxing. Most of them have the word 'deluxe' somewhere in their title, and aren't deluxe at all. The better ones are located in quiet backwaters offering fine views of the lake, and are run not by 'managers' but by local families. There are lots of relaxing boats like this up at Nehru Park, and on Nagin Lake. Boats in Dalgate/Boulevard area, tend to be very noisy.

Don't take the first boat you're shown. First, check who else is on board. Out of season, it's easy to have a whole boat to yourself; in season, you may have to share.

The best boats are about 30m long, so you don't lead a cramped life. They have a verandah/sun-lounge to sit out on, a spacious sitting-room with exotic wall-to-wall carpeting, a dining room with plush cushions and magazines, and three double-bedrooms, each with dressing-room and bathroom. Servants pad noiselessly about (except when trying to sell you something) and the furniture is handcrafted in the style of 80 years ago. For entertainment, there may be a colour TV and a stereo.

Before you agree the rate, make quite sure that it includes a) free *shikara* rides from boat to shore; b) all meals (usually breakfast and supper, with a packed lunch thrown in for daytime sightseeing); c) hot water for showers whenever required; d) free Kashmiri tea (though this tends to arrive all day long anyway); e) laundry service (worth a try). The golden rule with houseboats is never to pay by the day. This gives you the upper hand if rascally houseboat owners slack off after initially impeccable service.

A big plus (or minus) of houseboats is the food. There is generally a grinning *khansamah* (cook-boy) in attendance, who will attempt practically anything you ask him. Steak and chips, apple pie, and banana cake are popular Western requests. But far better to go for authentic Kashmiri food and drinks. Endless cups of sweet green-black Kashmiri tea (spiced with cinnamon, lemon and cardamom) and tasty breakfasts of fresh Kashmiri bread and boiled eggs arrive without asking. But try to persuade the cook to prepare you a traditional Kashmiri 'wedding-feast' meal. This might cost you extra, but is well worth it, especially if eating in a group.

There is an official charge list issued by the tourist office, setting out the allegedly 'fixed' prices for the five main categories of houseboat. In practice, nobody pays any notice to these rates. To start with, there's no way of knowing what category any particular boat belongs to: if they have a listed rating, they don't seem able to prove it. Thus a 'five-star' advertised houseboat may have facilities just as bad as a D class 'donga' boat. Alternatively, a well-run C class boat may be far better equipped and more comfortable than a poor A class boat. Another reason why the official rates are ignored is that houseboat owners are so keen for business. There are 1300 houseboats on the rivers, and, even before the onset of political unrest, not enough tourists to go round. This means that you can bargain yourself a very nice discount, particularly in the off-season. Be prepared to haggle quite firmly with the houseboat owner. Afterwards you can be the best of friends.

Since 1991 many of the hotels have either closed their shutters or been requisitioned by the security forces. On dry land, the five-star **Oberoi Palace Hotel** (tel 75651, 71241, tlx 0375-201 LXSR IN) is an ex-Maharajah's palace with 20 acres of landscaped gardens and unrivalled views over Dal Lake. Situated 7 km (4½ miles) from the city centre, it has charming olde-worlde rooms (with antique furnishings and light, bright decor). Ask for a lake-view room on the 1st floor. The one hotel that is anywhere like fully operational during the troubles is the **Centaur Lake View**, Cheshma Shahi, 9Tel 77601, 73135, tlx 0375-205). Situated on the eastern shore of Dal Lake the hotel continues to provide regular service. **Hotel Broadway**, Maulana Azad Rd (tel 75621-3, tlx 0375-212), overlooks the golf course and is very convenient for shopping centres and the tourist office. Centrally air-conditioned, with good pool and marvellous restaurant. Rooms are good value at Rs650–900. **Hotel Shangri-La** (tel 72422) has a quiet, out-of-the-way location at Sonwar Bagh, 2 km (1¼ miles) from Dalgate.

EATING OUT

If you tire of houseboat cooking, and wish to try the authentic, Persian-influenced, and spicy Kashmiri cuisine, go in search of *Wazwan*, the Grand Feast. In its original form, it comprised a basic *pilaf* (rice platter) with which were served up to 17 meat courses. Many of these were lamb dishes like the *guzhtaba* (meatballs cooked in yogurt, curd sauce and spices), *tabaq-mazh* (grilled spare ribs cooked in cashew-nut, poppyseed and onions), birianis and kebabs.

In better times, you should find these dishes either at the **Oberoi Hotel** or the **Broadway Hotel**; also a small selection of favourite local dishes—mutton roganjosh, *rishta* lamb dumplings, and *guzhtaba* meatballs. The Shahenshah Hotel's **Kohinoor** restaurant is also worth a try. The most authentic local-style restaurant is still **Mughal Darbar** on Residency Rd (near the post office) with a wide range of *Wazwan* dishes, including *rishta, guzhtaba, roganjosh* (mutton cooked with ginger and yogurt), and *marchwangamqurama* (mild korma curry), plus a variety of tasty sweets. Lots of cheaper restaurants do Kashmiri mutton or the traditional *kanti* (mutton or chicken cooked in spices and onions), but take care. Even in the best of times, many places reheated old food when business was slow, and stomach bugs were a common result.

GENERAL INFORMATION

J & K Government Tourist Reception Centre, Shervani Rd, Dalgate (tel 77303, 77305, 734568) is the largest tourist complex in India. Everything you need—post office, Indian Airlines (tel 73270, open 10 am to 5 pm, airport tel 31521-29), bookshop, restaurant, houseboat/hotel reservations, fishing/wildlife/sports information—is located here. Open 24 hours a day (in season, in peace time) for information and assistance, but only a skeleton service operates outside the normal 10 am–5 pm working hours.

The post office, on the Bund, is open 10 am to 5 pm daily; *poste restante* open 10 am to 5 pm Monday to Friday, 10 am to 1 pm Saturday, closed all day Sunday. The Foreigners' Registration Dept, Shervani Rd (just behind post office) is open 10 am to 4 pm.

Ladakh

Ladakh, the Land of the Passes, is perched in the cold deserts of the Karakoram ranges, at the crossroads of China, India and Central Asia. It may be part of India, but is less like India than anything you could imagine. A dry, mountainous moonscape, it is most often referred to as the 'little Tibet'. The surrounding Himalaya

Thikkse Monastery, Ladakh

let in very little rain, and for as far as the eye can see, the terrain appears to be a succession of flat, dust-ridden plains and barren mountains, occasionally enlivened by brilliant pink flowering dogrose bushes. The road winds snakelike round these massive folds of ancient rock, and only unravels itself into an arrow-straight line as it approaches **Leh**, the capital of the region. Behind this grim, forbidding façade, however, Ladakh is the 'last Shangri-La'—an exotic land of rich art treasures, inhabited by a gentle, benign people. The drab exteriors of gompas (Tibetan Buddhist monasteries) conceal colourful tantric frescoes, thangkas, and exquisitely carved statues of gold and stone. The tough, resilient people are a fascinating mix of native Ladakhis and refugee Tibetans, only recently exposed to the outside world and still steeped in magic and mysticism. Renowned for their devout, peace-loving ways, the great majority of them adhere to the Tibetan religion and culture. After the hardships of the extreme winter, they bring the land alive during summer with festivities, pageantry, mask dances and mystic plays. Their animals are delightfully odd—diminutive mules, yak/cow combinations called dzos, and hairy little sheep which look like overgrown Cairn terriers. Outside Leh, the practice of polyandry (whereby many men are married to one woman) is still a way of life, and the population of Ladakh has remained more or less the same since the year dot.

WHEN TO GO
Situated in one of the most elevated regions on earth, Ladakh has an arid cold climate throughout the year. In the depths of winter, when the passes are blocked by snow, the thermometer plummets as low as minus 35°C. Between May and November, when the valley is open to tourist traffic, daytime temperatures can reach a pleasant 20°C. But it's the nights you have to watch out for—bring some warm clothing and (if trekking) a heavy-duty sleeping bag.

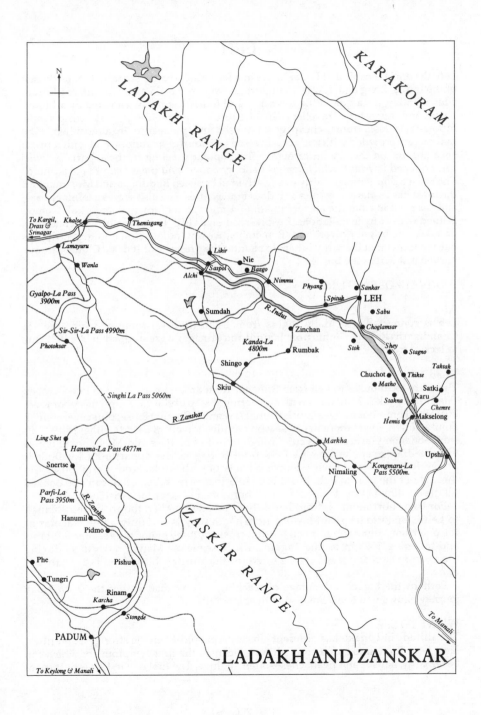

LADAKH AND ZANSKAR

LEH

Leh, the ancient capital of Ladakh, lies in a fertile side-valley some 10 km north-east of the Indus. Long ago, it was an important stop on the old caravan 'silk road' from China. Today, it's a quiet little township and tourist centre, overlooked by a hilltop palace and monastery. Travellers like it for its old royal buildings, rustic curio shops, hippie-style restaurants, cheap guest-houses and pioneer-town atmosphere. The markets are crowded with Ladakhis dressed in colourful splendour, and with tourists sneaking up on them with cameras. The popular greeting in these parts is *'julle'* (pronounced jew-lay), which means hello, goodbye, and please can I take a photo? The town's population is fairly evenly divided between Buddhists and Muslims, and the town has as many mosques as it does monasteries. Leh also serves a military base, and the road in from the airport 10 km (6¼ miles) out of town, near Spitok Gompa is lined with army installations. Despite road-signs like 'India, one brilliant bouquet, Ladakh, one bright flower' and 'Remember, we are Indians first and foremost', it's hard to forget that the army is here to counter the presence of 100 000 Chinese troops parked just across the border.

ARRIVAL/DEPARTURE

Air
Leh is connected with daily flights from Delhi (Rs1348) some of which are via Chandigarh (Rs876). Flights from Jammu and Srinagar were stopped in late 1992 due to lack of traffic.

Road
There are local buses to Leh from Srinagar from around early June to late October. The journey takes 2 full days with an overnight stop at Kargil. Kargil has poor food, but fair accommodation—a Tourist Bungalow and a Circuit House, plus several small family hotels. To get there in pre-season months, travellers used to either hitch a lift from Sonamarg (army trucks cut through to Leh as early as mid-May), or tag onto a trek heading over the Zoji La Pass from Srinagar. The opportunity for both is presently limited, and such a course is really not advisable. From Kargil buses run throughout the year to Leh. Buses back to Srinagar from Leh often can't be booked till the evening before departure—ask your hotel manager for assistance.

For two short months, from late July to late September, the road from Manali to Leh is open to jeep and bus traffic. The journey is certainly as spectacular as the one from Srinagar but much harder, crossing three major ranges of mountains and touching 5325 m on the **Taglang La**. Buses leave Manali most days during the short season and jeeps can be hired for the journey. Little food is available *en route*.

Perhaps the biggest advantage of reaching Leh by road is that the 2- to 3-day journey allows you to acclimatise to the high altitude.

WHAT TO SEE
The altitude in Ladakh has different effects on people. Even the strongest and fittest have been known to suffer from altitude sickness the first symptoms of which can be lethargy, nausea and headaches—often all three. The first day in Leh is best spent

relaxing in your hotel. At most, go for a short walk in the evening. Many doctors advise at least two days to acclimatise—this is especially important if you fly into Leh.

Central Ladakh occupies a large part of the Upper Indus Valley, and its 40 or so gompas are widely spread. Getting out to them is easy because the roads are so good (because the army uses them). Tourists aren't allowed to wander more than a mile off the main roads, on pain of arrest, and you can only visit about a dozen of the monasteries. Most of these are locked, and you will have to ask to be shown around. Your escort is usually a friendly if inscrutable monk who sticks to you like a shadow, to stop you wandering off. His attempts to illuminate the beautiful frescoes and murals with candles are often fruitless: most of the chambers are gloom-laden, and you'll need a powerful flashlight to see anything. All the gompas charge admission; most hold prayers from 5–9 am, and 4–7 pm; a few (Hemis, Thikse, Alchi, Rizong, Lamayuru) put up travellers overnight. Staying in cold, draughty gompas is spartan (you sleep on the floor, and pray for more blankets), but it's cheap and there's certainly no better way of absorbing the mystic, ascetic Ladakhi lifestyle. A good alternative is to walk in the valley—strolling from village to village, staying up in family houses or in the occasional travellers' lodge. For the time being, Ladakh is so new to tourism (it only opened up to outside visitors in the mid-70s) and is so thinly populated (9000 people in Leh, only 20 000 in the whole valley) that such nomadic ramblings are an out-of-time experience— you can walk all day, and not see another traveller. The only thing you have to watch out for is the climate. Leh is on a high-altitude plateau of 3500 m, and the thin, dry air takes some getting used to. Avoid strenuous walking or climbing the first couple of days (especially if flying in from the hot plains of Delhi) and always keep your water-bottle topped up. Even locals drink a minimum of 2 litres a day, to keep dehydration at bay. To avoid sunburn (the sunlight can be incredibly intense), don't expose legs and arms, and protect your face and neck with a wide-brimmed hat. If hiking out to remote monasteries, take along adequate supplies of food; eating the local fare of *tsampa* cakes (made from pan-roasted barley flour), *holkur* (Ladakhi biscuits) and *gurgur* (salted butter tea) can because monotonous after a while. All water should be boiled, and all fruit and vegetables peeled and washed.

From Leh's rather chaotic bus-stand, buses run out to all the major gompas, and the fare is rarely more than Rs10 one-way. Most buses leave around 7.30 am (get a timetable from the tourist office), and you should board them half an hour before departure, to be sure of getting a seat. From Leh, it takes 45 minutes to Stok (17 km) and to Shey (15 km), 1 hour to Thikse (20 km), 2 hours to Hemis (43 km) and 6 hours (taking the Kargil bus) to Lamayuru (127 km). It's impossible to visit Alchi (67 km) and Likir (61 km) in a day by bus—you'll have to stay overnight in Saspol (62 km, 3 hours from Leh). To cover Ladakh's main attractions in just 2 days, hire a jeep—day one, drive south to Shey, Thikse, and Hemis; day two, head west to Alchi, Likir and Rizong. Jeeps are expensive but take up to 6 passengers. Taxi rates (posted at the tourist office) are fixed, but you can often bargain a 10–15% discount. The big advantage of taking a jeep is that you can get out, stroll about, and take photos whenever you wish. When you get home, however, depends a lot on how often your jeep overheats or breaks down.

Gompa Tour (1) (by jeep/bus, full day)
Shey–Thikse–Hemis

This is the most popular *gompa* circuit. If travelling by jeep, set out early morning, see the monasteries in the order given, and expect to be back by lunch. Alternatively, catch the first bus out to Shey (for 7.30 am prayers), proceed straight on to Hemis (bus stops here for 2/3 hours sightseeing), and backtrack to Thikse. This way, you can easily be back in Leh by sunset. Even if going by jeep, take a packed lunch from your hotel and have the flexibility to spend the whole day out.

Driving out to Shey, the road is lined with *mani* walls (carved with the Tibetan Buddhist mantra 'Om Mani Padme Hum', or Hail to the Jewel in the Lotus) and conical stupas called chortens (symbolising the mind of the 13 rings representing the 13 realms of human consciousness). Like the *gompas* or monasteries, these *chortens* are made of unbaked earth or clay, and appear to be a natural extension of the surrounding desert. Some 14 km (8¾ miles) upstream from Leh, you'll come to **Shey**, a 15th-century palace *gompa* built by Lhachen Palgyigon, the first king of Ladakh. The old summer palace of the royal family, it houses in a back chamber of the *gompa* the largest golden Buddha in Ladakh, 7.5 m (22 ft) high. Making three anti-clockwise circuits of the image cleanses you of past sins, and solicitous signs outside prevent you committing any new ones. Views over the Indus plain from the palace roof are superb. The *gompa* is open from 7 to 9 am, and from 5 to 6 pm. At other times, you may have to walk over to Sabu, the nearby village, to ask Shey's only monk for the key. Sabu is also the favourite home of Shey's famous oracle.

From Shey, it's only 3 km (2 miles) down the road to **Thikse Gompa**. This is a spectacular 10-storey congregation of buildings perched atop a rocky crag. Built some 500 years ago, Thikse has the largest number of lamas and nuns of any *gompa*, houses the greatest collection of ancient Buddhist scriptures and books in Ladakh, and is a masterpiece of construction. The lower eight monasteries are heaped one on top of the other in perfect symmetry, their blank slit windows staring across the plain like empty eyes. The top two levels, which house the head lama, are painted in gay colours. It's a stiff climb up there, but you get an enthusiastic welcome and you can 'enjoy cold drink and postcard' at the small refreshment shop. The views from the upper levels are amazing. Just beyond the temple courtyard, a seated Buddha surveys the largest library in Ladakh. In the rooms behind, there's an intricately carved statue of the 'white Tara' (a female Buddhist deity) and a painting of Yamaraja (the Hindu god of death), both showing the early influence of Hinduism over the religion of these hills. But Thikse's most striking structure, three floors further up, is the 15-m high, heavily bejewelled, and colourfully adorned statue of Maitreya Buddha, the eighth incarnation of Buddha anxiously awaited by Tibetan Buddhists. Behind this, in a small back-annexe, a line of dusty old Buddhas gaze astonished at weird tantric wall-paintings—mainly of chickens flying off with antelope livers. This is a hotel-restaurant at Thikse, and if you get up at 6.30 am you will witness two monks blowing conch shells on the roof, followed by 7 am prayers. Staying overnight, you'll also see far more. Casual visitors, unless accompanied by a persuasive guide, are often shown only two or three rooms.

The drive on to **Hemis**, 25 km (15½ miles) further south, reinforces the barrenness of the landscape. Past the checkpoint at **Karu** (have your passport handy), you ford the Indus and wind your way up into the desolate mountains. At the base of one of these, tucked away in a beautiful valley overlooking a creek, is **Hemis Gompa**.

Founded some 350 years ago by Stagshang Rinchen (a visiting Tibetan lama), this is the largest monastery in Ladakh, and the richest. It has a 1000-sq-metre courtyard, a 9.5-m high statue of Guru Padmasambhava (his expression as ferocious as his teachings), and the largest *thangka* (scroll) which is embroidered and not painted as most are. This item is exhibited once every 12 years—the next display will be in 2004. After poking round the various dim chambers (look out for a brace of airborne stuffed antelopes, and for a 700-year-old tortoise guarding holy books), visit the delightful Middle Ages kitchen, where monks make *tsampa* dumplings and churn butter. Hemis is a great place to stay over—either in the monastery or at the newly built guest-house. It has jolly monks and lots of atmosphere. Hemis is the one major *gompa* to hold its festival during the summer months (most other gompas hold theirs during the quiet winters) and is consequently one of the better known. Each June/July a 2-day festival of dance-dramas are performed in the central courtyard. This event celebrates the birth of the Buddhist reformer Padmasambhava, and is getting so popular they charge for balcony seats. An hour's climb above Hemis, there's an older 13th-century monastery affording magnificent views down over the valley.

Gompa Tour (2) (by jeep, full day)
Alchi–Likir–Saspol–Rizong

One of the best reasons for visiting Alchi is the drive out there. This starts in a humorous fashion, with a series of PWD road-signs strung out along the airport road. 'Dozing is injurious to health' informs one. 'Accidents are *prohibited* on this road!' warns another. 'I will miss you—come again' pleads a third. Beyond the airport, past more massive *mani* walls, all signs of civilisation suddenly drop away and you're driving through a flat, moonscape. The thin, straight road cuts through bleak, scorched terrain relieved only by low ochre hills (left) and snow-capped mountains (right). Dead ahead, there's absolutely nothing. About an hour out of Leh, look out (left) for the wide **Zanskar river** flowing down into the **Indus**. The confluence of these two mighty rivers is spectacular. A little further on, you'll pass **Nimmu**, a large stack of mountains with an ancient city and an army camp at its base. Then you reach **Saspol**, a small oasis of greenery in the middle of the arid plain. The orchards of Saspol provide most of the delicious apricot jam found in Leh. There's a couple of travellers' lodges here—**Green View Guest House** (good food) and **Tourist Bungalow** (clean rooms, expensive food); also a modest **fort** and some interesting cave dwellings. Saspol is a popular base from which to discover Alchi and Likir gompas, which are situated 5 km (3 miles) on either side of it.

The ancient monastery of **Alchi**, built during the 11th century, is recognised as a major artistic site and has recently been declared a World Heritage Site under the UNESCO programme. Dedicated to the great Buddhist interpreter Rinchen Zang-po, who had come to Ladakh from Tibet in the late 11th century during an interlude in Kashmir-Tibet relations, it is now primarily important as a place of pilgrimage. Its heyday came after 1337, when Islam strengthened its position in Kashmir and Rinchen's ascetics fled their homeland, armed with their artistic skill, and went to Ladakh. They painted the walls of Alchi in fabulous miniature frescoes. The painting of 'thousand Buddhas' (actually 1000 representations of Shakyamuni Buddha) inside the main chamber is a true example of the influence of Indian miniature painting on Ladakhi art. Some of Alchi's tantric paintings, however, lean more towards the art of Gandhara, which in turn was heavily influenced by Greco-Roman forms. To fully appreciate them, and the 11th-century mandala walls, you'll need a powerful flashlight.

If Alchi is famous for its ancient large *Bodhisattva* images and wall-paintings, then nearby **Rizong** is most notable for its 'lady monks' (nuns). Founded in 1829, this sprawling seven-storey *gompa* is built on a sheer rock face and looks out on a stunning landscape. It has an interesting library, lots of old thangkas, and some amazing wall-paintings. If staying overnight, men sleep in the *gompa*, and women join the nuns in the associated Julichen nunnery. As a woman traveller, you won't be allowed inside the *gompa* itself after 4 pm. And nobody is allowed to smoke, drink alcohol or eat meat past the gateway *chorten*.

Back past Saspol, you'll come to the great **Likir Gompa**, a multi-storeyed edifice in white. Founded in the 11th century, the original monastery was destroyed by fire and the present one (often compared to the Potala in Lhasa) dates from the 18th century. A large community of 150 yellow-cap lamas study at Likir's famous school, and the best time to arrive is 4 to 6 pm, when prayers take place. Of the three or four rooms on view to the public, the oldest one has a triumvirate of giant clay statues of Buddha. Likir is to statues what Alchi is to paintings, and the small village below the *gompa* is home to some of Ladakh's most distinctive indigenous crafts. If staying overnight at the monastery, you can enjoy fantastic dawn views from the open roofs.

The scenery on the drive home from Likir is uniformly beautiful. There are often phenomenal sunsets, which throw a strange, surreal glow over the 'Death Valley' terrain, transforming it into a land of fairies and giants. Some of the rock formations are straight out of *Lord of the Rings*—in places, it's as though some leviathan of yore has taken the mountain in both hands, and squeezed it together like a crumpled blanket. Looming Tolkienesque cliffs, multi-coloured plateaus, and vast, empty plains vie for attention.

In and Around Leh (on foot, half-day)
Leh Palace–Tsemo Gompa–Sankar Gompa

Having toured Ladakh valley, it's time to explore Leh and its surrounds. This tour involves some stiff climbing, and is best left to last—the two earlier jeep excursions should have comfortably acclimatised you to high-altitude walking.

In Leh town, walk to the end of the main street, head up the alley by Tibetan Crown Curios (overlooking the market square), and follow the trail all the way up to **Leh Khar Palace** (15 minutes). Situated atop **Tsemo Hill**, overlooking the town like a silent sentinel, this is the old palace of the kings of Ladakh, and was built in the mid-16th century by King Singe Namgyal. It has never been the same since the Kashmiris shelled it in 1815—which was soon after the royal family moved down to Stok (the royals still live at Stok palace). This bombardment inflicted heavy damage on the towering eight-storey palace, and left lots of holes in the floors for tourists to fall down. For this reason, you'll only be shown a few bottom-section rooms. These house a three-headed Buddha with 1000 arms, a 700-year-old image of Avalokitesvara (an important disciple of Buddha), Hindu figures such as Kali and Durga, some 600-year-old thangkas, and an assortment of dead antelope masks. The palace is open 6 to 9 am, 5 to 8 pm, and if the resident monk is out shopping you need only knock on the door and cough a bit for an enterprising young tout to let you in. After a cursory tour of the palace, he'll direct you to the courtyard below, where a nodding lama bangs drums, clangs cymbals, and intones everlasting prayers without drawing breath. This is undoubtedly impressive, and you may wish to give a donation. But, be warned, this will encourage your guide to lead a lung-wrenching assault on Tsemo Hill—guiding you at breakneck speed up to **Tsemo Gompa**, above the palace. His favourite wheeze, if no more 'donations' are forthcoming, is to leave you a crippled wreck at the top. But don't worry; it's actually far easier to get down again than it looks. The *gompa* itself was built in 1430, and contains a fine three-storey seated Buddha. It is open only from 7 am to 10 am. The main reason for climbing up here (20 minutes from the palace, if fit) are the views. From the top, you can see right across the valley, and down into Leh town. Photography is generally best in the early morning or late afternoon, when there is least glare.

Back in Leh, take a pleasant half-hour (3-km, 1¼-mile) stroll—past Ali Shah's Postcard Shop, turning left at Antelope Guest House, and up to **Sankar Gompa**. This is a fairly active monastery, inhabited by some 20 monks of the Gelugpa or yellow-hat sect. You'll probably be shown only three rooms. One has an impressive figure of the 1000-armed, 1000-headed Avalokitesvara; another has a *Tara*. There are fine views over the valley from the roofs, and if you arrive at 6.30 am you may catch the monks blowing mournful trumpets to summon fellow lamas to prayer. The best time to visit, however, is the early evening (5–7 pm) when the well-run, well-lit monastery lays on refreshments for visitors.

Stok

Ten km (6 miles) south of Leh and on the opposite bank of the Indus is the small village of Stok. Home to the local royal family who moved here after the Dogra invasion of Ladakh. The palace was built in the early 19th century by Tshespal Namgyal and part of it is today a marvellous museum (open 7 am to 6 pm during the summer) and charges Rs25. A jeep taxi will take you to Stok, or you can walk along the Indus until you reach **Choglamsar** where there is a Tibetan settlement, and take the road bridge across the river. Stok is a good base for day treks and the starting point for longer treks to the Markha Valley.

TREKKING

From Leh, there are any number of trekking and mountain-climbing possibilities. The most popular trek destination—well off the beaten track—is the long, narrow **Zanskar Valley** running between Kargil and Lamayuru in the north, and Kishtwar and Manali in the south. Zanskar has superb mountain and valley scenery, friendly and hospitable local people, and a near-absence of military bases and police patrols. Unfortunately, this is no place for beginners: rough trails, deep rivers, and high passes make personal fitness and advance preparation essential. Zanskar receives particularly heavy snows, and trekking in this area is only possible from July to September. Even then, you have to go easily through the passes. Strolling off on your own can be dangerous. People do it, but they often hit major health problems. Walking 10–15 km a day, living on country food like *tsampa* and butter tea, it's easy to lose energy and fall sick. And if you collapse, it'll cost at least US$2000 for a helicopter to fly you out. If you're new to high-altitude trekking, go in an organised group. If you have some experience, buy survival equipment, and hire guides and porters and ponies in Leh. And take plenty of food—you'll need it!

A good short 4-day trek is out to **Lamayuru Gompa**, 124 km (77½ miles) from Leh. This is another of Rinchen Zang-po's creations, built at the end of the 10th century. Of the five original buildings, only the central structure is still standing. It houses some 30 monks (of the so-called yellow-hat sect) and has a famous statue of Chenrezig, with 11 heads and 1000 eyes. To get there from Leh, either take the daily Kargil bus (5 hours, Rs25–30) or hire a jeep (3½ hours Rs600–650). At Lamayuru, you can stay overnight in a wonderful 'glass room' with lots of large old windows. The charge (Rs15) includes blankets and refreshments. On day two, you can walk over to **Khalse** (25 km; 15½ miles, 5 hours), a pretty village famous for its dried apricots. Khalse is also a popular rest-stop for buses, and has some good little restaurants. On day three, you can hop on a bus from Khalse to **Saspol**, and make the short 2- to 3-hour walk up to **Rizong** *gompa*. On Day four, after an early morning hike to **Likir**, you can return by bus from Saspol to Leh.

Lamayuru is a favourite starting point for long-range treks down the valley into Zanskar. From Lamayuru, it can take anything from 8 to 11 days to reach **Padum**, the capital of Zanskar. There's nothing very exciting about Padum—it's a small settlement of some 100 houses on a low hill, inhabited by shy, friendly Zanskaris who (a rare phenomenon) worship Allah rather than Buddha. Padum has a small post office, a few restaurants, a camping ground, and a few half-decent lodges—notably a Dak Bungalow and Padumkar Guest House. From Padum, you can take on hard, rewarding 7-day treks to Kishtwar or to Manali, or settle for a short one-day excursion to the old castle of the King of Zangla.

A marvellous mid-range trek is out to **Markha Valley**, an 8- to 10-day roundtrip from Leh. Most people set out from Stok 7 km (4½ miles) from the Leh-Hemis road, and return via Hemis. The going is fairly easy as long as you are reasonably fit, and you don't need guides or porters—local people point the way, and may even offer to put you up overnight. Markha is an amazingly green and fertile valley—it has dense forestation, several high peaks between 5000 m and 6000 m, and a great variety of interesting wildlife (bear, jackal, fox, wolf, ibex and the occasional snow leopard). This trek is only recommended for the second half of August.

Leh town has several trekking agencies, most of them offering organised treks to Zanskar, Markha and Manali, at US$40–50 (inclusive of porters, ponies, food and mountain equipment). Their river-rafting treks from Leh to Lamayuru (June to August only) are almost as expensive. But you can get cheaper deals by shopping around. Qurban Ali at Hotel Choskor, for example, offers much cheaper Markha valley treks. At the same hotel, M. Javad operates fun one-day raft trips on the Indus between Spituk and Hemis.

RECREATION

During summer there are often polo tournaments, starting at 4 pm at the polo ground in Leh town centre. Tourists can join in. On Sunday afternoons, also at the polo ground, Leh's favourite sport—cricket—plays to delirious crowds. Once a month, cultural shows are held in the auditorium hall near the polo ground.

SHOPPING

Good places to shop are the bazaar in Leh town centre, and the **Tibetan Refugee Handicrafts** centre at Choglamsar (6 km out of Leh on the Shey road). Look out for beautiful Ladakhi coats in corduroy or velvet, silk belts and scarves, chhang and tea cups, hand-knitted Tibetan carpets (cheaper in Dharmsala), or prayer-flags. These can be specially made up for you for about Rs5, and stamped with wood-blocks at the *gompa* in Leh town. Most jewellers in Leh town are Kashmiri-owned, and a rip-off. For gems, jewellery and curios, go to **Leh Art Palace** or **Dragon Curios**, two fixed-price Ladakhi places. Their Chinese pearls are of reasonable quality and incredibly cheap: as low as Rs600 for a typical 400-pearl necklace.

WHERE TO STAY
There's a wide choice of accommodation in Leh. Prices of hotels vary greatly according to the season. Three good hotels with rooms from Rs300/400, are **Kangla Chen** (tel 144), **La-Ri-Mo** (tel 101), and **Shambala** (tel 67). The first two are quite central. In the mid-range (Rs200/300), stay at **Lungse-Jung** (tel 193), **Bijoo** (tel 131) or **Ibex** (tel 212).

Stok, 10 km (6¼ miles) south of Leh has two of Ladakh's most interesting properties. **The Ladakh Sarai** (tel 181) was established in the late 1970s and is a series of independent yurts with a central dining and recreation area set in a green meadow amid a grove of willow trees. From US$ 80 Book through **Mountain Travel India**, 1/1 Rani Jhansi Road, New Delhi 110055 (tel 7525357, 7525032, 7533483).

Popular guest-houses charge about Rs40 for a single room, Rs65 for a double. Many long-term travellers stay very cheaply with families at Changspa, a lovely little village on the river, 3 km (2 miles) east of Leh.

EATING OUT
Local restaurants in Leh offer a variety of cuisine—Ladakhi, Chinese, Tibetan and Continental. The ever-popular **Dreamland Hotel** has a wonderful restaurant—lovely staff, tasteful decor, and lots of gentle charm. The speciality *gyathuk* (a 'variety pot' meal of mutton, egg, shrimps, vegetables, steamed *momo*, rice and dessert) costs Rs450 serves six people. If full, try the **Snow Lion** restaurant opposite. South Indian food is good at the **Nandita** near the taxi-stand—huge helpings of curry and rice for just Rs10. **Hotel Pamposh** is well known for its fresh bread, curd and coffee, and **Tibetan Friends Corner** is where all the locals go for Tibetan-style cuisine. For evening drinks, drop in on **Ibex Bar**, just up from Dreamland.

GENERAL INFORMATION
J & K Tourist Office (tel 297) is located 1.5 km (1 mile) out of town, on the airport road. It's only worth visiting for the useful bus timetable. You'll find much better maps, guides, backround reading at Arturo Books in front of Dragon Hotel.

Post office (and *poste restante*) is in Leh main street, open 10 am to 1 pm, 2 to 5 pm (except Sundays). It's the most efficient post office in India—letters posted here get to Europe in just 4 days. Leh has two banks: The State Bank of India (tel 2520) and the Jammu & Kashmir Bank (open 10 am to 2 pm, except Sundays); an Indian Airlines office (tel 276) and a Foreigners' Registration Office (tel 236).

JAMMU

Gateway into Kashmir, Jammu is also the winter capital of the state. Situated on the banks of the river Tawi, this busy, prosperous town is surrounded by lakes and hills, temples and fortresses. Little is known of the city's origin. According to legend, it was founded by the 9th-century King Jambulochan on the site of Bahu Fort, which stands on the left bank of the Tawi. In AD 1730 it came under the rule of the Dogra chiefs of Rajput descent, and it was they who merged Jammu and Kashmir into one state in AD 1832 and continued to rule it until it acceded to India in 1947. Jammu has a fine artistic tradition, which culminated in the miniature court paintings of the 18th and 19th centuries.

ARRIVAL/DEPARTURE

Air
Indian Airlines flies daily between Jammu and Delhi (Rs1394), Chandigarh (Rs945), and Srinagar (Rs543). Jammu airport is 7 km (4½ miles) from the city centre. Taxis and auto-rickshaws are available.

Rail
Two quickest trains to Delhi (12/13 hours) are the Jammu Mail and the 172 DN Superfast Express, leaving Jammu Tawi rail station at 2.50 pm and 4.40 pm daily. Railway Enquiries (tel 31085, 30047; reservations 43836).

Bus
Very regular buses to Delhi (12 hours), to Srinagar (10–14 hours) and to Pathankot (2/3 hours). There are also 2 buses a day to Dharmsala (5 am and 6.10 am), and one bus a day to Shimla (6 pm). Buy all tickets as early as possible. Current bus/rail timings are posted at the Broadway Hotel. General bus-stand enquiries (tel 47475).

WHAT TO SEE
Travellers often arrive in Jammu tired and late at night, following the marathon bus journey from Delhi or Srinagar. Most of them move out the very next morning. Jammu (and Pathankot, the next point on the route) is very close to the Pakistan border and a major staging post for supplies to Kashmir and the long border. Not a very comfortable situation, but don't be in too much of a hurry to leave. Jammu has at least a morning's worth of decent sights.

Most buses drop passengers by the tourist office, which is close to all the better hotels and lodges. To your left, you will see the spires of the Raghunath Temple. Left of the temple, down some steps, is the main bus-station. All this is in the old part of town. The railway station, several kilometres away across the river Tawi, is in the new town. To get to it, take a 'tempo' minibus from outside the main bus-station (the stand is at the top of the bazaar). These leave about every half-hour.

For sightseeing, and getting round town in general, use either auto-rickshaws or taxis. Both have meters, but have the usual allergy to using them. Hiring cycles is not practical in Jammu—its few sights are very spread out, and there are many hills.

City Tour (by rickshaw/taxi, 3–4 hours)
Raghunath Temple–Kali Temple–Bagh-i-Bagh–Amar Mahal Museum–Dogra Art Gallery

Start with a short walk down to the **Raghunath Temple**, just below the tourist office. It is the centrepiece of a sizeable complex of small temples (built 1835) situated in the heart of the busy city. Make a short tour of the lively surrounding bazaars (there are some really strange things for sale here), then catch a rickshaw/taxi up to the old

Fort, 5 km (3 miles) above the town. This is best visited on a Tuesday or a Sunday, when pilgrims gather in swarms to offer *puja* to the tiny black-faced goddess in the **Kali Temple**, and to hire out a goat. In the old days, the goats used to be sacrificed. Now, they are rented by the hour, earnestly prayed to in a small pen, then sent back to live another day.

Below the fort lies Jammu's most pleasant feature, the lovely **Bagh-i-Bagh gardens**. This green, relaxing spot is constructed on a series of terraces, and gives fine views of the Tawi bridge and the river. You can pause here for tiffin at the small restaurant, before moving on to the **Amar Mahal Museum** (only open 5–7 pm Tuesday to Saturday, 8 am–noon on Sunday), situated on a hill overlooking the Tawi River. Built in 1907, this French-designed palace houses the art collection of Dr Karan Singh, the last Maharajah of Kashmir. The collection consists mainly of family portraits, though there are some rare Pahari paintings and excellent soft-toned Kangra-school illustrations too, and the palace is beautifully furnished.

Finally, visit the **Dogra Art Gallery**, Gandhi Bhavan, opposite the New Secretariat. Set up in 1954, this houses an important collection of nearly 600 paintings (poorly lit and presented, but of fine quality), plus ancient tarleaf manuscripts, terracotta, sculpture and arms. Many of the miniatures on view depict scenes from the Krishna legend, and are the work of the skilled Basholi and Pahari schools of painting which developed from the 18th century on. The schematic use of colours, with detailed Kangra brushwork, are the main characteristics of this delicate and refined school of art. Only a sample are represented, ask to see more. Open 11 am–5 pm winter, 7.30 am–1 pm summer, closed Mondays. Inside, discourage uninvited 'guides'.

WHERE TO STAY

Jammu has yet to shake off its reputation as a one-night tourist stopover, and there is a marked shortage of good accommodation. For mod cons and a cool pool try the four-star **Asia Jammu Tawi** at Ram Nagar, to the north of town (tel 49430, 43932, tlx 0377-224). Rooms are from Rs850. The best mid-range deal is **Hotel Mansar**, Denis Gate (tel 46161, 43610), a short walk from the bus-stand. A smart little place, with nice air-conditioned bar/restaurant and comfy room for about Rs200 (without air-conditioning) and Rs300 (with). The **Tourist Reception Centre** is a disappointment. The **Jammu Ashok**, opp Amar Mahal (tel 43127, 43864, tlx 0377-227) has both air-conditioned and ordinary rooms from Rs650.

EATING OUT

There isn't a great deal of choice. Most people eat at the **Cosmopolitan** and **Premier** hotels, which both have dining halls, jazzy sounds, and mid-priced Continental/Chinese menus. Of the two, the Cosmopolitan has the better service and atmosphere, and good Italian pasta too. Next to the Premier, the fast-food **Chinese Room** does very nice pastries and cakes, in addition to a roaring trade in take-away burgers, chop suey and ice-cream. For expensive quality fare, go to **Hotel Mansar**. For cheap and best vegetarian food, try **Trimurti** *dhaba* near Broadway Hotel.

GENERAL INFORMATION

Main tourist reception centre is in Mir Chowk (tel 8803), above the main bus-stand. The Mir Chowk office houses Indian Airlines (tel 42735, 47088, 47577 airport tel 5745). Jammu's Post Office is inside the railway station.

DALHOUSIE

One of the least visited and quietest of northern India's hill stations, Dalhousie has retained much of its original character. It is located on a spur of the Dhauladhar range of the Himalaya at about 2000 metres, amid still well-forested hills. To the north there are spectacular views of the Pir Panjal mountains, and to the south, the rivers and plains of Punjab. When Punjab came under the control of British India in 1848 Dalhousie was developed as a sanatorium and later a permanent military base. The land was leased from the Raja of Chamba, a nearby hill state, for an annual rent of Rs2000. By the 1860s Dalhousie was also a flourishing summer resort for the elite of Lahore (now in Pakistan).

Since partition in 1947 and the loss of her traditional summer residents, Dalhousie has remained a relatively undisturbed station; a good place to avoid the heat and commotion of the plains in relative peace.

ARRIVAL/DEPARTURE

Air
The nearest airports are Kangra (135 km; 85 miles) serviced by Vayudoot and Amritsar (188 km; 118 miles) connected by Indian Airlines with daily flights to/from Delhi (Rs1003) and Srinagar (Rs865). Cars can be hired from both airports and regular buses also operate.

Rail
Pathankot, which has excellent train links with Jammu and Delhi, is 80 km (50 miles) south-west of Dalhousie and there are regular buses plying the route. Taxis are also available.

Road
Apart from buses linking Dalhousie with Pathankot, Kangra and Amritsar there are regular links with New Delhi (from the Interstate Bus Terminal), Shimla, Chandigarh and Kulu.

WHAT TO SEE
Dalhousie is spread over five hills ranging from 1523–2378 m, the most important of which are Pottreyn, Bakrota and Tehra or Moti Tibba. Linking and encircling Pottreyn and Tehra is the Mall on which many of the houses, hotels and shops are located. Part of the mall remains closed to vehicles and is a popular walking area which winds through oak and conifer forest.

Dalhousie is not a town with great historical monuments or sites—for that you have to go to nearby Chamba— but it is a wonderful base for both short and long walks into the nearby forest. Five kilometres (3 miles) from the post office is the small village of **Lakkar Mandi** from which paths lead to Dainkund Peak and the nearby **Pholani Devi** temple (from which there are spectacular views). A small wildlife sanctuary at **Kalatope** 8.5 km (5½ miles) from Dalhousie has a small rest house set amid the forest which can be booked from the local forest officer. The sanctuary has a good population of barking deer, a few Himalayan black bear and the occasional leopard, in addition to a great variety of birds.

Khajjiar, 18 km (10½ miles) away is a large meadow with a small lake and nearby 14th-century temple in the centre. The surrounding forest, part of the Kalatope Sanctuary, still has plenty of wildlife. There is a small forest rest house nearby.

Chamba

From AD 550 to Independence in 1947 the small hill state of Chamba was ruled by the same family. The original capital was at Bharmour but shifted to Chamba about 1000 years ago. Chamba is 53 km (33 miles) from Dalhousie and can be easily reached by car, bus or Himachal Pradesh Tourism Development Corporation (HPTDC) tours. It is worth visiting for its ancient temples and fine, although small, museum. The main temple complex, on the banks of the river has recently been restored by the Archaeological Survey of India. The large **Lakshmi Narayan Temple** and two others are dedicated to Vishnu, while the other three are dedicated to Lord Shiva. The **Bhuri Singh Museum** has a fine collection of 18th- and 19th-century miniatures from the local *Pahari* schools plus local stone carvings and brass images.

WHERE TO STAY
Himachal Tourism (HPTDC) runs the mid-range **Hotel Geetanjali** (tel 2136), with rooms from Rs150 to Rs350 and a **Youth Hostel**. The two better properties are the Khanna's family-owned and run Hotel **Aroma-N-Claire**, Court Road, The Mall (tel 2199) and the new **Grand View Hotel** (tel 2123, 2623, 2194) in addition to which there are numerous budget hotels.

At Khajjiar, *en route* from Dalhousie to Chamba, is the **Hotel Deodar** with rooms from Rs250. Chamba has two HPTDC hotels. The **Hotel Iravati** (tel 2671) with rooms fron Rs175 to Rs400 is certainly better than the **Champak** with rooms at Rs75. Of the private hotels the **Hotel Akhand Chandi**, College Road (tel 2371) next to the palace, has great potential, if only it were better run.

EATING OUT
Neither Dalhousie nor Chamba have any great restaurants, and hotel food cooked to order is probably as good as any in the bazaar. Dalhousie has a **Kwality** at Gandhi Chowk with meals from about Rs35. **The Snow Lion**, a small Tibetan restaurant behind the cinema between the bus-stand and the Mall, serves reasonable Chinese food and some Tibetan dishes.

GENERAL INFORMATION
Tourist information is available from the Area Manager, HPTDC, Dalhousie (tel 2136).

DHARMSALA

Like Dalhousie, this picturesque hill station lies on a spur of the Dhauladhar range, some 18 km (11½ miles) north-east of Kangra. Surrounded by snow-capped mountains, deodar and pine forests, hills and tea gardens, it offers beautiful scenery and some lovely walks. Dharmsala began life as a typical British sanatorium, but suffered a major tragedy in 1905 when levelled completely by an earthquake.

In 1960, it gained a new lease of life when adopted as the temporary headquarters of the Dalai Lama, Tibet's spiritual leader. In 1959, after 8 years of trying to compromise with the Chinese in Tibet, he had fled—with 100 000 of his subjects—into exile in India. The journey was hard, and tens of thousands perished *en route*. Granted sanctuary by Pandit Nehru, some 3000 Tibetans made their new home in Dharmsala, on McLeodganj. Since then, the hill station has risen to international fame as the 'Little Lhasa in India'. The Dalai Lama has become a major spokesman for world peace, with a central policy of perpetuating Tibetan religion and culture in Dharmsala itself. Here, children continue to be ordained as monks, senior lamas and reincarnates teach, and Tibetan medicine, education, arts and crafts are thriving once again.

Over the past 30 years, the Tibetans of Dharamsala have carved out one of the most successful stories of the rehabilitation of a people, vigorously maintaining their own identity whilst harmonising with their new environment. They see the crisis which Tibet has undergone (25 000 Tibetans imprisoned in Chinese jails, all but 45 of Tibet's 6000 monasteries destroyed, only 1300 of their half-million monks and nuns still alive) as the result of bad karma from the past. In exile, their primary aim is to build up a collective fount of good fortune (or compassion) which will reinstate Tibet and oust the Chinese invaders.

Dharmsala is most pleasant from March to June, and from September to November. October is the best month of all—no rains, clear views, marvellous scenery. Whenever you come, bring some woollen clothing—it can get chilly at night.

ARRIVAL/DEPARTURE

Air
The new airport at Gagal, 20 km (12½ miles) below Dharmsala, is connected by Vayudoot with Bhuntar (for Kulu/Manali) andconnects by with Delhi.

Road
Dharmsala has buses to Kulu/Manali (see p.244), to Pathankot (3 hours), to Dalhousie, to Delhi (13 hours) and to Shimla. The Delhi-bound buses leave at 5 am and 6 pm from Dharmsala, at 4.30 am and 5.30 pm from McLeodganj.

To get to Dharmsala *from* Delhi, either take the Jhelum Express from New Delhi (dep 9.40 pm, arr 7.55 am) or the Jammu Tawi Mail from (Old) Delhi (dep 9 pm, arr 7.25 am) up to Pathankot, or the popular 7.40 pm night bus (10/11 hours) direct to Dharmsala from Delhi's Interstate bus-stand, Kashmir Gate (gate 7a).

WHAT TO SEE
The hill station divides neatly into two separate parts. Lower Dharmsala (1250 m) is a dullish Indian-style township, with civic buildings, a bazaar, a few hotels, the tourist office and the main bus-stand. Upper Dharamsala (1982 m) runs up from Forsyth Ganj to McLeodganj, and is anything but dull. McLeodganj has Tibetan temples, chatty monks, way-out travellers, curious curio shops, psychedelic restaurants, good music, second-hand bookshops, lots of *ganja*, and some interesting walks which people (eventually) get around to. For a few McLeodganj is the definitive freak centre of India—even more so than Manali, Goa or Pushkar. Travellers come here for enlightenment, Western food, alternative medicine, and dope—but mainly for rest and relaxation. The Dalai Lama is a big draw, and if you make a

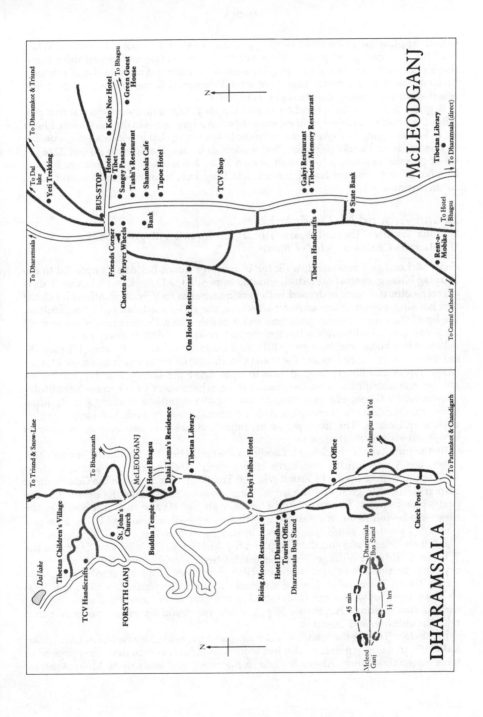

McLEODGANJ

To Dharamkot & Triund

To Bhagsu

Koko Nor Hotel

Green Guest House

To Dal lake

Yeti Trekking

Hotel Tibet

Sangey Passang

Tashi's Restaurant

Shambala Cafe

Tapoe Hotel

BUS-STOP

To Dharamsala

Friends Corner

Chorten & Prayer Wheels

Bank

TCV Shop

Gakyi Restaurant

Tibetan Memory Restaurant

Tibetan Library

To Dharamsala (direct)

Om Hotel & Restaurant

Tibetan Handicrafts

State Bank

To Hotel Bhagsu

Rent-a-Mobike

To Central Cathedral

DHARAMSALA

To Triund & Snow-Line

To Bhagsu

McLEODGANJ

To Bhagsu

Dal lake

Tibetan Children's Village

St. John's Church

Hotel Bhagsu

Dalai Lama's Residence

Tibetan Library

TCV Handicrafts

FORSYTH GANJ

Buddha Temple

Dekyi Palbar Hotel

Rising Moon Restaurant

Hotel Dhauladhar

Tourist Office

Dharamsala Bus Stand

Post Office

To Palampur via Yol

Mcleod Ganj

45 min

Dharamsala Bus Stand

1¼ hrs

Check Post

To Pathankot & Chandigarh

serious application at the main temple, you may well get a personal interview. When resident, he often gives public addresses in the mornings, and if you miss these, there's normally a video of him playing somewhere around town in the afternoons. Mcleodganj is in fact much more than a freak centre: it is one of the most pleasant, relaxing and, for many, spiritual places in India.

Regular buses ply between Lower and Upper Dharmsala from 6.30 am to 8 pm. After that, you've a choice of an expensive taxi or a long walk in the dark (over 1 hour up to McLeodganj, 45 minutes down to the lower town). Up in McLeodganj, you can hire mopeds or Suzuki 100 from Rent-a-Mobike in Buddha Temple Rd (tel 2246). A lot of people bike down to Manali, which takes around 6/7 hours return. Rent-a-Mobike is also a useful travel agency, handling bus/train reservations and flight confirmations.

In and Around McLeodganj (full-day, on foot)
Buddha Temple–Tibetan Library–Tibetan Children's Village–Dal Lake–TCV Handicrafts Centre–St John's Church

From McLeodganj bus-stand, walk for 10 minutes down Buddha Temple Rd to the **Tsuglag Khang**, central cathedral, situated opposite the Dalai Lama's house. This is a lively, colourful temple draped with exotic thangkas (religious paintings on cloth) and housing a giant image of Avalokitesvara, the 100-armed deity of Tibet. Built on the lip of the ridge, it commands fine views of the valley. Prayers take place around 4 am and 8 pm, and there's a Tibetan monastery and a small nunnery nearby.

Below the main temple, a steep hill-road leads down to the **Tibetan Library**. To get there, you can either follow the road (45 minutes) or cut across it using goat tracks (20 minutes). The library is open 9 am to 1 pm, 2 to 5 pm (except Sundays). It has an ancient manuscript room on the ground floor, where you can ask to see beautifully illustrated 1000-year-old volumes, containing the complete teachings of Buddha. Upstairs, there's a small museum with a nice collection of Buddhist images, ritual objects and crafts. The library also arranges lectures and can advise on courses long-term visitors might like to undertake.

By the time you get back to McLeodganj, it should be time for lunch. But don't sit down too long—lunch often turns into supper. Back at the bus-stand, a steep 15–20-minute hike up the hill-road (via Yeti Trekking) brings you to the Government Primary School, high up on the ridge. Here, you can either take the up-road to the pretty picnic spot of **Triund** (17 km, 4 hours' walk), or stay on the route and take the down-road—following the water-pipe all the way—down to Dal Lake. This is a pleasant 15-minute ramble, occasional breaks in the tree line revealing spectacular views over Dharmsala and the Kangra valley. Just before the lake, you'll come to the **Tibetan Children's Village**. This was established in 1960 to care for the numerous orphans, semi-orphans and destitute Tibetan refugee children who flooded into India. Today, it provides Tibetan-style education and upbringing for some 1300 children, many of whom have individual sponsors from Europe and the US. The best time to visit is from 7.30 am to 1.30 pm, when you can drop in on classes and chat with the children and teachers.

Just below TCV is the small, scummy pond surrounded by cedars which is **Dal Lake**. It's amazingly popular with local tourists—a local Hindu deity is supposed to have materialised here. Above the lake, a metalled road leads up to **Mehr Ashram**, the only Hindu ashram in Dharmsala. A lot of Westerners stay round here, studying yoga and meditation. Austerities start with the 4-km (2½-mile) climb up there. From the ashram, you can walk across to **Dharmkot**, a popular picnic spot affording panoramic views of the Dhauladhar range and Kangra valley. Dharmkot has a lovely old-colonial British house, and a rabbit farm.

If you're feeling lazy, take the main road (left) from Dal Lake back to McLeodganj. Ten minutes' walk down the road, **TCV Handicrafts Centre** appears on your left. This was founded in 1974, to give crafts training and employment to Tibetan children who could not continue formal schooling, or who had a talent for manual trades. At present, the centre has some 200 workers, and is fast achieving self-sufficiency. It specialises in Tibetan hand-knotted woollen carpets, and there's a good workshop layout where you can see them and other crafts being produced. A short walk below the centre, there's the unexciting village of **Forsyth Ganj**. Here you have a choice of a bus-ride or a 45-minute walk back to McLeodganj. If walking it, you'll pass by **St John's-in-the-Wilderness** Church, a typical old-English church in a peaceful glade of deodar cedars, which has fine stained-glass windows and a cemetery with a monument to Lord Elgin, one of India's viceroys. The pastor has a good sense of humour. He enjoys visitors, shows them his photo collection, and talks a lot about his plans to open a restaurant in the grounds. It's largely thanks to him that the old stone church is in such good condition.

TREKKING

Situated so close to the snowline, Dharmsala offers many possibilities for trekking and mountain climbing. The best seasons are April to June, and September to November. The going is generally tough, but there's a wealth of beautiful scenery to take your mind off tired muscles. And trekking in this region is far less exploited than at Manali. With a good pair of walking shoes and a supply of water and biscuits (refreshments are limited in the hills), you can head off in any direction and be alone. One warning: if you stroll off the beaten track, don't go wandering into any dark caves where animals may be sheltering, even bears. For the best views, set out in the early morning. By around noon, the valley is often obscured by dense mist. For short walks—say, up to Triund at the foot of the snow-clad Dhauladhar—you don't really need a guide. Beyond this point, however, you do. And any treks you make above 3400 m, you'll need to take it easy—altitude sickness is a common problem. For organised treks, contact **Yeti Trekking** just up from McLeodganj bus-stand, which offers year-round (except Jan/Feb) 4- to 5-day hikes to Kareri Lake, and marvellous 7-day treks (May to November only) over the Dhauladhar range to Bharmour, via the high Inderhara Pass (4610 m). Charges are most reasonable: about Rs250–300 inclusive of food, guide/porter, and equipment.

SHOPPING

Between McLeodganj and Forsyth Ganj, **TCV Handicrafts Centre** (tel 2592, open 8 am to 5 pm except Sundays) had the best range and quality of Tibetan produce. Nice buys include handwoven shoulder bags, earrings, woollen jackets, brass-button cotton shirts), colourful thangkas on silk or cloth (Rs200 to 20 000), rice-paper prints, postcards, semi-precious jewellery, hand or machine-woven cloth, and bright prayer-flags. TCV is particularly well known for its Tibetan woollen carpets, incorporating attractive tantric or dragon designs. The 'speciality' carpet measures 9 × 9 metres, depicts the sacred Kalchakra mandala, and can only be made on special permission from the Dalai Lama. There's another TCV shop in Temple Rd, McLeodganj. Like the main branch, it's fixed-price. Shopping anywhere else, be prepared to bargain hard. Because Tibetans aren't allowed to take jobs from native Indians, they can only sell handicrafts for profit—and prices are correspondingly high.

One of the more interesting shops in McLeodganj is **Nowrojee's Wine and General Merchants**, a fascinating old-fashioned general store which is one of the few genuine relics of the Raj to be found in any hill station.

A few restaurants in McLeodganj, notably Shambala and Darjeeling Cafe, sell Tibetan music/prayer cassettes. A small group of government handicraft shops down in the lower town (below the tourist office) sell mainly Kulu produce at fixed prices.

WHERE TO STAY

To avoid disappointment, it's not a bad idea to take rooms in Lower Dharmsala on your first night. McLeodganj is ridiculously popular, and there's often a host of travellers sleeping on the floor of restaurants waiting for a room to come up. If you're determined to stay here, arrive on a very early bus and ask around in the Shambala, Friend's Corner or Passang restaurants—there's nearly always someone about to check out, reluctantly. If nothing works, don't fret. Staying in the lower town has one big advantage—you get an extra hour's sleep when it comes to getting a bus out.

In **Lower Dharamsala**, the comfy option is HPTDC's **Hotel Dhauladhar** (tel 2107-9, 2256), just up from the bus-stand. This has a nice restaurant/bar, a relaxing garden patio (with views), tolerant staff, a cheap dormitory, and large clean double rooms with balconies from Rs200 to Rs375. A few minutes walk up the road, **Rising Moon, Tibet United Association** and **Dekyipalbar** are three cheap Tibetan-style hotels with rooms. A little less basic is the **Sun-n-Snow**, just down the hill from the bus-stand.

Up at McLeodganj, HPTDC's **Hotel Bhagsu** (tel 2290) has rooms from Rs225 and one cottage for Rs550. Far better is **Hotel Tibet** (tel 2587), behind the bus-stand. This has spacious, spotless 'super-deluxe' doubles at Rs350 (cheaper rooms from Rs150), a classy restaurant, pleasant roof-top patio, friendly staff and good information. It's always full. Good cheaper places include **Om Guest House** (below the main street), **Green Hotel, Koko Nor Hotel, Tibetan Himalayan Restaurant**, and **Namgyal Guest House** (all above Tibet Hotel), **Toepa Hotel** (on the main street), and **Ashoka Lodge** below the bus-stand (ask for Dr Ashoka's clinic). **Glenmoor**, a 20-minute walk up the hill from St John's Church, is McLeod's old residence—where he lived when he was Collector for the region. In its heyday, this vast Scottish-style villa was the social hub of the hill station, the scene of many balls and tea-parties. Today, it's divided up into four sections, ranging in price from Rs45–100. The best section (which can be shared between 3 couples) takes in the drawing room, lounge, verandah, sunroom (with French windows) and bathroom. Round the back, there are a few cosy cottages (originally servants' quarters). They are beautifully located in the forest.

EATING OUT

Down in Lower Dharmsala, **Hotel Dhauladhar** has memorable Continental food and forgettable Chinese food. The viewpoint patio is good for sunrise breakfasts and

FORTS, TEMPLES & THE TAJ

Old Delhi, a medieval city of forts, mosques & bazaars

The Taj Mahal.
Emperor Shah Jahan's passion for building bankrupted the country & led to the collapse of the Moghul Empire

The exquisite sculptures of Khajuraho celebrate life through the beauty of medieval art

Gwalior's fort dominated trade routes through Western India for almost four centuries

Detail of Pietra dura from Taj Mahal

Bharatpur Bird sanctu - ary

sarus crane

Diwan-i-Am.
Fatephur Sikri.
Akbar built the city as homage to a Sufi saint who predicted the birth of an heir

spoonbill

egret

An iron pillar at Lohagarh fort records the family tree of the Bharatpur rulers

Cadgan Books J. Robinson 1992

RAJASTHAN

Dilwara, Mt Abu. One of the finest examples of Jain temple architecture, constructed entirely of marble

Ganesh, "Remover of obstacles, Lord of Beginnings"

Jaipur's Hawa Mahal rises above the hectic life of Maharaja Jai Singh's planned city

Handprints beside the gateway of Jodphur's Mehrangarh Fort celebrate the faith of women who committed themselves to their husband's funeral pyre

The Shekavati region is famous for its 19th-century murals

Sleepy Pushkar attracts pilgrims, traders & nomads at Kartik Purnima, the festival at the November full moon

The exquisite Lake Palace, Udaipur, once served as a refuge for Shah Jahan, after he took up arms against his father

The Ganesh Gateway at hill-top Amber Fort, which glows golden at dawn & dusk

"eacock Doorway", Jaipur's City Palace, eads to the Maharaja's private apartments

The turbans of Rajasthani men indicate their ancestral village. Their wives wear dowry jewellery on their arms & ankles

e delicately carved stone screens of Jaisalmer's velis keep the interior naturally cool

Cadogan Books. J. Robinson 1992

THE WESTERN HIMALAYAS

Tibetan prayer wheels at Dharamsala, the home since 1960 of the Dalai Lama

Monasteries are the focal point of village life in Ladakh

Scandal Point, Shimla, takes its name from the Maharaja of Patalia, who supposedly abducted an English girl

House boats on Dal lake

All Sikhs bear the name Singh or "Lion"

18 million people are employed on Indian Railways, the 2nd-largest passenger network in the world

DELHI-JAMMU

CHAI

EASTERN INDIA

Belvedere House, Calcutta, once the Governors residence and now the National Library

Lion Capital, emblem of modern India, from the Ashoka Pillar in Sarnath

There are many followers of the "Yellow Hat" sect of Tibetan Buddhism in Sikkim, a remote Himalayan state

Tea plantations in Darjeeling were developed in the 1840's using bushes smuggled from China

Kali, goddess of Calcutta's ancient Kalighat Temple, from which the city takes its name

Varanasi on the banks of the sacred river Ganges, India's most ancient religious centre, & a city of learning

Cadogan B Russel Robinson 1992

SOUTH INDIA

Some of South India's wildlife parks are the best in Asia. Periyar Sanctuary is one of India's Project Tiger Reserves

Kovalum, one of India's most beautiful beaches

Fishing village in Kerala state

Ceremonial Charminar Gateway, Hyderabad

The elaborate Kathakali dance form employs a uniquely expressive language, compiled from an "alphabet" of 24 separate gestures

Kerala's backwaters are carpeted with water hyacinth & lichen in the spring

rom the time of the omans, the Malabar oast has been made, ich by its spice trade

CARDAMON तेजपा.ता
CLOVES
CASHEWNUTS काच
GINGER कपडे सिमेंट
NUTMEG
CASSIA
GREEN
WHITE ... ER

Elegantly decorated gopurams, temple gateways, are a feature of the South

chinese fishing nets, Cochin

Trichur's Pooram Festival is celebrated with temple elephants who carry the gods, trumpets & fireworks

Gadogan Books J. Robinson 1992

FROM GUJARAT TO GOA

Victoria Terminus, Bombay, reflects the confidence of the British Raj

Goa fell to the Portuguese in 1510, & remains strongly Roman Catholic

Ellora, site of the finest rock-cut caves in India, includes temples to Buddhi, Hindu & Jain faiths

Bombay is also known as "Bollywood" because of its film industry

JURRAT

Cows are often adopted, & parade through the streets supporting itinerant fortune-tellers

Market at Diu, a sleepy island off the coast of Gujarat, until 1961 a Portuguese enclave

Traditional fishing methods off the beaches of Goa

Cadogan Books J. Robinson 1992

sunset beers. The **Rising Moon** and **Dekyipalbar** hotels are okay for cheap Tibetan-Chinese meals, but the service is notoriously slow.

In McLeodganj, the favourite recreation is eating. A regular favourite, **Shambala Cafe**, is a second home to many travellers. It's just below the bus-stand, and has a Sony sound system, a microwave, a small book exchange, a useful noticeboard, hot apple pie, fresh doughnuts, great muesli, curd, shakes and chips. **Tapoe Hotel**, right next door, plays soft classical music and has soft seats. Come here for delicious chocolate cake and lemon tea. **Hotel Tibet** has good Tibetan-Indian food and there are 76 *Szechwan* dishes on its Chinese menu. It sells alcoholic drinks and runs popular Saturday night discos. So does **Friends Corner** by the bus-stand, well known for its lethal Thunderballs beer. Cheaper Punjab beer is available from the off-licence at the bus-stand. **Om Restaurant** is good for Chinese food, **Cafe Kangra** does tasty Swiss rostis, and **Yak Restaurant** is where to try *momo* soup and other Tibetan specialities.

GENERAL INFORMATION
HP Tourist Office (tel 2363) is just up the steps from the main bus-stand in Lower Dharmsala. It's open 10 am to 5 pm (except Sundays) and is only worth visiting for the current bus/rail timetable. Tibet Hotel in McLeodganj has far better information.

Main post office, open 10 am to 5 pm Monday to Saturday, is 1 km (¾ mile) below the tourist office. There's a small sub-post office in Kotwali Bazaar, near the tourist office. Foreigners' Registration Office, open 10 am to 5 pm weekdays, is 1 km below Dharmsala bus-stand. It's apparently a good, quick place to extend your Indian visa.

Taragarh
Approximately mid-way between Dharmsala and Kulu and set in a 15-acre estate, surrounded by tea gardens is the beautifully located **Taragarh Palace Hotel**. Built in the 1930s as a private resort the hotel now belongs to the royal family of Jammu & Kashmir. The 12 rooms are all well-furnished and facilities provided include a swimming-pool, a tennis court, fishing in nearby rivers for mahseer (the greatest-fresh-water game fish in the world), pony trekking through the foothills of the Dauladhar range and hang-gliding for the truly adventurous. Or you can just laze in idyllic surroundings. In short, Taragarh offers everything one needs to escape from the bustle of city life—but for those who need to stay in touch with the world, the hotel has 24-hour BBC World Service TV. The rate for room and full board is approximately Rs1500 per person depending on the room booked. Bookings can be made direct to Taragarh Palace Hotel, PO Taragarh, Dist Kangra (tel 3034) or at 3 Nyaya Marg, Chanakyapuri, New Delhi (tel 3015291, 3011744, tlx 031-61635, fax 011-343703).

KULU

Kulu town is situated on the banks of the winding River Beas, looking down the beautiful 'Valley of Gods' from a cool altitude of 1200 m. Unlike Manali it has not been developed for tourism but the town of Kulu is the administrative centre of the district. This means less facilities, but more peace and quiet. In fact the whole valley is often referred to as the Kulu Valley although this title is not strictly correct.

Kulu is mentioned in Hieun Tsiang's travelogue, and changed hands many times over the centuries before coming under British rule in the 19th century. Much of its history is tied up in its principal landmark, the temple of Raghunath, dedicated to Lord Rama. The story goes that in the mid-17th century, the Rajah of the area fell sick, and took advice from his holy men to send out to the locality of Iyudya for the murtis (sacred images) of Raghunath (Rama). In thanks for his prompt recovery, he donated the entire valley to the gods, and made Kulu the permanent home of the holy icons, erecting the present temple for their safekeeping.

Like Manali, Kulu has a wide variety of hill and mountain people. The women wear mainly traditional costumes—woollen homespun dresses (usually cord-belted), embroidered shawls and leather moccasins. The men, compromising with Western fashions, wear a strange combination of Kulu caps and wool jackets, and Levi jeans and plastic anoraks. Unlike in Manali, where there are so many tourists it is common to be 'blanked' by locals, the people of Kulu are very open, friendly and keen to talk to foreigners. They are also urbanised—a thriving chain of hi-fi, camera and electrical shops (plus several video parlours) have sprung up between the old, tumbling wooden houses manned by grizzled tailors, dentists and fruit-and-nut men. Surprisingly, few of the 'locals' are local at all but come from neighbouring valleys and other parts of Himachal.

The valley stretches northward for almost 80 km (50 miles) from near Mandi at only 760 m to the Rohtang Pass at 3978 m. Kulu is prettiest from April to June, and is best for mountain treks and views from September to November. But the town itself really comes alive only during the important **Dussehra festival**, which takes place in October after the monsoons. The festival starts on the 10th day of the rising moon, and continues with mounting vigour (and increasingly competitive dance competitions) for 7 days. All over India, Dussehra is celebrated to commemorate Rama's victory over the demon king Ravana. But in Kulu, it is Raghunath as 'main man of the valley' who is the focus of festivities: some 200 gods from temples all over the valley are brought here to pay him tribute. Hadimba is brought down from Manali to commence proceedings, and celebrations continue until she goes away again.

ARRIVAL/DEPARTURE

Air
Vayudoot offer daily flights between Bhuntar (10 km from Kulu) and Delhi (Rs2040). Jagsons Airlines also has daily flights from Delhi to Bhuntar, which continue to Shimla.

Road
Kulu has regular buses to Manali (see p.248), and hourly buses to Shimla from 6 am to 9 pm (8/9 hours). The fast deluxe bus to Delhi (16/18 hours) originates in Manali and arrives in Kulu at 8 am and is often full. Advance-book this one. All buses out of Kulu start from the new town bus-stand (by the tourist office) and then pick up from the old town bus-stand across the river. There are also buses to Chandigarh (12 hours) and Dharmsala.

Taxis are available, and can be shared to Chandigarh, Shimla, Manali and occasionally Delhi.

WHAT TO SEE
Most of Kulu's 'sights', as in Manali, are natural ones. They are best seen on foot, a short 2- to 3-hour expedition being sufficient to gain the finest local mountain and valley views. The town is divided into two parts by the winding Beas River. The 'new' town, with its modern bazaars, main bus-stand and tourist office, lies above the quiet, archaic village of the 'old' town. The long, narrow street connecting the two towns is a fiesta of Tibetan dhabas, Sikh jewellers, Hindu tailors, astrologer-palmists, bootmakers, and scores of shawl industries. In high season, the hi-fi/electronic shops keep a deliberately low profile. Handicrafts, not modern technology, is Kulu's main earner.

Unless you plan to stay overnight, a practical plan is to come into Kulu on an early bus from Dharmsala, drop your bags in a cheap hotel room or leave them with old 'Baba' at the Shiva Temple, spend a few hours looking around Kulu, and then hop on a late bus to Manali. Gruelling perhaps, but there are much better hotels and food in Manali.

Kulu Tour (on foot, 2–5 hours)
Shiva Temple–Raghunath Temple–Vaishno Devi Temple

This is a beautiful walk, offering some of Himachal's finest scenery. Start at the small pink-domed **Shiva Temple**, situated on the riverbank clearing which separates old from new Kulu. Opposite it is the **Kailash**, the only cinema in the whole valley (although there are now video parlours in Manali). The temple is a charming, modest affair with a small Nandi bull (wearing silk scarf) facing into a tiled shrine. The five-headed marble image of the deity within is surrounded by fine floral wall-carvings. In a little hut facing the shrine, you'll find the resident priest, usually in a huddle of assorted mystics and musicians. The eerie 'music' played here is the nearest thing to a recital you'll find in Kulu.

Walk back to the main road, and cross over. A steep stairway on the far side takes you up onto a cobbled path, which eventually rises above the town and right up into the hills. A few minutes walk, up the path, within a small courtyard left of a stone archway, is the **Raghunath Temple**. You can't enter the shrine, or take photographs of the deity, but you can peer through the grid window and see Lord Raghunath sitting on his velvet-cushioned silver chariot, under four huge ceiling mirrors. By the grid, there's a charming sentiment (donated by the Sapna Sweet Shop!) which invokes Shiva: 'As the fruit when ripened detaches itself from its limbs, so grant us the immortality liberating from the chain of transmigration.'

A few minutes further up the road, on the right, there's a wonderful old Transylvanian-style mansion called **Rapa Rupi Kulu**. It's a private house, guarded by Baskerville hounds, and with astonishing local architecture. Ask permission to visit but be careful, there may be dogs.

A minute further up the road, drop in on Ambika Shawl Industries. Here, in his small family-house workshop, the hospitable Lalchand Sharma produces beautifully embroidered Kulu shawls on wooden handlooms. Visitors are welcome to watch him at work, and to hear him explain how modern machinery will never replace his handloom: chiefly because the complicated 'flowering' (coloured patterning thread) must be woven in by hand. He generally begins work on a shawl at 7 am, finishing it at 5 pm. If you're lucky, you may be able to order the shawl he's working on at the time, and return to pick it up on the way back from your mountain walk. It's considerably cheaper than buying in town.

A steep ascent for some 20 minutes further up the cobbled trail, a major pilgrim and trekking route, brings you out above the village and onto the high ridges, with stupendous views down over Kulu valley, the River Beas running along its length like a silvery snake. A misty mountain range, enclosing the narrow valley on both sides, provides the perfect backdrop. The view from here is certainly the best reason for coming to Kulu. If you have the energy, another 45 minutes' climb (3 km: 2 miles) further up the rocky hill-path, following the other pilgrims, brings you to the small, quaint **Vaishno Devi Temple**, where the image of the goddess Vaishno (Durga) is enshrined in a small cave. The walk is a beautiful one, and along the way you will meet many friendly local families, hill-people and gaily chattering women casually handspinning wool on wooden spools. Look out for wiry villagers carrying barn-door beams up the mountain on their shoulders.

Returning down into the village (a complicated descent: mark your passage on the way up to avoid getting lost), try to be back at the Shiva Temple around dusk. The perfect way of ending your day in Kulu is to witness the priest and his friends as they perform the 7 pm evening *puja* to their Lord. Join the mystic circle in Baba's (the priest's) hut as the sacred coals are sprinkled with holy incense, the silver-topped conch shell is blown, and Shiva is praised to the accompaniment of ringing bells and rattling drums. The whole place is full of dense, perfumed smoke, and the atmosphere comes pretty close to the idea of 'mystical India' we have in the West.

SHOPPING

Kulu is famous for its fine, light woollen crafts—especially handloom shawls (*khaddi*). Almost every house spins and weaves, and the whole town is a living cottage industry. Kulu weavers produce shawls in varying grades. The cost of a standard 1.5 × 3 m shawl ranges from Rs100–1000: from those using plain 'raffle' (Australian wool) to patterned raffle, to 50% raffle with 50% pashmina wool, to the most expensive pure pashmina. If buying from a shop rather than a family-run 'factory' add 10–15% to the prices. All grades of shawl are beautiful, but the best buy are the 50:50 mixed-fabric variety—they last the longest.

To see the full range of Kulu crafts (small family shops only have a limited selection), go to **Bhutti Weavers Cooperative Colony**, 5 km out of town on the road to Mandi. This sells everything—caps, mufflers, gloves, jackets at wholesale prices; there is also a retail outlet in the town. Otherwise, try **ARR Fancy Kulu Shawls** on the bridge connecting old to new Kulu. This sells top-quality *chaddars* (pure pashmina wool lengths: the main wintertime wrap for Kulu men) and *pattus* (pashmina wool dresses for ladies, in striking designs and colours). It also has a representative selection of shawls. Down in the old town, the **Akhara Bazaar** is an interesting, and photogenic place to shop with many shawl shops and weavers, several antique wooden buildings, a **Govt Handicrafts Emporium**, and **HP Khadi Emporium**.

WHERE TO STAY AND EATING OUT

Kulu is not geared to European tourism to the extent Manali is, and has few lodging places and restaurants.

Mid-range (US$10–25/Rs250–750 per room night)
The two comfortable options—both well-run by HPTDC—are **Hotel Sarvari** (tel 2471) with double rooms at Rs250/300, and **Hotel Silver Moon** (tel 2488) with double rooms at Rs350, two suites at Rs500. The Sarvari, a short 10-minute walk from the tourist office, does the best Indian food in town. The **Silver Moon**, 2 km (1¼ miles) out of town (you can ask the bus to put you off here, if coming in from the south), is a well-furnished place, with a lovely situation and more good food. The new **Hotel Rohtang**, between the Sarveri and the tourist office, looks promising and apparently has a good restaurant. All the above hotels heavily discount their rates in the low season (November to mid-April).

Budget (Under US$10/Rs250 per room night)
The **Bijaleshwar View Guest House**, right behind the tourist office, is run by a wry old gent called Bhagwat Guru who looks on all guests as family. He offers clean rooms (with bath) at Rs40 single, Rs50 double. The garden's nice, and you meet a lot of people. Other, less good places are **Kulu Valley Lodge**, opposite old Kulu bus-stand, and **Fancy Guest House**, at the bottom of the maidan.

For cheap eats and coffee, try the tourist office's **Monal Cafe**. The speciality here is a plate of *channa bhatura*—a kind of chickpea pancake.

GENERAL INFORMATION
HP Tourist Office (tel 2349) is on the ridge above the new-town bus-stand. It's open 10 am to 5 pm, except Sundays, and is very helpful. The officer issues fishing permits for Katrain (20 km: 12½ miles) but doesn't handle trekking—you'll get full trek information (and guides) at Raison, 14 km (8¾ miles) from Kulu on the way to Manali. Raison is the base for many good short-range treks in this region.

MANALI

The small, picturesque hill-town of Manali lies at the head of the Kulu valley. Enclosed on three sides by calm mountains, it is surrounded by some of the loveliest meadows and orchards, rivers and terraced fields in Himachal Pradesh. Though a modern-day resort, it has been a holy site for over 1000 years and pilgrims still come in large numbers, both to visit the shrine of the saint 'Moni' in old Manali village, and to have a sacred dip in the nearby sulphur springs of Vashisht.

The name 'Manali' was a British creation. The Irish Banon family arrived in the 1870s and up until 1938 it was known as Dana Bazaar. Later, in the 1960s, the hippies found it (more accurately they found its high-quality dope), but it remained just a sleepy backwoods village until the late 1970s, when its tourist potential was discovered. Then a new town grew up, built downstream from Old Manali village, and a small iron bridge was built to connect them. Today, the new Manali is rapidly developing into a full-blown Indian holiday town, with 'Hot Byte' fast-food joints, noisy video parlours, screeching tannoyed music, and convoys of cars and jeeps full of party people. The tourist office, inundated with tourists from all over India, has little time for foreigners. It does them all a big favour by packing them off to Old Manali, where it supposes 'hippies' belong. Nobody objects. Out of the noisy new town, Manali is still one of the most picturesque spots in India—a peaceful vista of dense woodland, yellow mustard meadows and red saffron rice paddies, inhabited by an exotic array of different hill and mountain peoples. In the spring, the valley is indescribably beautiful: there are rippling streams, pine-scented forests, meadows of violets and blue speedwell, and fields full of wild raspberries and strawberries. There is a lot to see, do and buy in Manali, and the walks and treks in this region really take some beating.

Manali has a long tourist season. The flowers and meadows are at their best from mid-April to June; the tourist season is during the school holidays from mid-May to the end of June. High-level trekking takes place between July and mid-November; mountain views are clearest during October and November, following the monsoons; and the skiing season is from December to February, culminating in the **Winter Carnival** of February. The most colourful occasion of the year is the big **Dussehra** festival of September–October—when people from all over the valley turn up, bringing their gods with them, for a riotous 10-day carnival of music, song and dance. Somewhat akin to an English country show, it's a great opportunity to see the wide variety of peoples inhabiting the Kulu valley, decked out in all their traditional costumes.

ARRIVAL/DEPARTURE

Air
Both Vayudoot and Jagson Airlines fly daily between Delhi (Rs2040) and Bhuntar airport, 50 km (31¼ miles) from Manali. At Bhuntar, you have a choice of a local bus (from bus-stop 50 m from the terminal building) or taxi (takes up to 5 persons) to Manali.

Road
In season, Manali has daily buses to and from Delhi. The journey takes a long 16/18 hours, and most buses have screeching videos. 'We supply video purely complimentary!', beams the Manali tourist officer. See p.205 for details of Manali/Shimla buses.

WHAT TO SEE
Manali new town has just one main street, **the Mall**, which contains the tourist office, market, better restaurants, and handicrafts shops. The road up to **Old Manali** (15 minutes on foot) starts from the top of the Mall, and is lined with hotels. There are a few taxis who take parties of visitors to Vashisht, Old Manali, and other local interest spots—off the meter. But Manali is essentially a place for bracing, beautiful walks and for relaxation. The suggested sightseeing routes can be done in two days, but everybody stays longer—either to trek, or to shop, or to do nothing at all. Old Manali has a large population of long-stay travellers, who have refined the art of doing nothing.

Vashisht Walk (on foot, half-day)
The small, unspoilt village of Vashisht is famous for its natural mineral springs, and especially for its hot sulphur baths. If coming in from Pathankot (a long, sticky bus ride) or returning from a trek, this should be your first port of call.

Vashisht is a very scenic half-hour walk from Manali town. Start out first thing in the morning, taking the road leading down the hill, from just above the tourist office. The road runs parallel to a rushing river, with **Old Manali Mountain** rearing up to the left. If you make it to the top of this 923 m peak (a stiff 3-hour climb), the reward is a 360° panoramic view of the whole valley. Further along the road, you'll pass some rustic old Manali houses, with intricate carvings on pillars, doors and balconies. Be careful when taking photos. The custom with these simple, easy-going farming folk is to introduce yourself first. About 3 km (2 miles) out of town, a series of steps runs up right of the path, to the **Vashisht Baths**. These are actually Turkish bath-houses, with bathroom-tiled cubicles for single people and for families. They are exceedingly popular with Indian honeymooning couples, who don't generally get a lot of privacy elsewhere. Westerners enjoy them because they're often the first bath they've had in the country—a chance to lie back and let the bubbling sulphur waters soak away all the grime, dust and tension. You get about 20 minutes in the bath-house, which is quite long enough for beginners: vertigo is a common after-effect. Charges are very reasonable for single bathrooms and for the deluxe family bathroom. They're open 7 am–1 pm, 2–4 pm, 6–10 pm, and it's best to arrive early when there are no queues and everything is clean.

To recover afterwards, enjoy a hot pot of tea at the friendly **Hira Lal tea shop**, just up the steps left of the baths. From here, it's a 15-minute walk (left) up to the village of Vashisht itself. On the way, you'll pass the highest mountain dairy in India, then several more of the charming old slate-roofed Manali houses. In the village, visit the quaint little **Vashisht Temple**. Ascending the slope behind this (be careful, it's a public toilet) gives you fine views over the village and its beautiful valley backdrop. Below the temple, at the springs, local women can be seen deftly folding, kneading and pressing clothes clean using just their feet.

Walking back into town, you'll see the **Tibetan Refugee Camp**. It's a small, poor community with rough huts made from planking and old ghee or kerosene cans, a few supplies shops (often with sleeves of wool drying over the entrances), lots of fluttering Buddhist prayer-flags, and flocks of mynah birds diving through the woodsmoke in search of refuse. Through avenues of tall willow trees, you'll return to new Manali. Finish off at the bottom of the Mall, at the **Tibetan Monastery**. This is a modern, colourful Buddhist *gompa*, site of a famous carpet-weaving industry—one of the better places in town to buy Tibetan carpets and handicrafts.

Old Manali Walk (on foot, half-day)

This is another scenic morning walk. Start early, at the top of the Mall. Take the uphill road, via the unremarkable **Nehru Aviary**, a so-called 'sanctuary' with a few pine, cypress and juniper tree species, and three unhappy Monal pheasants in cages. From here, it's a 10 to 15-minute 'short cut'—striking left behind Hotels Marble and Pineview, across the yellow-blossom mustard fields, and up into the dense pine forest—until you come to a sign reading 'Dungri population 140 souls'. You are now within a short distance of Manali's holiest shrine, the **Hadimba Devi Temple**. This famous pagoda temple, built in the 16th century by Raja Bahadur Singh, is constructed in the local architectural style of rough-cut stones alternating with bands of wood. The overhanging rock is capped by a four-tiered pagoda roof made up of beautifully fitted slats of deodar. The plinth is high and the pillars, door-posts, and lintel—all exquisitely carved—are superb examples of the fine craftsmanship for which this valley is famous. Deer and Markhor horns, donated by local hunters, flank the entrance, lending a certain air of wild eeriness. The interior is a natural rock cave and the shrine itself is a simple, unadorned slab of stone, on which sacrifice is offered. Under this is the shallow cave, where you can just about discern a faint footprint of the resident *devi* (goddess). There is no other icon. The temple is located in a peaceful wooded glade, and is dedicated to the goddess Hadimbadevi. According to popular myth, she was a mountain belle rescued from her evil demon-brother by the god Bhim, whom she later married. Today, she is revered as the 'mother goddess' of the whole valley, and is regularly consulted in times of natural hardship or calamity (and by prospective marrieds). Most important, every Dussehra festival for centuries has been customarily opened and closed by Hadimba, in the presence of her *rath* or image. If (and this has happened recently) riots break out during the festival, it is taken as a sign that Hadimba is not amused, and the whole show is summarily cancelled.

Going back down, cut across to your left. This will bring you back to the main road leading out of new Manali, just by John Banon Guest House. Continue up this road a couple more minutes, and you'll come to the small bridge connecting the new and old towns. The landscape here is a pastoral delight of colourful meadows, brick-house water-wheels, rushing mountain streams, and snow-capped peaks. Five minutes up the shepherds' path at the far side of the bridge, you'll come into the village of **Old Manali**. Here life proceeds today much the same as it has for several centuries. Bales of hay hang out to dry from barnyard rafters, smoke drifts up from stove-chimneys poking out from slate roofs, stacked woodpiles prop up the sides of ornately carved traditional village houses. Look out for the old **temple of Moni** after whom the town was named. Head up to the top of the village, via damp cobbled paths, until you reach the ridge to the left. Below stretches a winding river valley of beautiful flowers and meadows. At the foot of the rushing river, you can see the simple but popular lodge, **Doloran's House**. The friendly owner offers cheap, very basic accommodation on a long-term basis.

RECREATION

Depending on the season Manali is a marvellous base for trekking, skiing and fishing. The most popular activity by far is trekking, though the trails are not well marked, there are no lodges or eating places *en route*, and you'll need to hire both equipment and a cook/guide. There are several trekking shops on the Mall, where you can pick up equipment and buy supplies. For maps and good information, contact Manali's **Mountaineering Institute** (tel 42), located 1.5 km (1 mile) out of town (take directions from the tourist office). This place also offers courses in mountaineering, skiing, water sports and high-altitude trekking. **Himalayan Adventurers**, c/o Mayflower Guest House (tel 104); **Paddy's Treks**, PO Box 32, Manali, run by the remarkable Capt Padam Singh; **Himalayan Journeys** (tel 2365); and **Ultimate Expeditions**, c/o Hotel Highland (tel 99) are three reliable—if expensive—trekking agencies. If you can't pay in excess of US$40 per day for long-range treks out to Lahaul, Spiti, Ladakh and Zanskar, then bargain yourself a private deal. Himalayan Adventurers will put together a marvellous 3- to 5-day 'local' trek up the valley for just Rs350 per head, inclusive of guide, porter, cook and ponies. Before you set off, let the tourist office know where you're going. There is no trekking permit required, but you'll want someone to look for you if you have an accident. Independent trekkers disappear with alarming regularity. If going solo, it's best to use Manali as a base-camp and just venture out on short 2- to 3-day mini-treks. The most popular expedition is up to **Rohtang Pass** (3915 m), which has the best mountain and valley views. Bear in mind, however, that after reaching the head of the valley (2 days) the steep inclines make crampons and full mountaineering gear obligatory. The pass is generally open only from June to November, but on the far side of it is a stark landscape of incredible beauty. If you haven't time to trek it, then take the bus from the tourist office, which plies up to the pass and over to the Buddhist village of Keylong, memorable for the resonant chanting of its monks, which echoes in a slow, deep rumble across the valley.

For a short, easy 3- to 4-day trek, head out to **Solang Nullah**—13 km (8 miles) out of Manali, at the head of the valley. It has spectacular mountain scenery, a comfy mountain lodge, and a fun ski lift. Shorter 1-day treks are to **Arjun Gufa** (5 km: 3 miles), a legendary cave near Prini village, and to **Nehru Kund**, (6 km (3¾ miles) from Manali on the Keylong road, a popular cold-water spring. A very easy, enjoyable 5- to 6-hour walk is to **Naggar**, 22 km (13¾ miles)out of Manali on the 'old road'. Scenery along the way is very pretty, and there are absolutely superb views from Naggar's **Hotel Castle**. You can stay here too for Rs30 (dorm beds) to Rs300, or at the cheaper **Hotel Poonam** down in Naggar town. Before going anywhere though, look out a copy of *Trekking in India* (Gianchand and Manohar Puri) and the revised Lonely Planet guide to *Trekking in the Indian Himalayas* by Garry Ware, in Manali market. The latter is the best book on trekking in Himachal Pradesh.

In the trekking season, Manali tourist office runs people out to popular jump-off points (like Solang Nullah, for Rohtang Pass) in small minibuses.

There's good fishing for trout on the Beas River at Katrain (22 km: 13¾ miles), Raison, Kasel or Naggar. Season: March to October. Fishing permits are issued by the Manali tourist office. Equipment hire (be warned) can be difficult.

Local entertainment is a bit thin. People go to bed early in Manali—it has a lot to do with the mountain air. There are no organised culture shows; to see traditional dance and music, you'll either have to be here for the Dussehra festival in September/October or hang around the Mall in the hope (often rewarded) of a local street festival.

Enquire at the tourist office about the small Manali 'Club'. This has a popular bar and indoor games, with nominal membership fee for visitors. There are now a number of noisy video parlours in the Mall—most showing Hindi movies to local tourists.

SHOPPING

Himachal Pradesh is famous for its handicraft skills, which find their expression in metalcraft, silver jewellery, bamboo products, dolls and carpets. Popular buys are the handloom shawls of Kulu and the woodwork and walking-sticks of Shimla. But Manali itself is famous for woollen goods—fancily embroidered Manali caps (circular box-hats, with Tibetan side flaps), gloves, socks, shawls and jackets. These are all reasonably priced and make excellent little presents.

Manali new town was only created in the 1970s and there is no bazaar tradition. The rather stark and offputting **Manu Market**, a modern arcaded bazaar, lies below the tourist office and is often half-closed. However, the 'fat man' at shop No. 2 sells some marvellous Tibetan produce, and the **Himachal Khadi Mandal** is the place to buy durable, well-tailored Manali woollen jackets which last for years. For Manali caps try first **Bea's Fancy Stores**, then **Gulati Traders**, both at the top of the Mall. They also sell nice gloves, socks, mufflers and pullovers. But don't buy shawls here—you'll find a cheaper, better selection in Kulu. What you won't find in Kulu, however, are fine-quality Tibetan curios and handicrafts. **Government Charitable Shop** on the Mall has a good selection—including some very unusual (if expensive) pieces.

The most amusing novelty buys in Manali are ayurvedic medicines. These are often foul-tasting concoctions sold by street doctors who beam in on sick tourists like bees to honey. Old gents sidle up in the bazaar to offer a 'love potion'. To endorse their sale they produce a booklet confirming:

This elixir benefits a man, can after use keep prolonged company with many a fair sex without feeling any sense of fatigue. He will have muscular energy like an elephant, he will be inflammable like fire, will have sweetness of voice like a peacock's, and will be noble like a horse. His eyes will be sharp as those of a vulture. His treasure of human potential fluid will be added in plenty. His heart would be amorous, and he would feel immense satisfaction after intercourse. It will bring him a sound undisturbed sleep. This may be taken by both the male and female partners. It is suitable in every season, and it will give them a healthy and handsome progeny.

WHERE TO STAY
Manali has boomed in recent years. In the 1970s, there were only five hotels. Now there are countless places to stay, nearly all of which, inevitably, are in the top or bottom brackets. If you want a decent room, and don't want to pay the earth, come in late March/early April. It's still officially low season then (even though the weather's fine), and many luxury hotels are still offering 30–50% discounts. The **Kulu Valley Hoteliers Union** has opened an office near the Tourist Information Centre (tel 2135, 2101) which can help make bookings. All rates quoted below are for the high season, and often include all meals:

Expensive (over US$35/Rs1000 per room night)
The new four-star **Hotel Picadilly** (tel 2113/4, tlx 03904-205) has a nice situation, good restaurant, and all mod cons. Rooms are well-furnished and centrally heated, and start at Rs500 single, Rs750 double. **Ambassador Resort Hotel** at Chadiyari (tel 2173, 2235) overlooks Old Manali and has rooms from about Rs1200. The **Log Huts** (tel 2439) run by HPTDC are beautifully located and cost between Rs1200 and Rs1500. The best run hotel is the **Span Resorts** at Katrain (tel 38) midway between Kulu and Manali. Rooms, including food, from Rs1200 and bookings can be made in New Delhi at GF-7 Surya Kiran, 19 Kasturba Gandhi Marg (tel 3311434).

Mid-range (US$10–35/Rs250–1000 per room night)
ITDC's **Ashok Traveller's Lodge** (tel 2331) is surprisingly good value for a government-run place. Rooms cost upwards of Rs350, the better doubles having superb

mountain views. Mr Negi's **Mayflower Guest House** (tel 2104) and **John Banon Guest House** (tel 2335) both offer friendly service, good food and superior rooms with a view from Rs500. Other HPTDC properties include the **Honeymoon Huts** and **Honeymoon Cottages** costing Rs500 per room. Hotels **Highland** and **Devidyar** are also good, with rooms from Rs175.

Budget (below US$10/Rs250 per room night)
Reliable cheaper places (priced around Rs150) are hotels **Meadows**, **Rising Star** and **Shivalik**. There are many small private houses, set in a pleasant apple-orchard, who take in paying guests. The Tourist Information Office keeps an informal list of what is available. Just over the bridge to Old Manali, there's **Him View Hotel** with basic, but clean, rooms, relaxing garden, and nice river views. The nearby **Manalsu Hotel**, up on the hill, is a quaint family house with rooms at Rs125. In the low season the rates drop but in May and June accommodation is so scarce that the hotels can charge any price, and many try to. This is also true at the nice **Bridge View** and **Riverside Cottage** guest houses, two other Old Manali favourites. Past these, moving up to Old Manali village, you can find cheap, simple rooms with families for absurdly little. Alternatively, put up at the charming little village behind Hadimba Temple. It's much quieter than Old Manali, and the people are welcoming.

EATING OUT
Manali's most popular restaurant, the **Mayur** behind the Mall, has an awesome menu (surely the longest in India) with some wonderful dishes like 'Poulet Saute Hengroise and bed of rice, garnished with chopyed mushrooms on top'. Actually, the Mayur has the best food, service, sounds and atmosphere in town. Most dishes are very reasonable (Rs15–25), and you often have to fight to get a seat. On the Mall itself, the high-class **Adarsh** restaurant has excellent Indian food; the more pleasant **Aashiana** is better for Chinese meals and has good sounds. Budget food is best at either the **Monalisa Restaurant**, or the **Mount View Restaurant** with good Tibetan dishes including over 30 soups.). Two good bakeries, just above the bus-stand, are **Super-Bake** and **New Rama Bakery**. The best bakery cum restaurant is **Peter & Tricia's** behind the taxi-stand, which serves pies, cakes and jams, and plays really good music. Over in Old Manali, the similar **Beas Cafe** just across the bridge has cakes and snacks, freaky sounds and freaked-out diners. If you've money to spend, **Hotel Picadilly** has a good reputation. For evening drinks, taxi out to **Span Resorts** (tel 38, 40) at nearby Katrain. This has one of the top hotel bars in India, with over 250 different varieties of Scotch.

GENERAL INFORMATION
HPTDC Tourist Office on the Mall (tel 2325, 2116, 2175) tries to assist, but is often deluged by tourists. Turn up in the late afternoon (it's open 9 am through to 8 pm) to ask any detailed questions. Printed information is poor, and the conducted tours to Rohtang Pass, Manikaran, and Naggar are geared to domestic tourists. Still, you'll want to come here to pre-book your bus on to Shimla, Kulu or Delhi.

State Bank of India is opposite the tourist office. Bookworm, down the lane behind the taxi-stand, is an excellent bookshop run by friendly Tibetans. Open 10 am–6 pm (except Sundays), it has new and second-hand books for rent, sale or exchange. If you want to get into the spirit of Manali, you'll be coming here a lot. Mountaineering courses are run by the **Mountaineering and Allied Sports Institute** (tel 2342).

SHIMLA (Simla)

Former summer capital of British India, Shimla is the largest hill station in the world and the one most associated with the 'old Raj'. Spread over a high 12-km (7 ½ mile) ridge on the lower spurs of the north-west Himalaya, its cool heights (2100 m) have always endeared it to foreign visitors. Favoured by politicians, army officers, writers (Kipling based his *Plain Tales of the Hills* on Shimla) and now tourists, it is a place designed for complete relaxation with lovely views, a pleasant climate, and more than just a memory of the Raj still clinging to it. It is the least 'Indian' of all hill stations, a probable hangover of the 'affectation that existed among officials of "being very English", of knowing nothing at all about India, of eschewing Indian words and customs' (P. Woodruff, *The Guardians*).

Shimla probably derives its name from 'Shyamla', a title of the goddess Kali whose temple was found in the thickly wooded hill region of Jackoo in the early 19th century. Another explanation traces of its origin to 'Shyeamalay', the blue-slate house erected by a fakir on Jackoo, the first nucleus of the settlement. However, 'Shimlah' or 'Shumlah' as pronounced by the local hill-people, is probably the actual word from which the station takes its name.

Presently a peaceful holiday resort, Shimla was born out of the turmoil of the early 19th-century Gurkha wars. Discovered by heat-weary British officers during the conflicts of 1819, its cool, healthy climate made it an ideal hill station on which to erect a summer-village of military tents and bivouacs. Then, in 1822, young Major Kennedy started the ball rolling by building the first permanent residence. Nurtured and popularised by the Government, the élite and the traders, a town rapidly grew up, and Shimla became a highly fashionable retreat—particularly for place-hunting young officers who wanted to 'get on' by ingratiating themselves with the military high-ups holidaying here. It was popular also with those who had been banished from India for misconduct, who escaped to Shimla to build themselves a substitute life of gay parties and revelry. Most notable as a place to escape the heat of the plains, it was only when Lord Lawrence visited Shimla as Viceroy in 1864 that it was at last accepted as the official summer capital of the Raj.

In 1904 the construction of the remarkable Kalka–Shimla railway finally provided easy access to the hill station. By this time, Shimla had become a thriving town of English red-roofed cottages, Georgian-style houses and Gothic government buildings like Barnes Court, Kennedy House, the old Viceregal Lodge, and Gordon Castle. The palatial residences of the Governor and the Commander-in-Chief were the sites of regular summer balls where frenetic dance and revelry were the order of the day. Polo, cricket and tennis tournaments gave way in the evenings to packed houses at the Gaiety Theatre (built to look like the old Garrick in London), while twice-weekly gymkhanas and races in the spacious playground occupied any remaining free time. In its heyday, Shimla represented the most sophisticated seat of British high society in India.

In 1966, having moved from humble hill-village to proud Imperial capital in just 150 years, Shimla received its final crown of success. The new state of Himachal Pradesh was created out of the reorganisation of the Punjab, and Shimla became its capital.

The days of the Raj may be over, but Shimla's attraction as a cool summer retreat, full of lovely walks and beautiful scenery, remains unimpaired. The town itself is busy, vital and very civilised—with marvellous hotels, restaurants and good tourist facilities—while outside it are calm, tranquil walks up into the green hills covered with fir, pine and Himalayan oak trees, red rhododendron and all kinds of mountain flowers, in between which are dotted the quaint old British houses and buildings which stand as a constant reminder of Shimla's Imperial past.

Best time to visit is mid-April to October, the official summer season. Wise travellers avoid the May/June tourist crush, and arrive late March–early April (bit chilly) for the cut-price accommodation. To see Shimla at its most colourful, full of wild flowers and greenery, come in September–October. Whenever you visit, bring some warm clothing: it can get pretty cold at night.

ARRIVAL/DEPARTURE

Air
Shimla is connected by Vayudoot and Jagson Airlines flights from Delhi (Rs2040) and Kulu (Rs545) (Bhuntar).

Rail
The *Himalayan Queen* leaves New Delhi station at 6 am daily, bound for Kalka, arriving at 11.15 am. The narrow-gauge mountain train leaves Kalka at 11.45 am, passes through 102 tunnels, and arrives in Shimla at 4.50 pm. The *Howrah-Kalka Mail* leaves Delhi at 10.45 pm, arriving at Kalka at 5.25 am the next morning in time to connect with the 6.30 RailCar or 7.10 am train to Shimla (arriving at 10.40 am and 12.15 respectively). See p. 207 for details of the return train to Delhi.

Road
Shimla has several buses daily to and from Delhi (see p.207), hourly buses from Chandigarh, Kalka and one deluxe bus to Manali (dep 8 am, from Interstate bus-stand).

WHAT TO SEE
Shimla is a lovely place, with lots to see and do, but it can be the very devil to get around. Like Darjeeling, the town sprawls out over a wide ridge in a many-layered wedding cake of winding, twisting streets and honeycombed houses. To reach each new layer involves steep, exhausting climbs or descents. The major roads have names, but where they begin or end is anybody's guess. Fortunately, most tourist facilities—hotels, restaurants, banks, the post office and tourist office—are on one level, the main thoroughfare called the Mall. Unfortunately, the Mall is right on the top of the wedding cake, and the bus and rail stations are way down below it, on Cart Road. In the day, there is no problem: the useful 'Tourist Lift' ferries people up and down between Cart Road and the Mall (near Oberoi Clarkes Hotel) for just Rs1. If arriving at night, there is a problem. Young lads meet tourists off night buses: 'Porter', they announce, proudly thrusting anonymous brass tokens in your face,

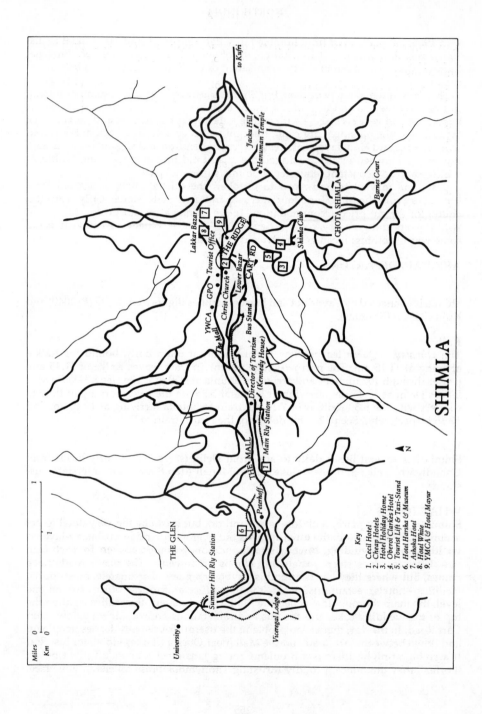

SHIMLA

Key
1. Cecil Hotel
2. Cheap Hotels
3. Hotel Holiday Home
4. Oberoi Clarkes Hotel
5. Tourist Lift & Taxi-Stand
6. Hotel Harsha & Museum
7. Ashoka Hotel
8. Hotel White
9. YMCA & Hotel Mayur

'Government porter!' Using them makes the gruelling 30-minute hike up to the Mall (if lodging there) far less arduous. They also locate the one or two hotels open this time of night.

You get round Shimla almost entirely on foot. The top two tiers of the ridge (the Mall and the level below it) are barred to all traffic. This makes for a very peaceful stay: no rickshaws, no taxis, no cows, no beggars, no mystics, no noise and no hassle,— but a leopard was seen on the Mall early one morning in July 1992. If you want to hire cars, taxis, rickshaws or take a bus, you'll have to go down to Cart Rd taxi-stand by the Tourist Lift. Hiring motorised transport can work out very expensive—largely owing to the very hilly terrain (slow going, high petrol consumption.).

Shimla is not a place for a whistle-stop tour. Life here proceeds at a slow, relaxed pace, and it is best just to go with it. Sightseeing is a low priority—people just stroll off to pleasant picnic spots, and don't much care, because the scenery is uniformly attractive, whether they reach them or not. The only high priority is a good pair of shoes.

The Mall and Surrounds (on foot, morning/afternoon)

Visitors often spend their first day in Shimla simply winding down. This is best done on the **Mall**, which is a sort of displaced Brighton, with bracing air, civilised promenades, English-style houses, ice-cream counters and bright souvenir shops.

At the top of the Mall, on the Ridge, is the tall, yellow painted **Christchurch** with a fresco over the chancel window designed by Lockwood Kipling. Its outward austerity conceals a rich interior of beautiful stained-glass windows (representing faith, hope, charity, fortitude, patience and humility) and murals, old oak pews and beamed ceiling, and interesting plaques to deceased army officers. It's worth attending the Sunday service if only to appreciate the rich, resonant organ.

The church leads out to **Scandal Point**, the large open area of levelled ground which is Shimla's main public meeting-place. Ever since a young equestrian Casanova (an Indian prince) absconded with a young high-born British maiden from this spot years ago, this has been the favourite rendezvous of people wishing to air their views or exchange the latest gossip. It is always packed, generally with happy tourists, and the views from this point are excellent—on a clear day, you can see the mountains.

In British days, it was *de rigueur* to sip a cool beer at one of the hotels overlooking the Mall, generally after a game of golf or billiards. Today, it is just pleasant to sit in one of its cafés or restaurants, and watch life going by. The lines of stately, oddly titled English houses always arouse comment, especially the present **Tax and Excise building**: a bizarre gothic towered mansion. After a few hours here most foreign visitors conclude that they are not in India at all, but in a bizarre Swiss-English village. The general effect, once you've got used to it, is one of total relaxation.

From the Mall, you can take a pleasant hour's stroll down to **Himachal State Museum** (tel 2357), just above the now closed Oberoi Cecil Hotel. Set up in 1975, it has a fine collection of hill arts and crafts, particularly of Himachal Pradesh. Famous for its Pahari-school miniature paintings, stone sculptures, and eye-catching embroidery and textiles, the museum is open 10 am–5 pm, except Mondays. The hill-path leading down below the museum gives panoramic views of the city skyline. It also takes you, in 5 minutes, to the new **Governor's Residence**. Beyond this, at the bottom of the hill, you can bear right (a 30-minute walk) for **Summer Hill**, the quiet and secluded suburb where Gandhi stayed on his visits to Shimla. It's also a very popular viewpoint. Follow the blue-and-white railings all the way up, until you reach the **University** at the top. Behind the last building (the Admin. Block), you'll find a forest trail leading back down to town (a 5-km, 1-hour walk). Before going down enjoy the views, generally best in the morning.

Jakhu and the Glen (on foot, full-day)

The early morning climb up to Shimla's highest point, **Jakhu Hill** (2438 m), is practically a tradition. Many travellers wish it wasn't. The ascent is relentlessly steep, and can take anything between 40 minutes (if fit) to 2 hours. Don't be shy of hiring a pony if you need one (about Rs45 return). To get there on foot, start up the slope alongside the church on the Mall, walk up to Hotel Dreamland, then bear right and follow the blue-and-white railings. These peter out near the place selling 'monkey sticks', but the path onward is clear. At the top, your effort is rewarded with spectacular views down over Shimla and environs, and across to snow-clad mountains.

Also at the summit is the **Hanuman Temple**. Inside, it's like Christmas—masses of bright, glittering tinsel, balls, decorations and streamers. The resident fakir sits warming himself at a single-bar electric heater, his hot-water bottle hangs on a rusty nail in the corner. The shrine is said to house the footprints of Hanuman, the monkey god, left when he paused here for a breather on his way over to Laxman, the injured brother of Rama, with some curative herbs. The temple itself is full of scampering very acquisitive brown monkeys. Writing of this place in 1837, the commentator Gerard wrote of the curious sight 'of the old fakir in his yellow garments standing in front of the temple, and calling "ajao, ajao" to his monkey children'. They all had pet names, and one it seems fell from a tree while feeding. The *jogi* seemed much concerned at this unusual occurrence, but lost no time in making his apologies. 'Forty years ago,' he remarked, 'when I first knew that monkey, she could climb as well as any here, but even a monkey can grow old in forty years. Alas, poor Budhee!' Mr C. J. French added in his 1838–9 journals:

'Mount Jakko seems to be the pivot around which the Simla community revolve in their morning and evening perambulations. While the evening is so often a scene of animation—sometimes the road is entirely taken up with conveyances—at this spot, in the morning it is generally one of perfect solitude.'

In the afternoon, try a pleasant walk down to **Glen Forest**. This is a pretty, secluded picnic spot located some 4 km (2½ miles) below the Ridge, beyond the cricket/polo-grounds of Annandale. One of Shimla's best walks, the Glen is famous for its lovely waterfall, best just after the monsoon, and for its rushing, ice-cold streams fed by melting mountain snows.

To get there, walk past the tourist office to the bottom of the Mall, take the right-hand turning just past Cecil Hotel, then follow your nose. Allowing for 'scenery stops', the return journey should take around 3 hours. On the way back, you can turn left at Cecil Hotel for a peek at the old **Viceroy's Lodge**. This huge six-storey building, once the site of so many elegant balls and festivities, is now the province of the Indian Institute of Advanced Study, with a fine reception hall and library.

Other good walks include **Prospect Hill** (5 km: 3 miles), down from Cart Rd to Boileauganj then a 15-minute climb, with its pretty temple of Karnana Devi affording excellent views of Shimla, Jutogh, Summer Hill and, if you're lucky, the toy train chugging past below. Views also of **Chadwick Falls** 2 km (1 mile) beyond Summer Hill, famous for its 67-m waterfall and deep gorge. A couple of places best seen by car or bus are **Wildflower Hall** (13 km: 8 miles) with spacious landscaped gardens and numerous varieties of wild flowers; and **Mashobra** (13 km: 8 miles) with famous apple orchards (best in April), oak and pine-forested picnic areas, and a big annual fair in June.

RECREATION
Shimla offers a lot more than just scenic walks. Go to Kulfri (16 km: 10 miles) for skiing (best in January/February, equipment for hire); to Chail (45 km: 281 miles) for tennis, squash and golf, and to see the world's highest cricket ground; and to Hatkoti (104 km: 65 miles) for trout-fishing. Best golf is on the scenic 9-hole course at Naldehra (23 km: 14½ miles). In Shimla itself, the better hotels arrange golf and tennis. In the winter (mid-December to mid-February only), try Shimla's famous ice-skating rink, the only natural rink in India, situated below the Mall adjacent to the bus-stand. There is year-round roller-skating in the old Regal cinema building. Both rinks hire out skates. There is a rank for pony-rides on the main square, below the church.

SHOPPING
Amongst Himachal Pradesh's handicrafts, woodwork pieces are special to Shimla. Visit **Lakkar Bazaar** along the eastern fork from the Ridge. Rolling pins are in great demand (husbands beware), as are exquisitely carved walking sticks, bowls, spoons and toys. Kulu shawls and dolls are other specialities. Try the **Himachal Emporium**, opposite the Telegraph Office on the Mall, or **Him Udyog**. Below the tourist office, just above Rivoli, is a makeshift **Tibetan Market** selling 'imported' jackets, woollens, and shoes, along with 'smuggled' articles like wrist watches and radios. A lot of unusual curios, often from the old Viceregal Estate or from the homes of long departed British officials, tend to make their way to this market. In the shops on the Mall, and in the Middle and Lower Bazaars, you can find rabbit-fur purses, jute handbags, woodwork items, handpainted wall-hangings, and attractive brass wall-plates. Chinese shoemakers can be found on the Mall, and are still good value. One interesting shop is the antiquarian bookseller on the Lower Mall. *Maria Brother* are notorious for their high prices but their fascinating stock is worth browsing through.

WHERE TO STAY
Shimla's hotels are very good, but there simply aren't enough of them. During the low season (November to mid-April), you should have no problem finding a 30–50% discounted room. By May, however, all hotels fill up rapidly and you'll be lucky to find a broom cupboard to sleep in. All prices quoted below are for the high season.

Expensive (US$35–75/Rs1000–2150 per room night)
Hotel Oberoi Clarkes on the Mall (tel 6091/5, tlx 351-206) has all the Oberoi tradition, and more, behind it. It launched M.S. Oberoi's career in 1934, and is still the hub of the city's social life. A pleasant combination of old-world charm and modern-day conveniences, it offers spacious and well-furnished rooms (with individual views of

the city) at US$48 single, US$91 double. Facilities, food, and in-house recreations are first-rate.

Two of Shimla's most pleasant places to stay are private homes. **Chapslee**, Lakkar Bazaar (tel 78242) is one of Shimla's oldest surviving buildings and was once the summer residence of the Maharajahs of Kapurthala and has rooms from Rs1500. The food, especially the afternoon teas, is excellent. **Woodville Palace** located in Chota Shimla (tel 72763, 6422) set in large grounds has attractive rooms from Rs1200 and a homely atmosphere.

Mid-range (US$10–30/Rs250–1000 per room night)
There are several good bets in this category. HPTDC's **Hotel Holiday Home** (tel 72375), is a short walk down Cart Rd from the Tourist Lift. It has a good restaurant, fine location, and double rooms (some with a view) from Rs425 to 1150. **Hotel Asia The Dawn** (tel 77522, 3141/4, tlx 0391-205), Tara Devi, although a few miles from the Mall has its own bus service to and from town. Rooms are from Rs750. **Hotel Harsha** (tel 3016/7) is quietly situated at the bottom of the Mall, near the rail station. Travellers recommend the **Hotel Mayur** on the Ridge, behind the church (tel 72392/3). It had an excellent dining hall (ask for the Mayur Chicken—it's special), very helpful staff, good transport information, and smart single/double rooms.

Budget (under US$10/Rs250 per room night)
Budget hotels and guest-houses are not confined to any one area. **Hotel White** (tel 6136) is in Lakkar Bazaar, and gets consistently good mentions. Friendly people, meals service, hot water, and very nice views. There are a few cheaper places on the Ridge, behind Christchurch. Best of the bunch are **Hotel Dreamland** (tel 5057), **Hotel Ridge View** (tel 3914) and **Ashoka Hotel**. All three have rooms from around Rs100. The Ashoka is most fun. It offers 'overlooking balconies with mounting, snowing view'. That's fine, but all the 'view' rooms have wire-grilled windows to stop the monkeys getting in. Finally, a special mention for the **YMCA** on the Ridge (tel 3341). This place is so popular, it's often booked out weeks ahead, partly because of the cheap rooms from Rs50; partly because of the superb recreation facilities (bridge, badminton, billiards, even a gymnasium); but mainly because it's such an unforgettable experience. Here you have lots of strange rules, an eerie boarding-school atmosphere, a fire-place that even in sub-zero temperatures is never lit, no water after 7.30 am, vast ex-Raj bathtubs, and a TV room permanently full of dusty old characters knitting things.

EATING OUT
Shimla's cuisine has, as one might expect, a distinctly British flavour. Lots of places have tiffin, 'English breakfasts' and china-service tea. There is also an American influence creeping in: hamburger stalls, fast-food joints and ice-cream palaces.

Quality multi-cuisine fare can be sampled (from Rs70) at **Oberoi Clarkes** or **Mayur** hotels. Around town, and outside of hotels, HPTDC's **Ashiana** and **Goofa** on the Ridge serve good pizzas, 'sizzlers', soups, and Chinese ginger chicken, but you wait ages for service, and they are far too crowded. **Fascination** is close to the fire station on the Mall. It's multi-cuisine with a sprinkling of Italian and Thai fare. **Embassy**, along the Mall, near the Tourist Lift, has popular fast-food combinations at mid-range prices. **Baljee's**, below the GPO on the Mall, has a very 'British' menu—come here for sausage, egg and chips, great cakes and ice-cream, fast service and good sounds.

The **Indian Coffee House** still offers dirt-cheap dosas, thalis and South Indian coffee. It's the most popular eating place in town.

GENERAL INFORMATION

HPTDC Tourist Office on the Mall (tel 78311, 77646) is open 8 am–7 pm daily. It's overworked, understaffed, and not much use. There's an Indian Airlines counter here, and a choice of local sightseeing tours (10 am–5 pm daily). The best tour goes to Narkanda (close-up views of snow mountains). The worst tour goes to Craignane (the much-publicised apple orchards are just a lot of dead trees till April).

The GPO is just up from the tourist office, on the Mall. It's open 10 am–7 pm, except Sundays. State Bank of India and better travel agents are nearby. A good bookshop is National Book Depot, near the Tourist Lift (Mall end).

A good map of Shimla is hard to find. The Rotary Club has posted a half-decent map down by the Tourist Lift (Cart Rd end). Both Vayudoot (tel 77646, 783110 and Jagsons Airlines (tel 5279, 201360) have offices in town..

Part V

WEST INDIA

Gateway of India

BOMBAY

Bombay is a dynamic, go-ahead city of tycoons, skyscrapers, film studios and big business—the nearest thing to the West in the East, and the modern Gateway to India. In just 40 years, it has mushroomed from a small, though thriving, coastal port-town of 500 000 inhabitants to a crowded industrial metropolis of 11 million people. A futuristic vision of India, with gleaming luxury hotels, high-rise business houses, and air-conditioned shopping centres, it is an irresistible land of opportunity for the masses of homeless, jobless poor, and refugees that flood in at an average rate of 6000 new families per day. They come in search of work or glamour or money, and most of them end up sleeping on the streets. The result is severe overcrowding and an appalling shortage of housing—a second city of ragged, squalid slum dwellings has grown up alongside the modern business capital of gleaming plate-glass buildings. Bombay is, like Calcutta, a city of powerful contrasts, though it's not just all the problems of modern India that are highlighted here, but all her potential and brighter prospects too. Here there is hope, optimism, and great prosperity—for Bombay handles half the country's foreign trade, manufactures the same percentage of her textiles, and pays a third of her income tax. The affluent rich—a hardworking cosmopolitan mixture of Hindus and Parsis, Jews and Jains, Arabs and Sikhs—divert surplus revenue to the philanthropic construction of hospitals, schools, museums and rest houses. But it is Bombay's 'action' that draws everybody here—this is a city bursting with life, colour, noise and vitality. And you can almost smell the money.

All this has happened since the Second World War, since the rise of India's new business class in the wake of Independence. Up until the 18th century, Bombay was just a marshy, diseased quag of seven islands, inhabited by a simple fisherfolk called the Kolis. Their name for the place was Mumbai or Bombaim, after their patron goddess Mumba Aai (Mother Mumba). This was later corrupted into Bom Bahia ('good bay') by the Portuguese. Ptolemy mentioned the islands as Heptanesia in the 2nd century AD, after which they faded from historical sight until occupied in the 13th century by the Hindu king, Bhimdev. The Sultans of Gujarat held the site briefly, and then the Portuguese arrived (1534). The first flush of Portuguese enthusiasm wore off—they saw its potential as a port, but the malarial swamps dissuaded them from developing it as a trading-post—and they offloaded it on the British, as part of Catherine of Braganza's dowry when she married Charles II of England (1661). Charles didn't see its possibilities either, and leased Bom Bahia, port and islands both, to the British East India Company for a nominal £10 per year in gold (1668). The Company's President, Gerald Aungier, became the founder father of modern Bombay, bringing in the influential Parsi merchant class and a host of assorted artisans and builders, to make possible the conversion of the port from pestilential swampland to thriving trading-centre. By his death, it was well on the way to becoming the centre of all west-coast trade in India. But it was in the mid-19th century that development suddenly became rapid—the railway arrived, so did the first textile mills and Bartle Frere's stately Victorian buildings. A series of large-scale land-reclamation projects took place (1862), the seven isolated mud-flat islands were joined into a single land mass, and Bombay's future success was assured. An excellent biography of Bombay, *City of Gold* by Gillian Tindall was reprinted by Penguin India in 1992.

Today, the city is a single, long, peninsula island, a dynamic commercial and industrial centre, and a major international port and city. For the foreign visitor, it is probably the easiest place to acclimatise to India. Westerners tend to like its bright, brash quality (it certainly has more character than colourless Delhi), also its fine international facilities—quality restaurants, shops, bars and real luxury hotels. Also, here there are so many other foreign visitors, you just don't get the same hassle, stares or curiosity as in many places elsewhere in the country. What you do get is a lot of noisy traffic, smells and garbage. As one Indian journalist warned: 'Whichever way you enter the city, you are face-to-face with streets pockmarked with rotting garbage dumps, sidewalks in ruins, and general confusion and chaos'.

Past the initial shock, however, Bombay is a fabulous place to be. Despite the chronic overcrowding and teeming traffic, the city boasts some fine parks, a cricket stadium, a couple of nice beaches, and a long sweep of seafront. It's always possible to escape from the madhouse inner city into quiet environs, and many wise arrivees do just that: heading straight for the peaceful, elegant surrounds of Colaba at the southern tip of the peninsula, to settle into India the civilised way—over a cocktail or a light meal at the famous Taj Mahal Hotel near the Gateway. After that, it's in with the earplugs, on with the smile and the money belt—Bombay is a pickpockets' paradise, and out into some of the most amazing street-life in the world.

WHEN TO GO
Best season is from October to February. It's very hot from March onwards (stay near the sea, to avoid boiling over), and the monsoon is from July to September. For a good

festival, come in the post-monsoon celebration of **Ganpati**, held in honour of Bombay's favourite god, money-lucky Ganesh. The February/March **Holi** festival is not a good time to visit—horrid crowds, lashings of red paint, and hapless tourists diving for cover all over the place.

ARRIVAL/DEPARTURE

Air
Bombay has two airports: Sahar International (tel 6366700), 26 km (16¼ miles) from the city centre, and used by all international airlines including Air India and for Indian Airlines flights to Karachi (Pakistan) and Colombo (Sri Lanka). The international carriers connect Bombay with Africa, the Gulf region, most of Europe, New York, South East Asia, Japan and Australia. The domestic airport is at Santa Cruz (tel 6126343), and is used by Indian Airlines (tel 6114433), Vayudoot (tel 6146583), East West Airlines and other domestic operators. There are two terminals. The newer (1992) handles Indian Airlines Airbus flights while the other, original terminal handles all other domestic traffic.

Airport–city Transport
a) EATS coach service (runs hourly, on the hour, from Sahar airport into city between 2 am and 11 pm; runs hourly, on the half-hour, from Santa Cruz into city between 2.30 am and 11.30 pm; returns hourly, on the hour, from Air India building, Nariman Point, to both airports all day, except 2 to 4 am; journey time can be anything between 1 hour and (in rush-hour chaos) 3–4 hours. If flying out from Bombay, aim for a night flight: traffic out to the airport is much lighter in the evenings.
b) Suburban train (auto-rickshaw from Sahar to Andheri station, from Santa Cruz to Vile Parle station, for cheap 1st-class, 2nd-class trip to Churchgate/Victoria Terminus stations in the heart of the city; best return trains to airports leave Churchgate station every 4 minutes, from platforms 1/2). Quick and comfortable, trains are much more reliable than buses: airport/city journeys by rail rarely take more than 45 minutes.
c) Airport taxi service (Sahar has a well-controlled meter-taxi booth open round the clock that provides pre-paid taxi services on the basis of fixed fares—an average Ambassador car ride to, say, Nariman Point, would be around Rs140). Having stated your destination, you purchase a coupon for the correct fare and amount of baggage you are carrying—this is handed over to the driver on reaching your destination. Alternatively, walk to the auto-rickshaw stand just outside Sahar airport concourse, and bargain a ride into town—officially auto-rickshaws are not allowed further into town than Mahim but are ideal if going to Bandra or Juhu. Travelling by airport coach, taxi or rickshaw, prepare yourself for horrendous traffic, grim slums and ripe garbage dumps lining the highway all the way into the city.

Leaving Bombay by Air
a) Make sure you have the right airport. An alarming number of people miss flights by sitting dreamily in Sahar lounge waiting for a domestic flight (which never comes) or in Santa Cruz coffee shop waiting for an international flight (likewise). Discovering your error at the last minute can be horrendous—the two airports are 5 km (3 miles) apart, and you'll have to forget about the leisurely EATS coach connection in favour of a frantic taxi-dash.

b) Late arrivals at airports can lose their reservations. For domestic flights, be at Santa Cruz a good hour ahead of check-in. For international flights, allow 2 hours—and have your Rs300 *departure tax* ready. You must pay this *before* checking-in your luggage.

Note: For Indian Airlines/Air India reservations, confirmations or cancellations in Bombay, avoid the Air India building in Nariman Point (open 8 am to 6.45 pm Monday to Saturday, 8 am to 5 pm Sunday—but the queues never move). Instead, either pay a travel agent to handle bookings for you, or wait until you reach a quieter centre (e.g. Goa, Cochin, Trivandrum) where you can do them quickly yourself.

Rail
Bombay has two separate railway systems, covering all major tourist destinations. **Central Railway** services the east and the south—Calcutta, Aurangabad, Goa, Gujarat, etc.—and a few places in the north. Reservations are from the special Tourist Booth opposite platform 9, Victoria Terminus (this is also the place to buy your Indrail Pass, if required). **Western Railway** services most places north and west—including Delhi and Rajasthan—and has booking offices at both Churchgate (next to Government of India tourist office) for 1st class, and at Bombay Central for 2nd class. The Victoria Terminus booking office has a Railway Tourist Guide, who handles a limited tourist quota of 1st and 2nd class tickets for all routes—he should be your very first option. In high season (October to February), it's essential to advance-book all rail tickets a few days ahead.

Some useful trains are the *Rajdhani Express* and the equally fast *AC Express* to Delhi from Bombay Central (17 hours, air-con seats and 1st class only); the *Calcutta Mail* (35 hours) from Victoria Terminus; and the *Dadar Madras Express* (24 hours), leaving Dadar station—seven stops up the main line from Victoria Terminus—at 2.45 pm daily.

Bus
The State Transport Bus Depot, opposite Bombay Central station, is the place to book long-distance buses. Places covered by road—MTDC luxury coaches are best—include Aurangabad, Panjim (Goa), Hyderabad, Bangalore, Madras, Delhi and Calcutta. MTDC also have booking desks at the Government of India tourist office, and at Air India building, Nariman Point. For destinations like Udaipur, Mt Abu and Ahmedabad, you may in the absence of state buses have to check out the private bus companies at 9th and 11th lane, Khetwadi.

Steamer
The boat for Goa has not operated since the the late 1980s but every year plans to reintroduce it are announced, and fail to materialise. If operable it should leave from Ferry Wharf, about 3 km (2 miles) from the city centre.

GETTING AROUND
For a major capital, Bombay is quite easy to negotiate. This is because most tourist facilities are concentrated in one place: a narrow 3-km (2-mile) strip running down from Churchgate to the bottom end of the island (Bombay is connected to the mainland by a series of bridges). This strip is bounded to the south-east by the Taj Hotel, Colaba, and to the south-west by the Oberoi Hotel, Nariman Point. The former hotel is in the area of most of the budget hotels, the latter is in the 'classy' end of

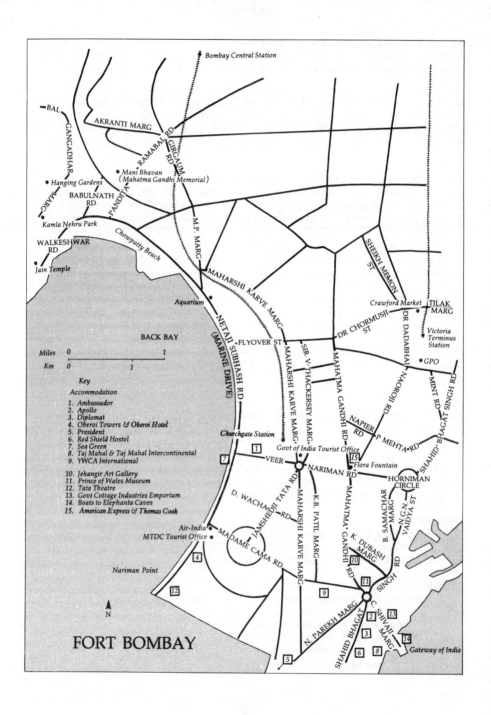

Bombay Central Station

BAL

GANGADHAR

AKRANTI MARG

RAMABAI RD

GIRGAUM RD

PANDITA

Mani Bhavan
(Mahatma Gandhi Memorial)

Hanging Gardens

BABULNATH RD

Kamla Nehru Park

WALKESHWAR RD

Jain Temple

Chowpatty Beach

M.P. MARG

MAHARSHI KARVE MARG

SHEIKH MEMON ST

Aquarium

Crawford Market

TILAK MARG

DR CHORMUSJI ST

DR DADABHAI NAOROJI RD

Victoria Terminus Station

BACK BAY

FLYOVER ST

NETAJI SUBHASH RD
(MARINE DRIVE)

MAHARSHI KARVE MARG

SIR V. THACKERSEY MARG

MAHATMA GANDHI RD

GPO

SHAHID BHAGAT SINGH RD

MINT RD

Miles 0 ———————— 1
Km 0 ———————— 1

NAPIER RD

P MEHTA RD

Key

Accommodation

1. Ambassador
2. Apollo
3. Diplomat
4. Oberoi Towers & Oberoi Hotel
5. President
6. Red Shield Hostel
7. Sea Green
8. Taj Mahal & Taj Mahal Intercontinental
9. YWCA International

10. Jehangir Art Gallery
11. Prince of Wales Museum
12. Tata Theatre
13. Govt Cottage Industries Emporium
14. Boats to Elephanta Caves
15. American Express & Thomas Cook

Churchgate Station

[7]

[1] Govt of India Tourist Office

VEER

NARIMAN RD

[15]

Flora Fountain

HORNIMAN CIRCLE

D. WACHA RD

JAMSHEDJI TATA RD

MAHARSHI KARVE MARG

K.B. PATIL MARG

MAHATMA GANDHI RD

B. SAMACHAR MARG

N.G.N. VAIDYA ST

Air-India

MTDC Tourist Office

MADAME CAMA RD

K. DUBASH MARG

[10]

SINGH RD

[4]

Nariman Point

[11]

[9]

[12]

N. PAREKH MARG

SHAHID BHAGAT

C. SHIVAJI MARG

[2]

[13]

[3]

[14]

[5]

[6]

[8]

Gateway of India

N

FORT BOMBAY

town, where you'll find many of the airline offices, banks and snobby hotels/ restaurants.

For transport round town, you're best off with (black and yellow) taxis. They normally know where they're going, and many carry electronic tamper-proof meters. Taxi rates in Bombay are revised every time there is a petrol price rise or devaluation in the value of the rupee. Consequently, while a meter may indicate a Rs2 fare the tariff card displayed in the taxi will show Rs10. Also, the meter clocks up time, not distance, so traffic jams can be expensive. As a general guide, a clear 2-km run from Colaba to Nariman Point (from the Taj to the Oberoi Hotels) should cost about Rs10.) Auto-rickshaws are on a similar metering system, and are usually restricted to airport/suburb routes. Horse-drawn carriages or 'Victorias' can be found at the Gateway of India— for an evening promenade up Marine Drive—also at Bombay Central and Chowpatty. Catching local buses is real pot-luck: drivers tear across town like men possessed, passengers tumble off like D-Day landing forces hitting the beaches, but it's all great fun, and very cheap. There's only one problem: how do you find the right bus and bus-stop when the numbers on both are so often in Hindi? For what it's worth, BEST bus depot in Colaba (next to Electric House) sell a decent local bus timetable.

WHAT TO SEE
Bombay's few conspicuous 'sights' are very spread out. To see everything in 2 days—which is what most visitors allow—requires a lot of stamina and a very energetic, knowledgeable guide. The alternative, as usual with a large Indian city, is to cover the main points of interest on a conducted bus tour, and then mop up the rest at leisure later on.

City Tour (conducted tour bus, 4 hours)
Gateway of India–Aquarium–Mani Bhavan–Jain Temple–Hanging Gardens– Kamla Nehru Park–Prince of Wales Museum

For a good introduction to Bombay, and to avoid the crowds, take the MTDC morning tour. Buses are comfortable, guides are good, and you are given some background history of the city. This said, insufficient time is allowed for each stop and you may well wish to backtrack to one or two places later.

At **Colaba**, named after the Koli, Bombay's original fisherfolk who are still here, you'll see **Apollo Bunder**—the traditional reception point for dignitaries visiting India in the days of sea travel. In 1911 a very important dignitary stepped ashore here—King George V, accompanied by Queen Mary. To mark the occasion (it was the first time a reigning monarch had made a state visit to India), a hasty decorative arch of white plaster was erected on the edge of Bunder pier. Later, in 1927 a proper monument—the present **Gateway of India**—was built to commemorate the historic occasion. Designed by a government architect, George Wittet, it is now Bombay's principal landmark. Built of local yellow-basalt, the 26-m high gateway is an architectural oddity: designed in the 16th-century Gujarat style, yet incorporating traditional Hindu and Muslim features, notably minarets and jalis (the trellis stonework in the side-hall arches which eliminate tropical sun-glare yet allow cool sea breezes in). Return to the Gateway in the evening—it's a popular after-work promenade spot for Bombayites, and a good relaxing place to end your day. The ebony-black equestrian statue you see facing onto the gate depicts the mighty Maratha emperor, Chhatrapati Shivaji, who became the bane of the Mughal Aurangzeb. It was set up soon after Bombay became capital of Maharashtra state in 1961.

From Colaba, the tour moves into the city via **Flora Fountain**. Situated at the top of Mahatma Gandhi Road, this is the business heart of downtown Bombay, the home of most of the city's major banks and offices. Nearby is the imposing Gothic structure of **Victoria Terminus** (or 'VT'), the largest railway station in the East. Also the Cathedral of St Thomas, begun in 1672 by Gerald Aungier, yet only opened in 1718. Then to the seafront, for a beautiful drive up **Marine Drive** (uninspiringly renamed Netaji Subhash Rd) which was built on land reclaimed from the marsh in 1920. It sweeps up, in a long elegant arc, from Nariman Point to Chowpatty at the top of Back Bay, and is another favourite promenade spot.

Below Chowpatty, the tour makes a stop at **Taraporewala Aquarium**. Opened in 1951, this aquarium (one of India's finest) houses a wide selection of interesting marine life—giant lobster, batfish, shark, sea-turtle, stingray and turbot—supplied with fresh sea water via an underground pipeline. Open 11 am to 8 pm daily, except Monday, the admission is money well spent.

At **August Kranti gardens**, 1 km (¾ mile) above Chowpatty, you'll find one of Bombay's most important buildings—**Mani Bhavan**, 19 Laburnum Road. This was Mahatma Gandhi's residence during his visits to Bombay between 1917 and 1934. From here, he launched both his *satyagraha* (non-violence) and civil disobedience campaigns (1919 and 1934 respectively), and you can see within an exact reconstruction of the room he lived in—his simple pallet-bed, spinning-wheel, walking-stick, sandals and quaint old telephone kept just as they were during his life, along with his few religious texts: the Koran, Bible and Gita. On the floor, there's a beautifully crafted tableau of 28 model panels depicting key events in the great man's history. If you want to see and learn more about Gandhi, return later to browse through the extensive library or to see one of the regular film-shows held in the auditorium. Open 9.30 am to 6 pm daily but closed on Sunday and Monday afternoons.

Next stop, at the top of Back Bay, is the **Jain Temple** on Bal Gangadhar Kher Marg. Take time out at this colourful shrine to study the marvellously intricate carvings on its exterior walls. Then climb to the upper storey and watch the monks (their faces masked to avoid swallowing insects) tracing complicated mandalas in powder and ash before the image of the god.

On the heights of nearby **Malabar Hill** are the famous **Hanging Gardens**. They are not as exotic as they sound—being simply a terraced garden landscaped in 1881 over three reservoirs supplying water to Bombay city—but they compensate with a truly bizarre topiary of trimmed animal-shape hedges. The popular flower-clock in the garden is near 'elephant'. Hidden behind a wall beside the Hanging Gardens is the **Tower of Silence**, where the Parsis leave out their dead to be consumed by vultures. Visitors aren't allowed. Across the road from the gardens, there's the pleasant **Kamala Nehru Park**. This was laid out in 1952 in memory of Pandit Nehru's wife, and is a colourful, touristy place with a children's playground and a giant Old Woman's Shoe. Ignore the jibes and climb it, for spectacular views down over Marine Drive and Chowpatty Beach—especially good around sunset.

The tour ends at the **Prince of Wales Museum**, off Willingdon Circle in Colaba. This beautiful Gothic structure—designed by Wittet in the Indo-Saracenic style, with imposing dome in the 15th/16th-century Western Indian style—was built in 1905 to commemorate the first visit of George V (then Prince of Wales) to India. It stands in oriental splendour in spacious palm-decorated gardens, and reminds many visitors of Monte Carlo. Within, you'll find one of the finest collections of art, archaeology and natural history in the country. Start off in the 'key gallery' just inside the entrance. This introduces all the other galleries in the museum, and exhibits the choicest specimens from each one. If your time is short (and it will be if you want to rejoin the tour bus: it stops here only 35 minutes), use this gallery to choose a couple of selected areas. Still better, leave the tour and do the whole museum properly. On the ground floor, you'll find sculpture and stonework, much of it Buddhist (Gandharan) and some huge ceiling slabs from Chalukyan temples in northern Karnataka, dating back to the 6th century AD; on the first floor, some excellent ceramics, pottery and necklaces; and on the third floor, the unmissable Purshottam Vishram Mawji collection of art, a worthwhile Tibetan/Nepalese gallery, and good exhibitions of Continental pottery/Victorian glassware. One of the jewels in this marvellous museum is the manuscript gallery with illustrations of Hindu texts, Mughal miniatures including the magnificent portaits of Jahangir and Dara Shikoh and the collection of later Pahari school painting from the hill states of Punjab and Himachal. The museum is open 10 am to 5.30 pm daily, except Monday. Entrance is Rs2, but free on Tuesdays.

Elephanta Island Tour (excursion boat, 4 hours)

This is a good way to occupy a Monday (when most other sights are closed), a Sunday (when the rest of Bombay is closed) or any other day when you need a break from the heat and noise of the city. What you're going to see are four rock-cut **cave temples**, dating from AD 450–750, situated on Elephanta Island some 10 km (6½ miles) north-east of Apollo Bunder. To get there, you've a choice of a 'Big Boat' (Rs40) or a 'Little Boat' (Rs25), tickets for which are sold from the small office opposite the Gateway of India. Take a 'Big Boat'—they have good guides (all archaeology graduates) who'll teach you a lot about Hindu religion, art and thought. Boats leave every hour, between 9 am and 2 pm, and take an hour to reach the island.

Elephanta has the longest historical pedigree of any of Bombay's seven islands. While the others were still boggy marshes, Elephanta was being developed anytime between the 7th and mid-8th centuries. The extent and quality of the rock-cut architecture and monumental sculpture is well worth the trip over. Much later, the Portuguese landed on the rear side of the island, found a massive stone elephant there (presently housed in Bombay's Victoria Gardens) and renamed it Elephanta. Later, as disenchantment set in, bored Portuguese gunners spent long, hot monsoon months using its beautiful cave temples for target practice.

The caves themselves are a testimony to the faith of those who excavated them. Some contain 7.7-m high friezes of astonishing workmanship and figurative detail. The quality, despite cannon-damage and loss of much of the original (beautiful) paintwork, is quite as fine as that of the more popular caves at Ellora.

Arriving at the island, it's a gentle climb up 125 sloping steps to the main cave, dedicated to Shiva. On the ascent, keep an eye out for acquisitive monkeys (don't display any food or bright jewellery). There are palanquins available for those who don't like exercise. At the top, pay your admission and follow the guide directly into the caves for his/her excellent half-hour lecture.

The main cave, carved out of the hard, durable blackstone around the middle of the 7th century AD, comprises a pillared hall and a small shrine (this has four entrance doors, flanked by *dvarapala* guardians). The architectural style is a combination of Chalukyan (cushion capitals and graceful sculptures) and Gupta (mountain, cloud, nature imagery) influences. The cave itself features a series of large sculptured panels, the finest of which, the 5.8-m high *Trimurti* monolith, depicts Shiva in a rare role as creator, protector and destroyer combined: *Mahesamurti*, or portrayal of the Hindu Trinity. He is shown first as a young man/Brahma/creator, holding lotus blossom (gentle, feminine face on right), then as a middle-aged man/Vishnu/preserver (wise, mature central face, wearing enigmatic smile comparable to that of the Mona Lisa), and finally as a wizened, ferocious old man (left panel), representing Shiva himself as destroyer, holding a skull. It's an exquisitely balanced piece of work.

Nearby is one of the finest sculptures in India—Ravana lifting Mount Kailash. This tells the epic story of the Lankan king, Ravana—often shown with 10 heads to denote superior intelligence—who took advantage of Shiva's deep slumber to try to displace his mountain home. But then Shiva woke up and, with just the gentle pressure of his toe, pressed the teetering peak back into place again, burying the demon king beneath it for 10 000 years. Such is the skill of the sculptor here, that you can actually see the strain on Ravana's rippling shoulder and back muscles.

To the left of the Trimurti is another masterstroke—Shiva as *Ardhanarisvara*, or half-man half-woman. This is a representation of the combined force of masculine spirit and feminine creativity. Viewed from the centre, the bisexuality of the figure's form and features appears quite harmonious: a remarkable achievement. The 'female' face is looking into the mirror of *maya* or illusion.

Other important panels show Shiva playing chess with Parvati on Mount Kailash, surrounded by awed domestic servants; performing the earth-shaking Tandava dance (*Nataraja*); and demonstrating the discipline of yoga (*Yogisvara*).

Sights Round-up
Kanheri Caves–Juhu Beach–St John's Church–Chowpatty Beach–Cross Maidan

If you enjoyed Elephanta, there's a second state-conducted tour out to **Kanheri Caves** (42 km: 26½ miles). This is one of the largest groups of Buddhist caves (109 in all) in western India. They are set high up on a hill, in a forest surround (in fact the edge of the Borivali National Park. Dating from around the 2nd to 9th centuries AD, the earlier (*Hinayana*) caves have been excavated from a huge circular rock. Most of them are simple monks' cells of limited interest, but caves 1, 2 and 3 are noteworthy for their massive pillars, sculptures and *stupas*. Cave 3 is the famous **Chaitya Cave** with icons and a long, pillared colonnade. This tour also includes a visit to **Juhu Beach** (18 km: 11 miles). This is a long beach (5 km: 3 miles) fringed with palms and coconut trees: a popular week-round picnic spot, with good beach entertainments at weekends. Juhu has lots of big hotels, but lousy swimming (highly unsanitary).

Back in Colaba, **Sassoon Dock** (1.5 km: 1 mile) down Shahid Bhagat Singh Rd from the Bunder is a great place to watch all the fishing boats unloading their catch around dawn. While you're in the area, walk 10 minutes further south to Colaba's most significant monument: the elegant **St John's (Afghan) Church**, built in 1857 in memory of British soldiers who died in the first Afghan War. Its tall spire has become a familiar landmark for sailors far out at sea.

For a good evening out, start with a high-rise cocktail at the Oberoi's roof-top restaurant, the **Malabar**, and watch the sun set gloriously over Back Bay. Then cruise up to **Chowpatty Beach** (4 km: 2½ miles) by cab. This is where tired Bombay businessmen come, with friends and families, to wind down after a hard day making money. After tucking into typical Bombay snacks like *bhel puri* (spicy mix of puffed rice, peanuts, onions, potatoes and chutneys) and *chaat* (fruit and veg tossed in a banana leaf—probably best after you have acquired enough immunities) they enjoy a relaxing evening massage. The beach is lined with expert masseurs. One end of the beach is a regular meeting area for Bombay's gay community. Come to Chowpatty for authentic local atmosphere, and for the popular view of Malabar Hill, beautifully lit after dusk. This is the renowned 'Queen's Necklace' around the 'throat' of Back Bay. Swimming, by the way, is not possible here.

Finish off at **Cross Maidan**, in the heart of the city. These urban gardens are overlooked by **Bombay University** (a wonderful gothic horror, dominated by the 80-m high **Rajabai Clock Tower**) and surrounding **High Court** buildings topped by Justice and Mercy figures. In contrast to this colonial austerity, the Maidan itself is a popular evening exhibition centre of twinkling lights and general jollification. There's nearly always something going on here. Perhaps an inflatable Taj Mahal at the entrance and a novelty fun-fair going on inside: stoical Brahmin families traipsing unamusedly through the 'Baby Diamond Laughing House', films about lion-taming playing to packed houses in the 'Family Planning Video Booth', and hordes of ticketless local youths clambering over the scaffolding of the '32-foot-height Ropeway'.

RECREATION

For another evening, choose from Bombay's good selection of music, dance and drama shows. Start by visiting the Government of India Tourist Office for the current culture events, listed in the *This Fortnight for You* handout. For classical dance recitals (including Bharatnatyam, Kathakali, and Odissi styles), pop along to Taj Mahal Hotel's **Tanjore** restaurant (6.15 pm performances most nights). For drama (Marathi, Gujarati and Hindi styles), there's the **Sahitya Sangh Mandir, Patkar Hall** and **Tata Theatre** at the National Centre for the Performing Arts (NCPA) at Nariman Point. The last two places also hold occasional music recitals. Performances start at 6.30 or 7 pm.

Regular exhibitions of art are held at **Jehangir Art Gallery**, adjoining Prince of Wales Museum and at the **Taj Gallery** in the Taj Mahal Hotel. The **Nehru Planetarium**, 8 km (5 miles) north of city centre, above the Race Course, has daily star-gazing shows in English at 3 pm and 6 pm (closed Mondays).

Going to the cinema in Bombay is a must—it's not only the film capital of India, it also produces more movies than any other city in the world, Hollywood included. There are literally hundreds of cinema houses here (although the video has resulted in some having to close), most air-conditioned and very comfortable. To tune in to Bombay movie-madness, buy any of the 'juicy screen gossip' mags peddled on the streets (*Star and Style* is a good one), then buy a newspaper to see what's on. Just head down the street opposite VT station, where three good cinemas—Excelsior, Empire and Sterling—show current epics (English, Hindi and Marathi) at 3, 6 and 9 pm daily, with a few extra matinees thrown in. Outside, there's a couple of good ice-cream parlours and fast-food places—handy for inter-film refreshments! Later, ask the tourist office to arrange a visit to one of the film studios, where you can have a chat with the stars and watch them playing three different parts in three different movies at the same time. Meet them again later in 'Studio 29' discothèque (the place to be seen) in Bombay International Hotel, junction of D. Vacha Rd and Marine Drive or RGs at the Nataraj Hotel on Marine Drive. Temporary membership at both places for foreigners is generally possible.

Bombay is rather exclusive when it comes to sports. For the best facilities, you'll either have to pay out for an expensive hotel (the Taj and the President for tennis, golf and swimming; the Oberoi for the best swimming-pool) or hover round in hope of an introduction to the two best social clubs—the **Bombay Gymkhana**, Mahatma Gandhi Road (tel 204101) and the **Willingdon Sports Club**, K. Khadye Marg (tel 391754).

Swimming in the sea round Bombay is not really on, the water is badly polluted. If you want a swim, go up to **Breach Candy Club** on Bhulabhai Desai Rd, 1 km north of Hanging Gardens. This has a large, fun swimming-pool in the shape of India before Partition—'Ceylon' is the kiddies' pool. Breach Candy has several other good recreation facilities too, but only lets foreign guests in on production of their passport.

Any good hotel should be able to arrange a game of golf at **Presidency Golf Club** (tel 5513670), about an hour's drive out of town, and worth it. The Taj and Oberoi hotels can arrange sailing, horse-riding, court games and buggy-rides round town—but only for their guests. Fishing is easier: apply to the Secretary of Maharastra State Angling Association (tel 571641) for temporary membership. Good katla, rahu, mirgil, bekti and gorami fishing at Powai Lake, 22 km (14 miles) by rail to Andheri and then 5 km (31 miles) further by road. A day's angling will cost you around Rs100, inclusive of boat-hire, tackle and bait.

Horse Racing at the Mahalaxmi Race Course, opposite Haji Ali Mosque, takes place every Sunday and public holiday between November and March. The big meetings are in February and March and the cream of Bombay society turns out to be seen.

SHOPPING

Here, as in Delhi, you can buy practically anything, and often a lot cheaper than anywhere else in India. For an idea of what's available and and how much it should cost, start at the **Central Cottage Industries Emporium**, 34 Chhatrapati Shivaji Maharaj Marg (tel 2022491), just up the road from the Taj Mahal Hotel. Although not as good as the main branch in Delhi, this fixed-price place stocks a wide range of regional crafts: silks from Kanchipuram, carpets from Kashmir, saris from Varanasi, marblework and jewellery from Agra and Jaipur. Probably the best general buy is top-quality Bangalore silk—either as material or in sari form (from Rs500 to 20 000.). Opening hours are 10 am to 6.30 pm Monday to Saturday (closed Sunday). To compare prices and quality, there's another good government emporium, **Khadi and Village Industries Emporium**, at 286 Dadabhai Naoroji Road. **Gujarat Government Handicrafts Emporium**, Khetan Bhavan, J.N. Tata Rd (tel 296292) has the best reputation for high-quality crafts—mainly silk, cotton, bright appliqué-work, brass and wood. Finally, before launching yourself into the high- street shops and markets, visit the shopping arcades at the Taj and Oberoi hotels. The Oberoi arcade is especially good for leather shoes and bags.

The old **Crawford Market** (1867), now renamed **Mahatma Phule Market**, is one of India's best. Raw, bloody, vital and colourful. Travelling in by taxi, keep your window wound up. Once there, resist the attentions of persistent 'guides', and be on your guard against pickpockets. Crawford Market is essentially a fruit, flower, vegetable, meat and fish market, but you can find many other things too, ranging from toy dogs and screeching parakeets to heaps of old machinery bits. The favourite anecdote in nearby **Chor Bazaar** (Thieves Market) is that you can be sold spare parts from your own car.

Visit Crawford Market around 6 to 7 pm, when crowds are thinner and shopping more civilised. Inside the covered warehouse, you'll find **Hakimi Stores**, which does a complete range of spices and curry powders: all the ingredients you need to reproduce good Indian cooking back home. Alternatively (and these make good little presents), you can buy small packs of ready-made curry powders.

Just outside the covered market, **Gulf Silk Centre**, 406 Shaikh Memon St, is a friendly shop—very useful indeed for picking up small, attractive last-minute presents before flying home. Choose from a wide range of silk/cotton saris, shawls and bedcovers, and from a marvellous selection of aromatic perfumes and spices. Men can pick up cool, practical 'Congress' outfits here (*kurta*/pant sets), which double up as jazzy pajamas. Across the road at **Chinubhai B. Shah**, 346 Abdul Rehman St, you can buy the Congress hat to go with them. For making fabric buys into pants, suits, saris etc., try **Mod Tailor** at 408 Shaikh Memon St. This place also has some nice outfits for the ladies—traditional three-part suits (*kameez* top, *churidhar* trousers, plus *dupata* scarf) at reasonable rates. Again, very cool and practical. Buy cotton clothes and materials at **M.G. Market**, just right of Crawford Market. For marvellous jewellery and antiques, visit **Zaveri Bazaar** off Mumbadevi Rd; for brass and copper, the adjoining **Brass Bazaar**; and for smuggled goods, leather and curios, the aforementioned Chor Bazaar.

Bombay shops are generally open from 10 am to 7 pm daily although many bazaars and most shops in the Oberoi arcade stay open till 9 pm, except Fridays.

WHERE TO STAY

Living in Bombay is very expensive, and good rooms are hard to come by. With housing such a problem, decent hotels are often fully booked, and the few habitable budget lodges packed out. In the former instance, make advance reservations; in the latter, arrive very early in the morning to snap up any rooms going. The most difficult time is the January/February high season.

Prices listed below do not include tax.

Luxury (US$100–250 per room night)
The top hotels are all central. More an institution than a hotel is the **Taj Mahal**, with its new addition the **Taj Mahal Intercontinental**, Apollo Bunder (tel 2023366, cable PALACE, telex 11-82442, 83837 TAJB IN, fax 022-2872711). The old building is one of Bombay's major landmarks: opened in 1903 and accorded (with its new skyscraper relative) the accolade of being one of the world's 12 best hotels. It is a major focal point of all visitors to Bombay. Rooms are US$155 for standard rooms and up to US$700 for a suite, and (if you have the choice) are best at the top of the new building, with views overlooking the sea, or in one of the large sea-facing rooms in the 'old Taj'. Guests also get the fine swimming-pool, the famous health centre, an excellent discotheque and the resident astrologer. Food

is superb. What the *Times* newspaper in London wrote in 1903 still applies, the Taj is '...the finest caravanserai in the East.'

Over at Nariman Point, the soaring **Oberoi Towers** (tel 2024343, cable OBHOTEL, tlx 84153 OBBY IN, fax 022-2043282, 2041505) is the tallest building in India, with 35 storeys. Efficient and personal, it has an opulent reception lounge and is superbly located for shopping centres and the airport. Overlooking the Arabian Sea on all sides, it offers elegantly furnished rooms (meticulously colour-matched) at US$155 single, US$170 double. For stunning views over Marine Drive and Back Bay, get one as high up as possible. Facilities include six speciality restaurants, massive swimming-pool, high-rise landscaped garden and vast shopping arcade. Only one other hotel comes close to this one and it's next door. Unmatched facilities and designer elegance are the keynotes of **The Oberoi Bombay**, Nariman Point (tel 2025757, cable OBBY IN, tlx 011-82337, fax 022-2043282, 2041505). This new structure (opened 1987) features an imposing 11-storey atrium, a high-level pool with cascading waterfall, a string quartet in the polished granite lobby, and a futuristic 'environmental unit' in the health club (lie back and computer-control your sauna, steam-bath, jacuzzi, sun-tan, even tropical shower). Geared to the top corporate business traveller, the decor may lack personality, but all standards are very high. There's a 24-hour business centre, an exclusive Supper Club, and every conceivable five-star amenity. In addition to three select restaurants and a roof-top bar, guests arriving in the dead of night are greeted by an immaculately turned-out butler bearing gifts. His first question will be: 'Does sir/madam prefer the juice or the champagne?' Rooms are priced at US$200 single, US$215 double. They are all beautifully furnished, and command prime views of the metropolis and the sea.

Fourth down the list, and probably more in the range of the general traveller, is Taj Group's **Hotel President**, 90 Cuffe Parade, Colaba (tel 2150808, tlx 011-84135, fax 022-2151201). This hotel remains one of the warmest, most pleasant upmarket hotels in India—a refreshing contrast to large businessman's hotels like The Oberoi. Many couples and families stay at the President: they like its informal atmosphere and relaxing pool, its famous service and food, and its cosy, stylish rooms—more reasonable at US$125 single, US$140 double.

Other luxury and five-star hotels are located in the suburbs and toward the airport. At Juhu Beach, 25 km (15½ miles) from the city centre but only 7 km (4¾ miles) from the airport are a range of properties. The **Centaur Hotel Juhu Beach** (tel 6113090, fax 022-6116343) has every conceivable facility and rooms from US$95. The **Holiday Inn** (tel 6204444, fax 022-6204452) has rooms from US$100. The **Ramada Inn Palm Grove** (tel 6112323, fax 022-6113682) has rooms from US$95. Nearer town is the **Welcomegroup Searock Sheraton** (tel 6425454, tlx 011-71230, fax 022-6408046) at Land's End, Bandra. The Searock has good restaurants and for those who overindulge, an excellent health club. Rooms are from US$120.

One of India's best hotels is located next to the international airport at Sahar. The **Leela Kempinski Bombay** (tel 6363636, tlx 011-79236, fax 022-6360606, 6341865) has excellent service, good rooms from US$150, good restaurants and a health club.

Mid-range (US$25–100 per room night)
The **Ambassador**, Veer Nariman Rd, Churchgate (tel 2041131, tlx 011-82918, 022-2040004), has a good central location, popular roof-top revolving restaurant, useful facilities, and attractive single/double rooms from US$75. A less expensive hotel on

Marine Drive is **Hotel Nataraj** (tel 2044161, fax 022-2043864) with rooms from Rs1200. Its advantage is the classiest disco in town—**RGs**—but otherwise lacks charm. At Santa Cruz (domestic airport) The **Centaur Hotel** has 24 check-in/check-out facilities and is only walking distance from the domestic airport. Rooms are from US$80. A Colaba option is **Fariyas**, 25 Arthur Street (tel 2042911) with good restaurants, including a roof garden, and rooms from Rs1200.

Budget (under US$25/Rs750 per room night)
In the downtown area of the city there are two particularly fine hotels offering mid-range standards at a relatively low price. **Hotel Apollo**, Lansdowne Rd, behind Regal Cinema, Colaba (tel 2020223) is well known for style and comfort. It has a nice restaurant, attentive service, and pleasant air-con rooms from Rs700. Ask for one with a sea view. Even better is **Hotel Diplomat**, 24–26 Merriwether Rd (tel 2021661), located just behind the Taj Hotel. It's in serious need of renovation, but travellers still love it. Friendly staff, quiet location, homely atmosphere, and cosy, livable rooms (with TV and balcony) at Rs550. For good views of the Arabian Sea, try **Sea Green Hotel** (tel 222294) at 145 Marine Drive. Staff can be po-faced, but the rooms are good value at Rs350 single and Rs450 double. Don't be fobbed off with one with (depressing) rear views of the cricket stadium. Another option is **Shelly's Hotel**, 30 P.J. Ramchandani Marg (tel 240229, 240270), still very friendly, with rooms at Rs350/500 with air-conditioning.

Moving up to the city, there's **Chateau Windsor Guest House**, 86 Veer Nariman Rd, next to the Ambassador Hotel (tel 2043376), a very friendly place with great roof views, useful facilities, and smart rooms (disinfected daily) from Rs250. A reasonable fallback is **Hotel Oasis**, 276 Shahid Bhagat Singh Rd, near the post office. This is a quiet, clean place with a good central location. Best rooms are the Rs350 air-con doubles.

Most budget travellers stay in the Colaba area, a number of 'cheapies' being situated just behind the Taj Hotel. Space and hygiene are at a premium. For maximum comfort, stay at **Whalley's Guest House**, 41 Merriwether Rd (tel 234206). Renovated, this old favourite offers huge rooms, complete with verandahs and Victorian tub-baths on pedestals, at low rates (Rs200) and breakfast is included. Ask for a top-floor room with balcony overlooking the street. If you're feeling more extravagant, splash out on one of the new air-conditioned double rooms with tiled bathrooms; they're the perfect antidote to hot, steamy Bombay. Needless to say, the average backpacker still makes a beeline for popular **Rex/Stiffles**, round the corner from the Taj Hotel. Just like its more fêted neighbour, this place has become an institution with rooms at Rs100. Despite its many drawbacks travellers love it, for the warm family atmosphere and the grim-faced security guards, keeping Colaba's relentless touts at bay. One place that will *never* change is Salvation Army's **Red Shield Guest House**, just across the road from Rex. It's the obvious shoestring fallback, with cheap dormitory beds at Rs75, inclusive of three meals (you have to get up for breakfast: a booming gong sounds at an unearthly hour in the morning until all guests are at table). It's a great place for meeting fellow travellers, but has poor luggage security. **Samson Guest House**, 2 minutes' walk from the Taj, is a useful alternative (Rs250). This place is run with efficiency by a tolerant ex-police officer, and has clean, comfy double rooms (with common bathroom). The nearby **Shilton Hotel** is tricky to find (look for the 'Sex and Alcohol Clinic' next to the movie theatre, by the circle) but is a real bargain with tiny, but spotless air-conditioned double rooms at Rs200. Equally good value is provided by **Seashore Hotel** at 1–49 Kamal Mansion, Arthur Bunder Rd (tel 2874237). Nice people and lovely large sea-view rooms.

Given the difficulty of finding rooms in Colaba at high season, you might do well to stay in the city instead. There are a few good places here, very well-located for the post office, tourist office, VT station and the better cinemas. Try first **City Lodge**, 121 City Terrace, W.H. Marg, opposite Victoria Terminus station (tel 265515), which is also a tailor's and cloth merchant's shop. Ask for either of the Rs150 roof-top doubles (rooms 5 and 6), which have first-rate city views. This place is run by a very pleasant family. Alternatively, there's **Rupam Lodge**, 239 P. D'Mello Rd, just past the post office (tel 267103/4), with 24-hour room service, telephones in rooms, and (a real rarity) thick mattresses on beds. It's rather run-down nowadays, but rooms are still cheap and it's often full. For a few rupees more, you can enjoy a much comfier stay at **Lord Hotel**, just off P. D'Mello Rd, at 301 Mangalore St. This has friendly staff, popular beer bar, and really nice rooms. With all the above hotels, don't forget the golden rule: the early bird gets the vacant room!

In **Bandra** and many of the midtown areas small guest-houses have recently become very popular. The tourist office also keeps a list of paying guest accommodation.

EATING OUT

When it comes to food, Bombay has no equal. It is the best place in India to enjoy good cuisine—not just Indian, but everything else. But food here is very expensive—Rs30 for a *thali*, and Rs35 for a *masala dosa*, may be cheap by Western standards, but seasoned Indian travellers would choke. This said, few people do complain, especially those who've just arrived lean and hungry from spartan travels in Tamil Nadu or Kerala.

The Taj Hotel is often the first place people head for when they want good food. It has a nice choice of air-conditioned restaurants, starting with the mid-range **Shamiana** coffee-shop with all-you-can-eat buffet breakfast for Rs100 and buffet lunch for Rs150, working up to the sophisticated **Tanjore** (*biriani* or *thali* suppers from Rs 250, tying in with cultural dance entertainment programmes at 7.45 pm, 9.45 pm and 10.45 pm), and hitting the heights up at the **Rooftop Rendezvous** superb Continental dishes, notably French, from Rs300. The **Menage à Trois** restaurant, also at the rooftop, offers designer dining from an exciting lunchtime menu created by London's well known chef and restaurateur, Anthony Worrall-Thompson. Well-presented, well-priced food from Rs300 and superb views from the 21st floor.

But it's the Oberoi Towers, Nariman Point, that has the prestige restaurant in Bombay. This is the **Cafe Royal**, a very select Parisian-style eatery where every item of food is specially flown in from France. Start with *escargots* or smoked salmon, move on to lobster, king prawn or steak for a main course, and conclude with *crêpe suzettes*. To wash it all down, you've a wide choice of vintage wines, or the speciality 'fruit punch'. Next door at the new Oberoi Bombay hotel, the French **Rotisserie** restaurant offers an Executive Lunch for Rs200, while the downstairs **Kandahar** serves authentic North-West Frontier food (huge portions) from about Rs250. It's a toss-up between the Kandahar and Oberoi Towers' **Mughal Room** (famous tandoori cuisine) for the best Indian restaurant in a Bombay hotel. The Towers also has a Polynesian restaurant, the **Outrigger**, which has a good-value lunchtime buffet for Rs165 and is certainly popular. Meanwhile, the famous **Samarkhand**—a 24-hour coffee shop overlooking busy Marine Drive—continues to enchant visitors and residents alike. It's one of the 'places to be seen' in Bombay.

Another good-value restaurant is the Taj-run **Rangoli** (tel 234678) at the NCPA , Nariman Point. Open every day with a good buffet lunch for Rs120, it's popular with local offices staff—reservations are needed at lunchtime and at weekends.

Nearly all Bombay's restaurants are more interesting than those of Delhi. This is because city residents eat out far more—their prime concern is making money, and they have little time for cooking. Bombay is not unlike New York in that people go out to be seen, and because most accommodation is so cramped they prefer the space of restaurants. If Bombayites choose a hotel restaurant, it's usually for something of value (like the buffet lunch at Taj Hotel's **Crystal Room**) or something fancy (like pizzas, home-made ice-cream, and serenading violinists at President Hotel's delightful **Trattoria**). But in the main, they stick to local restaurants like the renowned **Shalimar** in Bhendi Bazaar. This place serves cheap, delicious North Indian specialities (a whole leg of lamb for Rs60) and has a real family atmosphere. For fast food, they favour **Open House** opposite Churchgate station (pricey, but good) or the nearby **Sahyadri** restaurant (not only burgers and hot dogs, but excellent Punjabi cuisine too). South Indian fare—local-style—is nowhere better than at **Sanmans** (behind Government of India tourist office) or **Sadkar** (opposite Churchgate station) restaurants.

Many travellers prefer to stick to tried-and-tested favourites. Places like **Talk of the Town**, 143 Marine Drive (top of Veer Nariman Rd), with its popular lunchtime buffets (Rs75) and breezy open-air section, overlooking the seafront. Or for the best Chinese food in town the **China Garden** (tel 8280842) at Kemp's Corner, 131 August Kranti Marg, offering hot 'n' spicy *Szechwan* cuisine for about Rs150 per head in a beautiful setting of cultured trees, greenery and marble. It's the place for spotting Bombay's glitterati and reservations are recommended. Or (for cheaper Chinese fare) **Kamling** in Veer Nariman Rd and the ever popular **Nanking** (tel 20205940) near the Taj —opposite Cottage Industries.

But it's Colaba that has the best cheap restaurants. At lunchtime, people still pack into friendly **Martin's** for Goan specialities like grilled fish and fiery pork vindaloos. Diplomat Hotel's **Silver Plate** has a good reputation for cheap, reliable vegetarian food—continental and Indian—and is well-patronised by locals. **Dipty's Juice Bar** opposite Rex Hotel has delicious lassis, juices, ice-creams and snacks. There's a line of popular eateries running up Shahid Bhagat Singh Rd, starting with **Food Inn** (a 'Catch and Carry' fast-food place, serving cheap North Indian, Hyderabadi, Chinese and Japanese fare); moving up to **Leopold's** (English breakfasts, chilled beer and dropouts—very seedy now, so watch your money); **Laxmi Vilas** (down alley past Leopold's, for good-value thalis); **Kamat** (opposite Leopold's, good for ice-cream and vegetarian snacks); and **Delhi Durbar** (best mid-range Indian restaurant in Colaba, specialising in tandoor dishes and Indian sweets). A surprising number of backpackers turn up in Taj Hotel's **Shamiana** lounge—word's got around that you can have unlimited coffee here.

An excellent booklet—*Flavours* was published in 1988 and available from *Nalanda*, the bookshop in the Taj. Although a few years old, this book is still a great guide; it not only lists 84 restaurants by cuisine and locale but gives details of the menus.

GENERAL INFORMATION

Tourist Offices
Government of India Tourist Office, 123 M. Karve Rd, Churchgate (tel 293144), is open 8.30 am–5.30 pm Monday to Friday, 8.30 am–12.30 pm Saturday, closed Sunday. Sadly understaffed, but helpful. Good handout information, including when in stock an excellent monthly city-guide called *Bombay Calling* (also available from any bookstore). Book your MTDC city tour here (they run twice daily except Monday 9 am–1 pm, 2–6.30 pm; tickets Rs35) and get your city map. Government of India also have tourist counters (24-hour service) at both airports.

Government of Maharashtra Tourist Office, Madame Cama Rd (tel 2026713). Government of Goa Tourist Office, Bombay Central Station (tel 396288) is useful if you're planning to do the Goa–Diu routes in this book. So is the Government of Gujarat Tourist Office, Dhanraj Mahal, Ch. Shivaji Rd, Apollo Bunder (tel 243886).

Airline Offices
The airport telephone number (apt) is usually only answered a few hours before and after a scheduled arrival/departure. **Indian Airlines** (tel 2023031, 2021441 apt 6144433, 6114433, 6112850, 142 and 143), **Air India** (tel 20224142, 2026464, apt 6329090, 6226767), and **Singapore Airlines** (tel 2023365, 2023316 apt 6327024, 6327861) are all in the Air India building, Nariman Point. **Cathay Pacific** (tel 2029112/3 apt 6321965/6), **Delta** (tel 2024024, 2029020 apt 6324769, 6349890) and **Air France** (tel 2025021, 2024818 apt 6328070) are located in the Taj Hotel, Apollo Bunder. **Aeroflot** (tel 221743 apt 6320178) and **Swiss Air** (tel 222402, 222559 apt 6326084) are both on Veer Nariman Rd. **Lufthansa** (tel 2020887, 2023430 apt 6321485) is in Express Towers, Nariman Point, and **British Airways** (tel 220888 apt 6329061/4) is in Vulcan Insurance Building, Churchgate. **Emirates** (tel 2871648 apt 6365730/1) Mittal Chambers, Nariman Point.

Travel Agents
The better ones are **SITA World Travel**, 8 Atlanta Building, Nariman Point (tel 2233155); **Mercury Travel**, 70 V.B. Gandhi Marg (tel 2023663) with a desk at Oberoi Hotel; **Cox & Kings,** 270/2 Dr D. Naoroji Road, (tel 2043065); **Thomas Cook**, Cooks Building, Dadabhai Naoroji Road (tel 2048556). **American Express** is at Majithia Chamber, Dadabhai Naoroji Road (tel 2046349).

Cheap Flights
For cheap flights, visa assistance, student travel service etc., contact **Space Travels**, Nanabhay Mansion, 4th floor, Sir P.M. Rd (tel 2864773), open 10 am–5 pm Monday to Friday, 10.30 am–3 pm Saturday. Spaceway also has agencies at Panjim and Calangute, in Goa. Discounted tickets are also offered by touts outside the American Express building, and from budget hotels around Mereweather Rd.

Consulates
Among the many countries represented in Bombay (listed in telephone directory) are **UK**, 2nd floor, HongKong Bank Building, M.G. Rd (tel 274874); **USA**, Lincoln House, 78 Bhulabhai Desai Rd (tel 8223611); **France**, N. Gamadia Road, off Pedder Road (tel 4949808, 4948277); **Netherlands**, 16 M. Karve Rd (tel 296840); Japan, 1B Dhanukar Marg (tel 4933857, 4934610); **Germany**, 10th floor, Hoechst House, Nariman Point (tel 232422); and **Australia**, Maker Towers, B Block, 41 Cuffe Parade (tel 211071/2).

Miscellaneous

Foreigners' Registration Department is at Annexe 2, Office of the Commissioner of Police, Dadabhai Naoroji Rd, near Crawford Market (tel 268111).

The **GPO** is on Nagar Chowk, near VT station. Open 8 am–8 pm (*poste restante* 8 am–6 pm) Monday to Saturday, 10 am–5.30 pm Sunday. For Colaba residents, there's a useful little sub-post office in Mandlik Rd, just behind the Taj Hotel. **The Central Telegraph Office** is located at Flora Fountain. **State Bank of India** has several branches (there's a handy one behind the Government of India tourist office, Churchgate) and banking facilities at the airport are surprisingly efficient. Good **bookshops** include Nalanda in the Taj Mahal Hotel, Strand (just off Sir P.M. Rd) and Wheeler's (branches at all three rail stations). A readable introduction to Bombay is Gillian Tindall's *City of Gold, the Biography of Bombay* (London, 1982, reprinted by Penguin India 1992).

Route 4—Golden Goa

Once the jewel of Portugal's eastern empire, Goa still retains many of the ways of the old Portuguese colony and is a firm tourist favourite. A lush, green territory with mile upon mile of beautiful beaches, the emphasis here is very much on fun and relaxation. Good food, good wine, song and dance and general merriment—just the place for winding down and enjoying life. Goa is famous for its beaches to suit every taste and pocket, from high-class Aguada and Bogmalo, to busy, bubbling Calangute and Colva, to party-going Anjuna and Chapora, to peaceful, palm-fringed paradise coves with not a soul in sight. But Goa is not simply beaches. Within striking distance of the capital, Panjim, one of India's prettiest cities, are a variety of historic temples, churches, lakes and parks, market towns and old-style Portuguese villas. A short drive away, there's the impressive ghost city of Catholic cathedrals, Old Goa. Peaceful and serene, full of things to do and see, Goa is a self-contained holiday spot where many travellers end up staying a lot longer than originally planned.

Season: October to May.
Monsoons: June to October.
Climate: 21° to 32°C.
Route duration: 7–14 days (or longer).

TRAVEL ITINERARY

Bombay—Goa 594 km (371 miles)

Air
Indian Airlines have at least two flights daily between Bombay and Goa (Rs945); during the peak winter months of December and January a third and occasionally a fourth daily flight are introduced. There is a daily flight from Delhi (IC467) (Rs2862)

Portuguese-style church, Goa

that continues to Cochin; (Rs1313) and returns on the same route (IC468). There are also flights to and from Ahmedabad (Rs1509), Bangalore (Rs1107) and Madras (Rs2862). At Goa's Dabolim airport, major hotels have reception counters and many operate free transfers by coach for prospective guests. Otherwise, it's an airport bus or a Rs200 taxi-ride (27 km, 7 miles) into the capital, Panjim. East West Airways are expected to operate from Bombay, and Vayudoot has flights from Pune and Hyderabad.

There are direct charter flights to Dabolim from Germany (Condor), England (Monarch and Air Europe), Finland (Emere) and Denmark (Time Air). Flights from Portugal, France, Sweden and Austria are also being negotiated. It may be possible to buy seats on these flights without the hotel expenses—it's certainly worth trying. The suspended Air India flights to Dubai and Kuwait may have been re-instated by the time you read this.

Sea

For the time being the Shipping Corporation of India steamer service between Bombay and Goa is suspended. With luck it will be reintroduced soon, for the journey is one of the most leisurely in India. When operating it leaves New Ferry Wharf, Mallet Bunder, Bombay (reservations from MTDC, Madame Cama Rd, Nariman Point (tel 2026713) 10 am–3 pm daily, except Monday). Return reservations from M/s V.S. Dempo and Co., Custom Wharf (tel 3842) opposite the steamer jetty in Panjim. The service is suspended altogether during the monsoon months (June to September), and when weather is rough. The journey each way takes 22 hours. If sleeping on deck, you can hire bedding. Prices are likely to range from Rs75 for the lower deck to Rs300 for a 2-berth cabin. With meals and iced beer served on board, the ferry can be the most pleasant way of getting to Goa. Keep a watchful eye on your baggage, though.

Rail

A 1-m gauge line links Goa with Miraj from where broad-gauge trains run to Bangalore, Bombay and Pune. Trains between Bombay and Vasco da Gama (for

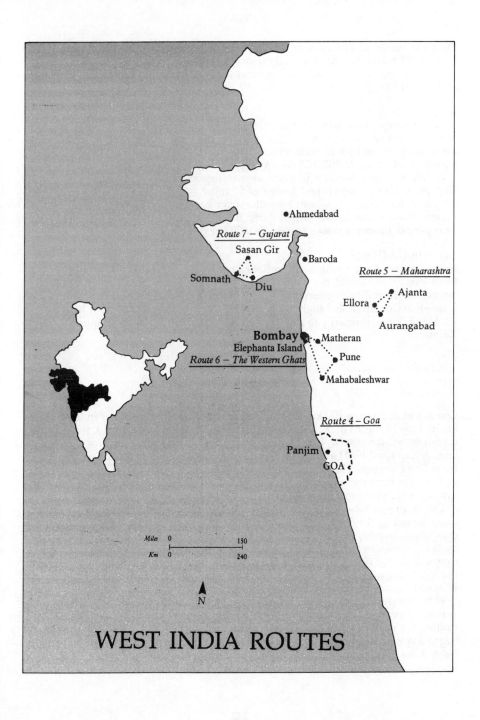

Route 7 – Gujarat

●Ahmedabad

Sasan Gir

Somnath

●Baroda

Diu

Route 5 – Maharashtra

Ellora ● ●Ajanta

Aurangabad

Bombay
Elephanta Island ●Matheran

Route 6 – The Western Ghats

●Pune

●Mahabaleshwar

Route 4 – Goa

Panjim ●

GOA ●

Miles 0   150

Km 0   240

N

WEST INDIA ROUTES

Bogmalo beach) and Margao or 'Madgaon'; (get off here for buses to Panjim) take a long 20/22 hours, and are generally uncomfortable.

Rail bookings can be made in Panjim at the KTC Terminal (tel 45620), at Margao Station (tel 22252) and Vasco Station (tel 2396).

Road

Several luxury buses daily (16 hours), both state and private, link Bombay and Goa. Most of them are the dreaded 'video' variety. The least unpleasant, by all accounts, are those operated by Maharastra State Transport Development Corporation. There's a particularly good MRSTDC bus leaving Bombay for Panjim at 3 pm daily.

If driving from Bombay in your own transport break your journey at the Taj Group's **Gateway Riverview Lodge** at Chiplun (tel 57, 59, 67 via Lote, 2853 via Chiplun). The Lodge is 267 km (165 miles) from Bombay and 226 km (140 miles) from Panjim. Rooms cost Rs595 single, Rs995 double except during the Christmas-New Year period when the rates go up to Rs1500 per double.

CONTINUATIONS

From Goa, you can continue on to Bangalore by air (IC524 Rs1077), rail (21 hours from Vasco), or bus (16-hour video coach). Or take a bus from Panjim to Hubli (7 hours), for the rail connection to Hospet/Hampi (4½ hours). A popular continuation is down to Cochin (IC467 flight daily (Rs1313), or crippling 22/24-hour haul by bus, via Mangalore—primarily to stay on the beach circuit, but also as an introduction to Kerala.

GOA

Goa is a long, narrow 100 km (62½ miles) of coastline running between the Arabian Sea and the Western Ghats. It has some of the best beaches in the world, and is India's favourite winter resort. The Mediterranean feel of the place (it was Portuguese territory up until 1961) adds to its charm, and many travellers come here for a break from India proper. There is a lot more to Goa than just its beaches—it is full of picturesque forts and churches, temples and towns, hills and mountains—and many visitors return time and time again.

The origins of Goa are lost in legend. The popular myth is that it was reclaimed from the sea by the sixth *avatar* (incarnation) of Vishnu. Historically, it is datable to the 3rd century BC, when it formed part of the Mauryan Empire. Later, it was ruled by the Chalukyan kings of Badami (580–750), and by the Kadambas (credited with first settling the site of Old Goa in the mid-11th century). In 1469 it was seized from the Vijayanagar kings by the Bahamani Muslims, and in 1510 it was taken from the Bijapur kings by the Portuguese.

With its natural harbours and broad rivers, Goa made the ideal base for the trading, seafaring, evangelical Portuguese, bent equally on spreading Catholicism and controlling the eastern spice route. They named it Goa Doirada, or 'Golden Goa', and began a systematic programme of building churches and destroying Hindu temples. Behind the conquistadors came Jesuit and Franciscan missionaries, who achieved spectacular success in converting most Goans from Hinduism to Roman Catholicism, largely an achievement of the Inquisition, which arrived in 1560. The Jesuits also introduced the first cashew saplings to Goa and Kerala, and developed the art of cultivating coconut trees, which became Goa's primary crops.

Portuguese control began in Old Goa, and gradually extended to include most of the territory, displacing a succession of local Hindu rulers in the process. Old Goa remained their capital until a terrible outbreak of plague in 1738 prompted a gradual move to Panjim. Portugal's power then began to fade in Europe in the late 18th century, during the brief spell of British occupation of Goa during the Napoleonic Wars. But all three pockets of Portuguese power in India—Goa, Daman and Diu—remained essentially intact right up to December 1961, when they finally returned to Indian control.

The last 30-odd years of Indian rule have hardly touched Goa's old Portuguese character and flavour (it is still a sleepy, laid-back Lisbon of the East), and has brought it considerable benefits. The Portuguese did little for Goa—until 1961 there were no bridges, no roads (just bullock tracks once out of Panjim) and no electricity. The Indians built bridges over Goa's principal rivers, the Mandovi and the Zuari, and Panjim was at last connected up with north and south Goa. They also developed Pilar Harbour—a vast natural harbour backing onto a rich mountain of iron ore—and Goa became wealthy practically overnight.

Finally, having constructed paved roads, modern buildings and hotels, and proper communications, the Indian Government prepared Goa for tourism. The potential was always there—the charming little villages with their sunny piazzas, the un-broken miles of wide sandy beaches, the pretty whitewashed churches and chapels, and the exotic combination of the Latin and Indian. But it was only in the 1960s, with the arrival of the hippies, that its vast tourist market was at last recognised.

The Goan people are not particularly keen on tourism, feeling it a threat to their culture and traditions. 'Tourism brings degradation', was one typical comment. 'Drugs, pimping, gambling, touting—all these things come around. Police are doing something now, but it is too little and too late.' There's an even fiercer reaction against 'Indian big business', especially since Goa finally gained her own identity, on 31 May 1987, and became the 25th state in the Union of India. As one aggrieved local remarked, 'The Indians are coming and taking all our land. Over the last ten years, our population has doubled—it's getting all crowded, not only with tourists but with financial sharks from elsewhere in the country buying up all our land. It's not good for the Goan people, you know. We'll be submerged as a minority. Even our culture is being wiped out. After twenty years, you'll find nothing of it.' The only thing that made this man smile was the news that police had just arrested some Western girls for topless sunbathing on Colva and Anjuna beaches.

Though the main industries of Goa are mining, fishing and tourism, most of her million or so inhabitants make their living from agriculture: the three main crops being rice, coconut and cashew. The population is pretty equally divided between Catholics and Hindus, both faiths coexisting in a state of pleasant harmony. The Goans are a basically simple, devout people, happiest when celebrating the feasts of their saints or deities. They love anyone who loves a good party.

The climate in Goa is most pleasant from November to February. Less crowded but hot from March to April. Avoid May—Indian annual holidays, when some beaches are packed with camera-clicking voyeurs. Monsoon is June to October.

GETTING AROUND

Goa is a surprisingly big place. It may look like just a dot on the map, but actually comprises 3702 sq km (1428 sq miles) of lush, attractive landscape dotted with hundreds of churches and chapels, fringed with an endless expanse of paddy fields and palm groves, all of it saturated with history. The unique mix of Portuguese and Indian cultures is apparent everywhere—stately Catholic cathedrals and charming terraced bungalows existing alongside traditional Hindu temples and Indian-style dwellings. While most of Goa's activities (swimming, water-sports, parties) take place on the beaches, most of her sights are inland—and they are well worth appreciating at leisure before getting out the sun-oil.

Goa has four main towns: **Panjim** in the centre (with its 'local' beaches of Miramar and Dona Paula); **Mapusa**, above the Mandovi River, which services the northern beaches of Vagator/Chapora, Anjuna/Baga, Calangute and Aguada; **Margao**, below the River Zuari, which connects to the southern beaches of Majorda, Colva/Benaulim, Betelbatim and Betul; and **Vasco da Gama**, near the Dabolim airport, the gateway to the exclusive luxury beach of Bogmalo. Some useful distances are: Panjim to Vasco (30 km: 18¾ miles), Panjim to Calangute (16 km: 10 miles), Panjim to Vagator (33 km: 20½ miles), Panjim to Tiracol (42 km: 26¼ miles), Margao to Dabolim (29 km: 18 miles), Vasco to Dabolim (3 km: 2 miles) and Vasco to Margao (30 km: 18¾ miles).

For short hops between these towns, there are either local buses (Rs1–5 to any destination, from Panjim's Kodamba bus terminal, near Patto Bridge) or shared taxis, which can work out just as cheap. Motorbike 'taxis' pi¨k up from the bus-stand and from the post office, offering cheap rides up to Altino Hill etc. Panjim, a convenient base for exploring Goa, is just 20 minutes (12 km: 7½ miles) from Mapusa, and 1 hour (33 km: 20½ miles via Courtillim) from Margao, for the northern and southern beaches respectively. To tour the beaches themselves, there are motorbikes for hire at Calangute and Anjuna, though these are expensive, and rather dangerous.

FOOD AND DRINK

A delicious mixture of Asian and Western cooking, Goan cuisine is a popular escape from the usual Indian diet of *thali*, *masala dosa* and curry. Long-term travellers flock here for the continental-style beach restaurants, with their pancakes, spaghetti, baked beans on toast, and chips. New arrivals, unaware of the pigs' diet, tend to favour the traditional Goan pork sausages (*chourisso*) or classic pork dishes like *vindaloo* (marinated in toddy vinegar, and very spicy) and *sorpatel* (pig's liver pickled in hot savoury sauce). *Xacuti* is a biting-hot coconut/*masala* preparation of chicken or mutton, and the rich, layered *bebinca* is a traditional, very filling Goan sweet made of coconut and jaggery. The other main fare is, of course, seafood. The Arabian Sea lapping Goa's coastline yields a variety of delicately flavoured fish and shellfish, including crab, oysters, king prawns, massive shark steaks and snapping-fresh lobsters.

Goa also has the cheapest beer in India as well as the famous *feni*, a raw, potent brew (usually distilled just once) made from either the cashew apple or the coconut palm. The local Goan wines are also popular and cheap, this being one of the few places in India where 'wine' shops actually sell wine, not just whisky.

Most of Goa's best restaurants are isolated from tourist centres. Authentic Goan food is nowhere better than at local homes but the **Oberoi** on Bogmalo beach prepares

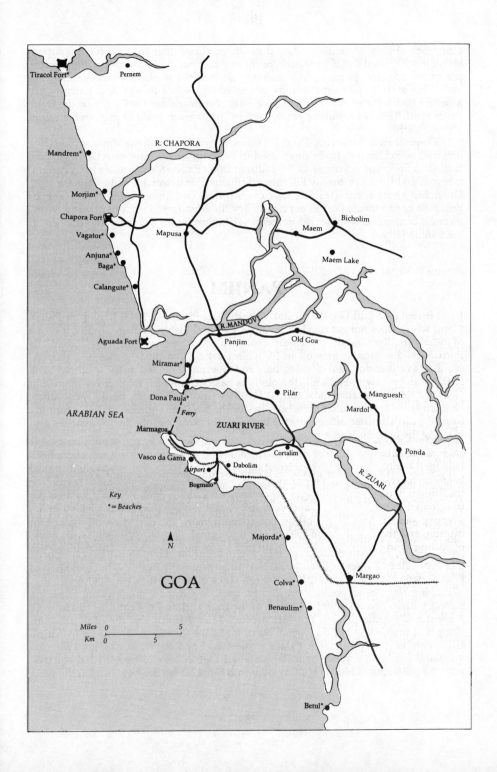

a number of local-style dishes found nowhere else. Either turn up for the superb buffet lunch (about Rs325 per head), or make a night of it—savouring grilled lobster, prawn *balchao*, and pomfret, followed by a visit to the poolside barbecue, dancing under the stars to romantic sounds of one of Goa's live bands. Alternatively, try **Martin's Beach Corner** at Caranzalem, a 3-km (2-mile) ride out of Panjim on the Dona Paula road. This is a fabulous place, famous for its fresh seafood prepared straight off the beach.

O'Coqueiro's at Porvorim, 4 km (2½ miles) out of Panjim on the Mapusa road (hire motorbike-taxi from Patto bridge), used to be *the* place for top-notch Goan cuisine. It still has a good atmosphere. **O'Pescador** at Dona Paula (8 km: 5 miles from Panjim) is better, and serves primarily Polynesian cuisine. For delectable Indo-Chinese food, **Goenchin** restaurant (tel 5718), near Mahalaxmi temple in Ponda serves generous.cheap meals (Rs150 per head). Try the Mandarin Fish, but go easy on the incandescent sauce. Another recommended Chinese restaurant is the **Riverdeck** near the Panjim jetty.

PANJIM

Until it replaced Old Goa as capital of Portuguese India in 1843, Panjim or Panaji ('land which does not get flooded') was only a small fishing village. Today, it is one of India's smallest and most pleasant capital towns, also one of the least 'Indian'. Its Portuguese heritage lingers on in its whitewashed, red-tiled houses and narrow, winding avenues dotted with cafés, bars and tavernas. Situated on the southern bank of the Mandovi river, Panjim is the obvious base from which to discover the rest of Goa, not simply because most tourist facilities (Indian Airlines, banks, post office, boat jetty) are concentrated here, but also for the two Goa sightseeing tours running from Panjim's tourist office—useful both for checking out the major beaches and viewing the better inland sights.

WHAT TO SEE
Panjim itself is a place for gentle, relaxing evening promenades and cosy evening drinks in jolly tavernas. You can visit its few sights in a couple of hours on foot or by auto-rickshaw. Start in the main thoroughfare, Dayanand Bandodkar Rd, at the **Tourist Hostel**. Opposite, you'll see the busy little **steamer wharf**, which services the Bombay ferry and runs evening river cruises. Strolling right, you'll pass the small sub-post office (with its distinctive striped postbox), then the statue of **Abbe Faria** (an 18th-century Goan churchman, believed to be father of hypnotism), and opposite this the **Idalcao Palace** or **Secretariat building** (originally built by the Adil Shah of Bijapur, later rebuilt, and unti 1759 the residence of the Portuguese viceroys).

Turning right here, you'll soon find yourself in Church Square (Communicada Street), with its beautiful white **Church of the Immaculate Conception**, built in 1600. A short walk behind this is the 18th-century **Jama Masjid** and the **Mahalakshmi Temple**, a interesting Hindu shrine. Next, make the 20-minute ascent up to **Altino Hill**, with its stately **Patriarch Palace** (where the Pope stayed during his 1986 Goa tour) and panoramic views over Panjim's red-tiled roofs and tree-shaded squares, with the glittering Mandovi spilling over into the Arabian Sea beyond. On the walk

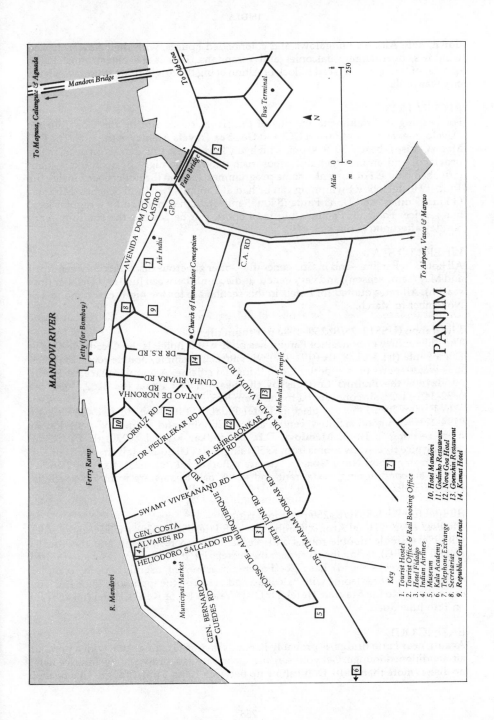

MANDOVI RIVER

To Mapusa, Calangute & Aguada

Mandovi Bridge

To Old Goa

Jetty (for Bombay)

Ferry Ramp

R. Mandovi

Bus Terminal

Pato Bridge

AVENIDA DOM JOAO CASTRO

GPO

Air India

Church of Immaculate Conception

C.A. RD

To Airport, Vasco & Margao

DR R.S. RD

ANTAO DE NORONHA RD

CUNHA RIVARA RD

ORMUZ RD

DR PISURLEKAR RD

DR DADA VAIDYA RD

Mahalaxmi Temple

DR P. SHIRGAONKAR RD

SWAMY VIVEKANAND RD

GEN. COSTA ALVARES RD

HELIODORO SALGADO RD

AFONSO DE ALBUQUERQUE RD

18TH JUNE RD

DR ATMARAM BORKAR RD

GEN. BERNARDO GUEDES RD

Municipal Market

N

Miles 0   250
m   0

PANJIM

Key

1. Tourist Hostel
2. Tourist Office & Rail Booking Office
3. Hotel Fidalgo
4. Indian Airlines
5. Museum
6. Kala Academy
7. Telephone Exchange
8. Secretariat
9. Republica Guest House
10. Hotel Mandovi
11. Godinho Restaurant
12. Nova Goa Hotel
13. Goenchin Restaurant
14. Kamat Hotel

down, note Altino's bungalows and colonnaded houses, with their flower-decked windows, overhanging balconies and verandahs. This is the oldest, most Latin, quarter of town, the terraced hillock of Altino being the original site round which the city was built.

RECREATION
For evening entertainment, try one of the river cruises run by the Goa Tourism Development Corporation (GTDC) and **Goa Sea Travels Agency** at the jetty. The Full Moon Cruise is best, 7.30–9.30 pm, with lively Portuguese folk dances on deck, meals provided, and an unforgettable moon rising above the night horizon like a giant tarnished penny. For current cinema programmes, look on the noticeboard inside the Tourist Hostel lobby. Swimming can be had at Panjim's two local beaches: Miramar (3 km: 19 miles) and Dona Paula (8 km: 5 miles), both connected by a regular local bus service. Football, Panjim's big local sport, can be seen at the stadium every Sunday afternoon (4 pm kick-off).

WHERE TO STAY
All hotels in Panjim—and in Goa generally—offer generous discounts between April and May (semi-season), and very generous discounts between June and October (low season). All rates quoted for hotels in this section are for the high season months of November to March.

Mid-range (US$10–25/Rs250–1000 per room night)
The only luxury option, since Panjim has no five-star hotel, is the **Cicade de Goa** at Dona Paula (tel 3301/8, tlx 0194-257) with attractive single/double rooms, marvellous water-sports plus superior Goan/Mughlai cuisine. A popular place for family holidays is the **Prainha Cottages by the Sea** at Dona Paula (tel 4162, 4004, fax 0832-3433) with air-conditioned rooms from Rs550.

In Panjim itself, the top place is **Hotel Fidalgo**, 18th June Rd (tel 46291/9, tlx 0194-213) with good facilities, central air-conditioning and swimming-pool. Rather more relaxing is **Hotel Mandovi**, D.B. Bandodkar Rd (tel 46270, tlx 0194-226), offering nice river-view rooms from Rs500 single, Rs 700 double (all air-conditioned). The two-star **Hotel Nova Goa**, Dr Atmaram Borkar Rd (tel 46231, tlx 0194-249) has central air-conditioning, restaurant and snack bar. Rooms are from Rs450 single, Rs550 double.

Budget (under US$10/Rs250 per room night)
Choose between **Hotel Aroma**, Cunha Rivara Rd (tel 3519, 4330), a well-located place with clean single/double rooms and pleasant air-con restaurant; and the **Tourist Hostel** (tel 3903), facing the river near the Secretariat. It's exceedingly popular (often booked out weeks ahead), has a good open-air restaurant, useful shopping complex and spacious rooms (some with balconies and views on the top floor). If it's full, you can either go to the **Mayfair Hotel**, Dr Dada Vaidya Rd or **Keni's Hotel** (tel 4581/3) on 18th June Road.

EATING OUT
Avanti, near Patto Bridge, is probably Panjim's favourite eating spot, with a popular air-conditioned lounge. Get your *sorpatel*, Goan sausage, prawn curry and rice here; no dish is more than Rs10. Don't show up between 1 and 2 pm, though—it's packed

out with local diners. Other typically Goan eating places are **Bar Godinho** (near the National Theatre in Cinema Square), **Bar George** (Communicada Square) and the slightly more expensive City Bar and Restaurant. Just across the street from Godinho's (the main backpackers' hangout), and round the corner, is **Hanuman Cold Drink House**, serving excellent shakes, ices and lassis. Nearby **Kamat Hotel**, at the top of Municipal Gardens, does delicious and cheap vegetarian food, while **Chit-Chat** at the Tourist Hostel has 'ravishing tandooris', and is a pleasant place to sit out in the evenings. **The Riverdeck**, near the jetty and on the waterfront, offers quality Chinese food/Indian snacks, and has a nice atmosphere. Despite the risky food, **O'Coqueiro** is still the nearest thing to night life in Goa, according to many locals. And despite poor service, **Hotel Mandovi** is still capable of producing excellent Goan and Portuguese cuisine, and there's a live band nightly. Of Panjim's numerous bars, try **Casa Olympia**, opposite the gardens in Communicada Square. It's owned by a real old pirate, and is a great place to meet the local people.

GENERAL INFORMATION

Government of Goa (Directorate of Tourism) Tourist Office is at Tourist Home, Patto Bridge, just below Panjim bus-stand (tel 45583, 45715, 44757). It's open 9.30 am–1.15 pm, 2–5.45 pm, Monday to Friday. Excellent printed information and helpful staff and a trained guide service for about Rs100 per day. Also regular launch cruises with cultural programme (departures 6 pm and 7.15 pm daily, 1-hour trip Rs35). Tourist taxis and luxury mini-coaches for hire. The **Goa Tourism Development Corporation—GTDC** Trionora Apartments (tel 64515) run various tours which are also available from the Tourist Hostel.

There are tourist information counters at Panjim bus-stand (tel 45620) and Dabolim airport (tel 2644), and at the Tourist Hostels in Margao (tel 22513) and Vasco (tel 2673).

Indian Airlines, Dempo House, D. Bandodkar Marg (tel 43826, 43831, 44067 apt 2788, 3251), lays on regular Rs20 buses to the airport. Air India is at Hotel Fidalgo, 18th June Rd (tel 44081, 45172). Vayudoot are handled by Alcon International, Delmon Caetano Albuquerque Road (tel 45917). The post office is midway between Tourist Hostel and Patto Bridge. State Bank of India, just up from the Tourist Hostel, is open 10 am–2 pm Monday to Friday, 10 am–noon Saturday, closed Sunday. Most shops closed Sunday too. Buy books/maps at Hotel Fidalgo's good bookshop.

The Foreigners' Registration Office is at the Police Headquarters in Panjim (tel 45360).

North Goa (by tour bus, full day)
Altino Hill–Mayem Lake–Bicholim–Mapusa–Northern Beaches

While this tour is worthwhile, if you're short on time or impatient to get to the beaches make the South Goa tour your priority: that one visits Old Goa, the main inland attraction. Both tours use buses, and you'll need a front seat to hear a word the guide's saying, but the sights and glorious scenery speak for themselves. Sufficient time is allowed at the beach spots to check out the current accommodation situation.

The North Goa tour winds up to **Altino Hill**, Panjim, for the spectacular view of the city, then proceeds inland through acres of paddy fields and palms to the natural lake resort of **Mayem**, a popular picnic spot with lovely gardens of bougainvillaea, crimson cana orchids, and china roses, together with peaceful lake views. Mayem is a wide basin lake encircled by green hills and dense palm groves. From here you'll move on to **Bicholim** to see a couple of **Hindu temples**, before arriving at **Mapusa** for lunch. Mapusa is the crossroads of northern Goa, and its main market centre. If possible, return to Mapusa for its Friday market. People from all over Bardez pour in to do their weekly shopping here, and you can buy anything from glass bangles to water-buffaloes. Open from around 8 am to 6 pm, Mapusa's bazaars are the cheapest and best place to shop in Goa. After the market, hang around for live music, folk dances and buffet at the Haystack (Friday-nights from 8.30 pm to very late). If staying in Mapusa, try the pleasant **Tourist Hotel** (rooms from Rs55) with nice attached roof-top bar/restaurant. Eat out either at **Sanbhaya** restaurant (superb seafood and Goan curry) or at the **Haystack**. Mapusa's useful little tourist office is housed in the Tourist Hostel.

In the afternoon, the tour covers the northern beaches—first **Vagator**, then the 'freak beach' of **Anjuna**, followed by the (spoilt) 'Queen Beach' of **Calangute** and the exclusive **Aguada** resort, marked by its 17th-century fort (now converted into a jail). There's just time at each place for a quick dip.

South Goa (by tour bus, full day)
Miramar–Dona Paula–Old Goa–Mangesh Temple–Margao–Colva–Marmagao

First stop on this tour is **Miramar Beach**, popular for its wide golden sands and lovely sunset views. Located just 3 km (2 miles) out of Panjim, it's the ideal place to come for a swim, if staying in the capital. Unfortunately, everyone else in town has the same idea. **Dona Paula**, a further 5 km (3 miles) up the road, is much quieter. A sheltered palm-fronted cove, with enchanting views of Marmagao Harbour and Zuari river estuary, this is another beautiful sunset spot. The sophisticated **O'-Pescador** restaurant and exclusive **Hotel Cidade de Goa** are both located here.

Driving into the cathedral ghost-town of **Old Goa** (9 km: 5½ miles from Panjim), you'll immediately detect the strong Latin influence. The priests of Rome were the real rulers here, not the Portuguese conquistadors, and the religious arrogance of the old conquerors is reflected in the grandiose complex of churches, monasteries and convents, many rivalling in size and scale the great cathedrals of Renaissance Europe. The Portuguese arrived here in 1510, bearing a sword in one hand, a crucifix in the other. Goa Velha, as Old Goa was then called, became a city of great splendour and power, dominated by the huge ecclesiastical buildings which replaced the old mosques and temples of former Muslim rulers. Then came a series of devastating plagues (1543, 1635 and 1735), decimating 80% of the population. In 1835 Old Goa was abandoned, and the administrative capital transferred to Panjim. Today, it is just a small village built round the ruined hulks of huge convents and churches dedicated to the zeal of Christianity. At present, only 6 of the town's original 14 churches remain in good condition, their red laterite structures eroded by centuries of wind and rain. They're a complete contrast to Hindu temples and shrines, though some find these haughty Catholic structures uncomfortably unlike India, much more reminiscent of Lisbon or Rome. If returning for a longer look, come in by local bus from either Panjim (10 minutes) or Margao (30 minutes). Old Goa really should be appreciated at leisure—one can spend hours wandering round the vast, deserted cloisters and corridors of these decaying old buildings. The Archaeological Survey of India has published an excellent 52-page guide, *Old Goa*, which is available locally and at their New Delhi office.

On tour, you'll first visit the **Basilica of Bom Jesus** ('good Jesus'), Goa's most popular and famous church. Built between 1594 and 1604, the rather dim interior is enlivened by the gilded baroque high altar, with elaborate screens and spiral columns, and by the huge, gaudy statue of Ignatius Loyola, the founder of the Jesuit order. To the right of the altar is the Basilica's big attraction—the silver casket enshrining the mummified **remains of St Francis Xavier**, Goa's patron saint, who spent his life spreading Christianity among the Portuguese colonies. Murals of events from the saint's life run round the walls of the Italian-marble sarcophagus enclosing the casket. One of the most well-travelled corpses in history, Xavier was taken all over the place after his death in China in 1552, and only came to rest here in 1613. During his posthumous travels, one of his toes was bitten off by a Portuguese holy-relic hunter (1554). Later, as the grisly process of dismemberment continued, he lost a hand to the Japanese Jesuits (1619), had various sections of intestine removed, and suffered a broken neck after being stuffed in an undersized grave. Today, what's left of his corpse is remarkably well preserved. If you don't believe it, you can peer at Xavier's bald, mottled head—illuminated within the casket by a naked bulb—or, for a donation, view his silver-encased toes. Every 10 years, the shrivelled cadaver is given a public veneration (the next occasion will be 1994) and the town becomes a stadium of hysterical devotees. The same thing happens, to a lesser extent, at the annual celebration on 3 December of the saint's death. Behind the casket, steps lead up to a small museum housing various portraits and relics attributed to Xavier, his life and times. The Basilica is open 9 am–6.30 pm daily; Mass at 7 am and 8 am weekdays, 8 am and 9.15 am Sunday. No photography is allowed.

Across the road is the huge **Se Cathedral** (1562–1652). Dedicated to St Catherine of Alexandria, a pagan girl who embraced Christianity and was beheaded on the same date (25 November) that the Portuguese took Old Goa from the Muslims, it is one of Asia's largest churches, having 15 altars. The harmony of its façade was destroyed in 1776, when lightning demolished one of its twin bell towers. The remaining tower houses the famous 'Golden Bell' which once announced the death-knell of burning heretics during the Inquisition, and now sounds over a deserted city (three times a day: 5.30 am, 12.30 pm, 6.30 pm) to a distance of 10 km (6½ miles). Walking up the crumbling staircase to view it is highly unsafe. The grand Renaissance Cathedral within is built in the Portuguese-Gothic style—the Corinthian interior being a baroque riot of carvings, with a vast barrel-vault ceiling and a glittering, gilded main altar (featuring painted scenes from the short life of St Catherine) which is the finest of India. Look at the 'miraculous' stone cross in one of the 14 side-chapels. According to the guide, it 'grew' so high over the centuries that the ceiling had to be raised. Nowadays it's protected by a sturdy wooden support to stop holy-relic hunters chipping away souvenirs. Undeterred, they chip away at the wood surround instead.

The nearby **Convent and Church of St Francis of Assisi**, notable for its two-storey façade crowned with twin octagonal towers, is one of Old Goa's most fascinating buildings. Originally a small Franciscan chapel (commenced 1517), the present structure was constructed in 1661. It is notable for its richly carved woodwork, ancient murals, and flooring of 16th-century gravestones. The **Archaeological**

Museum to the rear (open 10 am–5 pm, except Friday; entrance free) has a model Portuguese caravelle (poorly lit), an entertaining gallery of ex-Portuguese viceroys, and sculptures from the Hindu temples recovered from Goan sites.

If you want to make a day of it at Old Goa, leave the tour at this point. There's no problem getting back to Panjim: buses run back there every 20 minutes or so (15–20-minute journey). When you've had enough of dusty old churches, it's time to visit **Diwar Island**. This is a wonderful little demi-paradise, with empty beaches, shady palm bowers, and rustic old Portuguese houses. To get there, walk down the road behind Se Cathedral to the pier, catch a ferry (regular service) over the Mandovi River, and hop on the connecting bus into the island interior. A short, strenuous climb takes you up to the top of the island, with memorable views from the church. Return down for a relaxing afternoon on the beach. Don't forget to bring a packed lunch.

Staying on the tour, you'll continue on to the **Ponda** district, to see the 15th-century **Shri Mangesh Temple**, one of the few Hindu shrines in Goa to survive Muslim and Portuguese iconoclasm. Attractively situated on a hillock surrounded by green hills, it's a simple yet elegant structure dedicated to Shiva. The temple musicians here are astonishingly good. Set in an open courtyard, the shrine is notable for its glass chandeliers and blue-china murals. At nearby Mardol, you'll see the **Shri Mahalsa Temple**, one of Goa's oldest temples, dedicated to Vishnu. It was shifted here from its original site when Muslim persecution threatened its survival. You may also see the **Shanta Durga Temple** at Kavlem, with its impressive idol of the Goddess of Peace (Shanta Durga) flanked by Vishnu and Shiva.

Lunch is taken at **Margao**, Goa's southern centre and a thriving commercial metropolis. It has parks, modern buildings, and a very Latin flavour. Here are some of the area's most beautiful old Portuguese mansions, with balconies, patios, terraces and red-tiled sloping roofs—still lived in by descendants of the families who built them 400 years ago. There is not much for the tourist here—most folk just pass through on their way to Colva Beach. But if you get stuck here (on your way in from the south by train, perhaps) stay at the cheap and pleasant **Tourist Hostel** (tel 22513) at the top of the main square, with rooms from Rs55. It has a clean, adequate restaurant. Another hotel is the **Goa Woodlands** (tel 21121) opposite the bus-stand on Miguel Loyola Furtado Road, with rooms from Rs250/300. **Casa Menino** and **Longhino's**, opposite the Municipality building are both excellent for Goan food. **Gaylin** is one of Goa's best Chinese restaurants. Margao's tourist office is in the Municipal Building. To get here from the airport, get a bus to Vasco, then another into Margao (total journey time 1–1½ hrs). Regular buses to Benaulim (5 km: 3 miles) and Colva (10 km: 6½ miles) from Margao.

A pleasant hour at **Colva Beach** is followed by a visit to **Marmagao**, one of India's finest natural harbours. Here you can see mountains of iron ore (crushed from the cliff directly over the harbour), and fleets of tankers loading up 1000 tons of crude oil per hour. Located close to busy, modern **Vasco da Gama** (the airport gateway to Goa), tourists are shown Marmagao's massive refinery and shipping port, ostensibly for its fine views over the surrounding coastline, but more (one suspects) to demonstrate the new-found industrial muscle of this previously poor, agricultural territory.

If you're not into such propaganda, leave the tour at Colva and spend an altogether more enjoyable afternoon on the beach.

GOA'S BEACHES

Goa's beaches are world famous—long idyllic sweeps of silvery sand overlooked by undulating palms and the calm blue Arabian Sea. The hippies discovered them in the early 1960s, domestic tourists flocked to them in the 1980s (mainly to see the hippies), and two or three of them (notably Colva) deserve the description of the best beaches in India. There are still miles of unspoilt strands, and an ever-increasing number of first-class resorts.

Because there's so much choice, the 'sneak previews' provided by the Panjim tours can be a real help in selecting the best beaches to visit. But if you're determined to hit the beaches first thing, here are a few tips. Owing to rapid development, Goa's beaches are constantly changing, but the following guide should hold true for a while. The three luxury beaches of Majorda, Aguada and Bogmalo may have the best facilities, but are short on social life and laughs; the northern beaches strung close together, easily negotiated by foot) are ideal for those who bore easily —they have the best parties, the cheapest accommodation, and the worst reputation for drugs despite regular police searches; Colva and Benaulim, the extensive southern beaches, are for those in search of complete peace and quiet: here you can walk the whole day without seeing a soul.

Beach preparations should include the right equipment—sun-oil, flip-flops, sunglasses, face-mask, etc. (all things people later regret not bringing)—and the right attitude—relaxed, yet not too switched-off (theft, sunburn and drugs are all risk factors). Good sun-oil and sunglasses are not readily available in Goa (although Ray-Bans are now made in India for those wanting to emulate Tom Cruise). Some of the oil sold on the beach will be local concoctions in discarded bottles. Sleeping on the beach is not a good idea. If you are on a really tight budget, local families let out rooms at several beaches for a few rupees per night.

Northern Beaches
Fort Aguada–Calangute–Baga–Anjuna–Chapora/Vagator–Arambol/Terekol

Fort Aguada

This jet-set resort, notable for its 16th-century fort and apparently endless expanse of white sand, has the best water-sports, the best coastal views and the most famous beach hotel in India. This is the Taj group's **Fort Aguada Beach Resort** (tel 0832-87501/7, tlx 0194-291 TAJ IN, fax 0832-87733). Rooms here start at US$50 single in the off season (July, August and September) rising to US$135 during the Christmas and New Year period. The best ones, with excellent views from large terraces, are in the main block. Good facilities for water-skiing, wind-surfing, para-sailing, fishing and scuba-diving. Right next door is the equally fine **Taj Holiday Village** (tel 0832-87514/7, above telex and fax) which offers charming beach cottages designed like Goan homes, in a private, romantic setting. Prices start at US$35 in the low season, for a non air-conditioned room in a cottage, and reach US$125 in the high season for air-conditioned rooms. Single-bedroom cottages, two-room villas and family units are also available. The high level of service, the excellent facilities and special areas for children make the Holiday Village one of Goa's best options.

Taj's 20-villa **Aguada Hermitage** (tel, tlx and fax same as the Beach Resort) was built for the Commonwealth Heads of Government conference in 1982 and is situated on the hillside above the beach resort overlooking the sea. There are four types of Villa with rates ranging from US$100 in the low season to US$425 in the Christmas–New Year period.

Calangute

The old Queen Beach of Goa, where coconut palms once shaded a mile-wide stretch of tranquil orange sands, has been overdeveloped and ruined by unsightly tourist hostels and souvenir stands. Busloads of Indian voyeurs turn up here daily, hoping to photograph Western women unclad on the beaches. Calangute is now a fully fledged Indian holiday resort with popcorn stands, iced-beer stalls, and shifty businessmen, and is both dirty and commercial. Most travellers head straight on to Colva or Vagator, but a few hang around for the 'action'. This includes a trio of useful travel agencies offering cheap international flights near the tourist office and various stalls selling cheap-and-nasty Indian crafts and good but pricey Tibetan/Rajasthani items. Also, some good eating places like **Souza Lobo Restaurant** (lovely setting, superb seafood and Indian wine), **Wilson's** (on the beach), **Alex Cold Drink House** (by the statue, with good sounds), **Modern Tavern** (cheap drinks) and **Dinky Bar & Restaurant** (nice Goan food, popular travellers' hangout). The best place to stay is the charming **Varma's Beach Resort** (tel 22, 77), behind the bus-stand, with lovely gardens and homely air-con rooms with verandahs at Rs250–400. The **Concha Beach Resort** at Umtawaddo (tel 56, 74, 78) has a good restaurant, decent rooms and all services (Rs200–35). The **Tourist Hostel** (tel 24) is good value at Rs55/70, but often full and noisy. If the various other cheapies (mostly unsatisfactory) that you will undoubtedly hear about on the travellers' grapevine don't appeal, stay in a family house behind the beach. Families often meet travellers off the bus, and offer clean, simple double rooms. Recommended, but have your mosquito net handy.

Buses for Calangute leave from Mapusa every half-hour or so.

Baga

As you head north, the beaches become better and better. Baga, overlooked by a high promontory, is a fine example. Just 2 km (1½ miles) north of touristy Calangute, it is far more secluded and pleasant. **Hotel Baia Do Sol** (tel 84–86, tlx 0194-303) offers superb recreations (river cruises, water-skiing, yachting and fishing), good entertainments (traditional folk dances and music), great food (at the renowned **Seafood Restaurant**) and lovely riverside cottages on the seafront at Rs450, and gives a 60% discount in the off-season. Many cheaper rooms too. A good fallback is **Riverside Hotel** (tel 62), with a charming lady owner, delicious home cooking, and recommended two-person cottages (again, much cheaper in the low season). For relative solitude plus good facilities (it even has a small wind-surfing school), Baga is still the best of Goa's northern beaches. If you get bored, head into Calangute on a Saturday night, and let off some steam at one of the popular discos.

Anjuna

Just 10 minutes' walk further north (cross the stream at the top of Baga, walk round the headland past the chapel) is the 'freak beach' of Anjuna. A marvellous place for meeting people, illegal nude bathing, just hanging out, it has big pros and cons. It's famous for its beach parties, where everyone flips out on psychedelic 1960s music and goes skinny-dipping. Also for its superb **Flea Market**, which takes place at the southern end of the beach every Wednesday between 2 and 7 pm. This is a great place to sell your unwanted jeans, watch, camera or Walkman. Or to shop around for Tibetan/Kashmiri jewellery, Rajasthani handicrafts, stylish cotton clothing and funky hippie handicrafts. The atmosphere is amazing. The whole of Goa seems to turn up, also loads of Arabs, Chinese and Indians, either to buy Western luxury items or just to 'see the hippies'. For accommodation, there are just two proper lodges: **Poonam Guest House**, with overpriced rooms (Rs100–150 and popular garden restaurant; and **Parma Sol**, on the beach, with two seaview double rooms and some cheaper but huge non-view rooms run by friendly 'Israel' Tony (Rs50–150). Most Anjuna residents are long-stay, and negotiate very cheap family rooms back off the beach. Between November and February, when all accommodation is booked weeks ahead, don't turn up on spec—unless you're prepared to sleep on the beach.

Anjuna itself is a small, attractive cove, backing onto swaying palms. The sea is very suitable for swimming—except in the afternoon, when it is swept by strong onshore breezes. At this time of day, walk round to the quiet, protected coves between Anjuna and Baga—these are beautifully secluded. In the town is the splendid 1920s **Albuquerque Mansion**. There are only a couple of decent eating places: either **Poonam's**, or the **Rose Garden Restaurant** on the beach. In the town is **O'Coqueiro** (tel 7271), at Porvorim with excellent Goan food. Service at all Anjuna's restaurants is notoriously slow.

The most common approach to Anjuna is via local bus or shared cab from Mapusa (Rs7–10). But some travellers hire motorcycles from Calangute, and bike up. These can be hired at Anjuna too, for about Rs750 per fortnight, and are a popular—if injury-fraught—method of beach-hopping.

Chapora/Vagator

An 11-km (10-mile) bus ride from Mapusa, these most northern beaches are the least spoiled and the most secluded. If you tire of Anjuna, they are just a 3-km (2-mile) stroll up along the headland. Vagator is strikingly beautiful, a small cove of rich orange sands embraced by green-gold coconut palms. The small sandy coves of Chapora adjoining it to the north are overlooked by the old **Portuguese Fort** (built 1717, now in ruins but worth a visit for the fine views from the ramparts), and back onto a charming little village. The quality place to stay is **Vagator Beach Resort** (tel Siolim 41), with friendly atmosphere, good restaurant and lovely red-tiled beach-view cottages in the garden (from Rs150/275). Cheapies like **Dr Lobo's** or **Noble Nest** are friendly and clean, but basic. Ask around on the beach for others. Eat either at the big resort hotel; or at **Lobo's** on the beach, not at the lodge of the same name in the village. Vagator is another popular haunt of long-stay travellers; most stay at the small ashram run by missionaries. The atmosphere is extremely peaceful: people only rouse themselves for mass bingo (with disco music) in the day, and for cosy open-air parties at night.

Arambol/Terekol

These two northernmost beaches are the final retreat of the hippies and the place to get really away from it all. Bring a sleeping bag, just in case you have to sleep on the beach. Arambol has a beautiful freshwater lake (ideal for washing-off after swims in the salty sea), lovely sands, free camping, also beach-huts, and expanses of empty beach. The friendly village close to the main beach has restaurants with reasonable food. Above Arambol, Terekol marks the northern boundary of Goa's coast, and has a fine fort (now converted to a rest house) with a small church and good views. Arambol is 3 hours by bus from Mapusa. A long trip, but worth it.

Southern Beaches
Bogmalo–Colva–Benaulim–Betul

Bogmalo

This is one of Goa's best beaches, a secluded crescent-shaped cove with calm, safe waters for swimming (a contrast to the powerful breakers of the more open beaches) and a friendly fishing village. Behind the beach rises the small upland of the Marmagao peninsula. It is an exclusive beach, presided over (as at Fort Aguada) by a single luxury hotel: the **Oberoi Bogmalo Beach** (tel 2191, 3311/5, 3291 tlx 0191-297 OBGA IN, fax 08345-2510). Only 5 minutes' drive from the airport, this is an excellent holiday option with marvellous water-sports, freshwater swimming-pool, quality multi-cuisine restaurants, breezy open-air barbecues, and elegantly furnished rooms (US$85 single, US$95 double in the high season, dropping to US$35 and US$55 in the low season), each one with a private balcony overlooking the sea. Few budget travellers make it out here: transport is too awkward (1 hour minimum by bus from Panjim, with a change at the 'Aerodrome' stop 3 km before Vasco) and there's nowhere cheap to stay. Oberoi lays on free transport from the airport for residents.

South of Bogmalo are the Velsao and Majorda beaches. Both remain fairly quiet but the **Majorda Beach Resort** (tel 20751,20203, tlx 0196-234) set slightly back from the beach has all facilities (from Rs1200).

Colva

Goa's longest beach is an unbroken 20 km (12½ miles) of virgin white sand. Unlike Calangute to the north, Colva has not been spoiled by progress. Here you need only walk a kilometre or two out of the main tourist drag to have the beach all to yourself. The waters are warm and calm, the only people you'll see are local fishermen, and (unlike anywhere else in India) you can take off all your clothes if you want to, and not attract unwanted attention.

Colva is a half-hour bus journey from Margao. At the bus-stand there are a few pleasant shops, including **Damodar**, the place to buy or sell second-hand books. Reading is the main occupation on the beaches, so stock up. **Navneeta Handicrafts** is the place to buy cool, practical beach clothes. Other good purchases on the beach are beautiful lacquer boxes/eggs and painted shells. Buy cheap, attractive jewellery at Colva's **Full Moon parties** which are better than Anjuna, some say, with an illuminated marquee, great music and dancing, and lots of atmosphere. Top-bracket accommodation has now arrived with the **Ramada Renaissance Resort** (tel 08342-23611/2, tlx 0196-211; in Bombay call 234672, 2042346) near the Varca Village. The hotel, supposedly designed by Hawaiian architects, has a 6-hole golf course, a series of swimming-pools and direct access to the beach. The sea-facing rooms are from US$95 in the high season. Another new five-star property is **The Leela Beach** at Cavelossim (tel 6263/70, tlx 0196-258, fax 08344-6352) with rooms in villas and 'pavilions' from US$115. Since renovation, prices of rooms at the air-con **Hotel Silver Sands** (tel 08342-21645, tlx 0196-239 SAND IN) have gone up to Rs650 single, Rs750 double, in the high season. Still, you get all the luxury facilities, including swimming-pool, health club, wind-surfing, travel office, free airport transfer. At the bottom end of the range, there's a choice between two fairly dismal places—the **Tourist Hostel** and **Whitesands Hotel** (tel 3253)—and one worthwhile one, **Hotel Vincy**, above Vincy's Bar. All three charge from Rs125. Many people are quite happy to put up at one of the many cheap lodges near the beach—after all, all you really need here is a bed for the night. A couple of goodies are **Fisherman's Cottage** (200 m from the bus-station with friendly people) and **Rose Cottages**. During the high season, when beach accommodation is very thin on the ground, try family houses like **Sabfran Tourist Cottages** (1 km before Colva beach, ask the bus driver to put you off) which charge less than Rs1000 per *month* for clean, livable double rooms.

Most Colva residents eat at one of the ramshackle (but good) beach restaurants situated right on the shoreline. Regular favourites—all serving excellent seafood in addition to the usual pancakes, chips and omelettes—are **Sunset**, **Lucky Star** and **La Mir**. This is where people come to enjoy tasty fish dishes, spaghetti 'sizzlers', and a nightcap *feni*, after a hard day's sunbathing. In the morning, they pile over to **Umita Corner Restaurant & Bar** (away from the beach, near Tourist Nest) for breakfast. There's always a small gathering around the kiosks by the roundabout at 9 each morning, when hot doughnuts arrive.

Benaulim

If mainstream Colva is too busy for you, stroll 2 km (1¼ miles) down the sands to quiet, secluded Benaulim beach. This has a pretty fishing village (about 1 km behind the beach) full of quaint, sleepy old Portuguese houses and buildings. Stay either at **L'Amour Beach Resort** (near the beach), which has nice, clean rooms with bath (but disappointing, overpriced food), or **Brito Tourist Corner** at the village crossroads, offering large rooms—like Spanish flats. There are lots of cheaper places, often full. On the beach, eat at **Splash Restaurant**, which has good service and nice seafood, but steer clear of the pork sausages. Or try **Xavier's** (superlative fish dishes, good sounds). **Pedro's** has gone into steep decline, but **Johncy's** still has jolly beach parties.

On the walk along the beach from Colva to Benaulim kids turn up to offer people 'family-house' accommodation. This can work out remarkably cheap as well as giving an enjoyable insight into the lifestyle of the locals.

Betul

This lovely beach, located on the estuary of the river leading off from the bottom of Benaulim, is serviced by buses from Margao. Completely untouched by tourism, Betul offers total seclusion, magical beaches, and lovely scenery. At present, there is just one decent place to stay—a small lodge cum restaurant, run by a friendly Goan, right next door to an ancestral summer-house. This is a very well-run establishment with rooms with a balcony overlooking the river from Rs100. It is tricky to find. If coming in by bus, you still have to walk across the river via the bridge. Another problem is lack of direct access from the lodge to the beaches. You either have a half-hour walk over the hills to a secluded, idyllic beach, or you take a ferry across to the main beach, which runs down from Colva. Betul represents—for the time being at least—the perfect little getaway for the peace-loving beachcomber.

Route 5—Lost Wonders in the Wilderness

The rugged state of Maharashtra, with over 500 km (310 miles) of coastline, is separated from the dry Deccan plateau by the Western Ghats. Forts dominate the coastal hilltops of this area, which was once the heart of the mighty Maratha empire which ruled much of central India and presented the Mughals with their stiffest resistance. Of the great towns of the Deccan, Pune was once a Maratha capital; later a major military cantonment and the British summer capital of Bombay Presidency.

Earlier, between the 3rd and 13th centuries AD, kingdoms rose and fell including the great Kalachuri, Rastrakuta and Chalukya dynasties. The Deccan was on major trade routes between central India and the coast, and received visits from communities of wandering monks—Buddhist, Hindu and Jain—who were among the most skilled sculptors and painters India had ever seen.With patronage from the local kingdoms they immortalised their devotion in stone, creating the most beautiful examples of rock-cut cave architecture, and then they left. For hundreds of years, their achievement lay buried and forgotten. Then, quite recently, they were rediscovered—living masterpieces in stone, completely untouched by time.

The main three centres of sculpture plot the history of religion and architecture in ancient India. **Aurangabad** has its own caves, raw and primitive, situated on a high hillside shelf—but is more noted as a historical city full of Mughal monuments, and for its famous silks. The caves of **Ellora** are the finest rock-cut examples in the world, and point to a singular harmony existing between the leading three faiths (Hindu, Buddhist and Jain) of the period. But it is **Ajanta's** caves, full of magical frescoes and wall-paintings—still fresh after all these centuries—which inspire the most wonder and admiration. Here, in the depths of a forgotten wilderness, an essential part of India's spiritual and cultural heritage lives on. Other caves dating from the 2nd century BC are found at various places in the Western Ghats.

Season: September to March.
Climate: 22°–39°C (summer); 12°–34°C (winter).
Route duration: 4–8 days.

TRAVEL ITINERARY

Bombay to Aurangabad 392 km (245 miles)

Air
One flight daily—IC492 from Bombay (Rs767) which continues to Jodhpur (Rs1480), Jaipur (Rs1503) and New Delhi (Rs1859). IC491 follows the same route in reverse.

Rail
Long, awkward train journey (8/9 hours, change at Manmad). In high season, unless you have an Indrail Pass you are wise to reserve tickets up to 4 days in advance.

Road
Long, dusty 10-hour bus trip. Take a good book or an entrancing travelling companion. From Bombay's State Transport bus-stand, your best options are the quick night buses: either the bumpy 'local' MTDC bus (dep 9.15 pm) or the two MRSTDC deluxe buses (dep 7.45 pm and 8.15 pm,). From Aurangabad, there are two good MTDC buses to Bombay—the local and the super-deluxe—both leaving 8.30 pm daily. Book tickets from MTDC Holiday Resort or from the central bus-stand.

Aurangabad to Ellora 29 km (18 miles)

Road
Daily conducted-tour buses—MTDC or ITDC. Alternatively, local buses (every half-hour) or taxi day-return trips.

Aurangabad to Ajanta 106 km (66 miles)

Road
Daily conducted-tour buses—MTDC or ITDC. Otherwise, local buses or taxi day-return trips.
From Bombay to Ajanta direct, there's the train to Jalgaon (7½ hours), then tonga to Jalgaon bus-stand, and local bus to Ajanta (2 hours). To backtrack from Ajanta to Ellora, there are regular buses daily, via Phulambari.

CONTINUATIONS
From Aurangabad, the daily IC492 flight heads into Rajasthan, landing at Udaipur (Rs1221), Jodhpur (Rs1480) and Jaipur (Rs1503), before hitting base at Delhi. To connect with the South India routes, take the 12-hour train from Aurangabad to Hyderabad.

AURANGABAD

Most popular as a base from which to explore nearby Ellora and Ajanta, Aurangabad is a city of historical renown with some very attractive caves of its own. Originally known as Khadke, it was later renamed after the Mughal emperor Aurangzeb. Situated on the

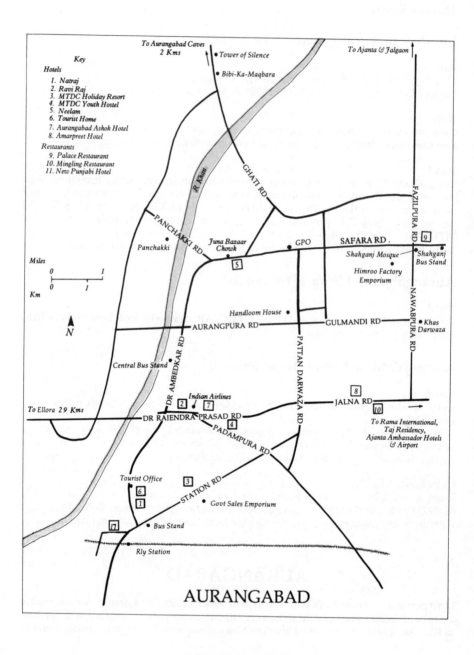

Key

Hotels
1. Natraj
2. Ravi Raj
3. MTDC Holiday Resort
4. MTDC Youth Hostel
5. Neelam
6. Tourist Home
7. Aurangabad Ashok Hotel
8. Amarpreet Hotel

Restaurants
9. Palace Restaurant
10. Mingling Restaurant
11. New Punjabi Hotel

Miles

Km

N

To Aurangabad Caves
2 Kms

• Tower of Silence
• Bibi-Ka-Maqbara

To Ajanta & Jalgaon

R. Khui

GHATI RD

PANCHAKKI RD

• Panchakki

Juna Bazaar
Chowk

GPO

SAFARA RD.

[9]

Shahganj Mosque

• Shahganj
Bus Stand

[5]

Himroo Factory
Emporium

FAZILPURA RD

Handloom House •

AURANGPURA RD

GULMANDI RD

• Khas
Darwaza

NAWABPURA RD

Central Bus Stand •

DR AMBEDKAR RD

PATTAN DARWAZA RD

To Ellora 29 Kms

• Indian Airlines

[2] [7]

DR RAJENDRA PRASAD RD

[4]

PADAMPURA RD

JALNA RD

[8]

[10]

To Rama International,
Taj Residency,
Ajanta Ambassador Hotels
& Airport

Tourist Office •

[3]

STATION RD

[6]
[1]

• Govt Sales Emporium

[11]

• Bus Stand

Rly Station

AURANGABAD

flat, dry Deccan plateau, the chequered history of the place is reflected in its several fine monuments, including some of the most beautiful sculptures in the country.

Best season to visit is October–November (post-monsoon, lush and green) or December–March (pleasantly warm, comfortable). During April/May, the thermometer leaps alarmingly and you'll need a full water-canister wherever you go.

WHAT TO SEE

Aurangabad is a small, relaxed town, alongside the Kham River. The relevant tourist points—rail station, budget hotels and tourist office—are all within 1 km (¾ mile) of the central bus-stand in Dr Ambedkar Rd. For local transport, use auto-rickshaws, but meters 'don't work' so agree on a price before starting. This is a sprawling, lazy place, best negotiated on foot.

Make Aurangabad your base on this route—food, accommodation and tourist facilities are all best here. Travel out to Ellora and Ajanta on (good) one-day conducted tours, and leave a day spare to pick up some shopping bargains in Aurangabad itself.

Aurangabad Caves

There are 10 of these—6 in the western group, 4 in the eastern group—and they are all Buddhist excavations of the 3rd to 7th centuries AD. Little patronised by tourists (owing to their hot, isolated situation 3 km (2 miles) out of town, plus the fact they were never completed), they compare favourably with the more popular caves of Ellora and Ajanta, and serve as a useful introduction to them.

Getting to the caves is best by auto-rickshaw—a bumpy 20-minute Rs10–15 journey across the arid, exposed desert plateau. Unless you're prepared to pay a stiff 'waiting charge', it's best to walk back—a very pleasant stroll.

Aurangabad's caves are hacked into a high hillside rock-cleft, and offer spectacular views down over the Deccan plains. Ask to be dropped at the **Western Group** (Caves 5–10), where there is usually a guide (an old boy with an 'illuminating' mirror) waiting. Start with a climb up the walkway leading off to the right. This takes you up to **Cave 10**, the last one to be worked on and the most incomplete (Buddhism was well on the way out by the 7th century). It is of interest only as an illustration of how each cave began its life—as a large chamber of rough-hewn pillars supporting a low rock-cut ceiling. All the sculptures came later.

Cave 9 features a large Buddha image (left-hand chamber), surrounded by large-breasted women, cobra-mantled attendants and fat, dissolute bodhisattvas (near-Buddhas)—all indicative of Buddhism's later period of decline. But the carvings are superb.

Cave 8 is just a hole in the rock. Pass on to **Cave 7**, the finest example of the whole group. This has the giant figure depicting Siddhartha as a near-Buddha on his way to enlightenment, praying for deliverance from eight fears—fire, sword, chains, shipwreck, lions, snakes, mad elephants and the demon of death. The theme of 'seven', recurrent throughout this cave, is most notable in the central shrine, with its seven handmaidens and seven bodhisattvas ranged round the large Buddha figure.

Cave 6 is a real curiosity: a mixed assortment of Hindu and Buddhist sculptures. The gradual reabsorption of Buddhism into mainstream Hinduism is here reflected by the sole Buddha figure (right) supporting elephant-headed Ganesh (centre) and seven other Hindu deities, including Shiva (left). The sculptures of women are

Cathedral Cave, Aurangabad

notable for their ornamentation and exotic hairdos. From the cave entrance, enjoy superb views over the surrounding plains.

Out of the western caves, it's a 20-minute walk right round to the other side of the hill. Here, at the top of a crumbling stone stairway, you'll find the **Eastern Group** (Caves 1–4). To appreciate most fully, start at the far end with **Cave 1**. This is incomplete, but has beautiful carvings (lotus designs) on its pillars, also imposing 'guardians' (bearing studded clubs) flanking the two humble Buddha figures in the side shrines. This cave also gives fine views down over the plateau. **Cave 2** has an army of exquisitely carved mini-Buddhas (each with two mini-bodyguards) set into the enclosing wall running round the main shrine. Within the shrine is a massive Buddha attended by supplicant spirits, animals and lesser deities.

The exterior simplicity of **Cave 3**—a square structure supported by 12 highly ornate columns—belies its inner charm and beauty. Within is an interesting series of sculptures depicting scenes from one of the jatakas (Buddhist fables); also the finest Buddha image of the whole Aurangabad group, attended by a large retinue of devotees kneeling in prayer. The walls are covered with figures of women (the whole group has a distinctly female emphasis), scantily clad yet heavily bejewelled.

Cave 4 is the only *chaitya* (temple) of the group, all the others being viharas (monasteries). A silver casket *stupa* containing Buddhist relics sits beneath an awesome ribbed ceiling, carved in the style of a gothic church. Outside the temple entrance a stone Buddha sits in his chair, enjoying the sun. **Cave 5**, the last in this group, is disappointing: the principal sculptures have all been plastered over.

The walk down to Aurangabad from the bottom of the cave steps is neither as long nor as daunting as it might first seem. One gets a real sense of desert isolation and timelessness in the 30-minute walk down over the flat, stark plains to the gleaming dome of the **Bibi-ka-Maqbara** at the northern end of town. From here, you can hire a Rs5 rickshaw back into **Aurangabad** centre, for a well-earned rest.

Ellora Caves (by tour bus, full-day)
Daulatabad–Grisheshwar–Ellora–Khuldabad–Bibi-ka-Maqbara–Panchakki

This useful tour covers not just Ellora, but a number of interesting spots in and around Aurangabad. If you decide you need more time at Ellora, stay overnight at the **Hotel Kailash** (tel 43, 46), with simple rooms Rs100, close to the caves. This has single/double rooms and good food in its attached restaurant.

First stop on this tour, halfway to Ellora, is the remarkable hilltop fortress of **Daulatabad**. Built by Bhilama Raja of the Yadava dynasty in AD 1187 and named Devagiri or 'hill of the gods', it later gained fame as the place selected by mad Mohammed Tughlaq (the unhinged Delhi Sultan) as his new capital. He force-marched all his subjects here in AD 1327, renamed the fort Daulatabad or 'City of Fortune', and then—just 17 years later—marched them all the way back to Delhi again. It was a long, long march (1100 km: 690 miles) and a good many of them didn't make it.

The only raised point in an otherwise flat wilderness, Daulatabad fort is perched on top of a 200-m high pyramidal hill. Surrounded by 6 km (3¾ miles) of thick walls, equipped with massive spiked gates (to deter elephant charges), dead-end ambush alleys, overhead channels (for depositing boiling oil on invaders), steep, gravelled slideways and, once, a crocodile-infested moat, Mohammed's new capital really was a masterpiece of security. The only trouble was, the water-supply gave out during a siege, and then (a very Indian device) the invading forces bribed the Sultan's guards to let them in by the front gate.

The tour round the fort is fascinating, but you'll need a flashlight. Just inside the entrance gate is the huge **Chand Minar** pillar. Built in 1435 as a Victory Tower, it soars to a height of 60 m and is only surpassed by Delhi's 72-m Qutb Minar. It faces onto a small mosque erected over an old Jain temple. Across the moat (now a dry gully), you begin a half-hour climb up to the fort. On the ascent look out for the **Chini Mahal**, the (blue-tiled palace where Golconda's last king spent his final 13 years imprisoned, and the massive 6-m **cannon** engraved with Aurangzeb's name and cast from five different metals. Near the top there's the pitch-black, spiralling tunnel used to unleash burning coals on invaders. This is where you need the flashlight. Enjoy fine views from the bastion summit.

The tour moves on next to **Grisheshwar**, an 18th-century Shiva temple housing one of the 12 ancient jyotirlingas (a symbol of Shiva's creative power) where 'visitors wishing to achieve *dharvana* with the deity must take off their clothes'.

Finally, you come to **Ellora**—site of the finest examples of rock-cut caves in all India. It is the meeting-point of three faiths, Jain and Hindu structures having risen alongside each other as the original Buddhist impetus slowly tailed off. There are 34 caves in all—12 Buddhist (*c*. AD 600–800), 17 Hindu (*c*. AD 900) and 5 Jain (AD 800–1000)—and they are numbered in that order, running south to north.

You'll probably see the **Buddhist caves** at the southern end first. Ten of these belong to the Mahayana sect (which favoured statue-worship) and contain images of the Buddha; the remaining two (**Caves 1 and 7**) are the work of Hinayana monks (who preferred relic-worship) and contain only stupas. They are all *vihara* monasteries, except for **Cave 10**, which is the only *chaitya* (temple) of the group. Known as the Carpenter Cave (owing to its ceiling ribs, which resemble wooden beams) it contains a gigantic Buddha figure, seated in meditation on a lion throne, flanked by attendants and flying figures. The image is fronted by a 9-m high *stupa*. To take any photos in the dimly-lit chamber, you'll need the services of a guide with a mirror. Moving on,

Cave 5 is the largest *vihara* in the group, its title of 'Assembly Hall' being suggested by the rows of stone benches within. **Cave 12** is a large three-storey enterprise, used as a training/sleeping area for student monks. The top floor has eight large Buddha figures, all exceptionally fine, and the walls are carved with attractive reliefs.

Cave 16 is the only **Hindu** example covered on the tour. This is the world-famous **Kailash Temple**, dedicated to Shiva and built to represent his Himalayan home of Mount Kailash. A stupendous edifice, with dimensions twice the area of the Parthenon in Athens—81 m long by 47 m wide and 33 m high—it was carved from one enormous rock. Unlike all the other caves, which were cut at ground level and took an average of 50 years apiece to fashion, the Kailash was begun from the top of the rock and worked slowly down to the floor—creating gateway, pavilion, courtyard, vestibule and tower along the way—in an amazing burst of creative energy which, according to one estimate, took 7000 labourers working in continuous shifts 150 years to build. Lavishly carved, and sculptured with epic themes throughout, it is the world's largest monolithic structure. Attributed to the Rashtrakuta kings of the mid-8th century the temple is a testimony to the skills and imagination of those who built it. Open from 9.30 am to 5.30 pm, admission Rs1 (all the other temples are open sunrise to sunset, free admission), the Kailash temple is best viewed during the late-afternoon sun.

Entrance to Kailash is via a bridge, leading through an enclosure to a large courtyard. To the front of the enclosure, two large stone elephants (with flagstaffs) flank the Nandi pavilion which faces into the main shrine. Of the many strikingly carved frieze panels, perhaps the most famous is that depicting the demon king Ravana trying to demonstrate his strength by lifting Mount Kailash, while Shiva (unimpressed) puts his foot down to replace it. There are many such episodes from the *Ramayana* epic.

The group of 5 **Jain temples** (slightly north of the others) mark the final phase of Ellora architecture. They lack the dynamism of the better Hindu caves, but compensate with exceptional attention to detail. You'll be shown **Cave 32**, the **Assembly Hall of Indra**, which is the best of the group. The ground floor is a simple (rather plain) imitation of Kailash, but has exceptional ceiling carvings. The upper storey, reached by a small stairway, is notable for its rich decorations. The shrine contains the seated Mahavira, last of the 24 tirthankars and founder of the Jain religion. The lotus design detail-work on the Jain columns is the finest of the whole Ellora complex.

After lunch you'll visit the small market town of **Khuldabad** ('heavenly abode'), 3 km (2 miles) out of Ellora. Once an important centre and fortified village (Aurangzeb built the battlemented wall around it), it remains the Karbala or holy shrine of Deccan Muslims, containing the tombs of many historical figures. Here you'll visit the simple bare-earth grave of Aurangzeb, last of the great Mughal emperors, surrounded by a decorative marble screen. Renowned for his puritanism, the emperor stipulated that only money that he himself had earned by copying out the Koran should be used to pay for his tomb. It was his way, it was said, of atoning for the financial excesses (including the Taj Mahal) of his spendthrift predecessors. Even the screen round his grave was a later addition, donated by the wealthy Hyderabad Nizam.

Back in Aurangabad, you'll get a closer look at the **Bibi-ka-Maqbara** built by Aurangzeb's son for the emperor's wife. Popularly known as the 'poor man's Taj', it was erected in 1679—just 25 years after the Taj Mahal itself—and pales in comparison. But its low cost of (68 000 rupees—300 times cheaper than the Taj, doubtless commended it to the parsimonious Aurangzeb. It differs from the Taj in three major respects: the four corner minarets are actually higher than the central mausoleum dome; it is built not of marble, but of plaster-covered common stone set on a marble base; finally, the carvings and decorations are far simpler, less ornamental, than those of the Taj Mahal.

Last stop is the **Panchakki**, overlooking Aurangabad's Kham River. Built in 1624 to honour the memory of Baba Shah Musafir, a Sufi saint who was Aurangzeb's spiritual mentor, it is a massive water-wheel which takes its name from a mill which used to supply grain for the masses of visiting pilgrims and holy men. A small dam releases water through the mill-gates into a large fish-filled tank, at the rear of which is a magnificent 500-year-old banyan tree.

Ajanta (by tour bus, full-day)

If the caves of Ellora are famous for their sculpture and carving, those of Ajanta take the honours for their beautiful frescoes and wall-paintings. Many travellers rave about Ajanta, saying it's the best thing they've seen in India. They add that an overnight stay is essential, since one day is insufficient to see everything here. Others, it must be said, just can't see what all the fuss is about—for the once-bright Buddhist frescoes and murals are rapidly fading away. Everybody suggests bringing a flash-light, for the caves are very poorly-lit—a deliberate device, to keep the sunlight from damaging the paintings any further. If you don't have your own lighting, you can buy a 'light ticket' (a group of up to 20 people can share this) whereby the caves with the most exciting paintings are illuminated. If here on your own, tack onto a group—guides are *most* reluctant to shine their lights on paintings for solo travellers. The caves are open 9 am to 5.30 pm, admission is Rs0.50, bags can be checked in at the 'cloakroom' for Rs1, and you can hire multi-lingual guides from the entrance. Only hand-held cameras are allowed, and flashes are prohibited. No tripods, probably because people would trip over them in the dark. If staying overnight, take a local bus down to Fardapur village 5 km (3 miles) from the caves, which has the best accommodation and food. The MTDC **Holiday Resort** has non air-conditioned rooms from Rs90. The government bungalow outside the caves is not recomended. Nor is the small café by the cave entrance, with its overpriced thalis. Be patient with local children trying to sell you bits of quartz and tacky moulded-plastic goods.

Visiting Ajanta after Aurangabad and Ellora is like saving your dessert for last. The 30 rock-hewn caves full of vivid sculptures and wall-paintings, many still glowing in their original colours, are the finest achievement of the Buddhist monks who arrived here in the 2nd century BC, and reflect the zenith of ancient Indian art and architecture. Chiselled into a steep horseshoe-shaped rock gorge, the caves appeared in two distinct phases over a 900-year period. Most were carved during a 400-year period from the 2nd century BC to the 2nd century AD), the remainder in the erratic bursts of activity from the 5th to 7th centuries. The site was then suddenly abandoned, the monks transferring their building activities to nearby Ellora. Only in 1819, after a millennium of obscurity, were Ajanta's beautiful cave-paintings dramatically rediscovered, by a British hunting-party out in search of tigers. Their isolation contributed greatly to the remarkable state of preservation in which they were found. Poor initial restoration work led to some sad deterioration in their quality, but expert Italian restoration in the 1920s halted their rapid decline. Today, work is constantly going on to ensure that as many visitors as possible will be able to enjoy this unique group of cave-paintings before they finally fade into obscurity.

The principal interest of the caves is their depiction of eight centuries of religious development, specifically Buddhism. Here can be seen the development of Buddhist art, thought and belief from the simple, ascetic Hinayana school reflected in the older, centrally located Caves 8, 9, 10, 12 and 13, with their emphasis on the abstract and symbolic, through to the popularist Mahayana 2nd century BC offshoot (the more modern caves, on either side of the older Hinayana structures, favouring the rich, realistic mode of art). The central theme of the frescoes and sculptures remains consistent, however, throughout the group: the life and times of the Buddha, along with tales of his previous earthly incarnations. He presides over a miniature cosmos of caparisoned warhorses and elephants, colourful monkeys and peacocks, bejewelled princes and princesses, spirited musicians and players—sometimes he is smiling, at other times meditating or dejected. The dominant theme of the paintings may be religious, but they are also a vivid portrayal of a bygone civilisation over 1000 years old.

As you tour the caves, you'll notice that most of them were carved to catch the full flood of sunlight at certain times of day. Also that the mood and meaning of each painting changes depending on which angle it is viewed from.

Like Ellora's Kailash cave, the Ajanta group are all monolithic each one carved from the bare rock alone, with no additions, and methodically chipped away from the ceiling down to reveal pillars, monks' beds, façades and massive back-room Buddhas. The technical feat is staggering—there was no room for the slightest error in carving.

You'll certainly need a guide for Ajanta (the tours provide good ones, but don't lose them), and detailed written information is not helpful because it is too dark to read inside. Briefly then, **Cave 1** is the biggest and best and most recent of the Ajanta caves, with the finest murals. Its large central hall has notable sculptures (including one of four deer with a single head) and fine paintings of the 'black princess', the 'dying princess', *jataka* depictions of the Buddha's previous lives, and portraits of various bodhisattvas. Along with Caves 2, 16, 17 and 19, it has the very best paintings. **Cave 4** is the largest *vihara* cave, supported by 28 pillars, with fine sculpture scenes of fleeing people seeking protection from Avalokitesvara (Buddha's disciple) against the 'eight great dangers'. Along with Caves 17, 19 and 26, it has the best sculptures in the group. The oldest cave of all, **Cave 10**, was also the first one stumbled upon by the British officers who rediscovered Ajanta.

The Archaeological Survey booklet on *Ajanta* is available at their site office for only Rs6 and gives valuable background to the site. ASI also publish a portfolio of prints from the caves.

SHOPPING

Aurangabad is famous for its *himroo* shawls, cotton brocade (still woven in gold and silver thread on silk, with motifs often derived from the Ajanta paintings), *bidri* ware and 'art' silk commonly known as 'Aurangabad' silk. Visit **Silk Loom Fabrics**, at the bottom of Station Rd near the rail station, which does a wide range of reasonably priced materials. Rs150 double-bedspreads are excellent value so are artificial silk saris. For quality silks and shawls, try the **Himroo Factory Emporium**, near the Shahganj bus-stand.

WHERE TO STAY

Expensive (from US$35/Rs1000 per room night)
Aurangabad's top hotels are reliable and close to each other in Chikalthana, halfway between the town and airport. They are the Welcomgroup **Rama International** (tel 83467/9, tlx 0745-212), the **Ajanta Ambassador** (tel 82211, tlx 0745-211). Both have swimming-pools, multi-cuisine restaurants, many facilities, and rooms around US$50 single, US$65 double. The Welcomgroup hotel has the slightly better reputation. More central are two mid-range hotels.

Mid-range (US$10–35/Rs250–1000 per room night)
Also with a swimming-pool, there is the popular **Aurangabad Ashok** in Dr Rajendra Prasad Marg (tel 24520/9, tlx 0745-229). This is one of the best mid-range options (very comfy, centrally air-conditioned, with good food) with well-priced rooms at Rs550 single, Rs750 double. Another central hotel is the **Quality Inn Vedant** (tel 26785, 25844, tlx 0745-304) in Station Road with rooms from Rs650.

Budget (under US$10/Rs250 per room night)
Cheaper hotels include **Amarpreet**, in Pandit Jawaharlal Nehru Marg (tel 23422, tlx 0745-307, fax 02438-2792) and the **Hotel Ravi Raj** (tel 3939) between the Youth Hostel (tel 23801) and Indian Airlines, in Dr Rajendra Prasad Marg. Both have rooms from Rs175. Most budget hotels are near the railway station. The **MTDC Holiday Resort**, Station Rd (tel 24259) rooms from Rs100 are good value. Perhaps the best budget hostel is the superb **Youth Hostel**, 10 minutes' walk right out of the bus-station, with an immaculate dormitory and useful meals service. The only drawback to this place is mosquitoes and the nets provided are useless. Either bring your own or, better, sleep up on the cool, breezy roof.

EATING OUT

The **Aurangabad Ashok** has a good restaurant with a mix of Indian and Continental cuisine with meals from Rs150. The **Rama International** offers a reasonable buffet, including live music. On Jaina Road, opposite Amarpreet Hotel, **Mingling Restaurant** dishes up some marvellous (mid-priced) Chinese food. There are several cheap eating places in Station Rd, including friendly **Pinky's**. A lot of people eat at the **Youth Hostel**, well known for its good-value *thali* suppers. This is also a great place to pick up information, and to meet other travellers.

GENERAL INFORMATION

Government of India Tourist Office, Station Rd (tel 24817) is short on information, but helpful. Opening hours are 8.30 am–6 pm weekdays, 8.30 am–12.30 pm Saturdays. MTDC Holiday Resort (tel 24713) do the best tours to Ellora/Daulatabad/Aurangabad (9.30 am–6 pm daily, Rs80), and to Ajanta (8 am–6 pm daily, Rs100). The cheaper, but quite adequate, ITDC tours are sold by **Ashok Travels & Tours**, Hotel Aurangabad Ashok (tel 24143). This hotel also hires out taxis and private cars, should you wish to tour in style.

Indian Airlines (tel 24864, 24008, apt 82223) is at Amikar Building, Adalat Rd; State Bank of India is at Kranti Chowk (tel 5386); GPO is in Juna Bazaar Chowk, at the northern end of town.

Route 6—The Western Ghats

The Western Ghats rise steeply from the narrow coastal plain of Maharashtra. For over 2000 years the region has been traversed by trade routes along which strategic fortifications were built, and monasteries and chapels were carved out of the rock by Buddhist communities as early as the 1st century BC. From the late 16th century the Maratha empire developed a chain of forts, each within sight of its immediate neighbours, almost all of which fell into disuse by the mid-19th century when British control over the area was consolidated. The British also left their mark here. **Pune**, the old Maratha capital, became an important colonial military centre and sanatorium. The ancient Hindu town of **Mahabaleshwar** acquired communications, a school and a race course. **Matheran** became a summer resort.

For travellers today, the region offers a contrast and a welcome escape from the bustle and hectic life of Bombay. You can visit the three main towns individually, and in any order. All are easily accessible by rail and road from Bombay. The Western Ghats receive the full impact of the monsoon and from late June to September many hotels are closed; they become packed with local tourists over Christmas and New Year. The best time to visit is in September or October, and from mid-January through to May.

PUNE

Pune has a chequered history, coming into prominence as the birthplace and one of the main estates of the Maratha hero Chhatrapati Shivaji. Earlier known as Punaka Wadi, 'land of a thousand villages', it went through several name-changes: Punyapura' (city of merit), Poona and finally Pune. It changed hands from the Khiljis to the Tughlaqs to the Marathas to the British, and each rule left its stamp on the place, the architecture and the people.

The earliest reference to the name Pune can be found on a copper-plate inscription of Krishna I of the Rashtrakuta dynasty, dated AD 768. Subsequently, Pune came to be ruled over by Yadava Kings and gradually deteriorated into a nondescript town. It was captured by the Khiljis in AD 1294 who destroyed the temples dedicated to Puneshwar and Nageshwar and built two dargahs (Muslim shrines) in their place. These dargahs still exist in the cantonment area under the names Great Shaikhsalla Dargah and Little Shaikhsalla Dargah. After the Khiljis came the Tughlaqs. The Muslim rulers appear to have begun building the forts of Sihagad, Purandhar and Lohagad.

While Pune was not considered sufficiently well-situated to be made into a garrison town or a commercial centre, it has always been a favoured seat of administration on account of the pleasant climate. The British chose Pune as one of the two summer headquarters of the Bombay Presidency.

However, it was under the Marathas that Pune's distinctive socio-cultural identity came into existence. Shahaji Bhonsle, the father of Shivaji, received Pune as a *jagir*, on condition that he campaigned in South India for the Bijapuri overlords while his wife and son remained in Pune. Thus started the 'Maratha period' in Pune's history. The Peshwas painstakingly transformed it from an obscure market town and the seat of a *jagir* into a thriving city with a population of around 100 000.

By the 18th century, Pune had become the nerve centre of the Maratha empire, ranging from Calcutta to Bombay and Attock to Madras. The various Peshwa rulers infused Pune with their typical Brahmanness and their faith, aspirations, intellectual abilities, and above all, pride. The Peshwas were pious to a fault, and they built many temples in the city: by 1811 over 400 existed in Pune City, the chief deities being the Ganesh in Kasba Peth and the Jogeshwari in Budhwar Peth.

Infighting among the Peshwas starting from 1772 weakened the Maratha Empire, which broke up and finally passed to British hands in 1817. Pune became an important military post for the British who built a cantonment to house the troops, as well as the headquarters of the military for the Deccan. To help run the military and civil administrations, the British encouraged the Parsis and Bohras to migrate to the city. These families stayed on in Pune and became part of the social structure.

Thus, the predominantly Brahman culture of Pune gave way to the more outward-looking cosmopolitan society that characterises the city today.

WHEN TO GO
Pune is only 598 m above sea-level, but the surrounding hills ensure a pleasant climate throughout the year, though April, May and October can be quite hot and dry.

ARRIVAL/DEPARTURE
Pune is well connected by rail, road and air.

Air
The Indian Airlines daily services to Pune from Bombay remain suspended at the time of writing, but both Vayudoot and Continental Aviation each operate two flights a day (Rs393). Indian Airlines operates a daily flight to and from Delhi (Rs2454) and on various days to/from Madras (Rs1928) and Bangalore (Rs1583). Vayudoot has flights to/from Hyderabad on certain days of the week. The East West Airlines daily service to/from Bombay should be up and running by the time you read this.

Road
Only 184 km (115 miles) from Bombay, there are several buses linking Pune with Bombay. While the Maharashtra State Transport Service runs an efficient service, there are luxury coach services, both air-conditioned and non air-conditioned, run by the Maharashtra Tourism Development Corporation, (MTDC) and other private operators. There are also private taxis for hire and sharing.

Rail
The *Deccan Queen* is one of four express trains shuttling between Bombay VT and Pune every day. The journey takes about 3 hours 20 minutes. The first train, the *Indrayani Express*, leaves at 6 am and arrives at 9.25 am. The Deccan Queen leaves at 5.10 pm, arriving at 8.35 pm. The return leaves Pune at 7.15 am and reaches Bombay at 10.40 am. Throughout the day and night trains between Bombay and Bangalore, Hyderabad and Madras pass through Pune, so getting a seat is rarely a problem.

GETTING AROUND
It is best to allocate at least 2 days to relax and take in the sights. However, for those just passing through there are conducted tours by both Pune Municipal Transport (PMT) and MTDC.

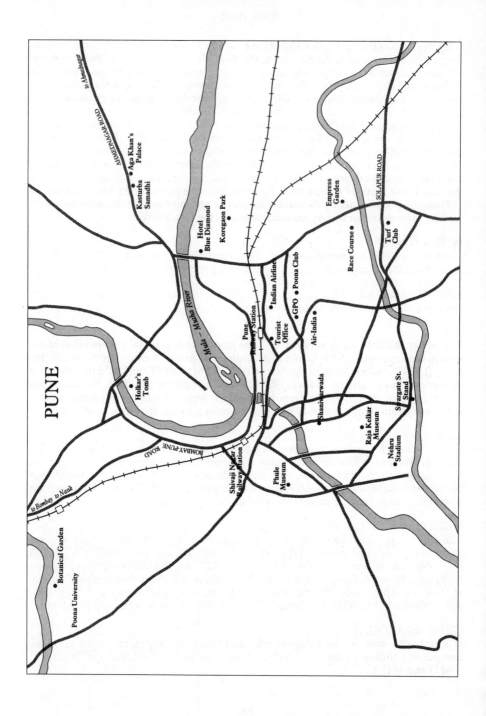

The conducted tour operates every morning and afternoon and lasts 2 hours. Reservations and tickets are available from the PMT office opposite Pune Railway Station or Deccan Gymkhana bus-stand. MTDC also runs a 2-hour city tour twice every day. Tickets and reservation can be had from Regional office, MTDC, Central Building. The best way to see the town is to hire a 3-wheeler auto-rickshaw for about Rs50 for 4 hours. The driver will often act as a guide and will have information about places of interest not on the usual tourist map.

WHAT TO SEE

Pune has several interesting sights, and most of them rate a detailed and leisurely visit. The **Empress Botanical Garden** is on the Prince of Wales Drive to the east of the racecourse. Spread over 60 acres, it has several varieties of plants and flowers, as well as a bandstand and a pond. This garden was originally known as the Soldiers Garden and was under British military management. The other major area of cultivated green is **Bund Garden** on the Mulla-Mutha rivers, about 2 km (1½ miles) north-east of the railway station. This opened to the public in 1869 and is a favourite with residents of the cantonment.

Shivaji Market, the lively local shopping area just west of the centre, was built in 1886 and was originally named The Reay Market after Lord Reay, the then Governor of Bombay. Its architectural design—a number of covered galleries projecting out like spokes from a central structure (in this case a 27-m tower), served as a model for subsequent Indian markets built during the British period.

The benign and universally revered Ganesh is regarded as one of the guardians of the city. The **Ganapati Temple** has grown from the original small temple built by Jijabai, Shahaji Bhonsle's wife, in about 1636. The east-facing **Omkareshvar Temple** of Mahadeva was built between 1740–60 on the bank of the Mutha river in Shanwar Peth, and is surrounded by a high and massive fortified wall built in the Saracenic style. **Panchaleshvara Temple**, also called Pataleshwara, is an 8th century rock-cut cave temple in Shivajinagar on the Jangli Maharaj Road. It has huge pillars and a shrine of Shiva in the centre, with the Nandi in front under a circular canopy, all apparently hewn from a single rock. **Parasnath Temple** is in fact a group of four temples situated in Guruvar Peth, and is dedicated to Lord Parasnath, the 24th Jain saint. Here Jains of both sects, Svetambara and Digambara, have separate temples for worship. The newest of the four temples, dedicated to Risabder, was built in 1834.

Other temples on **Parvati Hill** to the south-east of Pune include the temple of Parvati and Devadevasnvara built in 1749. Additional structures were built by successive Peshwas, including an unfinished large multi-storeyed palace by Bajirao II, the last Peshwa, which was destroyed by lightning in 1816.

Shanwarwada Palace of the Peshwas was built in 1736. Located in the old city near the Mutta river and enclosed by massive walls, this fortress-like structure was destroyed in a fire in 1827. Now a garden stands in its former place with small signs indicating where the various structures stood. The Archaeological Department undertook the task of excavating the whole site, and the foundations, courtyards and other structures give an indication of the splendour of the palace. From the remains of the several fountains, particularly the huge lotus-shaped fountain with over a hundred pipe outlets, one can visualise the magnificent spectacle they must have made when operative. The best view of the whole enclosure inside can be obtained from the balcony of the Nagarkhana.

The **Raja Kelkar Museum** in Shukrawar Peth houses various historical records and relics bearing on Maratha history. Of particular interest are the recreated rooms of the erstwhile Peshwas' Palace, notably the bedroom of Peshwa Bajirao I and his mistress Mastani. Open daily from 8.30 am–12.30 and 3pm–6.30 pm.

Rajneesh Ashram is situated in Koregaon Park, an oasis amidst the urban sprawl of Pune, set in 4 acres of grounds containing all varieties of lush tropical plants. The late, controversial godman Bhagwan Rajneesh had his Indian headquarters here and this was the place he retired to after the problems in Oregon. Beyond the Fitzgerald Bridge on the road toward the airport is the **Aga Khan's Palace** built in 1860 by HH Aga Khan III, the spiritual head of the Ismailiah Khoja Community. This palace was where Mahatma Gandhi, his wife Kasturba and his private secretary Mahadev Desai were kept imprisoned during the 1942 Quit India movement. Both Mahadev Desai and Kasturba Gandhi died here, and two marble samadhis have been built in the ground in their memory.

Excursion

Within a short distance of Pune proper there are several interesting sights, many of which are quite easy to reach. Local buses go to most of these places or a car can be hired locally—the drivers are usually good guides, although their standard of English varies and fantasy often embellishes historical fact.

Raigad Fort is famous as the capital of Shivaji during the last years of his reign and is located about 51 km (32 miles) south-west of Pune at a height of 869 m. The fort comprises 3 terraces—Padmavati, Sanjivani and Suvela, with the inner fort being centrally located. Only a few structures remain intact in this fort: the Padmavati temple, Ambarkhana, the Ramesvara temple and a number of carved stone figures on the Suvela terrace. A visit to the temple can fit into a trip to Mahabaleshwar.

The caves at **Karla**, 465 km (28 miles) from Pune, within the boundary of Vehergaon village, lie on a spur in a range of hills and are the finest surviving example of Hinayana Buddhist architecture. They consist of a large chapel (*chaitya*) and several dwelling places (*vihara*). Cave 8, the *chaitya*, is the finest and best preserved in the western Deccan and dates back to 80 BC. In and around the caves, there are several inscriptions.

Another group of early Buddhist caves are to be found at **Bhaja**, 6 km (4 miles) south of Karla and 8 km (5 miles) east of Lonavala (about 64 km from Pune). Set in a village in the Maval taluka, these caves date back to the 1st and 2nd centuries BC and are among the earliest examples of Buddhist art in the Deccan. More than 20 rock-cut monasteries are set into the west face of a steep hill about 140 m above the village. Starting from the north, the first cave is a natural cavern about 10 m long. This is followed by 10 plain cells. Cave 12 is a chapel (*chaitya*) about 20 m by 10 m. The structure of this cave, with its 27 octagonal shafts, arched roof and remains of wooden girders leaves no doubt about its importance. The other cave of note is Cave 19.

At the source of the river Bhima lies **Bhimashankar**, famous for its Mahadeva temple. Said to house one of the 12 jyotirlingas of India (symbols of Shiva's creative power), this temple was built in the 19th century by Nana Phadnavis. The original temple is built of dark stone with a vaulted roof. In the hall (*mandap*) lies a rough stone Nandi and in the shrine a metal cast of five heads representing the god Bhimashankar.

RECREATION AND SHOPPING
Pune is famous for its horses; racing as well as breeding. There are several stud farms around Pune and the owners are a dedicated lot. Most of them have inherited

fortunes or run parallel businesses and have hired professionals to run the stud farms, leaving them free to indulge in the sport.

Races are held at **The Royal Western India Turf Club**. Serious racers come to Pune for the major events; Pune has its own keen followers of the sport.

One of Pune's major shopping arcades is the M.G. Road which has shops selling most things, from Shrewsbury biscuits (a Pune speciality!) to walking sticks and solar topis (often found in old colonial towns), to basic necessities. Other spots to shop are the Deccan Gymkhana and Laxmi Road areas. However, the smaller markets in the city area are perhaps more interesting to browse in, with shops selling old brassware and local handloom saris of a silk-cotton weave. Pune jewellers are an enterprising lot and can quickly copy almost any design. Two shops selling gift items of traditional craft items are the **Attic** on Dhole Patil Road and the **Orchid** on Ferguson College Road.

WHERE TO STAY

There are many hotels to suit every pocket and taste in the cantonment and city areas. In Koregaon Park are numerous guest-houses which originally catered to visitors to the Rajneesh Ashram. Those who wish to experience traditional urban Pune are advised to seek a hotel in the city. For those arriving in Pune by train, the MTDC has a special hotel reservation chart as well as a booth at the railway station. A similar service is expected to be installed at the airport soon.

Note: Places to stay in the cantonment tend to get crowded, particularly during racing weekends; at other times, the atmosphere in these hotels is relaxed and friendly.

Expensive (Over US$35/Rs1000 per room night)

Hotel Blue Diamond (tel 663775, tlx 0145-7369, fax 0212-666101) in Koregaon Park offers five-star luxury with the attendant frills like business centre, swimming-pool, several restaurants. Room rates from US$45.

Mid-range (US$10–35/Rs250–1000 per room night)

Hotel Sagar Plaza on Bund Garden Road (tel 661880, 661585, tlx 0145-7645) is another favourite with rooms from Rs700. **Amir** on Connaught Road, near the railway station (tel 661840/9, tlx 0145-7292, fax 0212-444253) is one of the biggest and best hotels in Pune although only rated with three stars. A businessman's hotel with 24 check-in/out rooms, reasonable rooms from Rs500 and a central location. **Ashirwad** (tel 666142), also on Connaught Road, offers services comparable to Amir. **Hotel Regency** (tel 669411, tlx 0145-7609) on Dhole Patil Road, **Hotel Ranjeet** (tel 345012, 345142) on Bhandarkar Institute Road and **Deccan Park** (tel 345065) on Ferguson College Road, have good rooms and services for Rs300 single, Rs350 double.

EATING OUT

Originally Pune was split into two distinct parts: camp and city. The camp consisted of upper-crust society: Parsi, Sindhi and Christian communities, plus the military, and acquired several Western and Irani eating places. The city area was predominantly Maharashtrian and therefore boasted few upmarket eateries. Industrialisation has evened out the distribution of wealth, and societies and in both sectors of town there are restaurants to suit every pocket.

Overall, however, food remains cheap: except at five-star restaurants, the prices are lower than in the rest of the country. There are many roadside vendors serving Indian fast-foods like *pani-puri, bhel-puri, kachori* and *mirchi-pakoda*. Though residents flock to these stalls every evening, the snacks they serve are not recommended for people with delicate stomachs.

Reputable, clean restaurants with mixed menus include: the **Coffee House** in Moledina Road which used to be a Parsi eatery and now serves South Indian delicacies like *dosa, idli*, etc., also Mughlai dishes. **Shabri** near Ferguson College has traditional Maharashtrian fare. **Cafe Mahanaaz** in M.G. Road serves Irani food and is the most popular among several others of its kind. **Dorabjee** in Dastur Meher Road has typical Parsi food and is a Pune institution. **Vaishali** near Ferguson College mainly caters to students and serves South Indian food while **Vrushali** in Karve Road is a simple Maharashtrian *thali* restaurant. Meals at any of these restaurants cost from Rs25–75.

If time is not a constraint, it is possible to explore and sample the wide culinary choice the city has to offer. The other eating places of the city are classified according to cuisine.

Gujarati: **Dreamland** near the station, **Chetna** in Budhwar Peth. *Konkani*: **Calcutta Boarding House** on J.M. Road (basically all varieties of fish dishes), and **Kinara** in Hotel Hill View. *Maharashtrian*: **Suvarna Rekha Dining Hall** on Prabhat Road, **Shreya's** in Deccan Gymkhana. Fast food: **Marz-o-Rin** on M.G. Road, **Poona Coffee House** in Deccan Gymkhana, the **Coffee Shop** in Hotel Blue Diamond.

Apart from the above, a choice of different culinary styles is available at **Kwality** in camp and **Portico** on J.M. Road. This section on food would be incomplete without a mention of the bakeries of Pune. For quite some time now, Pune has enjoyed the reputation of having some of the best bakeries in the country and no Indian tourist returns from Pune without a bagful of Pune biscuits. The major bakeries include **Spices Health Foods** which sell excellent brown bread and jars of crunchy peanut butter, and **Royal Bakery** both on M.G. Road, **Baker's Basket** in Hotel Blue Diamond, **Kayani** on Dr. Coyaji Road and **Cake-N-Counter** in Thackers House on East Street.

GENERAL INFORMATION
Airline offices are; Indian Airlines (tel 664189, apt 665312), Continental Aviation (tel 6123390) and Vayudoot (tel 6121397, 6121405).

MAHABALESHWAR

Mahabaleshwar is one of the most popular hill stations of western India, and at 1372 m, the highest of the region. Situated in the Sahyadri range of the Western Ghats, Mahabaleshwar is also blessed with spectacular views of the Krishna and Koyna valleys.

For centuries this has been known as a holy place. The Sahyadri range is the source of many rivers including the Krishna which, as a main river of the Deccan, is considered to be one of India's seven sacred rivers. Near the old village, a 5-km

(3-mile) walk from the main post office, several temples, some dating from the 13th century, have been built near the source of this river. The Mahabaleshwar Temple dedicated to Lord Shiva, and from which the town has derived its name, and Atibaleshwar Temple (roughly meaning the 'Great Powerful God') are but two where worship still takes place.

The famous Maratha leader Shivaji visited the temples at the source of the Krishna in 1653 and later built Pratapgadh Fort on the nearby Par Ghat. The fort passed to British hands after the last Peshwa was defeated in 1818. Subsequently, the fort and the hill were handed over to Raja Pratap Singh of Satara, a descendant of Shivaji. Although Sir Charles Malet in 1791 was the first Briton to visit Mahabaleshwar, the development of this place did not take place until over 30 years later. Sir John Malcolm, the then Governor of Bombay, visited Mahabaleshwar in 1828 at the invitation of Rajah Pratap Singh, and took an immediate liking to the place. The Rajah had already started developing the hill, encouraged by successive British residents, and after Malcolm's visit, the new station was named Malcolm Peth. The name lasted for several years. Malcolm had the first Government House built there, and this is still known as Mount Malcolm. In fact Mahabaleshwar became the summer seat of the Bombay Government mainly because of the interest Sir John showed. All attendant facilities like telegraph and roads were quickly built, and several bungalows with names like Lily Cottage and Barchester sprang up, as well as churches, a polo ground, racecourse (now converted to a golf-course), Mahabaleshwar Club and Bazaar.

Some of the building and development work was accomplished through convict labour. Soon after the sanatorium was completed, a jail was built to house some 120 Chinese and Malay convicts. These convicts were allowed to move with complete freedom, and in their spare time they introduced potatoes and other English vegetables, and were instrumental in developing the various gardens of the resort. The jail was abolished in 1864 and some of the prisoners were allowed to stay on here. One of the several nearby waterfalls is still known as Chinaman's Waterfall.

WHEN TO GO
The season is October to June, and peak timings are during the school summer holidays, Christmas and the Indian festival of Diwali. Mahabaleshwar closes down during the monsoons of July to September and only a few hotels stay open.

ARRIVAL/DEPARTURE

Air and Rail
Mahabaleshwar is connected by road to nearby tourist centres and major towns. The nearest convenient airport and railhead is Pune, 122 km (77 miles) away (see p.309).

Road
MTDC operates direct buses from Bombay during the season either via Pune (290 km: 181 miles) or via Mahad (247 km: 154 miles)—book at the MTDC office, CDO Hutment, Madame Cama Road, Bombay (tel 2026713). Regular buses, and taxis are available from Pune.

GETTING AROUND

Mahabaleshwar has several miles of good road as well as a number of lovely walks. Ponies are available for hire, for the bridle-paths and gallops. It is essential to carry a map of all the main points and paths (available from Treacher & Co in the main bazaar). Alternatively, a guide can be hired for Rs100 a day.

WHAT TO SEE

The Maharashtra Cultural and Tourism Development Corporation (MCTDC) runs conducted tours every day during the season. One tour lasts about 4 hours (Rs55) and covers very briefly the major sights of Mahabaleshwar. The MCTDC also runs tours to Panchgani, a small satellite hill station nearby (see below), and to Pratapgadh Fort. Similar conducted tours are available from the State Transport Undertaking. Taxis with local guides can be hired for a full day's sightseeing for Rs250. All distances quoted hereafter are from the post office.

Hill Station Tour (on foot, selectively over a few days)

Yenna Lake–Lingmala Waterfall–Kate's Point–Connaught Peak–Old Mahabaleshwar–Marjorie Point–Arthur's Seat–Elphinstone Point–Hunter's Point–Dhobi Waterfall–Lodwick Point–Elephant's Head–Bombay Point–Chinaman's Waterfall–Babbington Point–Helen's Point–Wilson Point

This is a region of heights and views, lakes and holy places, for quiet wanderings and contemplation. Take a picnic.

Yenna Lake, 2.4 km (1½ miles) from the post office, has boats for hire. Fishing is possible here although not very good and permission needs to be obtained in advance from the local forest officer. The **Lingmala Waterfall** is at the top of the Yenna valley (6 km; 4 miles). It tends to dry up in high summer, but the sight during and after the monsoon is quite spectacular. **Kate's Point** (3.6 km; 2 miles) is 1291 m above sea-level, and a lovely view of the Krishna valley can be obtained from here. **Connaught Peak** (4 km; 2½ miles), formerly known as Mount Olympia, is 1385 m high and offers lovely views of the Yenna Lake and the Krishna Valley.

The village of **Old Mahabaleshwar** (5 km; 3 miles) looks out over the Krishna valley and has a number of temples: the **Mahabaleshwar Temple**, dedicated to Lord Shiva, and nearby **Krishna Temple** which according to tradition is the source of seven rivers—the Krishna, the Yenna, the Koyna, the Gayatri, the Savitri, the Saraswati and the Bhagirathi (the last two rivers exist only in the Hindu Scriptures). **Marjorie Point** (9.8 km; 6 miles) is at a height of 1292 m above sea-level. **Arthur's Seat** (12.4 km; 7¾ miles) is even higher and is Mahabaleshwar's most famous point. **Elphinstone Point** (10 km; 6 miles) is on the extreme west of the plateau and is a popular picnic spot. **Hunter's Point** (3.6 km; 2 miles) is at a height of 1290 m and overlooks the Koyna river valley. **Dhobi Waterfall** (3.2 km; 2 miles) is on the bridle path leading to Lodwick Point from Elphinstone Point and is a scenic spot. **Lodwick Point** (4.8 km; 3 miles) has a monument to General Lodwick and a lovely view of the rugged landscape. **Elephant's Head** (6 km; 3¾ miles) takes its name from its cliff, shaped like an elephant's head and trunk. **Bombay Point** (5 km; 3 miles), at 1294 m looks over the Pratapgadh fort and has the most extensive view. Visit in the evening, for the spectacular sight of the setting sun. During colonial rule, this point had a large carriage-park, and a band played from the bandstand. **Chinaman's Waterfall** (2.4 km; 1½ miles) is a popular picnic spot. The waterfall itself and the Koyna Valley are best seen from **Babington Point** (3.2 km; 2 miles). **Helen's Point** (3.2 km; 2 miles) offers a beautiful view of the Blue Valley. **Wilson's Point** (2.2 km; 1¼ miles), the highest point in Mahabaleshwar at 1435 m, was named after Sir Leslie Wilson, Governor of Bombay from 1923 to 1928, and has an enchanting view of the sunrise.

RECREATION
Apart from the numerous rides, gallops and bridle-paths to be walked or explored on pony-back, Mahabaleshwar offers facilities for fishing and boating at Yenna Lake, golf at the Mahabaleshwar Club, which offers temporary membership; tennis, badminton and indoor games at the Hindu Gymkhana.

SHOPPING
Strawberry jam and honey are the main produce. Honey in different flavours is best bought from the Government-owned Madhu Sagar Company which has a retail counter on Mahad Road, close to the bazaar. The main shopping centres are located on the main street and Malcolm Peth. The best general stores are Treacher's and Imperial.

EATING OUT
Most notable restaurants are attached to hotels. Non-vegetarian preparations are available at **Dina Hotel, Frederick Hotel, Race View Hotel** and **Silverene.** Vegetarian food is served at **Aram, Paradise Hotel, Poonam** and **Shalimar Hotel.**

WHERE TO STAY
Mahabaleshwar has over 100 hotels ranging from luxury to utilitarian—some are only open seasonally. The best hotel is probably the **Valley View Resort** (tel 445) with rooms from about Rs1200. Other major hotels are **Hotel Anarkali** (tel 336) with clean rooms and modern facilities, open throughout the year; **Frederick's** (tel 240) with a splendid view of the Yenna lake; **Dina's Hotel** (tel 246) also overlooking Yenna has an old-world charm about it; **Shreyas** (tel 365) is an Indian vegetarian hotel. Some of the other mid-range hotels are **Paradise** (tel 236), **Dreamland** (tel 228) and **Race View** (tel 238, 278). The MTDC has several cottages for hire at the site of the Old Government House.

A word of caution here is appropriate. During peak season, most hotels operate strictly on bed-and-board basis, during the off-season rates are cut by as much as half.

GENERAL INFORMATION
The **Roman Catholic Holy Cross Church** near the bus-stand holds regular services; the much more impressive **Anglican Christ Church** behind the Makharia Garden is now deserted. For Muslims, there are the **Deccani** and **Jama masjids**; and for Hindus, the **Hanuman, Krishnabai, Ram** and **Mahabali** (also known as Nahar) **temples.**

The **Tourist Information Bureau** (tel 271) near the bus-stand and the **Holiday Camp** (tel 7318) usually have a stock of maps of Mahabaleshwar showing bridle-paths, walks and rides. Since there is partial prohibition in Maharashtra, an **All India Liquor Permit** should be obtained from Indian missions abroad or from Government of India Tourist offices in Bombay, Calcutta, Delhi and Madras. Beer can be purchased without a permit.

PANCHGANI

Panchgani is a close neighbour of Mahabaleshwar and is considered to be a satellite station for the larger and more famous hill station. Situated at 1335 m on a ridge of the steep Parasni Ghat, Panchgani takes its name from the five (*panch*) hills surounding it. The development of this station is attributed to the efforts of John Chesson in the 1850s.

WHEN TO GO
Panchgani has an advantage over Mahabaleshwar with regard to the monsoon, or rather the lack of it, as it is in the rain shadow. The station remains open throughout the year.

ARRIVAL/DEPARTURE
Panchgani is only 19 km (12 miles) from Mahabaleshwar and is well connected with Pune (100 km; 62 miles) and Bombay (277 km; 172 miles) by regular bus services. Taxis are available from Pune for Rs350.

GETTING AROUND
Panchgani is spread over an area of 3.4 sq km, and has lovely views of the Krishna valley, and the huge reservoir formed by the Dhome Dam. All the places of interest can be visited on foot, though ponies are also available for hire.

WHAT TO SEE
The most interesting sight is the **Tableland** above the Panchgani ghat. This flat expanse of rock has superb sunrise and sunset views and is a favourite playground for the school-children from the many boarding schools in the area.

Several pleasant walks lead from the Tableland into the valleys. The countryside round here is beautiful and all the walks listed below provide gentle exercise punctuated by wide views and quiet picnic spots. **Sidney Point** and **Parsi Point** are the most popular. There is a walk down to the **Dhome Dam** from Sidney Point. The **Meherbaba Caves** and **Rajapuri Caves** are interesting sights, and **Harrison Point, Bombay Point, Kachhawari Point** are favourite spots for picnickers and visitors.

The other favourite sight is **Wai** (12 km; 7 miles), a small town on the bank of the Krishna river with several temples to Shiva and Ganpati. It is best to take a taxi (Rs50) although the walk is interesting. The Buddhist Caves at Lonara are a further 7 km (4 miles) away (see below).

RECREATION
The **Panchgani Club** offers temporary memberships to visitors, who can make use of the card-room, table-tennis and other indoor games.

WHERE TO STAY
There are several Western-style hotels as well as cheaper lodges and boarding-houses to suit all budgets. Among the better hotels are **Aman** (tel 211, 392), a modern and rather ugly hotel but the staff are pleasant. **Prospect** (tel 268), **Il-Palazzo** (tel 226) and **Jerroz** (tel 238) are small family-run hotels.

GENERAL INFORMATION
The **Tourist Information Centre** on Dr Billimoria Road provides general information and maps. There are two churches, Roman Catholic and Protestant. There is also a Parsi Fire Temple.

MATHERAN

Matheran on the Sahyadri (Western Ghats) range was discovered in 1850 by Hugh Poyntz Malet, the then Collector of Thane district. He climbed the hill now known as **One Tree Hill** and liked the general area enough to subsequently have a house built for himself. This house, 'The Byke', was the first house to be built here. Matheran became a popular resort through the patronage of Lord Elphinstone, Governor of Bombay in the 1850s. Elphinstone visited in 1855 and chose a site for the bungalow, still known as 'Elphinstone Lodge'.

WHEN TO GO
The season is October to May. Over the years, because of deforestation and global climatic change, there has been an appreciable increase in temperature and summers can be uncomfortably hot. The monsoon is quite heavy and by the third week of July when the rains slacken off, Matheran is at its prettiest, with the dark green mountains slashed by a number of freshets and waterfalls.

ARRIVAL/DEPARTURE

Air
The nearest airport is Bombay, 102 km (64 miles) away.

Rail
One of India's four and least well-known, hill railways links Matheran with the outside world. Take a Pune train from Bombay VT and change at **Neral** for the narrow-gauge train to Matheran. Several trains a day cover the 20-km (12½ -mile) climb in about 2 hours. During the monsoons, the train service is reduced to one a day, and during heavy rains the service stops altogether because of the possibility of landslides. This is perhaps one of the best introductions to the Western Ghats, and one of the most leisurely train journeys in the world.

Road
Motorised transport is banned in Matheran; the closest cars can approach to the town centre is the car park 4 km (2½ miles) away. Shared taxis are available from the nearest mainline rail-head at Neral.

GETTING AROUND
Matheran covers an area of 8 sq km (3 sq miles). Most visitors move around on foot; ponies and hand-pulled rickshaws are available for hire.

WHAT TO SEE
There are several places of interest at Matheran. Some of the major ones are **Cathedral Rock** and **Charlotte Lake**. **Rambagh Village** is 2 km from the post office at the start

of a pleasant walk to **Bhorgaon** and back to One Tree Hill via Shivaji's Ladder. A plethora of points offer lovely views of the plains or the ghats; their names pay homage to, amongst others, Artists, King Edward, the Landscape, Marjorie, One Tree, the Panorama and a Porcupine!

Panorama Point 5 km (3 miles) from Matheran post office has spectacular views of Neral, Bombay and the ghats. This is a popular point to watch the sun rise. **Porcupine Point** is where most people go to view the sunset.

RECREATION AND SHOPPING

The **Olympia Race Course** holds annual sports and riding competitions. A band plays on Pandey Playground in high season. Honey, footwear and decorative grasses are the local products offered for sale in Matheran's main bazaar on Mahatma Gandhi Road.

WHERE TO STAY

Matheran's hotels and guest-houses are mostly tree-shaded old bungalows with slate or tin roofs. There are several hotels, to suit all budgets. Better hotels are **Rugby** (tel 291/2) on Kotwal Road with rooms and full board for Rs1200, and **Lord's Central** (tel 228, Bombay 318008) Mahatma Gandhi Road. **Royal Hotel** (tel 247, 275, Bombay 352784) on Kasturba Road has rooms from Rs450, **Hotel Regal** (tel 243, 287) also on Kasturba Road charges Rs500 per room night. **Maldoonga Resorts** (tel 204, Bombay 6269981) in a secluded area between Louisa and Por-cupine Points charges Rs450 for a single room without food. **Brightlands Resorts** (tel 244, Bombay 6423856) is an efficient hotel in 7-acre grounds, dotted with bungalows for the guests, with tennis court, dairy and a stable for the horses. Rooms are from Rs550 single, Rs700 double.

Among the budget hotels **Gujarat Bhavan** (tel 378, 278) on Maulana Azad Road charges between Rs200 and Rs300 including meals.

EATING OUT

Matheran offers no great variety of culinary styles, since most tourists are Gujarati and Maharashtrian. Most hotels include meals in their tariff and many are strictly vegetarian in order to cater for the majority. **Divadkar's Hotel** (tel 223) and **Pramod's Restaurant** have permit bars.

GENERAL INFORMATION

The post office and the Tourist Information Bureau are situated on M.G. Road opposite the railway station. Ponies and rickshaws are hired by the hour, for Rs30.

LONAVALA AND KHANDALA

The twin hill resorts of Lonavala and Khandala are at a greater distance from Bombay than Matheran, but are much more accessible and hence more popular— practically a city suburb. Many wealthy Bombayites have built houses here and drive down for the week-end when the resorts become overcrowded. However, during the week they are quiet and extremely pleasant. Lonavala and Khandala have existed since the 1850s, but little is known about how they developed.

WHEN TO GO
Lonavala and Khandala stay open all year even though the monsoon is quite heavy.

ARRIVAL AND DEPARTURE

Rail
Lonavala, and to a lesser extent Khandala are connected to Bombay VT by a regular service. The ghat section before Lonavala is picturesque particularly during the monsoon. A local train service operates between Pune and Lonavala (64 km; 40 miles).

Road
Regular bus services operate between Bombay and Lonavala (100 km; 64 miles) as well as Bombay and Khandala (96 km; 62 miles). Buses also ply between Pune and Lonavala. The Maharashtra Tourism Development Corporation (MTDC) runs buses from Lonavala station to the MTDC Holiday Resort near Karla Caves.

GETTING AROUND
MTDC operates conducted tours to the Karla Buddhist Caves, as well as those at Bhaja and Bedsa, although most people prefer to take a taxi or a taxi 3-wheeler (approximately Rs75 return) for independent trips.

WHAT TO SEE
A half-day at the Karla caves or at the forts of Lohagad and Visapur (see below) is likely to cost in the region of Rs30 by taxi. For more hedonistic enjoyment the following beauty spots could be visited in a day, if you are not inclined to linger or picnic. Valvan Dam, Ryewood Park, Tiger's Leap, Tungarli Lake, Bhusir Lake, Rajmachi Point, Kuna Point, Duke's Nose, Lonavala Lake.

The most important sites of historic and religious significance in the area are the rock-cut caves of **Karla**, 4 km (2½ miles) away, which include the largest and best preserved chaitya cave in the country; **Bhaja**, a further 3 km, and **Bedsa**; these date back to the 2nd century BC. Detailed visits are recommended and an enjoyable half-day can be spent in the area. For a fuller description, refer to Pune. There are two forts, at **Lohagad** and **Visapur** 4 km west of the Bhaja and Bedsa caves. Both were occupied by the British in 1818 but have long since been deserted. Access to both is quite difficult and walking shoes are recommended if you are going to climb the 600 m to the Visapur fort.

RECREATION AND SHOPPING
The Municipal Sports Club (tel 2285) at Lonavala offers indoor games. Yoga enthusiasts can visit the **Kaivalyadham Yogashram** in Valvan. There are two swimming-pools—**Biji's Ingleside Inn** and **Gajanan Mahimtura** both in Lonavala, which are open to the public on payment of a fee (Rs35).

WHERE TO STAY
Both Lonavala and Khandala have a range of resort hotels and lodges. At weekends they are generally booked out but during the week rooms are available without too much difficulty—and at a discount rate. Lonavala's five-star hotel is the well-established **Fariyas Holiday Resort** (tel 2701/5, Bombay 2042911) which charges five-star prices but has all facilities. **Biji's Ingleside Inn** (tel 2966, 2638, Bombay 296352) on New Tungarli Road has rooms from Rs600.The **Span Hill Resort** (tel 3685, Bombay

6145166) charges Rs600 for a double room and Rs1150 for a suite. **Khandala Hotel Girija** (tel 2062, 3426) on the Bombay–Pune Road charges Rs400 for a room. **Hotel Vallerina** (tel 3410, Bombay 2863372) has rooms from about Rs500. There are smaller hotels at both Lonavala and Khandala which are reasonably clean and cheap.

EATING OUT
Among the good restaurants **Bijis Ingleside Inn** where meals would be from Rs125. **Cafe Gulistan, The Chancellor, Lonavala Restaurant** and **Tandoor House** are in the same price bracket and can be recommended.

GENERAL INFORMATION
Prohibition laws of Maharashtra apply. Beer is exempt, but for hard liquor, a permit must be obtained. The **Tourist Information Bureau** (tel 2428) is near the Lonavala Railway Station.

Route 7—Gujarat

Gujarat is a stronghold of Jainism, and for many it is seen as the home of Gandhi and his message. Though one of the nation's most industrially advanced states, it is equally well known as the home of traditions and religion, drawing thousands of pilgrims each year. Its lifestyle is colourful with bright textiles, handicrafts, folk-dances and festivals that are vivid splashes of bright sapphire blues, rich reds and lush emerald greens. Its people are gay, gentle, hard-working and inquisitive; many have never seen a foreigner before. Gujarat exists out of time. Untouched by tourism, it extends a warm, rather surprised, hand of welcome to the visitor who really wants to get away from it all.

Nowhere is this more true than on the southern coast of the state. Here a small triad of nascent resorts provide the visitor with the best beaches, wildlife and historic temple architecture that Gujarat can offer. The central attraction, the 16th-century ex-Portuguese port of Diu, is a small idyllic town of Mediterranean charm, with relaxing bars and tavernas, two glorious beaches, Catholic cathedrals and an imposing fort. Life here is slow and peaceful, a complete contrast to the normal hustle and bustle of India. Close by is Somnath, a major Hindu pilgrimage centre, with a famous shore temple (seven times destroyed and rebuilt) and another fine beach. At Sasan-Gir, one of the finest wildlife sanctuaries in the country, the Asian lion roams his last natural refuge on earth. Travelling this virgin territory, frequented by few foreign visitors, you will feel like a stranger in paradise.

Season: October to March
Monsoons: June to September
Climate: 27°–41°C (summer); 14°–29°C (winter)
Route duration: 5–10 days (far longer if pinned down on sunkissed beaches)

TRAVEL ITINERARY

Bombay to Diu 930 km (580 miles)

Air / Road
Vayudoot offers one flight daily to Keshod (PF325, Rs1540). It's wise to book a return as Keshod–Bombay flights are heavily subscribed. From Keshod to Diu is 150 km (94 miles) by road: local buses to Veraval (1½ hrs), to Oona (2½ hrs) and to Ghoghla (30 mins). Then either ferry or, when the new bridge is completed, auto-rickshaw over to Diu.

Rail
There are daily trains from Bombay Central to Ahmedabad (9 hours); and the *Gurdinar Express* from Ahmedabad down to Veraval (dep 8.45 pm daily, arr 10 am next morning).

Road
The daily 'luxury video' bus runs direct to Diu (22 hours). Book from Goa Travels/Hirup Travel Service, Prabhakar Sadan ground floor, Khetwadi Back Rd, 12th lane (tel 358186, 359856) or Pawan Travels, 103 Auto Commerce House, Kennedy Bridge, near Nana's Chowk Post Office (tel 356887, 357907). This is a notorious Indian bus journey: a whole day of excruciating disco music/video films, potholed roads and arguments over double-booked seats, plus the occasional breakdown. Take earplugs, two seat-cushions, and a crash helmet. One way on this bus is quite enough. It's popular though, and much quicker than the train. There's also a cheap state bus (about Rs100) from Bombay to Oona—less comfortable, but no video! Book from MTDC office, Bombay. It leaves 12.30 pm daily.

Diu to Somnath 54 km (34 miles)

Road
Buses to Oona (Rs4) and Veraval (Rs12); then a Rs15 rickshaw or Rs3 bus for the final 7 km (4½ miles) up to Somnath.

Somnath to Sasan-Gir 46 km (28.8 miles)

Road
Bus from Veraval (2 hours, Rs6). Do check timings for Sasan-Gir buses before going up to Somnath: it's an irregular service.

Sasan-Gir to Diu 105 km (65.6 miles)

Road
Two express buses daily to and from Oona (3 hours). Then bus to Ghoghla.

Rail
Daily train to Oona (9 hours). Slow.

Diu to Bombay

Road/Air
Buses from Ghoghla, Oona and Veraval to Keshod; one Vayudoot flight daily to Bombay (PF326, Rs1540).

Rail
Daily trains from Veraval or Somnath (13/14 hours) to Ahmedabad; night train to Bombay (dep 10.35 pm, arr 7 am).

Road
Two 'luxury video' buses daily (22 hours): 11.30 am departure from Diu, booked from Goa Travels, opposite jetty (tel 44, 87); 10.30 am departure from Ghoghla, booked from Rajasree Travels, Main Rd, Ghoghla (tel 98). Reserve your seats well in advance.

CONTINUATIONS
From Ahmedabad, you can connect with the Rajasthan itinerary via quick bus journeys up to Mt Abu (6/7 hours) or Udaipur (8 hours).

DIU

The small ex-Portuguese island of Diu is a perfect escape from modern India. In fact, it is hardly like India at all, more like a displaced Greek island. The clean, cobbled streets, the pastel houses, the Catholic churches and the old bastioned fort, the colourful fishwives in the elegant market square and the sleepy, relaxed atmos-

Diu Badminton Club is housed in a converted church

phere—everything about Diu is pleasantly Mediterranean. It makes the perfect base from which to explore south Gujarat, and offers some marvellous beaches.

Diu derives its name from the Sanskrit word 'Dweep'. Between the 14th and 16th centuries it was a busy and important seaport and naval base, used by merchants all over the world as a trading point with India. When the Portuguese set their heart on it, in the mid-16th century, Diu was under the rule of the Sultans of Oman. Their first offensive, led by Nunho da Cunha (the Portuguese governor), was launched in 1531, but failed. A short time later though, Bahadur Shah (the Sultan of Gujarat) was forced to let the Portuguese build a fortress on the island, in return for their armed help against Humayun, the Mughal emperor. The massive Diu Fort was completed in 1547 and gave the Portuguese the foothold they needed to seize the whole island from the Shah, as well as the opposite coastal village of Ghoghla. For the next 350 years, Diu was administered by a Portuguese governor. Only on 19 December 1961 did it return, along with the other Portuguese pockets of Goa and Daman, to Indian rule, after 450 years of foreign rule.

Now, Diu is a tidy, neat and attractive town. Since liberation, it has gained a number of new schools, roads, bridges and communications which have brought it slowly back into line with modern India. Yet it retains much of its old Portuguese charm, and is never anything less than completely relaxing. As a coastal fishing-town, the first thing you'll notice here is the powerful reek of fish—perfectly natural, since most of Ghoghla/Diu's population make their living from the sea. They are a happy, colourful and multi-national people, most of whom speak Gujarati and follow the Hindu faith. They are tuned in to Westerners, and you won't for once feel either odd or conspicuous. The only time you'll remember you're in India is at weekends when busloads of Gujaratis from far and wide come over for a party. Diu is the only place in 'dry' Gujarat they can get a drink

For comfort, visit during the comparatively cool season of November–February. It's still pleasant in March–April, but a bit too warm for most. Avoid coming in May–June at all costs: a swarm of tourists hit the beaches, and you can forget all about peace and quiet.

WHAT TO SEE
Not many people visit Diu with the idea of sightseeing. They come for the beaches. As soon as they find one they like, they lie down and go to sleep, sometimes for weeks. Yet Diu Town itself is an interesting place, well worth exploring by push-bike (there are good bike hire places near Nilesh Guest House) or on foot. The tourist office sometimes operates sightseeing tours, but Diu is one place to see on your own initiative. Off the jetty, the Old Fort Rd leads off left to the fort, churches, and some budget hotels. The town itself lies behind the small market square opposite the jetty. Within the square is the stop for the small, irregular local bus service, which is useful for the beaches, and for out-of-town forays. Diu has a handful of auto-rickshaws, whose drivers charge a fair Rs3 per km. From around noon to 4 pm it's siesta time (another Portuguese legacy) and the town clears.

Diu Town Tour (by cycle, 3–4 hours)
Diu Fort–Ancient Diu Church–Ruined Churches–St Paul's Church

It's best to start touring in the cool of the morning, but this can be difficult. Cycle hire shops open around 9 am, and it's nearly impossible to get breakfast before this time anywhere in town (try the Hotel Mozambique, if stuck). You'll quickly notice Diu's dominant characteristic: nobody is in a hurry to do anything.

Cycle down to the jetty. Opposite this, there's often an early-morning covered fish/vegetable market, little to buy but lots to see. From the market square, proceed down Old Fort Rd which runs out along the seafront. A cool, refreshing 10-minute ride takes you to the huge, battlemented **Diu Fort**. This is the double-moated 16th-century Portuguese bastion, largely ruined today but worth an hour-long wander. Within, walk up to the vantage-point Lighthouse, approached by a stone ramp, which gives prime views of the town, churches and coastline. From here, you can well appreciate the fort's strategic importance to the Portuguese; though rapidly crumbling today, it was in olden days near-impregnable. Round the lighthouse quadrant, looming over the stone buttresses, are some beautiful old cannon with reliefs of human faces moulded into the cast. Returning down into the courtyard of the sub-jail, you'll find the arrogant, strutting statue of **Don Nunho da Cunha**, a bronze life-size oddity surrounded by heaps of old cannonballs. Several have been employed as decorative borders to the flower-beds.

Behind the fort, visit the three old Catholic churches on view from the lighthouse. They can be seen in any order. Only a handful of Christian families remain in Diu, and these churches are no longer places of worship, little visited and largely ruined. Of the three, the **Ancient Diu Church** has been turned into a school—the imposing architectural style of its façade plus intricate interior woodwork contrasting strangely with the gleaming lunar module in the courtyard playground; the second, though notable for its stone springs and depictions of phases in Christ's life, has for the past 300 years doubled up as the town's **Hospital Building** (convenient for casualties of the cricket games going on in the square below); and the third—most peculiar of all—has now become the **Diu Badminton Club**.

Cycling back into town, drop in on the small but lively town **bazaar** (tucked away behind the market square), then take directions for nearby **St Paul's Church**. This is a towering structure, built in 1691, and dedicated to Our Lady of the Immaculate Conception. It is notable for its magnificent carved gates, and for its beautiful altar made of solid Burma teak.

The Beaches (by cycle/bus/rickshaw)
Nagoa–Ahmedpur Mandvi

These are two of the most pleasant beaches in India; not the best maybe, but certainly a couple of the quietest and, so far, the least spoilt. Both have decent food and lodging facilities, and after exploring Diu you'll just want to put your feet up at one or the other and mellow out for a few days. Don't feel guilty. Where else in India can you do this kind of thing?

Nagoa
Nagoa beach lies 7 km (4½ miles) out of Diu town and is best approached by local bus (2 per day, at 7 am and 11 am) or by push-bike (30 mins). Auto-rickshaws ferry couples; agree on the rate first. It shouldn't be more than Rs10–15.

An idyllic spot, Nagoa is a long crescent-shaped beach nestling within a quiet, protected cove, fringed by lazy palms and facing onto the Arabian Sea. It's a beautiful setting: the white, clear sands are ideal for sunbathing, the calm blue sea is very safe for swimming. Out of the tourist season, there are rarely more than a dozen people here. These are often travellers, perhaps like yourselves, taking a break from so-called 'real' India.

At the end of a hard day's sunbathing, admire spectacular sunsets from the small rock viewpoint at the top of the beach. For a cool, pleasant diversion from the beach itself, visit the small sleepy village of **Bucharvada** just behind it. Shoestring travellers can rent huts here but they're pretty spartan and often infested by insects.

The obvious place to stay at Nagoa is the excellent **Ganga-Sagar Guest House**, run by friendly Haridas Samji. He lets out clean, simple and airy single rooms very cheaply (ask for cool sea-view top rooms). Common bathrooms only, but with the Arabian Sea on your doorstep who needs a private one? Good meals service (squid, lobster and prawn, right off the beach), good bar and shop, and relaxing garden patio. Lots of animals, including two useless watchdogs (asleep/dead), the only fat cat in India, and an itinerant toad.

Ahmedpur Mandvi

This is the jet-set beach, overlooked by a luxury resort hotel. It faces onto the island of Diu from the mainland, and is approached from Ghoghla by rickshaw (2 km; 1¼ miles) or by walking along the beach (1 km; ¾ mile). Head right from Ghoghla jetty. Unless you have lots of money, keep Diu as your base and visit this beach as a day-excursion. The local bus from Oona to Ghoghla will if requested make a stop here, which is very useful for those in need of a cool swim when returning to Diu from hot, sticky Sasan-Gir or Somnath.

Ahmedpur Mandvi may have more people (generally rich Indians) than Nagoa, but it also has better food, accommodation and facilities. **Samudra Beach Resort** (tel 2216) has attractive two-bedded cottages at Rs400–600, a fine restaurant and, what a pity, a video parlour. A wide range of water-sports include boating, water-skiing, para-sailing, surfing and 'water-cycling'—jet-skiing—and great fun.

For details of other beaches and day-excursions, contact the tourist office.

SHOPPING

There is little to buy here, but few people care: Diu is quite free of insistent touts wanting to drag you off to dubious silk shops or gem factories. Visit the very small bazaar behind the market square for trinkets and novelties. The islanders once produced attractive items made of tortoiseshell and ivory, but trade in both materials is now banned by Indian and international law.

RECREATION

The best water-sports at Ahmedpur Mandvi; the best swimming at Nagoa Beach. Entertainment is limited. If you can penetrate the maze of tiny, narrow and non-signed backstreets to locate its one cinema, the Aradhana, then you're doing pretty well. The cinema apparently shows English films once a month.

In the evenings, you make your own amusement. This generally means a visit to one of Diu's many bars, tavernas or cafés. Treat the popular local 'hooch'with respect.

WHERE TO STAY

For luxury, stay at the **Samudra Beach Resort**, Ahmedpur Mandvi; book through Gujarat Tourism. There's nothing else. There's also precious little in the middle range—in fact, just one room. This is the VIP Suite at the **Hotel Mozambique**, off the

Bunder. It is well-furnished, quiet and sophisticated, and excellent value at Rs70. The hotel's sun-roof (offering nice sea views) is an added bonus. So is the pleasant restaurant. **Baron's Inn** on Old Fort Road has non-air-conditioned rooms with attached baths for Rs50.

The best economy lodge is still the **PWD Rest House**, next to the fort. Nearly always full, but if you get one of the Rs15 doubles with bathroom and private balcony, you're sitting pretty. Ask for a room overlooking the gardens. The restaurant does good food—usually thalis, and seafood on request. The best alternative is **Apna Guest House** in Old Fort Rd (off the ferry, walk for 2 minutes left along the seafront). It offers prime double rooms with bathroom, balcony and sea views for Rs85 and cheaper ones for Rs35–50; a pleasant sun-roof, an adequate restaurant and a useful car hire service for sightseeing. **Nilesh Guest House**, near the fish market, is an interesting place. It has the hardest beds in town, in spartan but clean 'cells' for Rs25–70 but has lots of character. Food, service and staff alternate wildly between sheer excellence and total failure. Its best feature is the bar cum restaurant where colourful locals inflict large quantities of *bevra* country liquor (Diu's favourite tipple) on unwary tourists.

EATING OUT
You eat in your hotel. When you want a change, you eat in a different hotel. Best hotel food is at the **Samudra** (pricey, but worth it) followed by the cheaper **PWD** and **Apna**. The only restaurant in Diu not in a hotel is opposite the bus-stand. It's called **Deepee**, and has marvellous tub ice-cream, good dosas and snacks. The **Saraswati Hotel** opposite has tasty sweets, and is where everybody goes for breakfast. In Diu, try the seafood, the Gujarati thalis and, especially, the *lassi*.

GENERAL INFORMATION
The Tourist Office, Marine House, Nagoa Road, near Bunder Chowk (about 185 m: 200 yds right, off the ferry) is poor, and tourist literature is decades out of date. It's supposed to be open 9.30 am–1.15 pm, 2–5.45 pm, but the tourist officer is often taking it easy on Nagoa beach. In season, there are minibus conducted tours of the island (11.30 am–1.30 pm daily, except Monday; Rs10), but it's very often 'off season'. The post office is next to Goa Travels, opposite the ferry jetty. In the road behind it, the State Bank of Saurashtra is the best place in town to change money.

SOMNATH

Somnath, also known as Prahbas Patan, is famous for its ancient Somnath Temple and is currently being developed as a home-tourist holiday resort. Here you can combine the business of visiting one of India's most revered temples with the pleasure of basking on an unshaded but lovely beach. **Somnath Temple**, the main tourist magnet, has one of the 12 sacred *jyotirlingas* (Shiva shrines) and is extremely old. Legend has it that the first temple on this site was built by Somraj, the Moon God, after Shiva kindly cured him of consumption. This first structure was built of gold. Subsequent versions were of silver (donated by Ravana); of wood, donated by Krishna to mark the spot where he 'lost his body'; and of stone, by Bhimdev.

By the 6th century AD, Somnath was the richest temple in all India. Its wealth was so great that when the acquisitive Mahmud of Ghazni descended on it in 1024, even his vast caravanserai of elephants, camels and mules couldn't take it all away. What he destroyed was probably the first historically recorded version of the temple, built in the 1st century AD. Over the following 700 years, Somnath Temple was built up, knocked down, and rebuilt. Finally, after Aurangzeb the Mughal iconoclast set his demolition team on it in 1706, the builders gave up and left it in ruins. Only in 1950, under the auspices of S.V. Patel whose statue you can see outside, was the temple finally restored. This present version is an interesting, if not quite successful attempt at a modern Hindu temple incorporating traditional styles.

For comfort, visit Somnath between November and February. After that, it's too hot. Festival-lovers will enjoy **Kartika Poornima** (November–December), a vibrant village fair and performing arts gala, with lots of folk theatre, dance and chanting of vedic hymns. Also worth a visit is the big festival of the year, **Mahashivratri** (February–March), patronised by thousands of pilgrims from all over India. Both celebrations take place at the historic temple.

WHAT TO SEE
Apart from the temple, there's not a lot. Somnath is situated 4 km (2½ miles) up the road from Veraval. From Diu, it's 30 minutes by bus to Oona, then 2½ hrs from Oona to Veraval. Regular Rs2 local buses ply back and forth between Veraval and Somnath, or you can take an auto-rickshaw for about Rs12. If you leave Diu early, you can cover Somnath and be in Sasan-Gir for the late afternoon. Sasan-Gir has better facilities, food and accommodation.

Temple Town Tour (on foot, 2–4 hours)
Prabhas Patan Museum–Jain Temple–Somnath Temple

Coming into Somnath from Veraval by bus, look out for the richly carved **Mai Puri**, which used to be a Sun Temple, and the **Junagadh Gate** (1 km; ¾ mile) further on. This is the ancient triple gate that Mahmud of Ghazni stormed to enter the temple town. Off the bus, bear left into **Somnath** town, a small relaxed place of quiet, narrow streets, with local traders selling tiny stocks of vegetables or making up clothes on vintage sewing-machines from tiny house-front shops.

On the right of the path leading down to the sea you'll see, opposite a large pink **Jain Temple**, the small government-run **Prabhas Patan Museum**. This is a small, grubby place, more like a warehouse than a museum, with lots of uncatalogued rubble lying around the central courtyard; but is the place to see what remains of the remains of Somnath. Enough is left of the 11th-century, fourth-version temple to give you an idea of its original magnificence, and you can climb onto the courtyard parapets for decent views of the sea. There's a strange collection of holy and not so holy waters in little bottles, collected from famous rivers all over the world—from the Nile to the Danube and the River Plate. Open 9 am–noon, 3–6 pm daily, except Wednesday. Admission is Rs0.50, and there's a charge for each photo taken which is not rigorously enforced.

For the best sneak-preview of the **Somnath Temple**, climb to the top of the Jain Temple opposite the museum. This is a clean, modern structure where temple musicians give impromptu recitals.

The Somnath Temple has a magnificent location, overlooking the Arabian Sea and a long stretch of grey but sandy coast. Just inside the entrance, a richly raimented Nandi bull faces onto the Shiva shrine, shielded by a pair of massive silver doors. A small fee gains you access to the upper storeys. Bypass the first floor with its boring wooden boxes containing faded photos, bits of rock, dusty neon tubes, and climb to the good second-floor museum. This has an interesting photographic exhibition describing the history and archaeological background to the seven versions of Somnath temple. Slip over to the balcony for fine views of the coastline, and of the temple's beautiful upper-storey carvings. These show a definite Orissan influence, especially the regal, now extinct Oriyan lion figures.

If you're staying over in Somnath, the best time to visit the temple is at sunrise or sunset, when Shiva is invoked in a lively, elaborate ceremony called *arti*.

WHERE TO STAY
As Somnath is not yet geared for tourism, there is still only one decent accommodation—the **Hotel Mayuram**, Triveni Road (tel Prabhas Patan 362, 268). This has clean and respectable double rooms with attached bathroom for Rs45. It also provides good Rs12 *thali* meals in its clean, popular restaurant. Other than this, it's a straight choice between the **Somnath Guest House** near the temple, with basic, simple rooms for Rs12–15, or a berth on the beach.

Many travellers opt to stay in the small port town of Veraval, just 4 km (2½ miles) down the road. It has a State Tourism **Toran Guest House** near the beach with adequate doubles for Rs80, and the basic, friendly **Satkar Hotel** near the bus-station with clean, basic rooms and air-conditioned rooms for Rs30–140. Veraval also has a couple of food places: the **Swati** air-conditioned restaurant and the **New Apsara**, both offering cheap vegetarian fare. Despite this, Veraval is a noisy, dusty little town; very unrelaxing. If you can, stay by the beach.

GENERAL INFORMATION
No tourist office. For information, contact the manager of the Somnath Temple Trust (tel 212). His office is right by the temple.

SASAN-GIR

This is one of the finest wildlife sanctuaries in India and the last natural refuge in the world of the majestic Asiatic lion *Panthera leo persica*. The Gir Forest is one of the largest continuous tracts of land in India reserved for the conservation of its wildlife, and contains an amazing abundance of animals, birds and flora. The terrain is extremely varied: open scrub country, dry deciduous and tropical thorn forest, and evergreen corridors along the river beds. Gir had an original spread of some 5000 sq km (1930 sq miles), but by 1969, when it was designated a wildlife sanctuary, this area had dwindled to just 1400 sq km (540 sq miles). The interior core of the forest (258 sq km; 100 sq miles) was constituted a national park in 1975.

Within historic times, the Asiatic lion roamed the forests and open grassland as far afield as Greece in the west and Bengal and Bihar in the east. But human pressures led to a sudden, dramatic decrease in numbers. By 1884 there were no sightings of

Asiatic lions outside the Gir Sanctuary. And by the turn of the century, the pitiful remainder of just 100 lions had been completely driven off their natural territory, the open scrub land, and confined to the very heart of the forest.

Then, in 1900, their fortunes revived. In that year, the Nawab of Junagadh invited Lord Curzon, then Viceroy of India, to join him for a lion shoot at Gir. Curzon accepted the offer, but soon had occasion to regret it. An anonymous protest in a British newspaper, angrily complaining of the impropriety of a VIP doing further damage to an already endangered species, not only persuaded Curzon to cancel his trip, but moved him to ask the Nawab to protect the remaining lions. The Nawab agreed, but it wasn't till much later that concerted conservation efforts began. In 1948 hunting in the area was banned but in 1974 there were still just 180 lions in the sanctuary. However, with continuing efforts to save the species, the numbers have climbed to about 300.

The sanctuary is open to visitors from mid-October to mid-June. November to February is best for lion spotting: in the hot months, lions retreat to the cool interior of the forest, and sleep a lot. The July–September monsoon season is best for observing the rich variety of bird life. Times not to come are May–June, the Indian holiday season; and the big **Diwali** festival of late-October/early November, when tourists and pilgrims arrive in busloads, and accommodation becomes impossible.

WHAT TO SEE

The main attraction at Gir is the Asiatic lion, a magnificent beast averaging a full 2.75 m (9 ft) in length, and with a larger tail tassel, bushier elbow tufts and more prominent belly folds than his African cousin. He also has a smaller mane, and is a lighter brown in colour.

The sanctuary is also home to many other predators (notably the powerful leopard, capable of climbing up a tree with a full-grown stag in its mouth) and animals like bear, langur, barking deer, chousingha (four-horned antelope), fox, hyena and blackbuck. There is a large population of nilgai or blue bull, a species of antelope which, like the peacock, has enjoyed a considerable degree of natural protection by virtue of its religious associations: it resembles the sacred cow. The forest is also known for its many reptiles, including cobra, python, viper and marsh crocodile.

Had Gir not been designated a lion sanctuary, it surely would have established itself as a major bird sanctuary. There is an incredible variety of bird life here including green pigeon, oriole, partridge, painted sandgrouse, rock bush-quail and paradise fly-catcher. In all, there are over 200 different varieties of birds to be seen, one of the most common being India's national bird, the peacock.

Rugged individualists can take their own vehicles into the sanctuary, provided they hire the obligatory guide to go with them. Alternatively, they can hire a private jeep, with guide, for about Rs400 per trip from the Forest Bungalow. If going in on your own initiative, aim to be in the forest interior either very early in the morning, or during the late afternoon. At these times, you'll see a lot more. During the heat of the day, most animals have gone 'deep' to keep cool.

The small village of Sasan-Gir is the main shopping market for the area (locals travel all the way in from the forest interior to buy supplies here) but, apart from a few unremarkable modern temples, is not of special interest. This said, just down the road from the bus-stand, outside the Forest Lodge there is something worth seeing—**Gir's Crocodile Breeding Centre**. Here, in a pleasant green compound around 700 sleepy crocs live, ranging in size from 13 cm (5 in) to 1.5 m (5 ft). The staff are very friendly, and will let you handle the little monsters, but watch out for those 66 baby teeth. This centre was established in 1976/7 to counter the sudden decline in numbers of Marsh Crocodile or 'Mugger'. Eggs are collected from the nearby Kamleshwar Dam, and brought to the breeding centre to be artificially hatched.

Another worthwhile visit is the Forestry Department's marvellous **Orientation Centre**. This is a very fine exhibition, employing maps, photographs and clear, descriptive panels to outline the history, background, and wildlife content of the sanctuary. It is the product of the Nehru Foundation for Development, Ahmedabad.

Until recently the park organised a 'lion show'. This allowed you to see Asiatic lions from very close quarters, as part of an organised jeep-safari party. These have now been discontinued—hopefully, they will start up again soon. However you enter the sanctuary—by jeep, by car or on a park organised tour in one of their jeep-minibuses, you must get permission from the Forest Ranger and pay the necessary entry (Rs25) and camera fees (Rs10). With the help of a good park ranger/driver you can be fairly sure of seeing lion.

Excursions

If you're not at Sasan-Gir just for the lions, you can hire a jeep and visit some interest spots further inside the forest. Of these, the most beautiful and the most difficult to get to is **Tulishyam Hot Springs** (96 km; 60 miles), a very scenic spot where you can bathe in natural sulphur springs, visit a very special temple to Bhim and his mother Kunti, and stay at the pleasant **Toran Holiday Home** (dorm and single/double beds Rs8–40). Much nearer is **Sirvan Village** (13 km; 8 miles), where *siddi* people of African origin live, retaining their own distinctive culture and way of life. The 1000 or so villagers have a fine tradition of dance, and can, for a donation, be persuaded to put on special shows for the benefit of visitors. If you want to see a tribal dance show, call in at **Jambur Village** 25 km (15½ miles) away, on a Thursday, when a weekly festival takes place at the tomb of a respected holy man. **Kamleshwar Dam**, a beautiful location with an area of over 3 sq km (1¼ sq miles), is worth visiting when there's water in it (October–December, after the monsoons), but is a wasted trip when there isn't.

WHERE TO STAY
There are two lodges, both state-owned and with good facilities. The three-star **Lion Safari Lodge** (tel 21) is good value at Rs300 for single rooms, Rs450 for doubles, and worth it if you can get one of the upper-storey suites with balcony overlooking the reserve. Ground-floor rooms are uncomfortably close to the noisy video parlour. Facilities include bank, post office, restaurant and laundry. The management arranges trips into the sanctuary and, on request, local folk dances.

The cheaper option is the **Forest Guest House**, set in a beautiful garden courtyard, and offering some of the best-value rooms in India: immaculate double 'chalets', some air-conditioned, from Rs40–150. All rooms have bath/shower room and mosquito nets. For shoestring travellers, there are Rs4 dorm beds. Also a cheap restaurant.

EATING OUT
The **Lion Safari Lodge** restaurant does reasonable Indian food and 'Continental Suggestions'. You can eat well here for Rs75. **Forest Guest House** provides cheap, good Rs14 thalis and vegetarian meals, but only does food at certain, awkward times of the day. If you're resident, on a budget, do not forget to order your meals in advance.

The **Milan Parotha** in the village main street serves good vegetarian breakfasts from 8.30 to 9.30 am.

GENERAL INFORMATION
For tourist information, contact the Forest Ranger. He is usually to be found in a small hut in the Forest Lodge compound between 9.30 am and 5.30 pm daily. If absent, he's probably playing ping-pong in the lodge reception area. Ask for xeroxed information sheets on the sanctuary, full of useful facts and figures.

The Gujarat State Tourism Corporation offers a special two-day package tour of the Gir Sanctuary. This includes reception at Keshod airport (80-minute flight in from Bombay), accommodation at the Forest Lodge, a tour of the sanctuary, and a visit to Somnath Temple. Trained guide supplied. Contact Government of Gujarat Tourist Office, Dhanraj Mahal, Apollo Bunder, Bombay (tel 2024925) for further information.

Sasan-Gir is 2 hours from Veraval/Somnath by local bus (about 6 departures daily); it is best approached from Diu via the 'express' bus from Oona (3 hours, 2 departures per day only—check timings at Diu tourist office).

AHMEDABAD

Legend has it that present-day Ahmedabad was built on the ruins of the ancient township of Karnavati, founded by King Karna Solanki in AD 1063–1093. Sultan Ahmed Shah. In 1411 he decided to build a town here after watching the rabbits on the banks of the Sabarmati river stand up to the royal hounds. Convinced that it was the site which made the normally timid creatures so brave, he founded a new city named after him.

Ahmedabad, with its rich pre-Mughal and Mughal architecture, most of which survive today, was rightly called 'The handsomest town in Hindoostan, perhaps in the world' by Sir Thomas Roe, an early British envoy to India. This city was a favourite of the great Mughal Emperors Jahangir and Shah Jahan.

During the 15th and 16th centuries a unique fusion of styles from Hindu and Muslim schools of architecture came together here to create what is now known as the Indo-Saracenic style. In Ahmedabad this is reflected in the mosques and mausolea in mellow, honey-coloured-sandstone built during this period: in the arches, domes, vaults, pillars, jharokas and trefoil designs. A few centuries later, rich merchants of the Jain and Hindu faiths had a number of large temples built, and these still form a distinct part of Ahmedabad's architectural landscape.

Modern Ahmedabad boasts of several public and private buildings designed by leading Indian and international architects like Charles Correa, Louis Kahn and Le Corbusier. This is a city where ancient architectural marvels survive among the modern; where traditional values and a modern outlook coexist in peaceful harmony; where progress hasn't meant the uprooting of all the ingrained customs and moral values.

WHEN TO GO
April through to June can be quite hot, rising from 23°C to 43°C. There is no particular high season, as this is the commercial and industrial capital of Gujarat and has a busy stream of visitors throughout the year.

ARRIVAL/DEPARTURE
Ahmedabad is well-connected by air, rail and road to the rest of the country.

Air
Indian Airlines connects Ahmedabad with the four metropolitan cities of Bombay (Rs1003), Delhi (Rs1509), Calcutta (Rs2935) and Madras (Rs2676); as well as Bangalore (Rs2488), Jaipur (Rs1083) and Jodhpur (Rs893). East West Airlines operates a daily flight to and from Bombay (Rs1003).

Rail
Western Railway links Ahmedabad to Bombay (492 km; 300 miles) and to Delhi (934 km; 583¾ miles). The **Ashram Express** via Ajmer and Abu Road is the most convenient train from Delhi with departures each evening at 6 pm and arrival in Ahmedabad at 11.15 the next morning. There are link lines from Ahmedabad to Jamnagar (256 km; 160 miles), Porbandar (467 km; 292 miles) and other centres in the Saurashtra peninsula.

Road
Ahmedabad is connected by national and state highways with the major cities of India. State Transport buses ply from many centres including Bombay (492 km; 301 miles), Palitana (217 km; 135½ miles), Sasan-Gir (219 km; 137 miles), Udaipur (287 km; 180 miles), Delhi via Udaipur and Jaipur (1076 km; 672½ miles).

GETTING AROUND
Ahmedabad was originally surrounded by a fortified wall built by Sultan Ahmed Shah but now the city has spread out and across the river Sabarmati. The newer portions of the city were built according to plan, so it is fairly easy to find one's way about. The walled city with its maze of lanes, is divided into self-contained quarters locally known as poles. Each comunity of weavers, merchants, jewellers or goldsmiths had their own *pole* and it is still possible to wander on foot through this area. Although not often visited by tourists, the narrow streets crowded with activity, colour and full of noise make a visit a rewarding experience.

WHAT TO SEE
The Tourism Corporation of Gujarat has several conducted tours for local sightseeing in Ahmedabad, as well as excursions to nearby places of interest like Gandhinagar, Modhera, Lothal and a host of other destinations. The Ahmedabad

Municipal Transport Service (tel 365610) also runs conducted tours for local sight-seeing. As their timings are constantly being changed, get up-to-date details from the **Gujarat Tourism** office in H.K. House off Ashram Road.

City Sights Round-up (on foot and by car; 4–5 hours)
Jumma Masjid–Teen Darwaza–Bhadra Fort–Sidi Saiyad Mosque–
Rani Rupmati Masjid–Hathee Singh Jain Temple–Shaking Minarets–
Dada Harini Dev Baoli–Matar Bhavani Baoli–Kankaria Lake–
Calico Textile Museum–Utensils Museum–Sarkhez Roza–M.K. Gandhi Ashram

Jumma Masjid situated almost at the centre of the walled city is a good place to start. This mosque, built in 1423 by Sultan Ahmed Shah in the Indo-Saracenic architectural style, is outstanding for its grand scale, superb proportions and exquisite workmanship. Fifteen domes of varying elevations are supported by over 300 pillars, and one of the achievements of the design is the successful filtering of light so no direct sunlight falls into the building. The 'shaking minarets' of this mosque were destroyed in an earthquake in 1818. (Similar minarets survive in the Siddi Bashir Mosque, see below.) Immediately to the west of the mosque is **Teen Darwaza**, a triple-arched gate, erected by Sultan Ahmed Shah to serve as the royal entrance to the Royal Square (Maidan Shah) of his eponymous city. Further west of Jumma Masjid is the ancient citadel now known as **Bhadra Fort**. The foundations of this fort were laid in AD 1411 but it takes its name from the temple to Goddess Bhadrakali, built by the Marathas within the fort when this came under their control in the 18th century. Beside the post office and court, which occupy an old palace next to the fort, is the **Sidi Saiyad Mosque** completed in AD 1472 by a slave. The mosque contains famous filigree stone windows; note particularly those on the west wall. A little to the north is the **Rani Rupmati Masjid**—just south of the Grand Hotel and south-west of the Delhi Gate. Built between 1430–40, this mosque was named after Rani Rupmati the Hindu queen of Sultan Mehmud Shah Beghara. Richly ornamented with carvings and finely crafted marble screens, it presents a fine example of the synthesis of Hindu and Muslim architecture. **Hathee Singh Jain Temple** just north of Delhi Gate was built in 1550 by a rich merchant. Of pure white marble and decorated with rich carvings, this temple rivals the beauty of the famous Jain temple of Mount Abu.

The **Shaking Minarets** which are part of the Siddi Bashir Mosque, 2.5 km (1½ miles) from the city centre, can be swayed by a little force applied to the top-most arch. When one minar is shaken, the vibrations are communicated to the other minar via a stone-bridge, and the second minar starts shaking. A similar pair of minarets existed in the Rajabai Mosque but were damaged in the 19th century.

A common architectural feature of Gujarat is the step-well or *baoli*. Many were built adjoining temples, and apart from being cool sources of water, they are often used as retreats in the hot, dry summer months. The **Dada Harini** step-well was built in AD 1501 by one of the ladies of Sultan Mehmud Shah Beghara's court. This has a spiral staircase leading down to the central reservoir. The walls' steps and supporting pillars are splendidly carved. A little to the north is the older **Mata Bhavani Baoli** and both are about 800 m north-east of the Daryapur Gate. Sultan Qutb-ud-din had the **Kankaria Lake**, to the south-east of the city, constructed in AD 1451. There is an island in the centre containing a summer palace known as Nagina Wadi and it is possible to hire a boat for a few rupees to reach it.

Ahmedabad has two excellent and unusual museums. The **Calico Textile Museum** in the Shanti Bagh Area, is only appropriate in a city which owes much of its prosperity to textiles. One of the finest such museums in the world, it was founded in 1949 and is open 10 am–12.30 pm and 2.30–5 pm every day except Wednesday. The other unusual museum is the **Utensils Museum** at the Vechaar Vishalla Environmental Centre on the Sarkhej Road 5 km (3¼ miles) from the city centre. The museum has an extraordinary range of items in daily use over the last couple of centuries throughout the country. Nearby is the vegetarian restaurant from which the museum grew (see below).

One of the architectural marvels of Ahmedabad is the **Sarkhez Roza** at Sarkhej about 8 km (5 miles) south-west of the city. This group of structures built around a large tank comprise the large tomb of Saint Ahmed Khattu Ganj Baksh the spiritual guide advisor to Sultan Ahmed Shah (built in 1445); an enormous but simply designed mosque constructed in 1454; and the tombs of Sultan Mehmud Shah Beghara and his queen Rajabai, built in 1460. Many years later the Dutch East India Company founded an indigo factory here.

About 6 km (4 miles) from the city, on the banks of the Sabarmati river, is the **Ashram** founded by Mohandas Karamchand Gandhi in 1917, on his return from South Africa. This quiet retreat was to grow into the nerve centre of the Indian freedom movement and was the starting point of Gandhi's 385-km (240-mile) march to Dandi in 1930, when 90 000 people demonstrated against the government Salt Tax.

Excursions

At a short distance away from Ahmedabad are several interesting sights. Among those are the **Adalaj Vav** (17 km; 11 miles), a fine example of the traditional step-well; and **Lothal** (80 km; 50 miles), where remains of Harappan Civilisation have been excavated recently. At **Modhera** (106 km; 60 miles) on the road north to Abu and Udaipur, are the remains of a fine Sun Temple built in AD 1026 by King Bhimdev I of the Solanki dynasty. **Nal Sarovar** (71 km; 44 miles) is a bird sanctuary which acts as the winter host to various species of migrant birds: rosy pelicans, Brahminy duck, flamingoes. **Patan** (130 km: 81 miles) is home to the families who weave the famous Patola silk saris which can be bought in Ahmedabad from **Gurjari**.

SHOPPING

Ahmedabad is famous for its textiles, gold jewellery and handicrafts. Various textile designs, as well as processes such as tie-and-dye, mirror-work and block-printing, are done locally and the products are of an excellent standard. Shops are located in the Teen Darwaza area. **Gurjari**, the Gujarat Handicrafts Emporium on Ashram Road and **Gramodyog Gandhi Hat** at Bhadra and Sabarmati Ashram are recommended for handicrafts.

WHERE TO STAY

Mid-range (US$10–35/Rs250-1000 per room night)
There are several Western- and Indian-style hotels. **Cama** (tel 25281, tlx 0121-6377) in Khanpur has rooms from Rs850 single, Rs950 double. **Karnavati** (tel 402161, tlx 0121-6519) on Ashram Road has rooms from Rs750. Other hotels in this price range

include the **Rivera Hotel** (tel 24201, tlx 0121-6598) in Khanpur with rooms from Rs450 single, Rs 600 double.

Budget (under US$10/Rs250 per room night)
Roopalee (tel 350814), and the **Ritz Hotel** (tel 353637-9) both at Lal Darwaza. The Ritz has a pleasant garden and helpful staff. Gujarat Tourism's **Gandhi Ashram Guest House** (tel 407742) is slightly out of town but is clean and functional.

EATING OUT
Gujarati cuisine is almost entirely vegetarian; an amazing variety of dishes are prepared for a meal accompanied by wheat breads and rice. Many dishes use a lot of chillies and and a little sugar. Small restaurants abound and the food in invariably well-prepared and fresh. A *thali* can cost as little as Rs15 but in an air-conditioned restaurant would be nearer Rs50. One of the finest restaurants in India is Vishalla on the road to Sarkhej, on the outskirts of the city, 5 km (3 miles) to the south-west. Meals are served in a village setting; at low tables and on leaf-platters. The associated Utensil Museum (see above) is open till 11 pm.

In the city there are many popular and inexpensive restaurants. Most hotels serve Gujarati food and other Indian dishes. **Woodlands** (tel 466310) on the 2nd floor of Shilp, C.G. Road, **Kalpi** near the Ritz Hotel at Lal Darwaza, and **Balwas** (tel 351135) on Relief Road are all independent of hotels and meals cost from Rs40 per person.

GENERAL INFORMATION
Liquor is completely prohibited in Gujarat but foreign tourists can get a liquor permit stamped into their passport by the main tourist offices in New Delhi and Bombay. This will enable you to buy liquor while staying in one of the bigger hotels—room service only.

Tourist information centres are at the Tourist Office, Ahmedabad Municipal Corporation, Danapath, and at the Tourism Corporation of Gujarat in HK House on Ashram Road. Indian Airlines (tel 353333 apt 67356) is at Khanpur. The Vayudoot office is at Sita Travels (tel 409105) opposite Jaihind Press, Mithakhali Underbridge, Ashram Road. Railway Enquiries (tel 131) are open from 8 am to 10 pm.

Part VI

EAST INDIA

Victoria Memorial

CALCUTTA

Calcutta is concentrated India—an intense, vital and overcrowded city of 11 million inhabitants. It is the country's largest city and one of the most populous in the world. Here are gathered India's finest artists and musicians, scholars and poets, and her most desperate, poverty-stricken slums. Full of holy men, gurus and street temples, Calcutta has been called the soul of India, but it is also her conscience. The contrasts between rich and poor, educated and ignorant, old and new, are here more stark and discordant than in any other Indian metropolis. The grand old monuments of the Raj—the Victoria Memorial, the High Court, even Writers Building—tower in frightening relief above a grey backdrop of shanty-towns and shattered pavements. Crumbling Georgian mansions look over narrow, festering bazaars. Dust-red London buses crawl alongside hand-drawn rickshaw carts through teeming highways. Busy coffee houses, buzzing with sophisticated literary debate, look out onto streets littered with uneducated poor. And just down the road from modern Chowringhee, with its glittering Western-style hotels and shopping arcades, there is primitive Kalighat, with its filth, ordure and animal sacrifices. Calcutta is the distillation, good and bad, of India—and no visit to the country is complete without seeing it.

The first settlement here was in 1690, when the East India Company—abandoning their earlier trading post at upriver Hooghly—sent their agent Job Charnock south to occupy the three fishing villages of Sutanati, Govindpur and Kalikata. The name of the latter was later corrupted to Calcutta. In 1696, with the construction of a small

338

fort here—Fort St William, near present Dalhousie Square—the British Empire in India was born. It grew steadily for a time, then was attacked by the Nawab of Murshidabad. The young Clive raced up from Madras in time to save the fort, but too late to save a number of its residents from suffocating to death in an underground cellar (later known as the Black Hole of Calcutta). In 1772 the strengthened fort and town became the capital of British India, and received its first Governor, Warren Hastings. During the later 19th century it advanced rapidly as a commercial and political centre becoming the Second City of the British Empire, then became a focus of agitation for Indian independence. This sparked off the move of the British Raj to Delhi in 1911, and Calcutta lost its political throne. Soon after, during the Second World War, it lost its trade supremacy also—to the industrial new-boy Bombay—and began to crumble and decay.

Today, all that remains of its glorious past is a series of yellowing classical palaces and more British clubs than any other Indian city. But Calcutta remains a major centre of art, letters and industry, and its vital colonial heritage of political/intellectual activity remains intact. The fundamental problem is one of overcrowding: hordes of new refugees pour in daily, and there is nowhere for them to live. They spill out onto the street, and traffic and communications grind to a halt. Municipal maintenance is a thing of the past, and Calcutta's reputation now rests not on the might of empire but on the horrors of over-urbanisation. Floods, famine, pollution, power-cuts, and unemployment are regular hazards tolerated, even expected, by the city's burgeoning population, yet few of them would prefer to live anywhere else. 'We're used to seeing Calcutta the way it is,' commented prominent city-poet Shakti Chattopadhyay, 'which means Calcutta will have slums, just like pockmarks on a face. There *will* be dirt, traffic jams, garbage, rickshaws, trams. . . If 40 000 people depend on garbage as a source of livelihood, then arrangements shouldn't be made to dispose of the rubbish. . . Actually, it is a blessing that the slums are still around; you can get cheap domestic help here—unlike in Delhi.'

Despite its notoriety, Calcutta comes as a pleasant surprise to many foreigners. Americans seem to enjoy it because it reminds them of New York—big, action-packed and very volatile. Australians tend to hate it, for precisely the same reasons! There are many long-stay travellers here, either working for Mother Teresa and her Sisters of Mercy in the slums, or receiving tuition from Calcutta's top sitar and tabla musicians. Tourists passing through find the noise and crowds either stimulating or overpowering, but they generally feel safe. The Bengalis are a civilised, friendly people; busy and familiar with foreigners, invariably polite and keen to help when you're in a spot. The only thing they don't like is visitors pointing cameras at the poorer sections of their community. Wandering the packed streets, you'll need to be sensitive to this; for alongside scenes of courage, laughter and simple natural beauty there are disturbing, harrowing scenes of human tragedy and suffering. Uniformed rich school children file down one side of the street on their way to a posh seminary, while on the other side lie ragged urchins living on the bottom, bottom line. Simultaneously beautiful and ugly, Calcutta leaves nobody unaffected.

WHEN TO GO
Close to the sea, and at low altitude, Calcutta suffers a lot of humidity. It is best visited from November to February, though for colour, spectacle and culture come for the

3-week **Durga Puja** festival of September–October. But Calcuttans hold festivals and holidays on any excuse, and it is rare to arrive without something going on. After the **Holi** feast of February/March, the city becomes uncomfortably hot. Later on, during the July/Sept monsoon, it is often subject to torrential floods. For the best coverage of routes in this guide, aim to arrive in late February, visiting Orissa first, then Bihar and perhaps a side trip to Varanasi, finally escaping up to Darjeeling and Sikkim, out of the heat around late March.

Note: Volunteers wishing to work for Mother Teresa are generally encouraged to come between September and March, when it's not too hot. If you write from London, you'll receive a letter back telling you when to go. Otherwise, simply turn up at the Mother House, 54a Lower Circular Rd, Calcutta (between 12 noon and 4 pm) to be employed on the spot.

ARRIVAL/DEPARTURE

Air

The centre for exploring Bengal and the East, Calcutta has a single airport for both international and domestic flights. Indian Airlines connects it with Bagdogra (for Darjeeling), Bangalore, Bhubaneshwar, Bombay, Delhi, Hyderabad, Madras, Port Blair, Patna, Varanasi and the many airports of Assam and north-eastern India. Air India connects it with practically everywhere via Bombay. Indian Airlines has international flights to/from Kathmandu, Bangkok, Dhaka and Chittagong in Bangladesh. International Carriers include Singapore Airlines, Thai, Royal Nepal, Aeroflot, KLM and Royal Jordanian. British Airways have announced that they wish to restart flights to/from Calcutta and may do so in 1993.

From Calcutta's Dum Dum airport (the bullet was invented at the cantonment near here) it's a 30-minute ride into the city centre (17 km; 10¾ miles) by EATS bus (regular Rs20 service from 8 am to around midnight), by taxi (about Rs50) or by air-conditioned private car (Rs200 but often negotiable) that can be booked on arrival. The EATS bus is convenient and makes drops at all major hotels, runs down Chowringhee via Sudder St, and ends up at the Indian Airlines office in Chittaranjan Rd. From here, it returns to the airport at fairly regular intervals.

Dum Dum airport has retiring rooms, and there's an **Airport Hotel** nearby, with five-star facilities and single/double rooms at Rs1550/1700.

Rail

There are two rail stations—sedate Sealdah station, north-east of the city centre (20 mins by taxi), which services Darjeeling; and bustling Howrah station, just over the Howrah bridge (a 40-min taxi ride from centre at offpeak times), which runs trains out to most major points, including Madras (fast *Coromandel Express* leaves 3.15 pm daily; 26 hours), Delhi (3 trains daily; 17–20 hours), Bombay (nippy *Gitanjali Express* leaves 1.50 pm on Mon, Tues, Wed, Fri and Sat; 32 hours), Varanasi (3/4 trains daily; *A.T. Express* is best, leaves 8.45 pm on Tues, Wed and Sat; only 9 hours) and Jammu (*Himgiri Express* leaves 11 pm daily; 25 hours). Rail reservations are now computerised. Quick, straightforward booking of tickets (anywhere, any class) from the Eastern Railway Booking Office, 6 Fairlee Place (tel 222789/4025). To tap the tourist quota, find the Railway Tourist Guide, who sits on the 1st floor of this building between 10 am and 5 pm, Monday to Friday. He's really your best bet—especially when the computers break down.

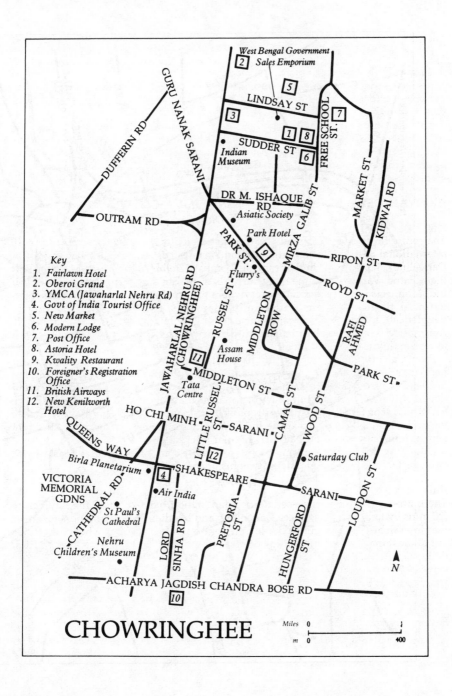

Key
1. Fairlawn Hotel
2. Oberoi Grand
3. YMCA (Jawaharlal Nehru Rd)
4. Govt of India Tourist Office
5. New Market
6. Modern Lodge
7. Post Office
8. Astoria Hotel
9. Kwality Restaurant
10. Foreigner's Registration Office
11. British Airways
12. New Kenilworth Hotel

West Bengal Government
Sales Emporium
LINDSAY ST
SUDDER ST
Indian Museum
DR M. ISHAQUE RD
Asiatic Society
Park Hotel
Flurry's
GURU NANAK SARANI
DUFFERIN RD
OUTRAM RD
PARK ST.
FREE SCHOOL ST.
MARKET ST
KIDWAI RD
MIRZA GALIB ST
RIPON ST
ROYD ST
PARK ST.
RAFI AHMED
MIDDLETON ROW
RUSSEL ST
JAWAHARLAL NEHRU RD (CHOWRINGHEE)
Assam House
MIDDLETON ST
Tata Centre
HO CHI MINH
LITTLE RUSSEL ST
SARANI
CAMAC ST
WOOD ST
QUEENS WAY
Birla Planetarium
SHAKESPEARE
Saturday Club
VICTORIA MEMORIAL GDNS
CATHEDRAL RD.
Air India
SARANI
LOUDON ST
St Paul's Cathedral
Nehru Children's Museum
LORD SINHA RD
PRETORIA ST
HUNGERFORD ST
ACHARYA JAGDISH CHANDRA BOSE RD

CHOWRINGHEE

Miles 0
m 0   400

N

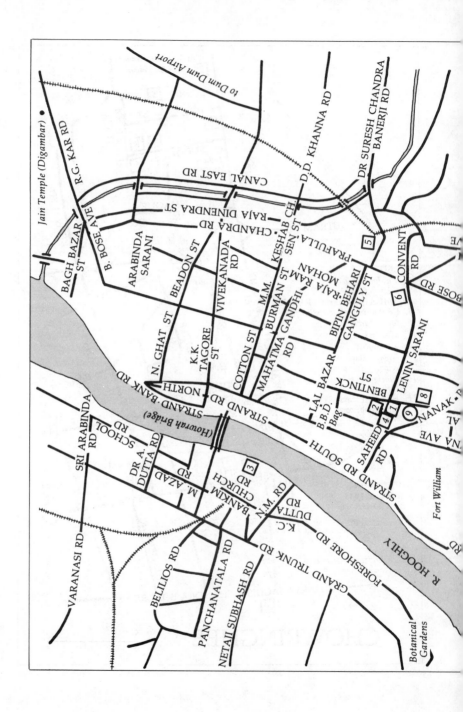

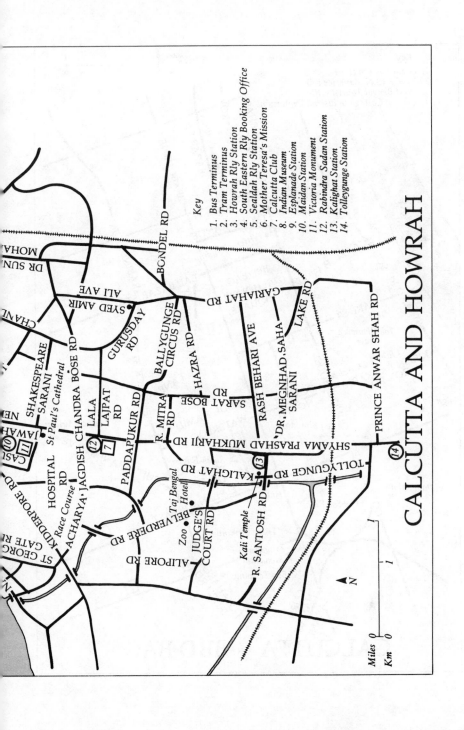

Key

1. Bus Terminus
2. Tram Terminus
3. Howrah Rly Station
4. South Eastern Rly Booking Office
5. Sealdah Rly Station
6. Mother Teresa's Mission
7. Calcutta Club
8. Indian Museum
9. Esplanade Station
10. Maidan Station
11. Victoria Monument
12. Rabindra Sadan Station
13. Kalighat Station
14. Tolleygunge Station

Miles
Km

N

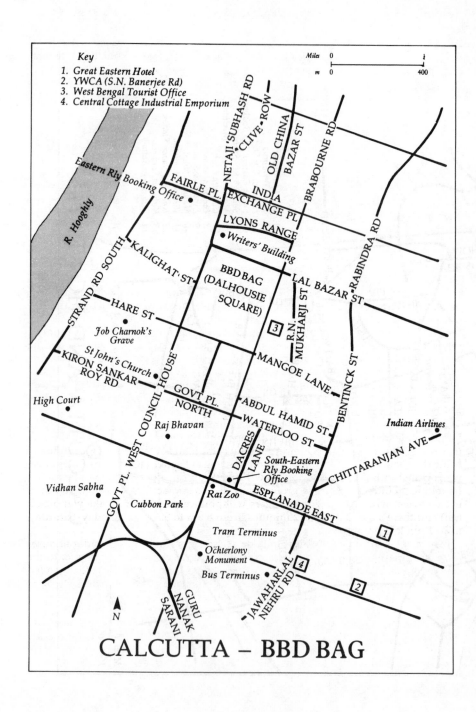

Key
1. Great Eastern Hotel
2. YWCA (S.N. Banerjee Rd)
3. West Bengal Tourist Office
4. Central Cottage Industrial Emporium

Miles 0
m 0   400

R. Hooghly

Eastern Rly Booking Office

NETAJI SUBHASH RD
CLIVE ROW
OLD CHINA BAZAR ST
BRABOURNE RD

FAIRLE PL.

INDIA EXCHANGE PL

LYONS RANGE

• Writers' Building

STRAND RD SOUTH
KALIGHAT ST

BBD BAG
(DALHOUSIE
SQUARE)

LAL BAZAR ST

RABINDRA RD

HARE ST

Job Charnok's
Grave

St John's Church

KIRON SANKAR
ROY RD

3

R.N.
MUKHARJI ST

MANGOE LANE

BENTINCK ST

WEST COUNCIL HOUSE

GOVT. PL.
NORTH

ABDUL HAMID ST

High Court
•

Raj Bhavan

WATERLOO ST

Indian Airlines
•

GOVT PL. WEST

DACRES
LANE

South-Eastern
Rly Booking
Office

CHITTARANJAN AVE

Vidhan Sabha
•

Cubbon Park

Rat Zoo

ESPLANADE EAST

1

Tram Terminus

Öchterlony
Monument

Bus Terminus

4

2

N

GURU NANAK SARANI

JAWAHARLAL NEHRU RD

CALCUTTA – BBD BAG

Road
Long-distance buses for Darjeeling, Orissa and Bihar leave from the Interstate bus-stand, Esplanade. It is essential that you advance-book tickets. The terminus is, however, impossibly congested, and finding the bus you want is a major achievement. This goes double for any buses outside the terminus. Whenever possible, use trains for out-of-town travel.

GETTING AROUND
Central Calcutta is a compact, congested area sprawling up along the west bank of the Hooghly River, from the Zoological Gardens in the south up to Howrah Bridge some 5 km (3 miles) north. Over the bridge are some of the worst slums, and the beautiful Botanical Gardens. In the city centre is the large open expanse of the Maidan, hugged by BBD Bag (West Bengal Tourist Office, GPO, American Express, etc.) on the north; by Chowringhee/Jawaharlal Nehru Rd (hotels, restaurants, airline offices, Government of India Tourist Office, etc.) on the east; and by the Victoria Memorial, Birla Planetarium and other major sights on the southeast.

Calcutta is notoriously difficult to get around. There are three reasons for this. First, like many Indian cities it suffers from a confusing duplication of street names, and nobody seems very sure whether to use the old (Raj) or new (post-Independence) names. Rickshaw-wallahs will continue to call Jawaharlal Nehru Road by its old title of Chowringhee Road for many years to come. Even maps aren't consistent. The second problem is lack of city planning. Calcutta was originally partitioned into a series of walled, self-contained jute mill or factory areas, with few surrounding streets. Roads today account for only 6% of the city's surface area, as compared to 25% in New Delhi. Third, and most relevant, hardly any of the city's main roads have pedestrian footpaths, and human traffic just spills over into motorised traffic. With a mind boggling average of 50% of Calcutta's population (against a national average of 20%) on the streets at any one time, it's a picture of sheer chaos.

The big plan is to displace 25% of this commuter crush off the streets and down into the new Metro railway which will hopefully by the mid-1990s run all the way up from Tollygunge to Dum Dum airport, but completion of this project is continually being deferred. A 4-km (2½-mile) section, starting at Esplanade south to Tollygunge, was opened in late 1985, and for a few rupees you can experience the pleasure of travelling on India's first underground railway. It's immaculately clean (if you drop even a sweet wrapper, other passengers will pounce on you and make you pick it up!) and there's a train every 12 minutes, from 8 am to 9.30 pm Monday–Saturday, from 1 pm to 7 pm Sunday.

Bus travel is to be avoided. Not only do passengers cling onto the sides of buses (regular Indian procedure), but passengers cling onto *passengers* clinging onto the sides of buses. Like the public city trams, this mode of transport is not recommended during the rush hours. If you do manage to get on, make sure you're near the door, or you'll never get off. And watch out for pickpockets.

Most people get around by taxi. Under the new fare structure, the minimum fare is Rs5 (for the first 2 km) and Rs1 for every subsequent 200 m. Most meters are calibrated to start at Rs4 so be prepared to pay extra—the driver should have a printed conversion chart. Owing to the shortage of auto-rickshaws (the few survivors hang around Sudder St/Chowringhee; Rs1.60 per km plus a 60% surcharge), many people use the old man-powered cart rickshaws. Calcutta is their last stronghold, and they are so keen for business you'll always get a cheap ride.

Calcutta's unique traffic situation is perhaps the main 'sight' of the city—a vast, heaving bedlam of rickshaws, cars, brightly painted lorries, double-decker buses, bullock carts, commuters and trolley buses. The combined impact of all this noise, dust, crowds and traffic is enough to put many sightseers off altogether. Persistence is the key. Expect to spend three times as long getting anything seen or done here as elsewhere in India, and start out slowly; spend the first couple of days just getting to know your immediate neighbourhood. If you don't have time to sightsee at leisure, allow 3/4 days to drift around town by hotel hired car, then brace yourself for a full-day city bus tour.

City Tour (sightseeing bus, half- or full-day)
Howrah–Botanical Gardens–Belur Math–Ramakrishna Temple–Dakshineshwar–Jain Temple (morning)–Indian Museum–Nehru Children's Museum–Victoria Memorial–Zoo (afternoon)

Purely for orientation, take one or both of the above bus (Rs75) tours. Neither is up to much: the guide's talk is drowned out by traffic, too much time is spent in the bus, too little at the more interesting sights, but at least you'll get out and about a bit, and certain sights, notably Howrah, are really best experienced from a bus window.

The morning tour leaves the bus terminal in the city centre via the **High Court** building (1872) and the oldest Catholic church in Calcutta, **St Mary's**. A half-hour later, it comes to the single-span cantilevered **Howrah Bridge** (1943), and grinds to a prolonged halt. Two million people cross this bridge daily, and you have to wait your turn. Originally a marshy swampland (the origin of its name), Howrah is now Calcutta's most congested area. A tidal wave of human and motorised traffic washes over and around the bus, and if this doesn't tell you what Calcutta's about, nothing will.

Across the bridge are the **Botanical Gardens**. The largest and oldest of their kind in India, they were laid out in 1787. Spread over 270 acres, and containing over 30 000 varieties of trees and plants, it is also Calcutta's principal lung. The gardens are famous as the place where Assam's and Darjeeling's famous teas were first developed, and presently house several species of bamboos, palms, succulents and exotic plants gathered from five continents. But their main attraction is the world's largest Banyan Tree, over 200 years old, with a circumference of 417 m (1367 ft). Despite the loss through decay of the 'mother' tree in 1925, the more than 1600 younger aerial roots continue to flourish, giving the tree the aspect of a forest. The tour bus spends exactly 4 minutes here, before leaving the gardens. Return to see them properly another day. Arrive by car or rickshaw (19 km; 12 miles from Chowringhee, 40-min drive, set out 7 am latest to avoid rush-hour Howrah crush) and use Nos 55/56 buses for the hour-long tour of the gardens.

Some 10 km (6½ miles) further north, still on the west bank of the Hooghly, the tour visits **Belur Math**, headquarters of the Ramakrishna Mission. This was established in 1898 by Swami Vivekananda, in memory of the popular Indian sage Ramakrishna, who preached the essential unity of all religions. Reflecting this ideal, the **Ramakrishna Temple** here looks like a church, a mosque or a Hindu temple, depending on where you view it from. The Mission itself is a medical help centre for the poor. Open to visitors 6.30 am to noon, 3.30 to 7.30 pm, daily. A short distance north, over the Hooghly via Vivekananda Bridge, a visit is made to **Dakshineshwar Kali Temple**, the place where Ramakrishna achieved his spiritual vision. Tour guides impress visitors by telling them that the saint's name has been invoked here continuously for 20 years. The great appeal of Ramakrishna's religion is its cosmopolitanism, its free and liberal tolerance, something which free-thinking Calcuttans can readily identify with.

Returning south, some 3 km (2 miles) from the city centre, the tour makes its final morning stop at **Parasnath Jain Temple**, arguably the most interesting temple in all Calcutta. An exquisite structure, built in 1867, it is accompanied by beautiful ornamental gardens. Dedicated to Sitalnathji, 10th of the 24 Jain tirthankars (prophets), it houses an elaborate, colourful blend of glass mosaics, mirror-inlay pillars, and stained-glass windows, and features a gilded dome ceiling, floral-design marble flooring from Japan, and ornate chandeliers from Brussels and Paris. For a Jain temple, it's unusually flamboyant. Opening times are 6 am to noon, 3 to 7 pm daily.

The **afternoon city tour** is altogether more worthwhile. It starts at the **Indian Museum**, at the junction of Sudder St and Chowringhee. Built in 1875 in the Italian style of architecture, this is the largest museum in India and houses one of the finest collections in Asia. There are presently six departments: archaeology, anthropology, zoology, geology, botany and art, arranged in dusty mothballed halls round a central garden courtyard. The archaeological section features the immense **Bharhut Stupa**, depicting the 500 incarnations of Buddha prior to his enlightenment. There is a fine collection of South Indian coins, dating back to the 5th century BC, and some beautiful terracottas. Also, a fine collection of Gandharan sculpture. Upstairs, there are giant prehistoric skeletons and a preserved goat with 8 legs and 4 ears; also the rare double-coconut tree, which blossoms only once every century, and takes a further 10 years to produce a fruit. The geology section has meteorites, also rocks and minerals. At the top of the building, there's an excellent display of miniature paintings. The whole place is dusty, dim and yellow with age, but this somehow adds to its appeal. The museum is open 10 am to 5 pm (summer), 10 am to 4.30 pm (Dec–Feb), except on Mondays, and there's a decent guidebook on sale at the entrance. Admission is Rs1.

The **Nehru Children's Museum**, at the bottom of Jawaharlal Nehru Rd, is a novelty stop. It has an overrated scale model of Amritsar's Golden Temple and various electronic/scientific games. But there's a fine collection of dolls, and a model exhibition depicting India's longest epic poem the *Ramayana*, in 1500 miniature models. This tells the story of the King Rama who defeated the many-headed demon king of Lanka, Ravana, to retrieve his abducted wife Sita. The museum is open 12 noon–7 pm, except on Mondays, and sells excellent ice-cream. Admission is Rs2.

The tour stops next at the majestic **Victoria Memorial**, picture-postcard symbol of Calcutta. Built between 1906 and 1921 at a cost of Rs7.5 m, this gleaming white marble palace stands at the southern end of the Maidan, a living reminder of the might of British India. It had been compared to the Taj Mahal, with its four rudimentary minarets, gleaming white dome and exterior of solid Macrana marble. It was conceived by Lord Curzon as both a tribute to Queen Victoria and a triumphant depiction of her reign in India. Playing on Henry James' lament on hearing of the Queen's death), 'We all feel a bit motherless today', Curzon appealed to popular sentiment and raised the money for this fabulous reliquary entirely from voluntary subscriptions. Fully reflecting the pomp of empire, the Empress of India sits at the entrance flight of marble stairs, enthroned in bronze, clad in the regal robes of the Order of the Star of India. Further symbol of her greatness is provided by the 49-m bronze Angel of Victory, spreading its wings skyward, high atop the central dome.

Inside is the finest collection of memorabilia relating to British India contained under one roof. The Royal Gallery on the first floor has paintings of the notable events in Victoria's life: her coronation, marriage to Albert, the christening of son Edward VII, celebrations of golden and diamond jubilees. Also, the museum's pride: the rosewood baby grand piano on which the young princess played, and her personal writing-desk and embroidered armchair. The largest painting in the gallery, indeed the largest oil painting in India, is the work of the Russian artist Vassily Verestchagin, and depicts all the pageantry of the Prince of Wales' (the future Edward VII) visit to Jaipur in 1876. The Portrait Gallery contains a rare collection of ancient Persian manuscripts, including some illuminated writings owned by the 'Tiger of Mysore', Tipu Sultan. The walls of the gallery are lined with pictures of key figures in the development of British India, including a pensive-looking Robert Clive, General Stringer Lawrence (father of the Indian army) and the Duke of Wellington. The adjoining gallery has an arms and armour collection dating back to the times of medieval Indian combat.

Beyond Robert Clive's cannon-fronted statue in the **Sculpture Gallery,** you'll find the Memorial's focal point, the magnificent **Queen's Hall,** with its graceful figure of the newly crowned girl queen. This is overlooked by 12 large frescoes depicting the main highlights of her life. The museum also has a very good collection of 18th and 19th century prints of India and portraits by British and European artists. The collection of prints by Thomas and William Daniell is the most complete in India. Back on the entrance balcony, you can enjoy a fine view out onto the Maidan.

Open 10 am–5 pm in the summer (only to 4 pm November to February), except Mondays, the Victoria Memorial demands an extensive visit. You can leave the bus here for the free guided tour from the memorial entrance which lasts 2 hours, and is highly recommended. The bus tour continues to the **Zoological Gardens** 2 km (1¼ miles) south, off Belvedere Rd (open 6.30 am–5 pm, entrance Rs1). The gardens house rare white tigers of Rewa, giraffes and exotic birds, and an odd reptilium with snakes living in little tiled bathrooms. From the zoo, cross the road and take tea in the fine, new **Taj Bengal Hotel.**

Finish off the day with a relaxing sunset stroll round the **Maidan.** This large area of not so green parkland was cleared from the jungle around the old **Fort St William** (not open) to allow cannon an unobstructed line of fire. Today it is a popular place to do early-morning yoga for city-dwellers preparing to do battle with another day of urban stress. If you want to see more than just joggers and cricketers, browsing sheep and goats, vendors and hangers-on, turn up on a Sunday for the **Dharamtolla ka Mela** fair. This takes place near the **Ochterlony Monument,** and features folk entertainers, quacks dispensing medicines, performing animals and children, and all sorts of strange goings-on. Just off the Maidan, on the corner of Cubbon Park, opposite the South-east Rail Booking office in Esplanade East, there's something *really* strange: a small hole-pocked triangular island affectionately known as **Rat Zoo.** It's rodent husbandry run amok.

City Sights Round-up (on foot, by taxi/rickshaw, full-day)
St John's Church–Writers' Building–Birla Planetarium–St Paul's Cathedral–
Kalighat Temple–Mother Teresa's Mission–Birla Academy of Art

For day two, see a number of places that should be but aren't included on the state conducted tours. Again, start early to miss the crowds. Take a pleasant promenade across elegant BBD Bag (opposite the West Bengal Tourist Office, north of Maidan). At the back of the square, walk for 10 minutes left down Council House St to find St John's Church, modelled on London's St Martin-in-the-Fields. Built in 1784, this old stone church served as a temporary cathedral (1814–47) until St Paul's Cathedral was completed. Things worth seeing inside include the *Last Supper* a painting by Zoffany and the charming wicker seats overlooked by marble memorials to imperial servants. The graveyard outside, Calcutta's first burial site, has the octagonal mausoleum of the city's founder, Job Charnock, also the tomb of Admiral Charles Watson who helped Clive retake Calcutta from the Murshidabad Nawab.

Twenty minutes' walk back up to, and just beyond, the rear of BBD Bag you'll find the remarkable Writers Building. Foreigners generally go there just to get a permit for Sundarbans Tiger Reserve (300 or so tigers here, who eat an average of 40 people a year), but others simply go for entertainment. Marvel here at the rows and rows of tables, piled with files, with a small space cleared by the occupant of each table for his newspaper and his cup of tea. One visitor remarked: It was classic India. I went for a Sundarbans permit and was told to apply to the 'rosy-coloured boy' upstairs. This turned out to be a middle-aged man wearing a rose-coloured shirt. He was sitting at his table, snowed under by papers, staring up at the ceiling in a mystic trance. So was everybody else. The building was full of people doing absolutely nothing, or just reading newspapers.

From here, take a rickshaw/taxi down to the Birla Planetarium, just below Victoria Memorial. It's the biggest planetarium in India, and the ideal place for an air-conditioned siesta out of the midday heat. There are at least two English-speaking programmes daily, at varying times between 11.30 am and 8.30 pm (except Monday). If you're waiting for a show, drop in on St Paul's Cathedral (open 9 am–12 noon, 3–6 pm), 2 minutes' walk down the main road. Built between 1839 and 1847, this distinguished Gothic structure is the oldest Church of England cathedral of the British Empire. It is notable for its striking murals and frescoes, stained-glass windows, and coloured altar reredos.

Another rickshaw/taxi ride south brings you to the notorious Kalighat Temple (open 5 am–8 pm). Dedicated to the 'black goddess' Kali or Kalika (another possible origin of Calcutta's name), and considered the chief Kali temple in India, the present structure is an 1809 version of an early 17th-century original. The gruesome legend attached to it is that Vishnu chopped up the body of Shiva's wife Devi, and one of her severed toes fell here. Today, it's goats and sheep who get the chop daily, the sacrifices taking place in the courtyard used for local cricket. The atmosphere is very unwholesome (even Gandhi couldn't take it) and it is not a place for the squeamish. People generally come to Kalighat not for the temple, but to visit Mother Teresa's Mission, 54a Lower Circular Rd, tel 24711 (open only early morning, and from 4 to 6 pm for visitors). The caring, unstinting help extended by this iron-willed yet gentle champion of the sick, poor and dying has provoked worldwide admiration. A short visit to see the results of her work is always rewarding.

Close by, at 108–9 Southern Avenue (another short taxi journey, or 15-minute walk), is the **Birla Academy of Art and Culture**. Open only from 4 to 7 pm (closed Monday), it's something to reserve for the end of the day. The ground floor has a good historical sculpture section, while upstairs there's contemporary art. The Indian Society of Oriental Art and other cultural bodies run regular exhibitions here, all the paintings being well lit, catalogued and presented.

RECREATION

Set aside an evening or two to enjoy Calcutta's rich heritage of music, dance and theatre. The principal culture halls are **Rabindra Sadan and Academy of Fine Arts**, both in Cathedral Rd. The **Nandan Theatre**, behind Rabindra Sadan, shows prizewinning English/Indian films. For programme details, pick up a copy of *Calcutta This Fortnight* from the Government of India tourist office, or buy a *Statesman* newspaper. *The Telegraph* newspaper on Sundays has a good local listing. All culture shows start at 6.30 pm. The *Dances of India* programme at the Oberoi's **Mughal Room** restaurant is convenient, if nothing special. Tickets are Rs35.

There's a wide selection of cinemas. In the Sudder St area, English films play regularly at the Lighthouse, the Globe and the New Empire. Current programmes are listed in the *Telegraph* newspaper.

Calcutta's close heat tends to discourage vigorous sport. But if you're pining for exercise and sightseeing hasn't worn you out, try joining one of the city's numerous clubs. The best one is the **Tollygunge Club**, 120 Deshapran Sasmal Rd (tel 463141), with golf, tennis, squash, swimming, riding and billiards. Set in over 100 acres of fine scenery, this is the premier country club of India. Alternatively, there's **Calcutta Cricket Club**, 19/1 Gurusaday Rd (tel 478721) for tennis as well as cricket; **Royal Calcutta Turf Club**, 11 Russell St (tel 241103), which holds regular race meets; and the **Royal Calcutta Golf Club**, 33 Tollygunge (tel 461288), best for 18 holes before lunch. This is the oldest Golf Club in the world outside Great Britain—founded in 1829. These all have excellent facilities, though their exclusive nature means you'll have to ring or write for temporary membership. To gain access to **Calcutta's Saturday Club**, 7 Wood St (tel 445411)—geared to the young 'jet-set' élite—you'll need an introduction. It helps to be young, pretty and/or rich. If you fit the bill, just hang around in the better hotel bars or restaurants (Fairlawns is a good bet) and use your charisma.

SHOPPING

Calcutta hasn't the choice or the variety of goods found in Bombay or Delhi, but there are some nice general buys to be found in the huge, covered **New Market**, behind Chowringhee. New Market is certainly the cheapest place in Calcutta to buy presents and souvenirs—silks, cottons, handwoven fabrics and silver in particular. You should also visit out the market's famous Chinese shoe-makers. Leather shoes, bags, belts and briefcases are cheaper in Calcutta than anywhere else in the country, and the quality is generally superb. Porters are available, as at all markets, for a couple of rupees.

For exclusive shopping, try **Bengal Home Industries Association (BHI)**, 57 Jawaharlal Nehru Rd (tel 441562). This sells stylish Bengal-style cotton (*tant*) saris, silk/cotton combination saris. Also a wide range of traditional Bengal crafts, like terracotta toys, bright jute furnishings (wall-hangings, pot-holders, bags and mats), conch-shell bangles and leather goods. For high-class menswear and fashion tailors, check out places like **Yak's** in Grand Hotel Arcade, or the clothing shops round New Market. Tailoring is extremely cheap in Calcutta, and again the quality of workmanship is high. If you're looking for silk by the metre, **Mayur** on Rafi Ahmed Kidwai Rd and **Indian Textiles** in the Great Eastern Hotel arcade have a large selection. Prices are high, but you're paying for class.

Two good fixed-price emporia, which are always useful if you don't know where to start and what's available, are **Central Cottage Industries Emporium**, 7 Jawaharlal Nehru Rd (tel 284139) and **West Bengal Government Sales Emporium**, 7/1D Lindsay St (tel 243990). Both places have a large stock of attractive handloom fabrics, textiles, silks and jewellery.

WHERE TO STAY
As is the case in the other gateway cities, accommodation in Calcutta is comparatively expensive. Mid-range hotels tend to be over-priced and, if travelling on a budget you should listen in hard to the travellers' grapevine. Cheap lodgings go up and down in quality. And do remember that the prices below do not include tax.

Luxury (US$100–250 per room night)
Calcutta's most opulent hotel is also a part of the city's tradition. **The Oberoi Grand**, 15 Jawaharlal Nehru Rd (tel 292323, tlx 5919, 5937, fax 033-291217), simply glows in the ambience of British Calcutta and must be the definitive Raj-style hotel of India. Packed with period furnishings and colonial character, it's a virtual museum of pre-war splendour, keeping alive the tradition of empire. Facilities include three speciality restaurants, an elegant pool, a business centre, and the best disco in Calcutta. In keeping with the Grand's policy of old-style charm blended with modern convenience, rooms are both elegant and functional, priced from US$160 single, US$175 double.

The Taj Bengal (283939, tlx 21-4776, 5988 TAJC IN, fax 033-281766, 288805), 34B Belvedere Road, is located in Alipur, a green part of the city, near the zoo. Opened in late 1989, impressively city, elegant and modern in style, the Taj has developed a reputation for good food and service, comfortable rooms and some excellent facilities. Rooms are from US$160 single and US$175 double.

Mid-range (US$25–100 per room night)
Calcutta's two other properties with five-star pretensions and prices are the **Park Hotel** (tel 297336, 297941, tlx 21-5867, fax 033-298027), 17 Park Street and the **Airport Ashok**. The Park Hotel is well located—almost all of central Calcutta is within walking distance, but rather uninspiring. Rooms from US$75 single and US$85 double. The **Airport Ashok** (tel 569111, tlx 21-5296) is only 1 km from the airport and a convenient place to move out to if you are taking a 5 or 6 am departure, but is inconvenient as a base during a stay in Calcutta. Rooms are from US$60 single and US$65 double. In terms of facilities, neither hotel makes it into the Big League.

Calcutta has many mid-range hotels of varying quality. **Hotel Hindustan International**, 235/1 A.J.C. Bose Rd (tel 442394, tlx 21-7164) is a useful fall-back, and very popular with Westerners. Rooms are a little overpriced at Rs1600 single, Rs1850 double, but food is good and so is the swimming-pool—pretty essential in sticky Calcutta. Better all-round value is **Great Eastern Hotel**, 1–3 Old Court House St (tel 282331, tlx 21-7571), a well-located place with superior food, adjustable air-conditioning, spotless carpets and large, quiet rooms at Rs900 single, Rs1050 double. Just renovated, **Hotel New Kenilworth**, 1–2 Little Russell St (tel 223403, tlx 21-3395) has a nice open-air garden bar and select single/double rooms at Rs950/1050. Ask for a room in the pleasant old wing.

The **Fairlawns Hotel**, 13A Sudder St (tel 244460, 241835) enjoys the reputation of the 'weirdest hotel in India'. A real period piece, with Noel Coward furnishings and wildly ostentatious lounges, it has a year-round clientele of real oddballs. The hotel has delightful air-con single/double rooms at US$45 single, US$60 double (all meals included), a restaurant full of po-faced waiters in peacock turbans, cummerbunds and white gloves, and a Barbara Cartland-esque manageress. The twinkling fairy-lights over the entrance (put up one Christmas, never taken down) only go off when the gong sounds for dinner. Travellers are fascinated, and enjoy playing out their parts in a kind of ongoing soap opera.

Budget (under US$25/Rs750 per room night)

Far less strange is the nearby **Astoria Hotel**, 6/2 & 6/3 Sudder St (tel 241359), with spacious, elegantly furnished double rooms. **Carlton Hotel**, 2 Chowringhee Place, near the Grand Hotel (tel 288853), is another peaceful place—clean and comfy. Rooms here are from Rs200 single. **Lindsay Guest House**, 88 Lindsay St (tel 248639) has popular air-con rooms at Rs350, cheaper non-air-con rooms are also available. Finally, the excellent **East End Hotel**, Kys Rd (off Free School St), offers huge double rooms with bath.

The cheaper hotels are concentrated in and around Sudder St—inevitable, because it's so convenient for bus/rail stations, tourist office and GPO. The backpackers' choice is the popular (and crowded) **Paragon Hotel**, 2 Stuart Lane, off Sudder St. This has good cheap meals, a nice sitting-out area and a handy sun-roof for drying clothes. Directly opposite, **Modern Lodge** has less space, but cleaner rooms and a better dormitory. The **YMCA** (tel 292192), 25 Jawaharlal Nehru Rd, has air-conditioned rooms at Rs400 single, Rs500 double. A sign reading 'Pets and Private Servants Not Allowed' sets the depressing, humourless tone. The **YWCA** (tel 297033), Gallway House is only for women residents and has rooms from Rs200. At Howrah station, the **Rail Yatri Niwas** is convenient for early starts and late arrivals at the station. Rooms are from Rs200 (non-air-con) and Rs350 (air-con).

EATING OUT

Because Calcutta families tend to eat in, there is a great shortage of restaurants serving typical Bengali cuisine: only **Suruchi** at 89 Elliot Rd (tel 291783) specialises in it. Suruchi closes on Saturdays at 5 pm and Sundays at 3 pm. Try its famous fish dishes (particularly the tasty smoked *hilsa*) and its sweets. Princess Anne visited on one of her Save the Children Fund trips, and tucked into *pati shapta*, a delicious coconut pancake from East Bengal. For the ordinary diner, Suruchi offers a daily choice of vegetarian, fish or meat meals. These are Rs25–35 standard meals inclusive of dal, vegetables, papadums and a sweet. Bengali sweets are famous—go to **Ganguram's**, 46c Chowringhee Rd (Everest House) for milk and curd-based *rosogolla*, *mishti doi*, *indrani* and *sandesh*, all made to melt in your mouth.

The Oberoi's **Mughal Room** restaurant does the best Mughlai/North-West Frontier food in Calcutta. Good-value Rs150 buffets at lunchtime, authentic Bengali-style atmosphere (packed with locals, great live entertainment) in the evening. The Grand also has an exclusive French restaurant, **La Rotisserie**, with select continental food and an impressive array of wines. This is where Calcutta's hardworked businessmen come for a Rs175–225 'express' lunch: you can be in and out in under an hour.

The Taj Bengal has developed a good reputation for its *Szechwan* restaurant, **The Chinoiserie**, and its Indian restaurant, the **Sonargaon** where meals would be from Rs250 per person. The Taj also has a very popular 24-hour coffee shop. Outside the hotels many locals go to the old Chinese restaurants in South Tangra Street (off the Eastern Metropolitan bypass). The area is a bit rough but the food is excellent; try the **Sin Fa** or the **Blue Diamond**. Calcutta used to have a large Chinese community and was famous for its restaurants. The meals at **Fairlawn Hotel** are exceedingly popular with travellers. Over at Sagar Hotel's **Amber Bar & Restaurant**, you can enjoy a lunch or dinner of Tandoori/Indian cuisine. Park Street has a number of good multi-cuisine restaurants serving meals from Rs125, including **The Skyroom** (tel 294362), **The Blue Fox** with a popular bar, **Waldorf** excellent for Chinese, **Vineet** for vegetarian specialities, **Kwality** and **Trinca's**. For tasty no-nonsense Indian meals, try **Mughal Durbar** in Free School St, or **Fiesta** in Hardford Lane, off Sudder St. An excellent bakery and fiercely air-conditioned restaurant is **Kathleen's** on Free School St.

GENERAL INFORMATION

Tourist Offices
Government of India Tourist Office, 4 Shakespeare Sarani (tel 221402), is open 9 am to 6 pm Monday to Friday, 9 am to 1 pm Saturday, closed Sunday. Very efficient and helpful staff, good handout information. Book your city tours here (8 am–noon, 1–5.15 pm, daily except Monday).

West Bengal Tourist Bureau, 3/2 BBD Bag (tel 288271) is mainly useful for gathering information on Darjeeling and the Sunderbans Tiger Reserve. From September to March, it sells 2-day organised tours (leaves every Saturday, at 6.30 am) to Sunderbans National Park. Both tourist offices have desks at the airport.

Airline Offices
Indian Airlines, 39 Chittaranjan Ave (tel 264433, 263390 apt 569841/5); **Air India**, 50 J. Nehru Rd (tel 222356); **most international airline offices** are between Nos 30 and 58, J. Nehru Rd. They include: Aeroflot (tel 229831), Air France (tel 296161), British Airways (tel 248181, 293453), Burma Airways (tel 231624), Japan Airlines (tel 298370), Royal Nepal Airlines (tel 243949, 244434), Lufthansa (tel 248611), and Delta (tel 295001). Cathay Pacific (tel293211) and KLM Royal Dutch Airlines (tel 441221/4) are at 1 Middleton St, Alitalia at 238 A.J.C. Bose Rd (tel 447394) and Thai International at 18G Park St (tel 299846). Druk Air (tel 441301) are at 1 Ballygunge Circular Rd. Singapore Airlines (tel 447783) are at 230 Acharya J. C. Bose Rd.

Note: The main Indian Airlines office is sheer mayhem. It's much quicker to buy IA tickets from (quieter) desks at the Great Eastern Hotel (tel 280073), at the airport (tel 569638) or through a travel agent.

Travel Agents
Try Travel Corporation of India (tel 445469) or Mercury Travels (tel 443555), both at 46C Jawaharlal Nehru Rd. Also good is Sita World Travels, 3B Camac St (tel 293003) and American Express (tel 288896) 21 Old Court House St.

Cheap Flights
For cut-price air tickets (also rail reservations/visa assistance) contact Crystal Travel
(tel 240599), c/o Paragon Hotel, off Sudder St.

Consulates
UK, 1 Ho Chi Minh Sarani (tel 445171); France, 26 Park Mansions, Park St (tel
240958); Japan, 12 Pretoria St (tel 442241); Netherlands, 18A Brabourne Rd (tel
262160), USA, 5/1 Ho Chi Minh Sarani (tel 443611). Nepal (tel 452024) 19 National
Library Ave takes 24 hours to issue a visa. Bangladesh (tel 444458) 9 Circus Ave. For
the rest, check a telephone directory.

Miscellaneous
The Foreigners' Registration Office is on 237 Acharya J. C. Bose Rd (tel 443301).
American Express is close by at 21 Old Court House (tel 280266). Central Telegraph
Office (great for international phone calls!) is at 8 Red Cross Place, the vast GPO is
at BBD Bag, and State Bank of India on Jawaharlal Nehru Rd.

Best bookshops are Oxford Book Co. on Park St (for new books), Bookmark on Free
School St and Mullick Book Emporium, just behind Sudder St (for 2nd-hand books).
Loads of second-hand bookshops and cassette shops in Free School St. For background
reading, look out for H.E. Busteed's *Echoes from Old Calcutta* (1882, reprinted by Shannon,
1972), J. London's *Calcutta and its Neighbourhood* (Calcutta, 1974) and G. Moorhouse's
Calcutta, the City Revealed (London, 1983). A spate of books were published in 1990 and
1991 to celebrate Calcutta's Tricentenary. Laura Sykes anecdotal *Calcutta through British
Eyes* (OUP 1992) is an affectionate collection of travellers' tales. For up-to-date information and topical reviews, pick up a copy of *Calcutta Skyline* from any street bookstall.

Route 8—The Eastern Triangle

Bastion of the ancient Kalingan empire, Orissa is a rural, riverine land of great Hindu
and Jain temples, of rich culture and colourful festivals, of attractive folk art and
charming, friendly villages. Undaunted by rapid industrial progress, the old and the new
coexist in perfect harmony. This is most true of **Bhubaneshwar**, the well-planned state
capital, where broad avenues and modern architecture blend in with 500 ancient temples,
dating back to the 7th century AD. This temple city is the base for visits to the popular
tourist triangle of Orissa, which includes **Konarak**, famous for its magnificent 13th-cen-
tury Sun Temple, and **Puri** by the sea, one of the four main pilgrim centres of India.
Blessed with some of the finest monuments, forests and beaches in the world, the 'Golden
Triangle of the East' is now on the brink of discovery. It only requires the opening of the
new international airport at Bhubaneshwar for it to compete with, then exceed in
popularity, the more fêted Golden Triangle of the North. This is one area that has not yet
been affected by tourism, yet has enormous potential and the basic infrastructure of
facilities and communications. It certainly deserves a visit soon.

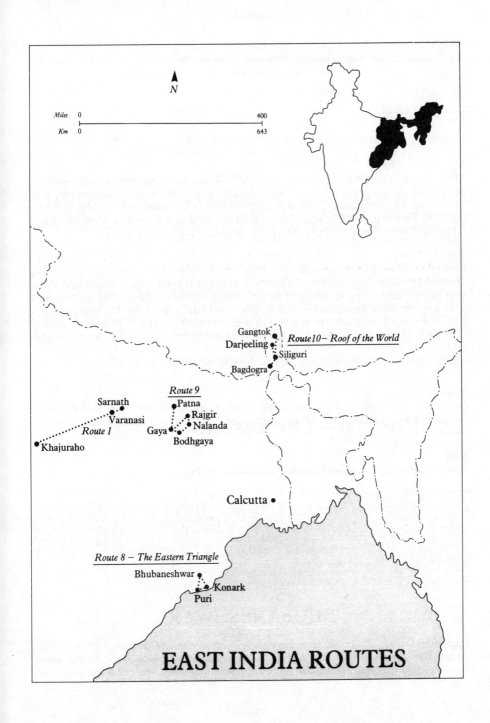

EAST INDIA ROUTES

WHEN TO GO
Best from October to mid-March, Orissa receives the monsoon from July to October. Temperatures from 27° to 49°C (summer), from 5° to 16°C (winter).

Route duration: 5 to 10 days.

TRAVEL ITINERARY

Calcutta to Bhubaneshwar 437 km (273 miles)

Air
At least one Indian Airlines flight daily (Rs893). The flight number and times vary depending on the plane's final destination and day of the week. Bhubaneshwar is also connected via Indian Airlines to Delhi (Rs2406), Varanasi (Rs1313), Hyderabad (Rs1796), Bombay (Rs2532) and Raipur (Rs1146). Bhubaneshwar airport is only 4 km (2½ miles) from town; a short ride by taxi or auto-rickshaw (Rs35/15).

Rail
The fast *Coromandel Express* leaves Howrah station at 2.30 pm daily, arrives Bhubaneshwar at 9.40 pm. On the return journey, this train departs Bhubaneshwar at about 4 am, arriving Calcutta 11.50 am. The *Howrah-Puri Express* leaves Howrah at 10 pm, reaching Bhubaneshwar at 5.40 am and Puri at 8.10 am. The return leaves Puri at 6 pm, Bhubaneshwar at 8.10 pm and arrives back in Calcutta (Howrah) at 5.30 the next morning. There are many other slower trains during the day and night.

Bhubaneshwar to Puri 65 km (40½ miles)/**Konarak** 64 km (40 miles).

Road
Good day-tour buses to both destinations; also regular private buses (1½ hours to Puri; 2/3 hours to Konarak). Minibuses connect Puri and Konarak (33 km; 20 miles, 1 hour).

Rail
Slower (2 hours) trains run from Bhubaneshwar to Puri.

CONTINUATIONS
For most other East India routes, you'll have to go back to Calcutta. However, you can join Route 1 and the side trip to Nepal on flight IC498 from Bhubaneshwar to Varanasi 4 days a week. Alternatively catch the *Coromandel Express* to Madras at 9.45 pm (reaching at 5.30 pm the next day and enjoy one of India's most beautiful train journeys along the east coast.

BHUBANESHWAR

Capital of Orissa, Bhubaneshwar is popularly known as the 'Temple City of India'. At one time, some 7000 sandstone temples are supposed to have stood on the site of the sacred Bindusagar Lake alone. Today almost 500 remain. Most of these were built between the 7th and 15th centuries, when Oriyan Hindu culture reached its zenith. Temple building began as a status activity of the wealthy (to ensure them a place in heaven) and was carried on with vigour by ensuing kings and rulers. But then came the Mughal conquest of the 16th century, and all but 500 or so of these distinctive beehive-shaped temples were destroyed. Today, there remain only 100 'living' temples (shrines where the gods' lifeforce is maintained by regular devotions), and only a small group of 30 of these can be said to be well preserved. Despite the ravages of time, these few noble survivors testify to the glory of an ancient civilisation that in terms of art and culture was perhaps the finest that India ever produced.

In ancient times, Orissa formed part of the powerful kingdom of Kalinga. At that time, Bhubaneshwar was known as Ekamrakshetra and was one of five religious centres in the state. It became a major place of pilgrimage, being considered a favourite resort of Lord Shiva, just as holy as his first preference, Varanasi. Here at Bhubaneshwar, Shiva was—and still is—worshipped as Tribhuvaneswara (Lord of the Three Worlds) or Lord Lingaraj. From this title, the city derives its name.

At the peak of their power, the Kalinga kings suddenly came into head-on collision with Ashoka, the powerful Mauryan emperor. Around 260 BC, Ashoka dealt the Kalingan forces such a crushing blow that—appalled at the resultant carnage—he turned his back on violence forever and embraced the Buddhist faith of peace and compassion. To mark this event, Ashoka left a famous set of rock edicts at Dhauli, 8 km (5 miles) south of Bhubaneshwar.

Buddhism quickly faded, and under the rule of Kharavela (the third Chedi king) Jainism was restored as the faith of the people. It was during his reign that the twin hills of Udayagiri and Khandagiri 8 km (5 miles) west of Bhubaneshwar became important Jain centres and the famous caves were created.

Under successive kings, the temple for Lord Jagannath was built at Puri (8th century AD), the worship of Shiva (Shaivism) replaced Jainism and many temples were erected at Bhubaneshwar (9th century), and the cult of Surya, the Sun God, became strong, resulting in the creation of the famous temple at Konarak (13th century).

Muslim incursions from both the north-west and the south (Golconda) led at last to the overthrow of the Hindu rulers. Thereafter, Orissa was held successively by the Muslims, the Afghans, the Marathas, and finally (in AD 1803) by the British.

Bhubaneshwar today is remarkably unlike a major state capital. It is clean, fairly free of traffic but spread out, and it backs onto large expanses of lush meadowland and green fields. A new city of modern buildings has recently sprung up to the north of the old temple town, but there is no real sense of contrast. Ancient sandstone temple spires soar above new hotels and restaurants, and modern paved roads fade into dusty old dirt-tracks. But Bhubaneshwar's progress is taking place in the context of its old traditions and culture, and it's almost impossible to believe that this small, relaxed, semi-rural city administers the affairs of 25 million people.

The best general time to visit is the cool season of October–February, though it is still very pleasant (and more relaxing) in March. After this, it's far too hot for comfort. The main festival of **Ashokastami** takes place over 5 days at the end of March at the Lingaraj. It's nothing like as grand as Puri's Rath Yatra, but you still get the spectacle of Lord Lingaraj being towed round town, visiting his relatives, by thousands of delirious devotees.

WHAT TO SEE

Bhubaneshwar new town, with its hotels, shops, restaurants and bus-station, lies to the north of the central railway line; the old temple town lies to the south. To tour the temples, hire a cycle-rickshaw from outside Panthaniwas Tourist Bungalow. Either hire a private car for about Rs300 for an 8-hour day (from OTDC and major hotels) or use cycle-rickshaws to get round town; taxis and auto-rickshaws seem only to ply the airport circuit. OTDC's conducted city tours are a cheap, convenient way of covering the widely spread out-of-town sights. Also use OTDC for quick, comprehensive day-outings to Puri and Konarak.

The Temples (by cycle-rickshaw/on foot, 3–5 hours)

Brahmeshwar–Rajarani–Mukteshwar–Parumeshwar–Lingaraj–Sisireswar–Vital Deul Temples

Though covered by the city conducted tour, Bhubaneshwar's famous temples are best first seen at leisure, and on your own. The quietest and coolest time of day to visit is the early morning.

From the new town, it's a short ride/walk down Bhubaneshwar Marg (south of the railway track) into the old city. Turn left into Tankpani Rd, and proceed straight ahead (10–15 mins on foot) until you come to the huge old banyan tree. Turn right here for short walk/ride to the 11th-century **Brahmeshwar Temple** 2 km (1½ miles) from the town centre.

Brahmeshwar is situated in the quietest of settings: a pastoral clearing right on the outskirts of the old city. Nearly all Bhubaneshwar temples are dedicated to Shiva, but this one is different. Shiva is the presiding deity, but the temple itself is the home of Brahma. A rickshaw man gave one explanation for this: 'Father Brahma live here to be quiet—all rest of noisy family [Shiva, Ganesh, Parvati, etc.] live in big Lingaraj temple.' Apart from the elaborate ribbed architecture of Brahmeshwar, a feature of the whole group of temples, appreciate the preponderance of dancing women, attractively carved in relief on the exterior walls; also, the beautifully sculpted Orissan lions on the higher levels.

Returning down Tankpani Rd, **Rajarani Temple** looms up on your left, just across the canal. This 9th-century monument is set in green gardens, and features unique erotic carvings of women and couples. The interior is very plain and the temple has long ceased to be in worship. It is however a fine example of the mature period of Orissan style.

A few hundred yards further up the road is the 9th-century **Mukteshwar Temple**, one of the most refined temples in Orissa. Small and compact, it is famous both for its ornate entrance arch and for its rare interior carvings. On the ceiling of the inner shrine can be seen lotus carvings, also representations of the whole pantheon of Brahman gods. Mukteshwar is set in a compound of several temples, ringed by mango and jackfruit trees and surrounded by most of Bhubaneshwar's small population of temple beggars.

The ancient **Parumeshwar Temple**, built in the 7th century, is located at the top of Tankpani Rd, near the northern edge of **Bindu Sagar Lake**. Ganesh lives here, along with his warrior brother Muruga (Parumeshwar). Renowned for its simple charm, and for the dense volume of its carvings (note the beautiful latticed windows) this is the best-preserved example of the early group of Orissan temples. It comprises a

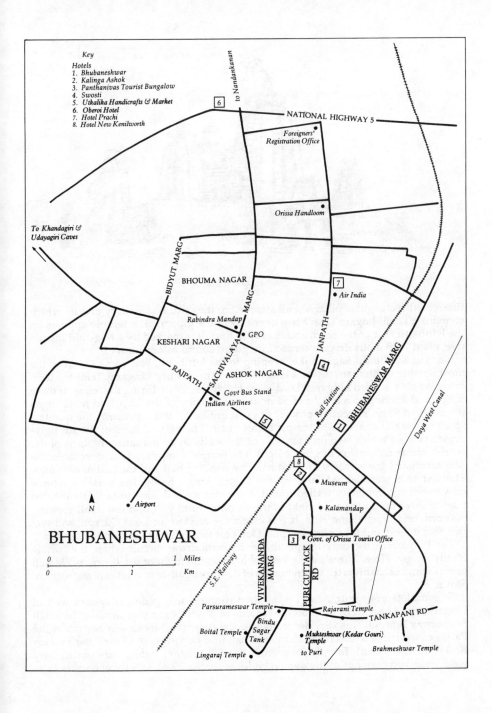

Key
Hotels
1. Bhubaneshwar
2. Kalinga Ashok
3. Panthanivas Tourist Bungalow
4. Swosti
5. Utkalika Handicrafts & Market
6. Oberoi Hotel
7. Hotel Prachi
8. Hotel New Kenilworth

6

to Nandankanan

NATIONAL HIGHWAY 5

Foreigners'
Registration Office

Orissa Handloom

To Khandagiri &
Udayagiri Caves

BIDYUT MARG

BHOUMA NAGAR

SACHIVALAYA MARG

7

Air India

JANPATH

BHUBANESWAR MARG

Rabindra Mandap

GPO

KESHARI NAGAR

4

RAJPATH

ASHOK NAGAR

Rail Station

Days West Canal

Govt Bus Stand

Indian Airlines

5

1

8

2

Museum

Kalamandap

Airport

N

BHUBANESHWAR

0   1   Miles
0   1   Km

S.E. Railway

VIVEKANANDA MARG

3

Govt. of Orissa Tourist Office

PURICUTTACK RD

Parsurameswar Temple

Bindu
Sagar
Tank

Rajarani Temple

TANKAPANI RD

Boital Temple

Muchteshwar (Kedar Gouri)
Temple

Lingaraj Temple

to Puri

Brahmeshwar Temple

Brahmeshwar Temple

flat-roofed rectangular pillared hall attached to the central sanctuary or *deul*, which contains a small lingam (don't trip over this in the gloom). The temple appears on the left-hand side of the road, and is easy to find. It is marked by a huge old mango tree, often with a bus driver or a security guard sound asleep under it.

Skirting the Bindu Sagar Lake, keeping to the left bank, you come at last to the most notable of Bhubaneshwar's temples, the 11th-century **Lingaraj Temple**, dedicated to Shiva as Lord Lingaraj (Lord of the Universe). Built during the reigns of three kings, and soaring to a height of 54 m, it contains one of the 12 prized jyotirlingas (symbols of Shiva's creative power) of great antiquity and represents the quintessence of the Kalinga style of temple architecture. The vertical lines of the strongly-drawn ribs, of which two on each side of the walls show miniature replicas of the whole, create an illusion of great height. The temple comprises four structures: the *deul* sanctuary, the *mandapa* or great hall, the dancing hall and the hall of offerings. The last two were added later by the Ganga kings. Sadly, the massive temple compound is completely walled round, and entrance is denied to non-Hindus. No matter, carry on up the road right of the entrance until you find the small viewing platform on the left–hand side. It was originally erected for Lord Curzon, and you can peer over it and take photographs. Don't let touts charge you for this service.

The Lingaraj is the only temple in the Bhubaneshwar circuit where the 'whole family' of gods live. There's a big festival here on the night of the February/March new moon, **Mahashivratri**, when hordes of devotees gather to celebrate the night of Shiva.

To complete your tour, head up the road running alongside the eastern wall of Lingaraj, then bear right until on the far side of Bindu Sagar you come to the small **Sisireswar Temple**. This very decorative 8th-century structure closely resembles the Parumeshwar in architectural form and has fine carvings. It adjoins the famous **Boital** or **Vital Deul Temple**, also from the 8th century, which has particularly well-preserved carvings of the demon goddess Durga. The name *boital* derives from

360

the word for 'spirit' and harks back to the days when a few temples were used for tantric practices, and when human sacrifices were made to the presiding eight-armed Chamundi deity. This is one of Bhubaneshwar's few non-Shiva temples, being dedicated to Durga.

City Tour (by sightseeing bus, full-day)
Khandagiri and Udayagiri Caves–Nandankanan Park–Dhauli–State Museum

The OTDC conducted tour covers the above spots plus the old town temples in any order, depending on the mood of the driver. If you've already seen the temples, suggest that they're made the last stop of the day so you can leave the tour early.

Some 8 km (5 miles) out of town you'll visit the **Khandagiri** and **Udayagiri Hills**, honeycombed with ancient caves. These were excavated by monks during the reign of Kharavela, the Kalinga emperor, around the 1st and 2nd centuries BC. Udayagiri has 44 caves, all carved out of sandstone. Their entrances are decorated with monkey (Hanuman) or elephant (Buddha) motifs, and are often adorned with Pali inscriptions. Several caves functioned as monks' sleeping quarters, and contain bare rockbeds. The central **Hathi Gumpha** (Elephant Cave) exhibits the best example of Pali records so far found in India: a full listing of Kharavela's religious, military and civil achievements during the first 13 years of his reign. An ingenious underground water supply runs right through the caves, originating from a central reservoir.

Above and to the left of Udayagiri, are the group of 19 Khandagiri caves. On top of Khandagiri hill, you'll find 24 Jain statues of great beauty in the 18th-century temple of **Mahavir** (founder of the Jain religion). There are nice views from the summit too.

The **Nandankanan Biological Park**, 20 km (12½ miles) out of Bhubaneshwar, is an attractive botanical garden and zoo set amid the forest and lakes of Chandaka. The largest lion safari park in India, it is also the first zoo in the world where white tigers have been bred naturally in captivity. The animals here live in semi-tropical splendour, often in quarters superior to those of their human visitors. They include rhinos, monkeys, gharials, pelicans, pythons, brown bear, and crocodile. In March, there's a colourful host of wild butterflies. For a quick orientation round the zoo grounds, take a ride on the toy train which circles the perimeter. Alight at the new **Lion Safari Park** at the top of the complex. Buses run visitors out every half hour or so (Rs3) to see African lions (often asleep) in the vast 20-hectare (50-acre) reserve. Otherwise, you can hire a pedal- or rowing-boat on the lake, or pay a brief visit to the **Botanical Gardens** north of the zoo, with its wide variety of indigenous and exotic plants. Nandankanan is open 7 am–6 pm (April–September), 7.30 am–5 pm (September–March) daily except Monday. Admission is Rs2. If not on tour, visit by local bus—there's an hourly service from Bhubaneshwar.

The bright-white Japanese peace pagoda on top of Dhauli hill 8 km (5 miles) from town can be seen for many miles. Bedecked with gilded lions, this **Santi Stupa** has five types of 'umbrella'—representing the five ancient Buddhist virtues of faith, hope, compassion, forgiveness and non-violence. It overlooks the vast plain where Ashoka destroyed the might of the Kalinga empire, and then dedicated himself to peace. At the foot of Dhauli hill, you may see the famous **Ashoka Rock Edicts**—inscribed by the repentant emperor after being converted to Buddhism by a resident monk. Above the edicts there is the earliest known sculpture in Orissa, the forepart of an elephant (representing Buddha) hewn out of a huge rock. Dhauli is a quiet, scenic spot with beautiful views in all directions. At the top of the hill, behind the white-domed pagoda, is a small Hindu temple of Lord Dhaveleswar which was reconstructed in 1992.

Orissa State Museum, just below the railway track in the old part of town, is a large sprawling building with a rich collection of tribal art and many interesting archaeological finds. The excellent Heritage of Orissa exhibition has a wide-ranging display of bronze images, tribal arts, stone inscriptions and anthropological specimens, also sculptures, coins, handicrafts, minerals and items of natural history. The old temple *dharani* inscriptions, mainly on stone tablets or blocks of wood, are of particular interest. The cultural Rainbow's Edge exhibition has a fine display of folk and traditional paintings, mostly inspired by legends, myths and folklore. Also many intricate tribal wall and floor paintings, similar to those that can be found in Oriyan homes even today. Despite poor lighting, and a rather gloomy, mothballed natural history section, this very representative collection is well displayed and worth a visit. Open 10 am–5 pm daily (except Monday). Free guide service.

Around sunset, try a relaxing rickshaw ride around **Bhubaneshwar** town. It's an interesting little place, which comes alive in the evening when the heat is down. Start with a pleasant ride north out of town. On your return, look out for the lines of patient egg-sellers seated by the roadside with their tidy little mountains of eggs lit by a single, flickering oil-lamp. Coconut, banana and nut vendors also have their small illuminated 'patches' here. Riding down the otherwise pitch-black highway, all these little lamps give the general effect of a deserted, flare-lit airport runway.

Puri/Konarak (by tour bus, full-day)

Puri is one of the four holiest Hindu cities in India, also an upcoming beach resort. It's a remarkable place, packed with atmosphere and pilgrims, which comes as close to 'real' India as you can expect. The religious and cultural life of the small, busy town centres round the huge 12th-century Jagannath Temple, home of the 'Formless God', Lord Jagannath, who is said to represent the primordial essence of the universe. At the spectacular **Rath Yatra** (Car Festival) of June–July, Puri is invaded by zealous armies of pilgrims who gather from all over India to worship the images of Jagannath, as they are dragged through town on massive wooden chariots. It's the most intense demonstration of religious fervour anywhere, an impossible madhouse of swaying crowds, but apparently great fun.

The ride out by OTDC coach to **Puri** is beautiful in spring—mile upon mile of lush, green paddy fields and violet water-hyacinths, interspersed with temples, semi-tropical jungles and lively farming villages.

Some 20 km (125 miles) out of Bhubaneshwar, you'll visit the small village of **Pipli**, internationally famous for its bright, colourful appliqué art and handicrafts. Here intricate mirror-inlaid tapestries are produced, and vivid prayer-flags and beach-umbrellas, saris and bedsheets, wall and table covers, canopies and lamp shades—all brilliantly coloured and often employing decorative motifs of birds, animals, flowers or leaves. Unfortunately, Pipli itself is not a good place to buy this produce. Most of its quality crafts are sent to Bhubaneshwar for sale. What remains, in grubby roadside shops and emporia, is largely substandard stuff. Ask to be directed to the houses of one of the few elderly artists who still remember how to make the delicate, elaborate work of the last century. Some of them are appointed costume-makers to Lord Jagannath.

At Puri, it's a 1-km (½-mile) walk up from the bus-stand to the **Jagannath Temple**. Even when there are no festivals, Puri's broad central avenue is total mayhem—packed solid with jostling beggars, bullock carts, cycle-rickshaws and pilgrims. Tin shacks and wooden stalls deal furiously in cold drinks, silverware, vegetarian food and all manner of cheap religio-tourist paraphernalia. All along the dusty thoroughfare, temple bells clang an insistent invitation to devotees.

The Jagannath Temple, built during the 12th century by the Kalinga ruler Chodaganga Deva, is the tallest and most magnificent monument in Orissa. Its pinnacle rises to a formidable height of 65 m (212 ft), and dominates the skyline for miles around. It is divided into four parts: the central main hall, the hall of audience, the dancing hall and the hall of offerings, and has four gates. Each of these has an animal theme: horse (south gate), elephant (north gate), tiger (west gate) and the lion (east gate). It is by the lion gate that pilgrims make their entrance, to visit Lord Jagannath and commune with his qualities of light, power and wisdom. In front of this main gate stands a 16-sided monolithic pillar called **Aruna Stambha**, which used to stand in front of Konarak's Sun Temple until brought here in the 18th century.

Non-Hindus aren't allowed into the Jagannath temple, but you can peer over the walls from a nearby viewing platform. This is located on the roof of the **Raghunandan Library**, opposite the Lion Gate. As you climb the stairs within, you are shown a sign reading 'Be Aware of Monkeys' and are given a big stick. From the open roof, you can marvel at the sheer power and majesty of this huge temple, which rather resembles a primitive spaceship. You also have a clear sweep of Puri town, the main street a veritable gauntlet of beggars and mendicants, ganja-sellers and hawkers, bullock carts and itinerant cows; scores of dazed Indian families weave a crazy, erratic path from tour bus to temple. Off the roof, stop in at the library's first-floor museum which has an interesting collection of rare palm-leaf manuscripts, some dating back 350 years. Many are written in ancient Sanskrit, scratched out by quill-pen, and beautifully coloured. The curator is keen to show you samples. He is even keener to sell you some copies.

Walking round the temple perimeter is interesting. You can see some of the original fine carvings on the exterior walls, buried until recently under a thick coat of lime plaster, but now being revealed as the result of patient conservation work. Note especially the four temple gates. These all have an animal theme—notably the main gate, with its portal pair of moustachioed lions. By the gates are the temple money-changers. Their job is to take Rs1 coins from visiting pilgrims, returning them 90 paise in small coins (for distribution to beggars within) and keeping the remaining 10 paise as commission. Many travellers use their services too: they are apparently the only people in India with a ready supply of small change.

The tour moves on to nearby Puri Beach for a pleasant *thali* lunch at the tourist bungalow. Afterwards, there's time for a walk along the long, sandy beach or a swim. The sea is rather brisk and very salty. You can shower off in the tourist bungalow afterwards but nothing deters pilgrims from their dip in the holy waters. If you decide to join them, be prepared to be adopted by local fishermen, who lassoo hesitant bathers with rubber rings. It's okay to change on the beach, leaving your togs with an Indian family, or pay a boy a rupee to mind them for you.

WHERE TO STAY/EATING OUT IN PURI

If you wish to stay over in Puri (which is worth it, even if only for the marvellous sunrises and sunsets), there are many decent hotels, restaurants, and seaside shops selling soapstone carvings, horn/wood articles and palm-leaf paintings situated along the seafront. Most of the **budget hotels** popular with travellers are at the east end of the beach towards the fishing village, along or off Chakra Tirath Rd. In the centre are most of the mid-range and top-end hotels. The best hotel is in fact 6 km (4 miles) from the town on the Konarak Road. **Toshali Sands** (tel 2888, 2999, tlx 0675-395) calls itself Orissa's Ethnic Village Resort and has rooms in the main block, also villas and a deluxe tented camp; room rates are from US$35. In town the best hotel is the **Nilachal Ashok** (tel 2968/80, tlx 0675-335) adjoining Raj Bhavan on VIP Road. In the winter rooms are from Rs450 single with a 10% discount from April to September. Other worthwhile options include **Hotel Prachi,** (tel 2638, tlx 0675-278) with comfortable rooms from Rs450 single; **Hotel Vijoya International** (tel 3705, tlx 6701-203) with rooms at Rs400/500; and the delightfully old-style **South-Eastern Railway Hotel** (tel 2062, 3005/9, tlx 6701-201) with air-con singles/doubles at Rs400/600 including all meals.

Budget hotels (below Rs250 per room night) include the fairly standard **Panthaniwas Tourist Bungalow** (tel 2562), and nearby the pleasant **Seaside Inn**. Other budget hotels include the **Hotel Sonali** (tel 2567) near the beach with both air-con and non-air-con rooms from Rs 150/250 respectively. On Puri beachfront, eat at **Mickey Mouse Restaurant** or **Xanadu's**—delicious seafood and Indian-style snacks. For Western food, you'll have to go into Puri town.

In the afternoon, the tour continues on to **Konarak** to see the famous **Sun Temple**. In its heyday, Konarak was the centre of Orissan culture and commerce. Today, it is a small village, with half an ancient temple standing in isolated splendour amongst desolate sand dunes. But it remains a major pilgrimage centre. Every year, at the important **Chandrabhaga Mela** festival of February, thousands of pilgrims arrive to honour the Sun God, Surya. At dawn on the 7th day of the festival, they all troop down to the beach, originally at the foot of the Sun Temple, but now 3 km (2 miles) distant from it, and take their ritual bath in the sea. Then they anxiously await the rising of the sun. Afterwards, they return to the Sun Temple to visit the nine planets installed there. This ceremony, which has been observed ever since the temple was constructed, is believed by all those who participate to erase the entire sum of their past misdeeds.

Konarak derives its name from the Sanskrit language, and roughly translates as 'sun's corner'. According to popular myth, it was here that the tradition of sun-worship began, some 5000 years ago. Krishna, offended by a negligent son-in-law called Samba, afflicted him with leprosy and advised him to do penance to the Sun God for 12 years. Cured of his disease, the grateful Samba erected a small temple to Surya, much added to and many times reconstructed in later centuries, by the banks of the sacred river. In the mid-13th century, after the Sun God granted his prayer for a child, Narasimha Devi I of the Ganga dynasty built the present massive structure. It is said to have taken a total of 1200 artisans assisted by 12 000 labourers 12 long years to complete (AD 1243–55).

First stop at Konarak is **Sun Beach**, a long unbroken sweep of golden sand considered by many to be Orissa's finest beach. The water is very suitable for swimming, and the beach is generally completely deserted except for a small fishing community. Of course, this can't last for long. The Oberoi hotel chain have already earmarked a large section of Sun Beach for development, but this is being disputed by conservationists as the site includes a wildlife sanctuary and a beautiful lagoon.

Konarak's Sun Temple itself is a masterpiece of design and construction: built in the shape of a huge chariot, pulled along by seven racing horses (one for each day in the week) on 24 intricately carved stone wheels (one for each fortnight of the Indian year). The idea of the sculpture was to recreate the magnificent progress of the Sun God, Surya, through the heavens.

It was designed so that the first rays of the morning sun, every single day of the year, would strike first the dancing hall, then the hall of audience, and finally the head of the Sun God in the main temple, charging it with new energy and lifeforce. Originally, the temple had a huge spire, projecting to a height of 70 m, but this collapsed some 400 years after its construction. In the past, this soaring beacon was an important landmark for mariners navigating the passage to Calcutta, and they named it the 'Black Pagoda' to distinguish it from the 'White Pagoda' of Puri's Jagannath Temple.

At the temple, start with a visit to the interesting little museum (closed Friday) and purchase its useful ASI guidebook (by Debala Mitra) on Konarak. Then hire a temple guide for about Rs20.

To appreciate further the educative function of this temple, take a circuit round the huge **Hall of Audience**, a 40-m leviathan which was filled in with sand by the British in 1903 to prevent collapse. The wall-carvings here divide into three distinct sections. Elephant and animal motifs run round the baseline and lower levels. On the central level, there are mostly erotic carvings. Finally, on the top layer, there are depictions of the various gods and goddesses.

There is a riot of carvings running right round the temple, most of the best work being concentrated within the massive spoked wheels of the chariot. Climb the stairs at the rear of the temple to see the three life-size images of the Sun God, carved out of polished blue-granite. These depict the rising, noonday and setting sun respectively; other explanations say that they represent youth, middle age and old age, or Brahma, Vishnu and Shiva. The empty dais in the sunken chamber once contained the seated statue of the Sun God, now housed in the British Museum. Note the beautiful elephant panels in this section, and return to admire the entrance doors of the **Hall of Audience**, which feature seven different carving styles, one for each spectrum of the rainbow (the Sun God's seven different 'lights'). Facing the doors is the **Dancing Hall**, still used on special occasions for classical Orissan dance displays. Standing here, look down at your feet. You are walking on a unique feature of this temple complex: its stone flooring, comprising solid massive blocks of stone joined with iron rivets. At no point was cement or mortar used. And the work still goes on. Industrious teams of stone-cutters are constantly at work on the site, carrying on time-honoured traditions of temple building and renovation. Despite the ravages of time, Konarak remains Orissa's finest achievement.

The Archaeological Site Museum has many finely carved chlorite panels and khondalite images from the monument; other pieces are in the National Museum, New Delhi and the Indian Museum, Calcutta. Open 9 am–5 pm, closed Friday.

Konarak has many cheap boarding lodges, plus a good OTDC **Tourist Lodge** (tel 23) and OTDC **Panthaniwas** (tel 31), but overnighters usually stay at nearby Puri.

Excursions

If you want to get off the beaten track, continue on by local bus/taxi to **Chilka Lake**, some 30 km (18¾ miles) south of Puri. OTDC luxury coaches/cars go there too, from Bhubaneshwar 96 km (60 miles) distant. Chilka is the largest lagoon in the country, spreading over 1100 sq km, and is an excellent venue for bird-watchers. During the winter season (October to February), it receives flocks of exotic and rare migratory birds, some from as far off as Siberia. From the small **Panthaniwas Guest House** at **Barkul**, one can take a boat into the lake at the crack of dawn, to float quietly for hours through the vast marshes, lowlands and backwaters of Chilka—perhaps visiting Nalaban Island, where great numbers of birds come to roost. Fishing, swimming and yachting is good in this area, and it's wonderfully quiet.

Further south is the rundown but charming beach-town of **Gopalpur-on-Sea**, 176 km (110 miles) from Bhubaneshwar. To get here, either take a night train from Calcutta to **Behrampur** (17 km; 10¾ miles by bus/taxi from Gopalpur), or a local bus that runs hourly from Bhubaneshwar to Behrampur. At this village, while arranging transport on to the beach, check out the silk-weavers lining the streets at the side of Behrampur's main temple. Gopalpur itself is a miniature seaside haven with a charming old British club-style hotel right on the beach. This is the **Oberoi Palm Beach** (tel 8121, 8123, tlx 673 261), the pre-World War Two resort choice of holidaying Calcuttans. A beautiful whitewashed building, it has good water-sports facilities, relaxing gardens, and an old-colonial flavour. Rooms rates from US$49 single and US$70 double. The beach itself is lovely, clean and very long. It looks out onto the Bay of Bengal, and borders a lush, green network of backwater creeks and sleepy lagoons. Gopalpur has very little infrastructure as yet, but there are a few government guest-houses and small hotels, ideal for people travelling on a budget.

RECREATION

For culture, visit the **Rabindra Mandap** in Sachivalaya Marg (town centre). There are good dance displays here, usually on Saturday/Sunday/Monday evenings at 7 pm. To sit in on training classes at **Odissi Dance Academy** and **College of Dance and Music**, first contact the tourist office. There are several good cinemas in town, notably the plush air-con **Kasori**, opposite Rabindra Mandap.

SHOPPING

Bhubaneshwar offers an extremely good choice of fabrics, textiles and crafts. The royal Mauryan textile workshops established over 2000 years ago began a lineage of spinners, weavers and embroiderers which has continued to the present day, with temple towns like Bhubaneshwar becoming the bases for several weaving communities. The result is a wide variety of silk, tussar and cotton fabrics, many with vibrant tribal, traditional or modern designs. Best buys are tie-and-dye textiles (particularly those incorporating the fine 'double ikat' cotton or silk weave), colourful appliqué work, silver filigree jewellery, stone and wood carvings, patta paintings on muslin, and animal-motif *papier mâché* masks. Most of these handicrafts originate from nearby Pipli.

You'll find the best handicrafts—really nice stuff—at **Utkalika Handicrafts Emporium,** (closed Thursday) near the government bus-stand in Rajpath. Attractive Oriyan-style silk saris or lunghis are good value at Rs300/1000, also palm-leaf illustrations and Pipli crafts. Both here, and at nearby **Handloom Cooperative**

Society, you can see skilled craftsmen at work. On your travels through Orissa, look out for palm-leaf paintings, prayer-sheets or horoscopes, often produced in local households, in temples or in astrologers' abodes. Even after printing paper became available in Orissa, important texts still continued to be printed on the sacred palmleaf.

WHERE TO STAY
Up till quite recently, superior accommodation in Bhubaneshwar was very limited. Now that Orissa is waking up to tourism, however, three five-star hotel groups have booked plots at Nayapalli, to the north-west of town. These are the Oberoi, opened November 1985, and the Taj and Welcomgroup hotels, yet to be built.

Luxury (from US$35/Rs1000 per room night)
The **Oberoi Bhubaneshwar**, CB-l Nayapalli (tel 56116, 56320 tlx 0675-348 HOB IN, fax 0674-56269) is the city's only five-star property. One of the nicest hotels in India with 12 acres of land, lovely gardens, floodlit tennis courts, poolside barbecues, good restaurants, and friendly management, it's 4 km (2½ miles) out of the city centre, but handy for the airport. Rooms are US$85 single, US$95 double.

Mid-range (US$10–35/Rs250–1000 per room night)
Apart from the comparatively expensive Oberoi, the other upmarket options are the **Hotel Kalinga Ashok**, Gautam Nagar (tel 53318, tlx 0675-282) with decent rooms in the old block at Rs450 single, Rs650/750 double. It's a friendly place, with large gardens and useful facilities. The **New Kenilworth** (tel 54330/1, tlx 0675-343) has rooms from Rs500 single and Rs750 double. Both hotels have swimming-pools, health club and bars in addition to their normal facilities.

In town, the best mid-range bet is **Hotel Swosti**, 100 Janpath (tel 54178, tlx 0675-321), with nice restaurant, pleasant bar (famous for its cocktails), travel counter and shopping complex. Here you have a choice of rooms—either noisy ones with a view, or quiet ones without. Tariffs are Rs450 single, Rs750 double. Across the road, find **Hotel Jajati**, Station Square (tel 50288). This place can be noisy (they're constantly building 'improvements'), but is otherwise superb value with non-air-con and air-con rooms from Rs100/200. Centrally located, two good restaurants, car park, travel counter and cosy bar. If you can afford it, take one of the Rs350 suites. In a class of its own, the decaying **Hotel Prachi**, 6 Janpath (tel 52689) is a wonderful relic of the Raj. Bags of Anglo-Indian character, an ancient lift, old-colonial rooms (Rs450 single, Rs650 double air-con) and the 'only regal billiard room in an Orissan hotel'. Nice swimming-pool too.

Budget (under US$10/Rs250 per room night)
At the top of the cheap range is the OTDC **Panthaniwas Tourist Bungalow** in Jayadev Marg (tel 54515, tlx 0675-335). Very convenient for tours, tourist office, temples, it has two decent restaurants and clean, comfortable rooms at Rs350 (air-con). Cheap hotels like the **Hotel Pushpak** and **Hotel Vagwat Niwas**, are near the railway station.

EATING OUT
Orissan specialities to look out for include *chena purda patha* (cheese-burnt-sweet), which tastes like caramel custard, also fresh seafood (lobster, prawns and crab). The

bekti and *rui* curries are good, as are traditional Oriyan thalis including local green vegetables of *potal* or *kara saag* (spinach).

For an evening of gracious dining, eat out at Oberoi's **Chandini** restaurant where a meal would cost from Rs150. This has fairly standard Indian cuisine, but also offers top-quality Oriyan dishes; prawns cooked in spinach, fish curry with mustard, aubergine and yogurt salad, sweet cottage cheese in cinnamon. Oberoi's other popular eatery, the **Pushpanjali**, has what is probably the best continental food in town, from Rs150 per head. The Ashok's **Ganjapati** is also known for the quality of its food.

The **Swosti Hotel** is renowned for its Oriyan food. This traditional fare, is cooked mainly in a very deep clay oven, much like tandoor. It's all pretty spicy stuff. The restaurant also has meat dishes prepared in pure *ghee*, rice is cooked just once, and dal is flavoured with caramel-flavoured jaggery. There is a problem: you have to order this food 8 hours in advance. But there's a wide range of standard Oriyan dishes ('typical home food') on the Swosti menu, in addition to the usual Indian fare. Many local people eat here and meals are from Rs125 per head. Those with less money patronise **Venus Inn**, near the Ashok hotel, famous for its inexpensive South Indian fare. If you're not feeling adventurous, try the Indian/Chinese restaurants at **Panthaniwas Tourist Bungalow**. Nothing exciting, but fairly cheap with meals from Rs60 per head.

GENERAL INFORMATION

OTDC Tourist Information Centre, 5 Jayadev Marg, behind Panthaniwas Tourist Bungalow (tel 50099) is small, but very helpful. Open 10 am–5 pm daily, except Sunday (and every second Saturday of the month). Other information counters (open 24 hours) are at the airport and rail station. OTDC city/temple tours (9 am–6 pm daily) and Puri/Konarak tours (9 am–6.30 pm daily) are sold at the tourist bungalow. You can also hire cars, coaches and even yachts for sightseeing here. The Govt of India Tourist Office (tel 54203) is at B/21 Kalpana Area and open Monday to Friday, 9.30 am–6 pm.

Modern Book Depot, Station Sq (tel 52373) is good for books and maps. Genesis Travel, at Jajati Hotel (tel 56493), handles air, rail and bus bookings. The GPO is just up from the bus-stand. Indian Airlines (tel 400544/33, apt 401084, 406472) is in Rajpath, opposite the bus-stand. While open till 5.30 pm it only issues tickets upto 4.15 pm. Many banks are in this area too. In Bhubaneshwar, most banks close on a Monday, most shops on a Thursday, and the whole town from noon to 4 pm every day, for siesta. Railway enquiries (tel 402233) are open 9 am–4.30 pm.

Route 9—In the Footsteps of the Buddha

India, birthplace of two major world religions—Hinduism and Buddhism—is a land of pilgrims. Joining the trail is a unique experience, one which no traveller ever forgets. Birthplace of Buddhism, and home of many aboriginal tribes, the north-eastern state of **Bihar** really is a holiday off the beaten track. The poorest state in India, Bihar has very limited tourist facilities, but compensates with the spiritual experience of a lifetime. Alongside the modern towns of industry stand the proud ruins of monasteries, temples and universities, reflecting the bygone might of a great world religion. From the major Hindu pilgrimage centre of **Gaya**, it's just a short drive down to **Bodhgaya**, where the Buddha achieved his enlightenment beneath the Bodhi Tree. Also close by are **Nalanda**, site of the world's oldest university, and **Rajgir**, capital of the ancient Magadha empire, where the Buddha and Mahavira (founder of the Jain religion) delivered their most important teachings.

Near Varanasi is **Sarnath** (see Route 1), a peaceful centre of stupas, shrines, monasteries and museums, where the Buddha came to preach his first sermon.

WHEN TO GO
Best season: October to March (monsoons: June to October).
Climate: 20°–47°C (summer); 4°–28°C (winter).
Route duration: 4 to 7 days.

TRAVEL ITINERARY

Calcutta to Gaya 458 km (286 miles)

Air
The closest airport is at Patna, 4 hours' drive to the north. Patna has daily Indian Airlines flights with Delhi (Rs1629), Ranchi (Rs681) and Calcutta (Rs1054) and 3 flights a week from Bombay (Rs2935) via Ranchi. If stuck overnight in Patna stay at the **Welcomgroup Maurya Patna** opposite Gandhi Maidan (tel 222061, tlx 022-352) with rooms from Rs1200. The **Pataliputra Ashok** (tel 226270, tlx 022-311) on Bir Chand Patel Path has rooms from Rs750. A budget alternative is the cheap, good **Hotel Republic** on Exhibition Rd (tel 55021).

Rail
Gaya is on one of the main lines between Calcutta and New Delhi so has a large number of trains passing through. The *AC Express* leaves Howrah at 9.15 am and reaches Gaya at 4.40 pm. A convenient night train is the *Doon Express* leaving at 8 pm and reaching Gaya at 6 am.

Varanasi to Gaya 220km (136¼ miles)

Rail
Daily train service (4–6 hours). Travel 1st class if you can—all trains are unbelievably crowded so advance-booking is required.

Gaya to Bodhgaya 13 km (8 miles)

Road
Auto-rickshaw/minibus (Rs3) from the Kacheri in Gaya city centre. If you find transport anywhere near the rail station, it's your lucky day. If staying overnight in Bodhgaya, there are 2 early buses at 4 am and 5 am running out to Nalanda.

Gaya to Rajgir 65 km (41 miles)

Road
Buses are fairly regular but often crowded (3 hours).

Rajgir to Nalanda 15 km (9½ miles)

Road
Rickshaw/tonga (30 mins, Rs8); also infrequent buses. From Nalanda bus-stand you can take a return-trip tonga up to the university ruins (3 km; 2 miles).

Nalanda to Gaya 66 km (41 miles)

Road
Only a few buses daily (3 hours). Check timings before exploring Nalanda. Cars can be hired in Gaya to do day trips to Bodhgaya, Nalanda and Rajgir as well as round trips with overnight stays. If returning to Patna by road a car from there can be advance-booked to meet you in Gaya and take in all the places. Book through a Delhi or Calcutta travel agency. A 4-day trip would cost approximately Rs3500.

CONTINUATIONS
Not easy. Your best option is the Darjeeling connection which means back-tracking to Calcutta and then connecting to Bagdogra. Otherwise, continue to Varanasi to connect with Route 1 (IC408 daily to Khajuraho, Agra and Delhi), the Eastern Triangle (IC497 flies to Bhubaneshwar), Delhi (daily IC498/9 flight or overnight train) or out Nepal (daily flight).

GAYA

Originally part of the ancient kingdom of Magadha, Gaya has long been a major pilgrimage centre—as sacred to the Hindus as Bodhgaya is to the Buddhists. According to legend, Gaya was a celestial being whom Vishnu endowed with the power to absolve all sinners and elevate them to heaven. Hundreds of thousands of pilgrims gather here each year to offer last rites for their departed ancestors, believing that offerings of pindas (funeral cakes) will free them from the Hindu cycle of rebirth. As in Varanasi, they must first perform a lengthy pilgrimage; in this case an arduous tour of the 45 or so Hindu shrines around Gaya, before the final purificatory bath in the sacred Phalgu river.

India's holiest places are often her poorest, and Gaya is no exception. In itself, it is just another dirty, noisy pilgrim centre, where sanctity (temples) and insanity (traffic) go hand in hand. But it does have vitality and atmosphere—also the only half-decent accommodation and food for many miles. Gaya does have some worthwhile sights of its own—good for a leisurely day's ramble—but is mainly useful as a base from which to explore nearby Bodhgaya, 13 km (8 miles) down the road.

The best months to visit this area are December to February, when there's a pleasant chill in the air and relatively few mosquitoes.

WHAT TO SEE

Gaya's few sights are best covered on foot. There are very few taxis and rickshaws, and they are invariably crowded. Very few people speak English here, and roads are not signed, so you'll have to use some initiative to get around. The bus-stand (for Bodhgaya) is in the centre of town, 15 minutes' walk away; turn right out of the rail station.

Pilgrimage Tour (on foot, 4/5 hours)
Vishnupad Temple–Surya Temple–Brahmajuni Hill–Akshyabat

This walk is best tackled in the morning when it is not so hot, dusty and crowded. Starting at the rail station, turn right for the centre of the old town. Ten minutes' walk brings you to the **Vishnupad Temple** (just follow the pilgrims), the main focus of the Hindu pilgrimage in Gaya. The original modest shrine, erected in ancient times over a 40-cm (16-in) long 'footprint' of Vishnu (imprinted in solid rock, ringed by a silver-plated basin) was completely renovated in 1787 by the revolutionary Rani Ahalya Bai of Indore, producing the present magnificent structure with its 30-m high octagonal tower and eight rows of beautifully sculpted pillars supporting the pavilion hall or *mandapa*. The temple is off-limits to non-Hindus, but the exterior makes fine viewing. So do the neighbouring ghats.

A short walk north brings you to the **Surya Temple**, dedicated to the Sun God. Situated on the banks of the river Sone, this is where the community of sun-worshippers gathers for prayers, mainly at sunrise and sunset. Continue 1 km (¾ mile) south-west to the foot of the **Brahmajuni Hill**. This is ascended via a steep series of 1000 stairs (40 mins/1 hour if fit; not at all if unfit) and offers fine views from the summit. Back at the foot of the steps, visit the 'immortal' banyan tree which pilgrims attend to complete the cycle of rituals begun for their ancestors back in Varanasi. This is the **Akshyabat** where the Buddha practised penance for 6 years before retiring to Bodhgaya, to commence the final meditation leading to his enlightenment.

There is a small **Gaya Museum** (open 10 am–5 pm, closed Monday) with a collection of bronzes, terracottas and sculpture.

The main excursions from Gaya are to Bodhgaya 13 km (8 miles), Nalanda 65 km (40½ miles) and Rajgir 64 km (40 miles). But there's an interesting day-outing possible to the **Barabar Caves** 20 km (12½ miles) north, which are the 'Marabar Caves' of E.M. Forster's *Passage to India*. The caves are very ancient, dating to at least 200 BC, and two of them bear original inscriptions of Ashoka the Great himself. But be warned: it's a very hot, exposed location. Take some covering for your head, and lots of water. To get there, hire a rickshaw or taxi.

WHERE TO STAY

At the new **Ajatsatru Hotel** (tel 22514) in Station Rd, just across from the rail station, basic but clean rooms are from Rs100. Just right out of the station is **Pal Rest House**, run by friendly Sikhs, with cheap but adequate rooms for Rs25. The **Railway Retiring Rooms** inside Gaya station itself are cheap and good. There are many other budget places in the station area.

EATING OUT
Bihari cuisine is very simple—boiled rice, breads, lentils and vegetables steamed with hot spices; *sattoo* (a mixture of seven grains made into dough) and popular 'snack' kachoris (deep-fried wheat or lentil-flour balls) often eaten with *kala chana* (black gram). It's all very cheap (Rs15–20), and best sampled at the Ajatsatru Hotel's **Sujata Restaurant** or at the Station View Hotel and Restaurant. The old town is full of cheap and friendly roadside dhabas.

GENERAL INFORMATION
The tourist information centre (tel 20155) is in the rail station, and apparently open 6 am–9 pm.

BODHGAYA

This is where Buddhism, one of the great religions of the world, was born. To this small secluded spot on the banks of the Niranjana came Siddhartha, the royal prince of Kapilavastu, after nine long years of searching for the Ultimate Truth. And here, under the holy Peepal or Bo tree (*Ficus religiosa*), he became Buddha, the enlightened one, and dedicated himself to the good of humanity.

Since this event, some 2500 years ago, Buddhists all over the world, and later Hindus who tried to bring Buddhists into their fold by regarding Buddha as an *avatar* or incarnation of Vishnu, have considered Bodhgaya a major pilgrimage place; the most important of the four holy places associated with the Buddha. The others are Lumbini in Nepal, where he was born; Sarnath near Varanasi, where he delivered his first sermon; and Kushinagar near Gorakhpur, where he died.

Bodhgaya is just as popular with Western travellers as with Indian pilgrims. Many foreigners come here to learn more about Buddhism or meditation; others just come in search of peace and solitude. The place has a serene, peaceful atmosphere, especially at dawn or dusk, which draws visitors back time and again.

But it is the annual Buddha Jayanti festival, held here each May, which brings Bodhgaya's unique spiritual presence into full play. It celebrates the anniversary of the day Buddha was born, the day he gained enlightenment, and the day he died, and attracts thousands of devotees from all over the world. Packed to capacity with people sleeping back-to-back on every roof top, the small hamlet generates a quite unbelievable atmosphere. If you can put up with the noise, the crowds and the mosquitoes, this is the time to come to experience Bodhgaya's special 'spiritual buzz', commented on by so many travellers.

WHAT TO SEE
Bodhgaya is a tiny place with one main street, one main 'sight', the Mahabodhi Temple and its Bodhi Tree, and several small international temples and monasteries. There are cycle-rickshaws for those short on time, but you can cover everything of interest at leisure and on foot in a single day. A second day can be profitably spent meeting with pilgrims, temple priests, and other travellers—a good way of getting the flavour of the place. For peace and quiet, spend at least one sunset on the banks

of the River Niranjana, where the Buddha bathed after gaining enlightenment. It flows gently just outside the town.

Pilgrimage Tour (on foot, 4–6 hours)
Mahabodhi Temple–Bodhi Tree–Tibetan Monastery–Wheel of Law–Museum

Bodhgaya has a very pleasant pilgrim circuit, best begun early in the morning when there are no crowds, no heat or noise. Arrive at the large, enclosed **Mahabodhi Temple** around 8 am, when it is peacefully deserted. The present brick structure is a relatively modern restoration (1882) of previous 11th- and 18th-century temples, yet remains more or less the same as the original 7th-century AD version. It is quite unique among other north-Indian temples in having a 50 m high pyramidal spire (capped with a *stupa*) instead of the usual curvi-linear summit contours. The four distinctive corner turrets erected round the base of the main temple were 14th-century additions of Burmese Buddhists, aimed at giving the structure balance. The original shrine on this site is believed to have been constructed by Ashoka in the 3rd century BC.

The Mahabodhi Temple lies within a large walled enclosure dotted with numerous sculptures and ornamented votive stupas, dedicated by pilgrims. The richly carved railings to the south and west of the enclosure are Bodhgaya's oldest remains. They are notable for their lotus, bird and animal motifs, also their *jataka* stories portraying the Buddha's previous incarnations.

Entering the temple complex by the main gate, turn right for the inner shrine. This contains a colossal image of the Buddha, brightly gilded and festooned with flowers, in his 'earth-touching' posture. Buddha had cited the earth as witness to the austerities he had practised on his long journey to enlightenment.

A saffron-robed monk will accompany you to the western side of the temple, where you'll find the famous **Bodhi Tree**. This sits on a small, elevated platform within a gated pavilion, and is surveyed by a small gilded Buddha. It is customary to make a donation of money, but not obligatory. The tree itself is gaily adorned with fluttering flags and streamers. It is also alive with chattering birds. For some reason, they only seem to settle and sing on this tree, and on no other. This is not the original *peepal* tree under which the Buddha sat to gain enlightenment, but is a direct descendant of it. Ashoka sent saplings of the original to Sri Lanka along with his son Mahinda, both to spread the message of Buddhism and to ensure that when the mother tree perished there would be saplings from grown Lankan trees to bring back and re-plant at Bodhgaya. Under the tree is the red-sandstone slab said to be the *vajrasan* or diamond throne on which the Buddha sat.

Leaving the tree, walk clockwise round the circumference of the temple. Pilgrims follow this circuit three times in succession to complete their ritual. On your round, look out for the beautiful Lotus Pond at the northern wall of the compound. This contains a life-size Buddha, shielded by the cobra which apparently saved him from drowning while he was in deep meditation. Just past the pond is the famous **Jewel Walk** (*chankramana*)—a raised platform, lined with small pillars, where Buddha paced up and down meditating on whether or not to reveal his knowledge to the world. Further on, you'll see the place of 'Buddha's footprints', often heaped with floral offerings. Elsewhere, sandwiched between all the tiny stupas and statues in the compound, keep an eye out for athletic ascetics, usually engaged in what look like very painful exercises. Outside the entrance to the inner shrine, up some crumbling steps, there's a small chamber containing a wreathed pile of rocks said to be 'Buddha's mother'.

Over the road from the temple you'll find the Tibetan **Mahayana Monastery**, built in 1938. The main attraction here, just left inside the entrance, is the massive **Dharma Chakra** or Wheel of Law. This is a 10-m high metal drum, painted in bright reds and golds, within a richly decorated chamber. To be absolved of all your past sins (if only it were so easy), simply revolve it three times from left to right. At the rear of the chamber, there's a showcase of sculpted Buddhas and near-Buddhas (Bodhisattvas). The largest one, Avalokiteshvara, *Bodhisattva* of Compassion and patron saint of Tibet.

A 10-minute walk up the hill brings you to the **Chinese Temple** (1945). Turn left here for the **Bodhgaya Site Museum** (open 9 am–5 pm daily) with its fine collection of archaeological exhibits recovered from the local area. The gold, bronze and stone sculptures of Buddha are especially fine. Finally, visit the nearby **Japanese Temple** (5 minutes' walk left, just beyond the **Thai Temple**). This houses a beautiful image of the Buddha, brought over from Japan.

SHOPPING

If you hunt around, you may come across some of the miniature paintings on paper or leaves, a traditional art of the villages round Bodhgaya. They generally depict scenes from the lives of Buddha and Mahavira. Nice little souvenirs are small packs of leaves from the Bodhi tree, sold along with the admission to Mahabodhi Temple. Small soft-stone images of the Buddha, carved in the nearby village of Patthalkatti are sold in a number of shops.

WHERE TO STAY

There is one reasonable hotel in Bodhgaya; the **Hotel Bodhgaya Ashok** (tel Gaya 22708, Bodhgaya 25). It's nothing special, and rooms are Rs750 single, Rs900 double, but at least it's air-conditioned and the food is good. There are also two **Tourist Bungalows**, with reasonable double rooms from Rs85, and dormitory beds. Most low-budget travellers stay at the **Burmese Monastery**, which now has comfy rooms with fans, in addition to the old very basic cells. This place has a pleasant garden, small library, and popular study courses. It's the best deal in town, but mosquitoes are especially fond of it, and you do have to behave yourself! Many of the national monasteries such as the Sri Lankan, Thai and Bhutanese, also have guest houses that welcome travellers.

EATING OUT

Plain but edible vegetarian fare including thalis, parothas and occasionally egg curries, is available at the **Kalpna Hotel** near Mahabodhi Temple; tasty Western-style food at the new **Shiva Restaurant**. During the season, a few Tibetan-style restaurants open up. If spartan living gets too much, lash out on a big meal at the **Hotel Bodhgaya Ashok**.

GENERAL INFORMATION

The tourist office (tel 26), close to Mahabodhi Temple, is open 10 am–5 pm. It's not very useful, but hires out decent guides.

RAJGIR

Rajgir lies in a pleasant valley enclosed by five hills, and was the first recorded capital of India. Known in ancient times as Rajagriha or 'home of royalty', it was already a flourishing metropolis of the Magadha empire when the Buddha arrived in the 6th century BC. It then became principally notable for its Buddhist associations. King Ajatshatru, the most influential ruler of his times, ascended to the throne of Magadha by murdering his father, and then gave the Buddha and his followers several years of aggravation. Later, he contracted a horrible disease and, in remorse for his evil acts, converted to Buddhism and supported the First Buddhist Council, held here at Rajgir. It was convened shortly after the Buddha's attainment of enlightenment, and many of his teachings were at this point written down for posterity. In all, the Buddha spent 12 years in and around Rajgir, delivering many of his more important sermons. The founder of the Jain religion, Mahavira, also spent several years here.

Today, Rajgir is being developed as a winter health spot. Little remains of the old city, it is largely in ruins, but there's enough for a pleasant day's sightseeing.

WHAT TO SEE
At the entrance of the site, buy a copy of the useful local guidebook, then a Rs275 return ticket for the Aerial Ropeway Chairlift. This operates daily, except Thursdays, and provides an entertaining ride up to the hilltop 6 km (3¾ miles) from the village. While airborne, you can see several ruins of the ancient fortress city dotted around the hills below, including the Jivakamarvana monastery with large elliptical halls, a favourite retreat of the Buddha. Off the chairlift, see the dazzling new **Japanese Vishwa Shanti Stupa** and its adjoining Buddhist monastery. A few minutes' walk below the chairlift is **Gridhakuta**, where Buddha is said to have spent much of his time in meditation, or delivering sermons.

Back down in the village, hire a tonga or cycle-rickshaw to see the remaining sections of the great **Cyclopean Wall**, which originally comprised 48 km (30 miles) of massive undressed stones, perfectly joined, girdling the entire circuit of ancient Rajgir. Note especially the few surviving entry and exit portals. Then make the short climb up **Vaibhara Hill** (ask the tonga to drop you here) to **Saptaparni Cave**, reputedly the site of the First Buddhist Council. Nearby are some of Rajgir's famous **Hot Water Springs**, and above these the rectangular natural-stone sculpture of **Pippla Cave**, originally a watchtower, now a hermit's retreat.

Finish off with a visit to the large **Ajatshatru Fort**, built in the 6th century BC by the same King Ajatshatru whom Buddha cured of a plague of boils.

WHERE TO STAY
The pilgrim circuit of Rajgir can take the better part of a day, and it is worth staying overnight. In addition to the expensive **Centaur Hokke Hotel** (tel 231, 245) which is primarily for the Japanese market with rooms from Rs1200 single, there are cheap rooms from Rs90 and dormitory beds at the **Tourist Bungalow**, the **PWD Rest House**, and the **Youth Hostel**.

GENERAL INFORMATION
The tourist office (tel 36) is in the Kund Market.

NALANDA

The ruins of the world's earliest known university can be seen here. Founded in the 6th century BC as a suburb of the Magadha capital, Nalanda later became a great centre of learning and one of the most famous university citadels of ancient times. Its importance as a monastic residential seat of learning continued unabated from the 5th century BC, when the university was established, right through to the 12th century AD. When Hieun Tsiang, the Chinese chronicler, spent 12 years here in the early 7th century AD, there were 2000 teachers and 10 000 monks and students in residence. His account of life in the *vihara* (monastery) is vivid:

> The day is not sufficient for the asking and answering of profound questions. From morning till night they [the students] engage in discussion; the old and the young mutually help each other. Those who cannot discuss questions out of the Tripitaka are little esteemed and are obliged to hide themselves for shame.

Nalanda produced some of the most prestigious and learned scholars of the ancient oriental world, and the university was heavily patronised by the Pala Kings of East India between the 8th and 12th centuries. Then, in AD 1199, the Muslim invader Bakhtiyar Khilji swept down from the north and attacked Nalanda. He massacred the priests, slaughtered all the residents, plundered the rich university, and burnt down the famous library. This wholesale destruction sounded the death knell of Buddhism in India.

Today, Nalanda lies in ruins. Careful excavations have uncovered a large area of stupas, stairways, decorated panels, lecture halls, dormitories, nine levels of occupation and six monasteries. Looking at them, one is hard pressed to imagine Hieun Tsiang's description of:

> ...precious terraces spread like stars and jade pavilions spired like peaks. The temple rose into the mists and the shrine halls stood high above the clouds. Streams of blue water wound through the parks, green lotus flowers sparkled among the blossoms of sandal trees, a mango grove spread outside the enclosure. The beams were painted with all the colours of the rainbow and were carved with animal designs while the pillars were red and white.

Yet, in its heyday, this was the greatest oriental centre of learning and art. Mahavira, founder of the Jain religion, lived here. So did Buddha, when he visited the university to preach his doctrine of *dharma*. And king after king built monasteries and temples on the site, adorning it with the most fabulous gifts and dedications.

WHAT TO SEE
At Nalanda bus-stand, arrange a horse-drawn tonga for the 10-minute ride up to the archaeological site. Here, call in on the **Nalanda Museum** (9 am–5 pm) with its fine collection of Buddhist and Hindu relics recovered from the ruins. Most exhibits are stone or bronze, and date from the 7th to 15th centuries AD. In addition to the **Great Seal** of the Nalanda University, there's an artistic 10th-century panel

depicting the 10 avatars of Vishnu, and a fun panel entitled *Mythical Wild Woodman Enjoying Wish-Fulfilling Dreams*. Also giant swastika carvings, copper-plate and stone inscriptions, coins and pottery. Open 9 am–5.30 pm daily, admission Rs1.

Entering the site of the university, make for the **Great Stupa**. This 31-m high ruin has terraces, steps and is surrounded by a number of intact votive stupas. Climb to the top for best view of the university complex. Only part of this vast area has yet been excavated. At the base of the stupa, scout round for the famous panel of an elfin-like Buddha which is Nalanda's finest surviving treasure.

On the other side of the open clearing, the only other raised point, visit the *chaitya* (temple) site. This is surrounded by a mass of small circular brick stupas, and features, near the top, a pair of beautiful portal pillars.

Now walk down to the monasteries. These were generally built on the ancient Kushana-age pattern, comprising a row of cells on four sides of a central court-yard. The best example, No. 11, has a distinctive central *chaitya* and a twin set of chambers with vaulted brick walls. Another has a beautiful brick well and a set of double-ovens chiselled into the courtyard floor. You'll notice that the site comprises parallel rows of temples and monasteries. This was a deliberate device, which allowed the disciples to move from one to the other, worshipping and studying alternately.

Although a couple of hours will be sufficient, wandering round these vast ruins gives only a faint idea of what their original splendour must have been. Yet Nalanda is the only monastery complex of its day not to have been completely destroyed. In view of its historical and archaeological importance, an international centre of Buddhist studies was established here in 1951.

WHERE TO STAY

It is best to stay in Rajgir, 15 km (9½ miles) away. If stuck, try the Burmese Rest House about 5 minutes by tonga beyond the museum. It's cheap but often full. There is a Youth Hostel, with rooms from Rs50, and it's sometimes possible to get rooms in the **Pali Institute**.

GENERAL INFORMATION

The tourist office (tel 29) is in new Nalanda (Bargaon), near the bus-stand.

Route 10—Roof of the World
Darjeeling and Sikkim

A mid-19th century creation of the Raj, Darjeeling is one of the major hill resorts of North India—and certainly the most spectacular. Perched literally 'on the roof of the world', this charming hill station lives in the shadow of the majestic Kanchenjunga peak and is surrounded by snow-capped mountains and dense conifer forests, plummeting down into an enchanting valley below. The busy little town is a maze of steps and terraces, a melting pot of exotic hill and village peoples, full of bazaars, markets and shops selling colourful handicrafts, and of course the famous Darjeeling tea.

Rich in flora and fauna, the surrounding countryside is a paradise for nature-lovers with over 4000 species of flowers, 600 varieties of birds, and many animals and reptiles. A major base for trekking in the eastern Himalaya, Darjeeling also has a variety of recreational facilities including golf and fishing. Nearby Tiger Hill offers unforgettable dawn views of Kanchenjunga, and even, on a clear day, of Mount Everest itself. At nearby Ghoom Monastery is enshrined the Tibetan 'Buddha to Come', Maitreya. Of all the hill stations of India, Darjeeling has perhaps the most to offer the foreign visitor with its cool charm, lovely scenery, a wide range of activities and truly unique atmosphere.

Darjeeling district was ceded to the British following a dispute with the then Rajah of Sikkim in 1828 and the small protectorate of Sikkim joined India as the 22nd State of the Union in 1975. Much of southern Sikkim is now open to tourists and a visit to Gangtok, the capital, or a short trek along the border with Nepal makes an interesting and worthwhile extension to a stay in Darjeeling.

Season: mid-April to mid-June (summer); September to November (winter).
Monsoon: from June to September, but sometimes continues into late October.
Climate: 6°–17°C.
Route duration: 5–7 days (if trekking, 14–21 days).

TRAVEL ITINERARY

Permits
Permits are currently not required to visit Darjeeling but it is a so-called 'sensitive area' and it would be best to check the prevailing situation before travelling. Permits are issued at the Foreigner's Registration Offices in Calcutta, Delhi, Bombay and Madras. When applying at the Calcutta office (237 Acharya J.C. Bose Rd, tel 473301), turn up at 10 am (it opens 10.30 am) and have your train ticket and passport handy. If travelling up to Darjeeling by air, you don't need a permit. Your passport is automatically stamped at Bagdogra Airport for a 15-day stay.

Permits are still required to visit Sikkim. Although these officially take 6 weeks to process, the Sikkim Tourist Office in New Delhi (New Sikkim House, 14 Panchsheel Marg, Chanakyapuri, New Delhi-110021) seems to manage in a few days. Permits are issued by the Ministry of Home Affairs, Lok Nayak Bhavan, Khan Market, New Delhi and applications can be routed through The Indian Diplomatic Missions abroad at least 6 weeks in advance of the intended visit. A copy of the application, endorsed to Sikkim Tourism, will ensure speedy sanction of the permit.

If permits are reintroduced for Darjeeling, extensions should be possible to obtain through Darjeeling's Foreigners' Registration Department in Laden La Road (tel 2261). In Gangtok the Police Headquarters (tel 2022) should be able to extend a permit for a maximum of 15 days. Trekking is the main, and most acceptable reason why an extension may be required.

Calcutta to Darjeeling   633 km (412 miles)

Air/Road
There is 1 flight daily from Calcutta to Bagdogra (IC221; Rs939). Then either a bus (4 hours) or shared taxi (Rs75, 3 hours) or even a toy-train (from nearby Siliguri) up to Darjeeling. Bagdogra also has daily flights to and from Delhi (Rs2406) and Guwahati (Rs629).

Rail
The quickest train is the overnight *Darjeeling Mail* (13/14 hours) from Calcutta's Sealdah station to New Jalpaiguri. Book a seat from Eastern Railway Booking Office, Fairlee Place, Calcutta. From New Jalpaiguri (or Siliguri, 2 km; ¼ mile south) you can travel on by toy train up to Darjeeling (about 3 departures daily), or take the quick 3-hour Rs40 express bus up there.

The toy train winds in and out of the scenic mountain valleys, a brilliant feat of engineering which culminates in the famous Batasia Loop, just short of Darjeeling: the bus is three times quicker on average, and since the road follows the train track almost exactly you get precisely the same views. The advertised time of the New Jalpaiguri–Darjeeling run is 7 hours, but what with the toy train crawling up the mountainside at 10 km (6 miles) per hour and making long pauses for water, it can take longer. If you don't have the time and want an experience of the miniature railway, wait until you're in Darjeeling itself and take the short but quite adequate half-hour run to or from Ghoom, the highest station on the line at 2222 m. The 88-km (55-mile) track is a feat of Victorian engineering. Work began in 1879 and the line was completed in 1881.

Road
In the possible absence of the toy train (the line sometimes gets blocked by landslides), it's wise to consider a direct bus from Calcutta to Darjeeling. A few such buses leave daily from Calcutta's Esplanade bus-stand. However, the 12-hour journey can now, owing to bad roads, take up to 16 hours. Buy a seat on the fast 'rocket service' bus which leaves Esplanade 8 pm daily (11 hours, Rs100), and hope for the best!

Darjeeling to Gangtok   110km (69 miles)

Road
There are regular buses plying between Darjeeling and Gangtok (5–6 hours). It is also possible to hire or share taxis (4 hours).

Darjeeling to Calcutta   663 km (412 miles)

Road/Air
The airport bus (3 hours; buy tickets in advance from Darjeeling Tourist Bureau) connects with daily IC222 flight from Bagdogra to Calcutta (Rs939).

Road/Rail
The quickest option is to bus down to New Jalpaiguri, for the Darjeeling Mail to Calcutta (recheck train timings in Darjeeling).

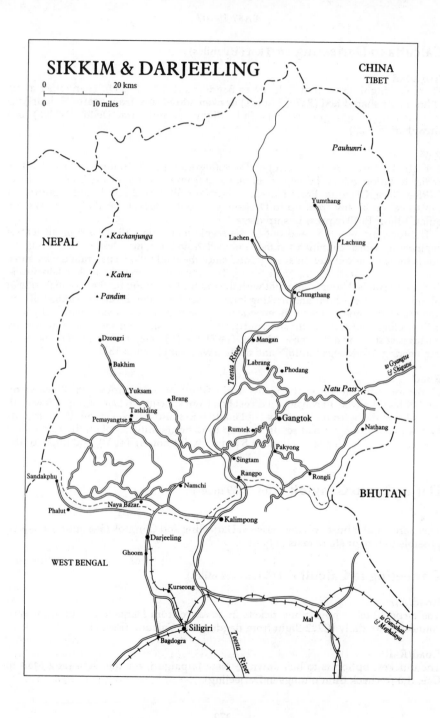

DARJEELING

Ruled first by the Rajahs of Sikkim (until the start of the 18th century), then by the Gurkhas of Nepal, who invaded Sikkim in 1780, and then returned to the Rajahs by the East India Company. Darjeeling had a chequered history before being 'discovered' in 1828 by two British officers on a fact-finding mission. At that time, Darjeeling was Dorje Ling or 'Place of the Thunderbolt'. This was the mystic thunderbolt of Lamaist religion, representing the sceptre of Indra (Lord of the Gods) said to have fallen here, on the site presently known as Observatory Hill. The town of Darjeeling grew up around the ex-Buddhist monastery of Dorje Ling, which had been built on this hill.

The two officers quickly appreciated Darjeeling's strategic importance as a possible access in Nepal and Tibet, and its recreational potential as a hill station resort. They reported back to the Calcutta authorities, who put pressure on the Rajah to grant the site to the British in return for an annual fee of Rs3000. Darjeeling quickly developed as a trading centre and a tea-growing centre, and despite much opposition from Tibetan lamas and merchants, whose own fortunes were threatened, the British hold on the area strengthened. In 1849, they annexed the whole territory between the present borders of Sikkim and the Bengal plains, making Darjeeling, previously just an isolated enclave within Sikkimese territory, part and parcel of other British territory further south.

The British arrived to find Darjeeling reclaimed by forest, the once large and busy village almost completely deserted. They began a rapid development programme, which by the early 1840s had produced roads, many houses, a hotel, a health sanatorium and several tea plantations using bushes smuggled from China. Not just British army officers and their wives, but also British families working and living down on the plains, mainly in Calcutta, began to use Darjeeling as a summer 'health' resort. The only problem was transport, visitors taking nearly a month to get up here from Calcutta by cruising up the Ganges, crossing the plains of Bihar and Siliguri, and proceeding up the old Hill Cart Road by bullock cart or buggy. The cost of such a journey (Rs2000) was also prohibitive. This led to the construction of the famous 'toy train' miniature railway, completed in 1881, which reduced the length of the trip up from Calcutta to just a couple of days.

Darjeeling has two tourist 'seasons'. The spring season of mid-April to mid-June is the greenest, most beautiful time to visit and a cool retreat from muggy Calcutta; the autumn season of September–November gives the best mountain views though a prolonged monsoon can have the rain still teeming down at the end of October. Take warm clothing at all times: evenings can be very cool. Buddha's birthday (1 May) is Darjeeling's biggest and best festival with colourful Tibetan Buddhist processions and the whole town celebrating.

Foreign visitors coming into Darjeeling are often struck by three things: first, the cool climate; second, the dense greenery of the place, not so much the tea plantations, which lie mainly off the beaten track but rather, the pine forests, mountain meadows and shrubbery; third, the incredible diversity of cultures and peoples. Darjeeling, like Kathmandu, is a real pot-pourri of different racial types and groups; Tibetan Lamas in their yellow robes and Tibetan ladies in striped aprons, ornaments and brocades; Gurung farmers from central Nepal and Gorkhas from eastern Nepal; fair-skinned Sikkimese, Lepchas and Bhutias, and Drukpas of Bhutan; also the famous mountaineering Sherpas and a great many local tourists either on holiday, or visiting their children being schooled here. Since Independence, much of Darjeeling's prosperity comes not from high-class British sponsorship or from its renowned tea trade which is greatly suffering today, due to soil erosion and little replanting of new tea trees, but from the local tourist market and from its schools, where well-to-do Indian children receive a 'proper English education'. In this queer quest for Western-style knowledge, they progress from kindergartens like Mini-land and Love-Bud to impressively named academies like North Point, St Paul's and Loreto.

Discounting the disturbing appearance of gum-chewing young Nepalis (a Michael Jackson look-alike brigade) and of Kung Fu video palaces, Darjeeling remains one of India's most pleasant, fascinating hill stations. The old guard, mainly restaurant staff or street-pedlars with fond memories of the Raj, still address Western women as 'memsahib' and invite foreigners into their homes for endless cups of tea. The atmosphere is relaxing and beguiling, a curious, intoxicating blend of British character and architecture interspersed with Tibetan/Nepali curio shops, jewellers, refugee camps and smoky tin–roofed wooden shacks. Here are lots of ponies, bright-green park benches, clean and civilised town squares, and rows of little wrinkled ladies selling woollen rugs, shawls and acrylic sweaters to shivering Indian tourists.

In the late 80s severe friction between the GNLF (Gorkha National Liberation Front) and the West Bengal government transformed this once-lovely queen of hill stations into something of a tourist wasteland. The situation has now settled with the establishment of the Gorkha Hill Council giving the people of Darjeeling and Kurseong Districts a level of self-government within the state of West Bengal.

WHAT TO SEE

Darjeeling is a large, widely-dispersed complex of steep steps, deep declines, heaped buildings and winding streets, few of which are properly sign–posted, strung out over a wide ridge like a flattened, many-tiered, wedding cake. As with Shimla, it takes days to figure out. Everywhere you go in Darjeeling is either a long way up, or a long way down, but the scenery takes your mind off the slog. There are some really pleasant walks in this area, though if you don't feel like the exercise you can hire taxis, jeeps and landrovers from the Tourist Bureau, or pick up a pony from Chowrasta square.

Orientation in Darjeeling is difficult and maps don't really help. A useful landmark is the small Lion's Club traffic island, on the town's top level. The taxi-rank is here, and it's a popular pick-up/drop point for buses to/from Calcutta/Bagdogra. The island sits at the junction of Nehru Road, leading up the hill to Glenary's restaurant, Tourist Bureau and Chowrasta, and Laden-La Rd which leads down the hill to Himalaya restaurant, Shamrock Lodge, and post office. Going down the steep steps behind Himalaya Restaurant, and heading right, takes you to New Dish restaurant on J.P. Sharma Rd. Just up from New Dish, a steep road leads down for Hill Cart Rd and the bazaar. Directly above the Lion's Club island (look out for Dekavas restaurant), Gandhi Rd leads off to Oberoi/Springburn hotels and the Tibetan/Japanese monasteries. The steep hill road going down from the traffic island, parallel to the taxi-rank, is the quick way to the bazaar.

Hardly anyone sightsees the first day here. The cool, crisp mountain air and the altitude makes most newcomers feel lethargic. After settling in, allow yourself 3 clear

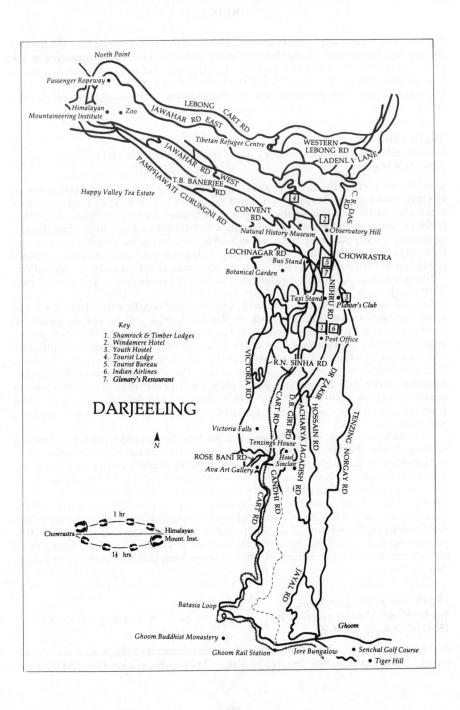

North Point

Passenger Ropeway •

Himalayan
Mountaineering Institute • Zoo

LEBONG CART RD

JAWAHAR RD EAST

Tibetan Refugee Centre

WESTERN
LEBONG RD

LADENLA LANE

JAWAHAR RD WEST

PAMPHAWATI GURUNGNI RD

T.B. BANERJEE RD

Happy Valley Tea Estate

C. R. DAS RD

4

CONVENT RD

2

Natural History Museum • Observatory Hill

LOCHNAGAR RD

Bus Stand

CHOWRASTRA

5

7

Botanical Garden

NEHRU RD

Taxi Stand

3

Planter's Club

1 6

• Post Office

Key

1. *Shamrock & Timber Lodges*
2. *Windamere Hotel*
3. *Youth Hostel*
4. *Tourist Lodge*
5. *Tourist Bureau*
6. *Indian Airlines*
7. **Glenary's Restaurant**

VICTORIA RD

R.N. SINHA RD

DR ZAKIR HOSSAIN RD

CART RD

D.B. GIRI RD

ACHARYA JAGADISH RD

TENZING NORGAY RD

DARJEELING

N

Victoria Falls •

Tenzing's House

ROSE BANI RD

Ava Art Gallery

Hotel
Sinclair

GANDHI RD

1 hr

Chowrastra

Himalayan
Mount. Inst.

1¼ hrs

CART RD

JAYAL RD

Batasia Loop

Ghoom

Ghoom Buddhist Monastery •

Ghoom Rail Station   Jore Bungalow   • Senchal Golf Course
• Tiger Hill

days to cover the main interest spots. Conducted tours are offered by the Tourist Bureau, but be warned, all sightseeing here is arduous. The walks suggested below cover the central, west and east sections of Darjeeling, and can be done in any order, though you should visit Tiger Hill at the very first sign of clear weather, to get the mountain views. All three walks take the Tourist Bureau, Chowrasta, as their starting point.

Walk One (on foot, 5/6 hours)
Natural History Museum–Botanical Gardens–Victoria Falls–Art Gallery–Tenzing's House

Coming up Nehru Rd to Chowrasta square, turn left for the **Bengal Natural History Museum** in Meadowbank Road. This was set up in 1903 to give visitors some idea of the wildlife of the district, and houses a comprehensive collection (4300 exhibits) of pattern-board butterflies and insects, hang-gliding Himalayan squirrels, worthy stuffed tigers and buffaloes, and an Indian elephant (tusks and legs only). It's an interesting display, very well-presented and describing mainly the fauna of Darjeeling, Sikkim, Tibet, Bhutan, Nepal and the Eastern Himalaya. Admission is Rs1, and it's open 10 am–4 pm (Wednesday 1–4 pm, closed Thursday).

Proceed on down Meadowbank Road, left into Cutcherry Road, and down into the main Cart Road. Ten minutes' walk to the left brings you to **Lloyds Botanical Gardens**, situated just below the Market Motor Stand. Opened in 1865, these pretty, peaceful gardens contain a representative collection of flora of the Sikkim Himalaya. The charming terrace has alpine plants, arum-lilies, geraniums, azaleas, rhododendrons, tree ferns and various conifers. There is a spacious **Orchid House** containing over 2000 different species of orchid and a herbarium. The hothouses are supposed to be a feature, but out of season contain just a few primulas, polyantha and cacti locked away under heavy guard. Open 6 am–5 pm daily; closed Sundays, admission free.

Take directions to leave the gardens into Victoria Road (south exit), and proceed left on a pleasant half-hour hike down to **Victoria Falls**. The falls themselves are often just a muddy stream running over an incredibly steep precipice (they only come into their own in the October/November post-monsoon season) but the walk is one of the most pleasant in the area. A short distance further down Victoria Road, turn up left into Uday Chand Road, then Cart Road. Just to your right is the **Ava Art Gallery** (tel 2469). This houses a fine exhibition of art and embroidery work belonging to Mrs Ava Devi. Open 8 am–noon, 12.30–6.30 pm; admission Rs1. Opposite the gallery, five minutes up D.B. Giri Road, finish off with a visit to **Tenzing's House**, the home of the famous mountaineer, before returning via the long Gandhi Road to the Tourist Office.

Walk Two (on foot, full-day)
Tea Gardens–Mountaineering Institute–Zoological Park–Passenger Ropeway–Tibetan Refugee Centre

Proceed down by the Cart Road, and follow the road signed 'Ropeway' leading off top of Chowrasta Square to the **Happy Valley Tea Gardens**, 3 km (2 miles) from the centre of town. The entrance is near the intersection of T.B. Banerjee Road, left off Cart Road, and Pamphawat Gurungni Road. It's best to arrive here early, since a full half-day is needed to tour the estate. Happy Valley is open 8–noon, 1–4.30 pm except Mondays, and Sunday afternoons. Of the 70 or so tea gardens in this hill region, this is one of the nearest to town. It still produces tea by the orthodox method, whereby the fresh tea leaves are placed in a withering trough and dried out with high-velocity fans, then successively rolled, pressed and carefully fermented on a conveyor belt. After a last drying process, the tea is sorted into grades of Golden Flowery Orange Pekoe (unbroken leaves), then Golden Broken Orange Pekoe, Orange Fannings and Dust (broken leaves).

Next visit the **Himalayan Mountaineering Institute** (tel 2438), on Jawahar Road West, some 10 minutes' walk down Pamphawat Gurungni Road (left out of the tea gardens), keeping to the right-hand side of the road. This unique institute, which exists to train mountaineers, has a marvellous museum (open 9 am–4.30 pm daily, closed Tuesdays in winter) full of photos, exhibits, and equipment relating to past mountaineering expeditions. The institute itself is open 10 am–1 pm, 1.30 pm–4 pm except Sundays, and Saturday afternoons.

The adjoining **Zoological Park** is a real anomaly. Its novelty value as a 'high altitude wildlife park' is spoilt by the quite awful conditions in which its animals, mostly Siberian tiger, Himalayan black bear, deer, panda and birds are kept. Even the prime exhibits, a beautiful snow leopard and red pandas, are not exempt. The anomaly is that the animals seem so happy, apparently thriving within their tiny, dirty little cages. Wildlife buffs and conservationists come away totally mystified.

On the way to the Mountaineering Institute from the Tea Gardens, one interesting possible diversion, for which you will need to take directions, is a visit to the **tomb of Alexander Körös**. This famous 19th-century Hungarian orientologist travelled to Darjeeling determined to prove that the Tibetan and Hungarian peoples shared a common root-race origin. His lasting monument was a dictionary and grammar of the Tibetan language. He died on the way to Lhasa in 1842, and was buried here at Darjeeling. His tomb, now a national monument, is in the cemetery.

A short distance right, out of the Mountaineering Institute, at North Point, is Darjeeling's famous **Passenger Ropeway**. The first passenger ropeway to be constructed in India, it is 8 km (5 miles) long and connects Darjeeling with Singla Bazaar, a beautiful picnic and fishing spot at the bottom of the valley. It's a lovely excursion, as long as you have a head for heights, and the perfect way of finishing off the day. Unfortunately, the ropeway is often closed for repairs. When fixed, it'll probably only be going down as far as **Tukbar Tea Estate**.

If you still have time, call in on the **Tibetan Refugee Self-help Centre** (closed Sunday) a sturdy half-hour trek back towards town along the Lebong Cart Road. Established in 1959 to rehabilitate displaced Tibetans who had followed the Dalai Lama to India, this large, very well-organised centre produces marvellous carpets, woollens, leatherwork, wood carvings and Tibetan curios and jewellery. Prices tend to be fixed, but bargaining with the friendly, hospitable Tibetan people is always fun. So is watching them at work weaving their carpets and making handicrafts. From here (take directions where you can find them!) it's a stiff, demanding half-hour climb back up to Chowrasta square.

Walk Three (by jeep/on foot, half-day)
Tiger Hill–Ghoom Monastery

Situated 11 km (7 miles) out of Darjeeling town, at an altitude of 2610 m, **Tiger Hill** is internationally famous for its dawn views over Mount Kanchenjunga and the great eastern Himalayan peaks, including Mt Everest.

Sightseeing buses and private jeeps ply up there each morning, but are unsatisfactory: you have to get up at 4 am, and you travel there and back in a horrid, noisy convoy of other tour vehicles. This is one trip to do completely on your own initiative. Set aside a full day, and stay overnight at the pleasant **Tiger Hill Tourist Lodge** with Rs20 dorm beds and rooms from Rs100 (tel 2813 to advance-book). This simple but friendly lodge is beautifully situated on a scenic plateau facing directly on to Kanchenjunga.

Set off early in the afternoon, taking a jeep to Ghoom from the rank at the bottom of Laden-La Road (regular departures but generally crowded). Alighting at **Ghoom's Jore Bungalow**, start up the hill road rising above the train track. A couple of minutes' walk up this road, strike left up the narrow, high path leading up to a small Buddhist temple; this is a short cut, taking you along the mountain ridge all the way up to Tiger Hill Lodge in 1 hour—far better than the dull 2/3 hour slog up the main road. The views along the ridge are spectacular: deep, dipping valleys of conifer, magnolia and rhododendron, against a dramatic mountain backdrop.

When dining at the lodge where they serve good *thali* suppers, request an early-morning call. You'll need to rise a good hour before dawn. In the lodge, have a flashlight handy since there's often no electricity at night. Dress warmly, it can get very cold.

In the morning, it's a stiff, steep 30-minute ascent up to Tiger Hill viewpoint. Walking up the dark road, keep your flashlight waving all the time, to avoid being mown down by fleets of tour buses and jeeps tearing up the highway. If exhausted, remember the big advantage of walking it to the top is that you arrive warm. Everyone else freezes solid.

The sunrise at Tiger Hill is spectacular. The massive peak of Kanchenjunga rears up flanked by Kabru and Pandim. To the far left, the central of three distant peaks, is Everest, surrounded by Markalu, Lhotse and several other summits. The observation point is swarming with Indian and Nepali tourists, all busily taking photographs. Before descending, call in on the small Shiva shrine just below. It's a charming little place, set on a small plateau in deep woodland, full of Buddhist prayer-flags and rows of tiny Shiva tridents decked with red arm-bangles. Return to the lodge along the hill path running above the busy main road swarming with departing tour buses. Back at the lodge, take breakfast, and return down the short-cut hill path to the **Jore Bungalow** (40 minutes).

The next stop is **Ghoom Buddhist Monastery**. Just right of the Jore Bungalow, turn left up Ghoom Monastery Road (signed–posted), and pass through the small, colourful village until some 10 minutes later you reach the open-air corridor of fluttering Buddhist prayer-flags which announce your arrival at the monastery. Ghoom Monastery is the oldest and most famous monastery in Darjeeling. Established in 1850 by a famous Mongolian astrologer-monk, it belongs to the Yellow Sect and houses a massive image of Maitreya (the 'Buddha to Come'). He sits in the dusty, atmospheric inner shrine, surrounded by flags, bells, drums and stacks of prayer-stools. A single beam of light from a ceiling window cuts through the gloom. It's the nearest thing to Tibet you'll see without actually going there. A small donation is customary, and there's a stiff Rs10 charge for each photo taken.

If it's running, return to Darjeeling by the toy train. There are usually regular departures from Ghoom station, 5 minutes' walk above Jore Bungalow. Even if the train is out of commission, enjoy strange station signs like 'Don't be afraid of Unnecessarily. Keep a strict watch around yourself.' The ride itself is a short, scenic half-hour 'taster' of the miniature railway, an ideal compensation for those who came up to Darjeeling by bus or jeep.

TREKKING

Darjeeling's treks are short, comfortable and very scenic. The most popular trekking months are April–May for seeing the flora of the region, and October–November when you have the clearest mountain views).

If you want an organised trek, complete with porter, guide and food, contact either Summit Tours, Indrani Lodge, 7 Chowrasta Road (tel 2710) or Tenzing Kanchenjunga Tours, 1/D.B. Giri Road (tel 3058). These agencies will set up everything.

Most people go off trekking on their own, however, for the trails are well marked and there are good tourist bungalows and lodges all along the way. A popular short trek is up to Sandakphu (3536 m), which gives fantastic views of Everest and the whole range of Kanchenjunga mountains. The return journey takes 4 days, starting with a jeep or taxi ride from Darjeeling to Manebhanjang (26 km; 16.3 miles) and proceeding to Sandakphu via Tonglu (3070 m), following the Nepalese border the whole way. The full trekking circuit takes 8 days: proceeding past Sandakphu to Phalut (3600 m) with its close-up views of Kanchenjunga, down through lovely terraced cultivations to the beautiful village at Lodhama River, and returning through several tea gardens, beautiful rhododendron, silver fir, camellia and magnolia forests via Bijanbari (762 m) down to North Point above Darjeeling.

For further details of these and other treks, contact the helpful Tourist Bureau in Darjeeling. You may need a permit to go trekking so check the current situation. If so, this is issued on the spot at the Foreigners' Registration Office in Laden-La Road. Potential trekkers are also advised to look in on the Darjeeling Youth Hostel before setting off: for cheap trek equipment hire, good information and maps, and lots of useful tips from previous trekkers in the visitor's book.

RECREATION

During the time of the Raj, Darjeeling residents spent their spare time collecting flora and fauna, creating botanical gardens, playing sports, laying out tea plantations and scaling mountains. Today, visitors have a choice of walking, trekking, pony-riding, or playing golf at the **Senchal Golf Course**, near Tiger Hill. This enjoys the reputation of being one of the highest golf courses in the world, at 2484 m. During the spring and autumn seasons, there is horse-racing at the **Lebong Race Course**. Good fishing can be had at the Rangeet River at Singla (8 km; 5 miles), permits being issued by the District Forest Officer. The **Darjeeling Gymkhana Club**, Bhanu Sarani West (tel 2002/2020) is apparently great fun. Previously a sophisticated social club, it is now where travellers drop in for pukkah games of snooker and billiards, while Indian children rumble around on roller-skates and clamber over tennis courts. Temporary membership is available on a daily or weekly basis for a nominal fee.

There are two cinemas, the Capital in Laden-La Road and the Rink in Dr S.M. Das Road. Both occasionally show English films. So do the masses of tiny backstreet video parlours, though these tend to favour kungfu and disaster films.

Cultural entertainment is thin, especially since the recent unrest put paid to the Nepali folk-culture programmes at **Kala Mandir Hall**, and the similar culture shows at the hotels. If you're desperate to hear authentic local music and song, phone Badri and Durga Kharel (tel 2231). They're the best home-grown talent in town, and even offer music lessons. Tibetan folk dances can be seen in the monasteries at festivals like the **Tibetan New Year** (mid-February), and local community groups hold their own celebrations, though these are rarely seen by tourists.

SHOPPING

The handicrafts of Darjeeling show marked influences of Tibetan, Nepalese, Sikkimese and Bhutanese art and culture. The main products are woollen blankets, hand-knitted garments and woven fabrics, also woodwork, bamboo fretwork, copper-plate curios studded with red and blue stone (or engraved with religious emblems), bedroom slippers and rope-sole shoes, hanzu coats (made from handloom cloth) and masks. All these goods are best purchased at the Tibetan Self-help Centre. This is also the best place to look for carpets.

The other main shopping centres are the **Bengal Emporium** in Nehru Rd, near the Tourist Bureau (good for Himalayan crafts and Bengal fabrics at fixed prices), **Hayden Hall** in Laden-La Road (for handknitted woollen goods), and the various tourist shops in Chowrasta (bargain hard for attractive wood carvings and local jewellery). The **Cart Road Market** sells novelty bamboo umbrellas and patterned woollen sweaters. Note that Darjeeling's main markets are closed on Thursdays, and its shops on Sundays and Saturday afternoons.

The best buy, of course, is tea. Real Darjeeling tea has a completely distinctive taste and aroma, greatly superior to the so-called 'Darjeeling' teas sold abroad, which are often mixed in with Assamese teas. The top-quality tea is unbroken leaves of (TP) Golden Flowery Orange Pekoe (about Rs200 per kilo). However, since untrained Western palates have great difficulty in distinguishing variations in the higher grades of tea, you are probably just as well off buying a good, reliable middle-range tea like ordinary Golden Flowery, at about half the price. The traditional way to grade tea, by the way, is to place a pinch in your closed fist, breathe on it to moisten the leaves, and then judge the quality from the aroma. The best place to buy tea is Chowk Bazaar, off Cart Road, near the Botanical Gardens. Try either **Arun Tea Enterpriser** or **Radhika & Sons**. Both stock hundreds of varieties, and can tell you all you want to know about Darjeeling's most famous product. The bazaar itself is full of all kinds of other goodies, including spices, jewellery, curios and handicrafts. For a pleasant rest from shopping, try some sweets and tasty samosas at the clean, friendly **Mehfil** restaurant (9E Chowk Bazaar), which also does excellent coffee.

WHERE TO STAY

Darjeeling has a fair range of hotels, the better ones offering lovely mountain and valley views (a prime consideration when choosing a room) and heating facilities, which are necessary in view of often chilly evenings. Insist on a room with 'a prospect'; there is nothing better than waking up in the morning and looking out onto sunlit Kanchenjunga and its surrounding ring of peaks. Tariffs at all hotels/lodges are heavily discounted, sometimes by as much as 60% in the low season.

Luxury (over US$35/Rs1000 per room night)
For comfort and style, stay at the **Windemere Hotel**, Bhanu Sarani, The Mall (tel 2397, 2841). This is a wonderfully eccentric place, much in the same mould as Calcutta's Fairlawns Hotel. Nearly a century old, once used as a British officers' club, it simply reeks of the Raj. Situated on the slopes of Observatory Hill, it offers spectacular views from the sundeck patio. Rooms have quaint functional furniture, log fires, quilted coverlets, and bags of rustic charm. Including all meals, they are fairly priced at US$50 single, US$80 double. Other features include bar, badminton court, miniature golf course and beautiful terraces of potted flowers. It's a real period piece!

Mid-range (US$10–35/Rs250–1000 per room night)
The **New Elgin Hotel** on H.D. Lama Rd (tel 3314, 3316) is another place in the British style and tradition—hot-water bottles and all. This hotel has a great reputation for food (you can get anything you want, if you order well in advance), with a superb location, and homely rooms from Rs750 single, Rs1150 double including all meals. The other good hotel with central heating is **Hotel Sinclair**, Darjeeling's most modern hotel, with good service and facilities. Single/double rooms are from Rs750 and Rs1150. The **Oberoi Mount Everest** has been closed for the last few years.

The government-run **Luxury Tourist Lodge**, Bhanu Sarani, The Mall (just behind the Windemere; tel 2611) is clean and comfortable, and all the rooms (Rs350–500, breakfast/dinner included) have outstanding Kanchenjunga views and good heaters. The **Bellevue Hotel** (tel 2129, 2221) on The Mall has some of the best views in town. The **Central Hotel** (tel 2033, 2746), Robertson Road has a good restaurant and rooms from Rs600 single, Rs1000 double.

Budget (under US$10/Rs250 per room night)
The most popular budget place is the **Youth Hostel**, Dr Zakir Hussain Road (tel 2290). A great place to meet fellow-travellers, it has a friendly manager, hot showers and prime morning views of the mighty Kanchenjunga. The hostel is a climb from either bus or rail station, but rooms are so cheap (singles only, at Rs25) it's worth it. The trouble is, this place is often full.

A good fallback is the homely **Shamrock Hotel** on Upper Beechwood Road (up stone steps adjoining Washington restaurant, turn right). Run in family-style, this is a very clean, comfy place with hot water, supplied by dunking live electric elements in buckets. Rooms are cheap (Rs30–65), and the two best ones (Nos 10 and 13) have the Kanchenjunga views.

EATING OUT
Local Tibetan-style food is cheap and simple. The most interesting items are Tibetan bread, which is delicious with honey or jam, and the traditional *momo* (mincemeat balls, flavoured with onion and ginger, cooked in steam). Finding good food is a problem, though, and many people eat in their hotel. Darjeeling has few restaurants, mainly just small speak-easies where patrons secretly consume their food in tiny partitioned boxes. Not only does this stop you meeting new people, but a curtain is often drawn to stop you even seeing other diners.

One exception to this is **Glenary's** restaurant (tel 2055) in Laden-La Road, which has a wide and open eating area. It's supposed to be the best eating place around, but isn't. Armies of cummerbunded waiters linger overlong in serving up very unpredictable over-priced Indian food. Glenary's is redeemed only by its superb ground-floor bakery. Just below it in the same road is the excellent **ice-cream parlour** affectionately known as the 'green pharmacy'. At the bottom of Nehru Rd, just above the Lion's Club traffic island, is **Dekavas Restaurant** ('the ideal place for fun and fast food'). Good veggie-burgers, pizzas, chow mein here, and the service is remarkably fast. Just up from the post office in Laden-La Rd, the ever-popular **Himalaya Restaurant** is where everybody goes for breakfast: Tibetan bread 'n' honey, recognisable porridge, non-greasy eggs). Down the steps behind this, **New Dish Restaurant** offers superb Chinese food, Japanese *sukiyaki*, 'speciality' dinners at US$10-plus which few can afford, and after-hours alcohol. The vegetable curries and the provocative menu deserve a particular mention. Opposite the Himalaya, both the **Washington** and **Lotus** restaurants continue to serve good, cheap Tibetan/Western-style fare. The Lotus is one of the few places in town which serves Darjeeling tea in the afternoons. Of the many good eating places up on Chowrasta, try **Chowrasta Restaurant** for South Indian food, and **Snow Lion Restaurant** for Chinese/Tibetan food. All Darjeeling's restaurants tend to close early, and late-nighters go either to the **New Dish**, or the **Golden Dragon Bar** just up from the Himalaya. At both these places, steer clear of the local *tomba* beer—it's made from non-purified water, and travellers have reported fearful after-effects.

GENERAL INFORMATION
The tourist Bureau, 1 Nehru Road (tel 2050) is located at the Hotel Bellevue complex at Chowrasta; open 10.30 am–4 pm, closed Sunday, and every second/fourth Saturday of the month). Friendly and helpful, but go armed with precise questions (they're extremely busy). Not much literature, but an adequate Darjeeling map. The bureau also sells bus tickets back to Bagdogra, for these returning to Calcutta by air; and hires out good guides, but trekking information is better at the Youth Hostel.

The Tourist Bureau offers three local sightseeing tours daily: Dhirdham Temple, Himalayan Mountaineering Institute (9.30 am–12.30 pm); the Zoo, Passenger Ropeway, Tibetan Refugee Centre, Lebong Race Course (1.30–4.30 pm); c) Tiger Hill, Senchal Lake, Ghoom Monastery, Batasia Loop (4–8 am). All tours cost Rs70, and are strictly for those who are short on time.

Indian Airlines (tel 2355) is next to the Tourist Bureau. The post office and Grindlays Bank are in Laden-La Road. So is the State Bank of India. The (good) Oxford Bookshop is up on Chowrasta.

SIKKIM

Sikkim is situated to the north of Darjeeling surrounded by Tibet in the north, Bhutan in the East and Nepal in the west. Although only 100 km (63 miles) from north to south and 60 km (38 miles) from east to west, the elevation ranges from 244 m to over 8500 m above sea-level, giving Sikkim an extraordinary range of flora and fauna within her borders. The most dominant feature of Sikkim is

Pemayangtse Monastery, Sikkim

Mount Kanchenjunga, the third-highest mountain in the world, soaring to a height of 8603 m. The Sikkimese consider the mountain to be their protective deity, the mother goddess.

People from the ethnic tribe of Lepchas and other small farmers were among the first to settle in Sikkim. Then came the Bhutias from Tibet to be followed by more immigrants during the 15th-century religious strife between various Buddhist sects in Tibet. The Nyingmapa sect of Buddhists thus became the dominant group in Sikkim; Buddhism was the state religion and the Chogyal (king) a devout Buddhist. In the early 19th century, Gorkhas from Nepal occupied a large part of Sikkim; they were eventually defeated by the British and signed the Treaty of Titaliya in 1827, by which they ceded all Sikkimese territories to the British. The British in turn handed back these territories to the erstwhile king but retained Darjeeling hill in return for an annual payment.

Unlike other parts of India, Sikkim displays very little evidence of the Raj. It was on Darjeeling that the British concentrated their attention. Sikkim became an independent kingdom in 1947 although, by agreement, India became responsible for its defence. However, by 1970, ethnic conflict between the minority Lepcha and Bhutia communities on the one side and the Nepalis on the other forced the king to rethink matters and in 1975, Sikkim merged with India to become its 22nd state.

WHEN TO GO
Best season: March to late May and October to end-December
Climate: 14° to 22°C (summer); 4° to 15°C (winter)

ARRIVAL/DEPARTURE
Because of the terrain, Sikkim is not accessible by train. However, its proximity to Siliguri and New Jalpaiguri railway stations as well as Bagdogra airport, ensures there are no major access difficulties.

Air

Bagdogra airport is 125 km (78 miles) from Sikkim's capital, Gangtok. There are several flights by Indian Airlines to Bagdogra from Delhi (Rs2406), Calcutta (Rs939) and Guwahati (Rs629). In 1990 the Sikkim Helicopter Service was introduced and operated daily flights which took only 25 minutes, but they were withdrawn after one season and, at the time of writing, have yet to be reintroduced.

Rail

Siliguri (114 km; 71 miles) and New Jalpaiguri (125 km; 77 miles) are the railheads nearest to Gangtok. These stations are well-connected with Calcutta, Delhi, Guwahati and other major cites of India.

Road

Sikkim Nationalised Transport (SNT) runs a Special Snow-Lion bus service from Bagdogra to Gangtok (124 km). Private taxis and buses also operate from Bagdogra, Darjeeling and Kalingpong to Gangtok. The Transport wing of Sikkim's Department of Tourism has a number of cars, luxury coaches and jeeps for hire.

ENTRY FORMALITIES

All foreigners intending to visit Sikkim must apply for an Inner Line Permit. This permit is issued by the Ministry of Home Affairs, Government of India, New Delhi and applications are to be routed through The Indian Diplomatic missions in the respective countries at least 6 weeks in advance of the visit. A copy of the application, endorsed to Sikkim Tourism, New Sikkim House, 14 Panchsheel Marg, Chanakyapuri, New Delhi-110021 will ensure speedy sanction of the permit. This permit allows visitors access to Gangtok, Phodang, Rumtek, Pemayangtse, Dzongri, Namchi and Naya Bazaar, and is valid for 15 days.

Restricted Areas

All of east Sikkim beyond Rongali and North Sikkim beyond Phodang are restricted areas for foreigners.

WHAT TO SEE

Gangtok is at a height of 1574 m above sea-level and became the capital of Sikkim in the 19th century. Built along a ridge by the side of the Ranipool river it is now a modern town and has lost much of its charm, but it offers spectacular views of deep valleys, rivulets and the majestic Kanchenjunga and has numerous places of interest nearby.

Sikkim Tourism runs guided tours out of Gangtok, covering local sightseeing as well as excursions to all nearby places of interest.

City Sights Round-up (on foot, 4/5 hours)

Royal Palace–Deer Park–Research Institute of Tibetology–Orchid Sanctuary–
Do-Drul Chorten–Orchidarium

Most of the town can be seen on foot, in a morning. Start at **Tsuklakhang**, the royal *gompa* (chapel) of the Chogyals (ex-rulers of Sikkim) in the grounds of the **Royal Palace**. This was once the most important *gompa* in Sikkim, site of the coronation ceremonies of the kings of Sikkim, of royal marriages and of celebrations to mark national and religious festivals. Appropriately, Tsuklakhang is a very elegant structure in typical Sikkimese style with carved and painted woodwork, murals, wall hangings and priceless Buddhist treasures. Among the important festivals still celebrated at Tsuklakhang are *Pang Lhabsol* held in mid-September in honour of Kanchenjunga the guardian deity of Sikkim; *Kagyat* in early December, which features a dance-drama enacted by Buddhist monks; *Loosong*, the Sikkimese New Year, also around this time; and *Losar* in February, to celebrate the Tibetan New Year.

The **Secretariat** building, hub of the state administration, is to the south of the Royal Palace. This is a recent structure but built in traditional style, blending very well with the surrounding areas. The **Deer Park** is spread out in the valley below the secretariat and has a gilded statue of Buddha in a teaching pose, a replica of the statue at Sarnath.

Established by the last Chogyal in 1958, the **Research Institute of Tibetology** is the only institute of its kind in India and contains several rare Lepcha, Tibetan and Sanskrit manuscripts, statues and thangkas, as well as other priceless objects. Located on a hill-top south of the palace and open 10 am–4 pm Monday to Saturday, except the second Saturday of the month. Next to the Institute is an **Orchid Sanctuary** containing over 200 varieties of orchids found in the Himalayan region. The **Do-Drul Chorten**, close by, was built in 1945 by the venerable Trulsi Riponche, head of the Nyingma order of Tibetan Buddhism. Around the large gold-topped *chorten* are 108 Prayer Wheels which are turned by devout Buddhists; some pilgrims may complete several circuits of the *chorten*, spinning each wheel as they pass. Flanking Do-Drul are **Chorten Lhakhang** and **Guru Lhakhang**, containing two huge statues of Mahaguru Padmasambhava, who took Buddhism to Tibet.

Peripheral Attractions (by bus/jeep-taxi, 3/4 hours)

In the afternoon take a bus or jeep-taxi 14 km (9 miles) south to the **Orchidarium** containing over 500 varieties of orchids found in the Himalayan region. Sikkim itself has over 600 species of orchid within its borders. At any one time almost half those in the sanctuary may be in bloom although the best time is April and May.

Back towards the town, near Siniolchu Lodge, about 3 km (1⅔ miles) south-east of the main bazaar is the 200-year-old **Enchey Monastery**. The monastery is an important centre of the Nyingmapa order of Buddhism, built on the site blessed by Lama Druptob Karpo who is believed to have been given the ability to fly by the tantric powers at his command. In January (coinciding with the twelfth month of the Tibetan calendar) every year, the masked dance (*chaam*) is performed in this monastery with a great fanfare.

Tashi View Point on the North Sikkim Highway about 8 km (5 miles) from Gangtok offers a spectacular view of the various monasteries on the surrounding hills, and the famous Siniolchu mountain peak. Take a jeep-taxi here to witness the sunrise or sunset.

Organised Tours and Excursions

The Tourist Information Centre on M.G. Road (tel 2064) runs 3 tours. One is a morning tour covering much of what is outlined above. The second, an afternoon tour, includes the Orchidarium and Rumtek Monastery. A third tour takes in Phodang.

The **Rumtek Monastery** is the largest of its kind outside Tibet and is the seat of the 'Kagyu' order of Buddhism. Situated 24 km (15 miles) south-west of Gangtok in a lower valley, it is an almost exact replica of the original Kagyu headquarters in Tibet. The Rumtek Dharma Chakra Centre, as the monastery is properly known, houses several unique religious art objects. If you wish to visit independently, a local bus leaves Gangtok each afternoon for Rumtek and returns early the following morning. Accommodation is available at the monastery and the bus timings are such that if you are going to enjoy the area two nights must be spent there—not a bad thing as the monastery life is fascinating, and the lamas welcoming.

Forty kilometres (25 miles) north of Gangtok is **Phodang Monastery**. Of Sikkim's 70 minor and major monasteries, Phodang is one of the 6 major monasteries. Though rebuilt in recent years, the **Labrang Gompa** retains the original structure and the old mural paintings and frescoes are fascinating.

TREKKING

For adventurous visitors, Sikkim is a delight as it offers several treks over a variety of terrain. Several package tours are organised by Sikkim Tourism and local trekking agencies. **Yuksam**, a 2-hour drive from Gangtok, is the base for many treks to the western mountain areas of the state, where the Himalayan Mountaineering Institute has a centre for its mountain climbing courses. This is also the place where the first ruling monarch of Sikkim was crowned by three lamas.

There are treks, from Yuksam to Bakhim (2740 m) and on to Dzongri (4030 m). Yuksam is also a day's trek away from **Pemayangtse** which is the premier monastery of Sikkim with over 100 lamas drawn from many of Sikkim's leading families. (Pemayangtse can also be reached by a full day's car journey from Gangtok.) Built in 1705, the monastery has a fine collection of sculpture and thangkas. The holiest shrine of all Sikkim is **Tashiding Monastery**, a further day's trek away from Pemayangtse. The mere sight of the monastery is supposed to absolve all sins, and each Spring pilgrims come to celebrate the festival of *Bumchu*.

Trekking equipment—haversacks, sleeping bags, tents, etc. are available for hire from Sikkim Tourism and leading travel agents.

SHOPPING

The best place to view and purchase the wide variety of traditional Sikkimese handicrafts is to visit the **Government Institute of Cottage Industries** on the opposite end of the town from the palace. Open 9.30 am–12.30 pm and 1.30–3.30 pm Monday to Saturday, closed on second Saturday of each month. Among the products for sale are carved Choktse tables and Lepcha shawls.

WHERE TO STAY

Mid-range (Rs250–1000 per room night)
The main hotels are centrally located. The **Nor-Khill** (tel 3186/7), Paljor Stadium Rd has rooms, including meals, from Rs 750 single and Rs1150 double. The other 'starred' hotel is the **Tashi Delek** (tel 2991, 2038) on M.G. Road. It has a nice roof-top garden and rooms from Rs450 single without meals, and Rs800 with full board. **Hotel Tibet** (tel 2523, 3468), Paljor Stadium Rd, has some Japanese dishes on its extensive restaurant menu. Rooms from Rs350.

There are two comfortable and reasonably priced mid-range hotels run by Sikkim Tourism. These are **Hotel Mayur** on Paljor Namgyal Stadium Road (tel 2825, 2752) with rooms from Rs300, and the **Siniolchu Lodge** (tel 2074) outside Gangtok, near the Enchey Monastery, with rooms from Rs250.

Budget (under Rs250 per room night)
The cheaper hotels are **Orchid** (tel 2381), **Kanchan View** (tel 2086) and **Sher-e-Punjab** (tel 2823), all on National Highway: and **Green** (tel 2554) on Mahatma Gandhi Marg. All have rooms from Rs150 single and Rs200–250 double.

Accommodation is provided on the treks either in tents or tourist huts. At Pemayangtse, **Hotel Mount Pandim** provides a spectacular view of the mountain range.

EATING OUT
The markets of **Gangtok Old Bazaar, Naya Bazaar and Lall Market** have several eating places, offering low-priced food primarily made up of Tibetan and Chinese dishes. The larger hotels serve continental and Indian cuisines. The native brew is called *chhang*, and made of fermented millet seeds. This is mildly intoxicating and is drunk in great quantities.

GENERAL INFORMATION
The Department of Tourism (tel 2064) on M.G. Road organises tours and can arrange car hire. Taxis are unmetered and rates should be negotiated before starting a journey.

Sikkim Tourism has offices in Delhi, Calcutta, Siliguri and will be happy to help visitors with information, guidance as well as help in securing permits: at New Sikkim House, 14 Panchsheel Marg, New Delhi-110021 (tel 3015346); Sikkim Tourist Information Centre, 4 Poonam, 5/2 Russell Street, Calcutta 700017 (tel 296717, 297316); and at SNT Colony, Siliguri (tel 24602). There is also a Sikkim Tourist Information Centre at Bagdogra airport.

From Gangtok it is possible to obtain train and air-tickets. Train tickets can be purchased from SNT Booking Office, Gangtok (tel 2016), and air tickets from Jossi and Jossi, Nam Nam Road (tel 2592).

Part VII

SOUTH INDIA

Valluvar Kottam, Madras

MADRAS

Capital of Tamil Nadu, Madras differs from the three larger Indian capitals of Bombay, Delhi and Calcutta in three major respects. First, it is the home of the ancient Dravidian civilisation, hardly touched by the invasions from the north, and often claimed to be 'pure' Indian. Next, it is still unusually spacious: a wide, green and airy 80 sq km (31 sq miles) of parks and gardens, beaches and esplanades with very few built-up areas despite a population of 5.5 million. (Although, in the last few years land prices have soared and a number of new high-rise buildings have started to spring up.) Last, it has managed to grow from rural village to modern metropolis in 350 years without losing much of its simple charm. All three factors have combined to give Madras and the south in general growing popularity as a tourist destination.

An important port, Madras has a long history of association with other cultures. The names of many of its streets—Armenian Street, China Bazaar Road, Portuguese Church St and so on—reflect its early days of international trade importance. Even before the British arrived, its precious cargoes of handlooms, fabrics, silk and hides had attracted European interest, leading to the establishment of a small Portuguese settlement at San Thome. Madras was also the first English settlement in India. The East India Company arrived here in 1639, and was granted by the Rajah of Chandragiri the small village of Chennapatnam (later the city of Madras), located between the ancient towns of Mylapore and Triplicane in the south and Tiruvottiyur in the north. On this site, in 1641, the Company constructed Fort St George and began exporting cloth home. To the north of the European fort arose a second town, called Madraspatnam or 'Black Town' for the Indian community, which later (following King George's visit in 1911) became the present Georgetown. Following its grant of a municipal charter in 1688 by James II making it the oldest Municipal Corporation in India, Madras became a battleground for competing French and British trading interests throughout the 18th century, and was even occupied by the French for a brief spell (1746–9) before the young Clive removed them at the 1751 Battle of Arcot. Though replaced a short time later by Calcutta as the primary British settlement (1772), it continued through the 19th century to be one of the four major seats of British Imperial power in India. Under the Madras Presidency, the city expanded rapidly outwards, giving birth to a relaxed, open garden city of clubs, churches, parks and elegant Victorian monuments. Today, Madras is moderating its traditional textile-based economy in favour of rapid industrial and technological development, but it still remains a pleasant, semi-rural town, a unique blend of the old and the new.

Many feel Madras to be the most pleasant introduction to India: it lacks the crowds, noise and pressure of Bombay and Calcutta, and it is possible to orient to the Asian way of life much more quickly. There is no cushioning effect here: you're face-to-face with 'real India' right from the start. Madras is a typical Indian city: one minute you'll be walking along an elegant main thoroughfare admiring well-to-do Madrassi women, sweet-smelling jasmine wound into their jet-black hair; the next, you'll turn into a dirty, crowded street full of thin men on the pavements in dusty sarongs, and even thinner mothers with ragged babies. But if the sights are contrasting, the people are uniform: dark-skinned, shock-haired; irrepressibly friendly and insatiably curious Tamils with an obsessive love of foreigners. Here, a casual enquiry for directions will get you a vast, swaying crowd of helpful locals within seconds. They'll even follow you down the road afterwards, just in case you want something else.

WHEN TO GO
The one big drawback to selecting Madras as an arrival point in India is the heat. The climate is tropical and despite two monsoons a year (June–Aug and Sept–Nov) it is *always* very hot and very humid. Remember, they've named a curry after Madras. Some like the hot humid atmosphere and slip easily into the calm, relaxed pace of life for which Tamil Nadu is famous; others simply melt, and regret not choosing a northern capital in which to adjust to Asian temperatures. The coolest season, but still rather warm, is Dec–Feb, and it's worth turning up for the Pongal (Spring Harvest) festival of mid-Jan. During this extravaganza, Madras paints itself and its sacred cows in bright colours, and goes singing, dancing and begging for a whole week. Though more sedate, the big Dance and Arts Festival of mid-December is also a major attraction. Madras has any number of festivals, and each one is a near-riot.

ARRIVAL/DEPARTURE
Madras is the Gateway to the south. The perfect base from which to commence one's discovery of southern India. Air, rail and bus connections are all superb.

Air
Meenambakkam airport is connected by Indian Airlines to Ahmedabad, Bangalore, Bombay, Calcutta, Cochin, Delhi, Hyderabad, Madurai, Port Blair, Trivandrum,

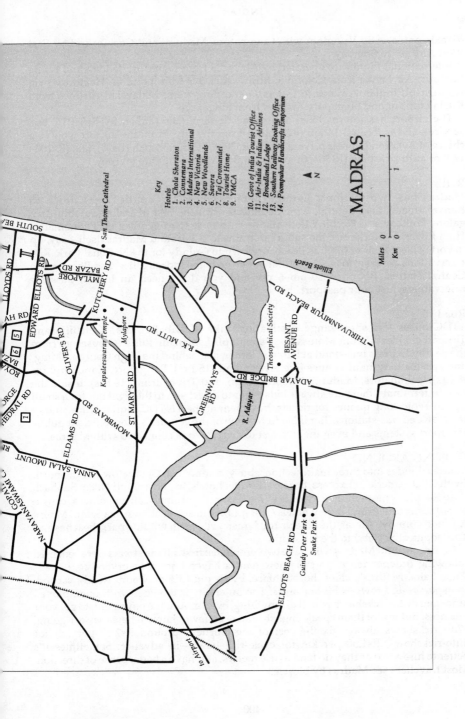

MADRAS

Key

Hotels
1. Chola Sheraton
2. Connemara
3. Madras International
4. New Victoria
5. New Woodlands
6. Savera
7. Taj Coromandel
8. Tourist Home
9. YMCA

10. Govt of India Tourist Office
11. Air-India & Indian Airlines
12. Broadlands Lodge
13. Southern Railway Booking Office
14. Poompuhar Handicrafts Emporium

N

Miles   0   1
Km   0   1

San Thome Cathedral

SOUTH BEACH RD

LLOYDS RD

EDWARD ELLIOTS RD

MYLAPORE BAZAR RD

KUTCHERY RD

AH RD

ROYA...BAZ...

FORGE RD

...EDRAL R...

Kapaleeswarar Temple

Mylapore

OLIVER'S RD

ELDAMS RD

MOWBRAYS RD

ST MARY'S RD

R.K. MUTT RD

GREENWAYS RD

ANNA SALAI (MOUNT)

NARAYANASWAMI...

GOPATI...

to Airport

ELLIOTS BEACH RD

Guindy Deer Park

Snake Park

R. Adayar

Theosophical Society

BESANT AVENUE RD

ADAYAR BRIDGE RD

THIRUVANMIYUR BEACH RD

Elliots Beach

Vizakhapatnam; by Vayudoot with Coimbatore, Madurai and Cochin; and by East West Airlines to Bombay.

International flights are operated by Air India from Frankfurt, Jeddah and Kuala Lumpur; Air Lanka from Colombo; British Airways from London (Heathrow) via Abu Dhabi; Indian Airlines to Colombo and Singapore; Malaysian Airlines from Kuala Lumpur and Singapore Airlines from Singapore.

The airport has international and domestic terminals (linked by Rs5 PTC bus service), and is located 14 km (8¾ miles) from the city. From the airport, you've a choice of Aviation Express private coach (Rs30), PTC mini-coach (Rs30), taxi (Rs100–120) or auto-rickshaw (Rs50–60) into town. It's a 40–60 minute journey.

Rail

Madras has two stations: Egmore, which serves the south (right down to Kanyakumari), and Central, which connects with the rest of India (notably Bangalore, Bombay and Cochin). Both stations are close to each other, off Poonamallee High Rd, and you can use the suburban trains to get around Madras itself—say, up to Fort St George or to Madras Beach, or down to Guindy for the National Park. Rail reservations are easy; to tap the tourist quota, go to the Indrail office, 2nd floor, inside Central station. It's open 10 am–6 pm and you don't need an Indrail Pass for reservations, just your passport.

Road

TTDC buses (for short-range destinations like Mahabalipuram, Kanchipuram, Tirupati etc.) leave from Mofussil bus-stand, off Esplanade Rd. TTC buses go from the nearby Express bus-stand at Parry's Corner, just behind the High Court building, and service long-haul venues like Hyderabad (15 hrs), Bangalore, Kanchipuram (3 hrs), Coimbatore, Madurai, Mysore (9 hrs), and Trivandrum (16 hrs). Inside the chaotic terminals, there are always kids eager to direct you to the right bus for a small tip. To avoid long queues for tickets, buy them at the TNTDC tourist office, and at the crowded bus-stations. Tamil Nadu has one of the country's most efficient public transport systems and even the smallest district town is connected with Madras.

GETTING AROUND

Madras divides into three main sections: busy, commercial Georgetown to the north (with GPO, American Express, bazaars, budget hotels, in and around Netaji Subhash Bose Road); Egmore in the city centre (for bus/rail terminals, airline offices, consulates, tourist offices and decent hotels/restaurants, in and around Anna Salai/Mount Rd); and Guindy/Adyar, the quiet, rural 'green belt' (with wildlife park, beaches and Theosophical Society) to the far south.

Getting around Madras, you have two problems: first, all the streets were renamed following Independence, and the new names haven't stuck (everybody still calls Anna Salai, Madras's chief thoroughfare, by its old title of Mount Road); second, transport round town is hit-and-miss. The inner city is crowded with unemployed auto- and cycle-rickshaws who'll do anything, even mount the pavement, to get your business. But few of them speak English, and even fewer know where they are going. With rickshaws always fix the cost of the journey—around Rs2.50 per km for auto-rickshaws, Rs1.50 per km for cycle-rickshaws—in advance. Sometimes it's better to hire a taxi as they do tend to use meters, and have a better sense of direction. Most travellers see Madras by bicycle.

WHAT TO SEE

Madras is a big, sprawling city and its few sights are very spread out. Take a conducted tour bus for quick, cheap orientation, then go exploring by car or cycle. Madras has one of the longest beaches in Asia, and this is where to head when sightseeing is over. There's also loads of 'street action', and good cultural entertainments, thus little danger of running out of things to do. Travellers tend to stay in Madras a good deal longer than originally intended.

City Tour (sightseeing bus, 4 hours)

Fort St George–St Mary's Church–Government Museum–National Art Gallery–
Valluva Kottam–Guindy Snake Park–Kapaleeshwara Temple–
San Thome Basilica

From the tourist office, it's a straight run up Anna Salai to the birthplace of Madras, **Fort St George**. Rebuilt several times between 1642 when its original bastions were completed, and 1749 when the French left, it remains—moats and all—pretty much today as when first made the seat of empire. Declared a national monument in 1948, most of its buildings have been converted into government offices, notably the Legislature and Secretariat. At various times the fort was home of Robert Clive, Elihu Yale and Sir Arthur Wellesley (later Wellington). Within the fort, visit the sturdy little **St Mary's Church** (open daily, 8.30 am–5.30 pm), the oldest Protestant church east of Suez and the first Anglican one in India. Built in 1680 from voluntary contributions of the Fort's English inhabitants, it gained its spire in 1710, and was completely renovated in 1759. Designed by a British gunner, and built to last with walls 1.2 m (4 ft) thick and a roof 0.6 m (2 ft) thick, this church is noteworthy for its total stone composition: no wood is used anywhere. The three aisles, arched with brick and stone, have a bomb-proof vaulted roof. The gallery has a finely carved nave, with two curved outer staircases. In the courtyard, you'll see some of the oldest British tombstones in India; some have been moved inside and are now beneath the altar. The Renaissance painting above the altar was painted by an unknown artist and brought here from Pondicherry in 1761. Famous people who married in St Mary's include Lord Cornwallis, Elihu Yale (early Governor of Madras, who later founded Yale University in the US) and Robert Clive. Clive House, behind the church, is another reminder of the great empire-builder who started out as a humble clerk within this fort. The nearby **Fort Museum**, now housed in the Fort's Exchange Office (1780–90), is open 9 am–5 pm but closed on Friday. The museum has 10 galleries with many exhibits telling the story of the East India Company's activities in south India. The top floor has some good French porcelain, clocks and glass, and most interestingly, some rare 19th-century prints of Madras. The ground floor has East India Company memorabilia, including officers' medals, tea-sets and cutlery. There is an old Arcot palanquin used by the pre-Raj Nawabs, a scale model of the fort, and a weird little iron cage in which a large, bearded officer spent a very long time after capture in combat. Admission is free.

Just north of the fort is the magnificent **High Court** (1861), reputed to be the finest example of Indo-Saracenic architecture in India. It's worth returning to later on, as you only get a fleeting glimpse from the bus, for a leisurely tour round its stately corridors, courts and staircases. There are several rare paintings here too, and a 'lighthouse' tower which was in use until 1977. You can climb to the top.

Returning to the city centre, the tour makes a worthwhile visit to the **Government Museum** in Pantheon Road. This is notable for its unequalled collection of fine bronzes, mainly from the early Pallava, Chalukya and Vijayanagar periods. One of the largest exhibits are the panels from the c. 200 BC **Amaravati Stupa**, said to have been erected over Gautama Buddha's relics. The collection, which occupies a whole gallery, was discovered, and later excavated in 1816, by Colonel Colin Mackenzie who found the panels being used as building material. The museum is open 8 am–5 pm daily except Friday. So is the attached **National Art Gallery**, a fine Indo-Saracenic building. The gallery has a good collection of Mughal and Rajput miniatures, glass-paintings from Tanjore and some 11–12th century metalware.

Down in Nungambakkam, the Hollywood of South India, and full of film studios, there's an overlong stop at **Valluvar Kottam**, a memorial dedicated to the poet-saint Thiruvalluvar. Opened in 1976, its massive auditorium is one of Asia's largest, containing 4000 seats, and is an important culture centre. 1330 of the poet's verses from his classic *Thirukkural* are inscribed on polished granite. Outside, there's a 'temple chariot' in stone, a vast rectangular terrace and extensive gardens.

Guindy Snake Park is 6 km (3¾ miles) further south, near Raj Bhavan (the Governor's House). It's a small, interesting reptilium of snakes, iguanas, crocodiles and spiders. Here you can go chameleon-spotting, investigate the curious 'Snake Worship Anthill', and watch the hourly (from 10 am) demonstration of unfanged-cobras being handled. You are also allowed to handle the snakes. Open 8.30 am–5.30 pm daily, admission Rs2. The Snake Park backs onto 300 acres of parkland supporting herds of blackbuck, many spotted deer or cheetal and monkeys. For a pleasant day here, return via urban train, or by No. 45 bus from Anna Square, city centre.

Off R.K. Mutt Rd, in the old Mylapore district, you'll come next to **Kapaleeshwara Temple**. Dedicated to Shiva, the temple's legend (Parvati as a peacock, praying to Shiva for deliverance after some domestic transgression) is portrayed in sculpture within. The tall, 40-m *gopuram* tower, festooned with richly-coloured deities, is a distinctive feature of Dravidian temple architecture. You'll see more of these throughout Tamil Nadu. Their principal purpose was to guard the inner shrine from attack, either spiritual or temporal. Considering how few south Indian temples suffered damage over the centuries, they seem to have been remarkably effective. Here, as with other 'living' temples in Tamil Nadu, non-Hindus are not allowed into the inner shrine.

After a brief visit to **Elliot's Beach**, and just enough time for a paddle, the tour finishes off at **San Thome Basilica**, South Beach Rd. This is a gothic-style Catholic church said to house the remains of St Thomas, the 'Apostle of India', who died at nearby St Thomas Mount in AD 72. The original church of AD 1504 was replaced by the present structure in AD 1893.

Beach Excursion (by cycle)
Marina Beach–Theosophical Society–Elliot's Beach–Golden Beach

This is the ideal follow-up to the hot, sticky city tour—a cool, relaxing ride by bicycle down Madras's long seafront towards some of the nicest beaches of the south. Except in Georgetown, Madras is ideal for cycling, being largely on the flat and relatively free of the usual capital-city traffic. Your hotel will usually know where to hire bikes.

From Anna Salai tourist office, a 15-min ride down nearby Woods Rd, left into Bharathi Rd) brings you out in the centre of **Marina Beach**, by the Aquarium. This long beach is an 11-km (7-mile) strip of fine sandy foreshore known as the 'pride of Madras'. A favourite evening resort of Madras citizens, it is fronted by garden-fringed promenades dotted with statues and parks dedicated to prominent Tamil writers and educators.

Turn right down South Beach Rd (the north part of the beach, round Georgetown, is too rough for safe swimming) until you come to **Gandhiji Statue** (2 km; 1¼ miles). Just behind this is the new **Lighthouse**, where you can climb 46 m for marvellous views of the coastline. If you want to go swimming here, the better stretches of Marina Beach are south of this point.

Continuing, it's a scenic half-hour journey via San Thome Basilica (turn off right here down San Thome High Rd) into the quiet, rural Adyar precinct. Past the derelict **Ayappa Temple**, which appears on the left some 2 km (1¼ miles) inland, you'll turn left into Dr Durgabai Deshmukh Rd, which takes you over the wide **Adyar Lake**. Over the bridge, turn left again into Besant Avenue Rd for the **Theosophical Society**. The approach along pretty country lanes is the perfect introduction to the 270 acres of beautiful gardens within the society's grounds. Established in New York in 1875 by Madam Blavatsky and Col. Olcott, the Theosophical Society moved to Madras in 1882. It was formed to promulgate the study of comparative religions, philosophy and science. After its move to Madras the society was run by Annie Besant. The vast campus houses a superb library with 17 000 manuscripts, has shrines to all faiths and also one of the world's largest banyan trees, which spreads over 3716 sq m (open 8–11 am, 2–5 pm Mon–Fri; 8–11 am Sat; closed Sunday). The gardens are open from sunrise to sunset.

Just 10 minutes ride past the Society, **Elliot's Beach** appears on your left. For a quick, quiet swim try the beach off V Avenue Rd. Then return to the main road, continue down to IV Avenue Rd for refreshments at the **Palace Tea and Coffee Centre**, which serves delicious samosas, ice-cream and snacks. The beach here is the best for miles, though be prepared for lots of local interest. Friendly fishermen take it in turns to 'guard' visitors, and mind your clothes and belongings while you're in the sea. There's lodging to be had here at Elliot's Beach too; for a few thousand rupees per month, you can get a beach chalet for two. Ask around in the quiet residential road backing off the beach, or ring Mrs Savitri (tel 479777/412134) for details of her furnished chalets and apartments in Besant Nagar.

Madras' best beach, **Golden Beach**, lies a further 10 km (6¼ miles) south. If this is too much to handle by cycle (and it probably is), then you can get there by bus from Elliot's Beach, and return here to pick up your bike afterwards. Alternatively, be at **Kapaleeshwara Temple** for sunset return over Adyar River, go straight ahead at the end of Dr Durgabai Deshmukh Rd, up R.K. Mutt Rd for 2 km (1¼ miles). The evening lights over the tank are beautiful, and so is the ceremony when the gods are brought out and shown the setting sun, to the accompaniment of bells, flutes, drums and invocations.

RECREATION
Madras is the centre of *Bharatnatyam*, possibly the oldest classical dance-form in India. Traditionally performed by young girls dedicated to south Indian temples (devadasis), it is today performed solo by women who describe not only passages

from religious texts, but also the varying moods of a maiden in love. Madras has a dozen good culture centres—notably **Kalakshetra Centre, Music Academy,** and **Raja Annamalai Hall**—and the day to go is Sunday. A great introduction to Tamil dance and music forms including *Bharatnatyam*, folk dances and shadow-puppet plays are the nightly cultural programmes (6.30–7.30 pm) at **Sittrarangam** mini-theatre at Island Grounds, near the fort. TNTDC tourist office often lays on free transport there, and admission is free. To plan your entertainment programme—dance and culture shows, cinemas, drama and tourist fairs, temple celebrations, music exhibitions, craft presentations and even circuses, buy a Friday edition of the *Hindu* or the *Indian Express* newspapers which carry a full listing of upcoming events.

For golf, apply to the **Cosmopolitan Golf Club**, Mount Rd (tel 849946) to use the sandy but shaded 18-hole course. The Race Course near Guindy rail station holds meets most weekends from November to March. Riding, including lessons, is possible throughout the year (apply to **Madras Race Club**, tel 431171, for temporary membership). There's instant membership for guests at the **Boat Club**. Swimming is possible, both at the **New Woodlands** (7.30 am–noon, 2–4.30 pm) and the nearby **Hotel Savera**, in luxury pools for a small charge. If you want to swim in the sea, the cleanest and safest stretch is at Mylapore Beach, near Mahatma Gandhi's statue on Beach Road, but avoid crowded Sundays. For squash, tennis and indoor games apply in writing to the Secretary of the **Madras Gymkhana** (tel 447863).

SHOPPING

For silk, the best buy, visit **Co-optex** just past the museum on N.S.R. Bose Rd. It's a huge place, with a whole ground floor of quality silks, and fabulous South Indian handloom fabrics. All prices are fixed. There are other branches of Co-optex throughout Madras and most towns in Tamil Nadu. If you find some nice material here, then have it made up into a dress or suit by Chandron, one of Madras's excellent tailors. You'll find him in the **India Silk House** (P) Ltd, 846 Mount Rd (tel 844930). India Silk House is one of many emporia on Mount Road that specialise in fabrics. Right next door, **Khadi Gramodyog Bhavan** has a fine range of handloom-cotton fabrics and furnishings at reasonable prices. For general handicrafts, try the interesting **Indian Art Museum**, 151 Mount Rd, which does nice jewellery and sandalwood carvings. Or the more exclusive **Cane and Bamboo**, 26 Commander-in-Chief Rd, Egmore, which deals in high-quality rosewood furniture, batiks and chess sets. Similar stuff, and rather cheaper, can be found at **Swallows Handicrafts Industrial Co-operative** society—a 10-minute bus ride (No. 56M or 56N) from Triplicane. Ask to be put off at 'Swallows Stop'. Open from 10 am–5.30 pm, Monday–Saturday, this little co-op often has sales of high-quality clothes. **Spencer's** offbeat department store on Mount Rd is being rebuilt after a recent fire. Latest-design leather articles are available at the in-house arcades of the **Taj and Connemara hotels** and in shops along Mount Road. Madras is a major centre of the leather boom and the city is full of *haute couture* leather boutiques, offering good quality briefcases, handbags, jackets, coats and shoes at knock-down prices. For flashy, flamboyant stuff, try **Iguana Boutique**, at the WelcomGroup Adyar Park lobby. For soft leather in more subdued styles, go to **Fashion 'N' Gems** on Nungambakkam High Rd. The best general market is the large **T. Mangaramteo** complex in Evening Bazaar, N.S. Bose Road, where you can buy practically anything, and a good deal cheaper than in emporia. But bargain hard. If you've only got time for one shopping outing, head for **Victoria Technical Institute** (VTI), 765 Mount Rd. This has practically everything under one roof, and prices are fair.

Shops and stores in Madras are open daily (except Sun) 9 am–8 pm.

WHERE TO STAY
As a Gateway City, accommodation in Madras is comparatively expensive. Yet, unlike in Delhi, Calcutta and Bombay, it is possible to find good, mid-range comfort at comparatively low prices. Madras is also one of the few big cities that has cheap, good budget hotels.

All prices quoted below are exclusive of tax.

Luxury (from US$100–250 per room night)
The five-star hotels of Madras do very well, mainly because their tariffs are so low. They are particularly cheap in the summer months (May to July) when rates are discounted. Three top-bracket hotels are very well located, near to the city centre. **Taj Coromandel**, 17 Nungambakkam High Rd (tel 474849, tlx 41-7194 TAJM IN, fax 044-470070), is a typical Western-style hotel of glitzy Singaporean design, but the upper-storey rooms (single US$95–105, double US$105–120) offer good views and the Indian restaurant is superb. The Taj have recently renovated the **Connemara** in Binny Rd (tel 860123, tlx 041-8486 CH IN, fax 044-860193), which has considerable charm and large, quiet rooms for US$80 single, US$90 double at the rear of the old building. It used to be an ex-Nawab's town house. WelcomGroup's **Chola Sheraton**, 10 Cathedral Rd (tel 473347, tlx 041-6660, fax 044-478779) has drab, overpriced rooms at US$100 single, US$120 double, but scores on cheerful, personalised hospitality.

Oberoi's venture, the **Trident**, 2393—1/24 G.S.T Rd, (tel 2344747, tlx 41-26055, fax 044-2346699) is a pleasant hotel with rooms from US$90 single, US$105 double. The hotel is a few miles out of town making it slightly less convenient for sightseeing but, being only 3 km (1¾ miles) from the airport, it is useful for an early morning flight departure. The new **Park Sheraton Hotel & Towers** is a totally renovated hotel in a quiet residential area at 132 T.T.K. Road (tel 452525, tlx 41-6868, fax 044-455913). Rooms are from US$95 single, US$110 double.

Expensive (US$35–100/Rs1000–2850 per room night)
The **Ambassador Pallava**, 23 Montieth Road, Egmore (tel 868584, tlx 41-7453, fax 044-868757) has rooms from Rs1200 single, Rs1300 double. The **Savera** 69 Dr Radhakrishnan Road (tel 474700, tlx 41-416896, fax 044-473475) is conveniently located, has a pool and rooms from Rs1000 single, Rs1250 double.

Mid-range (US$10–35/Rs250–1000 per room night)
Two central, moderately-priced hotels are **New Victoria**, 3 Kennet Lane, Egmore (tel 8253638, tlx 041-7897) with single air-conditioned rooms for only Rs450, doubles for Rs700; and **Hotel Madras International**, 693 Mount Rd (tel 861811, tlx 041-7373 ARU IN, fax 044-861520) with single rooms from Rs400, doubles from Rs700) Both have good Indian, Chinese, continental cuisine, and useful facilities. Slightly better and in quiet, downtown Mylapore, is **New Woodlands Hotel**, 72–75 Dr Radhakrishnan Rd (tel 473111, cable WOODLANDS). This is very

reasonable with rooms from Rs300 single, Rs450 double, a swimming-pool and an excellent restaurant.

Budget (under US$10/Rs250 per room night)
Far and away the best budget bet is **Broadlands Lodge**, 16 Vallabha Agraham St, opposite Star Cinema, Triplicane (tel 845573, 848131). Run by the genial Mr Kumar, it has all sorts of attractions: beautiful gardens, sun-roof, swing-seats, filtered water, good information and noticeboard, even room service. Here you can hire out a cycle, use the library, and meet lots of people. All this and more for just Rs75 single, Rs100 double. Ask for the two prestige rooms: No. 18, with the famous graffiti wall paintings; No. 44, the élite roof cottage. If Broadlands is full, and it often is, you can usually sleep on the roof until a room comes vacant.

Other good economy options are **Tourist Homes**, 21 Gandhi Irwin Rd (tel 8250079), with single rooms for Rs200, doubles from Rs250; **YWCA Guest House and Camping Ground** (tel 39920), 1086 Poonamallee High Rd, with rooms from Rs75; and the **YMCA** in Westcott Rd (tel 811158), opposite Royapettah Hospital, with clean, spacious doubles for Rs100. Both the latter take men and women. **Hotel Kanchi**, 28 Commander-in-Chief Road (tel 471100) has rooms from Rs350.

EATING OUT

Madras cuisine is essentially vegetarian and the food is extraordinarily cheap. The staple diet is the tray of assorted vegetables and spices, often served with a dollop of rice, called *thali* or 'meals'; also the folded pancake filled with spiced vegetables called *masala dosa*. Both are cheap (around Rs5) and although it takes a while to get used to them, extremely nourishing. There's also the famous south Indian coffee, generally served in two beakers. The idea here is to 'cool' the scalding brew by pouring it back and forth between the two utensils from increasingly high elevations until it's fit to drink. Losing half of it down your lap is an appalling loss of face, and very painful.

Since thalis and dosas may be all you'll find elsewhere in Tamil Nadu, it's worth eating as well (and as much) as you can in Madras. The Rs115 buffet lunches at the Taj Coromandel's **Pavilion** coffee-shop (12.30–3 pm daily) are ideal for budget travellers; arrive early, to be sure of a seat. For authentic *chettinad* south Indian cuisine (very hot and pungent, but it wakes up the jaded palate), try the Connemara's **Raintree** restaurant. It's an open-air establishment, set in 'sylvan surroundings', where a meal will cost upward of Rs200 per head and local people love it. Slightly out of town, the Oberoi's **Trident** has a fine Indian and stylish Chinese restaurants. A final upmarket option is Chola Sheraton's **Peshawri**—the only restaurant in the city serving meaty North-west Frontier food: a last repast of tasty tikkas, tandooris, birianis or marinated meats before you plunge into the vegetarian heartland. Peshawri is open 12.30–3 pm, 7.30 pm–midnight, and meals cost from Rs200 per head.

Cheaper 'kwality' fare is available at Spencer **Fiesta** restaurant (tel 810051). Local rich Indians come here to savour baked beans on toast and chilled glasses of filtered water. Westerners turn up for Indian/continental food, milk shakes and ice-cream and to sit in the shade! They often move on to **Dasaprakash** ice-cream parlour, 100 Poonamallee High Rd, which is open until after midnight.

Of the many restaurants in Mount Rd, the adjoining **Delhi Durbar** and **Sri Krishna Vilas** (patronised respectively by Westerners and local Indians) are among the best places for cheap, reliable south Indian, continental and Chinese food. The former has a roof garden. The latter is famous for vegetarian cooking. Also worth a visit is the **Agra** near TTDC tourist office, another popular local eaterie, specialising in inexpensive south Indian food. **Chung-King Chinese Restaurant**, 67 Mount Rd (tel 840134), is good for chicken, chips, springs rolls, for under Rs50 per head. The nearby **Southern Chinese Restaurant** at Whites Road junction is of similar quality.

Up in Triplicane, there are a couple of interesting eating places near to Broadlands Lodge. Best is **Hotel New Maharaja**, 307 Triplicane High Rd (opposite Star Cinema), with a cool air-conditioned lounge and perhaps the cheapest and best vegetarian food in Madras. Ask for the 'limited meal' (served lunchtime only, and not on the menu), which is actually unlimited and costs less than Rs10. The Maharaja also offers good tandooris, ice-cream and Indian sweets.

GENERAL INFORMATION

Tourist Offices

Tamil Nadu Government Tourist Office, 143 Mount Rd (tel 849803, 840752), is open 10 am–5 pm daily, and right round the clock for tour bookings. It's still the most useful and helpful tourist office in India. Walk in to find culture-show videos playing, staff fighting to answer ringing phones, brochures and maps readily available, and everybody doing something. Here you can pick up a complimentary copy of *Hello Madras* (full of useful information), buy a decent city map (Rs5), advance-book TTDC accommodation throughout Tamil Nadu, and watch a film. Also come here to book your tours—for Madras city (8.30 am–1.30 pm, or 2–6 pm, daily; Rs45); or for Kanchipuram, Thirukalikundram and Mahabalipuram (7.30 am–6 pm daily).

TTDC also has an information counter (open 6 am–9 pm) at Central railway station.

Airline Offices

Air India (tel 474477, apt 2347500) and Indian Airlines (tel 477977, 478745, apt 2343131) both at 19 Marshalls Rd, Egmore; Air France, 769 Mount Rd (tel 88377); Air Lanka, 758 Mount Road (tel 861777, apt 2340577); British Airways, 26 Commander-in-Chief Rd (tel 477388, apt 2344921); Delta Airways, 163/4 Mount Rd (tel 88493); East West Airways (tel 477007, 866669); Lufthansa German Airlines, 171 Mount Rd (tel 81483); Malaysian, 189 Mount Road (tel 868625, apt 2344888); Qantas, 112 Nungambakkam High Rd (tel 478680); and Singapore Airlines, 167 Mount Road, (tel 862404, apt 2343860)

Consulates

USA, 220 Mount Rd (tel 473040); UK, 24 Anderson Rd (tel 473136); Germany, 22 Commander-in-Chief Rd (tel 471747); France, 26 Cathedral Rd (tel 476854); Netherlands, 739 Mount Rd (tel 811566); and Japan, 6 Spur Tank Rd, Chetpet (865594). Note that all consulates are closed at weekends.

Miscellaneous

Most major **banks** (open daily 10 am–2 pm; Saturday 10 am–noon) are located in Mount Rd. You'll find State Bank of India at 103 Mount Rd (tel 840393). ANZ

Grindlays Bank, Padmanabha Nagar, Adyar is open Sundays 8.30-10.30 am) and closed Mondays.

Travel agents include Trade Wings Ltd, 752 Mount Rd (tel 864961), Sita World Travel (P) Ltd, 26 Commander-in-Chief Rd (tel 478861), and Travel Corporation India (TCI), 734 Mount Rd (tel 868813).

Bookshops (closed Sun) include Higginbothams, 814 Mount Rd; Landmark, Apex Plaza, 3 Nungambakkam High Road; Pai & Co, 152 Mount Rd; Kennedy Book House, 1/55 Mount Rd; and Giggles Book Boutique in the Connemara Hotel. All are useful, and should stock S. Muthiah's excellent *Madras Discovered* guide. Higginbotham's is especially good.

Many Indians you befriend in Tamil Nadu will hand you a visiting card. It's only polite to return the favour and Madras is one of the cheapest and best places to have personalised cards done. There are many small **printers** including Friends Offset Calendars, 39 Bunder St (tel 29419) and Vasantha Achagam, 4 Vallaba Agraharam St, opposite Broadlands Lodge (tel 844476). Use them.

Language

Phrasebooks/dictionaries are sold in the above bookshops, but the *Hello Madras* booklet has a useful 'Tamil for Tourists' vocabulary. Tamil is completely different from Hindi, so it's no good practising here the words you learnt in the north. Try out the following Tamil words—it's fun and worth the effort.

I/me—*Naan*	Why—*Ean*	Sleep—*Thoongu*
You—*Nee*	What—*Yenna*	Come—*Vaa*
Who—*Yaar*	Eat—*Sappidu*	Go—*Po*
When—*Yeppothu*	Drink—*Kudi*	Stop—*Niruthu*
One—*Onru*	Six—*Aaru*	Yes—*Aam*
Two—*Irandu*	Seven—*Eezhu*	No—*Illai*
Three—*Moonru*	Eight—*Ettu*	Good—*Nallathu*
Four—*Naangu*	Nine—*Onpathu*	Bad—*Kettathu*
Five—*Ainthu*	Ten—*Paththu*	Excuse me—*Manniyungal*
	Hundred—*Nooruu*	How much—*Ennavillai*
		Good morning/night—*Vanakkam*
		Thank you—*Nandri*

For sweet revenge on all those precocious infants whose only English is the dreaded 'Wot is yor nem?', reply with the same question '*Ungal pear enna?*'

Route 11—Temple Towns of Tamil Nadu

Relatively unspoilt by foreign invaders, or by tourism, Tamil Nadu is home of the ancient Dravidian people who today consider themselves the only true Indians. Here many of ancient India's customs, dances and literature survive in their purest form.

The pace of life here is more leisurely, more traditional than elsewhere, and the people are both warm and hospitable. Glorious temples, richly woven silks, extravagant festivals, cool hill stations and pleasant beaches are all attractions of Tamil Nadu, which is also one of the country's main agricultural and industrial states.

Tamil Nadu is essentially a land of temples, thousands of them. On this route, you can see some of the best and note the course of their evolution: from simple, unadorned beginnings at **Mahabalipuram**, with its famous Shore Temple and prototype Pallava sculptures (plus a lovely beach); to sophisticated, towering Chola and Vijayanagar examples at **Kanchipuram** (also famous for its silk); to the culmination of the sculptor's art at **Madurai**, the Sri Meenakshi Temple complex achieved by the 17th-century Nayak kings. To cool off from Madurai's palaces and bazaars, handlooms and handicrafts, there's the scenic hill station of **Kodaikanal**, followed by the Land's End of India, **Kanyakumari**, site of some of the most beautiful sunrises and sunsets in the world.

Season: November–March.
Monsoon: October–December; in the western hills, also June to September.
Climate: 18°–43°C.
Route duration: 7 and 10 days.

TRAVEL ITINERARY

Madras to Mahabalipuram 45 km (28 miles)

Road
Regular buses (Nos. 19a, 19c and 68) from Mofussil bus-stand, near Esplanade (2 hours, Rs10). Take care—this route is now notorious for bag-slashers!

Mahabalipuram to Kanchipuram 65 km (41 miles)

Road
Regular buses from 5 am to 7.30 pm (2½ hours). From Madras direct to Kanchipuram, there's bus No. 141 (2½ hours) or daily trains.

Kanchipuram to Madurai 410 km (256 miles)

Road
The night bus is best (10 hours). From Madras direct to Madurai, there are buses and trains (8 hours) and one morning flight (IC501, Rs945).

Madurai to Kodaikanal 120 km (75 miles)

Road
Regular buses (4.45 am to 6.15 pm) from PRC bus-stand (4 hours). Good mountain scenery and alarming road signs. The TDC bus-stand sells a special one-day tour to

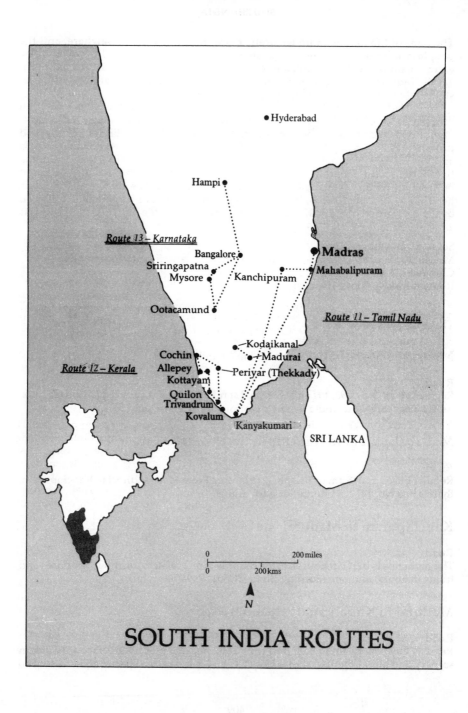

SOUTH INDIA ROUTES

Kodai, leaving 7 am daily. It's okay if you're in a hurry, but you only get 3 hours for sightseeing.

Madurai to Kanyakumari 150 km (94 miles)

Road
Several buses throughout the day (5/6 hours), but again it's best to travel by night: that way you reach Kanyakumari in time for the sunrise, instead of having to get out of bed for it.

Madurai to Madras 440 km (275 miles)

Air
One daily flight (IC501, Rs945).

Road/Rail
Regular buses and trains (8 hours).

CONTINUATIONS
From Madurai, you can continue on to Bangalore in Karnataka (IC503, Wed/Fri/Sun, Rs847). From Kanyakumari, the most obvious continuations are up to Trivandrum (many buses from 5.30 am to 9.30 pm) or even direct to Kovalam beach (10 am bus is best; 2½ hours).

MAHABALIPURAM (MAMALLAPURAM)

This is a small, quiet seaside resort with a unique 7th-century Shore Temple, a lovely beach, and some of the most beautiful rock-cut temples in the world. Situated on the shore of the Bay of Bengal, Mahabalipuram was already a famous seaport in the 1st century AD at about the time Tamil Nadu's recorded history begins. It was later adopted by the empire-building Pallava kings (AD 600–800), who turned it into a major trading port to service their nearby capital of Kanchipuram. They also used the town as a workshop for their temple-building schemes. The 7th century AD marking a move away from monolith rock-cut cave architecture to free-standing, structural temples. The seven 'rathas' or temple chariots, and the seven pagoda-style shore temples they built here at Mahabalipuram are the earliest known examples of Dravidian architecture, and were constructed in a single century-long burst of creative enthusiasm, starting in the reign of Narasimhavarman I (AD 630–68). For some reason, the large complex of caves, temples, bas-reliefs and friezes covering a huge hump-back hillock in the town centre was never finished. As at Ajanta and Ellora, the architects suddenly and inexplicably deserted the site, and its rich treasure of ancient art and sculpture lay lost and forgotten.

Now a small, thriving township, Mahabalipuram has become very popular with tourists needing a break from busy Madras; it is an ideal spot to wind down, switch off and relax. It has a year-round season, but is most pleasant from November to February.

The Five Rathas, Mahabalipuram

ARRIVAL/DEPARTURE

From Mahabalipuram, there are regular buses from the bus-stand opposite Mamalla Bhavan hotel to Kanchipuram (from 5 am to 7.30 pm; 2½ hours) and express buses to Madras (6 am, 12 noon, 2.30 pm, 3.45 pm and 5.15 pm; 1½ hrs). There are also buses daily to Bangalore (7/8 hrs) and one bus to Madurai (10 hrs). There's no need to advance-book tickets; you can buy them on the bus.

WHAT TO SEE

This is an ideal tourist situation, with lots to see, all of it interesting, and everything within walking distance. You can hire out auto-rickshaws, private cars (Rs5 per km, from JRS Travels opposite tourist office) and motorbikes (also from JRS), but few people bother. For sightseeing, allow a full day to wander round Mahabalipuram, then just flop on the beach. Doing it the other way round (relaxation first, sights second) is absolutely fatal—it'll take you a week to see anything.

Temple/Cave Tour (on foot, one full day)
Shore Temple–Krishna Mandapam–Descent of the Ganga–Cave Complex–Five Rathas

Time and especially tide has washed away all but one of Mahabalipuram's seven famous seashore temples. To see the single surviving example, take a 5-minute stroll down Beach Rd (left out of the bus-stand). Though built in the final phase of Pallava art by Rajasimha (700–28), the **Shore Temple** is the first thing most people head for. This, one suspects, is partly because nobody expects it to last much longer. It sits perched on the very edge of the angry sea, constantly battered by the pounding surf, and is almost certainly doomed. All of this, of course, only adds to its romantic charm.

A simple, elegant structure with layered pagoda roof, this shore temple is one of the oldest temples in South India. It's unusual in that it houses shrines for both

Vishnu and Shiva. The Shiva temple faces east and opens out on the sea, allowing the first rays of the sun to enter the shrine each morning to pay homage to the god. The smaller shrine faces west. Between the two shrines is the Vishnu temple, without a *shikhara* tower. This is the oldest part of the temple.

For a proper appreciation of this spectacular monument, hire a guide at the entrance—they speak good English, and treat their subject with warmth. Entering the temple enclosure, note the series of guardian bulls (Nandis) on the surrounding walls. Then, within the frontal shrine the bas-relief of Shiva, attended by Parvati (his wife), Brahma (as wisdom) and Vishnu (as eagle-god). Parvati's good-fortune son, Ganesh, is present, but not his brother Muruga (god of beauty and war). Left, in the second chamber (there's one on each side of the temple), you'll find the 2.5-m monolith of Vishnu in the attitude of repose. The rear chamber has the ancient, much-prized lingam, just a part of which now remains. Facing the lingam is the carving of a cow, representing a permanent sacrifice to the presiding deity. In the last chamber, you'll see the female symbol, a circular recess in the floor.

Walk down the beach to get the full effect of the shore temple; it is best viewed from a distance, and in the subdued light of late afternoon. If going in for a swim, be careful—the waves are invigorating but the current very strong. Drying off, be prepared to entertain the 'lobster-man', the 'coconut man' and a procession of hopeful youngsters hawking seashells and stone-carved images. The coconuts are refreshing. To get some peace, stroll down the beach, either side of the temple, until you find a quiet stretch of sand.

Back at the top of Beach Rd, bear left for Krishna Mandapam. Mahabalipuram has eight such mandapams (rock-cut cave temples), each one an exquisite study in bas-relief portraying various vivid episodes from Hindu legend or mythology. This one depicts Krishna using the umbrella of Mount Govardhan to shield his flocks of cows and shepherds from the rage of the rain god, Indra. It is noted for its realistic representation.

Nearby is the world's largest stone bas-relief, **The Descent of the Ganga**. This amazing piece of sculpture represents the earliest work of the Pallava sculptor, undertaken during the reign of Narasimhavarman I after whom the town is also named (this king earned the title of Mamalla or 'The Great Wrestler'). The Penance itself is a massive whale-back shaped rock, split down the middle with a fissure, the whole face of which is covered with relief sculptures. Measuring 27 m long, 9 m high, this vast stone frieze faces out to the sea. It pictures over a thousand sculpted deities and animals, each one a work of art. Dominated by a procession of elephants, two of which are 5 m, it portrays a dynamic world of gods, demi-gods, angels, men, animals and birds, all apparently rushing towards the cleft in the rock's centre. It is said either to represent the *Mahabharata* fable in which Arjuna, the emaciated figure seen standing on one leg, did penance to Shiva after fighting alongside Krishna and killing many fellow human-beings; or the 'descent of the Ganga' from Mount Kailash, the holy river seen flowing down from Shiva's matted locks. In this story Bhagiratha, a mythical hero, beseeched the gods to send down the celestial waters of the Ganga (the Ganges), to carry the ashes of his ancestors to *nirvana*. But he unleashed a mighty flood, only contained when Shiva mopped up the waters with his hair. Whatever the sculpture means, it's a masterpiece.

A huge granite hillock overlooks the *Descent of the Ganga*. The path up there leads past a number of interesting rock-cut caves, and peters out near **Krishna's Butter**

Ball, an immense boulder which is delicately poised on the crest of the hill. Like the Shore Temple, you can't imagine it staying there much longer. Behind it, pause for the beautiful view over **Koneri Lake**, a pretty inland lagoon with one of the ancient rathas situated on the far bank. Then proceed, via the colonnaded **Sthalasayana Perumal Temple**, to the high **Lighthouse**. You can climb to the top provided you arrive before noon, for a glorious view over the town and surrounds. Officially, no photos are allowed from the top. Below the lighthouse is the **Mahishasuramardhini Cave**, with a famous frieze of Durga (Kali) destroying the buffalo-headed demon Mahishasura. In the background, oblivious to all this activity, there's Vishnu in one of his famous 'cosmic sleeps'.

From the hillock, it's a 15-minute (1.6-km; 1-mile) walk down to the enclosure of the **Five Rathas**. These five monolithic 'temple cars' (four named after the Pancha Pandava hero brothers of the *Mahabharata* epic, the fifth after their wife, Draupadi) are the 7th-century prototypes of all Dravidian temples to come. Five differing monolith miniature temples, they display the familiar gopurams (gatehouse towers), and vimanas (central shrines), mandapams (multi-pillared halls) and sculptured walls so characteristic of later temple architecture. The rathas themselves are simple, unadorned structures, each of a different style, but all are viharas or monastery buildings. They are either square or oblong in plan, and pyramidal in elevation. Adorned with rampant lions, elegant pillars and sculpted divinities, they stand (unfinished) in lonely, isolated splendour, guarded by three life-size stone animals: a lion facing north, a central giant elephant looking south, and a bull to the east.

End your tour with a visit to the pleasant open-air **Museum** in town, and be sure to return to the Shore Temple on a moonlit night.

Tirukkalikundram (by bus, taxi or motorbike, half-day)

This semi-interesting little Shiva temple, situated atop Vedagiri Hill, is located 16 km (10 miles) out of Mahabalipuram. It's covered on the 1-day tour to Mahabalipuram sold by TTDC in Madras, but is a worthwhile little excursion from Mahabalipuram itself.

Tirukkalikundram has a famous popular eagle sanctuary at the temple, where two white eagles (apparently the reincarnations of two famous saints) fly in around noon daily, ostensibly for a rest on their flight between Varanasi and Rameshwaram, but in fact to grab a free lunch issued by the temple priest. Before you make the wearisome climb up 565 steps to the hilltop sanctuary (in bare feet) check that the birds have actually made it. Other attractions at Tirukkalikundram include a large tank, to the south-east of town, with alleged curative powers, and a marvellous temple complex at the base of the hill.

RECREATION

During the day, you can hire out four-log fishing boats down by the Shore Temple. For around Rs50 per head, fishermen will take you about 3 km (1¾ miles) out to sea—and then demand another Rs30 to take you home again.

In the evening, pop along to Silver Sands hotel classical dance performances and music concerts that are held here nightly from 9.30 pm onwards. The admission charge of about Rs40 is steep, but it's the only show in town.

SHOPPING
Mahabalipuram doesn't have much to offer. Real leather shoes often turn out to be real plastic, and cost twice as much as in Madras. The town's stone masons, drawing on the skill of centuries, produce some decent Indian images in marble and a lot of tourist tat in alabaster (which scratches, by the way). If you're going to do any shopping at all, save your money for **Poompuhar Government Emporium** on Shore Temple Rd. This has an interesting assortment of ceramics, handicrafts, perfumes, cut glass and dolls at more or less fixed prices. It's closed on Tuesday.

WHERE TO STAY

Expensive (over US$35/Rs1000 per room night)
The best hotel is in fact 12 km (7½ miles) to the north at Kovelong. The Taj Group's **Fisherman's Cove** (tel 04128-2304, 6268 Madras 474849) set in a beautiful cove has an excellent pool, wind-surfing, sailing and cottages in addition to rooms from US$65.

Mid-range (US$10–35/Rs250–1000 per room night)
At Mahabalipuram the resort hotels include the **Shore Temple Bay Resort** (tel 235), 3 km (1¾ miles) out of town, but ideal if you just want to snooze on a private beach. It has a good pool and restaurant, and large, bright rooms at Rs400. There are also a few air-conditioned cottages. Nearer town, **Silversands** (tel 228, tlx 41-8082, fax 04113-280) in Kovelong Rd is a simple, comfortable place with good facilities but excellent food. Single rooms here run from Rs350 in the off season (May–July) to Rs495 single and Rs750 double in the high season (Dec–Jan). The **Temple Bay Ashok** (tel 251) has cottages, some with attached kitchenettes, from Rs450 single and Rs850 double.

Budget (under US$10/Rs250 per room night)
Cheaper lodgings are fairly basic, but since most people spend all day on the beach and only go home to sleep, nobody appears to mind. **Mamalla Bhavan** (tel 250) by the bus-stand had adequate double rooms for around Rs60. The best room—No. 16—is light and airy, and has a lovely balcony. Downstairs of course, there's the famous restaurant. **TTDC Youth Hostel and Cottages**, situated on the way to the Shore Temple, is another favourite. It's a well-run place, with clean rooms at Rs125 and a nice Rs10 dormitory. If you don't mind sleeping in the open, covered with mosquito repellent, lads at the bus-stand will offer you a place to stash your gear for just Rs70 per week.

WHERE TO EAT
Silversands still has the best food in town—Indian, Chinese and continental—with fresh grilled lobster the speciality. Seafood is very good in Mahabalipuram, as is the usual travellers' fare of pancakes, chips and lassis. **Sunrise** restaurant, on the way down to the Shore Temple, offers tasty grilled/boiled lobster with all the trimmings at Rs100, grilled jumbo prawns at Rs75, and a whole giant swordfish at Rs200. It's a popular meeting-place. Nearby, the **Rose Garden** is popular for toasted sandwiches and choc milkshakes, while **Village Restaurant** offers fresh lobster from Rs50, Madras Chicken at Rs20, and Western breakfasts at Rs20. **Bamboo Hut**, near Sunrise, has a regular clientèle of laidback gourmands, though less patient diners head up to **Shore Temple Bay Resort** to get some food in under an hour.

TOURIST INFORMATION
TTDC (tel 232), East Raja St, near the post office, is friendly and helpful. Indian Overseas Bank is in the town centre, near the police station.

KANCHIPURAM

Kanchipuram is one of the oldest towns in India, famous for both its temples, many of them remarkably well preserved, and for its handwoven silks. Known as South India's 'Golden City of Temples', it is a major pilgrimage centre and the perfect introduction to anyone seeking a crash course in Hindu religion, mythology and architecture. Kanchipuram is one of the seven sacred cities of India (the others are Varanasi, Mathura, Ujjain, Hardwar, Dwarka and Ayodhya), and it is the only one associated with both Shiva and Vishnu.

It was the empire-building Pallavas (6th to 8th centuries AD) who turned the ancient holy town of Kacchi into the wealthy capital of 'Kanchi'. Under the artistic Mahendravarman I (600–630), a sudden surge of cultural and building activity took place, starting the traditions of silk-weaving, temple building and Bharatnatyam dance for which Kanchipuram later became famous. In this period, Dravidian architecture developed from modest simplicity, as exemplified by the Mahabalipuram rathas, to wildly extravagant maturity. The development of the *gopuram* temple-towers into soaring stone leviathans dripping with tiny dancing deities was particularly dramatic. All this zealous religious activity attracted flocks of artists, educators and musicians to Kanchipuram, and it became a major centre of art and learning. But then, in the 9th century, the Pallava dynasty fell, and the city's power and influence rapidly faded. Under subsequent rulers—the Cholas, the Vijayanagar kings, the Muslims and eventually the British—it returned to being just a typical country town, enlivened by constant parades of devout pilgrims.

Kanchipuram today is a noisy, dusty place, with a definite shortage of good hotels and restaurants. But the temples are unmissable, and the priests invariably friendly. The fever-pitch noise and bustle may come as a bit of a shock after tranquil Mahabalipuram, but like Varanasi, the authentic spirituality of the place lies just beneath the surface.

The cool season to visit is November to January, but many brave the heat for the big **Car Festival** of February–March. Subsequent festivals in April–May are hot, crowded and uncomfortable.

ARRIVAL/DEPARTURE

Road
There are regular buses in and out of Kanchipuram from both Madras and Mahabalipuram. All buses are a mad scramble, and you'll have to fight tooth-and-nail for a seat.

WHAT TO SEE
There are around 1000 temples in and around Kanchipuram. About 200 of these are in the city itself, and with one exception the best examples are all conveniently close

to the bus-stand. If you're short on time, hire an auto-rickshaw for a quick morning tour of the temples for around Rs45/50. If you've a full day to spare, do your sightseeing by cycle; there are many bike-hire places around, charging only Rs10 per day. Most of the temples worth noting are open only from sunrise to 12.30 pm, and from 4 pm to sunset. At the temples, be firm in turning away uninvited guides, and be prepared for the notorious temple beggars.

Temple Tour (by cycle/rickshaw and bus, 4–6 hours)
Kailasanathar Temple–Ekambareshwara Temple–Kamakshiammon Temple–Vaikuntha Perumal–Varatha Temple

A short 15-minute cycle ride down Nellukkara and Putteri Streets takes you to the west of town, and the 8th-century **Kailasanathar Temple**. This lies in a garden clearing, and the giant Nandi bull in the grounds tells it's a Shiva temple. The structure itself is very early Dravidian architecture—apart from the front, which was added later by Mahendra Varman III. Delightfully simple and elegant, it has none of the decorative ostentations which were the hallmark of the later Chola and Vijayanagar building styles. Built of sandstone, it has some beautiful carvings and sculptures (some well-renovated), and remnants of bright fresco paintings still cling to a few of the 54 small shrines running round the inner courtyard, giving an idea of the temple's original magnificence.

Just left of Nellukkara and Putteri Street junction, you'll find **Ekambareshwara Temple**, marked by its towering 57-m high *rajagopuram*. Inside, there's an extensive temple compound surrounded by a massive stone wall, added by Krishna Devaraja (a Vijayanagar king) in AD 1500. Ekambareshwara probably derives its name from 'Eka Amra Nathar'—Shiva, as 'Lord of the Mango Tree'. The ancient mango tree in one of its compounds, which according to local tradition is over 2500 years old, is where Parvati is said to have done penance to Shiva, after misguidedly closing his eyes and plunging the whole universe into chaos. Pilgrims troop around the tree all day long, and will (after you've paid your camera fee) urgently insist that you join them. Actually, you are not allowed to see much more—Ekambareshwara is a living temple (the god still lives here, in the mango tree) and many of the other shrines are off-limits to tourists. No matter, you can still climb the central *gopuram* for marvellous views down over the temple complex. Permission is granted by the temple curator, who is found behind the **Thousand Pillar Temple** inside the compound. This particular temple has a thousand pillars, a colourful display of temple chariots, and images of the various animal carriers who accompany the gods of the Hindu pantheon. Allow yourself a good hour at Ekambareshwara.

The most popular temple, **Kamakshiammon** (5 mins left out of Ekambareshwara), is dedicated to Parvati and is the site of the February/March Car Festival. As one of the three holy places of Shakti (Parvati as bride of Shiva), it is considered particularly auspicious for marriage-blessings, and up to 25 000 people show up at the larger festivals to supplicate the goddess for happy nuptials. Show up around 8 pm on Tuesday or Friday evening for fireworks and music, caparisoned elephants and vast, swaying crowds—the Golden Chariot cruises slowly round the temple grounds, and the moaning hordes part like the Red Sea in the Cecil B. de Mille movie. It's a spectacle. By day, Kamakshiammon is surprisingly quiet and relaxed; a few visiting pilgrims stare appreciatively at the resident elephant, and you're free to wander around unmolested. In its present form, the structure is a 14th-century temple of *chola* construction, its central ghat overlooked by watchtower gopurams.

A short ride away, you'll come across **Vaikuntha Perumal**. This is one of the oldest temples in town, dedicated to Vishnu and built by Parameswar Varman in the 7th century AD. It is most notable for its cloisters within the outer wall which are prototypes of the 1000-pillared halls seen at later temples like Ekambareshwara. There's an interesting bas-relief circling the main shrine, which portrays battle scenes between the Pallavas and the Gangas/Chalukyas, also various depictions of Vishnu sitting, standing and lying down.

A rather alarming bus ride from the Nellukkara St stand, just up from Raja's Lodge takes you 4 km (2½ miles) across town to **Varatha Temple**. Recently renovated, this temple is in fine condition and features one of Kanchipuram's finest gopurams, and the views from the top are stunning. There's also an agreeable temple elephant contributed by the Elephant Shed Foundation, which will take you for a short ride round the grounds.

Pay your camera fee, and head for the central 100-pillared **Marriage Hall**. The pillars are notable for fine base-carvings, of Vishnu (warrior-horses), Parvati, Ganesh, Brahma, Shiva and Buddha. The raised plinth within is the marriage platform, with seating space for wedding guests. In the corner lives the gloriously painted wooden chariot of Varatha (Vishnu). It is carried round town on festival days. Beyond the marriage hall is the large temple ghat, and two small shrines. The small stone marquees dotted round the marriage hall are for pilgrims to relax under, tucking into popular temple sweets like lemon-rice *laddoo*.

SHOPPING

With a weaving tradition dating back to the Pallava era (when silk was the royal cloth, Kanchipuram is justly famous for its particularly fine silk saris, embellished with stunning zari patterns. There's no problem finding shops—over 5000 families are currently engaged in the weaving industry—but there is a problem finding ones which speak English or don't rip off tourists. Avoid expensive private emporia, and stick to the cheap government co-operatives. Places like **Murudan** in Railway Rd; **Srinivas & Co**, 135 Thirukatchi Nambi St; **Thiruvallur Co-operative Society**, 207 Gandhi Rd; or **Kamatchi Co-optex**, 182 Gandhi Rd, have a good name. For shopping advice, and to see top-quality Kanchi silk being produced on the looms, call in on the **Handlooms Weavers Service Centre** at 20 Railway Rd, just up the road from the post office. Open 9.15 am–5.45 pm on weekdays only.

WHERE TO STAY

Kanchipuram is a typical temple town, with lots of pilgrim dharamsalas and hardly any tourist hotels. But the **TTDC Hotel Tamil Nadu**, 78 Kamatchiamman Sannathi Street (tel 2953, 2954) is a pleasant place, with rooms from Rs200, and a nice restaurant. Cheap alternatives are **Raja's Lodge** and **Rama's Lodge**, adjoining each other in Nellukkara St, close to the bus-stand. Both charge Rs40 for clean rooms with hard beds and boisterous Indian neighbours. The Rama is the better deal, with a pleasant sun-roof and a vegetarian restaurant.

EATING OUT

There is not a great choice: *Masala dosa* (the traditional south Indian snack of spiced vegetables within a thick pancake envelope), thalis and precious little else. For something slightly more thrilling, take a rickshaw over to **New Madras Hotel** or

Pandiyan Restaurant. The latter is in Station Rd, and attempts Chinese food. If you're happy with local food, try either **Hotel Tamil Nadu** or **Sri Rama Cafe** (opposite Raja's Lodge). The little restaurant next to Raja's has good-value Rs5 *dosa* dinners and an air-conditioned lounge where you can practise 'cooling' coffee the Tamil way.

GENERAL INFORMATION

The tourist office is at the Hotel Tamil Nadu. The Archaeological Survey of India office opposite Kailasanathar Temple is helpful, but often closed.

The post office, Kossa St, is just below the bus-stand. State Bank of India (tel 2521) is on Gandhi Road.

MADURAI

One of the most pleasant Indian cities, Madurai has a charming situation on the River Vaigai, fringed by lush paddy fields and coconut groves. It is both the home of Tamil culture (poets, artisans, artists, scholars and saints have used it as their base for centuries) and the special abode of the goddess Meenakshi, the 'one with eyes like fish'. The vast temple complex built here in her honour is perhaps the finest achievement of the Dravidian architects and still remarkably intact. The nine soaring gopurams of Madurai are the first thing most visitors see, whether coming in by air, rail or road.

Over 2500 years old, Madurai takes its name from *mathuram*, the nectar which Shiva let fall from his flowing locks after Kulaskera, a Pandyan ruler, began praying for a new capital. The Pandyas, great patrons of Tamil art, architecture and learning, ruled 'Nectar City' from as early as the 6th century BC, right through to the 13th century AD, apart from a short period of Chola rule during the 11th/12th centuries. After the Pandyas came the Delhi Sultans and the Vijayanagar kings, but it was left to the enlightened Nayak rulers, who governed Madurai from AD 1559 to 1781, to build the city in its present form. It was laid out in the shape of a lotus flower, with the impressive Meenakshi temple at the centre, in accordance with the Shilpa Shastras (ancient laws of architectural science). In AD 1781 the British ousted the Nayaks, razed the old fort, and converted the surrounding ditches into broad avenues known as *veli* (outer) streets. The growth of the modern town outside the temple walls was thenceforth rapid.

Full of colourful bazaars, itinerant street tailors, thronging pilgrims and academics, and joyful religious processions, Madurai today is a small, bustling town which attracts up to 10 000 visitors from outside each day. For fun and spectacle, come for the month-long **Chithrai Festival** of April/May. People have been known to pass out in the heat and crowds, but it really is a glorious pageant. Otherwise, there's the cooler **Teppam** (Float) **Festival** of January/February. Madurai is popular all year round, but the climate is most pleasant from October to January.

ARRIVAL/DEPARTURE

Air

Indian Airlines flies Madras–Madurai daily (Rs945) and returns via Trichy (Rs376), and to Bangalore (Rs847) a couple of times a week. From Madurai airport it's a 6-km (3¾-mile) ride into the city centre by airport bus (Rs15) or taxi.

Rail

The fast *Vaigai Express* from Madras gets to Madurai in just 8 hours, stopping at Trichy on the way. The morning Madras–Quilon Mail takes 8 hours to reach Quilon, and crosses the scenic Western Ghats. You can't advance-reserve seats on either train, but they're often half empty. If you don't fancy taking the chance, contact the TTDC information counter inside the station.

Road

Madurai has two main bus-stands, adjoining each other off West Veli St. The PRC stand is for Kodaikanal and for local city buses. The TDC stand is for Kanyakumari, Madras, Trichy, Trivandrum and Kottayam. With TDC buses, you must buy your tickets in advance.

WHAT TO SEE

Two small cities in one, Madurai is easily negotiable by foot or by cycle. The central Meenakshi Temple, aptly named a 'city within a city', is enclosed by the old town, which is itself enclosed by the four Veli Streets. The newer town, a couple of kilometres (a mile) north over the river Vaigai, is of little interest but has the better hotels. All the budget lodges, restaurants and tourist office are in the old town, and so is all the action. Whenever possible sightseeing is best done on foot. But don't jaywalk round the temple area unless you want to be mown down by crazed cyclists. You can hire auto-rickshaws or cycle-rickshaws for around Rs10 for short hops, but most people only use them for out-of-town trips. Allow at least 2 days to see the sights, and don't worry if you miss something. You can always try again, when you return here from Kodaikanal.

City Tour (on foot or by rickshaw/taxi, full-day)
Sri Meenakshi Temple–Thirumalai Nayak Palace

From either the bus or rail station, it's a 15-minute walk up Town Hall Road to the **Sri Meenakshi Temple**. This is one of the biggest temple complexes in India—258 m long and 241 m broad. Most of it was built in the reign of Thirumalai Nayak (1623–55), though it was substantially added to by later rulers. It is a rectangular twin shrine: the southern temple dedicated to Meenakshi (a Pandyan princess who lost her embarrassing third breast when she met Shiva up on Mount Kailash), the other dedicated to Sundareswarar (Shiva himself). Dominated by four enormous outer gopurams, the common entrance point is the Ashta Sakthi Mandapam on the east side. Within, are five smaller gopurams, enclosing the two small golden vimanas or central shrines.

Meenakshi temple is a constant buzz of noise and activity, especially around the East Tower Bazaar, full of exotic stalls selling bright clothes, jewellery, incense, and spices. Enter the temple by the main gate, at the end of Town Hall Rd, and remember to deposit your shoes before entering. Just inside the entrance, bearing right, there's usually a row of fortune-tellers. Just past these are a couple of 'classrooms' where, in the early evening, you can hear tuneful songs and prayers being practised. Turning left, you'll find the **South Tower**. It used to be possible to climb to the top of this soaring *gopuram*, and to enjoy spectacular views over the whole temple complex. But then came a bomb scare, and the tower was temporarily closed to the public. It is worth asking if it is again open.

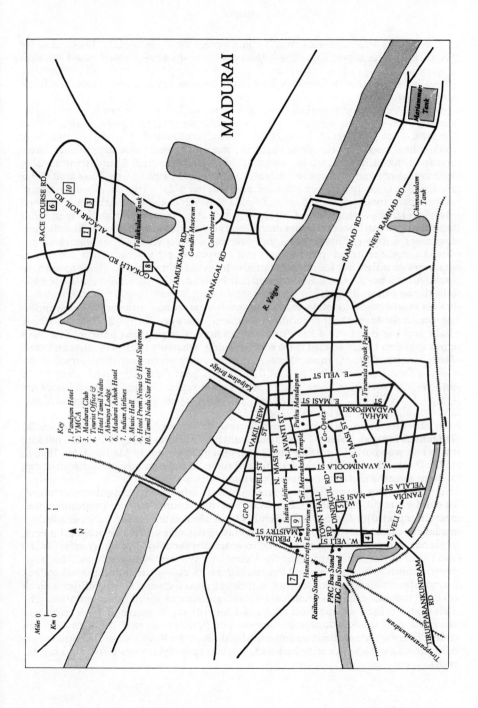

MADURAI

Key
1. Pandyan Hotel
2. YMCA
3. Madurai Club
4. Tourist Office &
   Hotel Tamil Nadu
5. Abinaya Lodge
6. Madurai Ashok Hotel
7. Indian Airlines
8. Music Hall
9. Hotel Prem Nivas & Hotel Supreme
10. Tamil Nadu Star Hotel

Miles 0   1
Km 0   1

N

RACE COURSE RD
ALAGAR KOIL RD
GOKALH RD
TAMUKAM RD
PANAGAL RD
Tallakulam Tank
Gandhi Museum
Collectorate
Mariamman Tank
Chinnakulam Tank
RAMNAD RD
NEW RAMNAD RD
R. Vaigai
Kaipalam Bridge
Tirumala Nayak Palace
E. VELI ST
E. MASI ST
MAHAL VADAMPROKKI
ST
S. MASI ST
Pathu Mandapam
Co-Optex
Sri Meenakshi Temple
N. AVANTI ST
W. AVANIMOOLA ST
VELALA ST
PANDIA
N. MASI ST
N. VELI ST
VAKIL NEW ST
GPO
Indian Airlines
W. PERUMAL MAISTRY ST
Handicrafts Emporium
Railway Station
PRC Bus Stand
TDC Bus Stand
TOWN HALL
DINDIGUL RD
W. MASI ST
W. VELI ST
S. VELI ST
TIRUPPARANKUNDRAM RD
Tirupparankundram

Continuing anti-clockwise, you'll come across the **Golden Lily Tank,** used by pious Hindus for sacred dips. The legend goes that any book thrown into it will sink if worthless (this guide is a rare exception). Surrounding the tank is a pillared portico, its walls decorated with paintings from Hindu mythology and verses from the Tamil classic, *Tirrukkural.*

Beyond the nearby mural of Meenakshi's wedding to Shiva are the two single-stone sculptures of the temple's 12th-century founder, and his chief minister. Behind the tank is the gate-facing shrine of **Sri Meenakshi Sannath,** guarded by two huge dwarabhalagas or doorkeepers. Past this, through the entrance gate of **Sundareswarar Sannathi,** you'll find the beautiful hall of **Kambathadi Mandapam,** notable for its excellent sculptures of Shiva. Next, wander over to the nearby **Thousand Pillar Hall,** which actually has only 985 superbly sculpted pillars. Two small temples stand on the space intended for the other 15 pillars. Much of the rest of the hall has been given over to the extensive **Art Gallery**—a fascinating, if poorly lit exhibition of Tamil temple art and architecture. Outside again, take directions for the **Puthu Mandapam,** opposite the Eastern Tower. Built by Thirumalai Nayak in honour of Sundareswarar, this is noted for its sculptures and for its imposing pillars, on which are carved representations of the four Nayak rulers. Just east of this is the **Rajagopuram,** a massive 53.5-m tower base which—had it been completed, would have been the tallest tower in south India.

Don't feel obliged to follow this route to the letter, people often enjoy just wandering round Sri Meenakshi at random. The temple is open 5 am–12.30 pm, 4–10 pm daily, and the day to avoid is Friday, when hordes of pilgrims pour in. The most enjoyable time of day to visit is the early evening, when it's relatively quiet and cool. There's normally some musical entertainment going on (informal, inspired) at the Golden Tank from 6.15–7.30 pm, 9–10 pm. If you're at the South Tower around 9.15 pm, you can see Shiva being 'put to bed'. Photographs are only allowed inside the temple from 1–4 pm daily (camera fee Rs5). But you can pick up some good black-and-white prints in the bazaar, very cheaply.

In the afternoon, take an auto-rickshaw (it's complicated on foot) down to **Thirumalai Nayak Palace.** This palace, built by Thirumalai Nayak in 1636, fell into ruins and was partially restored by Lord Napier, Governor of Madras from 1866 to 1872. The original palace was four times larger than the existing building, though enough remains to make a visit worthwhile.

Enter via the magnificent granite portico into the rectangular courtyard, flanked by huge, tall colonnades. Walk up to the north-west of the building, to see the splendid Main Hall. Originally Thirumalai Nayak's 'bedroom', it measures 41.5 m long by 20.9 m wide. It was also used as a theatre, where dancers, musicians and court magicians used to entertain the king and his guests. On the west side of the courtyard, visit the Celestial Pavilion (Swarg Vilasa). The large central dome is supported by 12 columns, but (a clever illusion) appears to lack any support whatsoever. The fine decorative stucco *chunnam* or shell-lime work on both the dome and its arches are a characteristic of Tamil ornamentation. The Celestial Pavilion is approached by a flight of steps guarded by a group of sculpted, damaged, mounted horsemen. The Palace is open 9 am–1 pm, 2–5 pm daily. There's an excellent sound-and-light show in English here, commencing 6.30 pm daily. Tickets are Rs2 or Rs3. The cheaper tickets are best—you see far more.

Sights Round-up (by local bus, full day)
Thirupparankundram–Mariamman Teppakulam Tank–Gandhi Museum–Government Museum

From the PRC bus-stand, catch a No. 5 bus (they leave every 10 minutes) for the remarkable rock-cut temple of **Thirupparankundram**, 8 km (5 miles) out of town. This temple, carved into the side of a mountain, is one of the six sacred abodes of Subramanya, second son of Shiva, and celebrates his marriage to Deviyani, daughter of the rain god Indra. Opening times are 5 am–12.30 pm, 4–10 pm daily, and admission is free.

Entrance to the innermost shrine cut from solid rock is denied to non-Hindus, but there's lots to see in the preceding series of mandapas or halls. These are generally packed to capacity with devotees preparing to go into worship. The head of each family distributes small lamp-lit bowls of coconut, fruit, rice and incense to his group, and marks their foreheads with the lines of Shiva in red or grey powder. You can follow them on their way into devotions, as far as the door leading to the inner chamber. Just beyond the door is a small courtyard, containing 'Shiva's Postbox', where incinerated prayers drift up to the god through the soaring wicker-tower roof. In the centre of the courtyard is a brightly-painted triumvirate of a Nandi (Shiva's bull), a peacock and a rat fashioned of black granite. The surrounding pillars are surmounted by fierce stone lions, and the ceiling decorated with beautiful murals. Following the pilgrims out of the shrine, you'll see them making offerings of boiled rice to the schools of leaping fish in the temple ghat. Out in the street again, sit awhile over a cup of *chai* and enjoy the colourful flow of people: pilgrims, priests, holy men and Indian families on their way to prayer.

Back at PRC bus-stand, catch bus No. 4 or hire a rickshaw to **Mariamman Teppakulam Tank**, 5 km (3 miles) east of the city. Measuring about 305 m square, this tank is almost as large as the Meenakshi Temple. Built by Thirumalai Nayak in 1646, it is the site of the big **Float Festival** held on the night of the January/February full moon. The central pavilion, **Mayya Mandapam**, houses a small temple and can be reached by boat, for a rupee or two. The tank is connected to the nearby Vaigai river by underground channels.

From here, take bus No. 6 to the **Gandhi Museum** (closed on Wednesday), 5 km (3 miles) north. It's a 5-minute walk from the Collector's Office in the new town. The museum contains various relics, photos and material relating to Mahatma Gandhi, a crafts exhibition of Khadi and Village industries, and a south Indian handicrafts display. Also here is a relatively new **Government Museum** (1981). Both museums are open daily 10 am–1 pm, 2–6 pm (the latter closed Fridays). To return to the old town, you'll need a bus No. 3 or 4.

RECREATION
Lakshmi Sundaram Hall, Gokali Rd, Tallakulam (tel 25858), and **Raja Sir Muthiah Mandram**, opposite the district court, hold regular dance and music programmes. Near Gandhi Museum, there's a yoga centre and a swimming-pool. Ladies' hours are 2–4 pm.

SHOPPING
Madurai is a living bazaar—there are shops, stalls and markets everywhere. Cotton and silk clothing are the best buys, followed by cheap costume jewellery. There is no

problem finding good clothes here. The streets are alive with salesmen carrying armloads of clothes and silver trinkets around, and they pester tourists with irresistible sales patter.

All the best tailors hang out opposite the East Tower of Meenakshi temple. Check out a guy called 'Paramount' in Shop 100—several travellers have found him of great help. Both here, and down by the South Gate, you can get clothes made up at very reasonable prices and in under 4 hours.

Poompuhar, the new government emporium opposite the rail station, has a good selection of fabrics, wood-carvings, stone-carvings, brass trays, and cotton lanterns at fixed prices.

WHERE TO STAY

Luxury (over US$35/Rs1000 per room night)
Madurai's most interesting hotel is the **Taj Garden Retreat**, Pasumalai Hill, (tel 88256, 22300, tlx 0445-205 located on a hill 6 km (3¾ miles) from the town. The house once belonged to the managing director of a large British company and the gardens include a swimming-pool and tennis courts. Rooms are from US$48.

Many of the other hotels are located in the new town, about 4 km (2½ miles) from bus and rail stations.

Mid-range (US$10–35/Rs250–1000 per room night)
The air-conditioned **Pandyan** in Race Course Rd (tel 42470, tlx 0445-214) has useful facilities, a good restaurant, and fine temple views from rooms (Rs450 single, Rs750 double). **Hotel Madurai Ashok** in Alagarkoil Rd (tel 42531, tlx 445-297) is rather more impersonal and expensive with rooms at Rs650 single, Rs800 double. TTDC's **Tamil Nadu Star Hotel**, Alagarkoil Road (tel 42461, tlx 445-238) has rooms from Rs250 and a couple of large comfortable suites for Rs500.

Budget (under US$10/Rs250 per room night)
Madurai attracts a good crowd of budget travellers, and there are many cheap lodges. A few favourites, with rooms around Rs50 single, Rs75 double, are **Hotel Prem Nivas** (tel 37531) at 102 West Perumal Maistry St; **Ganga Guest House** opposite it; **Abinaya Lodge**, 198 West Masi St; **P.S.B. Lodge**, West Veli St; and **Aftab Lodge**, 12 Kakka Thopu St. TTDC's **Hotel Tamil Nadu**, West Veli St (tel 37470) is rather a disappointment with uncomfortable rooms from Rs130 single, Rs200 double.

EATING OUT
Pandyan Hotel's **Jasmine** restaurant offers a superb Rs95 buffet lunch between 12 noon and 3 pm daily. The à la carte is good too—a fine range of Indian, continental and (after 7 pm) Chinese dishes at between Rs30 and 55. Helpings are huge. Three popular restaurants, all close together in Town Hall Rd, are the **Taj**, the **Mahal**, and the **Akbar**. They all serve Western-style food in addition to standard Indian fare, but the Akbar has an air-con lounge upstairs, and gets the best mentions. Old favourites like the **Indo-Ceylon** and the **Amudham**, also in Town Hall Rd, are fairly drab now, but the **New College House** continues to turn out the cheapest, best south Indian thalis in town. Similar fare can be had at the **Ashok Bhavan** opposite the tourist office, which serves 'special' lunches for Rs15–25 from 12 noon–2.30 pm daily.

GENERAL INFORMATION
TTDC, West Veli St (tel 22957), has good information and is very helpful. There are also tourist information counters at the rail station and at the airport.

The post office is in Scott Rd, near the rail station. Indian Airlines (tel 22795, apt 37433) is at Pandyan Building, West Veli St. State Bank of India is also in West Veli St. Higginbotham's bookshop, selling a useful city guide and map, is in the rail station.

KODAIKANAL

Kodai is a quiet, charming hill station situated 2125 m up in the scenic Palani Hills. It's the ideal place to cool off from hot, dusty travels down in the plains of Tamil Nadu. Currently being developed as a health resort, it's only just being discovered by Western tourists. This is perhaps surprising since Kodai has more attractive reminders of the Raj—churches and colleges, bungalows and parks, a golf course and an artificial lake—than other more popular hill stations. And it is the only hill station in India that was developed by American missionaries. The bus trip up there across rugged mountains, plummeting valleys and terraced coffee plantations is spectacular. Kodai is famous for its hill-fruits and plums, and its pride is the rare Kurunji flower, which blooms just once every 12 years. Unfortunately, it last flowered in 1992. The two tourist seasons, when the place is rampant with holidaying school-children, are mid-November to mid-January, and mid-April to end June. For better weather and 20–30% discounts at larger hotels come February/March or August/September. If visiting between November and February, bring warm cloth-ing—it gets very cold at night.

ARRIVAL/DEPARTURE
From Kodai, there are regular buses to Madurai; one bus daily to Coimbatore (4.30 pm); and one bus daily to Bangalore (6 pm). It's wise to advance-book seats.

WHAT TO SEE
The emphasis here is on light exercise and recreation; walking, pony-riding and boating on the lake. The small town overlooks the lake, and is easily negotiated on foot. You can hire out cycles by the hour or for the day down by the boat club, which is ideal for leisurely tours round the vast artificial lake. There are also taxis, but few people take them. Kodai is really just a place for long, invigorating rambles. Allow 2 full days for the best walks, and have a decent map handy (try Higginbotham's bookshop in Madurai).

Walk One (full-day)
Coaker's Walk–Sacred Heart Church–Kodai Lake–Bryant Park–Golf Club–Green Valley View–Pillar Rocks

Rise at 5.30 am, dress warmly and take a blanket, for Kodai's main attraction: the sunrise over the mountains. A 15-minute walk up **Coaker's Walk** from the market-place brings you out on a plateau running along the steep southern face of the Kodai basin. The early-morning scenery is glorious but latecomers be warned: the views are often gone by 9 am.

After breakfast, proceed east from the market-place down to the lake. On the way, divert right for a brief visit to **Sacred Heart Church**. It has a touch of Surrey with stained-glass windows, gothic arches, a mock-Tudor tower, and a small English cemetery. If not for the Tamil hymn books and alarming fresco of Christ rescuing a flock of anxious Indian villagers from a watery grave, you wouldn't know you were in India at all. Kodai's famous star-shaped **Lake** was formed in 1863 by Sir Vere Levenge and nestles in a wide range of dense wooded slopes. Covering an area of 243 hectares (60 acres), it is the focal point of all life on the hill station. Clean, tranquil and scenic, it is very 'English'. The small Boat House here (tel 315), on the left, coming down from the Church, hires out four-seater rowing boats from Rs20 per hour. For choice of boats, and no crowds, turn up early. Nearby, you can hire out ponies for about Rs40 per hour from the curiously named Horse Riding Forward Association. It doesn't accept any responsibility for 'any accident those who riding themselves without horse man'. From the pony rank, it's a 10-minute walk to the east of the lake, where you can enjoy a picnic lunch in pleasant **Bryant Park**, noted for its flowers, hybrids and grafts. There's a popular horticultural show here each May.

Even if you are not a golfer, the walk up to the **Golf Club** (tel 323, 6 km: 3¾ miles) is one of the best in the station. Take the road leading off the northern end of Bryant Park, ascend to the top of the ridge from which there are fine views down over the lake, and whenever you hit a major fork, keep to your left. The walk is a continuous joy. Young boys may turn up to suggest 'short cuts' and they are reliable. You'll reach the golf club in around an hour. The course itself is beautifully kept, and spans a succession of undulating meadows and hills. Cows are employed to keep the grass down. It's hardly ever used, except in May, when the 300 club members turn up for the annual tournament and for a small green fee of Rs75 you get clubs, balls, temporary membership and the course practically to yourself. An extra Rs20 will hire you a good caddy and for another Rs10 you get a spare set of balls.

Alternatively, take directions at the club for adjoining **Green Valley View**, which commands a beautiful view of the entire Vaigai Dam. Or walk 1 km (⅔ mile) further on past the golf course for **Pillar Rocks**, three massive boulders standing shoulder to shoulder, measuring a total of 122 m and providing a plummeting view down into the valley plains. There's a pretty waterfall here too.

Walk Two (full-day)
Observatory–Bear Shola Falls–Museum–Telescope House

For day two, try a pleasant 40-minute stroll up to the **Solar Physical Observatory** 3 km (2 miles) from town, approached via Observatory Rd, located 5 mins north of the Boat House. Founded in 1898, situated at the topmost point of Kodai at a height of 2347 m, it gives panoramic views of the town, lake, and surrounding Palani Hills. Check opening times (normally 10 am–noon and 7–9 pm, April to June) at the tourist office before visiting. On the return walk, take the rugged, picturesque path left for **Bear Shola Falls** 1.5 km (1 mile) from the lake, another popular view point and picnic spot.

In the afternoon, stroll back up Coaker's Walk for the **Shenbaganur Museum** near the top of the rise, on left. This is famous for its collections of flora and fauna including

300 varieties of orchid, and is well maintained by the Sacred Heart College. It is open 10–11.30 am and 3.30–5 pm. The **Telescope House** at the nearby observatory is a good place to be at sunset. If it isn't free, and it often isn't, enjoy the sun going down from the small knoll below which it is a sheer drop of 670 m, with privacy guaranteed.

There are several other nice walks, notably **Prospect Point** (6 km; 3¾ miles), **Fairy Falls** (5 km; 3 miles) and **Silver Cascade** (1 km; ⅔ mile), behind the Sacred Heart Church.

RECREATION
Apart from golf, boating and pony-riding, Kodai is a good area for fishing. Licences are issued from the Fisheries Officer (enquire at the tourist office), and charges are Rs5 per day for carp, Rs25 per day for trout-fishing in local hill streams.

Short treks around the Kodai hills for about Rs100 per day are offered by **A School in Nature Education**, c/o Greenlands Lodge, Coaker's Walk. These are easy-going nature rambles, geared to students and youth hostellers, which take place between May and June, September and November.

SHOPPING
There's a reasonable selection of weavings and local crafts at the **Cottage Craft Shop** near the bus-stand. It's open 9 am–12.30 pm, 2–6 pm, Monday to Saturday. You'll find attractive Tibetan produce and local coir mats for sale on the road leading down to the lake.

WHERE TO STAY

Expensive
There's elegance and lake-view rooms (singles Rs1200, doubles Rs1450) at **Carlton Hotel** on Lake Rd (tel 561, tlx 04412-210 CARL IN, fax 04542-570). The room rate includes meals and during the low season of mid-January to March and July to mid-October discounts of 25% or more are given. This 'warmhearted luxury hotel you and your family deserve', has good food and good facilities which include a health club with jacuzzi, sauna and massage, billiards and tennis. But it's often full.

Mid-range (US$30–35/Rs250–1000 per room night)
Mid-range properties include **Hotel Kodai International** (tel 649, tlx 04412-205) with rooms from Rs500 and cottages from Rs750. **Sterling Resorts**, 44 Gymkhana Road (tel 760, tlx 0441-2209) has cottages from Rs750–1100.

Budget (under US$10/Rs250 per room night)
Among the budget hotels is the **Hotel Jai** in Lloyds Rd (tel 344) which has the rather alarming advertisement: 'Be our cosy guest tonight—wake up Gay in the morning'. If that sounds too much of a risk try **Hotel Clifton** in Bear Shola Rd, and **Hotel Anjay** (tel 489) near the bus-stand. All three have clean, comfy rooms from Rs150 to Rs350. The **Holiday Home**, Golf Links Road (tel 257) has rooms from Rs200. **Hotel Tamil Nadu**, Fernhill Rd (tel 481) has double rooms at Rs250. Budget lodges up on Coaker's Walk are generally squalid, though the **Yagappa Lodge** has a few adequate rooms at Rs60 single, Rs80 double. Backpackers still favour the excellent **Greenlands Youth Hostel** right at the top of Coaker's Walk. Beautiful situation, lovely gardens, pleasant rooms from Rs80.

EATING OUT

There is a good range of Indian food at either the **Carlton Hotel** or the **Hotel Tamil Nadu** for about Rs100 and Rs75 respectively. The **Hotel Jai** does reputable non-vegetarian cuisine. The **Boat-Club** restaurant is okay for snacks. Just below the market square are three good places: **Lala Ka Dhaba**, a *proper* Indian restaurant offering delicious Punjabi food in tasteful setting; **J.J.'s Fast Food**, a busy pizza-burger joint run by jolly Vincent; and **Tibetan Brothers** with delicious vegetable momos (deep-fried dumplings), fair Chinese food, and homely service. After dark, there is the **Manna Bakery and Restaurant** run by Israeli Bhoonji and his English wife, at Keith Lodge near the Clifton Hotel. Famous for its banana cake and custard, wholewheat bread and pies.

GENERAL INFORMATION

TTDC tourist office is near the bus-stand, open 10 am–5 pm daily. The post office is between the market square and the lake. State Bank of India (tel 468) is just above the bus-stand.

KANYAKUMARI (CAPE COMORIN)

Kanyakumari is the Land's End of India, a staggering 3300 km south of Jammu. It is named after the Kumari (virgin) goddess whom the gods tricked out of a marriage with Shiva because they needed a virgin to defeat the powerful demon Banasura. It's just the kind of poignant, tragic love story that devout Hindus adore, and they turn up here in their thousands to console the dejected goddess in her temple, and to seek her help. They also come because Kanyakumari is the meeting-point of three great seas: the Indian Ocean, the Arabian Sea and the Bay of Bengal, and bathing in the waters is believed to wash away all sins. Local tourists and foreign travellers come for the unique sunrises and sunsets which are most spectacular at full moon, when sunset and moonrise take place simultaneously. It's otherwise a small, unremarkable place which has somehow developed in the short space of a few years from a modest fishing village into a full blown Indian-style resort. And of all Indian resorts, this one is the most full of cheap tourist junk. It sells grass hats, funny masks, plastic whistles, plastic tropical plants, and bags of coloured Kanyakumari sand. It has crowds of well-to-do families clambering over rocks, taking invigorating walks, and paddling around in the shallows dressed in their best suits and saris. It even has a drive-in restaurant chicken corner. The high season months are November–January and April–June. For peace, quiet and a chance of a decent room visit between February and March. It's fairly cool then, and you can enjoy the full moon.

ARRIVAL/DEPARTURE

Road

Kanyakumari has a swish new bus-station, with rest rooms, a restaurant and a shopping complex. It's inconveniently situated, a long 1-km (¾-mile) walk up the hill from Vivekananda boat-pier. From here, buses go to Trivandrum/Kovalam, to Madras (at 9.45 am, 12.45 pm, 4.45 pm, and 8.45 pm; 16hrs), to Madurai (at 7 am, 2.30 pm, and 9.30 pm), to Coimbatore and to Trichy.

WHAT TO SEE

This is a tiny seaside town, with one main street. Sights are few, but walks are interesting. Stay for at least one sunrise and one sunset, and during the day try the following jaunt.

Beach Tour (on foot, 3/4 hours)
Sunrise Point–Kumari Amman Temple–Gandhi Mandap–Fishing Village–Vivekananda Memorial

Try to be up around 5 am for the sunrise. This is best seen either from **Sunrise Point** down on the beach, or from your hotel roof. Every hotel near the shoreline has a roof, and each one will be choc-a-bloc with jostling tourists. The sunrise itself takes place against an atmospheric background of Muslim muezzin-calls, Catholic prayers and picturesque fishing boats putting out to sea. Afterwards, you can go straight back to bed.

Later, take a walk down to the beach. Here you'll find **Kumari Amman Temple**, dedicated to the virgin goddess who is now the nation's protective mother-figure. The deity sits in a small dark pavilion, flanked by four attendants. She used to look out to sea, but her glittering nose-diamond lured so many sailors to their deaths (including the British vessel which purloined the original jewelled nose-ring) that the temple door was closed in her face. The temple is open from 4.30–11.30 am and 5.30–8.30 pm but the sanctum is closed to non-Hindus.

Just west of the temple is **Gandhi Mandap**, the rather bizarre monument erected to commemorate the spot where the Mahatma's ashes were kept before being immersed in the sea. It's worth a visit (have 10 paisa handy, or you'll never get in), if only for the coastline views from the top-storey balconies.

A total contrast to the touristy new town is the quaint little **Fishing Village** just down the beach. Here you'll find a warm and friendly community of fisherfolk living in the same way they have for centuries. Give them a hand with a fishing line, or help push out a dugout to sea, and you'll be their friend. For around Rs20, they run parties of 3/4 people out to sea for 'fishing trips'. You don't get to do a lot of fishing, but you do get stunning views of mainland India and Sri Lanka from a mile or so out. Sitting for 2 hours in a primitive five-plank catamaran you also get very damp so take a spare pair of trousers.

Beyond the village are lovely palm-fringed beaches: great for sunbathing, fatal for swimming. The coastal currents are generally dangerous. To swim in safety, use either the sheltered bathing ghat back in town, or the new pool on the shore built for visitors.

Above the village is the clean, white **Catholic Church**, established by Francis Xavier in the 16th century. It's massive. So is the Disney-ish image of the Virgin Mary inside. She is patron-saint of the fishing community, afforded just the same reverence as is given the Kumari deity by the Hindu pilgrims across the bay. Since the congregation prefer to squat in the church, there are no pews.

Returning to the bathing ghat, take a boat (Rs6 return, regular departures from 7–11 am, 2–5 pm daily, except Tuesday) out to **Vivekananda Memorial**, which lies on the two rocky islands 200 m offshore. Dedicated to the philosopher-saint Swami Vivekananda, who came here in 1892, meditated on the rock, then set out to become one of India's leading religious crusaders. It is a relatively recent structure (1970) which attempts to blend all the architectural styles of India. There is over-strict security here, in part to highlight the sanctity of the site. Smoking and eating are prohibited and shoes must be removed. The views of the mainland from it are excellent. Pilgrims visit the rock to view the Kumari goddess's footsteps.

Try to be back at the ghat around 6 pm for sunset. This is often low tide, and best views can be obtained by wading over to the small observation rock opposite. Take care coming back though, as the rising tide has a nasty habit of leaving unwary tourists stranded. At the April full moon the setting sun and rising moon appear side by side on the same horizon.

RECREATION
For entertainment, there is good sea-fishing (but nowhere to hire tackle); also one cinema. At sunset, pop over to **Suchindram Temple**, a 10-minute auto-rickshaw ride away for the evening *arti*.

SHOPPING
Apart from seashells, plywood toy racing-cars and 'precious sand of three seas', there's nothing local that is worth buying.

WHERE TO STAY
TTDC Hotel Tamil Nadu (tel 257, tlx 0430-3202) is just below the new bus-stand. Clean and friendly, it has the prime beach situation, with some lovely rooms (Rs150) overlooking the sea. Food is good, and so is the dormitory accommodation. **Hotel Cape** (tel 222) is also run by TTDC and has rooms from Rs175. TTDC also run a **Youth Hostel** next to Hotel Tamil Nadu with rooms from Rs50. The better budget lodges are located down by the old bus-stand. **Manickam**, North Car St, and **Lekshmi**, East Car St, have the best roofs for sunrise/sunset views, and charge Rs40 for clean, adequate rooms. The brand-new **Hotel Saravana**, opposite Vivekananda pier, is a little more expensive but worth it.

EATING OUT
Again, you won't find anything exciting. **Hotel Saravana** has the best vegetarian restaurant in town. Hotels **Sangam** (tel 351) and **Manickam** offer reasonable non-veg food. Otherwise, it's back to thalis.

GENERAL INFORMATION
TTDC tourist office (tel 276) is near Gandhi Mandapam, open 10 am to 5.30 pm (except weekends). Staff regard Western visitors with undisguised shock. Post office and State Bank of India are both near the old bus-stand.

Route 12—Kerala

A tropical paradise of undulating palms and warm, sandy beaches, Kerala is a narrow strip of coastal territory sloping down from the Western Ghats in a riot of green, luxuriant vegetation. Said to have been carved out by axe-wielding Parasurama, an *avatar* of Lord Vishnu, it is still a land of ancient charm and mystery. Kerala is also one of the richest states in India with forests and plantations of rubber, cashew, and coconuts everywhere. The meeting place of many cultures, Hindu and Muslim, Christian and Jewish, Kerala has a particularly rich heritage of dance and drama (Kathakali, Koothu and other temple arts originated here) and her people are among the most industrious and well-educated in the country.

Kerala's appeal lies in its calm, relaxed style of living, combined with its wide variety of scenic attractions. **Kovalam** is a picturesque beach resort which every traveller is loath to leave; nearby **Trivandrum** is capital of the state, with temples, palaces, art gallery and a good zoo. **Quilon** is the start of Kerala's famous inland waterways, where ancient 'pagoda' boats still ply the lagoons and Chinese fishing nets stand at the water's edge. Leisurely yet spectacular boat-trips up the backwaters to **Alleppey**, the Venice of India, and to **Kottayam**, age-old pilgrim centre of the Syrian Christians, lead on to **Periyar Lake**, one of south India's finest wildlife sanctuaries. Finally, at the old Portuguese/Dutch port of **Cochin**, the modern city of **Ernakulam** (centre of Kathakali dance-theatre, and handicrafts) vies for attention with Fort Cochin, the oldest European settlement in India—the site of historic churches, synagogues, museums and pastel Mediterranean buildings.

As with so many places in India, many of Kerala's towns have recently adopted new names. However, at the time of writing they have not yet been adopted by Indian Airlines, Indian Railways or most people in their daily conversation. Officially, Cochin is now Kochi, Trivandrum is Thiruvananthapuram, Quilon is Kollam, Trichur is Thrissur, Palghat is Palakkad, Cannanore is Kanoor, and Alleppey is Alappuzha. In this guide we use the old, familiar form.

Best season: November–April.
Monsoon: June–September/October.
Climate: 21°–35°C.
Route duration: 10–20 days (it's so restful. . .).

TRAVEL ITINERARY

Madras to Trivandrum   920 km (575 miles)

Air
One flight 4 days a week (IC529, Rs1250).

Rail
The daily *Trivandrum Mail* (18 hours).

Trivandrum to Kovalam   18 km (11 miles)

Road
Bus No. 9D (every half-hour, 6 am–10 pm) from the city bus-stand at East Fort (40-minute journey, Rs4 fare). Sometimes, auto-rickshaws offer cheap 'share' rides (Rs25 per head) from the bus-stand. The normal point-to-point rickshaw fare is nearer Rs60. Taxis and hire cars regularly ply this route.

Trivandrum to Quilon 71 km (44 miles)

Road
About 6 buses daily (2 hours). If you can find the right bus at Trivandrum's chaotic bus-station, fight hard for a seat and prepare yourself for a very bumpy ride.

Rail
Several trains daily. Less crowded than buses, and if you catch the 6.15 am *Pareswarum Day Express* (1½ hours) the journey is also quicker.

Quilon to Alleppey 83 km (52 miles)

Backwater
The Alleppey Tourism Development Co-operative Society ferry leaves Quilon on Tuesday and Saturday at around 9.45 am, arriving Alleppey some 7/8 hours later. The fare is Rs70 and tickets can be bought on the boat. Other ferries leave most mornings at about the same time. You may have to pay a few rupees extra to sit on the boat roof, which has the views. For a seat down below, arrive 30 minutes before departure. Wherever you sit, it's an unforgettable journey.

Road
There are some buses to Alleppey daily but the boat journey is recommended.

Alleppey to Kottayam 29 km (18 miles)

Backwater
A number of local ferries daily (3 hours, Rs10). For maximum comfort and best views, get an early-morning boat.

Kottayam to Kumily 110 km (69 miles)

Road
Only 4/5 buses daily (4½ hours), so you'll need to check timings. It's a crowded, uncomfortable ride, but the views as the road ascends to a 905-m plateau crowned with tea-plantations more than compensate for any discomfort.

Kumily to Periyar 5 km (3 miles)

Road
Hire cycles (30 mins) or take a local jeep taxi.

Kumily to Cochin 190 km (119 miles)

Road
One early-morning express bus (4/5 hours). Other buses are slower 'locals' (6/7 hours).

Cochin to Madras 560 km (350 miles)

Air
One flight via Trivandrum most days a week (Rs1325) and direct flights on other days.

CONTINUATIONS
From Cochin, you can connect with **Bangalore** (IC538, Rs842; or the *Island Express* train, 14 hours); and with **Goa** (IC468 daily, Rs1313). The usual continuation from Cochin, however, is up to **Ootacamund** (via Mettapulayam/Coimbatore) on the 9.25 pm *Tea Garden Express*. The final leg of this 15-hour journey, as the pretty blue steam train huffs and puffs its way up the mountainside on the narrow-gauge track, presents some memorable scenery. Get a window seat on the right-hand side of your carriage, and have your camera ready.

TRIVANDRUM

Though many travellers head straight for Kovalam, 13 km (8 miles) away, there are several good reasons for making Trivandrum the starting point of your Kerala tour. This is the state capital, and has been so from the days of the old princely families. Yet, having retained much of the stately, unhurried broad-avenued ambience of that regal era, it doesn't look or feel like a state capital at all. It is, perhaps even more than Cochin, the home of Kathakali dance, of the Kalarippayat martial art, of yoga therapy, and of ayurvedic massage. Many travellers stay in Trivandrum for weeks on end studying one or other of these ancient arts and sciences. There are some interesting sights which, even if you only come into the city for the day from Kovalam, make a pleasant change from the beach.

Life on the backwaters

Trivandrum is a busy, friendly seaside city built on seven hills, many of its buildings overlooking peaceful valleys. It derives its name from *Thiru-Anantha-Puram* (Home of the serpent), and is believed to be the home of Anantha, the sacred snake on which Vishnu reclines. Trivandrum is also known as the City of the Sacred Geese.

ARRIVAL/DEPARTURE

Air
From Trivandrum airport (6 km/3¾ miles from city centre, Rs1 by No. 14 local bus) there are daily flights to and from Bombay (IC168, Rs 2362), Cochin (IC468, Rs525), Delhi (IC468, Rs 3757), and Goa (IC468, Rs1313). Also less frequent flights to Bangalore (IC530, Rs1192), Hyderabad (IC516, Rs2043), and Madras (IC530, Rs1250).

Trivandrum is also an international airport with Air India flights to cities in the Gulf including Dubai and Muscat. Some of these flights continue to Europe and New York. Indian Airlines operates flights to Male in the Maldives and Colombo in Sri lanka. Air Lanka also operates to and from Colombo. Gulf Air operates from and to Abu Dhabi, Bahrain, Doha and Muscat with onward connections to Europe.

Rail
From Trivandrum rail station (opposite the bus-station), there are a number of trains daily to Ernakulam (Cochin), via Quilon. The fastest train is the 6.15 am *Pareswarum Day Express*, which gets to Quilon (70 km; 3¾ miles) in 1½ hours, and to Ernakulam in just 3 hours. It's a wonderfully scenic ride, cutting right through the eight creeks of Ashtamudi Lake. Best of all, you don't even need an advance-reservation: just hop on, and pay for your 2nd-class air-conditioned seat on the train.

The best train for Goa leaves Trivandrum at 11 pm, arriving in Mangalore 10 am next morning. Proceed immediately by auto-rickshaw to Mangalore's government (not private) bus-stand, in order to catch the 11 am express bus (10 hours) to Panjim. Don't miss this early bus as the next one bound for Goa is in the evening.

Road
Trivandrum has two bus-stands. Buses for Kovalam leave from the Fort bus-stand. Buses for all other destinations leave from the city bus-stand, opposite the rail station. Points covered include Madurai (many buses from 4.30–10 am, from 5–11 pm; 7 hours), Kanyakumari (9 am, 3 pm, and 10.15 pm; 2½ hours), Coimbatore (6.30 pm; 12 hours), Madras (12.30 pm and 7 pm; 17 hours) and Kumily (8 hours). For all these long-haul destinations, you'll have to advance-book tickets: a real pain, in view of the awesome queues. Try to find a boy to queue up for you for Rs3–4 while you go sightseeing.

Fortunately, there's normally no need for advance reservation on the hourly, from 5 am–midnight buses to Ernakulam (4 hours), via Quilon (2 hours) and Alleppey (3 hours). Just toss your bags in the window, and pay on the bus.

WHAT TO SEE
Trivandrum city is bisected by a single long thoroughfare, M.G. Road. To get to the museum, zoo, art gallery, main tourist office and Indian Airlines (all at the top of M.G. Rd) from Padmanabhaswamy Temple or the Kovalam bus-stand (opposite each other, at the bottom of M.G. Rd) is a long 15-minute ride by auto-rickshaw (Rs7–8)

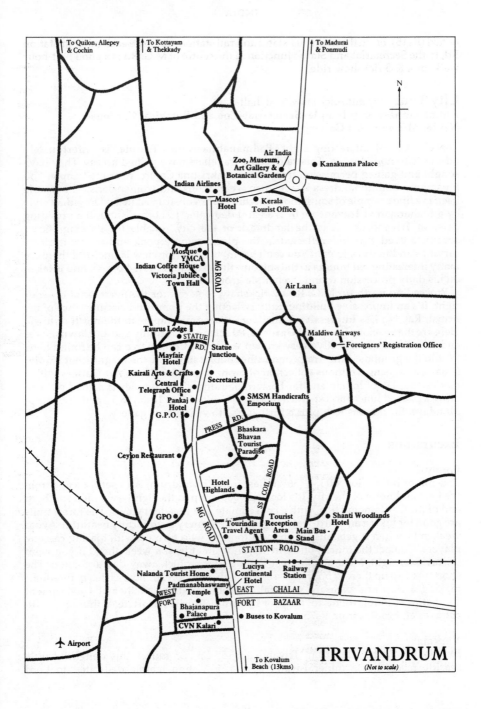

To Quilon, Allepey & Cochin

To Kottayam & Thekkady

To Madurai & Ponmudi

N

Air India
Zoo, Museum,
Art Gallery &
Botanical Gardens

Kanakunna Palace

Indian Airlines

Mascot Hotel

Kerala Tourist Office

Mosque
YMCA
Indian Coffee House
Victoria Jubilee
Town Hall

MG ROAD

Air Lanka

Taurus Lodge

STATUE RD.

Statue Junction

Maldive Airways

Foreigners' Registration Office

Mayfair Hotel

Kairali Arts & Crafts
Central Telegraph Office

Secretariat

Pankaj Hotel
G.P.O.

SMSM Handicrafts Emporium

PRESS RD.

Bhaskara Bhavan Tourist Paradise

Ceylon Restaurant

SS COIL ROAD

Hotel Highlands

GPO

MG ROAD

Tourindia Travel Agent

Tourist Reception Area

Main Bus Stand

Shanti Woodlands Hotel

STATION ROAD

Nalanda Tourist Home

Luciya Continental Hotel

Railway Station

Padmanabhaswamy Temple

EAST CHALAI

WEST FORT

FORT BAZAAR

Bhajanapura Palace

Buses to Kovalum

CVN Kalari

Airport

To Kovalum Beach (13kms)

TRIVANDRUM

(Not to scale)

or taxi (Rs15). From the main bus-stand and rail station, opposite each other in Station Rd, to the Secretariat and Statue Junction at the centre of M.G. Rd is a good half-hour walk, or a Rs5 rickshaw ride.

City Tour (by auto-rickshaw/taxi, half-day)
Padmanabhaswamy Temple–Secretariat–Zoo and Botanical Gardens–Napier Museum–Art Gallery

The city's most interesting sight, **Padmanabhaswamy Temple**, is unfortunately off-limits to non-Hindus. This said, some travellers have gained access. They have sought and gained permission from the Ramakrishna Centre, near the temple. You must wear traditional dress inside; men wear dhotis and women saris. The temple itself is a fine example of south Indian architecture, constructed in the Dravidian style by a Maharajah of Travancore in 1733 and dedicated to Lord Vishnu, the presiding deity of Trivandrum. It is the landmark of the city, notable for its magnificent seven-storeyed *gopuram*, reflected in the placid temple pool, and for its intricate carvings and murals. Even if you can't get in, the exterior view is fine, and there are many interesting old houses in the surrounding backstreets. At 4 pm Vishnu is taken on his daily procession round the temple grounds.

Proceeding north up M.G. Rd by rickshaw, look out for the **Secretariat** on your right. It's an impressive building, fully reflecting the pomp and circumstance of the British Raj. No less impressive is the large museum complex to the north of town. Here are the spacious **Botanical Gardens**, 80 acres of beautifully laid-out lawns, lakes and woodlands. Practically every known variety of tropical tree can be found here. Within the grounds is the dingy and rather depressing **Zoo**, the magnificent **Napier Museum** housing a famous collection of bronzes and **Sri Chitra Art Gallery** with a modest display of Indian and far-Eastern paintings. The complex is a good place to bring a packed lunch, and spend a relaxing day. It's open 10 am to 5 pm daily, except Mondays. Entrance is Rs1, plus a further Rs2 to visit the art gallery.

Excursions

Ponmudi
This minor hill station, 60 km (56¼miles) from Trivandrum, is a useful escape from the heat and noise of the city. It's located 1000 m up in the lightly-wooded southern end of the Cardamom Hills, with a cool climate and excellent views. The forest trails are good for hiking and bird-watching, and the scenery is uniformly beautiful. Avoid weekends, when it gets busy with local tourists who turn up with blaring cassette players. Contact the tourist office in Trivandrum at least a week ahead if you want to stay overnight. Most people treat Ponmudi as a quick away-day excursion. The short bus-trip up there (2 hours) passes through good forest, and then tea plantations, making a stop at a pleasant waterfall. Accommodation is either at **Government Bungalows** (double rooms for Rs60) or **Ponmudi Tourist Resort** (tel Vithura 30), with cottages and rooms from Rs75.

Varkala
Exactly 1 hour by train from Trivandrum (55 km; 35 miles), this delightful little seaside resort has a mineral-water spring, a Vishnu temple dedicated to Lord

Janardhana with fascinating rituals, a beach that is empty except at weekends, with good swimming, and lovely country scenery. Cheap places to stay include the **Tourist Bungalow** a 5-minute walk up hill from the bus-stand; clean Rs75 doubles, **G.A. Lodge** (near bus-stand), and **Donkey Lodge** (on the way to the beach). There are several long-stay travellers at Varkala, mainly in the area of the Krishna temple. A famous saint called Sri Narayana used to live here and many followers have stayed on.

RECREATION

Two troupes, Kathakali Club and Drisyavedi, give displays of traditional Kathakali 'story-play' dance twice monthly, usually at the **Karthikathirunal Theatre**, near to Padmanabhaswamy temple. Both outfits draw their players from the Margi School of Kathakali, near the West Fort, and if you turn up at the Fort High School behind Padmanabhaswamy temple in the early morning, you can make an appointment to 'sit in' on classes the following day.

Kalarippayat, the martial art of Kerala, is best seen in the **C.V.N. Kalarisangam**, East Fort (just below Padmanabhaswamy temple), where maestro C.V. Govindkutty Nair normally holds classes between 6.30 and 8 am. Kalarippayat is being increasingly recognised as the parental martial art of Asia; the forerunner of Thai kick-boxing, karate, kendo, judo, and kung fu, using 14 weapons and the whole range of unarmed combat methods. It also teaches an advanced system of massage therapy. For more information, contact G.P. George, himself a Master of Kalarippayat, at Taurus Lodge, Statue Rd.

Instruction in yoga and ayurvedic massage is given by Dr Pillai at the Yoga Therapy Hospital in Bazhuthacaud Junction. The doctor prefers you to take the full 3-month course, but if you've only a week to spare, he may decide he can do something for you.

From the sublime to the mundane, the **Veli Tourist Village** has just opened up 9 km (5¾ miles) out of Trivandrum. This has landscaped gardens, sculptures, wading pools, water-sports, motor boats, even a hovercraft; the full range of Indian-style 'fun' recreations. Earplugs are a must on busy weekends. Accommodation here is at the village (Tel 71364) or **Hotel Lakeside Tourist Home** with rooms from Rs85.

SHOPPING

Popular buys in Trivandrum are carvings and curios, bell-metal lamps, screw-pine items, handloom fabrics, and Kathakali masks and dolls in *papier mâché* or wood. The two (good) government emporia are **Kairali** (tel 60127) at Statue Junction, and **SMSM Institute**, behind the Secretariat. Both are fixed-price establishments, offering the full range of local produce. Although some shops still offer ivory items the sale and export of ivory is banned by both Indian and international law.

WHERE TO STAY

Mid-range (US$10–35/Rs250–1000 per room night)

Although the Taj Group have a proposal to develop one of Trivandrum's old palaces into a hotel by the end of 1993, there are at present no five-star hotels in the city. The better properties are near Kovalam. The most interesting hotel is the renovated KTDC **Mascot Hotel** (tel 68990, 68475, tlx 0435-229), a well-located hotel at the top of M.G. Road, near museum complex, with a pool, a sauna, and rooms from Rs700. Similar standards at the new **Hotel Luciya Continental**, East Fort (tel 73443, tlx 435-330, fax 0471-73347), offering swish air-con rooms at Rs450 single, Rs800 double. Opposite the Secretariat, **Hotel Pankaj** (tel 76667, tlx 0884-323 PNKJ IN) is the least 'Indian' of Trivandrum's big hotels. It can be snobby (*very* reluctant to show backpackers rooms) and food is pricey, but there's good service, stylish rooms from Rs375 single, Rs500 double and a nice roof-top restaurant. **Fort Manor**, Power House Junction (tel 70002, tlx 435-246) is centrally located, has good facilities and rooms from Rs450 single, Rs600 double.

Budget (under US$10/Rs250 per room night)
At the budget end, a good place to stay is **Taurus Lodge**, located down Statue Road. It's run by 'George', one of those polite, informative lodge-owners who help make travel in India a joy, rather than a continual struggle. Rooms are clean and quiet and the best ones (Nos. 21, 24 and 25) are spacious, with good views. Whatever you want to know about Trivandrum, its culture, transport, entertainments or shopping, ask George. The KTDC **Chaithram** in Station Road (tel 75777) has rooms from Rs300 single, Rs350 double. The central **Highlands**, Manjalikulam Road, Thampanoor (tel 78440, 78466) has rooms from Rs250 single, Rs275 double.

EATING OUT
The best upmarket restaurants are at **Hotel Shanti Woodlands** (Thycaud) and **Hotel Pankaj**. Both offer mid-priced quality fare in air-con comfort. For great grills (burgers etc.) and Indian food, try **Kalabara Restaurant** near Taurus Lodge. The opposite **Mayfair Hotel** has a good bar. Two popular restaurants with more local food are **Ananda Bhavan** and **Athul Jyoti**, both in M.G. Rd, just along from the Secretariat.

GENERAL INFORMATION
KSTDC Tourist Office (tel 61132) is at Parkview, opposite the museum complex. It has very friendly, helpful staff and excellent published information, including a useful festival list for Kerala.

KSTDC Reception Centre (tel 75031, near the bus-stand in Station Rd), is open 6 am–10 pm, also very helpful, and sells a number of tours: Trivandrum city sightseeing, Rs60; Kanyakumari; Thekkady (Periyar), Rs150. There is also an information counter at the airport (tel 71085).

GPO is just off M.G. Rd, between the bus/rail stations and the Secretariat. Indian Airlines (tel 66370, apt 72228) is at Mascot Junction. Air India (tel 64837, apt 71426) is at Vellyambalam. Gulf Air use Jet Air, Saran Chambers, Diamond Hill (tel 68003, 67514). Two good travel agents, for air tickets and for tours, are Sherif Travel, Patan Palace Junction, and Tour India (tel 79407) in M.G. Rd.

KOVALAM

Kovalam, 15 km (9¼ miles) from Trivandrum, was once the Arabian Sea beach resort of the court of the Rajahs of Travancore. Today, its scimitar-sweep of sand between two high headlands is a popular tourist beach catering not only to hippy-dippy backpackers but also, since it began developing into south India's premier beach resort, to international yuppie jetsetters. Kovalam is famous for its soft white sands, its warm, clear waters, and its panoramic views extending to the ocean-line. Small beach restaurants provide the laid-back tourist community with fresh seafood and delicious Western-style cuisine. It's a lovely place as yet undefiled by tourism; villagers still cultivate their paddy fields, pawpaw, bananas and coconuts, fishermen still put out to sea in their catamarans each morning and most visitors find it very difficult to leave. The coolest and best months to come are December–March. In April, the heatwave arrives driving many people north. The result (if you don't mind sunburn and a few pre-monsoon showers) is empty beaches and cheap accommodation.

Kovalam has two popular beaches, separated by a large rock outcrop extending into the sea. The luxury beach, overlooked by the five-star Ashok Beach Resort Hotel, is just below the bus-stand. The main beach, with all the budget accommodation and beach restaurants, is a 15-minute walk (through shady palm groves) from the bus-stand. The end of this 'budget' beach is marked by the lighthouse up on the headland.

Popular beach activities at Kovalam include snorkelling (easy to hire equipment), water-skiing (contact the Ashok Hotel), and body-surfing the big waves. Semi-nude bathing is still allowed, but do respect local sensibilities and the inevitable attraction created by topless bikinis. Swimming is very pleasant in the shallows, but don't go out of your depth as the currents are dangerously strong. Also, try not to swim underwater. Recently, fishermen have taken to lobbing hand-grenades into the sea to knock out the fish, and have knocked out or deafened quite a few bathers as well. In high season, sun-worshipping on the tourist beach is quite impossible as hordes of grinning salesmen come selling fruit, seashells, sarongs and soft drinks. For peace and quiet, try the quieter cove directly behind the lighthouse, or wander up to the bay above the big Ashok hotel. This bay is often quite deserted, and one lucky swimmer went far enough out to be taken for a ride by a dolphin!

The only real problem with Kovalam is sloth. Too much sun, sea and sand makes people careless. They either doze off on the beach and wake up, badly sunburnt, to find all their belongings gone, or they get bored and begin experimenting with the infamous 'Kerala grass'. Drugs may be freely available in Kovalam, but don't be fooled: police informers are all over the place.

WHAT TO SEE
If inertia or boredom does set in, and you need a break from the beaches, it's time to get out and about. For many people, this just means a leisurely stroll up onto the headland, to visit Kovalam Town. For something more rewarding, try the following short excursion:

Fishing Village (morning)

This walk is a treat. Be down on the beach at 7 am, to watch the fishermen putting out to sea, then take the high road running up from the lighthouse to the top of the headland. From here, it's a scenic 2-km (1¼-mile) stroll, offering beautiful views along the coastline, to the small decorative Muslim shrine perched on the cliff edge. There's a path here, which takes you down to the beach again. Keeping to your left, you'll shortly arrive at the fishing village. Here is a friendly community of simple fisherfolk who continue to make their living from the sea. The beach is lined with the hulks of long, primitive wooden dugouts and the way to introduce yourself (they don't see a lot of tourists) is to lend a hand with a fishing rope, net or boat. At the back of the beach, you'll see the charming tiered Catholic shrine housing a red-faced Jesus and Mary, the community's patron saints. Climb the rise behind this for a cold drink and stunning coastline views. Then drop in on the village, an interesting collection of thatched dwellings and narrow, cobbled streets, with wide courtyards for drying out the fish. Behind the village, back on the main road, you'll find the modern seaside town, with Portuguese-style bungalows, little knick-knack shops, a couple of cafés and lots of locals on holiday. From here, it's a leisurely 45-minute walk back up the headland to Kovalam Beach for a well-earned rest in the sun.

SHOPPING
The most common buys at Kovalam are sun-oil, beach clothes and mosquito repellent. You can find all this stuff, plus cigarettes and confectionery, at the small general stores by the bus-stand. Seashells, sarongs and (fake) jewellery are hawked by children on the beach, but Kovalam just isn't a buyers' market. Like Goa, it's a place to sell things. Unload any unwanted film, cameras, Walkmans, and even snorkel equipment here. You'll have no problem swapping books either. Most people, remember, spend all day on the beach reading!

WHERE TO STAY

Luxury (over US$35/Rs1000 per room night)
The prestige place to stay is the five-star **Kovalam Ashok Beach Resort** (tel 68010, 65323, tlx 435-216, fax 0471-62522), with its superb location, water-sports, yoga and massage facilities, but the standard of service and food fluctuates. The beach cottages are pleasant, but as the air-conditioning rarely works, are not recommended in the hotter months. The large balcony rooms from Rs1300 single, Rs1450 double in the low season and 25% higher between mid-December and the end of February, have the famous sunset view. A new wing opened in late 1992 and the old Palace guest-house on the hill above the resort has four suites from Rs2800.

Mid-range (US$10–35/Rs250–1000 per room night)
Try the well-appointed **Hotel Rockholm** (tel 584306) up on the lighthouse headland. This has some lovely, breezy rooms (Rs375 single, Rs450 double) overlooking the cliffs, and an excellent restaurant with open-air patio. KTDC's pleasant **Hotel Samudra**, (tel 62089) a 15-minute walk north of the luxury Ashok hotel, is a modern building, tastefully done, commanding a quiet stretch of beach. In season, it has a good restaurant on the roof. Rooms include Rs550 doubles, with balconies and sea views.

Budget (under Rs250 per room night)
Directly behind the Rockholm on Lighthouse Road, is **Syama Lodge** with huge, well-furnished rooms at Rs150 single, Rs200 double (half the price in low season). There are a few rooms from Rs250, with sea-view balconies, at **Hotel Seaweed**, near the lighthouse (tel 60806, 63452) and like all Kovalam's hotels you can bargain discounts of up to 50% in the low season (any time apart from November to February). At the budget end, there are now so many small, cheap, and generally

comfortable lodges, either right on the beach, or set just back from it that recommending any one over another is a difficult exercise: they're changing all the time. Many have rooms from Rs50 per night and it is also possible to rent rooms with local families for Rs250 a week.

EATING OUT

Kovalam has some excellent restaurants although some of the old favourites on the beach have been closed down. Good Italian, French, Chinese and Malabar dishes plus the local seafood are all just a short, lazy stroll up the beach. Two popular beach restaurants are the **Black Cat** and **Coral**. The **Rockholm** (tel 306) has excellent fish dishes, depending on what's available that morning in the market. While the menu includes some European dishes it is their seafood that excels. Lobster, crab, mackerel can be prepared to order. Meals cost anything from Rs60 to 250 a head depending on how many dishes of crab curry you can eat. The **Searock** restaurant has a menu of Indian and continental dishes and meals are from about Rs50. No restaurant is in a hurry to serve you in Kovalam. If the laid-back service gets to you, eat out at the **Rockholm** or the **Eden**.

GENERAL INFORMATION

The nearest tourist office is in Trivandrum. So is Indian Airlines, State Bank of India, and the post office. To change money, use the bank at Kovalam Ashok Beach Resort. To post letters, buy aerogrammes, etc., use the small sub post-office in Kovalam Village (a 20-minute climb up the back of the beach, near the top of the headland).

QUILON

The gateway to Kerala's beautiful backwaters, Quilon is situated on the edge of the Ashtamudi Lake, 'lake of eight creeks', amid luxuriant coconut groves and cashew plantations. It is an ancient commercial centre, used by the Phoenicians, Persians, Greeks, Romans, Arabs and the Chinese. Even today, you can see the Chinese fishing nets, more commonly associated with Cochin further north dotted round the lakes here. Quilon city, established in the 9th century, is associated with the origin of the Malayalam-era 'Kollavarsham', which began in AD 825. In more recent times, its commercial wealth made it a bone of contention between Portuguese, Dutch and English trading interests. Today, it is just a sleepy market-town of red-tiled wooden houses and winding backstreets, an interesting study of a typical Keralan township. But few people linger here more than a day and the big attraction in these parts are the famous backwaters, best visited from December to February. By March, the heat and the mosquitoes are oppressive.

WHAT TO SEE

Arriving in Quilon, go straight to the boat jetty, a minute's walk below the bus-stand, to check the departure time of the morning backwaters' boat. You'll need to arrive early to get a seat. Use any free time in Quilon to stroll around the pretty town, or to visit **Thangasseri Beach** (3 km; 2 miles) for its sands, lighthouse and Portuguese/Dutch fort ruins. For a short while Thangasseri was a British trading outpost.

Kuttanadu Backwaters are unforgettable. The 8½-hour boat journey takes you from narrow canals canopied by dense foliage out into large inland lagoons framed by dense tropical palm groves. Fishermen stand waist-high in the waters and cast their nets. Families of river-dwellers pass by in narrow punted dugouts. Wooden vessels with primitive Chinese sails drift up the waterways, stately and silent. Children run down from Portuguese churches and schools to welcome your approach. In the lush season (February), the boat carves a plough through canals carpeted with blossoming water-hyacinths and lichen. At sunset, you chug into Alleppey along a corridor of gently swaying coco-palms, backing onto brilliant-green meadows. The trip is a perfect delight. Take plenty of camera film (the views cry out to be photographed) and lots of food, because there are only two stops, at about 1 pm and 4 pm, for local thalis. Try to get a berth on the boat roof; you're generally allowed up, depending on the mood of the crew, a short while after departure from Quilon. A couple of rupees baksheesh may be in order, but it's well worth it.

WHERE TO STAY
In Quilon, there's the popular **Government Guest House** (tel 76456), a former British Residency with lovely gardens and charming rooms from Rs100. It has pleasant Keralan-style food and a useful jetty with boat-hire from 10 am to 4 pm daily. Rickshaws run out here from Quilon jetty or rail station. The more central **Hotel Sudarshan**, Parameswar Nagar, 10 minutes' walk up from jetty (tel 75322, tlx 0886-292 HSN IN) has single rooms at Rs200, doubles at Rs250 and is a good place to eat. There's similar quality at **Hotel Karthika**, Paikada St (tel 76240, tlx 0886-284) with ordinary rooms from Rs35 single, Rs60 double, and five air-conditioned rooms at around Rs175. All hotels have a problem with mosquitoes, so bring lots of repellent.

EATING OUT
For good Indian, Chinese and continental food, try the **Hotel Sudarshan** (two restaurants, plus air-con bar); for cheaper vegetarian meals, visit the **Hotel Guru Prasad** on Main St. For a big breakfast before the boat trip (you may not eat again all day) try **Mahalaxshmi Lodge** opposite the bus-stand. The **Indian Coffee House** on Main Street is good for snacks and coffee.

GENERAL INFORMATION
There is a tourist information desk at the Government Guest House (tel 76456). The post office and Bank of India are both at the top of Parameswar Nagar, 1 km (2/3 mile) above the bus-stand. Boats can also be hired from the **Quilon Boat Club** (tel 72519) or through the tourist office.

ALLEPPEY

Another small market town, Alleppey's curious maze of bridges and canals has earned it the title 'Venice of the East'. The centre of Kerala's famous coir products: mainly yarn, mats and rope, it is otherwise unremarkable. It comes to life once a year, for the spectacular Nehru Cup Snake Boat Race, held on the second Saturday of August.

WHAT TO SEE

For travellers, Alleppey is simply a jumping-off point for another amazing trip up the Keralan waterways. Many find the shorter 2½-hour journey from here to Kottayam far more satisfactory than the preceding trip from Quilon: you don't tend to get jaded with the scenery.

Furthermore, being so near to the extensive Vembanad Lake stretching north to Cochin, Alleppey is a major centre of inland water transport, so there's a good deal more to see on the lakes. It's a very scenic run, with many country craft, laden with coir goods and cashew, gliding up the canals. Also some lovely inland lagoons, fringed by thin green necklaces of vegetation. The narrower stretches of water are often covered with a purple-green blanket of blossoming water-lilies. The final approach into Kottayam is down picturesque avenues of lush tropical trees.

There are a number of boats leaving for Kottayam daily. But for maximum comfort and superior scenery, an early morning or mid-afternoon departure is best.

WHERE TO STAY

Alleppey Prince Hotel (tel 3752, tlx 0883-202) has flexible rates; do not hesitate to bargain. Situated on A.S. Rd, a long 2 km (1¼ miles) from the town centre it works hard for custom. Touts selling this hotel board your boat just as it drifts into Alleppey. Rooms are from Rs325 single and Rs400 double. The Prince has a swimming-pool, a superb restaurant and a boat.

The **Komala** (tel 3631), opposite the jetty has clean rooms and a good restaurant. The old travellers' haunt, **St George's Lodge** (tel 3373), in C.C.N.B. Rd has rooms from Rs40, and it's useful for money-exchange (Canara Bank is in St George's Buildings), but the food is quite bad. **Kerala Hotel**, across the bridge from the jetty, has cleaner rooms with bathrooms attached at Rs50 single.

EATING OUT

Far and away the best place for food, drink and relaxation is the **Indian Coffee House**, 1.5 km (⅔ mile) south of the boat jetty, near Hotel Ashoka, with Raj-style waiters and decor, cheap non-vegetarian food and excellent coffee. For good Rs5 thalis, try **Vijaya Restaurant** in Jetty Rd. Otherwise, check out the inexpensive vegetarian places near Raja Tourist Home. The **Arun Restaurant** at the Komala Hotel is considered by some the best in Alleppey.

KOTTAYAM

Of principal interest as a jump-off point to nearby Periyar Wildlife Sanctuary, Kottayam is a prosperous commercial town, famous for its cash crops of rubber, tea, pepper and cardamom. In the old days it was developed as an educational centre by English missionaries, while even earlier it was patronised by St Thomas (1st century AD). The descendants of some of the wealthy Brahmins he converted later helped build some lovely old churches here, including **Vallia Palli Church** some 5 km (3 miles) north-west of the railway station. It is notable for its Pahlavi inscriptions and for its Nestorian cross, which is said to have come from St Thomas's original church at Cranganore. Kottayam is an important centre for Syrian Christians in Kerala, as well as being the place where many of Kerala's leading newspapers are published.

WHERE TO STAY
Stay at either the **Anjali Hotel**, K.K. Rd (tel 3661-6, tlx 888-212 ANJL IN) with clean, comfy air-conditioned rooms for Rs245 single, Rs300 double; or the off-beat **Tourist Bungalow**, a tricky but rewarding 15-minute walk/climb from the boat jetty. It offers spacious double rooms (originally British officers' quarters) with period furnishings for just Rs50. The **Hotel Greenpark**, Nagampadam (tel 3331) has rooms from Rs195 single, Rs225 double. Twelve km (7½ miles) from Kottayam, on the shores of the Vembanad Lake is the KTDC **Kumarakom Tourist Complex** (tel 258), an old building in extensive grounds. The woodland and lake attract extensive bird life and rooms in the complex are Rs 70 single, Rs85 double.

PERIYAR (THEKKADY)

The Periyar Wildlife Sanctuary (Tiger Reserve) at Thekkady is one of the main sanctuaries of southern India and one of the largest in India. Comprising 777 sq km (300 sq miles) of lush, tropical forest, with a vast artificial lake in the centre, it is the natural habitat of an extensive range of wildlife. The huge Periyar Lake, measuring 24 sq km (¼ sq mile) in area, was formed in 1895, with the completion of the Periyar Dam by the British government in Madras. Its original purpose was irrigation, but its conservation potential was soon recognised.

The first game warden was appointed in 1923, the area was constituted a sanctuary in 1934, and it came under **Project Tiger** management in 1978. The rapid decrease in the population of tigers (from 40 000 at the turn of the century to just 1830 in 1972) led to the creation of Project Tiger, and the immediate management of 7 parks. Eighteen now come under the Project, and the tiger population had increased to 4334 in 1989, 48 of them at Periyar.

Situated at a high altitude of between 914 m and 1828 m Periyar has a comfortably cool climate between November and January. But to see the wildlife at close quarters, it is best to come during the 'dry' months of February to June, when the animals, deprived of the forest water-holes, come to water down by the lake.

WHAT TO SEE
Periyar has a rich variety of wildlife, notably leopard, gaur, wild dog, sambar, wild boar, monkey, and a few Malabar flying squirrels, among many mammal species. It is especially good for observing the Indian wild elephant. The extensive bird life to be seen includes heron, hornbill, jungle fowl, kingfisher and egret. The forests are dense jungles of creepers, spices and blossoming trees interspersed with some grassland.

Sanctuary Tour (by tour boat, ½-day)

To see the wildlife to best advantage, take the early 7 am boat onto Periyar Lake (Rs10 tickets from the Wildlife Office, above jetty). This is your best chance to see elephants, bison, deer and, sometimes, tiger at close quarters; they come to water only very early in the morning, and in the late afternoon. You will not see many animals taking a boat out at any other time of day. At weekends, a motorboat full of tourists will send most animals on the banks scurrying for cover, so you may be better off hiring a private launch, from the Wildlife Office at about Rs60 per hour.

The boat tour lasts 1½ hours, and is a useful introduction to the sanctuary's flora and fauna. To follow up, it is necessary to explore the surrounding forests on foot. The Wildlife Office runs 3-hour 'forest group treks' (Rs20 per person) which if the group is small and disciplined is worthwhile. These walks are often good for bird-watching. Some people, disregarding the injunction not to wander into the forest unescorted, report alarming experiences, returning with tales of unexpected eyeball encounters with bull elephants. The wisest course is to hire a private guide from the Wildlife Office (Rs20) who'll take you to the best hides in complete safety, enabling close sightings of elephants, bison, snakes, monkeys and a rich array of bird life.

Other possible activities include elephant-rides, bookable from the Wildlife Office. Cycling is very pleasant in this region, and bikes can be hired in Kumily but cannot be used in the park.

Persuade the wildlife officer at Periyar that you're not a typical tourist, that you've come here specifically to study wildlife, and he may just let you stay at one of the observation watchtowers. These stand in the heart of the forest, on stilts, and elephants come to rest in their shade. To get to them, you take the tour boat out onto the lake, then walk a couple of miles into the jungle along with the park ranger. Since there are only two watchtowers available, it's worth booking 3/4 days in advance. Secondly, since these observation huts are poorly equipped, you need to buy in supplies. A flashlight, drinking water and mosquito repellent are essential.

WHERE TO STAY

Mid-range (US$10–35/Rs250–1000 per room night)
The **Government Rest House** in the forest has three rooms from Rs200 single to Rs300 double. Check availability with the tourist office in Kumily. The plush **Lake Palace** (tel Kumily 24) is an island bungalow with nice gardens, a prime lake-shore situation, in the heart of the park, and pleasant rooms at Rs450 single, Rs600 double. **Aranya Nivas Hotel** (tel Kumily 23) is a fair fall-back with dodgy food, but good facilities. Rooms face the lake, and are reasonably priced at Rs150 single and Rs200 double. Both can be advance-booked through the KTDC office in Trivandrum (tel 61132).

If staying in the nearby village of Kumily (a short bike-ride from Thekkady; 3 km 1⅔ miles from the lake), stay at **Spice Village** a new resort with well-furnished cottages from Rs 600 single, Rs800 double (book through the Casino Hotel, Cochin tel 340221, tlx 0885-6314, fax 0484-340001).

Budget (under Rs250 per room night)
Budget places include the **Lake Queen Tourist Home** opposite the tourist office (Rs50 single, Rs80 double), or **Hotel Vanarani** (tel Kumily 71) with excellent Rs75 singles, Rs100 doubles, and a dormitory. The Lake Queen has some nice 1st-floor rooms with views of the hills, but guests complain of the alarming 6.30 am 'breakfast calls'. The Vanarani arranges boating, sightseeing, trekking, elephant-rides, and has a marvellous restaurant. The Ambadi (tel 11) at the checkpost, near the sanctuary entrance,

offers well-furnished, homely cottages at Rs100 double, also 4-bed dormitory accommodation.

EATING OUT
The best eating places are in Kumily. **Hotel Vanarani** offers a fine range of south Indian cuisine, very cheaply; **Hotel Paris** is the best for Western food, with quick service; and **Hotel Ambadi** often lays on displays of Kathakali dance in its popular open-air restaurant. All the hotel restaurants are open to non-residents.

GENERAL INFORMATION
Kumily tourist office is located at the top of the main street, opposite Lake Queen Hotel. When open, it dispenses boat-trip tickets, maps and walking/trekking permits. The Wildlife Preservation Office (tel 27) is at Periyar, overlooking the boat jetty.

COCHIN

Cochin is one of Kerala's most beautiful places. A lagoon of islands and peninsulas separated by the backwaters of the Arabian Sea, connected by bridges and ferries. It comprises the mainland town of **Ernakulam**, the southern peninsula of **Fort Cochin and Mattancherry**, and the islands of **Willingdon**, **Bolghatty**, **Gundu** and **Vypeen**. The scenic setting of its famous natural harbour, surrounded by palm groves, green fields, inland lakes and backwaters, has earned it the title 'Queen of the Arabian Sea'
Cochin has a rich maritime history, and still ships Kerala's coir, rubber, seafood and pepper products off to foreign ports. Influenced at various times by the Arabs, the Chinese, the Dutch, the British and the Portuguese, it was Cochin's Jews who founded the first strong community here, over 1000 years ago. Seized for the Portuguese by Vasco da Gama in 1502, the port was also the first European settlement

Kathakali dancer

in India. Lured by its spices and ivory, the Dutch arrived (1602) and displaced the Portuguese (1663). In 1795 Cochin passed into British hands. All of these conquerors left their mark, and present-day Fort Cochin/Mattancherry is a curious pot-pourri of Jewish synagogues, Chinese fishing-nets, Portuguese churches, Dutch palaces and British cricket greens. The atmosphere is perceptibly Mediterranean. But the climate is sub-tropical; hot and sticky for much of the year. The official season is October to March, but for comfort visit in December or January.

ARRIVAL/DEPARTURE

Air
Cochin airport (Willingdon Island) is 6 km (3¾ miles) from Ernakulam town centre, a Rs30 taxi-ride, or Rs1 by bus (to or from Ernakulam's Kallor city bus-stand, just above Ernakulam Town railway station).

Indian Airlines flies 3 times daily between Cochin and Bombay (Rs2026). There are also flight connections with Bangalore (Rs842), Delhi (Rs3757), Dabolim in Goa (Rs1313), Madras (Rs1325) and Trivandrum (Rs525). East West Airlines operates a daily flight to and from Bombay (Rs2026).

Rail
Ernakulam has two rail stations—Ernakulam Junction and Ernakulam Town—both some 2.5 km (1½ miles) from the main boat jetty. Ernakulam Junction is easier to deal with: the Area Manager here (office open 10 am–5pm) may be able to get you tickets at short notice, if you've failed to advance-book. There are daily trains to Kottayam, Quilon, Bangalore, Trivandrum, Bombay and New Delhi. For Ooty, take the daily 9.25 am *Tea Garden Express*.

Road
Buses for Alleppey and Trivandrum (regular), Quilon (one express bus daily), Thekkady (6.30 am and 8.15 am buses, 6 hours), Kottayam (regular, 2 hours), Bangalore (few Interstate express buses, 15 hours) and Madurai (regular, but 8.15 am is best; 10 hours; superb scenery) all leave from the KSRTDC bus-stand in Ernakulam.

WHAT TO SEE
Fort Cochin and Mattancherry have the historical sites; modern Ernakulam has the bus and rail stations, the hotels, shops and restaurants; Willingdon Island is the site of the airport, the two top hotels, and the tourist office; Bolghatty has its famous palace hotel; and Gundu its interesting coir factory. Most travellers stay in Ernakulam. It may be a busy, unrelaxing commercial centre, but it's certainly the best base for sightseeing. All Cochin's islands are linked by a regular ferry service, operating from Ernakulam's three jetties. The main jetty charges Rs1 for trips over to Willingdon, Vypeen, Vallarpadam and Fort Cochin (*either* to Chinese Fishing Nets, *or* to Dutch Palace) islands. The High Court jetty, at the top of Shanmugham Rd, has ferries to Bolghatty island. And the Sealord jetty, near Sealord Hotel, is the venue for twice-daily KSTDC boat trips round *all* the islands (see General Information below). These latter excursions are an excellent way of covering Cochin's many sights in a single day.

To get around Ernakulam itself, you have a choice of auto-rickshaws, which don't use meters (establish your fare in advance) or taxis.

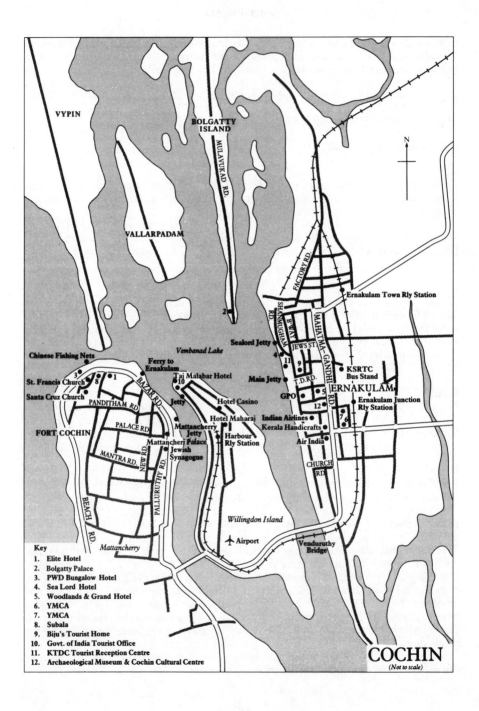

Key
1. Elite Hotel
2. Bolgatty Palace
3. PWD Bungalow Hotel
4. Sea Lord Hotel
5. Woodlands & Grand Hotel
6. YMCA
7. YMCA
8. Subala
9. Biju's Tourist Home
10. Govt. of India Tourist Office
11. KTDC Tourist Reception Centre
12. Archaeological Museum & Cochin Cultural Centre

COCHIN
(Not to scale)

If staying at Fort Cochin, which has limited but pleasant accommodation, the most enjoyable way of getting round is by cycle. There are several bike-hire places, charging around Rs10 per day.

Cochin Islands Tour (conducted tour boat, half-day)
Mattancherry Palace–Jewish Synagogue–Chinese Fishing-nets–
St Francis Church–Santa Cruz Church–Bolghatty Palace–Gundu Island

Get a sun-deck seat aboard the 9.30 am KTDC sightseeing boat leaving daily from Sealord jetty. (This is cooler than the 1.30 pm departure.) The tour passes by Willingdon Island, off which are moored giant cargo ships loaded with fertiliser, chemicals and palm oil, and makes its first stop at **Mattancherry Palace** in Fort Cochin. Presently administered by the Archaeological Survey of India, this large white, red-roofed structure has an interesting history. Built by the Portuguese around 1555 and presented to Raja Veera Kerala Varma (1537–61) as a goodwill token in exchange for trading rights. It was later renovated by the Dutch in 1663 and gained the misnomer of the 'Dutch Palace'. An interesting combination of Kerala and Dutch building styles, it stands in a walled garden enclosure fronted by a tank, backing onto mango groves and three Hindu temples. The palace is built on two floors and around a central quadrangle. Inside the palace, see the large central Durbar Hall, where the Cochin royal family held their coronation ceremonies. Here you'll find an assortment of their palanquins, weapons, dresses and turbans. The adjacent series of royal bedrooms and other chambers have some fine murals. Covering a wall area of nearly 305 m, the 45 murals date from the 17th century and depict scenes from the *Ramayana* epic, also the Puranic legends relating to Shiva, Vishnu, Krishna, Kumara and Durga. Vigorous, fresh and delightfully sensual; one can't help but notice Shiva's eight arms busily at work on eight grateful handmaidens. Unfortunately you cannot photograph them without permission from the Archaeological Survey, and there are no books or postcards for sale. The Dutch Palace is open 10 am–5 pm daily, except Friday.

Just a few hundred yards south is the oldest **Jewish Synagogue** in the Commonwealth. The present structure was built in 1568, destroyed by the Portuguese in 1662, rebuilt by the Dutch in 1664, and donated its distinctive clock tower by Ezekiel Rahabi, a wealthy Jewish trader, in the mid-18th century. He also provided its exquisite willow-pattern floor tiles, each handpainted in a different design, brought over from Canton in 1776. The synagogue interior is fascinating: 19th-century Belgian chandeliers, interlocking pews, a ladies' gallery, and a superbly crafted brass pulpit. The curator, Jacky Cohen, shows visitors around and gives full information. He can also sometimes be prevailed upon to show the synagogue's two most prized treasures: the Great Scrolls of the Old Testament, and the copperplate grants of privilege made by the Cochin Maharajahs (962–1020) to the Jewish merchant Joseph Rabban. Nowadays, the place has a rather empty feel: all but 27 of Cochin's Jews have left; many have migrated to Israel. The Synagogue is open 10 am–noon, 3–5 pm, daily except Saturday. Admission is Rs1.

The tour boat proceeds to the northern tip of Fort Cochin, where huge, cantilevered fishing-nets proclaiming the ancient trade connections with China are ranged along the water's edge like a string of filigree lace handkerchieves. Probably introduced by traders from the court of Kublai Khan, these fascinating nets are still an efficient method of fishing. While not unique to Cochin, the nets flanking the opening to the harbour are perhaps the best place in Kerala to see them at work.

A short walk below the nets is **St Francis Church**, believed to be the first European church to be built in India. The original structure, presumably built by Portuguese Franciscan friars in 1503, was of wood. Later, during the mid-16th century, it was rebuilt in stone. Over the years it has experienced a number of 'conversions' from Catholic Portuguese, to Protestant Dutch, to Anglican before achieving its present status as the Church of south India. The exterior is notable for its impressive façade, and there's an array of interesting Portuguese and Dutch tombstones including that of Vasco Da Gama, who died here in 1524 although his body was taken to Portugal 14 years later. Should you wish to leave the tour at this point, a short walk inland brings you to **Santa Cruz Cathedral**. This is a Roman Catholic structure, built in 1557, with a brilliantly-painted interior. Nearby, locals play polite games of cricket on the Surrey-style village green. Beyond this, walking up Calvetty St, you'll find a medieval settlement of pastel houses, 16th-century Portuguese bastions and narrow alleys, and still more Catholic churches.

The tour continues on to **Bolghatty Island**, to visit the **Bolghatty Palace Hotel**. Set in 15 acres of lush green lawns, this palatial structure started life as a Dutch palace, built 1744, and later became home of the British Resident to the Rajah of Cochin after 1799. Presently run as a hotel by the Kerala Tourism Development Corporation (KTDC), it has a golf course, a bar and a restaurant. From here, it's just a short chug across the harbour to **Gundu Island** (look out for leaping dolphins), for shopping at its small **Coir Factory**. Here a busy co-operative workers' society produce doormats handwoven from rough coconut fibre (coir) (Rs50–200). The weaving process is worth seeing.

Back in Ernakulam, off the boat, it's a short walk to Durbar Hall Rd for **Parishath Thamburan Museum** in the old Durbar Hall. This has 19th-century paintings, copies of murals, old coins, delicate chandeliers, sculptures, musical instruments and lovely chinaware. The main attraction is the collection drawn from the Cochin royal family treasury. Open 9.30 am–12 pm, 3–5.30 pm daily, except Mondays.

RECREATION
No visit to Cochin is complete without seeing a performance of **Kathakali**, the famous dance-drama of Kerala. Kathakali started out some 2000 years ago as a temple art-form, depicting themes from the *Ramayana* and *Mahabharata* epics. More an elaborate sequence of yogic exercises than a dance-form, Kathakali may seem slow and stylised compared to say, Bharatnatyam, but it has a grace and a charm all of its own. A unique 'language' of 24 separate gestures has evolved over the centuries, any combination of which conveys a definite meaning. The eyes are especially important, suggesting an immense range of differing moods and emotions. The costumes, wigs and masks used are bright and flamboyant, all made from natural materials. Make-up is distinctive with several layers of paint being applied to the dancer's face to accentuate lips, eyebrows and eyelashes. The overall effect is highly dramatic.

At present, Cochin has three Kathakali dance companies. They are **Cochin Cultural Centre** (tel 353732), Durbar Hall Ground, D.H. Rd; **See India Foundation** (tel 369471), Kalathiparambil Lane; and **Art Kerala** at Ravipuram Rd. All three places charge the same (Rs30, pay at the door), and shows start at either 6.30 pm (Cultural Centre) or 7 pm (See India and Art Kerala). Turn up early to see the dancers applying make-up backstage which you can photograph, and bring mosquito coils to place under your chair. Of the three, the Cultural Centre has the best reputation, though Art Kerala puts on a wide range of Keralan dances (not just Kathakali), and See India gives the fullest, clearest explanations preceding each dance.

Other recreations include golf (9-hole course, Rs40 green fees include caddy, balls and clubs) and horse-riding at Bolghatty Palace Hotel; and English films in air-conditioned comfort at the **Sridhar** cinema, near the KSTDC reception centre in Shanmugham Rd.

The cool air-conditioned **Devi** cinema (Cochin's best) in Mahatma Gandhi Road, Ernakulam, is the ideal escape on hot, sticky afternoons. So is the swimming-pool at the Malabar Hotel on Willingdon Island, open to non-residents (except Tuesday and Friday) for a daily charge of Rs50.

SHOPPING
Buy teas, spices (ginger, turmeric, cardamom, cumin and cloves) and cashew-nuts along the roadside leading down to Ernakulam main market. Because these pavement vendors sell their produce in the open, they can't (unlike shops) adulterate them. Another good place to buy the famous Cochin spices at local prices is **Grand Bazaar** supermarket, at Abad Plaza Hotel in M.G. Rd. For fabrics, rosewood, walnut, Kathakali props and masks, and assorted jewellery, try the various emporia and shops along M.G. and Broadway roads.

WHERE TO STAY

Luxury (over US$35/Rs1000 per room night)
The two top hotels are on **Willingdon Island** near to the airport. The **Taj Malabar Hotel** (tel 340010, tlx 885-6767 TAJN IN, fax 0484-340297) has an excellent location on the north-western promontory of the island, overlooking Mattancherry and the Chinese fishing-nets, with good first-floor balcony rooms in the original building, a nice swimming-pool, and the Government of India tourist office on your doorstep. Rooms are from US$75. The **Casino Hotel** (tel 340221, tlx 885-6314, fax 0484-340001) has air-conditioned singles from US$38, doubles from US$50, a brand-new pool, informal (yet stylish) ambience, and two excellent restaurants. Both hotels have been recently renovated.

Mid-range (US$10–35/Rs250–1000 per room night)
Over on Bolghatty Island, the KTDC **Bolghatty Palace** (tel 355003) is a rather run–down Raj-style hotel with large grounds, good recreational facilities, and lots of character. The massive old-wing rooms are not air-conditioned (single Rs165, double Rs220), while the newer air-con rooms (Rs340 single, Rs400 double) are not so attractive. The cottages down by the water's edge (Rs385 single, Rs600 double) are often plagued by mosquitoes.

In Ernakulam, stay at **Sea Lord Hotel**, Shanmugham Rd (tel 352682, tlx 0885-6643 TOUR IN) with air-conditioned singles from Rs350, doubles from Rs475. The hotel has a good roof-top restaurant. **Hotel Presidency**, Paramara Road (tel 363100, tlx 885-6201) has air-conditioned rooms from Rs450 single, Rs650 double. **Hotel Abad Plaza** (tel 361636, tlx 885-6587, fax 0484-369729) on M.G. Rd has comfy singles and doubles for Rs350 and Rs500 respectively and is well-located with seafood restaurant and attached supermarket.

A new **Gateway Hotel** overlooking the harbour and near the KTDC office in Ernakulam is due to open in 1993.

Budget (under US$10/Rs250 per room night)
Woodlands Hotel (tel 361372), also on M.G. Rd, has rooms from Rs165 single, Rs250 double. It's a reasonably clean hotel, if tacky, with air-con veg restaurant and ice-cream parlour. Many budget travellers enjoy **Biju's Tourist Home** in Market Rd, opposite the main jetty (tel 369881), with a friendly and informative management and bright, spacious rooms just Rs50 single, Rs80 double. There are also a few air-conditioned rooms at Rs150. As a second string, try Hotel Luciya in Stadium Rd, next to the bus-stand (tel 354433). Rooms cost from Rs80.

In Fort Cochin, the **Hotel Sea Gull** (tel 28128) in Calvetty Rd has a pleasant location between the two ferry stops, overlooking the harbour, and nice air-conditioned singles and doubles from Rs200 and Rs250 respectively. The restaurant and bar are very popular. Facing the Chinese fishing-nets, there's KTDC's **Subala**, a nice friendly place with cheap restaurant, helpful staff and comfy rooms at Rs50 single, Rs75 double. It's very convenient for the boat jetty and bus-stand. Other decent cheap lodgings are **PWD Tourist Rest Home** near the beach (spacious, spartan rooms at Rs80) and **Hotel Elite** near St Francis Church, with decent Rs60 double rooms on the ground floor but grim rooms upstairs.

EATING OUT
On Willingdon Island, Casino Hotel has one of the most prestigious eateries in town, a seafood speciality restaurant called **Fort Cochin**. Service and food are excellent, and the lobsters unbelievably large. An average meal including dessert comes to around Rs200 per head. The Casino's other restaurant, the multi-cuisine **Tharavadu** features a daily lunch buffet for Rs120 and live music performances nightly. The Taj Malabar's **Rice Boats** prepares some excellent Malabar food from Rs250 per head.

In Ernakulam, there's a wide choice of eating places. **Sealord Hotel** has a popular air-conditioned restaurant, with tasty Indian/continental food at around Rs40 per dish. For fast food and superb North Indian fare, try **Pandhal Restaurant** opposite Woodlands Hotel on M.G. Rd. This is a relaxing air-con place, with good lunchtime specials; thalis and Kerala-style curries from Rs18, 12 noon–3 pm daily, except Sundays. For seafood, try the Rs50 buffet lunch (12 to 3 pm) at **Abad Plaza Hotel**, which serves squid, lobster and prawns in Ernakulam. At **Subhiksha**, the stylish vegetarian restaurant attached to B.T.H. Hotel in D.H. Rd, you can enjoy amazing lunchtime thalis for about Rs25 and incredibly cheap south Indian food with most dishes only Rs8 in air-conditioned comfort. Next door, there's a popular little coffee shop. Ernakulam has two **Indian Coffee Houses**; one opposite the main jetty in Cannon Shed Rd, the other below the rail station in M.G. Rd, which do good cheap breakfasts. Two reliable Chinese restaurants are **Malaya** on Bannerjee Rd, and **Golden Dragon** opposite Park Hotel. Chinese food is also available at the Sealord's roof-top restaurant and The Hotel Presidency. Two good bakeries are **Cochin Bakery** opposite Woodlands Hotel, and **Ceylon Bake House** near the tourist office on the Broadway.

In Fort Cochin, **Hotel Seagull** is good for non-vegetarian food, doughnuts and porridge, and KTDC's **Subala** has a nice breezy restaurant by the water, with cheap if unimaginative meals. The best treats are still at **Hotel Elite's** famous Parisian-style café. This has patisseries, fancy cakes and refrigerated cheese.

GENERAL INFORMATION
The Government of India Tourist Office, Malabar Hotel, Willingdon Island (tel 340352, tlx 885-6847) is open 9 am–5 pm weekdays, 9 am–12 noon Saturday, closed Sunday. It still enjoys the reputation of being the 'best tourist office in India'; hires out good approved guides (Rs50 half-day, Rs80 full-day) and the staff are invariably helpful. KTDC's Tourist Reception Centre, near Ernakulam jetty (Shanmugham Rd, tel 353234) is open 8 am–6 pm daily, and sells the boat tours (9.30 am–1 pm, or 1.30–5 pm; Rs20) round Cochin and its islands. It also sells Jaico's monthly *Timetable*; an excellent little publication with up-to-date city information and local air/rail/bus timings.

All useful tourist addresses are in Ernakulam: Indian Airlines at Durbar Hall Rd (tel 353901, 353826, apt 364433), East West Airlines tel (361632, 355342, apt 340041). The main post office in Hospital Rd (8 am–8 pm Mon–Sat, 10 am–6 pm Sun). There is a useful travel agent for bus/rail reservations at Woodlands Hotel on M.G. Rd (tel 351372) (9 am–7.30 pm).

Route 13—Empires of the South

The Muslim conquest of India in the 13th and 14th centuries moved the power-centres of the south up to the Deccan. Present day Andhra Pradesh, is a historic land of temples and mosques, combining the age-old traditions of the south with the Muslim cultural heritage of Western and Central Asia. **Hyderabad**, modern capital of the state, took over from Golconda, ancient capital of the Qutb Shahid kings, as the symbol of Muslim imperialism in the south. Today, it boasts glorious palaces and mosques, peaceful lakes and picnic spots, and the most outstanding zoological park in India.

The modern state of Karnataka comprises large parts of the princely state of Mysore, the Berar territories of the erstwile Nizam of Hyderabad's kingdom and a few areas that were controlled by the British. The area was unified in the 1950s on the basis of common language; in this case Kannada. In Karnataka, the Hindu kingdom of Vijayanagar resisted the Deccan Sultans for 200 years, before being overpowered in 1565. Its capital was **Hampi**, perhaps the finest and certainly the largest complex of ruins in the country today. In earlier centuries the area was the seat of powerful dynasties like the Kadambas, Hoysalas, Chalukyas and Vijayanagars. Under British influence in the 19th century the cool garden city of Bangalore was developed.

South of Karnataka are the Nilgiri hills; although in Tamil Nadu they are best reached from Bangalore and Mysore. In these hills, Ootacamund (Ooty) and Coonoor became summer resorts of the Raj. Ornate palaces, glorious parks and beautiful buildings appeared, often sponsored by local princes and maharajahs, and reflecting the might of empire. **Bangalore**, once a staid cantonment city, became the glorious 'Garden City of the South', and then a booming commercial capital of cinemas, restaurants, night clubs and fun activities. **Mysore**, famous 'City of Incense', gained the spectacular Maharajah's Palace and numerous public buildings, a magnificent zoo, and the famous Brindhavan Gardens. The lovely hill station of **Ootacamund**, bordering Karnataka and Tamil Nadu states, gained its large, scenic lake, its botanical gardens, and the coveted title 'Queen of the South'.

For relaxed, sophisticated elegance, away from the usual heat of the Indian plains, this route provides the perfect introduction to the south.

Bangalore is the most convenient base from which to see this lovely area. However, transport is such in the region that the city will inevitably become a base for excursions to the neighbouring places of interest, rather than a jumping-off point for a route. The travel itinerary on p.471 makes your options clear. Hyderabad, although central in terms of influence and importance, is relatively isolated and should be visited separately at the beginning or end of your trip round the empires of the south. But whatever you do, don't miss it out.

Season: October–April.
Monsoon: June–October.
Climate: 26°–35°C (summer); 14°–25°C (winter).
    Ootacamund: 12°–16°C (year round).
Route duration: 7–15 days.

HYDERABAD

Now capital of Andhra Pradesh, Hyderabad is a beautiful city surrounded by lakes of great charm and tranquillity, and is itself sometimes known as 'The Lake'. It was founded in the late-16th century by the Qutb Shahi dynasty, a line of Muslim rulers famed for their magnificent monuments and mosques. The city was laid out in 1591 by Mohammed Quli when Golconda, the fortress city from which the Muslim rulers had ruled their Hindu subjects since 1512, fell prey to epidemics of plague and cholera, caused by poor water supplies. It was planned out on the grid system, and comprised two broad intersecting streets with the famous central Charminar Arch (described as the outstanding architectural monument of the Qutb Shahi period) at the crossing, and space for some 14 000 shops, schools, mosques and baths.

Successful trading in diamonds, pearls, printed fabrics and steel rapidly made Hyderabad one of the richest cities in India. Then, in 1650, the Mughal emperor Aurangzeb captured Golconda, and Hyderabad's short period of prosperity came to an abrupt end. Its importance as an administrative and financial centre declined, and the city fell into partial ruin. In the 18th century, with the disintegration of the Mughal empire, the Mughal Viceroys or Nizams of the Deccan seized power and in 1763 Hyderabad again became the capital of the area (under the Mughals, power had been wielded from Aurangabad). Commerce and construction rapidly resumed, and the city once more became a major business concern. The Nizams soon became some of the wealthiest individuals in the world, a position they maintained right up to, and for a decade beyond Independence in 1947.

Today, while Hyderabad, together with Bangalore, is the fastest-growing city in Asia, it has yet to find itself as a tourist centre. Its obvious attractions, its beautiful sights, good shopping, unique cuisine are largely offset by its remote location. But you can expect big changes in the near future. Hyderabad is rapidly equipping itself with tourist facilities, luxury hotels, better transport, shopping complexes, even a Rs100 *crore* Disneyland project around the Hussain Sagar lake—and is now patiently awaiting the expected boom.

Situated 610 m above sea-level, Hyderabad has a very equable climate through much of the year. The coolest (best) time to visit is from October to February. From March onwards, it is not so much the heat as the very dry air that has visitors reaching for the water bottle.

ARRIVAL/DEPARTURE
Indian Airlines offers daily flights between Hyderabad and Bangalore (Rs1083), Bombay (Rs1394), Calcutta (Rs2534), Delhi (Rs2362) and Madras (Rs1106); less frequent flight connections with Bhubaneshwar (Rs1796), Nagpur (Rs1054), Trivandrum (Rs2043) and Visakhapatnam (1129). Vayudoot connects Hyderabad with Pune.

Hyderabad's airport is some 10 km (6¼ miles) from the city centre; a Rs25 auto-rickshaw ride *if* you persuade your driver to set his meter to zero before setting off!

Rail
Trains to and from the south use Hyderabad Station while those from the north, the west and east use Secunderabad Station. This is where you will arrive if you come from Madras (510 km: 319 miles). For southern-bound trains to Bangalore (the 3 pm *Hyderabad-Bangalore Express*, arriving 7.30 am, is best) you can board at Hyderabad rail station in Abids area. Advance-reservation is essential for all long-hauls.

Road
From Hyderabad's central bus depot, Gowliguda Rd, there's one state bus daily to Madras (704 km; 15 hours) and to Bombay (739 km; 17 hours); plus 3/4 buses daily to Bangalore (566 km). The above destinations, together with places like Aurangabad (599 km) and Hospet, are also handled by private bus companies. You can and should advance-reserve seats.

WHAT TO SEE
Hyderabad is effectively two cities in one, though the new city of Secunderabad (to the north) is of minimal tourist interest. All the sights, the hotels, the action and the bazaars are concentrated in the Abids area of Hyderabad town, directly south of Hussain Sagar, and north of the Musi River.

The city itself is a busy, bustling and sprawling complex where new multi-storeyed buildings and wide modern streets contrast strongly with narrow medieval lanes and backstreets, and where the smoke of modern industrial factories meets the dust of busy roadside cottage workers, turning out some of India's finest handmade crafts. It is a friendly, active place, with a great deal to see and do.

But the traffic is suicidal. In the city centre, you need nerves of steel to get around on foot. 'Daydreaming is dangerous', cautions one traffic sign.

Hyderabad has overcrowded city buses, crazed auto-rickshaws which stop for absolutely nothing (Rs2.5 per km), and a few maniacal taxis (Rs5 per km, metered).

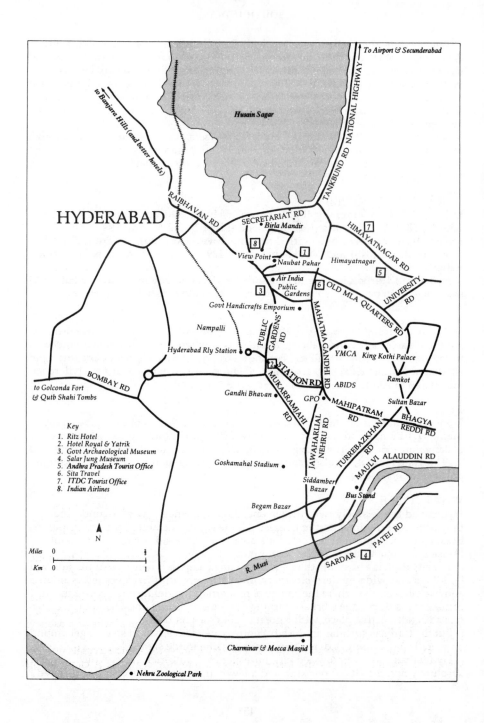

HYDERABAD

To Airport & Secunderabad

to Banjara Hills (and better hotels)

RAIBHAVAN RD

TANKBUND RD NATIONAL HIGHWAY

Husain Sagar

SECRETARIAT RD

● Birla Mandir

HIMAYATNAGAR RD

View Point

8

1

Naubat Pahar

7

Himayatnagar

5

● Air India

Public
Gardens

3

6

OLD MLA QUARTERS RD

UNIVERSITY RD

Govt Handicrafts Emporium ●

PUBLIC GARDENS RD

MAHATMA GANDHI RD

Nampalli

Hyderabad Rly Station

YMCA ●

King Kothi Palace

BOMBAY RD

2

STATION RD

ABIDS

Ramkot

to Golconda Fort
& Qutb Shahi Tombs

MUKARRAMIAHI RD

Gandhi Bhavan ●

GPO

MAHIPATRAM RD

Sultan Bazar

Key
1. Ritz Hotel
2. Hotel Royal & Yatrik
3. Govt Archaeological Museum
4. Salar Jung Museum
5. Andhra Pradesh Tourist Office
6. Sita Travel
7. ITDC Tourist Office
8. Indian Airlines

JAWAHARLAL NEHRU RD

TURREBAZKHAN RD

BHAGYA REDDI RD

MAULVI ALAUDDIN RD

Goshamahal Stadium ●

Siddamber
Bazar

Bus Stand

Begam Bazar

Miles 0

N

Km 0

1

R. Musi

SARDAR

PATEL RD

4

Charminar & Mecca Masjid

● Nehru Zoological Park

For worry-free travel, use the tourist taxi service offered by A.P. Travel & Tourism Dev. Corp., Gagan Vihar, Mukhram Jahi Rd (tel 556493, 556303) or your hotel. For out-of-town trips, cycling is pleasurable and cycles can be hired for Rs10–15 per day from several places; your hotel can advise). If biking around in town, make sure you have some decent insurance. City conducted tours are far too hurried, but they are a useful introduction and orientation. Then you should tour Hyderabad independently, allowing a minimum of 2 days for sightseeing and shopping. The traffic in the old city is often chaotic, and downright dangerous; ride wherever possible, and avoid walking across main roads. If you need a badge-carrying guide, contact A.P. Dept of Tourism, Lidcap Building, Himayatnagar (tel 223384, 223385).

Old City Tour (by auto-rickshaw/taxi, 4–6 hours)
Golconda–Mecca Masjid–Charminar–Salar Jung Museum–
Birla Mandir Temple–Birla Planetarium

Set out for **Golconda Fort** early in the morning. It lies 11 km (7 miles) west of Hyderabad, and takes about 40 minutes by rickshaw (Rs60–70 return, plus a waiting charge of Rs5 per hour while you sightsee). Going by taxi takes slightly less time but doubles the cost. The fort lies in a very dry, exposed situation, so wear a hat/scarf and long-sleeved shirts. There are about a dozen good English-speaking guides at the fort entrance. It's not a bad idea to establish their fee in writing before you set out; you can pay them more if they're worth it, which they usually are. The inner fort of Golconda is 25 km (16 miles) around, and you can tour its various palaces, audience rooms, baths, armoury and mosques comfortably in 1½ hours. If you wish to wander round on your own, buy the good little Golconda guide book with map, printed by Commercial Book Depot, Charminar, and available in many Hyderabad bookshops.

Golconda is the biggest fort in south India. It is made of solid limestone, and took several thousand labourers, working day and night, 62 years to build. Founded in the 13th century by the Kakatiyas of Warangal, it was originally just a small hilltop fort with mud walls. Its name derived from the words *Golla* meaning 'shepherd' and *Konda* meaning 'hill'. In 1512 it became the capital of the Persian Qutb Shahi kings, who expanded the original structure into a massive fort with battlements and crenellated walls of granite some 5 km (3 miles) in circumference. Like so many Indian forts, Golconda finally fell to treachery rather than to arms, a treacherous Qutb Shahi general letting the Mughal emperor Aurangzeb in the front ('victory') gate in 1687 after a siege lasting 8 months. Thereafter the legendary fort and its famous diamond market went into decline, and power passed to the new capital of Hyderabad.

Though partly in ruins today, this monumental fortress erected on a picturesque granite hill some 123 m high, and surrounded by three tiers of loopholed and battlemented ramparts, remains the major tourist attraction of the Hyderabad area. Of its eight original gates, four are still in use. They are studded with iron, some wrought into long, pointed spikes to deter elephant charges. The fort also has 87 semi-circular bastions, each 15.4 m high, and each built of huge blocks of masonry weighing several tons apiece.

Start your tour at the **Grand Portico** (entry gate). Here you'll come across its unique system of acoustics, one of the fortress's most interesting features. A clapping of hands in the centre porch can be heard at the fort's highest point, the Bala Hissar, 380 steep steps above. This device was contrived, it is believed, to convey any message regarding visitors to the topmost guards. Behind this echo chamber is a purple-blossomed tree, very popular with local people. They use its hard-wood bark for cleaning their teeth.

Your guide will take you up into the fort via the 'common passage', leading past the armoury on your left; the mortuary bath where dead royals had a ceremonial dip before being buried, to your right; and the bodyguard barracks, with adjoining two-storeyed building used by the court ministers Akkanna and Madanna, also to your left. An ascent of 360 steps now begins, leading up to the **Bara Dar** (General Assembly Hall). On the ascent you'll see various deep wells, water reservoirs and watering canals.

Halfway up, you reach the **Ramdas Kotha**, an old storehouse which became the 12-year prison of Abdul Hasan Tanah Shah's chief cashier, Ramdas. He was interred for dipping into official revenue to renovate a nearby temple. It's a dark, gloomy place, full of the handmade deities (Ram, Lakshman, Hanuman) and faded carvings/paintings of animals and plants which the bored Ramdas made to fill in his time.

Past the jail, and just above the **Barood Kotha** (gunpowder store), there's a charming little Hindu temple cut into a large natural boulder the shape of a Nandi bull. A little further up is the simple, elegant **Mosque** of the royal family, built by the third king of the dynasty, Ibrahim Quli Qutb Shah in 1550. In those days, the king prayed in the mosque and his Hindu chief minister in the small rock-cut temple below; it was an age of practical religious tolerance. From the eastern side of the mosque, there's a beautiful view down over Golconda and across to Hyderabad city. From the northern side, you can see the Qutb Shahi Tombs, fully reflecting the glory and pomp of the rich sultans of Golconda, whose last resting-place these are.

Finally, you'll reach the **Baradari** or Durbar Hall at the summit of Golconda. This is a 12-arched, three-storey pavilion, with a top terrace giving panoramic views of the surrounding fort, and an open-air stone throne called Shah Nashin. Here, the Qutb kings used to sit out on the open terraces, or hold meetings with the royal family or court ministers. The Durbar Hall also has an 8-km (5-mile) long secret underground passage which was used in times of emergency or danger. It is here, from the topmost point of the fort, that your guide will show the effectiveness of the 'clapping' technique, signalling down to the entrance gate for a demonstration.

You'll probably return down via the **King's Way**, which leads to the royal palaces and harem area. In olden days, the king was transported down this path by palanquin. You won't be, but the descent on foot is a pleasant one. On the way, look out for the fort's unique water-supply system. Huge tanks filled with water diverted from the Banjara hills 6 km (3¾ miles away, and ingeniously raised to the fort by a system of laminated clay pipes and Persian wheels, which moved it all the way up to the gardens, waterfalls and hanging gardens near the fort's summit.

Below, in the beautiful **Rani (Zanana) Mahals**, the first thing you're likely to be shown are the royal bathrooms. Only then will your guide point out the other attractions of the site. This series of crumbling, complex ruins used to be full of painted, jewelled palaces, arcades, Turkish baths, flower gardens and bubbling fountains. Little remains either of the lovely harem palaces nearby, though the royal kitchen, on the site of the old Camel Stable, is still in good condition. Return via the armoury to the entry gate.

Before going back to Hyderabad, take some time to explore the old town of Golconda, situated within the outer fort walls. In times past, this small bazaar town was a splendid fortress city, famed for its cutting, polishing and marketing of diamonds. The unique *Koh-i-noor*, now part of the British crown jewels, is said to have come from here. Today, the town is small, yet well-populated, and there are lots of cheap knick-knacks and trinkets being sold.

From Golconda, return to Hyderabad city centre for the impressive **Mecca Masjid**. This huge white mosque is the finest in south India, and the seventh largest in the world. It was begun in 1614 by Mohammed Quli Qutb Shah, and completed in 1687 by Aurangzeb, the Mughal invader. It derives its name from the few bricks brought from Mecca (and the stone apparently brought from Mohammed's birthplace) which are embedded in its walls.

Entering the mosque, beware of unsolicited guides. Most are difficult to understand but if you take one on, he should charge about Rs5. Just inside the wide courtyard, on the left, you'll see a long enclosure full of small marble tombs. This is where many of Hyderabad's wealthy Nizams are interred. The mosque itself is a marvellous structure. Its huge entrance façade is built of a single block of stone, richly inscribed with sayings from the Koran. Within can be seen Portuguese chandeliers, an antique French clock, and inlaid marble flooring. This mosque is the principal place of Muslim worship in the city, and every Friday up to 50 000 people gather for prayers. The huge interior 21.5 m high can accommodate 3000 worshippers, the grounds a further 7000. On important religious days and festivals even the streets outside are filled with kneeling devotees.

Just across the road from the mosque you'll find the **Charminar** (Four Tower Arch), Hyderabad's definitive landmark. This imposing arch, deriving its name from its four 56-m high slender minarets, was built in 1591 by Mohammed Quli Qutb Shah, reputedly to commemorate the end of a terrible plague. It stands a watchful guardian over the old city, serenely overlooking the surrounding chaos of anarchic traffic and crowded thoroughfares. A climb of 149 steps up a winding staircase brings you out near the top of the arch, at the tiny second-floor mosque. The high terraced balconies, notable for their profuse stucco decorations, balustrades and noble arches, offer superb bird's-eye views over the heart of Hyderabad city—busy, bustling scenes of battling rickshaws, thronging pavements, teeming mosques, and colourful bazaars of silversmiths, bangle makers, embroidery shops, perfume merchants and antique dealers. The Charminar is open 9 am–4.30 pm daily, and is beautifully illuminated from 7 to 9 pm in the evenings.

Continuing on by rickshaw or taxi, visit the **Salar Jung Museum** on the south bank of the Musi River. This rather ugly building houses the superb private collections of three Nawabs Salar Jung, successive wazirs or prime ministers of the Nizam of Hyderabad. Salar Jung III died in 1949 without an heir, and the collection was handed over to the Government of India in 1956. The 35 000 exhibits, gathered from all over the world, now fill 35 large rooms. The ornate entrance hall, with its beautiful chandeliers, leads into the ground-floor collection of textiles, Mughal glass, ivory, miniatures and a fascinating bell clock. On the first floor are Kashmir, Burmese, Chinese, Japanese and Western art, and a good selection of bronzes. The prize pieces of the museum are the ivory chairs and the turban of Tipu Sultan, and the swords and daggers of the Mughal emperors. Also of special interest are the small collection of Indian miniature paintings and the fine exhibition of jade. The collection is vast and only a small portion is on display. Open 10 am–5 pm daily (except Friday). Admission Rs2. Free guide service. Photographs not allowed.

If you still have the energy, finish off with a sunset visit to **Birla Mandir Temple**. Set atop a rocky hill overlooking the southern end of Hussain Sagar, this modern Hindu temple, constructed from pure white marble, offers memorable setting-sun views over the city. It's open 4–9 pm Monday to Friday, 7–11 am and 3–9 pm on Saturday/Sunday. Nearby is the **Birla Planetarium**, arguably the best in India with its 'Japanese Technology Sky Theatre'. Admission Rs5. English programmes at 3.30 and 6.50 pm daily, plus an extra 11.30 am show at weekends. Pleasantly air-conditioned, it's the perfect place to cool off after a steamy day's sightseeing.

Wildlife Excursion (by taxi/rickshaw, 4–8 hours)

Nehru Zoological Park

Hyderabad has the best zoo in India. It lies in a huge 121-hectare (300-acre) expanse of undulating, semi-tropical landscape, and is the home of some 1600 animals. Famous for its Lion Safari Park and for its many birds (over 240 species), its extensive grounds vary from attractive landscaped gardens to peaceful picnic bowers, from lush jungle forests to still, serene inland lakes. A Rs25 rickshaw ride from the town centre, the **Nehru Zoological Park** is located just outside the old city walls on the Bangalore Rd, quite near to Charminar. Open 9 am–6 pm daily (except Monday), admission Rs0.50.

Visit early in the morning, when all the big cats are still fairly alert (by noon, they're comatose), and spend all day wandering around. There's enough here to justify it. Inside the entrance, you'll find a useful map. Straight ahead, there's the small toy-train track that runs right round the inner park perimeter, and the Rs1 ride is a good way of orienting yourself quickly within the large grounds. Back at the park entrance, head left on foot. This takes you via the tiger, cheetah and camel compounds, and over to the ever-popular elephants and white rhinos. You'll note that all the animals are very well kept, and live in near-natural surroundings separated from their human visitors only by the most unobtrusive of barriers.

At the top of the park, some 20 minutes' walk from the entrance, you'll come to the **Lion Safari Park**. Crowded but cosy minibuses speed off in search of lions every 15 minutes or so, from 9.30 am to 12.15 pm, from 2 to 4.30 pm, daily. For Rs1, it's good value. When the bus finds some lions, it generally screeches to a halt for photographs, sometimes it breaks down, and the lions wander over to stare at the tourists instead.

Out of the Lion Park, strike left down the outer perimeter path to find deer, bison, gnu, monkeys. Just past the waterbuck compound, head into the centre of the park for sambhar, crane, nilgai, bear, water-birds and more lions. There's a couple of snack restaurants here, and a pleasant picnic area where you can enjoy a relaxing lunch. During the hottest part of the day (1–4 pm), while the animals rest, visit the **Natural History Museum and Aquarium**, both by the entrance ticket-gate (open 9 am–1 pm, 2–5 pm daily). Then the **Prehistoric Animals Park** and nearby **Ancient Life Museum**, both a short walk from the entrance. Otherwise, visit the monkeys who never go to sleep.

RECREATION

Dance, drama and musical concerts featuring both Indian and foreign performers take place nightly at **Rabindra Bharathi**, a beautiful air-conditioned auditorium. Good painting and sculpture exhibitions are held at the **A.P. Lalit Kala Academy**, Kala Bhavan, Saifabad (tel 34794). Full details of current events are given in the *Deccan Chronicle* newspaper.

SHOPPING

Not for nothing is Hyderabad known as the City of Pearls. In olden days, the Nizams would settle for nothing less than the best of Gulf pearls. Today, while connoisseurs are content with beads from China and Japan, Hyderabad remains the only centre for their trade in India.

At a reputable pearl dealer like **Mangatrai**, Bashir Bagh (tel 235728) or **Mangatrai Ramkumar**, Pathergatti (tel 521405, 524339) or the Gateway Hotel, you can pick up old pearls from the Persian Gulf (known as Basra pearls) for as little as 20% of current London prices. The cost of pearls varies depending on type and shape. Both the above dealers offer rice pearls, seed pearls, round pearls and drop pearls. A medium-sized string of pearls weighs about 30 to 35 grams. But don't have pearls strung and set in Hyderabad. Have them done in Bombay where it is far cheaper.

If you can't afford pearls, shop around for the famous, sparkling Hyderabadi bangles, nagans. Often embedded with semi-precious stones, they are made from pure lac, a resin secreted by beetles, and are extremely lustrous and durable. Prices range from Rs15 to Rs500 per pair, and you can find a wide selection at the **Chudi Bazaar** near the Charminar.

Charminar's many bazaars are among the most varied, lively and colourful in India; an exotic pot-pourri of antique shops, bangle makers, jewellers, chemists, *bidri*ware craftsmen, pearl dealers and silversmiths. You can find practically anything here, and the atmosphere is quite remarkable. There are whole streets covered in old books and clothes, intriguing hairdressers and lots of local people wandering around in green Viking helmets and pilot goggles. Things to buy include traditional *bidri* work—shiny silver inlay designs on black gun-metal, *nirmal* lacquerware toys, picture–frames, trays and furniture, *Himroo* fabrics and brocades, gun-metal statuettes, and *kondapalli* sandalwood toys.

There are some good fabric shops on Nampali Rd, and an interesting **Flea Market** every Thursday morning near the Charminar which starts early. Prices on all goods are variable, and you're best advised to get a idea on what is fair at a reliable government emporium. Good ones are **Lepakshi Handicrafts Emporium** at Gun Foundry (top of Abid Road, tel 235028), **APCO Handloom House**, Sundar Estate (also Abids, tel 222807) and **Handloom House**, Mukharam Jahi Road.

There are good opportunities in Hyderabad to see traditional craft processes. The ancient process of *bidri*ware may be seen at **Mumtaz Bidri Works Co-op Society**, 22-1-1042 Darush Shifa (tel 845843) or **Yaqoob Brothers**, 995 Habeeb Nagar (tel 234273). To see *nirmal*ware being made, visit the factory and showroom of **Nirmal Industries**, Raj Bhavan Road (tel 232157); left off the main road between Panjagutta and downtown Hyderabad in Khairatabad. When at the factory, ask for directions to the nearby *Himroo* weaving centre.

WHERE TO STAY

In Hyderabad, you stay either in isolated splendour up in the Banjara Hills 6 km (3¾ miles) from the rail station, or in the seedier, but atmospheric Abids area of the town centre. Here, as in many large Indian cities, top hoteliers appear to think that foreign visitors need protection from the din and dust of town centres. Hence most of India's best hotels are often away from the city centre, whilst the budget lodges have the premium locations right in the heart of the city.

Luxury/Expensive (over US$35/Rs1000 per room night)

The **Krishna Oberoi**, Road No. 1, Banjara Hills (tel 222121, tlx 0425-6931 OBH IN, fax 0842-223079) is set in 9 acres of beautifully landscaped gardens, with many rooms (US$100 single, US$110 double) overlooking the Hussain Sagar lake. Its palatial-style architecture is perhaps over-emphasised by the presidential suites that have their own swimming-pools.

The Taj's **Gateway Hotel on Banjara Hill** (tel 222222, tlx 0425-6947 GATE IN, 2115 TAJH IN, fax 0842-222218), just down the road from the Oberoi, has been completely renovated, has good food, and choice of lake-view or Golconda-fort rooms. Tariffs are US$49 single, US$85 double, and most rooms have balconies. **Basker Palace**, Road no 1, Banjara Hill (tel 226141, tlx 425-6182) has all facilities and rooms from Rs1200 single, Rs1500 double.

Mid-range (US$10–35/Rs250–1000 per room night)

Like Madras, Hyderabad has many hotels in the mid-range. The **Quality Inn Green Park**, 7-1-26 Ameerpet (tel 228610, tlx 425-2154 has well-maintained rooms for Rs450 single, Rs800 double.

The fine old **Ritz Hotel** (tel 233571, tlx 0425-6215), well-situated on Hill Fort Rd, Basheer Bagh, is an ex-palace with Raj-style charm, lovely views, attentive service, tennis courts and massive pool. Rooms are Rs450 single, Rs600 double, and you'll want one with individually controlled air-conditioning.

At the bottom, more basic end of the range there are a number of hotels to choose from. **Rock Castle**, Road 6, Banjara Hills (tel 222541) is a small family hotel with pleasant rooms from Rs500 and a large garden. **Hotel Dwaraka**, Raj Bhavan Rd (tel 237921), **Hotel Jaya International**, Nehru Rd, Abids (tel 232929) and **Hotel Taj Mahal**, King Kothi Rd (tel 237993) all have rooms around Rs250 single, Rs350 double.

Budget (under US$10/Rs250 per room night)

Hyderabad has many budget lodges, some of which should be avoided. The **Yatri Niwas**, S.P. Road, Secunderabad (tel 847603) has rooms from Rs125 single, Rs150 double. Also in Secunderabad is the **Youth Hostel**, near the Boat Club (tel 220121) with rooms from Rs75. In Station Rd, 5 minutes' walk (right) out of the rail station, choose between **Sri Brindavan Hotel** with large, breezy singles and doubles at Rs80 and Rs100 respectively and **Hotel Imperial** with stuffy but clean rooms from Rs60.

EATING OUT

Hyderabad does fine southern Indian cuisine: tray-meal thalis, pancake-like dosas, rice and dal idlis, and flour-wafer pappadams. But the speciality dishes are *baghara baigan* (small eggplants stuffed with spices, cooked in tamarind juice and sesame oil) and *mirchi ka salan* (stuffed green chillies). Both are a bit hot for Western palates, so you may care to try the city's famous birianis or tikka kababs instead. Particularly recommended is *haleem*, a mildly spiced mutton and wheat preparation, followed by *khobani* (dried apricots cooked to a purée). Finish off with a pot of good, rich south Indian coffee.

The city has a rich culinary heritage, and the **Dakhni** in the Gateway hotel has an excellent menu with meals costing from Rs200 per head. The menu at the Oberoi's **Firdaus** restaurant includes dishes culled from the personal collection of the city's most renowned gourmet, Salar Jung. Eat well à la carte at around Rs250 per head, or sample the good-value Rs135 lunchtime buffet (12.30–3 pm).

The Gateway's **Kabab-E-Bahar** is a lake-side open-air barbecue open each evening. The **Abhiruchi** in Sarojini Devi road (tel 822547) serves non-vegetarian Andhra food and a meal would cost from Rs75 per person. In town, two good restaurants are **Palace Height**, 8th floor, Triveni Building, Abid Rd, a stylish place, with great continental, Mughlai and Chinese cuisine at around Rs100 per head; and **Peacock Restaurant**, Basheer Bagh (similar quality, less expensive). In the Abids area, you'll find cheap and tasty vegetarian fare at Emerald Hotel's **Sapphire Restaurant**, Royal Hotel's **Laxmi Restaurant**, and **Annapurna Hotel's** air-con restaurant. The Annapurna is particularly well known for its ice-cream.

GENERAL INFORMATION
Andhra Pradesh Tourist Office, 1st floor, Gagan Vihar, M.J. Rd (tel 556493, 556523) is extremely helpful and well organised. Its city sightseeing tours run from 8 am to 6 pm daily, and cost Rs45.

A.A. Hussain Bookshop, Abid Rd, stocks Avion Escort's good city map/guide (Rs4). The tourist office sells M.A. Mahmood's excellent *Glimpses of Hyderabad*. *City of Legends* by Ian Austen (Viking, Penguin India 1992) is a popular history of the city. Another excellent book is *The Days of the Beloved* an oral history of life in Hyderabad under the last Nizam collected by Harriet Lynton and Mohini Rajan; originally published by California University Press (1974), a local reprint by Orient Longman is available. The small pocket guide and map published by Sangam Books (Rs50) is locally available.

Reliable travel agents are Sita World Travels, Hyderguda and Chapel Rd (tel 233638, 235549) and Sheriff Travels, Basheer Bagh (tel 237904). State Bank of India is in Bank St, and the post office is near the railway station, Abids. Indian Airlines (tel 236902, apt 842051) and Air India (tel 232858) are both in Saifabad near the Secretariat building; Vayudoot, 2nd floor Samrat Complex, Saifabad (tel 234717, apt 842855).

BANGALORE

Capital of Karnataka state, Bangalore is a clean, spacious and well-planned city of beautiful parks, long avenues and magnificent buildings. One of Asia's fastest-growing cities, it has lost many of the trees, gardens and quaint bungalows that gained it the soubriquet 'Garden City of India', but it still remains the nation's tidiest and greenest capital. A busy commercial and cosmopolitan centre, Bangalore is rapidly advancing towards Nehru's vision of it as India's 'City of the Future', yet retains its old summer-resort charm and sophistication. It is an ideal base from which to discover the south of India.

This 'town of boiled beans' (the derivation of its name) began as a small mud fort, built in 1537 by a feudal chieftain called Kempe Gowda (1513–1569). He predicted a great future for his new town, and built four watchtowers at four elevated points around it, to demarcate what he envisaged to be its future boundaries. These have now been far exceeded. The small fort was ruled by various dynasties over successive centuries, before being enlarged and rebuilt in stone by Hyder Ali in the late 18th century. Significant improvements to the new structure were made by his son, Tipu Sultan. The arrival of the British (1809) spelt further changes, and a spacious cantonment town, with parks and gardens, museums and churches, gothic bungalows and colleges sprang up. Encouraged by the enlightened Maharajahs of Mysore, Bangalore swiftly became a leading educational and industrial centre and eventually replaced Mysore as the state capital.

Now, Bangalore is a city of the 90s. Many *hi-tech* industries have been developed here; India's huge computer software industry operates from Bangalore, jet fighters and helicopters for the airforce are made here and some of the country's largest garment exporters make the city their manufacturing base. Yet, 'beautiful Bangalore' still has a wealth of colourful vegetation; notably its two lungs of Cubbon Park and Lal Bagh, and is one of India's most attractive cities. Despite the crowds, there's a refreshing sensation of space created both by the broad open-plan avenues, and the orderly sophistication of the city's inhabitants. These are a well-educated, invariably polite people, who even form queues outside cinemas. And Bangalore has an awful lot of cinemas.

Situated on a high, cool plateau above the plains, Bangalore has an all-year tourist season but is most pleasant in October–November and February–May. To see the gardens, parks and flowers at their best, come in January or August.

ARRIVAL/DEPARTURE

Air

Indian Airlines offers daily flights between Bangalore and Bombay (Rs1675), Calcutta (Rs3000), Cochin (Rs842), Coimbatore (Rs600), Delhi (Rs3057), Goa (Rs1077), Hyderabad (Rs1083), Madras (Rs727), Pune (Rs1583), and Trichy Rs847). There are less frequent flights to centres like Madurai (Rs847) and Trivandrum Rs1192). Bangalore airport is 13 km (8 miles) from the city centre and is connected by taxi or auto-rickshaw.

Rail

There are several trains daily to and from Madras (6/7 hours) and to Mysore (about 3 hours). From Madras the two best trains are the (*Brindhavan Express* and *Bangalore Mail* from Madras Central station (7 hours). The *Hyderabad Express* leaves Bangalore 5.15 pm daily, arriving Hyderabad around 8 am the next day. The *Hampi Express* leaves 9.40 pm daily, getting in to Hospet around 6 am the following morning. The *Bangalore–Trivandrum Express* leaves daily at 6.15 pm (journey time 18 hours) and the fast *Karnataka Express* goes daily (journey time 38 hours) to Delhi. A faster *Shatabdi Express* has been proposed between Delhi and Bangalore but probably won't be introduced until late 1993. There are various express trains to Bombay (24 to 27 hours), some of them requiring a change of train at Miraj.

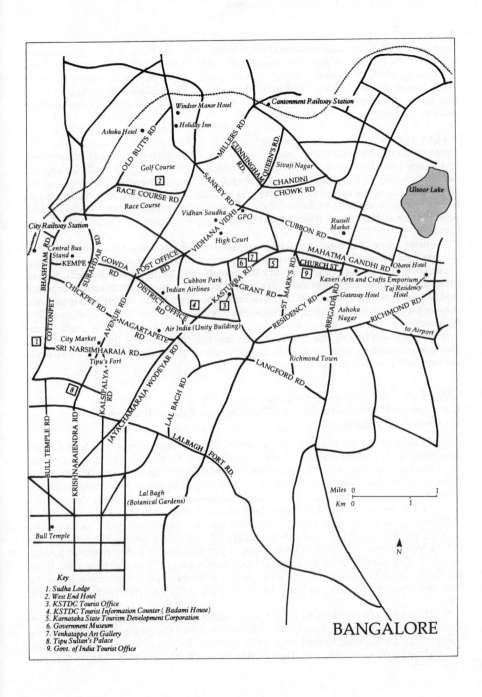

BANGALORE

Key
1. Sudha Lodge
2. West End Hotel
3. KSTDC Tourist Office
4. KSTDC Tourist Information Counter (Badami House)
5. Karnataka State Tourism Development Corporation
6. Government Museum
7. Venkatappa Art Gallery
8. Tipu Sultan's Palace
9. Govt. of India Tourist Office

Road

Bangalore's efficient central bus-station, directly opposite the city rail station, offers superb connections to Mysore (express buses every 15 minutes from 6 am to 9.30 pm; 3½ hours), to Madras (many departures throughout the day; 9 hours), to Bombay, via Belgaum (buses at 8 am and 2 pm; 24 hours), to Ernakulam and to Hospet (plus two buses direct to Hampi; journey time 8/9 hours). There's also at least one bus daily to Ootacamund and to Goa (Panjim).

WHAT TO SEE

Because Bangalore has few sights of its own, and these widely dispersed, travellers tend to spend just a couple of days here, resting up and cooling off before heading to Bombay, Goa or further south. But if there's little to see in the city, there are some marvellous spots just outside it. A number of good tours run out to Hampi and Ooty, to Belur/Halebid, to Bandipur Tiger Reserve and Nagarhole National Park, and (best of all) to Mysore, Sriringapatna and Brindhavan Gardens.

For orientation in Bangalore itself, use taxis or auto-rickshaws. The latter are Rs2.50 per km, and generally use the meter. Trying to get around on foot is a disheartening experience: this is a big city, with very long roads (few of them well-signed), and all interest spots miles away from each other. The 'budget' sector, with the cheaper hotels and restaurants, is around the bus and rail stations on the east of town, and is perhaps the easiest area in which to acclimatise to the busy city. The best time for independent sightseeing is the afternoon, when Bangalore goes into siesta. For a quick, comprehensive overview of the city take a conducted tour. Follow this with a day of shopping (excellent here) or discover the beautiful parks. Out-of-town excursions are optional extras.

City Tour (by sightseeing bus, morning or afternoon)
Government Museum/Art Gallery–Tipu Sultan's Palace–Bull Temple– Lal Bagh–Ulsoor Lake

A short tour of the palatial buildings round Cubbon Park brings you to the three museums in **Jayachamarajendra Park**. Best of these is **Government Museum**, one of the oldest museums in India (established 1866). It has 18 sections, housing fine collections of miniatures, inscriptions, coins and sculptures recovered from the neolithic-period Chandraval excavation. The **Venkatappa Art Gallery** forms one wing of this museum, and has well-presented exhibitions of water-colours, plaster-of-Paris sculptures, bronze antiquities and various contemporary works of art (by famous artist Venkatappa and other court painters). There are regular modern-art exhibitions on the third floor. Open 10 am–5 pm daily (except Wednesday), admission Rs1. The adjoining **Technological Museum** is generally unexciting. Just down the road, opposite Queen Victoria's statue, is the **Aquarium**. It's not covered by the tour, but is worth returning to (open 10 am–7.30 pm daily, except Monday, admission Rs1).

South of town (1 km; ½ mile from City Market), you'll visit **Kempe Gowda Fort**, Hyder Ali's stone construction (built 1761) on the site of the original mud fort. While the fort interior is closed to the public you can enter the first two courtyards and pass through an impressive gateway. The exterior view of the lovely 16th-century **Ganpati**

Temple within the walls merely whets the appetite. Much more satisfying is **Tipu Sultan's Palace**, started by Hyder Ali in 1781, completed by Tipu in 1789. One of three summer palaces built by the two Mysore rulers, it is (like the others) made entirely of wood, except for the internal pillar-supports. Within are gloriously painted walls, ceilings, balconies and soaring pillars of green, red, black and gold; also elaborate arches, surrounded by minarets and family paintings. As at Daria Daulat, the palace here has a small museum, illustrating the life and times of Tipu Sultan, who presented the British with their most stubborn resistance in the south. Open 8 am–6 pm daily.

Near the palace you'll see the **Venkataramanaswamy Temple**, built by the Wodeyars in the 17th century. An attractive example of Dravidian-style architecture, it was restored for the use of the Wodeyar kings who recovered their throne after Tipu's death in 1799.

From the palace, it's a 1.5-km (1-mile) drive south to the **Bull Temple** up on Bugle Hill. Here you'll find the fourth-largest Nandi bull in India, made of black granite and measuring 6.3 m across by 4.6 m high. Credited with miraculous 'growing' power, the Nandi is chiefly notable for being so much larger than its 'master', Shiva. You'll find Shiva's tiny image in the small temple at the foot of the hill. Also here is the strange **Ganesh Temple**, with its large elephant made of 110 kilos of butter. Donated by wealthy devotees, the butter is broken up every four years and distributed to pilgrims. Local philanthropists are then 'buttered up' to donate a fresh coating.

The beautiful botanical gardens of **Lal Bagh**, 2 km (1¼ miles) south-east of the City Market, were laid out by Hyder Ali in 1760, and substantially added to by Tipu Sultan. Smaller than Cubbon Park, they are in every way superior—97 hectares (240 acres) of trees and plants (1000 tropical and sub-tropical varieties, many of them rare), 19th-century pavilions and lamps, landscaped gardens and avenues, fountains and flower-beds, even an elegant glasshouse modelled on London's Crystal Palace! The best time to see the dahlias, marigolds, rose gardens and many flowers here is either January or August. Just up from the entrance, overlooked by Kempe Gowda's statue, is the flower-bordered **Lawn Clock** (completed 1983), accurate to three seconds each month. Just right of this is the area where visiting dignitaries/state leaders are invited to 'dedicate a tree' (in olden days, they had expensive monuments erected to them, now they get a shrub).

Ulsoor Lake, last stop of the day, is on the eastern edge of town (3 km; 2 miles from the bus-station). A pleasant boating lake with eagles, islands and rose-pink water lilies, it has a small **Boat Club** (rowing boats for hire at Rs15 per hour) and a peaceful 'Kensington Gardens'. Open 9.30 am–5.30 pm daily.

Around sunset, take an enjoyable promenade down **Vidhana Vidhi** (Bangalore's finest avenue) and admire its attractive selection of Greco-colonial style buildings. Start with the palatial post office (India's grandest) and walk down the tree-lined boulevard to **Attara Kacheri** ('18 Courts'), the stately red-brick structure housing the High Court. Recently saved from development and now restored to its original splendour. Opposite this is the magnificent post-Independence **Vidhana Souda**, housing the Secretariat and the Legislature. Built in 1954, this is a four-storey ornamental structure of solid granite, designed in the neo-Dravidian style. It is notable for its soaring columns, charming frescoes and excellent carvings. Visitors are only allowed inside between 3.30 and 5.30 pm, and must get permission from the

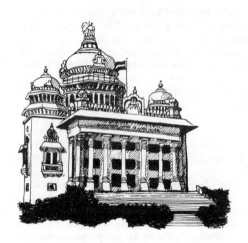

Vidhana Souda

public relations officer in the entrance lobby. If you're around on a Sunday evening (between 7 and 9 pm), you can see Vidhana Souda beautifully illuminated. Just down the road, at the bottom of Vidhana Vidhi, **Cubbon Park** has nightly illuminations and features a popular 'Fairy Fountain'.

RECREATION

Bangalore is one of the few Indian cities with any real claim to nightlife. There's a wide selection of bars and restaurants, clubs and discotheques, and your hotel will always have some recommendations. Otherwise try one of the 100 or so cinemas here; Bangalore is a film-making capital. A few theatres along M.G. and Brigade Roads show recent English-speaking releases.

Cultural entertainments are best in March–April, when regular shows of Karnataka dance and music are held at **Chowdiah Memorial Hall**, Sankey Rd and **Bharatiya Vidya Bhavan**. For details of current programmes and events (there's something going on most evenings), buy a *Deccan Herald* or *Indian Express* newspaper. The cultural shows held at **State Youth Centre**, Nrupathunga Rd, are supposed to be especially good.

For outdoor recreation, there's horse-racing at Bangalore's beautiful race-course (November–March, mid-April to July), fishing at Hesaraghatta Lake or Chamarjasagar Reservoir (enquire at the tourist office), and good golfing at the 18-hole course in the city centre (nearby Windsor Manor or West End hotels arrange games for visitors).

SHOPPING

Next to Madras, Bangalore is the prime shopping centre of the south. It is famous for its fine silk, particularly traditional Mysore silk saris. Other good buys include rosewood, sandalwood, lacquerware, *bidri*ware and wooden-inlay items. Many people go for (cheaper) imitation silks, attractive bangles, handloom fabrics and jewellery. A good place to see the range is the **Cottage Industries Emporium** on

Mahatma Gandhi (M.G.) Rd, alternatively the **Cauvery Arts & Crafts Emporium**, 26 M.G. Rd. The latter is particularly good for hand-crafted rosewood furniture and sandalwood carvings.

For quality silks, try **Janardhana Silk House**, located in the main general shopping complex of **Unity Buildings**, Jaya Chamaraja Rd. For cheaper silks and textiles and amazing atmosphere, there's the **City Market** in Chickpet, or the big shopping centre in M.G. Rd. For gold and silver jewellery, the best shops are in Commercial St.

WHERE TO STAY

Luxury/Expensive (over US$35/Rs1000 per room night)

Three of the best properties in Bangalore are managed by the Taj Group but in August 1992 an Oberoi hotel opened making the city one of the few with hotels run by all India's major chains. The oldest hotel in Bangalore, the Taj Group's magnificent **West End Hotel** in Race Course Rd (tel 269281, tlx 0845-2337 WEND IN, fax 0812-200010), is set amid 20 sweeping acres of landscaped gardens, splendid trees and bird life. Rooms start at US$90 single, US$100 double, and vary depending on their layout and location. Welcomgroup's **Windsor Manor Sheraton**, 25 Sankey Rd (tel 269898, 296322, tlx 0845-8209, fax 0812-264941) is a first-rate hotel, with exquisite decor, immaculate service, nice restaurants, and well-furnished rooms from US$85 single, US$110 double. The **Taj Residency**, 14 M.G. Rd (tel 544444, tlx 0845-8367 TBLR IN, fax 0812-544748) caters more to business than to general travellers, and has rooms from US$60 single, US$75 double. The new **Oberoi Hotel**, M.G. Road (tel 542220, tlx 845-8696 OBBL IN, fax 0812-544118) opened in August 1992 and has rooms from US$100 single, US$110 double. The **Ashok Hotel**, High Grounds (tel 269462, tlx 845-2433, fax 0812-260033) has rooms from Rs1000 single, Rs1200 double.

Mid-range (US$10–35/Rs250–1000 per room night)

Perhaps the best value of any hotel in India is the Taj Group's **Gateway Hotel on Residency Road**, 66 Residency Road (tel 544545, tlx 845-2567 LUX IN, fax 0812-544030) with rooms from Rs825 single, Rs 950 double. **Comfort Inn Ramanashree**, 16 Raja Ram Mohun Roy Road (tel 235250) has rooms from Rs525 single, Rs800 double including breakfast.

Cauvery Continental, 11/37 Cunningham Rd (tel 266966, tlx 0845-8112 HCC), is a favourite spot for Sai Baba devotees, with cosy rooms at Rs300 single, Rs400 double and a cheap vegetarian restaurant ('Executive Lunch—limited *thali*' for Rs20).

Budget (under US$10/Rs250 per room night)

Budget hotels are mainly in the city market area. **Hotel Luciya International**, 6 OTC Rd (tel 224148, tlx 0845-8360 LUCY IN), has a popular restaurant, tourist bus service, and smart rooms at Rs150 single, Rs200 double. At the cheaper end of the range is **Sudha Lodge**, 6 Cottonpet Main Rd (tel 605420), with central situation, good information, hot and cold running water, and clean rooms at Rs50 single, Rs70 double. It's a great meeting-place, often full. The next-door **Hari Priya** restaurant does the cheapest Indian breakfast (Rs3.50 for *masala dosa* and coffee). **Sudarshan Hotel**, near the bus-station, is a friendly place with rooms at Rs40. The **Tourist Hotel** on Race

Course Rd has many rooms at Rs50, but is often packed out with local tourists. Further into the city centre, **Hotel Ajantha** (22 M.G. Rd) and **Hotel Brindhavan** (40 M.G. Rd) are reliable cheapies: Rs40–50 for single rooms, Rs80 for doubles.

EATING OUT

Food in Bangalore is excellent and it is one of the few cities, Bombay is another, where there is a wide range of cuisine available outside major hotels. In order to compete, the hotels themselves have good restaurants.

Among the Indian restaurants, the **Coconut Grove**, Church Street (tel 579132) and the **Karavati** at the Gateway Hotel both serve excellent Malabar, Konkan and Coorg food from Rs75 per head. The **Windsor Manor Hotel** has the best NW Frontier food.

For continental food there are excellent non-hotel restaurants; the exclusive **Prince's Restaurant**, 9 Brigade Rd (tel 580087, wise to book) with amazing steaks, popular Indian food, lovely decor, great service, and attached 'Knock Out Disco' (Bangalore's only one, free to restaurant customers Tuesday–Thursday, otherwise Rs75 per couple). **Peacock** in Residency Rd has top-notch Indian/Western cuisine; **MTR Restaurant**, by the main entrance of Lal Bagh, has a famous bar and a solid reputation for good mid-bracket food. It's open 7 to 11 am, 4 to 7 pm.

For Chinese food, try the **Rice Bowl**, 215 Brigade Road (tel 572417) or **Memories of China** in the Taj Residency Hotel where a meal would cost Rs150. The **Paradise Island** at the West End Hotel serves Thai food and a multi-cuisine buffet at lunch time for Rs135 per head.

Most restaurants in Bangalore serve draft beer and there are numerous pubs throughout the city. Tasty snacks are served at **Excel Restaurant** in Tank Bund Rd, behind the bus-station. This place also has a well-stocked bar, and lots of 'local' character. Over in Gandhi Nagar, Kempe Gowda, travellers favour **Hotel Blue Star** (opposite Tribhuvan cinema) for its 'well-experienced cook' and tasty chicken dishes. Nearby **Sukhsagar Food Complex** (opposite Majestic Theatre) has Gujarati/Punjabi food on the 3rd floor, south Indian meals on the 1st floor, and mouthwatering ice-creams, sweets and juices on the ground floor. Finally, there's **Chit-Chat** on M.G. Rd one of the ritziest ice-cream parlours in India. It has chandeliers, musical fountains, and toffee-nosed waiters who won't serve you unless you sit on the ground-floor and look very rich.

GENERAL INFORMATION

KSTDC Tourist Office, 10/4 Kasturba Rd, opposite the Aquarium (tel 212901, 578753) gives information in slow motion (essential to visit with precise questions) but is generally helpful. It's open 10 am to 5.30 pm daily, except Sunday. A second KSTDC office, at Badami House, N.R. Square (tel 215883), sells the useful Bangalore city tour (7.30 am–1.30 pm, 2–7.30 pm daily), the comprehensive day tour to Mysore, Sriringapatna and Brindhavan (7.15 am–10.45 pm daily), and the over-ambitious tour out to the famous temple spots of **Belur** and **Halebid** (7.15 am–10.30 pm daily). There are several other 'tourist offices' dotted round Bangalore.

If visiting Nagarhole Wildlife Sanctuary (see also Mysore section) you can advance-book accommodation at Jungle Lodges and Resorts, Shrungar Shopping centre, M.G. Road (tel 575195).

Higginbotham's bookshop on M.G. Road and inside the rail station, does a good range of TTK city/state guidebooks. Another bookshop on M.G. Road is Gangarams who have the widest selection of both books and magazines.

The post office is at Vidhana Vidhi (but *poste restante* at the old GPO by Bangalore International Hotel, Crescent Rd), State Bank of India is in St Mark's Rd, and Indian Airlines is at K.G Road (tel 211211, 211914, apt 566233) and Cauvery Bhavan complex, District Office Rd (tel 572605). A useful listing is *Bangalore This Fortnight*, available from most hotels and bookshops.

EXCURSIONS FROM BANGALORE
There are no flights to and from the important sites in the region, but distances are comparatively short and all can be easily negotiated by road and rail within a day. From Bangalore it's a short hop to Hampi and back again by the excellent overnight *Hampi Express*. Ooty is reached via Mysore, to the south. From there, you can connect into Tamil Nadu or Kerala (see Connections, below).

Bangalore to Hampi   350 km (219 miles)

Rail/Road
The *Hampi Express* leaves at 9.30 pm and arrives in Hospet at 6.20 am the following morning. From Hospet to Hampi 13 km (8 miles) away, there is a regular local bus service. Taxis, auto-rickshaws and bicycles are available for hire. The return train leaves Hospet rail station at 9 pm daily, reaching Bangalore at 8 am the following morning.

Road
Ten express buses daily ply the Bangalore-Hampi route (9 hours).

Bangalore to Mysore   140 km (88 miles)

Rail
Fairly regular train service (3½ hours). The line has been relaid as broad gauge and new services started in late 1992.

Road
Several buses daily (3 hours). Quick, popular.

Mysore to Ootacamund   159 km (100 miles)

Road
There are two good early buses, 8 am and 9 am (4/5 hours). Also, many local buses. For Madumalai Wildlife Sanctuary, disembark at Theppukady (halfway to Ootacamund).

Ootacamund to Madras   525 km (328 miles)

Rail/Air
Train to Coimbatore via Mettupulayam (5½ hours), then IC534 daily flight to Madras, Rs1031.

Road/Rail
Bus (a treat) to Coimbatore (3 hours), then choice of several trains to Madras (8/9 hours).

CONTINUATIONS
The most popular option is up from Mysore to Goa by rail (3 pm daily train, 16 hours, to Londa; then 3-hour bus to Margao/Vasco). Others prefer to join the Kerala circuit at Cochin, from Ootacamund (14 hours by rail, via Coimbatore). Less obvious, but feasible, is to backtrack to Bangalore (9 hours by bus from Ootacamund) for IC579 flights to Madurai, Rs847.

HAMPI (Vijayanagar)

About 190 km (119 miles) east of Belgaum and 350 km (219 miles) north of Bangalore lie the ruins of Hampi, once the greatest of all medieval Hindu capitals. Founded in 1336 by two local princes, Hari Hara and Bukka, it became the seat of the mighty Vijayanagar empire, which held sway over south India for more than two centuries. By the reign of Krishnadeva Raya (1509–29), generally considered the golden period of the empire, its rule extended from the Arabian Sea to the Bay of Bengal, and from the Deccan plateau to the tip of the peninsula. The Vijayanagar kings built up Hampi as a showpiece of imperial magnificence, and a definitive Vijayanagar style of architecture emerged, typified by lofty gopurams, stylised sculptures (often depicting scenes from the *Puranas* and the *Ramayana*), intricately carved columns, and separate shrines for goddesses. The city itself had a spectacular natural setting, enclosed on three sides by the Tungabhadra river and by rocky gorges. The addition of seven concentric rings of massive fortifications made it almost invulnerable to attack. Hampi had a series of enlightened rulers who patronised the arts and education, cultivating it as a centre of learning and culture. Meanwhile, a growing trade in spices turned its busy, colourful bazaars into an international centre of commerce. In its heyday, the city had a population of half a million, bolstered by a powerful mercenary army of one million soldiers. Such a large force was required to defend the supremacy of Vijayanagar against rival Muslim sultans and Hindu kings. In 1565, however, it was finally overcome by five allied Deccan sultans in the disastrous battle of Talikota. The king fled southwards, and the invaders spent six long months systematically sacking and looting the abandoned city, burning and pillaging without mercy. The empire lingered on for another century, but Hampi itself was never occupied again.

Hampi's ruins are well worth the 2-day side trip from Bangalore. So well preserved are the relics, and so vividly do they reflect a vanquished past, that Hampi has been termed 'The Pompeii of India'. Spread over a vast area of 26 sq km, including temples, pavilions, baths and palaces, the ruins are on a very grand scale. You can really sense a mighty civilisation at work here; with only the slightest effort of imagination, you can really visualise it. At present, the Government of Karnataka and the Archaeological Survey of India are trying to restore the capital to something of its past glory. An ambitious project perhaps, but not impossible. A great many of the ruins are in surprisingly good condition.

Hampi has a very dry, exposed location and is best visited in the cool months of December to February. Travellers do trickle in as early as August and September, when the river is swollen by the monsoon and the surrounding countryside a rich lush green, and as late as March, but after that it's too hot for comfort.

ARRIVAL/DEPARTURE
Hampi can be reached within a day from both Bangalore and Hyderabad.

Rail
From both cities there is one overnight train daily taking 8 and 13 hours respectively. From Bangalore the *Hampi Express* overnight train leaves at 9.30 pm and reaches Hospet at 6.20 am the following morning. The return departs Hospet at 9 pm and reaches Bangalore at 8 am. From Hyderabad you have to change trains at Guntakal.

Road
There are 10 express buses daily from Bangalore (9 hours) and 2 from and to Hyderabad(11–12 hours). Two buses a day to Mysore (10½ hours), and a few morning buses to Hubli, for Goa (4/5 hours). Hubli has one express bus to Panjim (dep 11 am, arr 3 pm), four slow buses to Panjim (7 hours), and one slow bus to Vasco (7/8 hours). There are also 2 trains (dep 7 am and 11 pm) from Hubli to Goa.

Hospet to Hampi 13 km (8 miles)

Road
A regular local bus service connects these two places. Otherwise, hire an auto-rickshaw, taxi, or bicycle.

WHAT TO SEE
Hospet, 13 km (8 miles) from Hampi, is the popular base for travellers. It has better food and accommodation, and offers frequent buses (Rs1) to Hampi Bazaar and Kamalapuram, the two main entry points to the ruins. From either point, you'll need at least 2 days to see everything on foot. The sights are very spread out and walking it can be exhausting. Wear comfortable walking shoes and be prepared to wander off the beaten track.

If you're touring on foot, bear in mind that the complete round-trip (from Hospet to Hampi, round the ruins, and back) is 42 km (26¼ miles). Most people take a bus to **Hampi Bazaar**, walk up to the **Vittala Temple** complex, return to the bazaar, strike south to **Kamalapuram** (via the Palace complex), and take a mid-afternoon bus from Kamalapuram back to **Hospet**. The few remaining sights can be seen on a second day's stroll.

To cover the ruins in just one day, you've a choice of bicycle, taxi or auto-rickshaw. A good many travellers take an early bus out to Kamalapuram, where they can hire cycles. They bike up to Hampi Bazaar (via the Palace complex), walk along the river to the Vittala Temple (leaving bikes at the bazaar), and finish off with a ride back to Kamalapuram, via **Ugranasimha** and **Sister Stone**. Starting out at 6.30 am, they can be back in Hospet by 2 pm—before it gets too hot. Alternatively, they hire an auto-rickshaw (Rs45 for up to 3 persons) or a taxi (Rs150–20) from Malligi Tourist Home in Hospet. This is the most comfortable option as you see everything in comfort, and in just a day.

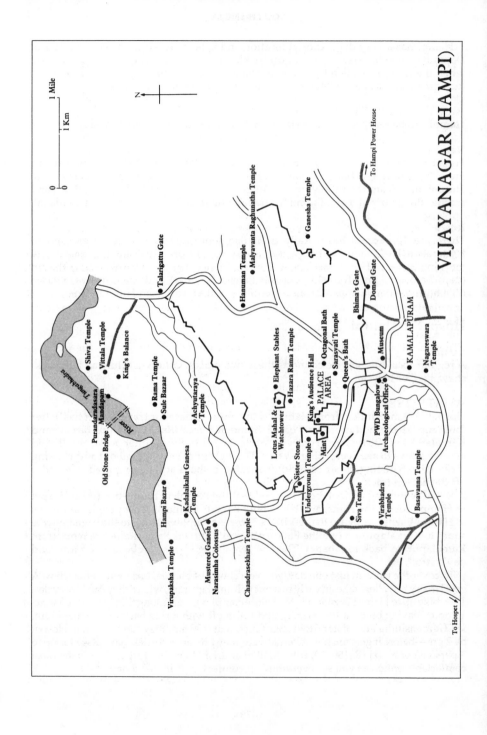

VIJAYANAGAR (HAMPI)

Hampi Tour (by auto-rickshaw/taxi, 6 hours; by cycle 8, hours)

**Virupaksha Temple–Vittala Temple Complex–Narasimha–Sister Stone–
Palace Complex–Kamalapuram**

Just up from Hampi Bazaar bus-stand, you'll find **Virupaksha Temple**, the only
sacred complex in Hampi still 'living' (still in worship). Dedicated to Virupaksha, an
aspect of Shiva, it has two main courts, each entered by a towered gateway or
gopuram. The larger *gopuram* is over 50 m high, and looks incredibly new and gets a
fresh coat of whitewash every year, at **Shivratri**. Inside the temple, look out for finely
carved columns with rearing animals. Also for hordes of acquisitive monkeys. If
you're here around 7 am, you can watch Shiva and other resident deities being woken
up by the priests.

Walking up along the river, you'll soon come to **Sule Bazaar**, ruined rows of arched
pillars, where fruit, gems and spices were once sold. Past this, up a low rise, is the
King's Balance. In ancient times, the king established the wealth of his kingdom by
sitting in one scale, while his rich vassals poured cash and jewellery into the other.
The proceeds went to the temple brahmins. Enjoy the views here, then walk down
to **Vittala Temple**, the finest achievement of Vijayanagar art. Constructed in the 16th
century and currently being restored by the archaeological department, this is a
delightful complex of structures set within a rectangular courtyard. A few guides are
available around the entrance. The main temple is famous for its rearing animals and
for its 'musical' columns. Each series of 16 columns is hewn from a single granite
block, and each one plays a different scale of musical notes or phrases when struck.
There are 250 pillars either side of a central path, which leads up to the Marriage
Hall. East of this hall is an exquisite **stone car**. A faithful reproduction of a real temple
chariot (as used in festivals), it is said to symbolise the ancient University of Gulbar-
ga, 300 km from Hospet. The miniature car houses Vishnu's vehicle, the *garuda*, and
is drawn by a pair of stone elephants. Traces of the original bright paintwork still
cling to the wheels. Out of the temple, walk down to **Purandaradasa Hall**, a low-ceil-
inged temple down by the riverside. According to legend, a famous 16th-century
musician, Purandara, was turned to stone here, for singing a particularly divine song.
A tiny figurine of him playing his mandolin is propped against one of the pillars.
Opposite, there's a spectral group of stone pylons spanning the river. These once
supported the old stone bridge which linked the two banks. You can cross over
Tungabhadra River in traditional 'coracle' boats (Rs4 per person), but don't go
swimming in it as whirlpools have claimed a few lives.

Back at Hampi Bazaar, a short walk south takes you up onto Hemakuta Hill. Best
views are from the **Kadalaikullu Ganesa Temple**, notable for its unusually tall
columns and huge image of the elephant god. Nearby, another Ganesh image stands
with an open hall known as **Mustered Ganesh**. Off the hill, **Badavi Lingam** is a
massive monolith Shivalinga within a chamber, fed with water from a narrow
roadside stream. Next to it is the famous figure of **Narasimha**, half man, half lion
avatar of Vishnu, carved out of a single boulder.

Driving south, keep an eye out for **Sister Stone**, two huge boulders propped
against each other like a pair of Siamese twins. They are apparently two of Shiva's
sisters, whom he petrified after a family squabble. Down at the **Royal Palace
Complex**, you'll find state archaeologists busily at work restoring the ruins. Walk
inside the palace walls to find a large raised dais from which the king observed
festival rites, various columned structures (for officers and guards), a roofless

subterranean chamber, possibly the state treasury, and various civic buildings and watchtowers. Past these is **Lotus Mahal**, a beautiful two-storey pavilion with distinctive arches. It was built for the ladies of the court, in a skilful blend of Hindu and Islamic architectural styles. Nearby, there's a large step-well, extremely well-preserved, which served as a royal bath. Behind this is the **Queen's Bath**, a square water basin surrounded by a vaulted corridor. It was originally covered by a large canopy, supported by four pillars. This is now gone, and the walls are defaced by graffiti. But there's nice stucco work, and the remains of a narrow moat. Also fine carvings, mainly monkey figures, on the ceilings of the corridor. The tiny niches in the ceilings were for candles which illuminated the baths at night. Just outside the enclosure, to the east, look out for the largest **elephant stables** in the world. A row of 10 chambers with high vaulted roofs, they are symmetrically disposed around a central two-storey pavilion. Back at the palace entrance, you can take refreshments at the small restaurant (near the archaeologists' camp) before driving down to **Kamalapuram**. Built as a fort with circular bastions, this small town has an interesting **Archaeological Museum** with many fine recoveries from the Hampi site. Open from 10 am–5 pm (except Fridays) it has a good scale model of the ruins which is useful for orientation, if you're starting out from Kamalapuram by bike. The museum also sells the useful ASI booklet on Hampi (Rs6).

SHOPPING
Hampi has no indigenous crafts. **Malligi Tourist Home** has its small 'curious' shop, which sells Karnataka handicrafts. **Aspiration Store** in Hampi Bazaar has a wide range of produce from Sri Aurobindo ashram in Pondicherry; marble, silk fabrics, hand-made paper, postcards, even herbal bath powder. Good books to buy here are R. Sewell's *Forgotten Empire* and Longhurst's *Hampi Ruins*. Though most people get by with Michell and Fritz's *Hampi*, issued free at the tourist office.

WHERE TO STAY
In Hospet, stay at **Malligi Tourist Home**, 6/143 Jambunatha Rd (tel 8101), a short rickshaw ride from the bus-stand. Friendly and comfortable, it has nice single/double rooms from Rs50 (plus air-conditioned doubles at Rs250), good restaurant, bakery and ice-cream parlour, running hot water till 10 am, laundry and money-changing facilities, small library and bookshop, TV lounge and cool gardens. Malligi can arrange all local sightseeing and advance-book all onward travel. As a fallback, try **Hotel Sudarshan** (tel 8574) on Station Rd. Service is poor, but rooms are reasonably priced from Rs35 (single, no bath) to Rs120 (clean doubles, with bath).

Also at Hospet is the new KSTDC **Hotel Mayura Vijaynagar** (tel 8270) which has the best facilities and rooms from Rs200. There is a second KSTDC unit at **Tungabhadra Dam**, 6 km (3¾ miles) away. For a budget stay you can usually get a room (basic but cosy Rs20 doubles) at **Hampi Power Station Inspection Bungalow**, 3 km (1¾ miles) out of Kamalapuram.

EATING OUT
Malligi Tourist Home has two nice restaurants. The indoor **Nirmal** does cheap vegetarian fare, including good standard thalis. The garden restaurant, the **Eagle**, is the perfect spot to cool off after a hot, dusty day in the ruins. It serves a range of tasty non-vegetarian meals, and has a bar with ice-cold beers. The Hotel Mayura has a restaurant and the **Shanbag Hotel**, next to the bus-stand in Station Rd, is famous for

its vegetarian food, and is always crowded. Another **Shanbag**, on the way to College Rd, offers North Indian cuisine in more relaxed surroundings.

GENERAL INFORMATION
KSTDC Tourist Office, behind Hospet bus-stand, is open 10 am–1 pm, 2–5 pm daily. It's fairly helpful and has a free map of the site, but Malligi Tourist Home has the better information.

There are post offices at Hospet, Hampi and Kamalapuram. State Bank of Mysore (for changing travellers' cheques) is next to Hospet tourist office.

MYSORE

The golden age of maharajahs and princes may be over, but Mysore remains a splendid city of palatial buildings, beautiful gardens and broad tree-lined boulevards. There are 17 palaces here in all, and even the most common public buildings are adorned with domes, turrets, pavilions and vaulting archways. No longer a princely state capital, it nevertheless retains its old charm, and its fame as 'Sandalwood City' of the south remains undiminished. A major centre for the manufacture of incense, the air here is fragrant and sweet with the perfume of musk and jasmine, sandalwood and rose.

Mysore derives its name from *Mahishasura*, the demon who wreaked havoc among the people in this area until destroyed by the goddess Chamunda. In the course of time, *Mahishuru*, town of Mahishasura, became 'Mysore', the cradle of many great dynasties in the South. During the rule of the Hoysalas, from the 12th to 14th centuries, art and architecture came to their peak resulting in the five famous sculptured temples of nearby Halebid, Belur and Somnathpur. Then, later in the 14th century, Mysore became the permanent capital of the Wodeyar Maharajahs. They lost it just once; to Hyder Ali in 1759, but regained it from the British after the death of Tipu Sultan in 1799. Under the protection of the Raj, the Maharajahs had nothing left to fear and went into palace-building in a big way. Yet the coming of Independence in 1947 spelt the end of their power, and of their many opulent palaces the finest, Amber Vilas, was turned into a museum, another into an art gallery, and three more into luxury hotels. The tourist revenue coming in from these establishments is sufficient to guarantee the present Maharajah just as rich a lifestyle as that of his predecessors.

Like Bangalore, Mysore is at a fairly high altitude (770 m), giving it a pleasant climate throughout the year. It is most pleasant from September to January, but travellers drift in right up to May. The best two months are September and October when the city is a post-monsoon spectacle of lush greenery and the 10-day festival of **Dussehra** takes place. This is the spectacular 'festival of nine lights', when many of the top musicians, dancers, and artists of Karnataka state turn up to give exhibitions and shows. It's best to arrive on the last (10th) day of the festivities, when a victory procession of elephants, cavalry and (real) gold and silver coaches, accompanied by bands, floats and parading soldiers, celebrate Chamundi's defeat of Mahishasura. Throughout October, the Maharajah's Palace is illuminated nightly.

ARRIVAL/DEPARTURE

Air
Although Mysore has a small airfield the Vayudoot service is suspended at the time of writing.

Rail
From Mysore, there are trains to Bangalore (6/7 daily, 3½ hours), to Goa (one train daily, changing at Londa Junction—from here, rather than wait many hours for a rail connection, proceed to Goa by bus), and to Bombay, Delhi and Calcutta.

Bus
The new Central bus-stand in Irwin Rd (north of Hotel Ritz) offers non-stop express buses to Bangalore (every 15 minutes; 3 hours) and Interstate buses to Ooty (scenic ride; 5½ hours), to Cochin (one night bus, departing 9.30 pm; no advance-booking so arrive early to grab seats) and to Coimbatore (14 hours) for Trivandrum (another 4 hours, by train). There's a useful cloakroom at the bus-stand where you can leave your bags if you're only visiting Mysore for the day.

WHAT TO SEE
Mysore is a small, relaxing place with a lot to see and do in town, and some worthwhile excursion spots (Sriringapatna, Somnathpur, Brindhavan, etc.) just outside it. Orientation is easy; you can walk from one end of the town to the other in 30 minutes. Auto-rickshaws are Rs2.50 per km, and because journeys are so short, you should never have to pay more than Rs10 anywhere. Local buses are useful for out-of-town destinations like Brindhavan, Chamundi, Sriringapatna, Government Silk Weaving Factory etc., and leave from the bus-stand near New Statue Square.

For a comprehensive viewing of the many sights, take one of the (good) city conducted tours. Allow a second day's sightseeing, either to return to certain places you want to see more of, or to do one of the wildlife excursions suggested.

City and Surrounds Tour (conducted tour bus, full-day)
St Philomena's Church–Art Gallery–Zoo–Maharaja's Palace–Chamundi Hill–Sriringapatna–Brindhavan Gardens

The first call is generally **St Philomena's Church**, at the north of town. This is one of the largest neo-Gothic style churches in India. Though built in 1931, its lofty grandeur and stained-glass interior are more suggestive of medieval than modern origin. Tour buses rarely stop long here and few of your Indian co-passengers will be Catholics.

The **Sri Chamarajendra Art Gallery**, just off New Statue Square, is of more general interest. It is housed within Jaganmohan Palace, and contains treasures of rare musical instruments, exotic wall decorations, original paintings of Ravi Varma, a couple of beautiful mother-of-pearl inlay sofas, and a marvellous French musical clock (each second marked by a drum beat, toy soldiers march out on parade every hour). Open 8 am–5 pm daily, admission Rs2, no photos allowed.

Mysore's **Zoological Gardens**, Lalitha Palace Rd (1 km; ⅔ mile east of the central bus-stand) are, apart from those of Hyderabad, the best in India. Over 1500 varieties of animals and birds live here, in near-natural surrounds. The brief tour stop is insufficient to see half what's available. Return on a separate occasion for a com-

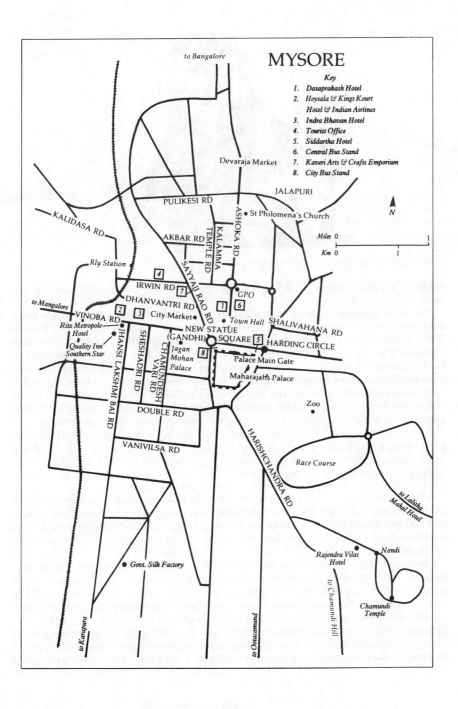

MYSORE

Key

1. Dasaprakash Hotel
2. Hoysala & Kings Kourt Hotel & Indian Airlines
3. Indra Bhavan Hotel
4. Tourist Office
5. Siddartha Hotel
6. Central Bus Stand
7. Kaveri Arts & Crafts Emporium
8. City Bus Stand

to Bangalore

Devaraja Market

JALAPURI

PULIKESI RD

KALIDASA RD

St Philomena's Church

AKBAR RD

ASHOKA RD
KALAMMA RD
TEMPLE RD

Rly Station

Miles 0   1
Km 0   1

N

4
IRWIN RD
7

SAYYAJI RAO RD

GPO

to Mangalore

DHANVANTRI RD

1 6

VINOBA RD
2 3 City Market

Town Hall

SHALIVAHANA RD

Ritz Metropole Hotel

Quality Inn Southern Star

JHANSI LAKSHMI BAI RD
SHESHADRI RD
CHAMUNDESH VARI RD

NEW STATUE (GANDHI) SQUARE
5 HARDING CIRCLE

8
Jagan Mohan Palace

Palace Main Gate

Maharajah's Palace

DOUBLE RD

Zoo

VANIVILSA RD

HARISHCHANDRA RD

Race Course

to Lalitha Mahal Hotel

Govt. Silk Factory

Rajendra Vilas Hotel

Nandi

to Karapura

to Ootacamund

to Chamundi Hill

Chamundi Temple

Nandi Bull, Chamundi Hill

prehensive visit (come early, when the big cats are awake). Open 8.30 am–5.30 pm daily, admission Rs2.

The **Indo-Saracenic Maharajah's Palace** in the town centre is Mysore's main attraction and the entrance by South Gate only. Built over a period of 15 years (1897–1912) after the old wooden palace was razed by fire, this imposing structure, a gleaming profusion of domes, turrets, archways and colonnades, was designed by the English architect Henry Irwin, with workmanship by local artists (the Hoysala-style wall decorations are especially fine). An immense structure, it measures 74.5 m long, 44 m high, 47.5 m wide. The interior is a Pandora's box of treasures: a Durbar Hall with jewel-studded throne, mosaic marble floors, crystal furniture, stained-glass domed ceiling (a miracle of art and design), hammered silver doors opening onto sumptuously furnished apartments, mirror-spangled pleasure rooms and a lovely portrait gallery. Hugely extravagant, but great fun. Open 10 am to 5.30 pm daily. Admission (Rs2 for each section) includes free guide service (tours every hour from 10 am). Cameras and shoes must be left at the entrance, unless you get permission from the Museum Director (office near ticket desk) to take photos. If you're in town on a Sunday evening (7 to 9 pm), return to the Palace to see it brilliantly illuminated with thousands of tiny bulbs. The atmosphere is amazing: teeming crowds of picnicking tourists, balloons, toys, snacks and food, fruit and sweetmeats, Indian music wailing out of loudspeakers, and of course the glittering backdrop of the fairytale palace.

Chamundi Hill (4 km; 2½ miles) out of Mysore, at an altitude of 1072m, is a popular beauty spot with panoramic views and elegant parks. Once a royal summer resort, the hill is now a major pilgrimage and tourist centre. At the top, visit the 12th-century **Sri Chamundeswari Temple**, built in the southern Dravidian style with a distinctive *gopuram*. Within, there's an interesting pillar with silver panels depicting Ganesh, Nandi, and Shiva's trident, facing into the solid-gold Chamunda figure. If visiting independently, note that the temple is only open from 9 am to noon, and 5 to 9 pm. In the open courtyard below it, you'll find the **Mahishasura Statue** (a giant technicolor pirate) erected in memory of Chamunda's slain demon. Behind it is the small **Godly Museum**. A third of the way down Chamundi Hill is the huge monolith **Nandi Bull**, the third-largest (49 m high) in India. To see Chamundi properly return by local bus and make the invigorating 1000-step pilgrims' climb.

Out at **Somnathpur** (45 km; 28 miles from Mysore) there's one of the most beautiful temples in the world. Built in 1268, dedicated to Keshava, it is one of the three great **Hoysala Temples** of Karnataka. Covered with beautiful carvings portraying various scenes from the *Ramayana* and other epics, also numerous fascinating depictions of Hoysala life and times—the temple is especially notable for the six horizontal friezes running round its baseline. Open 9 am–5 pm daily. The Rs1 admission includes a free guide service. There's a tourist canteen cum rest house in Somnathpur, should you wish to stay overnight.

The next stop is the ruins of **Sriringapatna**, 16 km (10 miles) out of Mysore. From this small island fortress-town straddling the river Cauvery came the two brilliant Muslim leaders Hyder Ali and his son Tipu Sultan, who ruled a powerful empire comprising much of southern India for 40 years. Tipu Sultan, the 'Tiger of Mysore', became the most dreaded foe of the British in the South, and inflicted two punishing defeats on the forces of the East India Company before at last being overcome in 1799. His beautiful fort was destroyed, but the elegant **Summer Palace** (Daria Daulat Bagh) remains intact. Set in beautiful gardens, approached via a corridor of sculpted trees, the stylish lime-green palace built in 1784 is mainly constructed of wood. The interior is beautifully painted in black, red and gold and features attractive floral decorations and various portraits of Tipu's contemporaries. Amongst the murals depicting battle scenes, there is one commemorating Tipu and Hyder Ali's victory at Polilur, the plaque beneath mocking the Deccan forces (who arrived too late to help the British) with the taunt 'they came like a boar and fled like a cow'. The superb little museum upstairs has a fascinating collection of engravings, family ink drawings, coins and prints illustrating Tipu's life and times, plus a number of his belongings. The palace is open 9 am–5 pm daily, admission Rs0.50. There are good guides for hire.

Beyond the Palace there's Tipu Sultan's mosque, the large and imposing **Jami Masjid**, notable for its tall minarets; also the **Gumbaz**, burial place of Tipu and Hyder Ali. Walking up to the extensive Fort ruins, note the small plaque, on your right, marking the spot where Tipu Sultan died in combat. Also, see the **Sri Ranganathaswamy Temple**, one of the oldest Dravidian temples in Karnataka, AD 894. A prominent white blockstone structure, supported by hundreds of monolith pillars, it houses a massive Vishnu reclining on a serpent and a soaring brass prayer column.

The ride back from Sriringapatna to Mysore is very picturesque, a continuous vista of palm-groves, rice paddies and sugar-cane plantations. For this journey alone, the bus tour is worthwhile. If you wish to stay at Sriringapatna, by the way, there are cheap riverside cottages for rent at the **Hotel Mayura River View** (tel 114).

Last stop of the day is at the fabulous **Brindhavan Gardens**. Situated 19 km (12 miles) north of Mysore, these are among the best known of Karnataka's attractions. Beautifully terraced below the recent (1937) Krishnarajasagar Dam, Brindhavan's ornamental gardens take their name from an original series in Mathura, south of Delhi. Taking as their theme the pastoral frolics of Krishna with his 16 000 gopis (handmaidens), they are of enormous popularity among young Indian couples. In high season (April/May) up to 400 tour buses per day swarm up here. Weekends are also excessively busy. Arriving here around dusk, you'll have time to view the landscaped lawns, rose gardens, flower bowers and conifers in the (vast) southern section before the mass exodus starts via the central boating lake (Rs3 boat trips) to see the pretty musical 'dancing fountains'. These are illuminated each evening from 7 to 8 pm Monday to Friday, 7 to 9 pm Saturday to Sunday. So are the gardens, which are transformed into a colourful fairyland of cascading fountains and twinkling lights. The walk back to the tour bus is delightful. For overnight stay, choose between the ex-palace **Krishnaraj Sagar Hotel** (tel Beluga 22) with rooms from Rs325 single, Rs450 double or the cheaper **KSTDC Tourist Home** (tel Beluga 52) with single and double rooms at Rs90 and Rs125. Both offer fine views, but are often full.

One sight rarely seen in Mysore is the marvellous **Rail Museum** in Krishnarajasagar Rd, just above the railway station itself. Almost as good as the one in Delhi, it houses antique engines, rolling stock, the Maharani's coach and a joyride mini-train. Open 9 am–5 pm daily, except Monday.

Wildlife Excursions
Bandipur Wildlife Sanctuary–Nagarhole Sanctuary

Mysore is the most convenient jumping-off point for two of India's best wildlife sanctuaries, and is well-connected to them by regular buses. **Bandipur Wildlife Sanctuary** (80 km; 50 miles south) is 690 sq km (266 sq miles) of mixed deciduous forest notable for its Indian bison, elephants, chital and spotted deer, macaques and numerous birds. Best seen between September and April. Elephant safaris can be arranged, along with all internal transport, via the Forest Lodge and Guest House officers. Accommodation *must* be advance-booked, via the Director of Project Tiger, Government House Complex, Mysore (tel 20901).

Nagarhole Sanctuary (74 km; 46¼ miles south-west) is 573 sq km (221 sq miles) of tropical and moist deciduous forests with a few swampy areas around the Kabini Lake shore, with tigers, elephants, leopards, sloth bears, wild boar and even more birds than Bandipur, visits to **Heballa Elephant Camp**, jeep and coracle trips and accommodation (forest lodges) can all be booked from the Asst Conservator of Forestry (tel Mysore 21159). The beautifully located **Kabini River Lodge** on the edge of the park has good rooms and a tariff that includes all meals and game-viewing from Rs1000 per person. Book through Jungle Lodges and Resorts, Shrungar Shopping Centre, Bangalore (tel 575195).

RECREATION
There's a good racecourse below Chamundi Hill, with popular meets on Wednesdays and at weekends (September to November only). Several cinemas, notably the Woodlands and the Ritz, show English films as matinees. Others, like the Shalimar and Sterling, show English films all day. Newspapers like the *Deccan Herald* and *Mofussil Diary* carry full details of current events and entertainments.

SHOPPING
Mysore is famous for its incense and its sandalwood, and these are the best buys. Other popular purchases are silk saris, printed silk, inlay work and jewellery.

To see the full range, visit **Kaveri Arts and Crafts Emporium** (tel 21258), Sayaji Rao Rd (closed Thursday), but avoid badly joined furniture and overpriced sandalwood. The best buys here are incense (*agarbathi*), rosewood (inlaid with deerbone, not ivory) and silk. For quality silks, catch a No. 4 or 5 bus out to the **Government Silk Weaving Factory** and **Karnataka Silk Industries Corporation Workshop**, both on Mananthody Rd. For pure 100% sandalwood; carvings, powder, paste, dust, oil, incense and even soap visit the small row of shops opposite the Zoo. Biggest and best is the **Handicraft Sales Emporium** (tel 23669), where you can buy small sandalwood Buddhas or Indian deities from Rs100 to 150, sandalwood oil by the vial or bottle, and sandalwood paste and powder by the gramme. The upstairs section does a fine line in gems and jewellery. Apart from Jaipur, Mysore is the best place to buy semi-precious stones and precious gems. The rubies, garnets and lapis lazuli are of particularly high quality. But take care when buying a 'line' stone; the orientation is all-important. With moonstones, sapphires and rubies alike, the line *must* be central.

Mysore's **Devaraja Market** is probably the best fruit and vegetable market in India. It's certainly one of the largest, running all the way down Sayaji Rao Rd from Dhanvantri Rd to New Statue Square. There's one section devoted exclusively to bananas and their many varieties. You can wander round here all day, and not get bored. Nobody returns empty-handed. Good purchases here include colourful bangles, lacquerwork and crafted silver jewellery. Marvellous little souvenirs are the packs of 10 assorted incenses, sold for around Rs30. But pack these carefully.

WHERE TO STAY

Luxury (over US$35/Rs1000 per room night)
The best of a generally poor assortment of luxury hotels is **Lalitha Mahal Palace**, T. Narasipur Rd (tel 26316, 27650, tlx 846-217), with some stylish rooms in the old building (Rs1300 single, Rs1450 double) overlooking the city.

Mid-range (US$10–35/Rs250–1000 per room night)
Quality Inn Southern Star, Vinobha Road (tel 27217, tlx 846-256) is a well-run mid-range hotel with comfortable air-conditioned rooms from Rs 500 single, Rs800 double.

Hotel Dasaprakash Paradise, 105 Vivekananda Rd, Yadavagiri (tel 266664, tlx 846-266 DASA IN) is the top Indian-style hotel, with single and double rooms from Rs275 and Rs335 respectively, a good restaurant and a pool. The **Hotel Metropole** (tel 20681) at 5 Jhansi Lakshmi Bai Rd, has recently been renovated; is popular for its spacious grounds, restaurant and bar, and colonial-style rooms from Rs300 single, Rs450 double. The Taj Group have recently taken over the **Rajendra Villas Hotel** on Chamundi Hill (tel 20690, tlx 846-230). When the renovation is completed toward the end of 1993, this old palace should rival Lalitha Mahal.

Budget (under US$10/Rs250 per room night)
Opposite the Metropole is the **Hotel Kings Court** (tel 25250) with cosy, personal atmosphere and big-bedded rooms (from Rs200 single, Rs250 double). An enjoyable Indian-style hotel is the **Siddhartha**, 73 Guest House Rd, Nazarbad (tel 26869). Well-located and quiet, with large carpeted rooms (single Rs150, double Rs220), tiled bathrooms and free newspapers/soap. KTDC's **Hotel Mayura Hoysala**, 2 Jhansi Lakshmi Bai Rd (tel 25349), is very much a case of pot luck with rooms from Rs100.

As a travellers' centre, Mysore has any number of budget guest-houses. Two on Dhanvantri Road are **New Gayathri Bhavan** and **Hotel Indra Bhavan**, with clean rooms (bathrooms attached) from Rs40. Over at Gandhi Square, **Hotel Durbar** (tel

20029) has okay rooms from Rs50, and two very popular restaurants. The nearby Srikanth Hotel (tel 22951) is also worth checking out: clean rooms with bath for Rs60.

EATING OUT
Hotel Metropole is where to dine in style: a stately, palatial restaurant offering well priced Indian, Chinese and continental cuisine and elegant service. After your meal for about Rs100 per head, relax in the air-con bar. At the Southern Star, next door to the Metropole, the main restaurant has extensive buffet lunches for Rs75 and a 24-hour coffee shop. Over at the Hotel Dasaprakash, there's a good cheap vegetarian restaurant, with meals from Rs50 per head and a memorable ice-cream parlour. Two popular roof-top restaurants in Gandhi Square are Shilpashri (consistently good veg and non-veg fare, nice bar) and Hotel Durbar (cheap Chinese, Mughlai and Indian food, tinny taped music). For good-value Rs8 south Indian thalis investigate the many cheapie restaurants in and around Dhanvantri Rd.

GENERAL INFORMATION
KSTDC Tourist Office (tel 22096) is in the Old Exhibition Building, Irwin Rd; waffly but helpful staff, poor handouts, but good information (hotels, tours) posted on various boards. Open 10 am–5.30 pm daily.

KSTDC Tourist Reception Centre (tel 2365) is in Hotel Mayura Hoysala, open 6.30 am–8.30 pm daily. It sells the Mysore city sightseeing tour which includes Somnathpur (Rs85, 7.30 am–8.30 pm) and the over-ambitious tour to Belur, Halebid and Sravanbelagola on Fridays and Sundays (Rs100, 7.30 am–8.30 pm).

Indian Airlines (tel 25349) is also in Hotel Mayura Hoysala complex, open 10 am–5.15 pm daily (except Sundays). State Bank of India is in St Mark's Rd. Central Post Office is in Ashoka Rd. Gita Book House, New State Square (near the bus-stand), is possibly the only place in town which sells a decent Mysore map.

OOTACAMUND (UDHAGAMANDALAM)

Former summer capital of the Madras Presidency (now Tamil Nadu), Ooty is popularly known as the Queen of Hill Stations. It nestles in the Nilgiris (Blue Hills) near the junction of Karnataka, Tamil Nadu and Kerala, at an altitude of 2308 m. Famous for its spectacular scenery and all-season climate, it is approached via the popular blue-train (cog railway) ride up from Coimbatore.

Ootacamund derives its name from a Toda term *Othakamanthu*, meaning 'village of huts'. The Todas, original settlers here before the British, are an aboriginal tribe who comprise most of the hill station's resident population. They still live in small barrel-shaped huts, and if invited in you'll have to crawl on all fours.

Ooty was first discovered by the Collector of Coimbatore, John Sullivan, who built first a residence (1819) and then created the lake (1823). The British quickly moved in, erecting stone cottages with flower gardens, laying the beautiful Botanical Gardens (1840) and developing facilities for golf, horse-racing, polo and tennis. In 1869, the hill station became the summer headquarters of the government in Madras.

Today, 'Snooty Ooty' is a rather rundown resort and retirement home for the rich. But it remains a popular watering hole for travellers, with a definite air of elegance and refinement still clinging to it. There are Raj reminders everywhere, notably in the terraced Botanical Gardens, the English public schools, the churches and, above the town, the tea-gardens and eucalyptus plantations. Even the climate is British; cool, even chilly, in the winter and one of the few places in India you'll need to bring warm clothing. Though most popular in September/October and April/May, it's far cheaper (low-season hotel discounts) and far less crowded in February/March. Ooty has its big **Summer Festival** throughout the month of May with tribal dances, live music and drama shows, held every evening at Anna Stadium. There's even a ballroom dancing competition when they can find enough people to participate!

ARRIVAL/DEPARTURE

Air
Indian Airlines has daily flights between Coimbatore (3 hours by bus from Ooty) and Bangalore (Rs600), Bombay (Rs1785) and Madras (Rs1031).

Rail
The toy train leaves for Mettupalaiyam/Coimbatore at 2.50 pm daily. From Coimbatore, there are regular trains for Madras, Madurai, Cochin etc. To reach Mettupalaiyam directly from Madras take the *Nilgiri Express* which leaves Madras Central at 9 pm and reaches at 7.20 am in time to connect with the waiting *Nilgiri passenger* to Ooty via stations with names such as Hill Grove, Coonoor, Ketti and Lovedale.

Bus
Ooty's smart, efficient bus-stand has a handy reservation desk for buses to Mysore (8 am, 9 am, 11.30 am, 1.30 pm, 3.30 pm; 4½ hours) and for Bangalore (6.30 am, 10.30 am, 12.30 pm, and 8 pm; 8 hours). There are also hourly buses to Mettupalaiyam (2 hours) and Coimbatore (3 hours).

WHAT TO SEE
Ooty is a place for pleasant walks, boating on the lake, and general relaxation. The air is very bracing, and, after the heat of the plains, you may need to take it easy the first day or two. There are some lovely walks in the area, and fine views over the Nilgiris, the surrounding hill stations and Ooty town itself. Owing to the spread-out nature of the viewpoints, you'll need some sort of plan. The suggested walking routes cover the main points of interest, but there are several other mini-treks available. In town, get around on foot, by cycle (hire bicycles in the market) or by auto-rickshaw (Rs10 for short trips). The focal point of the small town is Commercial Street, with its tourist office, banks, and many shops.

Walk One (on foot, full-day)
Botanical Gardens–St Stephen's Church–Ooty Club–Lake–Golf Course–Wenlock Downs

From either bus or rail station on the east edge of the lake, it's a winding 2-km (1¼-mile) walk north-west (via the racecourse, up Commercial St) to the **Botanical Gardens**. Created by the Marquis of Tweedale in 1847, these are 51 acres of terraced gardens and extensive lawns housing 650 varieties of plants. There's a big **Flower Show** here each May, and visitors can buy flowers and seedlings from the Curator's office. Just below the mini-lake, check out the intriguing 20 million-year-old fossil tree. Ascending through gardens of ornamental plants, orchids, ferns, conifers and rockplants keep an eye out for the local Toda community on the top levels. About 2000 of them live up here, almost exclusively engaged in the cultivation of potatoes and weaving. As a race, they are supposed to date back to Alexander the Great's Greeks. The women are tattooed, wear bright handwoven clothes, keep their hair in distinctive plaited loops, and are very feminist. They have up to four husbands apiece (all of them henpecked) and won't give male visitors the time of day, considering men a sub-species. Nearby, you'll see the **Raj Bhavan** (Government House), still used by the Tamil Nadu Governor as a summer residence.

Out of the gardens, turn right at the end of Garden Rd, then make a hairpin turn left into Higgins Rd to **St Stephen's Church**; a 20-minute ascent. The creation of a Captain John Underwood (1829), it is a typically English parish church, with Gothic exterior and Tuscan interior. Just below it is the select **Ooty Club**, well worth a visit for its amazing collection of Raj memorabilia (contact manager for permission to view) and famous as the place where snooker was invented in 1875. From here, it's a straight walk down to **Ooty Lake**: small (4 km; 2½ miles circumference), picturesque, with good boating and fishing facilities. This is Sullivan's artificial lake, chosen for its scenic surrounds, and still, despite silting and incursions of water-hyacinths, the perfect place to spend an afternoon messing about in boats. The **Boat House** here (open from 8 am to 6 pm) hires out rowing boats at Rs35 per hour (plus Rs25 deposit). Next to it is a pony-rank.

In the afternoon, try a lovely walk (6 km; 3¾ miles, 3 hours return) up to the **Golf Club**, bear right at the top of the Lake, then left at Finger Post into Golf Links Rd. The scenery is very varied and picturesque, and if you turn up at 9 am sharp, you can usually get a game of golf (Rs100 green fee including hire of clubs and balls) on the expansive 18-hole course. Walking on a further kilometre, you'll come to **Wenlock Downs**, offering spectacular views down over the Coimbatore plains, Ketti Valley, the Mysore plateau, and the tea estates. Alternatively, visit **Hindustan Photo Films** (also a kilometre from the golf course) for its interesting model room demonstrating the manufacture of sensitised photographic materials. You may need prior permission to visit so enquire at the golf course.

Walk Two (bus, then on foot; 5/6 hours)
Dodabetta Heights

This is a very pleasant excursion, best done in the afternoon. Take a bus (20-minute journey, regular service from Ooty bus-stand) up to **Dodabetta Heights**, the highest peak (nearly 3000 m; 9750 ft) in the Nilgiris. There's an observation point with telescope at the top, and on a clear day the views down over the hill ranges, plateaux and plains are superb. But the walk back down's a 3-4-hour descent (10 km: 6¼ miles) through tea-gardens, terraced fields, wooded glades and pretty valleys. If you get tired, you can always hitch a bus for a quick lift back to town.

Other good viewpoints in the area include **Snowdon Peak** (panoramic view of Mysore), **Cairn Hill** (overlooking Avalanche River) and **Elk Hill**, which is just an hour's walk from Ooty. Further information, plus details of the many local treks available from the Trek Director, Department of Tourism, Government of Tamil Nadu, Madras (tel 849803).

Wildlife Excursion
Madumalai Wildlife Sanctuary

From Ooty, it's a 2½-hour express bus journey (60 km; 37½ miles) to **Madumalai Wildlife Sanctuary**. Before leaving, be sure to advance-book accommodation; there is a choice of either Rs20 dormitory beds or twin-bedded rooms from Rs75 in forest lodges (contact the Wildlife Warden in Ooty on Coonoor Rd, tel 3114). There are two private lodges at Masinagudi. **Jungle Hut** run by Joe and Hermie Mathias has comfortable rooms, great bird-watching, game-viewing and elephant rides for Rs1000 per person, including food. Contact Mathias, Masinagudi PO, Nilgiris 643223 (tel Masinagudi 240—via Ooty, Bangalore 578686). **Bamboo Banks Farm House**, nearer Masinagudi village (tel Masinagudi 222) has rooms from Rs450.

Madumalai is 322 sq km of dense, varied deciduous forest over undulating terrain; thick jungle is interspersed with open areas which eventually connect with Bandipur and Nagarhole Parks. The animals in the sanctuary include gaur (often called bison in south India), sambhar, spotted deer, tiger, leopard, wild boar, pangolin (a type of scaly ant-eater) and many birds. Jeeps and vans can be hired, but the best way of seeing the reserve is on elephant-back. You can hire an elephant from Theppakadu village, in the heart of the sanctuary, from 6 to 8 am, 4 to 6 pm. The charge for a 4-person howdah-load (1-hour trip) is Rs80. It's an amazing experience, for the elephants crash through the undergrowth, stopping for absolutely nothing; if there's a tree in their path, they simply root it up. An early-morning ride is recommended.

RECREATION
If walking, pony-riding, boating and golfing are not enough, there's good fishing to be had (carp and trout) at Avalanche (25 km; 15¾ miles away) Emerald and Parson's Valley, and in Ooty Lake itself (contact the Assistant Director of Fisheries near the bus-stand (tel 2232) for a licence). For indoor games: badminton, table tennis, visit Anna Stadium, below the Botanical Gardens. Of the several cinemas in town, the Liberty in Commercial Rd is most popular.

SHOPPING
Tribal Toda jewellery, shawls and silver can be found at **Suraaj** in Main Bazaar, or **Suraaj Paradise** in Commercial Rd. Prices are not cheap, so bargain hard. **Vimal Gems & Jewellery**, next to Nahar Hotel in Charing Cross, has a good selection of silver jewellery, semi-precious stones and Nilgiri spices and honey. Two government emporia nearby, **Poompuhar** and **Chellarams**, sell the full range of Ooty handicrafts at fixed prices. Buy tea and eucalyptus oil, the two most famous local products, at **Idco Tea** next to the tourist office.

WHERE TO STAY

Luxury (over US$35/Rs1000 per room night)
There is a choice of deluxe rooms or cottages with verandah, from US$50 single, US$55 double at Taj Group's reputable **Hotel Savoy**, 77 Sylks Road (tel 4142, telex 8504-207) which also arranges golf and horse-riding. The Taj have also recently taken over the **Fernhill Palace** (tel 3910), built in 1842 by the Maharajahs of Mysore and set in a large estate. When renovation is complete this will be a superb property.

Mid-range (US$10–35/Rs250–1000 per room night)
Quality Inn Southern Star Havelock Road (tel 3601, tlx 850-4213) has rooms from Rs450 single, Rs850 double. **Hotel Lake View,** West Lake Rd (tel 3904, 3580) has a nice location, many useful facilities, double rooms only at Rs340. As with all Ooty's hotels, rates are heavily discounted in the low season but charge 25% more during the Christmas-New Year period and in the May–June holidays.

Budget (under US$10/Rs250 per room night)
The best value in the budget range is **Nahar Hotel,** Charing Cross (tel 2173), run by jolly Babuji. A well-run, well-located place this, with a bakery, a vegetarian restaurant, and cosy, livable rooms at Rs100 single, Rs175 double. **Hotel Tamil Nadu** (tel 2543) up on the hill is comfortable, with communal dining hall, and rooms from Rs150 single, Rs250 double. The dormitory beds in the attached **Youth Hostel** are a good deal but are nearly always taken.

    YWCA (tel 2218) on Anandagiri Ettines Rd near the bus-stand takes men and women and has a few charming cottage rooms at Rs100. **Vishu Lodge** in the bazaar has nice clean rooms, with bath, at Rs75.

EATING OUT
For a real taste of the Raj, try to get invited to lunch or dine at the Ooty Club. If this is not possible dine out at **Fernhill Palace.** The palatial 'restaurant' features elegant but painfully slow service, romantic lighting, and well-priced Mughlai/continental cuisine. Eat well for around Rs100 a head, and have a chuckle over the menu.

    Punjabi food is good at **Paradise Restaurant** in Commercial Rd, and the nearby **Tandoor** is reliable for non-vegetarian fare. Both cost from Rs60 per head. **Nahar Tourist Home** has a cheap vegetarian restaurant, popular with *thali*-lovers. **Shinkows** in Commissioner's Rd (near Collectorate) is best for Chinese food, while town residents favour **Kurungi** (near the tourist office) for local-style Indian meals. Of Ooty's many bakeries, **V.K. Bakery,** 148 Commercial Rd, still makes just about the best piping-hot fresh bread, mutton puffs, coconut balls, pies and cakes in India!

GENERAL INFORMATION
The tourist office at the Super Market building, Charing Cross (tel 3964) organises tours. There's far better information (and good sightseeing tours) at **King Travels** (tel 3137) across the road, and **Blue Mountain Tours,** Nahar Shopping Centre, Charing Cross.

    The post office is near the Collectorate, and State Bank of India overlooks Commercial St. Higginbotham's bookshop is opposite Chellaram's department store in Charing Cross area.

Part VIII

THE KATHMANDU VALLEY
NEPAL

Durbar Square, Patan

The history of Nepal goes back a long way. Its name is attributed to the 7th-century Chinese traveller Hieun Tsiang. He never visited, but during his travels in India he recorded all he heard about the land of 'Ni-Po-La'. However, until the 18th century the history of the present kingdom has centred on Kathmandu Valley. Even now, hill-people travelling to Kathmandu say they are going to Nepal. It is difficult to believe that barely 200 years ago Nepal extended as far west as the Kangra Valley of Himachal Pradesh and east to Bhutan.

Kathmandu Valley is thought to have been settled from prehistoric times. This is supported by Neolithic artefacts, and the fact that the region is extremely fertile. Rich in flora and fauna, it would have been a favourite place for hunter-gatherers; eventually farming communities settled here.

The Myth

Legend has it that a long long time ago, the Kathmandu Valley was a holy lake some 22.5 km (14 miles) in circumference. Vipasuri, the first Buddha, visited the lake and tossed a lotus seed into its deep blue-black waters from the top of Nagarjung mountain. The seed blossomed some 80 000 years later, into a thousand-petalled flower carrying the dazzling light of *swayambhu* (self-born). Many worshippers came in pilgrimage to the lake to pray to the sacred flame. Among them was the Buddha Manjushri, who came from China to see this marvel. Wishing to make the *swayambhu* more accessible to the pilgrims, he circled the lake to find the lowest point, which he struck with his Sword of Wisdom. The lake waters drained away, and the newly created valley became a sacred place of pilgrimage for the devout. Centuries later, a Buddhist priest hid the sacred light in a hole under a precious stone, to save it during the present Age of Sin (Kali Yuga), and built a shrine and *stupa* on it. The *stupa* of Swayambhunath is now one of the holiest shrines in Nepal.

Interestingly, geologists who have studied the area confirm that there indeed was a lake at the site of present day Kathmandu. Also that the Kotwal Gorge, which drained the lake, and through which the Bagmati river flows was created as the result of a massive earthquake several thousand years ago.

The Early Dynasties: 700 BC–AD 1200

Recorded history begins with the **Kirati dynasty** of the 8th and 7th centuries BC. A Kirati king, Yalambar, is mentioned as having fought the great 'Mahabharata' battle. During the reign of the seventh Kirati king (there were 28 in all), Gautam Buddha and his favourite disciple, Ananda, are believed to have visited the valley and rested in Patan. Emperor Ashoka, after his conversion to Buddhism, visited Lumbini and Kathmandu valley in the 3rd century BC when he erected Patan's five ancient stupas which still bear his name.

While historians are divided on the origin of the Kirati kings—some say they were indigenous to the valley, others that they hailed from the East—there is no doubt that the Lichhavis who displaced the Kiratis were Rajputs from North India. Around AD 300 the last Kirati King, Gasti, was defeated by the Lichhavis, who were to reign for over 550 years.

The Kiratis had ruled the valley for over a thousand years, and under them Kathmandu had become a prosperous commercial centre, centred on the trans-Himalayan trade route between Tibet and India with a thriving export trade in woven woollen carpets and blankets, musk, yak tails, iron and red copper.

The **Lichhavi dynasty** is credited with having introduced the Hindu religion, with its attendant caste system and other socio-religious traditions which have lasted to the present day. (By this time, Nepali Boddhish art and architecture was quite highly developed, as expressed is several viharas (monasteries), chaityas (chapels) and stupas.) The Lichhavi kings also brought about the first Golden Age of Nepalese arts, through patronage.

The **Thakuri dynasty,** which followed the Lichhavis, is said to have started with King Amsuvarman in AD 602. Amsuvarman's palace, as described by the 7th-century Chinese traveller Wang Hsuan Tse, gives an indication of the king's immense riches, and the architectural abilities of the Nepali craftsmen of the time. His chronicles describe the royal palace as having a seven-storey copper-roofed tower, ornamented with precious stones and pearls; golden fountains shaped like dragons that spewed forth clear water; and a king who sat upon a lion throne wearing golden ear-rings, jade, pearls, crystal, coral and amber. Wang Hsuan Tse also describes the royal court, guards and more importantly, the people; their jewellery and their love of music and theatrical performances. Trade was highly developed using copper coins. People lived in carved and painted wooden houses.

The valley also remained a centre for Buddhist monks, teachers, translators and pilgrims and became a conduit in the 7th century through which Buddhism spread to Tibet. Amsuvarman's line was displaced by other Thakuri dynasties, notably the **Thakuris of Nuwakot** in AD 1043 and then in 1082 by a **second Rajput dynasty**. Such political upheavals mark what has become known as Nepal's Dark Ages, which continued till the **Malla dynasty** took firm control in AD 1200. Yet trade and commerce flourished in the valley during this time, and settlements expanded all along the trans-Himalayan trade routes. Among the several kings who ascended the throne for brief periods during this time, Gunakamadeva (10th century) is believed to be the founder of Kartipur, today's Kathmandu. Gunakamadeva started the practice of holding three great religious festivals: Indrajatra, Krishna Jayanti and Machhendranath Jatra. According to legend, a powerful god came in disguise to watch one of these festivals and could not return because of the spell cast by some tantrics. He was finally released in exchange for the boon of a celestial tree. A large wooden building or *kasthamandap* was constructed out of the wood of this celestial tree and the name Kathmandu seems to have been derived from this.

The Malla Epoch: AD 1200–1500

By the beginning of the 13th century, the valley was divided into the three small kingdoms of Kathmandu, Patan and Bhaktapur, which were periodically at war with each other over the control of the lucrative trans-Himalayan trade route. Ironically, this political turmoil marks the beginning of the **Malla ('Wrestler')** epoch, which lasted for 550 years, and was a period of artistic creativity and unity. The first king to hold the title Malla was King Ari Deva in AD 1200, who presided over the laying of Kathmandu Valley's rich cultural and artistic foundations. For the next half century there were explosions of creative activity in all fields: architecture, sculpture, wood carving, and painting. The best surviving examples of the artistic expression of this wood-carving era are the gilded statues of three great Malla rulers in the Durbar Squares of Patan and Kathmandu.

The Malla kings also laid the socio-religious fabric of the valley kingdoms. One of the rulers of the period (early 14th century) was Raja Hari Singh from Tirhut, a small kingdom in the foothills to the south of Kathmandu. He brought with him the image of the goddess Taleju Bhawani from south India, who is still the royal deity. The kings themselves ruled by Divine Right, and were considered to be incarnations of the Hindu god Vishnu. Despite being Hindus they were tolerant of Buddhism, the Vajrayana sect of which was widespread at the Royal Court as well as among the people in the valley.

The Malla epoch was marred by foreign invasions and infighting among the royal houses. Shamsuddin Ilyas, the Muslim Sultan of Bengal invaded Kathmandu and destroyed several temples. His army damaged and desecrated Buddhist and Hindu images including that of Lord Pashupatinath, still the most important Shiva temple in Nepal, and greatly damaged the Swayambhunath Stupa of the Sacred Flame . In the aftermath of the invasion, the Brahman empire of the valley broke apart. About this time, various Rajput families fleeing the Muslim rulers in India settled in the mountains of Nepal and established small independent kingdoms. (Among these was the kingdom of Gorkha which was to play a major role in the political scene some four centuries later).

By the end of the 14th century, King Jayasthiti Malla brought together the three kingdoms of Kathmandu, Patan and Bhaktapur as well as several smaller kingdoms located nearby. A period of stability and prosperity followed during which the caste system was strengthened within the larger framework of Hinduism. The Malla kings remained tolerant of Buddhism and worship of both Hindu and Buddhist deities continued.

The Flickering Flame AD 1500–1700
King Yaksha Malla (1428–82), Jayasthiti's grandson, was the last great king of his dynasty. He expanded his territory northwards up to the border with Tibet, south of the Ganges, east to Sikkim and west to the Kali Gandaki river. On his death, however, the kingdom became divided, and for the next 200 years his descendants fought among themselves, primarily for the largest cut of the revenue from passing caravans on the trade route, but also for the profits to be made from the minting of coins and the collection of taxes in the valley.

Paradoxically, as during the first 200 years of the epoch, these two centuries of political instability were a golden age for the arts. Rivalry between the three cities of Kathmandu (Kanitipur), Patan (Lalitpur) and Bhaktapur (Bhadgaon) resulted in the construction of fine palaces, pagodas and temples. Many of the magnificent buildings now seen in the three cities date back to this period.

The Making of Modern Nepal

Of the 46 rival kingdoms in the mountains of western Nepal, the **Shah dynasty** of the Gorkha kingdom emerged as the most powerful. The ninth king of the Shah dynasty, Prithvi Narayan Shah was bold, powerful and ambitious. Over 26 years of preparations, sieges and battles, he and his army of Gorkhas conquered all the independent kingdoms. Kathmandu fell in 1768 and the Shah dynasty was established at the Royal Palace in Kathmandu.

Prithvi Narayan Shah's descendants continued their expansionist policies and by 1814 had brought under Shah rule a large area stretching from Sikkim in the east to beyond Garhwal in the west.

Nepal signed a commercial treaty with the British in the early 19th century, but this could not prevent a full-scale war between the parties in the *terai* region (1814–16) as a direct result of Nepal's forays into areas linked by treaty to British India. The Gorkhas were defeated and were forced to sign the 'Treaty of Friendship' of 1816, by which Nepal was stripped of all the newly acquired territories including Sikkim, and had to accept a British Resident at Kathmandu.

The 1816 treaty also made Nepal a political dependant of the Raj, because it stipulated that contacts with all eastern nations had to be made through England. However, as Nepalis cite with some pride, Nepal was never colonised, nor ruled by outsiders. After signing the Treaty of Friendship, it closed its borders to all foreigners except for the British Resident and his successors. The Resident had no function at all, except for an annual meeting with the king; the Nepalese rulers retained full control of the country and maintained a standing army of some 19 000 men. Gradually, however, power passed from the hands of the king to the prime minister, and successive Shah monarchs were relegated to the background. Intrigue, plots, counterplots and murder were the order of the day. Finally, in 1846, after the bloody Kot Massacre, where armed soldiers killed dozens of Nepal's leading nobles and over a hundred lower officials attending a meeting summoned by the queen, an army general named Jung Bahadur Kunwar engineered himself into the post of prime minister.

Fall and Rise of the Monarchy

Jung Bahadur later took on the title Maharajah and called himself Jung Bahadur Rana. He made the office of the prime minister hereditary and thus began what is known as 'Ranocracy', Prime Ministers being the supreme rulers of Nepal in all but name. The Shah kings remained very much in the background as figureheads. Jung Bahadur Rana is credited with progressive steps such as the abolition of *sati* (the ritual suicide by a widow on her husband's funeral pyre) and the restriction of capital punishment; his successors abolished slavery and reformed the forced labour system; but the Ranas enriched themselves at the cost of Nepal, and did little to modernise the kingdom and to ease the living conditions of its poorer citizens. The 104-year long reign of Ranas ended when King Tribhuvan fled Nepal in November 1950. Confrontations intensified between the Ranas on one side and the King and the Nepal Congress Party, with active support from India, on the other. In 1951, a compromise brokered by the Indian Government sent the Ranas into relatively comfortable exile in India, and King Tribhuvan returned to Kathmandu.

King Tribhuvan opened the doors of Nepal to the world in 1951, but democratic government was not established until 1991 during the present reign of Tribhuvan's grandson, King Birendra. Under the new constitution, Nepal is declared to be 'a multi-ethnic multilingual, democratic, independent, indivisible, sovereign, Hindu and Constitutional Monarchical Kingdom'. The King is the constitutional monarch of Nepal and a symbol of Nepalese unity. Members of the 205-seat Legislative Assembly are chosen directly by the electorate.

The Present

Nepal now faces several major problems. It is one of the poorest countries in the world; average per capita annual income is less than US$160. Economic development is extremely slow, hampered by rapid population growth and other restraints like an antiquated land-ownership system, transportation difficulties and lack of natural resources. The bulk of the population is dependent on agriculture as their only source of livelihood, and Nepal's main source of foreign exchange is from tourism and foreign aid. Imports are extensive; the costliest being petroleum for energy. Yet Nepal's abundant hydel potential remains largely untapped.

For the visitor, however, this is a land rich with natural beauty. The three cities of the Kathmandu Valley have retained much of their traditional way of life; they celebrate festivals throughout the year, old skills have been handed down through generations of craftsmen and a vibrancy remains in their day-to-day activity. Whether in the bazaars of Kathmandu or on a trekking trail in the far west of the country, the people of the Kathmandu Valley almost always have a warm smile for a stranger, and often extend an invitation to join their family for a meal, a celebration, or just to share a cigarette.

WHEN TO GO
The best time to visit Nepal is during the winter: October to March. The tropical low lands are very hot and humid in summer (April to June). The rains start in June and generally last for 3 months. Winter nights are rather chilly, but the sun warms up the atmosphere quickly and daytime is cool and pleasant with clear skies and lovely views of the Himalaya.

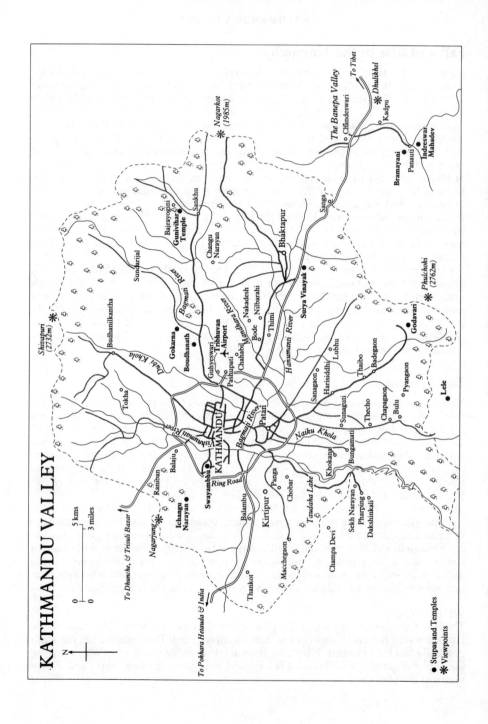

The Lie of the Land

Nepal is a land-locked country situated along the axis of the central Himalayan range: 800 km (497 miles) long and from 90 to 220 km (56 to 137 miles) wide. The altitude varies from near sea-level to 8848 m above sea-level at the summit of Mount Everest. (Including Everest, Nepal has 8 of the world's 10 highest mountains.)

Nepal's topography can be broadly divided into four ecological zones: lowland, midland, highland and trans-Himalayan. The lowland zone comprises a narrow strip along the southern border with India. This is the *terai*; an area of thick forests and riverine grassland ranging in altitude from 60 m to 300 m above sea-level. The climate is tropical and temperature varies from 38°C in summer to 10°C in winter. Heavy rains fall between June and September.

The midland zone occupies two hill ranges running from Pavaley to the Himalaya, the Mahabharata Lekh and the Shivalik Hills. The valleys between these ranges are often called inner *terai* or *duns*. The midland zone used to be impenetrable with thick forests. Now most of the trees have been cleared and the area is densely populated. The climate is subtropical and varies according to the altitude, which ranges from 1000 m to 3500 m.

The highland zone comprises almost all northern Nepal, and the eight major Himalayan peaks higher than 800 m: Everest, Kanchenjunga, Lhotse, Makalu, Cho Oyu, Dhaulagiri, Manaslu and Annapurna. The terrain ranges from coniferous forests at around 3000 m, to alpine meadow-zone, to the barren rocky slopes and perpetual snowline between 5000 m and 6000 m. The area is extremely difficult to traverse and south faces of the mountains are steep (inhibiting formation of glaciers), and several rivers have cut deep gorges on their way to the lower valleys.

The trans-Himalayan ranges in north-western Nepal, about 50 km north of the main Himalayan range comprise several peaks between 6000 m and 7000 m, and marks the boundary between Tibet and Nepal.

ARRIVAL/DEPARTURE
Kathmandu, the capital of Nepal is well connected to all major international cities by air, and accessible from neighbouring India and Tibet by road.

Air
Nepal's flag-carrier **Royal Nepal Airlines** links Kathmandu with Bombay, Calcutta, Delhi, Dhaka, Dubai, Hong Kong, Bangkok, Singapore, Frankfurt, London, Colombo, Karachi and Lhasa. **Indian Airlines** has daily flights from Delhi (Rs1616/US$140 and Varanasi (Rs788/US$72) and four flights a week from Calcutta (Rs.1276/US$105). **Thai Airways** operate several flights a week between Kathmandu and Bangkok. **Singapore Airlines** has a weekly flight between Kathmandu and Singapore. Other international airlines with services to Kathmandu are **Lufthansa, Pakistan International Airlines (PIA), Biman Bangladesh, China Southwest Airways, Burma Airways Corporation and Druk Airways**.

Tribhuvan Airport is 4 km (2½ miles) east of Kathmandu. Most major hotels have courtesy pick-up services for their guests. Metered taxis are available, though it is cheaper to opt for Sajha Yatayat's Deluxe Bus service which links the airport with central Kathmandu. This bus service touches major hotels. For the adventurous, the city bus service provides an even cheaper, though more crowded, alternative.

Overland from India

For those travellers for whom time is not a constraint, and particularly for those travelling in north-eastern and eastern India, there are several entry-points to Nepal. The main crossings are Sunauli, Birganj (Raxaul) and Kakarbhitta.

Sunauli is the most popular crossing from Delhi via Lucknow and Gorakhpur. The Delhi–Gorakhpur leg of the journey takes 16 hours by train, and Gorakhpur to Sunauli is an hour's ride by bus. From Sunauli, there are several buses to Kathmandu, leaving morning and evening, which take 12 hours. There are also buses to Pokhara. **Raxaul** on the India-Nepal border is 3 hours by bus from Muzaffarnagar, which you can reach from Calcutta by train (12 hours). Muzaffarnagar can also be reached from Patna (1½hours). Across the border from Raxaul is **Birganj** from where buses ply the 200 km (125 miles) to Kathmandu regularly. Birganj has an airport and there are daily flights to Kathmandu.

For visitors wishing to enter Nepal from Darjeeling and Sikkim, **Kakarbhitta** is the nearest crossing: an hour's ride away by taxi from Siliguri, the nearest major town to Darjeeling and Sikkim. From Kakarbhitta, buses ply to Biratnagar from where there are daily flights to Kathmandu. The hard way from Kakarbhitta to Kathmandu is by road, a distance of 541km (338 miles).

Overland from Tibet

It is possible to travel from Lhasa to Kathmandu by road, but the journey takes 3 days and lack of adequate overnight resting places as well as difficult road conditions make this an uncomfortable trip. However, the terrain and the views make it a memorable one. Starting from Lhasa, the road crosses several 5000-m passes and the second Tibetan town of Shigatse. A brief glimpse of the north face of Mt Everest is possible at Tingari village. After Tingari comes the Lalung La pass at a height of 5050 m, after which it is mostly downhill. Within a few hours you reach the pine forests surrounding the Sun Kosi river gorge which contrasts strongly with the frigid Tibetan plateau. Beyond the river lies the border outpost of Zhangmu or Khasa. Across the border is the Nepali village of Kodari, connected to Kathmandu by a 114-km (71¼-mile) highway.

Customs

Travellers who are using their own transport need a *carnet de passage en douane* to show at the border before crossing over to Nepal. This exempts the owner from having to pay customs duty for a period of 3 months. This can be obtained from the AA in the UK and India, the RAC in the UK only; and from the AAA in the US.

GETTING AROUND

Air

The easiest and least time-consuming way to travel within Nepal is by air. Royal Nepal Airlines (RNAC) has the monopoly on the domestic routes. Its fleet of 19-seat Twin Offers and smaller Pilatus Porter aircraft fly to 41 destinations from Kathmandu; some of the airstrips are nothing but grassy landing strips perched high on mountain-sides. Flights are dependent on weather conditions and may be cancelled at short notice.

The RNAC also has a 3 times daily flight (except on Saturdays) between late September to May, for visitors wishing to see the eastern Himalaya and Mt Everest. The plane flies within 20 km (12½ miles) of Khumbu Himal and the views are spectacular. The first flight of the day provides the clearest views and the best photographic opportunities.

Road/Rail
Nepal's roads are poor and there is only about 100 km (62 miles) of railway line. The southern *terai* region has the major share of the country's road network while the mountainous interior, north of the Kathmandu–Pokhara road, is accessible only on foot.

Because the steep mountain trails are difficult even for pack-animals, most of Nepal's goods are shifted by manpower. Generations of porterage as well as travellers have created between 15 000 km and 20 000 km (12 500 miles) of footpaths, linking hamlets, villages, towns with each other and with Kathmandu. Nepal now has some 6300 km (4000 miles) of road including two major highways built with foreign assistance, compared with 376 km (235 miles) in 1952.

Bus
Nepal's state transport service, Sajha Yatayat, runs regular and deluxe buses to various destinations from Kathmandu. Night services are slightly better, faster and less crowded. There are several privately owned tourist buses to popular destinations, tickets and reservations for which can be got from travel agents in the Thamel area. For the Sajha Yatra buses and private buses, tickets and reservations are available at Central Bus Park on the east side of Tundikhel in Kathmandu, and also at Sundhara, near the post office.

Car
For leisurely travel, both within Kathmandu and outside, Hertz and Avis provide rental-cars and drivers, through Gorkha Travels and Yeti Travels respectively. Private cars and taxis are also available for short/long trips.

Motorcycle
Another way to travel in Nepal is to rent motor-cycles. This can be fun, but the traffic in the valley tends to be quite chaotic and the highways/roads rather tough-going. International Driving Licence-holders can obtain a temporary Nepali Driving Licence from the Police Station at Hanuman Dokha. Most rental shops are located on Dharma Path, south of the New Road.

Bicycle
It is possible to rent a bicycle from any of the several shops in Thamel, Freak Street and Bhotahiti. Many tourists opt for a bike because it frees them from the restraints of organised tours of Kathmandu, and to venture outside the city.

Scooters and Rickshaws
Within Kathmandu, apart from taxis and private-cars, short-distances can be covered by scooters (3-wheelers) and rickshaws. Scooters have meters, but it is best to settle a price before boarding a rickshaw.

KATHMANDU

Old Kathmandu city is located at the confluence of the Bagmati and Vishnumati rivers, and within a core of some 5 km lie the most interesting areas. It can be confusing to find one's way about, but the best way to experience the city is on foot.

City Tour (gentle walking, 3–4 hours)
Durbar Square–Kumari Bahal–Kasthamandap–Jaishi Dewal–Hanuman Dokha–Indrachowk–Asantol–Rani Pokhari

Through the ages and successive dynasties Kathmandu synthesised religions, cultures and peoples to its present distinct character. Because of the closed-door policy of Nepal's rulers from the mid-19th century to 1952, it and its sister cities of the valley, Patan and Bhaktapur, retain their unique culture. Added to this, natural beauty and artefacts created over centuries make the valley a living museum.

Kathmandu takes its name from **Kasthamandap**, a wooden pagoda near Hanuman Dokha and this is the best place to start a leisurely walk through the old city. Take a taxi or rickshaw from your hotel, down New Road to the junction with Indrachowk. New Road connects the ancient. **Durbar Square** with the parade ground of Tundikhel and was laid after the 1934 earthquake levelled part of the old city. The old trade route to Tibet began from Kasthamandap and the city grew along it. Walk westward through **Basantapur square**. The old Royal Palace appears on your right dominated by the nine-storey **Basantapur Tower** decorated by some of the finest wood carving in the valley. The square is now used by street-sellers but was earlier used as elephant stables.

At the far end of the square you reach the richly decorated **Kumari Bahal** on your left. The tradition of the Kumari, or living goddess, is unique to Nepal; a symbol of the peaceful coexistence of Hinduism and Buddhism, and the merging of one into the other. The Kumari is said to be the living incarnation of the Hindu Goddess Durga, as invested in a young virgin Buddhist Newari girl chosen after a search conducted by five high priests. After a series of tests, the new Kumari is installed in a secret ritual held at the Taleju Temple (see p.499). She is revered and worshipped by the royalty as well as ordinary citizens, living in her 18th-century palace on the edge of Durbar Square. She makes rare public appearances during festivals. Her own 3-day festival of Kumari Jatra is held within the longer Indra Jatra, when her chariot is dragged by worshippers through the streets of Kathmandu.

Non-Hindu devotees are not allowed beyond the courtyard of her palace, but you can occasionally see her when she appears on her elaborately carved balcony. Photography is strictly prohibited. A new girl is chosen when the Kumari attains puberty. The ex-Kumari receives a small pension from the state and is free to marry and live a normal life, though in reality she finds it difficult to find a husband because of the belief that a man who marries an ex-Kumari has an early death. Apart from the Royal Kumari of Kathmandu, there are at least 11 different Kumaris throughout Nepal who are worshipped in the same manner.

Just beyond the Kumari Bahal is the **Kasthamandap**, said to have been constructed from the wood of a sacred tree, during the reign of King Laxmi Narsingha Malla in the beginning of the 16th century. The Kasthamandap is also known as Maru Sattal and houses images of the four Vinayakas, or guardian deities of Kathmandu valley:

Surya Vinayaka, Jala Vinayaka, Karya Vinayaka and Ashok Vinayaka (also known as Kathmandu Ganesh or Maru Ganesh). Five minutes away, down a side road, is the Shiva Temple of **Jaishi Dewal**, famous for its erotic carvings. This area was the nucleus of the valley during the Lichhavi period.

Back in Durbar Square, you are surrounded by small shrines, bells, temples and statues. Often known as **Hanuman Dokha**, after the entrance to the Royal palace guarded by a statue of Hanuman the monkey-god caked in red vermilion paste, Durbar Square with its temples and palaces used to be the centre of all political, social and other activities. To a large extent, this remains so. It is worth climbing the steps of **Maju Deval Temple**, a three-tiered pagoda-roofed shrine. From the top steps you can sit and take in the excitement and life of the square. Nearby is the **Statue of King Pratap Malla** on a lotus-topped column.

Opposite the temple are models of **Shiva and Parvati** leaning out of the top window of another temple. To one side of the square is the **Kal Bhairav**, a huge bas-relief of the God Bhairav with six arms and a garland of human heads. To your right is the entrance to the **Hanuman Dokha Palace** with the guardian statue on the left. The palace can be visited between 10.30 am and 4.15 pm (3 pm in winter and closed on Tuesday). There is a Rs10 entrance fee. The first courtyard is **Nassal Chowk** which was originally used by the Malla kings for dance dramas but subsequently the Shah kings of Nepal were crowned here. The palace was once much more extensive than it is today with almost 50 courtyards. Much of the building was destroyed in the 1934 earthquake but what is left was well restored under a UNESCO project in the early 1970s. Around the courtyard is a gallery with portraits of the Shah kings wearing their fantastic plumed crowns. Other parts of the palace are open to visitors and you can climb up one of the towers for a fine view both into the palace courtyards and out over the city. Also in Durbar Square is the **King Tribhuvan Museum** dealing exclusively with the life of the king. Admission to this is included in the entry ticket for the Palace complex.

The **Taleju Temple**, which houses the royal goddess Taleju Bhawani, is one of the largest and best preserved in the city. Located behind the palace, it has a distinctive three-tiered pagoda roof on a 12-stepped platform, rising behind locked gates. The secret investiture ceremony of the Kumari takes place here. Otherwise, entry is restricted to members of the royal family and their priests.

Before leaving the square, look left into the small **Kot Courtyard** where the 1846 massacre took place (see p.492). From the north-east corner of the square the old trade route runs through what is now a crowded bazaar. The old city is a maze of narrow streets and side alleys crowded in by three-storey houses. At the base of many of these buildings are stalls selling vegetables, fine woollen shawls, caps, household items, building material and almost anything that can be traded. The first major crossing you reach is **Indrachowk** beside which is **Akash Bhairav Temple**. During the Indra Jatra, there is week-long festivity around the temple and the image of Akash Bhairav is displayed outside. Follow the road in a north-easterly direction keeping a three-storey temple on your left, the steps of which are covered in a display of fine shawls. On your right are women selling coloured glass beads strung into fine necklaces.

A little further on a small alley leads to the **Machhendra Nath temple**. Although Nepal is a Hindu Kingdom, Buddhism is widespread and centuries of mutual tolerance has resulted in the worship of common deities. The temple of Seto (white)

Machhendra Nath is situated between Indrachowk and Asan, and dedicated to Padmapani Avalokiteshwar (also known as Janmadyo or Machhendra) who is worshipped by both Hindus and Buddhists. The temple has a two-tiered bronze roof and is surrounded by various stupas and statues.

Beyond Machhendra Nath is the other major intersection in the bazaar area. Known as **Asantol**, or more simply as Asan, this is one of the most active and congested markets, with spices, vegetables, cloth, lentils. It is possible to climb onto the first floor of a couple of the shops and look down into the market-place.

From Asan two roads lead out of the bazaar onto Kanti Path, the main north–south road through the city. From here you can hail a taxi back to your hotel, hire a bicycle to explore more of the city, or walk north along the road before cutting in to Thamel. Opposite the exit from the by-lanes of the bazaar is **Rani Pokhari**, a tank created by King Pratap Malla in 1670 to console one of his wives. If you cycle or walk south along Kanti Path, the road passes the large parade ground, locally know as **Tundikhel** on your left. A short way down is the **Mahankalsthan**, or temple of Mahankal, one of the most popular shrines of the city. To the Hindus, Mahankal is a form of Shiva/Bhairav; to Buddhists he is a protective deity, said to have been created by the great Indian sage Nagarjuna for the protection of the Swayambhunath Stupa. The image of Mahankal is made of black stone with silver eyes, and is one of the masterpieces of ancient Nepali sculpture. At the base of the temple is a small bookshop.

Kanti Path passes the end of New Road, the ugly headquarters of Royal Nepal Airlines and the main post office (including *poste restante*). Just after the post office is a road leading into the southern part of the old town. A short way in is the tower of **Dharahara**. At first glance this can be mistaken for a Muslim minaret. The tower was built in AD 1832 by Prime Minister Bhimsen Thapa and originally had 11 sections but the top two have been destroyed in an earthquake. Close by, **Sundhara** (Golden Water Tap) also built by Bhimsen Thapa, is used by the local people as a public bath.

A few hundred metres in front of the post office is the **Shahid Gate**, a memorial to the group of revolutionaries who plotted to restore King Tribhuvan to power in 1940. There are bronze busts of five ringleaders of the plot, centred around a statue of the king. Cycle or walk past the marble gate and continue towards **Bhadrakali Temple**. Also known as Lumarhi, this is one of the main Bhagavati temples of the valley. Located on the eastern edge of Tundikhel, the road leading to Singha Durbar skirts it and then decends a gentle slope; fun to cycle down. The huge **Singha Durbar** was built in 1901 by Prime Minister Chandra Shamsher Rana as his private residence. At one time containing over 1700 rooms and 17 courtyards, this was the largest private residence in Nepal until 1951 when it became the headquarters of the new Government. In July 1974, a 2-day fire destroyed large portions of this immense structure, but the façade remained and parts of the building have been rebuilt. Only the State Rooms are open to the public, and on a limited number of days. These rooms give an idea of the labour and expense which went into the construction and decor of the whole building, particularly at a time when the Carrera marble, Belgian chandeliers, mirrors in gilt frames and a thousand other opulent fittings had to be carried over the mountains by teams of porters.

If you have walked to Singha Durbar you will be able to get a taxi nearby to return to your hotel. If you cycled, you can continue to Patan or back towards one of the small restaurants in Thamel at the northern end of the old city.

Thamel and New Kathmandu

At the top end of Durbar Marg, the road that runs parallel with Kanti Path, is **Narayanhiti Palace**, the official residence of the King of Nepal, King Birendra Bir Bikram Shah. Unfortunately it is not open to the public except on the tenth day of Dasain. The Palace takes its name from the Narayan Temple, which was built in 1793 and is close by, and Narayanhiti, a famous tank which has been restored recently. From the top of Durbar Marg, walk or cycle left. After a couple of hundred metres you cross Kanti Path; on the right is a large gateway leading onto a drive flanked by tall fir trees full of fruit bats. The drive leads to one of the many splendid Rana Palaces. **Kaiser Mahal**, as this one is known, is no longer a private residence but houses the Ministry of Education and the magnificent **Kaiser Library**. The library contains the private collection of Gen. Kaiser S.J.B. Rana who brought together over 35 000 rare books and manuscripts. The collection is open to the public (on a non-borrowing basis) and visitors have a chance to see the interior decorations of a typical 'Nepali neo-classical' palace, with its sweeping formal staircases, chandeliers and over-stuffed furniture. In the library are some paintings of tiger and rhino shoots that took place in what is now the Chitwan National Park during the 1930s.

From Kaiser Mahal the road leads into the top, northern, end of the old city and bazaar area. Known as **Thamel**, it was popular with hippies in the late 60s and is still the place for cheap lodgings and an extraordinary range of restaurants. Thamel has also become a popular shopping area with shops selling yak wool sweaters, Tibetan carpets, mountaineering and trekking equipment. This is an unashamedly tourist patch but at the same time distinctly 'Kathmandu'.

From Thamel the lanes and streets lead through an area known as Thahiti, south towards Asan and Indrachowk. Thahiti has a Tibetan-style *stupa* dating back to the 15th century, which it is said was built over a fountain bringing forth gold. Along this road is the small **Ikhu Narayan Mandir**, a small temple with a 10th-century Vishnu image. Close by, set on a wall is a Buddha statue thought to be about 1500 years old. Further along the road, there is an exquisite statue of Uma-Maheshwar (Shiva and Parvati) in a small shrine. A short distance still further on, the **Srigha Chaitya** or **Kathesimbhu**, which means Kathmandu's Swayambhu, was said to have been constructed out of the building material left over from the Swayambhunath Stupa. Situated in a courtyard off the road leading from Thahiti, a visit to Kathesimbhu, particularly for the elderly or those unable to negotiate the 365 steps leading up to Swayambhunath, is said to acquire as much merit as visiting the original. The *stupa* was constructed around the 17th century; the Lichhavi inscriptions and a statue of Padmapani Lokeshwara nearby indicate that the site has been sacred from ancient times. A little further on is a large chunk of wood embedded with thousands of nails; known as **Washya Deo** after the Newari 'Toothache God', the nails pin down evil spirits and thus relieve the pain. The area is called Bangemudha (crooked stick) after a legendary large piece of wood of which Washya Deo is a small fragment. Continuing along the road to Itum Bahal and finally back into Indrachowk, is the pottery pagoda or **Kel Tol Mandir**.

Valley Sites Tour (Full-day by cycle, half-day by car)
Swayambhunath–Budhanilkantha–Boudhanath–Pashupatinath

A long day's cycling, or a few hours by car, can link four of the valley's most interesting and diverse sites. All are individually extremely important and revered by those who live in the valley. If leaving the city through the old town, visit the **National Museum** at Chhauni, 2 km (1½ miles) west of the city. It contains a splendid array of weapons, artefacts and sculpture, some dating back to ancient times. The **Natural History Museum** close by has a collection of 14 000 specimens of flora and fauna unique to Nepal, as well as some recently found fossils.

Swayambhunath, situated 3 km (1⅔ miles) west of Kathmandu across the Vishnumati river on a hillock 77 m above the valley floor, is one of the most important Buddhist sites in the world. There are 365 steps leading up the hillside to the *stupa* and painted on the four sides of the spire-base are the all-seeing eyes of Lord Buddha. Although you can use a back staircase leading up to the *stupa* from the parking area, it is better to use the main stairs and circle the monument in a clockwise direction. Past the main gate at the base of the staircase are three giant Buddhas, the oldest of which is Buddha Akshobya dating back to 1750. All around the main Swayambhu Stupa are various smaller shrines and temples: **Vasupur** (dedicated to Buddhist earth-goddess Vasundhara), **Vayupur** (Place of the God of Wind), **Amitabha** (Buddha of Boundless Light). Also **Tara, Harati and Sitala Mandir** (Buddhist and Hindu names respectively). For the Buddhists, Harati or Ajima as she is popularly known is the protector of the valley children as appointed by Buddha. For the Hindus, Sitala is the Goddess of Smallpox and needs to be placated. Other shrines and temples include **Agnipur** (Place of the God of Fire), **Shantipur** (Abode of Peace, which is said to contain the still-living 8th-century tantric master Shantikar Acharya—who had hidden the Swayambhu light at the approach of Kali Yuga, behind a locked door guarded by two fierce tantric deities and a pair of painted eyes); also the shrine of **Buddha Amoghasiddhi**, and finally **Nagapur** (The dwelling place of Naga). Close by is a Tibetan Temple containing a huge image of Shakyamuni and a small **Stupa of Manjushri**, the legendary *Bodhisattva*.

From Swayambhunath, drive or cycle around the ring road, past the industrial area of Balaju to join the road north of Kathmandu at Maharajgunj. At the crossroads, turn left and follow the road up a gentle slope toward **Budhanilkantha** 8 km (5 miles) north of Kathmandu. Here there is a colossal Vishnu statue reclining on a bed of snakes, dating back to the 5th century AD in the Lichhavi period. If you go in the morning try to reach the site by 9 am when a *puja* is performed.

From Budhanilkantha there are many walks to Shivpuri on the northern slopes of the valley, through a small sanctuary which is good for birds and the only place in the Valley that the spiny babbler, Nepal's only endemic bird, is found. If you have brought food with you this is a great area for a picnic.

Return from Budhanilkantha to join the ring road and turn left for a 4-km (2½-mile) drive to the Buddhist *stupa* at **Boudhanath**. In contrast to Swayambhunath Stupa, Boudhanath has a much simpler architectural style, though it is much larger. Unlike Swayambhunath also, whose worshippers are Vajrayana Buddhists and local Newari Buddhists, Boudhanath's worshippers are almost exclusively Tibetan Buddhists from Tibet, Bhutan and Ladakh. Boudhanath Stupa, 8 km (5 miles) to the east of Kathmandu, is built on flat ground which emphasises its massive size: a diameter of over 100 m and height of 36 m. It was built in the Lichhavi period (5th century AD) by King Mana Deva I, and is said to contain the remains of Kashyapa, the Buddha of a previous age. The *stupa* is built to represent a *mandala* with eyes painted on the four sides of the harmika to symbolise the guardians of the four directions. Boudhanath was the first stop on the old trade route from Kathmandu to Tibet and always had a Tibetan settlement. After the Chinese invasion of Tibet a large number of refugees settled here. The nearby **Guhyeshwari temple** can be reached on foot in about 20 minutes from here.

There are several other shrines in the Boudhanath complex as well as six major Tibetan Monasteries (gompas), which although constructed in the last 30 years have priceless woodcarvings, thangkas, statues and murals. These gompas are **Tarik Rinpoche, Ka-Nying Shedrup Ling, Jamchen Yigghe Choling, Nyingma** and **Shechen Tennyl Targye**. The Jamchen Yigghe Choling Gompa contains a 35-m tall statue of Maitreya, the Buddha to be; and the Nyingma Gompa contains the sacred remains of the head of the Nyingmapa sect of Buddhism, Dudjom Rinpoche.

From Boudhanath, return and rejoin the ring road. Three kilometres away, near the junction with roads leading back to Kathmandu and the road swinging left toward the Royal Kathmandu Golf Course and the airport, is the most sacred of all Nepal's Shiva shrines. **Pashupatinath** (Shiva as Lord of the Animals) attracts thousands of devotees from all over Nepal and India throughout the year, but particularly for the festival of Mahashivratri on the 'night of no moon' in the month of Phalgun (February–March).

The temple is situated 5 km (3 miles) east of Kathmandu, on the bank of the sacred Bagmati river. Around the site are several other shrines including one to **Bhandareshwara**, Treasury Keeper of Lord Pashupatinath, **Jaya Bageshwari**, and the abandoned town of **Deoparan** (Abode of Gods).

Pashupatinath itself is a two-tiered gilded pagoda dating back to the reign of King Pratap Malla. The site, though, is quite ancient; inscriptions dating back to 477 AD have been found here. Non-Hindus are not allowed to enter the temple proper, but the courtyard has enough sculptures, carvings and sculptural detail to keep visitors busy for hours.

Other sites and shrines around the main temple of Pashupatinath include **Aryaghat**, the cremation platform reserved for the Royal family, on the bank of the Bagmati river, and also the area marked for cremation of common citizens. The shrines include images of Lord Vishnu, Bachaleshwari and Lakshmi, a 6th-century Buddha in the Raja-Rajeshwari Ghat and across the river the shrine of Gorakhnath. Most important of all is the temple of Guhyeshwari, one of the most sacred sites where Shiva's wife Sati is worshipped. According to Hindu religious texts, Sati immolated herself in protest over her mother's insulting attitude towards Shiva. When he came to know of this, Shiva became angry and with Sati's dead body flung over his shoulder, started his famous Tandava (Dance of Destruction). As there was no way to stop him, Lord Vishnu had no option but to use his famous weapon Sudarshan Chakra to chop the body of Sati into pieces. These pieces fell at 51 sacred pithas of which Guhyeshwari is one of the most important.

PATAN AND BHAKTAPUR

The two other cities in the valley each deserve a full day's visit but can be seen in a morning or afternoon (even though this is not recommended). Both can be reached by cycle, bus or taxi.

Patan (Lalitpur)

Patan, an ancient city, was once a kingdom by itself and is situated about 5 km (3 miles) south of Kathmandu. The two cities were earlier separated by farmland but are now contiguous, although divided by the Bagmati river. In contrast to Kathmandu, Patan has preserved much of its tranquillity and charm despite modernisation and urbanisation. It is the third-largest city of Nepal and 80% of its inhabitants are Newars. The city is famous for its craftsmen, particularly metalworkers. Previously, it was known as Lalitpur and was one of the major Buddhist cities of Asia. Most of the city's major temples, palaces and public buildings date back to the late Malla period.

Ask your taxi driver to drop you at Patan's own Durbar Square. Getting a taxi back should not be difficult. The city is very roughly divided into four quarters by north–south and east–west roads that meet at the **Durbar Square**. This is much lovelier than the squares in Kathmandu or Bhaktapur. Each structure is meticulously planned, and there is a wonderful sense of cohesion, balance and proportion among the various buildings. The centre of attraction is the ancient **Royal Palace** with three chowks or courtyards: Mul Chowk and Sundari Chowk; and Mani Keshap Narayan Chowk, the Taleju Bhawani temple, also a temple to Degu Taleju. Durbar Square owes much of its splendour to the Malla Kings Siddhi Narsingh (17th century) and his son Shrinivasa. Apart from the lovely structures in the square, Siddhi Narsingh built the **Krishna Mandir Temple** of Lord Krishna which holds the pride of place at the northern end of the palace complex. This temple was the first to be built according to the Shikhara style of architecture; its walls bear major scenes from the Hindu epics *Ramayana* and *Mahabharata* engraved on stone.

Any young child in Durbar Square will try to direct you to the **Hiranya Varna Mahavihar**. The local Newari name for this is Kwa Bahal but the children and tour guides refer to it as the Golden Temple. This Buddhist temple to Lord Lokeshwar (Lord Buddha) is a three-storey golden pagoda built by King Bhaskar Varma in the 12th century, and maintained to this day with donations from Newari merchants. In the upper storey is the golden image of Lord Buddha on a pedestal, and a large prayer wheel. The highlight of Kwa Bahal is the fine Newari metalwork, and the wonderful carvings which should be examined in detail. There is a tiny 3-cm frieze of Buddha's life which is exquisitely rendered.

North of the square, past the imposing Bhimsen Mandir is Patan's oldest surviving temple, the **Kumbheshwar**. Built during the reign of King Jayasthiti Malla (late 14th century), this is one of the two examples of five-roofed temples in the valley, the other being the Nyatapola temple in Bhaktapur. The local people believe that Lord Shiva spends the six winter months at Kumbheshwar and migrates to Mount Kailash (in western Tibet) during the summer months. On Janai Purnima day, usually in August, a fair is held here.

Take the road going south-east of the square, past the three statues of Narasimha, Ganesh and Hanuman, and a 5-minute walk takes you to the 14th-century **Mahabouddha**. This clay-brick temple with thousands of terracotta Buddha images is a landmark of Nepali architecture of that era. Its conception and construction is credited to an architect called Avay Raj. A few metres beyond the entrance to the temple is the **Rudra Varna Mahavihar** or Uku Bahal, a Buddhist monastery dating back to the Lichhavi era with a fine collection of images and statues in metal, stone and wood. It is said that kings of earlier times were crowned here.

Due south of the square is the **Raato Machhendranath Mandir**, perhaps the most beloved deity of Patan. His origins are obscure and an examination of the folklore reveals a curious mixture of Buddhism and local religious beliefs. As the local deity Bunga Dyo (God of Bungamati), Newari Buddhists have worshipped him from the 7th century. Soon after, Bunga Dyo seems to have been associated with *Bodhisattva* Padmapani Lokeshwara, who is said to be the originator of the world and the teacher of all the gods of the Hindu pantheon. By the 18th century, Bunga Dyo was known by his other title, Machhendranath or 'Lord of the Fishes'. Machhendranath resides for six months (December to June) in a 17th-century pagoda in the locality of Tabahal. After a chariot festival lasting several weeks and culminating in the major festival of 'Bhoto Jatra', the deity is carried in a palanquin to his 'family home' in Bungamati, a Newari village 6km (3¾ miles) south of Patan.

Across the street from the Machhendranath Temple, is the **Minnath Temple**, believed to be Machhendranath's son, and fondly called Saano (little) Machhendranath. However, Minnath pre-dates Machhendranath, and local folklores indicate that he must have been an ancient local deity. In appearance, Minnath is identical to Machhendranath and accompanies the latter in a smaller chariot during the annual chariot festival.

The **Tibetan Centre** at Jawalakhel on the south-western edge of Patan is the largest in the valley and a major centre for carpet weaving. Ten kilometres (6¼ miles) south-east of Patan at **Godavari**, is the **Royal Botanical Garden**, established by botanists from Kew with a wide variety of Himalayan flora. Above Godavari rises **Phulchowki** a 2739-m high mountain with a Buddhist shrine at the top which can be reached either on foot or by jeep. In March and April the mountainside is ablaze with rhododendrons of different varieties and the bird life on the hill is extraordinarily diverse. It is best to be dropped at the top of the hill early in the morning and follow the road down.

Bhaktapur (Bhadgaon)

The third major city of the valley and once an independent city-state, Bhaktapur lies along a ridge above the sacred river Hanumante, 14 km (8¾ miles) east of Kathmandu. Bhaktapur grew from a string of villages along the Tibetan trade route and used to be the capital of the valley when King Jayasthiti Malla moved here from Patan in AD 1382.

Bhaktapur is the most isolated and unchanged of the three former kingdoms of the valley, and has retained much of its original character. Though most visitors 'do' Bhaktapur in the course of an afternoon, the place deserves a longer visit in order to truly appreciate its medieval ambience. Bhaktapur is economically self-sufficient, 60% of its people being farmers, and has remained a purely Hindu community in contrast with mixed Kathmandu and Buddhist Patan. The city is pure Newar: the inhabitants speak a Newari dialect distinct from Kathmandu's, and until the main road was built with Chinese assistance in 1966, a trip to Kathmandu meant a 14-km (8¾-mile) walk along a dirt-track. Bhaktapur is earthquake-prone; more so than Kathmandu and Patan. The 1934 earthquake destroyed about 70% of the city but the sacred temples and the town centre have been rebuilt meticulously. And when the 1988 earthquake took place, the rebuilt town houses withstood the tremor. Bhaktapur is laid out according to a deceptively simple, but sophisticated system of tols, neighbourhoods, according to caste. The public courtyards, water sources and temples speak volumes for Newari town planning abilities. The city has received help and major funding from Germany by way of the **Bhaktapur Development Project** (BDP) aimed at protecting the special atmosphere and unique character of this city, even while the quality of life improves with urbanisation.

The road from Kathmandu passes through a small pine wood and then past the 16th-century reservoir, **Siddha Pokhari** on your left. This large tank serves as a water source for many people, and the Shiva and Vishnu shrines on its bank are still under worship. After the tank the road forks and the left-hand fork leads to Bhaktapur's Durbar Square.

Before the 1934 earthquake took its toll, the Royal Palace of Bhaktapur was the most splendid of those in the three kingdoms, and its **Durbar Square** was the most picturesque. Though several buildings have been reconstructed, the gaps where missing structures once stood and the lack of the bustle and crowds make this a forlorn scene. The surviving structures include the **Lion Gate** built during the reign of King Bhupatindra Malla, whose statue in the act of worship sits on a column facing the **Sun Dokha** or golden gate that leads to the Taleju Temple. The Gate is richly adorned with carvings and the door has figures of Goddess Kali and Garuda, the *vahana* (carrier) of Lord Vishnu. The Golden Gate is generally considered the most important single piece of art in Nepal. To the right of the gate are the remains of the old Royal Palace and the **Palace of 55 Windows** built in 1697 by Bhupatindra Malla, although only 53 windows survive today after the reconstruction made necessary by the 1934 earthquake.

Opposite the Sun Dokha is the **Batsala Devi Temple** with its wonderful stone carvings, a fine example of Shikhara-style architecture. The bronze bell of this temple, cast in 1737 by order of King Ranjit Malla, is known as the 'bell of the barking dogs' as it sets the local dogs barking when it is rung every morning for the *puja* of Goddess Taleju.

An important recent addition which helps to restore the harmony of Durbar Square to some extent is the **Chysalin Mandap**. This structure was reconstructed by local craftsmen in 1990 using old etchings, with financial support from Germany. Behind the Mandap, the **Pashupati Mandir**, built by King Yaksha Malla in the 15th century, has a replica of the sacred *linga* of the original Pashupati Mandir. By bringing the image to Bhaktapur he was spared the daily 12-km (7½-mile) trek for his morning *puja* at Pashupatinath. The struts supporting the temple roof are richly carved with images of Lord Shiva on one level and erotic scenes below.

A lane running behind the Pashupati Temple leads to another great square. A short 5-m (3-mile) detour, however, leads to an area called **Talako** where potters make and bake their wares; clay lamps, bowls, small animal figures and pots. The second great square of Bhaktapur is **Taumadhi Tol**, largely restored by the Development Project. One of the old pagoda buildings in the middle has been rebuilt and now runs as the **Nyatapola Cafe**; you can look out from the first floor over the bustle of the square. The most imposing structure here is the **Nyatapola Temple**. It was built in 1702 by Bhupatindra Malla and this five-storey pagoda is so finely balanced that it has survived several earthquakes. The five terraces are adorned by a pair of figures, each said to be ten times stronger than that below. The pair on the lowest terrace is wrestlers Jai and Patta Malla (who were ten times stronger than ordinary men), then come two elephants, two lions, two griffins and finally Baghini and Singini (the tiger and lion goddesses). The goddess worshipped within is not clearly identified; while some say she is Siddhi Lakshmi, some say she is Bhairavi or Durga, and others believe that the goddess resides in spirit form and there is no image inside. The high priests, who alone see the deity during the nightly *puja*, are tight-lipped about her identity.

The **Kasi-Bishwanath (Bhairavnath) Temple** was originally a one-storey structure built during the reign of King Jagat Jyoti Malla, but the temple was expanded into a three-storey pagoda in 1718 by King Bhupatindra Malla, who brought the powerful deity Bhairava from Varanasi in India for installation here. The finely proportioned pagoda, with the top-most roof gilded, has elaborately carved struts and a rich gilt-inlaid façade. According to local legend the powerful and troublesome Lord Bhairava is counter-balanced by the secret goddess of Nyatapola Mandir. Yet the popular local festival of Bisket Jatra is associated with Bhairavnath and although he is worshipped unseen, with offerings pushed through a small opening in the temple-façade, his gilded mask is set in a massive chariot every spring and pulled through the Bhaktapur streets by a joyous crowd. Dattatreya, the three-headed image of Brahma, Vishnu and Maheshwara (Shiva), resides in the **Dattatreya Temple**, said to have been built from the trunk of a single tree in 1427 during the reign of King Yaksha Malla, and refurbished in 1458 by King Bishwa Malla.

The **Pujari Math Monastery**, with exquisitely carved peacock windows, was built by King Yaksha Malla, and has also been restored to its earlier glory with German assistance. The 'Math' houses the National Art Gallery's **Woodcarving Museum** which has several specimens of exquisite wooden statues and struts. Still in Tachapal Square an important Vishnu temple, the **Til Madhaba Narayan Mandir**, dates back to 1080. Though the deity in the sanctum sanctorum is definitely Vishnu, the metal *torana* depicts the dancing Shiva and the bull Nandi, his mount. Two important events on the calendar of this temple are the **ihi** ceremony held on certain auspicious days, when nubile local Hindu girls are wedded to the deity; and the annual *puja* when the deity is massaged with ghee and offered *til* (sesame seeds)—in memory of his discovery in a merchant's mound of sesame seeds, which did not subsequently diminish, despite brisk sales. (An echo of the biblical parable of the loaves and fishes.

If time allows, go beyond Tachapal Square toward the fields and a fine view of Nagarkot Ridge. A short walk to the left leads to a path heading uphill and back into the town. After a few hundred metres, near the top is the **Navadurga Temple**, dedicated to the fierce Navadurga (nine Durgas), depicted on the toranas of the temple. On the first floor, the painted masks used in the ritualistic masked dances are stored and offered blood sacrifice.

Beyond Bhaktapur

There are several interesting sights close to Bhaktapur which can be reached on foot, with bicycles, or by rented car or taxi from Kathmandu. Most of these places are connected by public transport, but the buses can be slow and crowded, and the service irregular.

Just beyond the edge of Bhaktapur, on the Nagarkot road, is **Kamal Vinayak**, literally Ganesh of the Lotus, with a large pond and a small Ganesh temple. **Nagarkot**, 20 km (12½ miles) north of Bhaktapur (32 km; 20 miles from Kathmandu), is a hilltop viewpoint and resort popular for sunrise and sunset views along the distant mountain peaks. From Nagarkot (2175 m) the peaks which can be seen clearly are Mt Everest (8848 m), Manaslu (8463 m), Ganesh Himal (7111 m), Langtang (7246 m), Choba Bhamre (6016 m), Gaurishanker (7134 m) and Nambur (6957 m).

Changu Narayan a hilltop temple complex only 4 km (2½ miles) north of Bhaktapur, has been called 'the most shining example of the culmination of the best in Nepali art and architecture'. Changu Narayan is Kathmandu valley's oldest proven religious site and the holiest Vishnu shrine. Built in AD 323 by King Hari Dutta Varma, the temple is richly decorated with stone sculptures, wood carvings and metalwork, all coming together in a wonderfully harmonious manner. The temple courtyard also contains the earliest recorded inscription in the valley, on a stone column: a recording made in AD 464 of the prowess of King Manadeva.

About 30 km (18¾ miles) east of Kathmandu (18 km; 11¼ miles from Bhaktapur) on the Arnika Rajmarga (Kathmandu–Kodari Highway), is the ancient town of **Dhulikhel**—famous for its scenic beauty, and panoramic view of the snowy mountain range from Karyolung in the east to Himalchuli in the west. Dhulikhel and the town of **Banepa** nearby are medieval townships that offer glimpses into the lifestyle, occupations, housing and mode of dress of the Nepali people.

Panauti, an ancient village off the Dhulikhel Road, has interesting old houses, as well as some examples of exquisite 14th-century wooden struts on the Indreshwar Mahadev, Brahmayani and Gorakhnath temples.

A 2-hour walk from Dhulikhel through paddy-fields, villages and pine plantations is the **Namobuddha Stupa**. For Tibetan Buddhists, this *stupa* is the third most important in Nepal , after Swayambhu and Bouddha.

Kirtipur

Kirtipur is a small town with an illustrious past, set atop a hill some 8 km (5 miles) south-west of Kathmandu—the last town in the valley to fall against the invading Gorkha troops of Prithvi Narayan Shah in 1768.

As well as **Tribhuvan University**, Kirtipur boasts of several old shrines, temples, and houses—and the sight of the local people dressed in traditional costume going about their daily chores. Among the shrines and temples, the important ones are **Chilamchu Stupa** built in the 16th century, and **Bagh Bhairava Temple.** Various images in the temple compound, particularly the series of five buxom earth-mother goddesses from the 4th century AD, and the equally ancient standing statue of Shiva-Parvati, are among the oldest in the Valley.

BEYOND KATHMANDU VALLEY

While the valley is the recognised centre of Nepali culture, there are several interesting sights beyond it which can be reached easily by road or air.

Kakani

Located 29km (18 miles) north-west of Kathmandu, at a height of 1982 m, **Kakani** offers panoramic views of the Himalayan range. The scenic **Trishuli Road** leading to Kakani passes through green forests and mountain ranges on one side, and fertile river flats and terraced cultivation on the other. The peaks which can be seen from Kakani are Gaurishanker, Choba Bhamre, Manaslu, Himalchuli and Annapurna.

Pokhara Valley

Pokhara is 200 km (125 miles) west of Kathmandu, and can be reached by air, road and on foot. The flight lasts half an hour, and for most of the time gives a magnificent view of successive ranges of mountain peaks. The plane lands at Nagdhunga Airfield, which has a spectacular view of the five Annapurnas with the Machhapuchhare peak right in the centre. The Kathmandu–Pokhara road can take between 7 and 9 hours, depending on the condition of the road. Public buses, tourist buses and taxis ply this route frequently.

Until recently, Pokhara could only be reached on foot, a gentle trek lasting 6 to 7 days starting from Trishuli 44 km (30¼ miles) north-west of Kathmandu. With the advent of the road it has become the biggest tourist destination in Nepal outside the Kathmandu Valley—a sub-tropical paradise with a balmy climate and a relaxed way of life.

Perhaps the best thing about Pokhara is the glorious views of the Himalayan mountains that one can obtain from any point in the valley. The choice of view and vantage points is wide, encompassing a 140-km (306-mile) section of the Himalaya including Dhaulagiri, the 56-km (35-mile) long Annapurna range, Manaslu, Himalchuli and Machhapuchhare.

Pokhara is also the starting point of several short and long trekking routes. The shorter treks include the 3-day walk to the village of **Chomrong** at the entrance of the Annapurna sanctuary; or the **Ghorepani** loop via **Ghandruk** which can be done in less than a week; **Birethni** and **Chandrakot** villages which are a further half-day trek from Ghandruk. Likewise, there are several other treks which lead to unspoilt villages, mountain summits, forts and religious sites.

Trekking permits can be obtained from the Immigration Office in Pokhara and equipment is available for rent at various travel agencies in the Lakeside and Pokhara Bazaar.

Lumbini

Lumbini is the birthplace of Lord Buddha and a major site of Buddhist pilgrimage. Situated in the western *terai* of Nepal, Lumbini can be reached in 3 hours by bus or car from Tansen via Bhairawaha. Bhairawaha is linked with Kathmandu by air.

Lumbini's **Mayadevi Mandir**, an ancient stone relief depicting Buddha's birth, dates back to the 2nd century. The marble copy close by depicts the new-born Buddha being blessed by Brahma and Mayadevi—Buddha's mother. Typically, the temple is looked after by Hindu priests who worship the goddess Mayadevi as Rupadevi.

Lumbini also has the oldest recorded relic in Nepal: the **Ashokan Pillar** erected by Emperor Ashoka when he visited Lumbini 20 years after his coronation. There are two modern monasteries: a **Tibetan Gompa** built in 1968 by Chopgye Trinzin Rinpoche, and **Theravada Monastery** built by the Government of Nepal.

The ancient city of Kapilavastu and Gautama Buddha's father, King Suddhodana's Palace have been recently excavated at **Tilaurikot**, 27 km (16⅔ miles) west of Lumbini, close to the village of Taulihawa.

Royal Chitwan National Park

Chitwan (Rapti Valley) is situated in the inner *terai* region of Nepal and can be reached in 6 hours by road or half an hour by flying from Kathmandu. There are two airports close by: Bharatpur and Meghauli; the latter is used by visitors booked in at Tiger Tops Jungle Lodge. The nearest bus-stop for the Royal Chitwan National Park is **Tadi Bazaar** on the East–West Highway, 15 km (9⅓ miles) from Narayanghat. From Tadi bazaar, there is a choice of transport—foot, jeep, bicycle, oxcart, the occasional elephant—to cover the 7 km (4⅓ miles) distance to Sauruha, the entrance to the Park.

Chitwan National Park is the most famous wildlife reserve in Nepal, and among the most important in Asia. Thousands of visitors come every year to see the wide range of wildlife. The greater one-horned rhinoceros was the prime reason for the park being established in 1961. Other animals include four species of deer, sloth bear, leopard, wild boar, crocodile, and tiger. Over 350 species of birds provide a major attraction for ornithologists.

Apart from Tiger Tops, there are several other safari camps including Machan, Temple Tiger, Island Jungle Resort, Gaida Wildlife, Chitwan Jungle Lodge and Jungle Camp. The last one is particularly good for bird-watchers. Visitors are taken into the park by experienced guides on elephant-back, in jeeps or on foot, to view the wildlife in their natural environment.

Because of its natural riches Chitwan has become quite crowded, but there are other more remote National Parks in Nepal. These are not so developed, and camps have a more natural atmosphere and surroundings. Most have luxury lodges and have developed their own infrastructure. Unfortunately, this does mean that individual tourists not booking safari trips with these lodges may find it difficult going. One of the best, **Royal Bardia National Park**, is also in the *terai*, but further west than Chitwan: 4 hours from Nepalganj airport, with headquarters at Thakurdwara, although the park office is likely to move to Motipur shortly. Accommodation is confined to **Tiger Tops Karnali Lodge** and its **Tented Camp** on the bank of the Churia river. Bardia has a good number of tiger, blackbuck, crocodiles and wild boar, an extensive bird life and the rare Gangetic freshwater dolphin.

RECREATION

Compared to the rest of the country, **Kathmandu** provides the best facilities for entertainment and recreation.

There are a number of **movie theatres** which mainly run Indian films. The video culture has caught on and most hotels have TV and video in their lounges; and, in the upper bracket hotels, in guest-rooms as well. Western films are also shown in European and American cultural centres. There is virtually no nightlife after 10 pm, barring in the large hotels where discotheques stay open till the small hours. Some bars in the Thamel area stay crowded till late at night.

Nepal also has **casinos**. The Soaltee Oberoi Hotel runs Casino Nepal on its premises; only Indian rupees and foreign exchange can be used to buy the chips and Nepalis are not allowed in. **Casino Anna** opened at the Taj Annapurna Hotel in August 1992.

Some hotels arrange **folk-dances and musical shows** by local troupes and invited artists. Everest Culture Society at Lal Durbar near Yak & Yeti Hotel, and New Himalchuli Culture Group of Lazimpat perform every evening. Some Indian restaurants, particularly Ghar-e-Kebab in Hotel de l'Annapurna and Far Pavilions in Everest Hotel, feature Indian classical music every evening.

Sports. Kathmandu has olympic-sized public swimming-pools at the National Stadium and at Balaju, but these are usually crowded. The hotel pools are much more exclusive, and the pools at Hotel de l'Annapurna, Shangri-La, Everest, Soaltee Oberoi can be used for a small fee. There are tennis courts, sauna, beauty and massage parlours and exercise facilities at major hotels like Hotel de l'Annapurna, Everest, Yak & Yeti and Soaltee Oberoi.

SHOPPING
Kathmandu is a buyers' market. Even without stepping into regular shops, visitors can buy all kinds of goods from traders and hawkers, who congregate in the tourist spots and tend to swoop down on unwary visitors.

Very often these vendors, and regular shops in the various bazaars sell fake or over-priced products. Shop around for the real thing and the right price. Government-run or controlled shops are the safest bet. The best buys include handicrafts, metalware, carpets, stone-sculpture, wood carvings, prayer wheels from Jawalakhel Tibetan camp, clothes, Tibetan trinkets, and Tibetan woollen jackets especially.

Some of the better stores are **Nepalese Handicrafts Centre** near Jawalakhel which has a selection of goods from all over Nepal, **Tibet Ritual Art Gallery** for antiques and rare art objects, **Patan Industrial Estate** and **Bhaktapur Crafts Centre** for wood carving, metalwork and thangkas.

WHERE TO STAY IN KATHMANDU

Luxury (over US$100 per room night)
At the top end of the range, hotels conform to international standards, each with shopping arcade, swimming-pool, business centre, restaurants, etc. Suites are the most expensive accommodation at around US$225. In this category: **Hotel Yak & Yeti** on Durbar Marg (tel 413999, 222635; fax 977-1-227782), **Hotel Soaltee Oberoi** in Tahachal (tel 272550, 272555; fax 977-1-227405) and **Everest Hotel** in Baneshwar (tel 220567, 220288, 220614; fax 977-1-226088). The Taj Group has recently taken over the management of the **Hotel de l'Annapurna** (tel 221711, fax 977-1-225236).

Expensive (US$50–100 per room night)
Slightly cheaper (US$70–100 for single and double occupancy), but offering practically all luxuries, are the **Hotel Himalaya** on Sahid Sukhra Marg, Lalitpur (tel 523900) under Japanese management; **Hotel Kathmandu** in Maharajganj (tel 413082, 418497; fax 977-1-416574); **Hotel Malla** on Lekhnath Marg (tel 413020, 418385; fax 977-1-418382:), **Hotel Sherpa** on Durbar Marg (tel 222585; fax 977-1-222026:), **Hotel Shanker** in Lazimpet (tel 410151, 410152) and **Hotel Shangri-la** also in Lazimpet (tel 410051, 412999; fax 977-1-414184).

Mid-range (US$20–50 per room night)
Kathmandu Guest House, the first of its kind in Thamel (tel 413632, 418733; fax 977-1-417133); **Hotel Vajra** in Bijayaswori, near Swayambhunath (tel 271545, 272719) and the Dutch-managed **Summit Hotel** in Kopundole Heights, Lalitpur (tel 521894, 522694) are all well run, clean and good value. The Summit has rooms for budget travellers in its Holland House wing and deluxe rooms in the Garden wing.

Budget (below US$10/NR500 per room night)
Low to moderately priced hotels and guest-houses are **Hotel Shakti** (tel 410121) and **Hotel Thamel** (tel 412744), both in the Thamel area. South-east of Thamel on Jyatha Tol several new hotels have come up including **Lhasa Guest House** (tel 213019), **Hotel New Gajur** (tel 226623), **Blue Diamond** (tel 226320, 226392), **Hotel Rara** (tel 226969; fax 977-1-419935) and **Mustang Holiday Inn** (tel 226794, 226538). South-west of Thamel in Chhetrapati, there is another string of moderately priced hotels including **Shambala Guest House** (tel 225986, 228524), **Potala Guest House** (tel 220467, 226566; fax-223256), **Tibet Guest House** (tel 214383, 215893) and **Trans-Himalayan Guest House** (tel 214683, 211211).

Similarly, in north Thamel, there are the **Hotel Garuda** (tel 416776, 416340; fax 223814), **Hotel Mandap** (tel 413321; fax 419734), **Hotel Marshyangdi** (tel 412129, 414105; fax 410008) and the ever-popular **International Guest House** (tel 410533).

There are several very cheap basic lodges throughout Kathmandu and the tariff ranges from Nepalese Rs40–200 (US$0.8–4). In the Thamel area, these include **Yeti Cottage** (tel 427089), **Cosy Corner** (tel 417799), **Lodge Pheasant** (tel 417416), **Om Guest House, Holy Lodge** and **Himal Cottage**. In the Freak Street area south of Kathmandu's Durbar Square, the prices are even cheaper, at **Century Lodge** (tel 215769), **Sayami Lodge** (tel 212264), **Friendly Home** (tel 220171), **Mustang Cottage, and Royal Guest House**. Slightly upmarket are the lodges around Durbar Square including **Kathmandu Lodge** (tel 214893) and **Kumari Lodge**.

Around Town. Outside the main Kathmandu areas, there is the **Taragaon Hotel** in Boudhanath, run by the Government of Nepal (tel 410409, 410634). This hotel also accepts reservation for the other hotels in the Taragaon chain, situated in Nagarkot, Kakani and Pokhara. Also in Boudhanath area is **Lotus Guest House** behind Tarik Rinpoche's Gompa, and **Hotel Stupa** (tel 470400, 470385) on the main road.

Note. While all these hotels and guest-houses officially charge for stay and services in foreign currency, and guests have to show a bank exchange receipt, the cheaper lodges accept payment in Nepali rupees.

Patan
Though visitors mostly stay in Kathmandu, Patan does have a few hotels including **Aloha Inn** near Jawalakhel (tel 522796), **Hotel Narayani, Hotel Summit** and **Hotel Greenwich** all on Kopundole Heights. The top-end of the range is the Japanese-managed **Himalaya Hotel** (tel 523900) on Sahid Sukhara Marg, while the cheapest accommodation is at the **Mahendra Youth Hostel** just before Jawalakhel.

Bhaktapur
A few visitors decide to stay overnight in Bhaktapur, so as to experience the ambience of the city without an early morning trek or cycle-ride from Kathmandu. Choice of accommodation is limited to basic amenities at **Golden Gate Guest House, Shiva Guest House, Traditional Guest House** and **Luna Guest House**, all on or close to the Bhaktapur Durbar Square.

Nagarkot
As Nagarkot is a popular place to view the Himalayan range, a number of lodges and hotels have sprung up to accommodate visitors wishing to experience early

morning or sunset views. There are several lodges scattered along the ridge line which offer spectacular views of the Himalayan range. **Hotel Flora Hill** (tel 226893, Kathmandu 223311) is the most expensive at US$38 for a double room, followed by **Taragaon Resort**, Government-run at US$18 for a double room. The cheaper lodges are **New Pheasant Lodge, Niwa Home, Peaceful Cottage** and the new **Hotel View Point**. About 4 km (2½ miles) away is an excellent hotel run by the Hotel Vajra, called **The Farmhouse.**

Dhulikhel

The most popular place, among several inexpensive lodges, is **Dhulikhel Lodge** (tel 225092 in Kathmandu) which was started in 1969 by converting an old five-storey Newar house. Also popular is the new **Hotel Himalaya Horizons** (tel 225092 in Kathmandu). The most expensive is **Dhulikhel Mountain Resort** (tel 220031 in Kathmandu) at US$60/US$55 for double/single occupancy, excluding meals.

Lumbini

Lumbini Garden Guest House and the new **Lumbini Hokke Hotel** offer decent accommodation; the latter though is quite expensive at US$70 and above and caters primarily to Japanese tour groups.

Chitwan

All the safari camps dotted throughout the Royal Chitwan National Park have booking offices in Durbar Marg in Kathmandu, and bookings include plane tickets (although this is charged extra), airport pick-up, food, lodging, guide fees, etc.

At the top end of the range is the first such camp to come up (in 1965), **Tiger Tops** (tel 222706 in Kathmandu). Apart from the **Tiger Tops Lodge**, this organisation also runs a tented camp on an island in the Narayani river, and a **Tharu Village Lodge**. The tariffs range from US$275 down to US$125, and reservation is a must, especially for the high season in autumn.

The other jungle camps include **Temple Tiger** (tel 221585), **Island Jungle Resort** (tel 226022), **Gaida Wildlife** (tel 220940), **Jungle Camp, Chitwan Jungle Lodge** (tel 228918) and **Machan Wildlife Resort** (tel 225001). Tariffs are slightly cheaper than at Tiger Tops, but services are similar.

For the budget traveller, there are several inexpensive lodges in the range Nepalese Rs40–180); **Hotel Park Cottage, Hotel Shiva's Dream, River View Hotel and Lodge, Rhino Lodge**. Semideluxe lodges include **Jungle Shangri-la, Jungle Safari Camp** and **Hotel Elephant Camp,** at about US$110 per night.

EATING OUT

Kathmandu has hundreds of restaurants, ranging from the exclusive to the cheap, to suit all pockets and all tastes. Food is cheap in Kathmandu, at least for those used to restaurant prices in the West. A big plate of quiche, assorted vegetables and salad will cost less than Rs80 in most standard restaurants. Set breakfasts are even cheaper.

With the exception of Newari cuisine which is very elaborate, spicy and available only in private homes, Nepal has not evolved a distinct cuisine. The dishes are by and large a variation of Indian food: rice, lentils (*dal*) and vegetables, either fried or cooked. Meat is eaten on festive days, barring beef which is banned in Nepal. Regional variations include *tsampa*, which is ground roasted barley and often mixed with milk, water or tea by the Tibetans and nomads in the hills. The sherpas are fond of *gurr* which is prepared by pounding raw potatoes with spices and baking the mixture into pancakes. Tibetans settled in Nepal favour *thupka* which is a thick soup of noodles; and *momo*, boiled or fried dumplings.

The indigenous population drink large amounts of tea brewed with milk, sugar and spices. Alcoholic drinks include *chhang* which is a popular drink in the hills, made with fermented barley or millet, *arak*, potato alcohol and *rakshi*, wheat or rice alcohol. Apart from these, local distilleries produce passable rum, gin and vodka, though the locally made whisky is very much below international standards.

For visitors, Kathmandu's restaurants offer several cuisines, and leading resturants are grouped below accordingly.

Nepali: The **Nepalese Kitchen** in Thamel serves a standard Nepali *thali* (set menu with helping of rice, *dal* and vegetables). **Sunkosi** on Durbar Marg and **Bhanchha Ghar** in Kamaladi both serve good Nepali food.

Indian: Ghar-e-Kabab at Hotel de l'Annapurna serves very good tandoori and other Indian dishes. **Naach Ghar** at Yak & Yeti Hotel has the same high standard amidst a plush 'period Rana' setting. **Himalchuli Room** of Soaltee Oberoi Hotel and Everest Hotel's **Far Pavilions** serve excellent Mughlai food. **New Kebab Corner** in Hotel Gautam, **Amber Restaurant** and **Moti Mahal** both on Durbar Marg serve good Indian Mughlai food in semi-deluxe setting. **Ghoomti, Shiva's Sky, Tripti Restaurant** and several other smaller eateries on New Road serve traditional Indian food.

Chinese: Chinese food is available from a number of places throughout the city both in hotels and independent restaurants. **Mountain City Chinese Restaurant** in Hotel Malla has an elegant setting. Shangri-La Hotel's **Tian Shan** serves Chinese dishes of very good standard. Cheaper than these are **Ras Rung** near Hotel Shanker, **Jasmine's** on Freak Street, **Nanglo's Chinese Restaurant** and **Beijing Restaurant** both on Durbar Marg and **Xue Shan** and **Mel Hua** both on Kanti Path. There are several smaller Chinese places around Thahiti Stupa which serve noodles and *jiaotze* (similar to the Tibetan *momo*).

Tibetan: **Utse Restaurant, Namkha Ding** and **Gombu's Restaurant**, all in Thamel, serve Chinese-Tibetan dishes like chow mein and *momo*.

Japanese: Kathmandu's Japanese restaurants are quite good and food is authentic. **Fuji Restaurant** on Kanti Path, **Tamura** in Jhamsikhel and **Kushifuji** and **Koto's** both on Durbar Marg are well patronised by visitors, and to a smaller extent by the Nepalis.

Continental: The pride of place is taken by **Chimney Restaurant** in Yak & Yeti hotel which belonged to the legendary Boris Lissanevitch. Apart from Boris's original European and Russian menu including chicken à la Kiev and baked Alaska, the restaurant also has the original copper fireplace from the bar of Boris's Royal Hotel. There are several other top-grade restaurants serving continental food, among which are **The Gurkha Grill** at Soaltee Oberoi Hotel, **Kokonor Room** at Hotel Shangri-La, **Al Fresco** also at Soaltee Oberoi for Italian food, **Le Bistro, K.C.'s Restaurant, Coppers Restaurant** and **The Old Vienna Inn** for Austrian cuisine, all in Thamel. In Durbar Marg and central Kathmandu, several restaurants serve Western and fast food, some of which are **Big Bell Cafe, Hotel New Crystal, Mike's Breakfast, San Francisco Pizza, Nirula's, Nanglo's Pub** and **Kwality.**

All big hotels have coffee shops open throughout the day and these serve snacks and meals across a range of cuisines.

Any list of restaurants in Kathmandu can neither be comprehensive nor complete, as new establishments open almost every other week and a few of the older ones down shutters. Ask around.

GENERAL INFORMATION

Money
Nepalese rupees = NR. At the time of writing NR50 = 1US$; NR97 = £1; and NR1.7 = Indian Rs1.

Visa Formalities
All visitors to Nepal must hold a valid passport and visa for Nepal. Visas can be obtained from the Royal Nepali Embassy or Consulate in your country for a period of 30 days. A 15-day visa can be obtained in King Tribhuvan airport or at the other entry points to Nepal, upon arrival, for a fee equivalent to US$10. (For British passport-holders, the fee is £20.) The 15-day visa can be extended for another 3 weeks, free, at the Central Immigration Office near the Royal Palace in Thamel, but a foreign currency encashment receipt of US$10 or equivalent, for each day already spent in Nepal, needs to be submitted. Visas can be extended for a second month at (Nepali Rupees) NR75 per week, and for a third month for NR150 per week. A Home Ministry recommendation is necessary for extending a visa beyond 3 months.

Tourist Information Centres
The Department of Tourism, His Majesty's Government, Nepal have offices all over Nepal. In Kathmandu, their offices are located in Tripureshwar (tel 214519, 211293) and Tribhuvan International Airport (tel 410537). The other Tourist information centres are at Pokhara Airport (tel 20028), Basantapur (Kathmandu) (tel 220818), Birgunj (tel 2083), Janakpur (tel 20755) and Kakarbhitta (tel 1304).

Consulates and Embassies
Countries that do not have a consulate or embassy in Nepal are represented by their Embassy in New Delhi. All those listed below are located in the greater Kathmandu area, or Patan.

Austrian Consulate, Hattisar (tel 410891)
Consulate of Belgium, Lazimpat (tel 414760)
Danish Consulate for Nepal, Kantipath, (tel 227044)
Finnish Consulate for Nepal, Khichapokhari, (tel 220939)
Consulate for Netherlands, Kumaripati, (tel 522915, 524597)
Norwegian Consulate, Jawalakhel, (tel 521646)
Sri Lankan Consulate, Kamalpokhari, (tel 414192, 416432)
Swedish Consulate for Nepal, Khichapokhari, (tel 220939)
Swiss Consulate Agency, Jawalakhel, (tel 523468)
British Embassy, Lainchour, (410583, 414588, 411281, 411789)
Embassy of Australia, Bhatbhatini (tel 411304, 411578)
Embassy of Bangladesh, Naxal, (tel 414265, 410566, 414943)

LANGUAGE

Though about half the population speak Hindi, it can't be called the official Indian language. In fact, there are over a dozen major languages in India, and hundreds of lesser local dialects and languages. What holds the lot together, strangely, is English—still spoken (to a varying degree of success) by Indians in all parts of the country. Attempts to phase it out in favour of Hindi have met with limited success—mainly because English is the main international business language, and in India business makes the world go round.

Because of this, you can expect to get around pretty well using just English. A smattering of Hindi never goes amiss, however, and can on occasion be extremely useful—especially when lost, when shopping, and when making Indian friends. In the south, Hindi won't work—the language there is Tamil, and a short phraseology has been included in the Madras section for travellers visiting this part of the country.

The following Hindi phraseology should cover most contingencies. If you're travelling by Air India, their free passenger booklet includes a useful words and phrases section.

Good Morning	*Shubh prabhat*	Train	*Gadi*
Good night	*Shubh ratri*	Excellent (Number One)	*Premiere*
Good	*Acha*	Shirt	*Kamiz*
Very good	*Bahut acha*	Trousers	*Pajama*
Bad	*Bura*	Laundry	*Dhobi*
Yes	*Han*	Bill, please	*Bill lao*
No	*Nahi*	Water	*Pani*
Perhaps	*Shayad*	Rice	*Chawal*
Please	*Meherbani se*	Fruit	*Phal*
Thank you	*Dhanyavad*	Vegetables	*Sabzi*
Hello/goodbye	*Namaste*	Bread	*Chapati/Roti*
What is that?	*Voh kya hai*	Husband	*Pati*
How much (cost)?	*Kitna (kitna paise)?*	Wife	*Patni*
Too much (cost)	*Jada hai*	Marriage	*Shadi*
Come lower (cost)	*Kum karo*	One coffee (without milk)	*Ek kafi (dudh nahi)*
Toilet	*Paikhana*	Two teas (without sugar)	*Do chai (chini nahi)*

High numbers in Hindi are measured by the 'lakh' (10 000) and by the 'crore' (10 million). There are no Hindi words for million or billion, just multiples of lakhs or crores.

One	*Ek*	Eight	*Aath*	Sixty	*Sath*
Two	*Do*	Nine	*Nau*	Seventy	*Sattar*
Three	*Tin*	Ten	*Dus*	Eighty	*Assi*
Four	*Char*	Twenty	*Bis*	Ninety	*Nubbe*
Five	*Panch*	Thirty	*Tis*	Hundred	*Sau, So*
Six	*Chhe*	Forty	*Chalis*	Thousand	*Hazar*
Seven	*Saat*	Fifty	*Pachas*		

However you pronounce these words, you're going to be wrong. Subtle variations in intonation and dialect from state to state (and even from one town to the next) mean that you can expect a high failure rate till you've adjusted to each local tongue. But it's worth persisting. Indians may find your *faux pas* humorous at first, but they'll always respect the effort you're making, and will help you pronounce things right. One helpful hint I can offer, which will reduce local chuckles by about half, is that the letter 'h' is nearly always (except when the first letter of a word) silent. Whether you win or you lose with Hindi, it's always fun trying.

FURTHER READING

Of the many books written on India, the following are recommended for the quality and accuracy of their observations, and for sheer readability. John Keay's well-informed travelogue, *Into India* (London, John Murray, 1973); Trevor Fishlock's down-to-earth *India File* (London, John Murray, 1983); V.S. Naipaul's *An Area of Darkness* (London, André Deutsch, 1964, now in Penguin) and *India: A Million Mutinies Now* (London, Heinemann, 1989); Mark Tully's *No Full Stops in India* (London, Viking, 1991); James Cameron's *Indian Summer* (London, Penguin, 1987); *Goddess in the Stones* by Norman Lewis (London, Cape, 1991); *Third Class Ticket* by Hilary Ward (London, Penguin, 1984); *On a Shoestring to Coorg (An Experience of South India)* by Devla Murphy (London, John Murray); *Krishnamurti (The Years of Awakening)* by Mary Lutyens (London, John Murray); *Family Web (A Story of India)* by Sarah Hobson (London, John Murray); *An Indian Attachment* by Sarah Lloyd (London, Eland, 1992); *Untouchable* by Mulk Raj Anand (London, Penguin); *Raj to Rajiv* by Mark Tully (London, BBC Books, 1989). Paul Theroux's *The Great Railway Bazaar* (London, Penguin, 1980) is essential reading for anyone who's going to be spending a lot of time on Indian trains (and nearly everyone does).

For health, there's John Hatt's *The Tropical Traveller: An Essential Guide to Travel in Hot Climates* (London, Pan, 1982), which is exactly what its title suggests. For historical background, F. Watson's *A Concise History of India* (London, Thames & Hudson, 1974) is a short and easy introduction. John Keay's *India Discovered* (London, Collins 1988) is a very readable account of the British 're-discovery' of India's history and natural history. *History of India* Parts I and II (London, Penguin, 1992 (first pub. 1950s), as well as *Lives of Indian Princes*, by Charles Allen (London, Century, 1985), *The Great Moghuls* by Bamber Gascoigne (London, Cape, 1972), and *When Men and Mountains Meet* and *The Gilgit Game* (The Explorers of the Western Himalayas 1820–75), by John Keay (London, John Murray, 1977/79) all provide interesting reads. For religion, try K.M. Sen's *Hinduism* (London, Pelican, 1961), the most intelligible of many long-winded volumes on this subject.

Books to Take with You

Unless you're going on a beach holiday (probably the only chance you'll get to do a lot of reading), pack a maximum of three fiction books. You can always buy more in India, or swap books with other travellers. Popular titles on the India circuit are: M.M. Kaye's absorbing saga *The Far Pavilions* (London, Penguin 1978), Salman Rushdie's mystical-cum-historical classic, *Midnight's Children* (London, Cape, 1981) and L. Collins' and D. Lapierre's riveting account of India's progress to independence, *Freedom at Midnight* (India, Vikas, 1976; London, Collins). If you can find it, Dr Paul Brunton's *The Search for Secret India* (London, Rider, 1930s) is also a good read. And J.G. Farrell's rumbustious *The Siege of Krishnapur* (London, Weidenfeld & Nicolson, 1973) remains the most entertaining account of the Indian Mutiny.

Specialist guides include Shobita Punja's illuminating *Museums of India* (The Guidebook Company, HongKong, 1991), and by the same author *Divine Ecstasy: The*

Story of Khajuraho (Penguin, India, 1992), Royston Ellis's *India By Rail* (Bradt Publications, UK, 1989), Gillian Wright's *The Hill Stations of India* (Hong Kong, 1991) and the *Insight Guide to Indian Wildlife* (Singapore, 1986).

All the above titles, and many more, should be available throughout India, where the range is impressive and prices are lower than those in the UK.

INDEX

Page numbers in **bold** refer to maps